Unless Recalled Earlier

To Estelle

# Preface

The common subject of the twenty papers assembled in this volume is input-output analysis and its application to a great variety of economic problems. They reflect the past development and the present state of the art in that general field and in particular the author's contributions to it. Written over a period of more than forty years, the material is arranged, with only a few exceptions, in chronological order.

The first chapter provides an introduction to the subject. It describes the construction of a national input-output table and explains several concrete examples of how the factual information contained in the table can be used to trace the direct and indirect interdependence among the many sectors of a complex modern economy. The second chapter is devoted to systematic description—with recourse to simple algebra—of basic static and dynamic input-output models. Written originally for the German *Handwoerterbuch der Socialwissenschaften*, it was revised for the *International Encyclopedia of Social Sciences* and quite recently was brought up to date for inclusion in the *International Encyclopedia of Materials Science and Engineering*. Chapter 3 takes up the problem of industrial classification, that is, the choice of variables to be employed in description of intersectoral relationships within the framework of a complex multisectoral economy. A similar, although not exactly the same, methodological problem comes up again in Chapter 13, in which it is shown how concise analysis of what is usually referred to as a dynamic economic process can be carried out within the framework of an enlarged, formally "static" input-output model extended over many successive periods of time.

The analysis of the mutual interrelationships among wages, profits, and prices presented in Chapter 4 is advanced in greater depth in Chapter 19. The structural significance and role of foreign trade is explored in Chapters 5, 6, and 7. That subject is taken up again in Chapter 15, the 1973 Nobel Lecture, in which a very simple multiregional input-output model is described, which served as a prototype of the large, multiregional, multisectoral World Input-Output Model constructed in the course of the next four years. Two special applications of that model are described in Chapter 16, devoted to an analysis of the relationship between population growth and economic development—and Chapter 17 in which detailed input-output projections of interregional commodity flows are used as a basis for the estimation of the future growth of maritime traffic and projections of port facilities needed to accommodate it.

Chapters 8 and 9 analyze the direct and indirect economic effect of arms spending. In the second of these papers a multiregional input-output model is employed to determine the regional distribution of these changes.

Concern for the environmental repercussions of economic activities, described in Chapter 10, required inclusion in the basic input-output model of the generation of various polluting agents on the one hand and, on the other hand, of their elimination by means of appropriate abatement activities. Chapter 11 places that model within the framework of the conventional system of national accounts, while an example of concrete empirical computations based on it is presented in Chapter 12.

Chapter 16 takes up the question of technological change. The argument introduced in it is carried further in Chapter 19, which contains a recently completed study of the relationships among the return on capital, wage rates, and technological change. The standard input-output analysis of cost-price relationships is refined in that paper through a separation of wage income from the returns on capital, thus opening the way for systematic cost comparison between "old" and "new" technologies and providing a firm basis for fundamental, that is, causal explanation of technological change.

Successful application and development of the input-output approach depends, more than that of any of the more speculative methods of economic analysis, on systematic, factual inquiry. Therefore, it seems appropriate to include in this volume, as its closing chapter, a paper that emphasizes the critical importance of systematic data gathering for efficient decision making in a complex modern economy.

Each chapter of this volume is self-contained. No attempt was made to eliminate overlaps or to fill the gaps among the different papers or to bring up-to-date statistical figures and bibliographic references. In advancing through these pages and occasionally moving back and forth to pick up this or that thread of thought at different stages of its development, the reader should be able to gain a deeper understanding of the input-output approach—not only as a formal theory but also as a research strategy—than could have been acquired by effortless advance through a smooth textbook presentation of the subject.

New York
January 1986

Wassily Leontief

# Contents

# Input-Output Economics

# 1

## *Input-output economics*

### ( 1 9 5 1 )

### I

If the great nineteenth-century physicist James Clerk Maxwell were to attend a current meeting of the American Physical Society, he might have serious difficulty keeping track of what was going on. In the field of economics, on the other hand, his contemporary John Stuart Mill would easily pick up the thread of the most advanced arguments among his twentieth-century successors. Physics, applying the method of inductive reasoning from quantitatively observed events, has moved on to entirely new premises. The science of economics, in contrast, remains largely a deductive system resting upon a static set of premises, most of which were familiar to Mill and some of which date back to Adam Smith's *The Wealth of Nations*.

Present-day economists are not universally content with this state of affairs. Some of the greatest recent names in economics—Léon Walras, Vilfredo Pareto, Irving Fisher—are associated with the effort to develop quantitative methods for grappling with the enormous volume of empirical data that is involved in every real economic situation. Yet such methods have so far failed to find favor with the majority of professional economists. It is not only the forbidding rigor of mathematics; the truth is that such methods have seldom produced results significantly superior to those achieved by the traditional procedure. In an empirical science, after all, nothing ultimately counts but results. Most economists therefore continue to rely upon their "professional intuition" and "sound judgment" to establish the connection between the facts and the theory of economics.

In recent years, however, the output of economic facts and figures by various public and private agencies has increased by leaps and bounds. Most of this information is published for reference purposes and is unrelated to any particular method of analysis. As a result we have in economics today a high concentration of theory without fact on the one hand, and a mounting accumulation of fact without theory on the other. The task of filling the "empty boxes of economic theory" with relevant empirical content becomes every day more urgent and challenging.

This chapter is concerned with a new effort to combine economic facts and theory, known as *interindustry* or *input-output* analysis. Essentially it is a method of analysis that takes advantage of the relatively stable pattern of the flow of goods and services among the elements of our economy to bring a much more detailed statistical picture of the system into the range of manipulation by economic theory. As such, the method has had to await the modern high-speed computing machine as well as the present propensity of government and private agencies to accumulate mountains of data. It is now advancing from the phase of academic investigation and experimental trial to a broadening sphere of application in grand-scale problems of national economic policy. The practical possibilities of the method are being carried forward as a cooperative venture of the Bureau of Labor Statistics, the Bureau of Mines, the Department of Commerce, the Bureau of the Budget, the Council of Economic Advisers, and, with particular reference to procurement and logistics, the Air Force. Meanwhile, the development of the technique of input-output analysis continues to interest academic investigators here and abroad. They are hopeful that this method of bringing the facts of economics into closer association with theory may induce some fruitful advances in both.

## II

Economic theory seeks to explain the material aspects and operations of our society in terms of interactions among such variables as supply and demand or wages and prices. Economists have generally based their analyses on relatively simple data—such quantities as the gross national product, the interest rate, price and wage levels. But in the real world things are not so simple. Between a shift in wages and the ultimate working out of its impact upon prices there is a complex series of transactions in which actual goods and services are exchanged among real people. These intervening steps are scarcely suggested by the classical formulation of the relationship between the two variables. It is true, of course, that the individual transactions, like individual atoms and molecules, are far too numerous for observation and description in detail. But it is possible, as with physical particles, to reduce them to some kind of order by classifying and aggregating them into groups. This is the procedure employed by input-output analysis in improving the grasp of economic theory upon the facts with which it is concerned in every real situation.

The essential principles of the method may be most easily comprehended by consulting Table 1-1, which summarizes the transactions that characterized the U.S. economy during 1947.[1] The transactions are grouped into 42 major departments of production, distribution, transportation, and consumption, set up on a matrix of horizontal rows and vertical columns. The horizontal rows of figures show how the output of each sector of the economy is distributed among the others. Conversely, the vertical columns show how each sector obtains from the others its needed inputs of goods and services. Since each figure in any horizontal row is also a figure in a vertical column, the output of each sector is shown to be an input in some other. The double-entry bookkeeping of the input-output table thus reveals the fabric of our economy, woven together by the flow of trade which ultimately links each branch and industry to all others. Such a table may, of course, be developed in as fine or as coarse detail as the available data permit and the purpose requires. The present table summarizes a much more detailed 500-sector master table which had just been completed in 1951 after two years of intensive work by the Interindustry Economics Division of the Bureau of Labor Statistics.

### III

For purposes of illustration let us look at the input-output structure of a single sector—the one labeled "primary metals" (sector 14).

---

[1]Preliminary data for Table 1-1 were compiled by the Bureau of Labor Statistics. Each number in the body of the table represents billions of 1947 dollars. In the vertical column at left the entire economy is broken down into sectors; in the horizontal row at the top the same breakdown is repeated. When a sector is read horizontally, the numbers indicate what it ships to other sectors. When a sector is read vertically, the numbers show what it consumes from other sectors. The asterisks stand for sums less than $5 million. Totals may not check due to rounding.

INDUSTRY PRODUCING

| | | agriculture and fisheries | food and kindred products | textile mill products | apparel | lumber and wood products | furniture and fixtures | paper and allied products | printing and publishing |
|---|---|---|---|---|---|---|---|---|---|
| | | 1 | 2 | 3 | 4 | 5 | 6 | 7 | 8 |
| agriculture and fisheries | 1 | 10.86 | 15.70 | 2.16 | 0.02 | 0.19 | | 0.01 | |
| food and kindred products | 2 | 2.38 | 5.75 | 0.06 | 0.01 | ° | ° | 0.03 | ° |
| textile mill products | 3 | 0.06 | ° | 1.30 | 3.88 | ° | 0.29 | 0.04 | 0.03 |
| apparel | 4 | 0.04 | 0.20 | | 1.96 | | 0.01 | 0.02 | |
| lumber and wood products | 5 | 0.15 | 0.10 | 0.02 | ° | 1.09 | 0.39 | 0.27 | ° |
| furniture and fixtures | 6 | | | 0.01 | | | 0.01 | 0.01 | |
| paper and allied products | 7 | ° | 0.52 | 0.08 | 0.02 | ° | 0.02 | 2.60 | 1.08 |
| printing and publishing | 8 | | 0.04 | ° | | | | | 0.77 |
| chemicals | 9 | 0.83 | 1.48 | 0.80 | 0.14 | 0.03 | 0.06 | 0.18 | 0.10 |
| products of petroleum and coal | 10 | 0.46 | 0.06 | 0.03 | ° | 0.07 | ° | 0.06 | ° |
| rubber products | 11 | 0.12 | 0.01 | 0.01 | 0.02 | 0.01 | 0.01 | 0.01 | ° |
| leather and leather products | 12 | | | ° | 0.05 | ° | 0.01 | | ° |
| stone, clay, and glass products | 13 | 0.06 | 0.25 | ° | ° | 0.01 | 0.03 | 0.03 | |
| primary metals | 14 | 0.01 | ° | | ° | 0.01 | 0.11 | | 0.01 |
| fabricated metal products | 15 | 0.08 | 0.61 | ° | 0.01 | 0.04 | 0.14 | 0.02 | ° |
| machinery (except electric) | 16 | 0.06 | 0.01 | 0.04 | 0.02 | 0.01 | 0.01 | 0.01 | 0.04 |
| electrical machinery | 17 | | | | | | | | |
| motor vehicles | 18 | 0.11 | ° | | | ° | | | |
| other transportation equipment | 19 | 0.01 | | | | | | ° | |
| professional and scientific equipment | 20 | | | | | | ° | 0.01 | 0.03 |
| miscellaneous manufacturing industries | 21 | ° | 0.01 | ° | 0.26 | ° | 0.02 | 0.01 | |
| coal, gas, and electric power | 22 | 0.06 | 0.20 | 0.11 | 0.04 | 0.02 | 0.02 | 0.12 | 0.03 |
| railroad transportation | 23 | 0.44 | 0.57 | 0.09 | 0.06 | 0.14 | 0.05 | 0.22 | 0.07 |
| ocean transportation | 24 | 0.07 | 0.13 | 0.01 | 0.01 | 0.01 | ° | 0.02 | ° |
| other transportation | 25 | 0.55 | 0.38 | 0.08 | 0.03 | 0.14 | 0.04 | 0.12 | 0.03 |
| trade | 26 | 1.36 | 0.46 | 0.23 | 0.37 | 0.06 | 0.06 | 0.18 | 0.03 |
| communications | 27 | ° | 0.04 | 0.01 | 0.02 | 0.01 | 0.01 | 0.01 | 0.04 |
| finance and insurance | 28 | 0.24 | 0.15 | 0.02 | 0.02 | 0.08 | 0.02 | 0.02 | 0.02 |
| real estate and rentals | 29 | 2.39 | 0.09 | 0.03 | 0.10 | 0.02 | 0.02 | 0.03 | 0.06 |
| business services | 30 | 0.01 | 0.63 | 0.07 | 0.10 | 0.02 | 0.06 | 0.02 | 0.06 |
| personal and repair services | 31 | 0.37 | 0.12 | ° | ° | 0.04 | ° | ° | 0.02 |
| nonprofit organizations | 32 | | | | | | | | |
| amusements | 33 | | | | | | | | |
| scrap and miscellaneous industries | 34 | | | 0.02 | | | | 0.25 | |
| eating and drinking places | 35 | | | | | | | | ° |
| new construction and maintenance | 36 | 0.20 | 0.12 | 0.04 | 0.02 | 0.01 | 0.01 | 0.04 | 0.01 |
| undistributed | 37 | | 1.87 | 0.30 | 1.08 | 0.73 | 0.27 | 0.17 | 0.50 |
| inventory change (depletions) | 38 | 2.66 | 0.40 | 0.12 | 0.19 | ° | 0.01 | 0.09 | 0.03 |
| foreign countries (imports from) | 39 | 0.69 | 2.11 | 0.21 | 0.28 | 0.18 | 0.01 | 0.62 | 0.01 |
| government | 40 | 0.81 | 1.24 | 0.64 | 0.38 | 0.34 | 0.11 | 0.50 | 0.34 |
| private capital formation (gross) | 41 | DEPRECIATION AND OTHER CAPITAL CONSUMPTION ALLOWANCES | | | | | | | |
| households | 42 | 19.17 | 7.05 | 3.34 | 4.24 | 2.72 | 1.12 | 2.20 | 3.14 |
| TOTAL GROSS OUTLAYS | | 44.26 | 40.30 | 9.84 | 13.32 | 6.00 | 2.89 | 7.90 | 6.45 |

## Table 1-1

Exchange of goods and services in the U.S. for 1947

PURCHASING

| chemicals | products of petroleum and coal | rubber products | leather and leather products | stone, clay, and glass products | primary metals | fabricated metal products | machinery (except electric) | electrical machinery | motor vehicles | other transportation equipment | professional and scientific equipment | miscellaneous manufacturing industries | coal, gas, and electric power |
|---|---|---|---|---|---|---|---|---|---|---|---|---|---|
| 9 | 10 | 11 | 12 | 13 | 14 | 15 | 16 | 17 | 18 | 19 | 20 | 21 | 22 |
| 1.21 |  |  | 0.05 | * | 0.01 |  |  |  |  |  |  |  |  |
| 0.79 | * |  | 0.44 | * | * | * | * | * |  |  | 0.01 | 0.02 | * |
| 0.01 | * | 0.44 | 0.09 | 0.03 |  | 0.01 | 0.02 | 0.05 | 0.15 | 0.01 | 0.05 | 0.08 | 0.07 |
| 0.03 |  | * | * |  |  | * | * | * | 0.10 | 0.01 | * | * | * |
| 0.04 | 0.01 |  | 0.02 | 0.02 | 0.06 | 0.06 | 0.09 | 0.05 | 0.05 | 0.03 | * | 0.06 | 0.06 |
|  |  |  |  |  | * | 0.01 | 0.10 | 0.03 | 0.02 | * |  | * |  |
| 0.33 | 0.11 | 0.02 | 0.05 | 0.18 | * | 0.09 | 0.04 | 0.07 | 0.03 | 0.02 | 0.08 | 0.07 | * |
| 0.02 |  |  |  |  |  | 0.01 | 0.01 | 0.01 |  |  | * |  | * |
| 2.58 | 0.21 | 0.60 | 0.13 | 0.12 | 0.18 | 0.13 | 0.08 | 0.20 | 0.11 | 0.02 | 0.05 | 0.17 | 0.06 |
| 0.32 | 4.83 | 0.01 | * | 0.05 | 0.90 | 0.02 | 0.04 | 0.02 | 0.03 | 0.01 | * | 0.01 | 0.47 |
| * | * | 0.04 | 0.05 | 0.01 | * | 0.01 | 0.13 | 0.03 | 0.50 | 0.01 | * | 0.04 | * |
|  |  |  | 1.04 |  |  | * | 0.02 | * | 0.01 | * | 0.01 | 0.01 | * |
| 0.26 | 0.05 | 0.01 | 0.01 | 0.43 | 0.21 | 0.07 | 0.07 | 0.12 | 0.19 | 0.01 | 0.03 | 0.06 | 0.02 |
| 0.19 | 0.01 | 0.01 | * | 0.04 | 6.90 | 2.53 | 2.02 | 1.05 | 1.28 | 0.43 | 0.07 | 0.20 | 0.05 |
| 0.13 | 0.08 | 0.01 | 0.02 | * | 0.05 | 0.43 | 0.62 | 0.34 | 0.97 | 0.10 | 0.07 | 0.04 | * |
| * | 0.01 |  |  | 0.01 | 0.07 | 0.28 | 1.15 | 0.17 | 0.63 | 0.22 | 0.03 | * | 0.03 |
| * |  |  |  | 0.01 | 0.05 | 0.24 | 0.58 | 0.86 | 0.62 | 0.12 | 0.03 | 0.02 | 0.02 |
|  |  |  |  | * | * | 0.03 | 0.03 | 0.01 | 4.40 | * |  |  | 0.01 |
| 0.01 |  |  |  |  |  |  |  | * | 0.01 | 0.30 |  |  | * |
| 0.01 |  |  |  |  |  | 0.04 | 0.04 | 0.01 | 0.07 | 0.02 | 0.18 | 0.02 | * |
| 0.03 |  | * | 0.02 | 0.01 | * | 0.02 | 0.05 | 0.11 | 0.02 | * | 0.03 | 0.16 | * |
| 0.19 | 0.56 | 0.04 | 0.02 | 0.20 | 0.35 | 0.08 | 0.10 | 0.05 | 0.06 | 0.03 | 0.01 | 0.03 | 1.27 |
| 0.29 | 0.27 | 0.04 | 0.04 | 0.15 | 0.52 | 0.13 | 0.16 | 0.07 | 0.23 | 0.04 | 0.01 | 0.03 | 0.15 |
| 0.04 | 0.09 | * | * | 0.01 | 0.08 | * | * | * | * | * | * | 0.01 | * |
| 0.10 | 0.47 | 0.01 | 0.02 | 0.07 | 0.16 | 0.03 | 0.04 | 0.03 | 0.07 | 0.01 | 0.01 | 0.01 | 0.03 |
| 0.17 | 0.02 | 0.05 | 0.06 | 0.05 | 0.36 | 0.20 | 0.26 | 0.14 | 0.06 | 0.07 | 0.04 | 0.05 | 0.05 |
| 0.02 | 0.01 | 0.01 | * | 0.01 | 0.02 | 0.02 | 0.03 | 0.02 | 0.02 | 0.01 | 0.01 | 0.01 | 0.02 |
| 0.02 | 0.13 | 0.01 | 0.01 | 0.05 | 0.06 | 0.04 | 0.05 | 0.04 | 0.02 | 0.02 | 0.01 | 0.02 | 0.05 |
| 0.03 |  | 0.01 | 0.02 | 0.02 | 0.06 | 0.03 | 0.04 | 0.03 | 0.02 | 0.02 | 0.01 | 0.03 | 0.05 |
| 0.42 | 0.04 | 0.02 | 0.05 | 0.01 | 0.03 | 0.05 | 0.09 | 0.06 | 0.08 | 0.01 | 0.05 | 0.06 | 0.01 |
| 0.01 | 0.01 | * | * | 0.03 | 0.01 | 0.01 | 0.01 | * | * | * | * | * | 0.02 |
|  |  |  |  |  |  |  |  |  |  |  |  |  |  |
| 0.01 |  | 0.01 |  | 0.01 | 1.11 | 0.02 | 0.05 | * |  |  | * |  |  |
|  |  |  |  |  |  |  |  |  |  |  |  |  |  |
| 0.04 | 0.03 | 0.01 | 0.02 | 0.03 | 0.10 | 0.03 | 0.05 | 0.02 | 0.04 | 0.02 | 0.01 | 0.02 | 0.27 |
| 1.49 | 0.65 | 0.27 | 0.27 | 0.47 | 0.32 | 1.14 | 1.71 | 0.89 | 0.41 | 0.34 | 0.19 | 0.87 | 0.25 |
| 0.14 | 0.01 | * | 0.03 | * | 0.11 | * | * | * | 0.01 | 0.01 | 0.05 | 0.16 | * |
| 0.59 | 0.26 | * | 0.04 | 0.14 | 0.62 | 0.01 | 0.05 | * | 0.02 | 0.01 | 0.05 | 0.14 | 0.01 |
| 0.76 | 0.78 | 0.11 | 0.14 | 0.32 | 0.82 | 0.48 | 0.77 | 0.40 | 0.66 | 0.12 | 0.13 | 0.19 | 1.14 |
| ARE INCLUDED IN HOUSEHOLD ROW | | | | | | | | | | | | | |
| 3.75 | 5.04 | 1.08 | 1.20 | 2.35 | 5.35 | 4.14 | 6.80 | 3.41 | 3.39 | 1.95 | 0.90 | 2.17 | 5.11 |
| 14.05 | 13.67 | 2.82 | 3.81 | 4.84 | 18.69 | 10.40 | 15.22 | 8.38 | 14.27 | 4.00 | 2.12 | 4.76 | 9.21 |

INDUSTRY PRODUCING

| | | railroad transportation | ocean transportation | other transportation | trade | communications | finance and insurance | real estate and rentals | business services |
|---|---|---|---|---|---|---|---|---|---|
| | | 23 | 24 | 25 | 26 | 27 | 28 | 29 | 30 |
| agriculture and fisheries | 1 | ° | ° | 0.01 | | ° | | | |
| food and kindred products | 2 | 0.08 | 0.01 | 0.03 | 0.07 | 0.01 | | | |
| textile mill products | 3 | | 0.01 | 0.01 | 0.03 | ° | | | ° |
| apparel | 4 | ° | ° | ° | 0.02 | ° | | | |
| lumber and wood products | 5 | | 0.01 | ° | 0.03 | ° | | 0.14 | ° |
| furniture and fixtures | 6 | | | ° | | ° | 0.04 | 0.08 | |
| paper and allied products | 7 | ° | | ° | 0.57 | ° | ° | | ° |
| printing and publishing | 8 | 0.04 | ° | 0.02 | 0.10 | 0.03 | 0.21 | | 2.45 |
| chemicals | 9 | 0.03 | 0.01 | 0.02 | 0.07 | ° | ° | | 0.01 |
| products of petroleum and coal | 10 | 0.27 | 0.09 | 0.45 | 0.20 | ° | 0.01 | 0.78 | ° |
| rubber products | 11 | ° | | 0.13 | 0.06 | ° | 0.01 | ° | |
| leather and leather products | 12 | | | ° | ° | | | | |
| stone, clay and glass products | 13 | 0.01 | ° | ° | 0.04 | ° | | | |
| primary metals | 14 | 0.20 | | 0.01 | | ° | | | |
| fabricated metal products | 15 | 0.03 | ° | 0.01 | 0.06 | ° | | | ° |
| machinery (except electric) | 16 | 0.06 | | 0.01 | 0.01 | | 0.02 | | |
| electrical machinery | 17 | 0.04 | | 0.01 | 0.01 | 0.05 | | | 0.01 |
| motor vehicles | 18 | ° | | 0.13 | 0.02 | ° | | ° | |
| other transportation equipment | 19 | 0.04 | 0.08 | 0.13 | | | | | |
| professional and scientific equipment | 20 | | | ° | | ° | | | 0.01 |
| miscellaneous manufacturing industries | 21 | ° | ° | ° | 0.01 | ° | | | 0.15 |
| coal, gas, and electric power | 22 | 0.44 | ° | 0.09 | 0.49 | 0.01 | 0.06 | 3.15 | ° |
| railroad transportation | 23 | 0.41 | ° | 0.06 | 0.08 | ° | 0.01 | 0.42 | 0.03 |
| ocean transportation | 24 | | | 0.22 | | | | | |
| other transportation | 25 | 0.19 | 0.04 | 0.25 | 0.31 | ° | ° | 0.13 | 0.03 |
| trade | 26 | 0.03 | 0.01 | 0.42 | 0.20 | 0.01 | 0.04 | 0.75 | 0.14 |
| communications | 27 | 0.02 | ° | 0.04 | 0.33 | 0.06 | 0.09 | 0.06 | 0.43 |
| finance and insurance | 28 | 0.02 | 0.12 | 0.30 | 1.00 | ° | 1.85 | 0.56 | 0.02 |
| real estate and rentals | 29 | 0.02 | 0.01 | 0.15 | 1.96 | 0.05 | 0.21 | 0.21 | 0.06 |
| business services | 30 | 0.02 | ° | 0.03 | 1.71 | 0.09 | 0.14 | 0.04 | 0.06 |
| personal and repair services | 31 | 0.11 | 0.01 | 0.26 | 1.42 | 0.02 | 0.11 | 0.03 | 0.07 |
| nonprofit organizations | 32 | | ° | ° | | | 0.02 | | |
| amusements | 33 | | | | | | | | |
| scrap and miscellaneous industries | 34 | | | 0.04 | 0.39 | 0.01 | 0.11 | 0.03 | 0.02 |
| eating and drinking places | 35 | | | 0.01 | | | | | |
| new construction and maintenance | 36 | 1.12 | ° | 0.13 | 0.18 | 0.18 | 0.03 | 4.08 | ° |
| undistributed | 37 | 0.10 | 0.04 | 0.03 | 2.59 | 0.01 | 0.71 | 0.36 | 0.31 |
| inventory change (depletions) | 38 | | | | | | | | |
| foreign countries (imports from) | 39 | 0.04 | 0.50 | 0.08 | | 0.03 | 0.10 | | |
| government | 40 | 0.91 | 0.26 | 0.77 | 3.30 | 0.44 | 1.11 | 4.00 | 0.21 |
| private capital formation (gross) | 41 | | | | | | | | |
| households | 42 | 5.70 | 0.90 | 6.20 | 26.42 | 2.15 | 7.93 | 14.06 | 1.08 |
| TOTAL GROSS OUTLAYS | | 9.95 | 2.29 | 9.86 | 41.66 | 3.17 | 12.81 | 28.86 | 5.10 |

## Table 1-1 (Cont.)

8

PURCHASING     FINAL DEMAND

Column legend (rotated headers, left to right):

- 31 — personal and repair services
- 32 — nonprofit organizations
- 33 — miscellaneous amusements
- 34 — scrap and industries
- 35 — eating and drinking places
- 36 — new construction and maintenance
- 37 — inventory change (additions)
- 38 — undistributed
- 39 — foreign countries (exports to)
- 40 — government
- 41 — private capital formation (gross)
- 42 — households
- Total — TOTAL GROSS OUTPUT

| 31 | 32 | 33 | 34 | 35 | 36 | 37 | 38 | 39 | 40 | 41 | 42 | Total |
|---|---|---|---|---|---|---|---|---|---|---|---|---|
|  | 0.12 |  |  | 0.87 | 0.09 | 0.17 | 1.01 | 1.28 | 0.57 | 0.02 | 9.92 | 44.26 |
| ° | 0.25 | ° | 0.02 | 3.47 | ° | 0.42 | 0.88 | 1.80 | 0.73 |  | 23.03 | 40.30 |
| 0.03 | ° |  | 0.01 |  | 0.05 | 0.52 | 0.06 | 0.92 | 0.10 | 0.02 | 1.47 | 9.84 |
| 0.02 | 0.02 | ° | 0.01 | 0.02 | ° | 0.15 | 0.21 | 0.30 | 0.28 | ° | 9.90 | 13.32 |
| ° | ° |  | 0.11 | 0.01 | 2.33 | 0.35 | 0.17 | 0.17 | 0.01 | 0.04 | 0.07 | 6.00 |
|  | ° |  |  |  | 0.20 | 0.20 | 0.08 | 0.03 | 0.05 | 0.57 | 1.46 | 2.89 |
| 0.06 | 0.03 |  | 0.68 | 0.06 | 0.17 | 0.31 | 0.04 | 0.15 | 0.06 |  | 0.34 | 7.90 |
| 0.03 | 0.17 | 0.01 | 0.01 | 0.03 |  | 0.68 | ° | 0.07 | 0.16 | 0.09 | 1.49 | 6.45 |
| 0.20 | 0.22 | ° | 0.03 | 0.04 | 0.64 | 1.25 | 0.30 | 0.81 | 0.19 |  | 1.96 | 14.05 |
| 0.06 | 0.06 | ° | 0.01 | 0.01 | 0.62 | 0.36 | 0.06 | 0.68 | 0.18 | ° | 2.44 | 13.67 |
| 0.07 | ° |  | ° | ° | 0.06 | 0.47 | 0.09 | 0.17 | 0.02 | 0.01 | 0.71 | 2.82 |
| 0.03 | 0.01 |  | 0.01 |  | ° | 0.29 | 0.11 | 0.08 | 0.03 | 0.02 | 2.03 | 3.81 |
| 0.02 | 0.01 |  | ° | 0.06 | 1.74 | 0.36 | 0.10 | 0.21 | 0.02 | 0.01 | 0.34 | 4.84 |
|  | ° |  | 0.15 | ° | 1.19 | 1.24 | 0.16 | 0.77 | 0.02 |  | 0.02 | 18.69 |
| 0.03 | 0.01 |  | 0.06 | 0.02 | 3.09 | 1.44 | 0.21 | 0.39 | 0.05 | 0.28 | 0.95 | 10.40 |
| 0.15 | ° |  | 0.07 |  | 0.51 | 2.24 | 0.37 | 1.76 | 0.18 | 5.82 | 1.22 | 15.22 |
| 0.09 | ° |  | 0.04 |  | 0.77 | 1.27 | 0.25 | 0.44 | 0.17 | 1.75 | 0.93 | 8.38 |
| 1.05 | ° |  | 0.07 | ° | 0.04 | 0.67 | 0.40 | 1.02 | 0.15 | 2.98 | 3.13 | 14.27 |
| ° |  |  | 0.01 |  | ° | 0.46 | 0.02 | 0.32 | 1.25 | 1.20 | 0.17 | 4.00 |
| 0.05 | 0.18 |  | 0.01 |  | 0.02 | 0.24 | 0.03 | 0.18 | 0.08 | 0.26 | 0.62 | 2.12 |
| 0.16 | 0.05 | 0.05 | 0.11 | 0.02 | 0.03 | 0.68 | 0.04 | 0.19 | 0.08 | 0.51 | 1.89 | 4.76 |
| 0.31 | 0.16 | 0.05 |  | 0.22 | 0.03 | 0.02 | 0.03 | 0.35 | 0.20 |  |  | 9.21 |
| 0.03 | 0.05 | ° | 0.03 | 0.25 | 0.71 | 0.30 | 0.08 | 0.59 | 0.33 | 0.27 | 2.53 | 9.95 |
|  |  |  | ° |  |  |  | ° | 1.16 | 0.31 |  | 0.10 | 2.29 |
| 0.01 | 0.02 | ° | 0.02 | 0.10 | 0.57 | 0.17 | 0.04 | 0.32 | 0.35 | 0.10 | 4.77 | 9.86 |
| 0.37 | 0.29 | 0.01 | 0.09 | 1.06 | 2.52 | 1.01 | 0.20 | 1.00 | 0.05 | 2.34 | 26.82 | 41.66 |
| 0.12 | 0.07 | 0.01 |  | 0.01 | 0.04 | 0.08 |  | 0.04 | 0.15 |  | 1.27 | 3.17 |
| 0.12 | 0.09 | 0.03 |  | 0.07 | 0.40 |  |  | 0.14 | 0.03 |  | 6.99 | 12.81 |
| 0.71 | 0.40 | 0.18 |  | 0.39 | 0.08 |  |  |  | 0.22 | 0.80 | 20.29 | 28.86 |
| 0.12 | 0.02 | 0.10 |  | 0.06 | 0.13 | 0.42 |  |  | ° | 0.04 | 0.18 | 5.10 |
| 0.56 | 0.08 | 0.02 | 0.03 | 0.23 | 0.82 | 1.17 |  |  | 0.08 | 0.27 | 8.35 | 14.30 |
|  | 0.09 |  |  |  |  | 0.16 |  |  |  | 5.08 | 8.04 | 13.39 |
|  | 0.01 | 0.39 |  |  |  | 0.01 |  | 0.13 |  |  | 2.40 | 2.94 |
| ° | ° | 0.01 |  |  | ° | 0.01 |  | 0.03 | ° |  |  | 2.13 |
|  | 0.15 |  |  |  |  |  |  |  |  |  | 13.11 | 13.27 |
| 0.06 | 0.34 | 0.02 |  | 0.07 | 0.01 |  |  |  | 5.20 | 15.70 | 0.15 | 28.49 |
| 1.13 | 0.91 | 0.22 |  | 0.59 | 0.43 |  |  |  |  |  |  | 21.60 |
|  |  |  | 0.40 |  |  |  |  | 0.02 |  |  |  | 4.43 |
|  |  | ° | 0.07 |  |  | 0.01 |  |  | 1.31 |  | 1.32 | 9.52 |
| 0.50 | 0.17 | 0.32 | 0.07 | 1.41 | 0.47 | 2.19 | 0.34 | 0.83 | 3.46 | 0.22 | 31.55 | 63.69 |
| 8.20 | 9.41 | 1.50 |  | 4.20 | 10.73 | 2.27 |  | 0.85 | 30.06 |  | 2.12 | 223.58 |
| 14.30 | 13.39 | 2.94 | 2.13 | 13.27 | 28.49 | 21.60 | 5.28 | 17.21 | 51.29 | 33.29 | 194.12 |  |

The vertical column states the inputs of each of the various goods and services that are required for the production of metals, and the sum of the figures in this column represents the total outlay of the economy for the year's production. Most of the entries in this column are self-explanatory. Thus it is no surprise to find a substantial figure entered against the item "products of petroleum and coal" (sector 10). The design of the table, however, gives a special meaning to some of the sectors. The outlay for "railroad transportation" (sector 23), for example, covers only the cost of hauling raw materials to the mills; the cost of delivering primary metal products to their markets is borne by the industries purchasing them. Another outlay requiring explanation is entered in the trade sector (sector 26). The figures in this sector represent the cost of distribution, stated in terms of the trade margin. The entries against trade in the primary metals column, therefore, cover the middleman's markup on the industry's purchase; trade margins on the sale of primary metal products are charged against the consuming industries. Taxes paid by the industry are entered in the row labeled "government" (sector 40), and all payments to individuals, including wages, salaries, and dividends, are summed up in the row labeled "households" (sector 42). How the output of the metals industry is distributed among the other sectors is shown in row 14. The figures indicate that the industry's principal customers are other industries. "Households" and "government" turn up as direct customers for only a minor portion of the total output, although these two sectors are, of course, the principal consumers of metals after they have been converted into end products by other industries.

Coming out of the interior of the table to the outer row and columns, the reader may soon recognize many of the familiar total figures by which we are accustomed to visualize the condition of the economy. The total outputs at the end of each industry row, for example, are the figures we use to measure the size or the health of an industry. The gross national product, which is designed to state the total of productive activity and is the most commonly cited index for the economy as a whole, may be derived as the grand total of the five columns grouped under the heading of "final demand," but with some adjustments necessary to eliminate the duplication of transactions between the sectors represented by these columns. For example, the total payment to households, at the far right end of row 42, includes salaries paid by government, a figure that duplicates in part the payment of taxes by households included in the total payment to government.

## IV

With this brief introduction lay economists are now qualified to turn around and trace their way back into the table via whatever chain of interindustry relationships engages their interest. They will not go far before they find themselves working intuitively with the central concept of input–output analysis. This is the idea that there is a fundamental relationship between the volume of the output of an industry and the size of the inputs going into it. It is obvious, for example, that the purchases of the auto industry (column 18) from the glass industry (row 13) in 1947 were strongly determined by the number of motor vehicles produced that year. Closer inspection will lead to the further realization that every single figure in the chart is dependent upon every other. To take an extreme example, the appropriate series of inputs will show that the auto industry's purchases of glass are dependent in part upon the demand for motor vehicles arising out of the glass industry's purchases from the fuel industries.

These relationships reflect the structure of our technology. They are expressed in input-output analysis as the ratios or coefficients of each input to the total output of which it becomes a part. A graph of such ratios in Figure 1-1, computed from a table for the economy as of 1939, shows how much had to be purchased from the steel, glass, paint, rubber, and other industries to produce $1000 worth of automobile that year. Since such expenditures are determined by relatively inflexible engineering considerations or by equally inflexible customs and institutional arrangements, these ratios might be used to estimate the demand for materials induced by auto production in other years. With a table of ratios for the economy as a whole, it is possible in turn to calculate the secondary demand on the output of the industries that supply the auto industry's suppliers and so on through successive outputs and inputs until the effect of the final demand for automobiles has been traced to its last reverberation in the farthest corner of the economy. In this fashion input-output analysis should prove useful to the auto industry as a means for dealing with cost and supply problems.

The graph of steel consumption ratios (Figure 1-2) suggests, incidentally, how the input–output matrix might be used for the contrasting purpose of market analysis. Since the ultimate markets for steel are ordinarily buried in the cycle of secondary transactions among the metal-fabricating industries, it is useful to learn from this table how many tons of steel at the mill were needed in 1939 to

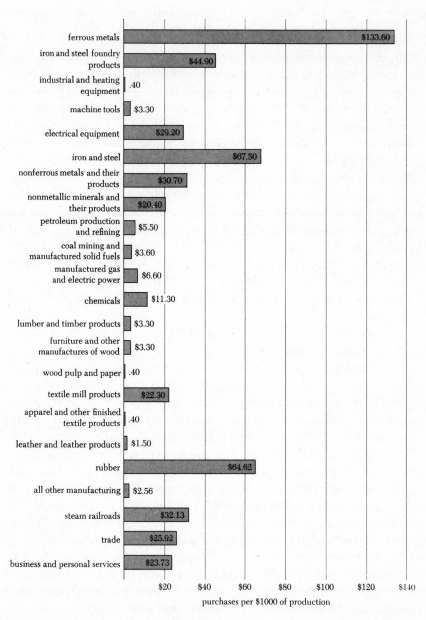

Figure 1-1

The input to auto industry from other industries per $1000 of auto production was derived from the 1939 interindustry table. Comparing these figures with those for the auto industry in the 1947 table would show changes in input structure of the industry due to changes in prices and technology.

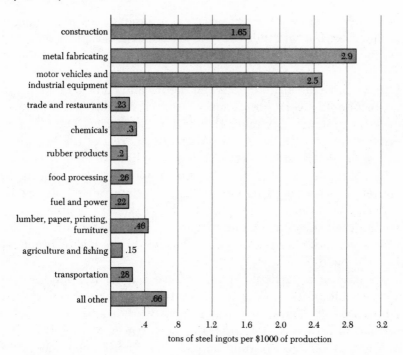

construction 1.65
metal fabricating 2.9
motor vehicles and industrial equipment 2.5
trade and restaurants .23
chemicals .3
rubber products .2
food processing .26
fuel and power .22
lumber, paper, printing, furniture .46
agriculture and fishing .15
transportation .28
all other .66

.4    .8    1.2    1.6    2.0    2.4    2.8    3.2

tons of steel ingots per $1000 of production

**Figure 1-2**

The output of the steel industry depends heavily on what kinds of goods are demanded in the ultimate market. This table shows the amount of steel required to meet each $1000 of the demand for other goods in 1939. The current demand for the top three items is responsible for the steel shortage.

satisfy each $1000 worth of demand for the products of industries that ultimately place steel products at the disposal of the consumer. This graph shows the impressively high ratio of the demand for steel in the construction and consumer durable-goods industries which led the Bureau of Labor Statistics to declare in 1945 that a flourishing postwar economy would require even more steel than the peak of the war effort. Though some industry spokesmen took a contrary position at that time, steel production in 1951 had been exceeding World War II peaks, and the major steel companies were then engaged in a 16-million-ton expansion program which was started even before the outbreak of the war in Korea and the subsequent rearmament.

The ratios shown in Figures 1-1 and 1-2 are largely fixed by technology. Others in the complete matrix of the economy, especially in the trade, services, and households sectors, are established by custom and other institutional factors. All, of course, are subject to modification by such forces as progress in technology and changes in public taste. But whether they vary more or less rapidly over the years, these relationships are subject to dependable measurement at any given time.

Here we have our bridge between theory and facts in economics. It is a bridge in a very literal sense. Action at a distance does not happen in economics any more than it does in physics. The effect of an event at any one point is transmitted to the rest of the economy step by step via the chain of transactions that links the whole system together. A table of ratios for the entire economy gives us, in as much detail as we require, a quantitatively determined picture of the internal structure of the system. This makes it possible to calculate in detail the consequences that result from the introduction into the system of changes suggested by the theoretical or practical problem at hand.

In the case of a particular industry, we can easily compute the complete table of its input requirements at any given level of output, provided we know its input ratios. By the same token, with somewhat more involved computation, we can construct synthetically a complete input-output table for the entire economy. We need only a known "bill of final demand" to convert the table of ratios into a table of magnitudes. The 1945 estimate of postwar steel requirements, for example, was incidental to a study of the complete economy based upon a bill of demand that assumed full employment in 1950. This bill of demand was inserted into the total columns of a table of ratios based on the year 1939. By arithmetical procedures the ratios were then translated into dollar figures, among which was the figure for steel, which showed a need for an absolute minimum of 98 million ingot tons. Actual production in 1950, at the limit of capacity, was 96.8 million tons.

## V

Though its application is simple, the construction of an input-output table is a highly complex and laborious operation. The first step, and one that has little appeal to the theoretical imagination, is the gathering and ordering of an immense volume of quantitative information. Given the inevitable lag between the accumulation and the collation of data for any given year, the input-output table will always be a historical document. The first input-output tables, prepared by the author and his associates at Harvard University in the early 1930s, were based upon 1919 and 1929 figures. The 1939 table was not completed until 1944. Looking to the future, a table for 1953, which is now under consideration, could not be made available until 1957.[2] For practical purposes the original figures in the table must be regarded as a base, subject to refinement and correction in accord with subsequent trends. For example, the 1945 projection of the 1950 economy on the basis of the 1939 table made suitable adjustments in the coal and oil input ratios of the transportation industries on the assumption that the trend from steam to diesel locomotives would continue throughout the period.

The basic information for the table and its continuing revision comes from the Bureau of the Census and other specialized statistical agencies. As the industrial breakdown becomes more detailed, however, engineering and technical information plays a more important part in determining the data. A perfectly good way to determine how much coke is needed to produce a ton of pig-iron, in addition to dividing the output of the blast furnace industry into its input of coke, is to ask an ironmaster. In principle there is no reason why the input-output coefficients should not be entirely derived from "below," from engineering data on process design and operating practice. Thus, in certain studies of the German economy made by the Bureau of Labor Statistics following World War II, the input structures of key industries were set up on the basis of U.S. experience. The model of a disarmed but self-supporting Germany developed in these studies showed a steel requirement of 11 million ingot tons, toward which actual output is now moving. Completely hypothetical input structures, representing industries not now operating, have been introduced into tables of the existing U.S. economy in studies conducted by Air Force economists.

# VI

This brings us to the problem of computation. Since the production level required of each industry is ultimately dependent upon levels in all others, it is clear that we have a problem involving simultaneous equations. Though the solution of such equations may involve no very high order of mathematics, the sheer labor of computation

[2]In November 1964 the U.S. Department of Commerce published a preliminary version and in September 1965 the final version of the newly compiled input-output table of the U.S. economy for the census year 1958. It contained 86 producing and 6 final demand sectors. In releasing these figures the Secretary of Commerce announced that in the future up-to-date input-output tables would be published "as an integral part of national income and product accounts."

can be immense. The number of equations to be solved is always equal to the number of sectors into which the system is divided. Depending upon whether a specific or a general solution of the system is desired, the volume of computation will vary as the square or the cube of the number of sectors involved. A typical general solution of a 42-sector table for 1939 required 56 hours on the Harvard Mark II computer. Thanks to this investment in computation, the conversion of any stipulated bill of demand into the various industrial production levels involves nothing more than simple arithmetic. The method cannot be used, however, in the solution of problems that call for changes in the input-output ratios, since each change requires a whole new solution of the matrix. For the larger number of more interesting problems that require such changes, special solutions are the rule. However, even a special solution on a reasonably detailed 200-sector table might require some 200,000 multiplications and a greater number of additions. For this reason it is likely that the typical nongovernmental user will be limited to condensed general solutions periodically computed and published by special-purpose groups working in the field. With these the average industrial analyst will be able to enjoy many of the advantages of the large and flexible machinery required for government analyses relating to the entire economy.

A demonstration of input-output analysis applied to a typical economic problem is presented in Figure 1-3, which shows the price increases that would result from a general 10 percent increase in the wage scale of industry. Here the value of the matrix distinguishing between direct and indirect effects is of the utmost importance. If wages constituted the only ultimate cost in the economy, a general 10 percent rise in all money wages would obviously lead to an equal increase in all prices. Since wages are only one cost and since labor costs vary from industry to industry, it can be seen in the chart that a 10 percent increase in wages would have decidedly different effects upon various parts of the economy. The construction industry shows the greatest upward price change, as it actually did in recent decades. For each industry group the chart separates the different effect of increases in its own wage bill from the indirect effects of the wage increases in other industries from which it purchases its inputs. Giving effect to both direct and indirect increases, the average increase in the cost of living is shown in the chart to be only 3.7 percent. The 10 percent money-wage increase thus yields a 6.3 percent increase in real wage rates. It should be noted, however, that the economic forces that bring increases in wages tend to

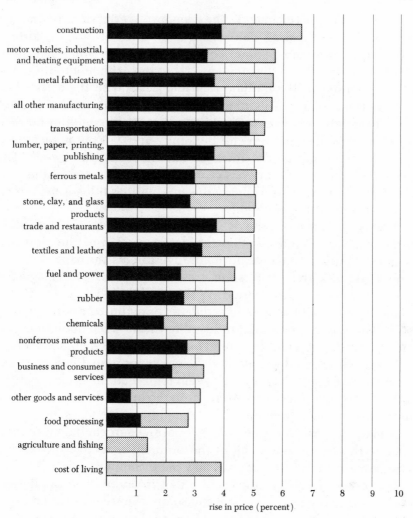

**Figure 1-3**

The price increases that would be caused by a 10 percent increase in wages were computed from the 1939 interindustry table. The increases include the direct effect of the rise in each industry's own wage bill (black bars) and the indirect effect of price increases on purchases from others (shading).

bring increases in other costs as well. The advantage of the input-output analysis is that it permits the disentanglement and accurate measurement of the indirect effects. Analyses similar to this one for wages can be carried through for profits, taxes, and other ultimate components of prices.

In such examples changes in the economy over periods of time are measured by comparing before and after pictures. Each is a static model, a cross-section in time. The next step in input-output analysis is the development of dynamic models of the economy to bring the approximations of the method that much closer to the actual processes of economics. This requires accounting for stocks as well as flows of goods, for inventories of goods in process and in finished form, for capital equipment, for buildings, and, last but not least, for dwellings and household stocks of durable consumer goods. The dynamic input-output analysis requires more advanced mathematical methods; instead of ordinary linear equations it leads to systems of linear differential equations.

Among the questions the dynamic system should make it possible to answer, one could mention the determination of the changing pattern of outputs and inventories or investments and capacities that would attend a given pattern of growth in final demand projected over a five- or ten-year period. Within such broad projections, for example, we would be able to estimate approximately not only how much aluminum should be produced but how much additional aluminum-producing capacity would be required and the rate at which such capacity should be installed. The computational task becomes more formidable, but it does not seem to exceed the capacity of the latest electronic computers. Here, as in the case of the static system, the most laborious problem is the assembly of the necessary factual information. However, a complete set of stock or capital ratios, paralleling the flow ratios of all of the productive sectors of the U.S. economy for the year 1939, has now been completed.

This table of capital ratios shows that in addition to the flow of raw pig-iron, scrap, coal, labor, and so on, the steel works and rolling mills industry—when operating to full capacity—required $1800 of fixed investment for each $1000 worth of output. This would include $336 worth of tools, $331 worth of iron and steel foundry production, and so on, down to $26 worth of electrical equipment. This means that in order to expand its capacity so as to be able to increase its output by $1 million worth of finished products annually, the steel works and rolling mills industry would have to install $336,000 worth of tools and spend corresponding amounts on all other types of new fixed installations. This investment demand constitutes, of course, additional input requirements for the product of the corresponding capital goods industries, input requirements that are automatically taken into account in the solution of an appropriate system of dynamic input-output equations.

# 2

## *Input-output analysis*

### ( 1 9 8 5 )

Input-output analysis is a method of systematically quantifying the mutual interrelationships among the various sectors of a complex economic system. In practical terms, the economic system to which it is applied may be as large as a nation or even the entire world economy, or as small as the economy of a metropolitan area or even a single enterprise.

In all instances the approach is essentially the same. The structure of each sector's production process is represented by an appropriately defined vector of structural coefficients that describes in quantitative terms the relationship between the inputs it absorbs and the output it produces. The interdependence among the sectors of the given economy is described by a set of linear equations expressing the balances between the total input and the aggregate output of each commodity and service produced and used in the course of one or several periods of time.

The technical structure of the entire system can accordingly be represented concisely by the matrix of technical input-output coefficients of all its sectors. It constitutes at the same time the set of parameters on which the balance equations are based.

## I. Input-output tables

An input-output table describes the flow of goods and services between all the individual sectors of a national economy over a

This article published as the entry on "Input-Output Analysis" in the *Encyclopedia of Materials Science and Engineering*, Oxford: Pergamon Press, 1985. Reprinted with permission of the publishers.

### Table 2-1

Simplified input-output table for a three-sector economy

| *from*                    | *into*  Sector 1: Agriculture | Sector 2: Manufacture | Sector 3: Households | Total Output         |
|---------------------------|:-----------:|:-----------:|:-----------:|----------------------|
| Sector 1:               |           |           |           |                      |
|   Agriculture  | 25        | 20        | 55        | 100 bushels of wheat |
| Sector 2:               |           |           |           |                      |
|   Manufacture  | 14        | 6         | 30        | 50 yards of cloth    |
| Sector 3:               |           |           |           |                      |
|   Households   | 80        | 180       | 40        | 300 man-years of labor |

stated period of time, say, a year. A simplified example of an input-output table depicting a three-sector economy is shown in Table 2-1. The three sectors are agriculture, whose total annual output amounts to 100 bushels of wheat; manufacture, which produced 50 yards of cloth; and households, which supplied 300 man-years of labor. The nine (3 × 3) entries inside the main body of the table show the intersectoral flows. Of the 100 bushels of farm products turned out by the agriculture, 25 bushels were used up within the agricultural sector itself, 20 were delivered to and absorbed as one of its inputs by manufacture, and 55 were taken by the households sector. The second and third rows of the table describe in the same way the allocation of outputs of the two other sectors.

The figures entered in each column of the table thus describe the input structure of the corresponding sector. To produce the 100 bushels of its total output, agriculture absorbed 25 bushels of its own products, 14 yards of manufactured goods, and 80 man-years of labor received from the households. The manufacturing sector to be able to produce the 50 yards of its total output, had to receive and use up 20 bushels of agricultural—and 6 yards of its own (i.e., of manufactured)—products as well as 180 man-years of labor from households. In their turn, the households have spent the incomes— which they have received for supplying 300 man-years of labor— to pay for the consumption of 55 bushels of agricultural and 30 yards of manufactured commodities and 40 man-years of direct services of labor.

All entries in Table 2-1 are supposed to represent quantities, or at least physical indices of the quantities, of specific goods or services. A less aggregative, more detailed input-output table describing the same national economy in terms of not 3 but of 50, 100, or even 1000 different sectors, would permit a more specific qualitative identification of all the individual entries. In a larger table, manufacturing would, for example, be represented not by one but by many distinct industrial sectors; its output—and consequently also the inputs of the other sectors—would be described in terms of "yards of cotton cloth," "tons of paper products," or even "yards of percale," "yards of heavy cotton cloth," as well as "tons of newsprint" and "tons of writing paper."

## Input-output tables and national income accounts

Although in principle the intersectoral flows as represented in an input-output table can be thought of as being measured in physical units, in practice most input-output tables are constructed in value terms. Table 2-2 represents a translation of Table 2-1 into value terms on the assumption that the price of agricultural products is $2 per bushel, the price of manufactured goods is $5 per yard, and the price of services supplied by the household sector is $1 per man-year. Thus the values of total outputs of the agricultural, the manufacturing, and the households sectors are shown in the new translated table as being equal to, respectively, $200 (= 100 × 2), $250 (= 50 × 5) and $300 (= 300 × 1). The last row shows the combined value of all outputs absorbed by each of the three sectors. Such column totals could not have been shown in Table 2-1 since the physical quantities of different inputs absorbed by each sector cannot be meaningfully added.

The input-output table expressed in value terms can be interpreted as a system of *national accounts.* The $300 showing the value of services rendered by the households over the period of the years obviously represents the annual national income. It equals the sum

### Table 2-2

Simplified input-output table expressed in value terms

| *from* | *into* | Sector 1: Agriculture ($) | Sector 2: Manufacture ($) | Sector 3: Households ($) | Total Output ($) |
|---|---|---|---|---|---|
| Sector 1: Agriculture | | 50 | 40 | 110 | 200 |
| Sector 2: Manufacture | | 70 | 30 | 150 | 250 |
| Sector 3: Households | | 80 | 180 | 40 | 300 |
| Total Input ($) | | 220 | 250 | 300 | |

total of the income payments—shown in row 3—received by the
households for services rendered to each sector; it also equals the
combined value of goods and services—as shown in column 3—
purchased by the households from themselves and from the other
sectors. To the extent to which the column entries (showing the
input structure of each productive sector) cover the current expenditures but not purchases made on capital account, the latter—
being paid out of the net income—should be entered in the households column.

All figures in Table 2-2—except the column sums shown in the
bottom row—can also be interpreted as representing *physical quantities* of the goods or services to which they refer. This only requires
that the physical unit in which the entries in each row are measured
be redefined as being equal to that amount of output of that particular sector that can be purchased for $1 at prices that prevailed dur-
ing the interval of time for which the table was constructed.

National input-output tables are now constructed in some 80
countries. Many regional and metropolitan input-output tables have
also been compiled. The number of sectors that describe the economic system has increased dramatically in recent years. Some of
the more detailed tables describe a national economy in terms of
500 or 600 separate sectors.

## II. Technical coefficients

Let the national economy be subdivided into $n + 1$ sectors; $n$ industries, that is, producing sectors and the $n + 1^{th}$ final demand sector,
represented in input-output Tables 2-1 and 2-2 by the households.
For purposes of mathematical manipulation, the physical output of
sector $i$ is usually represented by $x_i$ while the symbol $x_{ij}$ stands for
the amount of the product of sector $i$ absorbed—as its input—by
sector $j$. The quantity of the product of sector $i$ delivered to the final
demand sector $x_{in+1}$ is usually identified in short as $y_1$.

The quantity of the output of sector $i$ absorbed by sector $j$ *per unit
of its total output $j$* is described by the symbol $a_{ij}$ and is called the
*input coefficient* of product of sector $i$ into sector $j$.

(2-1)                          $$a_{ij} = \frac{x_{ij}}{x_j}$$

A complete set of the input coefficients of all sectors of a given economy arranged in the form of a rectangular table—corresponding to
the input-output table of the same economy—is called the *struc-*

### Table 2-3

Simplified structural coefficient matrix of three-sector economy

| *from* into | Sector 1: Agriculture | Sector 2: Manufacture | Sector 3: Households |
|---|---|---|---|
| Sector 1: Agriculture | 0.25 | 0.40 | 0.133 |
| Sector 2: Manufacture | 0.14 | 0.12 | 0.100 |
| Sector 3: Households | 0.80 | 3.60 | 0.133 |

*tural matrix* of that economy. Table 2-3 represents the structural matrix of the economy whose flow matrix is shown on Table 2-1. The flow matrix constitutes the usual—although not necessarily the only possible—source of empirical information in the input structure of the various sectors of an economy. The entries in Table 2-3 are computed according to formula (2-1) from figures presented in Table 2-2:

$$(2\text{-}1) \qquad a_{11} = \frac{25}{100} = 0.25 \qquad a_{12} = \frac{20}{50} = 0.40 \qquad \text{etc.}$$

In practice the structural matrices are usually computed from input-output tables described in value terms, such as Table 2-2. In any case, the input coefficients—for analytical purposes described below—must be interpreted as ratios of two quantities measured in physical units. To emphasize this fact, we derived the structural matrix (Table 2-3) in this example from Table 2-1, not Table 2-2.

## Static input-output system

The balance between the total output and the combined inputs of the product of each sector, as shown in our example in Tables 2-1 and 2-2, can be described by the following set of $n$ equations:

$$
(2\text{-}2) \qquad
\begin{aligned}
(x_1 - x_{11}) &\quad -x_{12} &\quad - \; \ldots &\quad -x_{1n} = y_1 \\
-x_{21} &+ (x_2 - x_{22}) &\quad - \; \ldots &\quad -x_{2n} = y_2 \\
\ldots &\quad \ldots &\quad \ldots &\quad \ldots \; \ldots \\
-x_{n1} &\quad -x_{n2} &\quad - \; \ldots + (x_n - x_{nn}) &= y_n
\end{aligned}
$$

A substitution of equations (2-1) in (2-2) yields $n$ general equilibrium relationships between the total outputs, $x_1, x_2, \ldots x_n$, of all producing sectors and the final bill of goods, $y_1, y_2, \ldots y_n$, absorbed by households, government, and other final users:

(2-3)
$$
\begin{aligned}
(1 - a_{11})x_1 &\quad - a_{12}x_2 - \ldots \quad - a_{1n}x_n = y_1 \\
-a_{21}x_1 &+ (1 - a_{22})x_2 - \ldots \quad - a_{2n}x_n = y_2 \\
\ldots &\quad\quad \ldots \quad\quad \ldots \quad\quad \ldots \quad .. \\
-a_{n1}x_1 &\quad - a_{n2}x_2 - \ldots + (1 - a_{nn})x_n = y_n
\end{aligned}
$$

If the final demand, $y_1, y_2, \ldots, y_n$, that is, the quantities of all the different kinds of goods absorbed by households and all other sectors whose outputs are not represented by the variables appearing on the left-hand side of equation (2-3), are assumed to be given, the system can be solved for the $n$ total outputs, $x_1, x_2, \ldots, x_n$.

The general solution of these equilibrium equations for the "unknown" $x$'s in terms of the given $y$'s can be presented in the following form:

(2-4)
$$
\begin{aligned}
x_1 &= A_{11}y_1 + A_{12}y_2 + \ldots + A_{1n}y_n \\
x_2 &= A_{21}y_1 + A_{22}y_2 + \ldots + A_{2n}y_n \\
.. &\quad \ldots \quad\quad \ldots \quad\quad \ldots \quad\quad \ldots \\
x_n &= A_{n1}y_1 + A_{n2}y_2 + \ldots + A_{nn}y_n
\end{aligned}
$$

The constant $A_{ij}$ indicates by how much the output $x_i$ of the $i$th sector would increase if $y_j$, that is, the quantity of good $j$ absorbed by households (or any other final users), had been increased by one unit. Such an increase would affect sector $i$ directly (and also indirectly) if $i = j$, but when $i \neq j$ the output $x_i$ is affected only indirectly, since sector $i$ has to provide additional inputs to all other sectors which in their turn—directly or indirectly—must contribute to the increase in the delivery $y_j$ made by sector $j$ to the final users. From the computational point of view, that means that the magnitude of each coefficient $A$ in the "solution" (2-4) in general depends on all the input coefficients $a$ appearing on the left-hand side of the system of equilibrium equations (2-3).

In mathematical language, the matrix

$$
\begin{bmatrix}
A_{11}A_{12} \ldots A_{1n} \\
A_{21}A_{22} \ldots A_{2n} \\
\cdots\cdots\cdots\cdots\cdots \\
A_{n1}A_{n2} \ldots A_{nn}
\end{bmatrix}
$$

of constants appearing on the right-hand side of the solution (2-4) is identified as the inverse of the matrix

$$
\begin{bmatrix}
(1 - a_{11}) & -a_{12} \ldots & -a_{1n} \\
-a_{21} & (1 - a_{22}) \ldots & -a_{2n} \\
\ldots & \ldots\ldots\ldots & \ldots \\
-a_{n1} & -a_{n2} \ldots & (1 - a_{nn})
\end{bmatrix}
$$

of constants appearing on the left-hand side of equations (2-3). The computation involved in finding such a solution is called the *inversion* of the coefficient matrix of these original equations. The inverse of the matrix

$$\begin{bmatrix} (1 - 0.25) & - 0.40 \\ - 0.14 & (1 - 0.12) \end{bmatrix}$$

based on Table 2-3 is

$$\begin{bmatrix} 1.457 & 0.6623 \\ 0.2318 & 1.2417 \end{bmatrix}$$

Inserted in solution (2-4), this yields two equations:

(2-5)
$$x_1 = 1.457y_1 + 0.6623y_2$$
$$x_2 = 0.2318y_1 + 1.2417y_2$$

which permits us to determine what total outputs of agricultural and manufacturing sectors, $x_1$ and $x_2$, would correspond to any given combination and the deliveries of their respective products, $y_1$ and $y_2$, to the exogenous sector, households. To verify this result by comparing them with the corresponding entries in Table 2-1, set $y_1 = 55$ and $y_2 = 30$ on the right-hand sides of the two equations, and they will yield $x_1 = 100$ and $x_2 = 50$ on the left.

Only if all elements $A_{ij}$ of the inverted matrix are nonnegative will there necessarily exist for any given set of final deliveries, $y_1$, $y_2, \ldots, y_n$, a combination of positive total outputs, $x_1, x_2, \ldots, x_n$, capable of satisfying it. A sufficient condition for this is that the determinant of the matrix,

$$\begin{bmatrix} a_{11} & a_{12} & \cdots & a_{1n} \\ a_{21} & a_{22} & \cdots & a_{2n} \\ \cdot & \cdot & & \cdot \\ \cdot & \cdot & & \cdot \\ \cdot & \cdot & & \cdot \\ a_{n1} & a_{n2} & \cdots & a_{nn} \end{bmatrix}$$

and of all its principal submatrices,

$$1 - a_{11} > 0 \quad \begin{bmatrix} (1 - a_{11}) & - a_{12} \\ - a_{21} & (1 - a_{22}) \end{bmatrix} > 0 \cdots \begin{bmatrix} a_{11} & a_{12} & \cdots & a_{1n} \\ a_{21} & a_{22} & \cdots & a_{2n} \\ \cdot & \cdot & & \cdot \\ \cdot & \cdot & & \cdot \\ \cdot & \cdot & & \cdot \\ a_{n1} & a_{n2} & \cdots & a_{nn} \end{bmatrix} > 0$$

should be positive. If this so-called Hawkins-Simon condition is satisfied for one arbitrarily numbered sequence of sectors, it is neces-

sarily satisfied for any other sequence too. The material interpretation of that condition is that if an economic system in which each
sector functions by absorbing output of other sectors directly and
indirectly is to be able not only to sustain itself but also to make
positive delivery to final demand, each one of the smaller and
smaller subsystems contained in it must necessarily be capable of
doing so too. If even one of them cannot pass that test, it is bound
to cause a leak that will destroy the sustainability of the entire
system.

A simpler sufficient, but not necessary, condition of sustainability
of an economy is that the sum of the coefficients of each column of
its structural matrix should be less than or equal to 1, with at least
one of the column sums strictly less than 1.

In most cases in which the structural matrix of a national economy
has been derived from a set of actually observed value flows such as
are represented, for example, in Table 2-2, the condition stated
above will be satisfied.

Since in an open input-output system the households are usually
treated as a final, that is, an exogenous sector, its total output, $x_{n+1}$,
that is, the total employment, usually does not appear as an
unknown variable on the left-hand side of system (2-3) and on the
right-hand side of its solution (2-4). After the outputs of the endogenous sectors, $x_1$, $x_2$, . . . , $x_n$, have been determined, the total
employment can be computed from the following equation:

$$(2\text{-}6) \qquad x_{n+1} = a_{n+1.1}x_1 + a_{n+1.2}x_2 + \ldots + a_{n+1,n}x_n + y_{n+1}$$

The technical coefficients, $a_{n+1.1}$, $a_{n+1.2}$, . . . , $a_{n+1,n}$, represent the
inputs of labor absorbed by various industries (sectors) per unit of
their respective output; $y_{n+1}$ is the total amount of labor directly
absorbed by households and other exogenous sectors. Such an
employment equation constructed for the three sector system with
the structural matrix shown in Table 2-3 is:

$$(2\text{-}7) \qquad x_3 = 0.80x_1 + 3.60x_2 + y_3$$

Households must not necessarily be considered to be part of the
exogenous sectors as they are in the example used above. In dealing
with problems of income generation in its relation to employment,
the quantities of consumer goods and services absorbed by households can be considered to be structurally dependent on the total
level of employment in the same way as the quantities of coke and
ore absorbed by blast furnaces are considered to be structurally
related to the amount of pig iron produced by them. With house-

holds shifted to the left-hand side of equations (2-2) and (2-4), the exogenous final demand appearing on their right-hand side will comprise only such items as governmental purchases and exports and, in any case, additions to or reductions in stocks of goods, that is, real investment or disinvestment.

When all sectors and all purchases are considered to be endogenous, the input-output system is called *closed*. A static system cannot be truly closed, since endogenous explanation of investment or disinvestment requires consideration of structural relationships between inputs and outputs that occur in different periods of time (see "Dynamic Input-Output Analysis," below).

## Exports and imports

In an input-output table of a country or region that trades across its borders, exports can be entered as positive and imports as negative components of final demand. If the economy described in Table 2-1 ceased to be self-sufficient and started to import, say, 20 bushels of wheat and to export 8 yards of cloth—while letting the households consume the same amounts of both products as before—a new balance between all inputs and outputs would be established, as described in Table 2-4.

The input coefficients of the endogenous sectors, and consequently also the structural matrix of the system and its inverse, remain the same as before. To form the new column of final demand, we have to add to the quantity of each good absorbed by the households the amount that was exported and subtract the amount that was imported (i.e., imports can be treated as negative exports):

$$(2-8) \quad y_1 = x_{1 \cdot n + 1} + e_1, \quad y_2 = x_{2 \cdot n + 1} + e_2, \ldots \quad y_n = x_{n \cdot n+1} + e_n$$

### Table 2-4

| from | into | Sector 1: Agriculture | Sector 2: Manufacture | Sector 3: Households | Exports (+) or Imports (−) | Total Final Demand | Total Output |
|------|------|------------------------|------------------------|----------------------|-----------------------------|--------------------|--------------|
| | | | | **Final demand** | | | |
| Sector 1: Agriculture | | 19.04 | 22.12 | 55 | −20 | 35 | 76.16 bushels |
| Sector 2: Manufacture | | 10.66 | 6.64 | 30 | + 8 | 38 | 55.30 yards |
| Sector 3: Households | | 60.93 | 199.07 | 40 | | 40 | 300 man-years |

The corresponding sectoral outputs can then be derived (see above) from the general solution (2-4). For the present numerical example, we can use directly equations (2-5). The total labor requirement of the economy—300 man-years—remains in this particular case unchanged after it enters foreign trade, because the total direct plus indirect labor content of the 20 bushels of imported wheat happens to be equal to the labor content of the 8 yards of exported cloth.

If the imports of good $i$—that is, the negative $e_i$—happens to exceed the final domestic consumption of that good $x_{in}$, the corresponding "net" final demand $y_i$ will turn out to be negative. As $y_i$ diminishes, the total output of all sectors and in particular the total output $x_i$ must (ceteris paribus) diminish. At some point, that output will be reduced to zero, which means that the entire direct and indirect demand for that particular commodity will be covered by imports. The corresponding domestic industry will be automatically eliminated from the endogenous part of the input-output table. The imports of such goods are called noncompeting, particularly when—as in the case of coffee and certain minerals—even a large increase in demand does not call forth their domestic production. The magnitude of total domestic demand for noncompeting imports can be computed in the same way as the total demand for labor can be derived from equation (2-6).

## Prices in an open static input-output system

Prices are determined in an open input-output system from a set of equations which states that the price that each productive sector of the economy receives per unit of its output must equal the total outlays incurred in the course of its production. These outlays comprise not only payments for inputs purchased from the same and from the other industies but also the value added, which essentially represents payments made to the exogenous sectors:

$$
\begin{aligned}
(2\text{-}9) \quad (1 - a_{11})p_1 && - a_{21}p_2 - \ldots && - a_{n1}p_n &= v_1 \\
&- a_{12}p_1 + (1 - a_{22})p_2 - \ldots && - a_{n2}p_n &= v_2 \\
&\ldots \qquad\qquad \ldots \quad \ldots && \ldots \\
&- a_{1n}p_1 && - a_{2n}p_2 - \ldots + (1 - a_{nn})\,p_n &= v_n
\end{aligned}
$$

Each equation describes the balance between the price received and payments made by each endogenous sector per unit of its product; $p_i$ represents the payments made by sector $i$—per unit of its product—to all exogenous (i.e., the final demand) sectors. These usually comprise wages, interest on capital and entrepreneurial revenues credited to households, taxes paid to the government, and other final demand sectors.

In analogy to the solution (2-4) of output equations (2-3), the solution of the price equation (2-9) permits the determination of prices of all products from the given values added (per unit of output) in each sector:

$$
\begin{aligned}
(2\text{-}10) \qquad p_1 &= A_{11}v_1 + A_{21}v_2 + \ldots + A_{n1}v_n \\
p_2 &= A_{12}v_1 + A_{22}v_2 + \ldots + A_{n2}v_n \\
&\quad \cdots \\
p_n &= A_{1n}v_1 + A_{2n}v_2 + \ldots + A_{nn}v_n
\end{aligned}
$$

The constant $A_{ij}$ measures the dependence of the price $p_i$ of the product of sector $j$ on the value added, $v_i$, earned per unit of its output in sector $i$.

Each row of the $a_{ij}$ coefficients appearing in the output equations (2-3) makes up the corresponding column of coefficients appearing in price equations (2-9); the $A_{ij}$ coefficients appearing in each row of the output solution equations (2-4) make up the corresponding coefficient column in the price solution equations (2-10).

Thus, inserting the inverse computed in the example used above in solution (2-10) of the price equation, we have:

$$
\begin{aligned}
(2\text{-}11) \qquad p_1 &= 1.457v_1 + 0.2318v_2 \\
p_2 &= 0.6623v_1 + 1.2417v_2
\end{aligned}
$$

From Tables 2-2 and 2-3 we can see that in our example the values added paid out (i.e., the wages) by agriculture and in manufacture per unit at their respective outputs amounted to $0.8 and $3.6. According to the two equations above, this yields $p_1 = \$2$, $p_2 = \$5$, which are the prices of agricultural and manufactured products used in deriving the value figures presented in Table 2-2 from Table 2-1, which described the input-output flows only in physical units.

The internal consistency of the price and the quantity relationships within an open input-output system is confirmed by the following identity derived from equations (2-4) and (2-9):

$$
(2\text{-}12) \qquad x_1v_1 + x_2v_2 + \ldots + x_nv_n = y_1p_1 + y_2p_2 + \ldots + y_np_n
$$

On the left-hand side stands the sum total of value added paid out by the endogenous to the exogenous sectors of the system; on the right-hand side are the combined values (quantities times prices) of their respective products delivered by all endogenous sectors to the final (exogenous) demand. This identity confirms, in other words, the accounting identity between the national income received and the national income spent, as shown in Table 2-2.

For the purposes of more detailed price analysis, the technical "cooking recipe" for producing, say, one ton of bread not only has to specify the requisite amounts of current inputs such as flour, milk, and yeast, but also has to list needed pots and pans and other kinds of capital goods required for that purpose. Thus the matrix $A$ of technical flow coefficients has to be supplemented by a corresponding matrix of capital stock coefficients, $B$:

$$B = \begin{bmatrix} b_{11} & b_{12} & \dots & b_{1n} \\ b_{21} & b_{22} & \dots & b_{2n} \\ \vdots & \vdots & & \vdots \\ b_{n1} & b_{n2} & \dots & b_{nn} \end{bmatrix}$$

A capital coefficient $b_{ij}$ represents the technologically determined stock of the particular kind of goods—machine tools, industrial buildings, "working inventories" of primary or intermediate materials—produced by industry $i$ that industry $j$ has to employ per unit of its output. In other words, each column of matrix $B$ describes the physical capital requirements (per unit of its total output) of a particular industry, in the same way that the corresponding column of matrix $A$ describes its "current inputs" requirements.

The price analysis outlined above can be advanced one step further by splitting each of the values added, appearing on the right-hand side of each equation in (2-9), into two parts: the returns on capital invested in buildings, machinery, and other stocks of goods required for production of the output in question on the one hand, and wages on the other. The return on capital can be represented as the value (price times quantity) of all productive stocks (used per unit of its output) in each industry multiplied by the given rate of return.

The relationship between wage rates, the rate of return on capital (i.e., the "price" of capital), and the price of different goods and services takes on the following form:

(2-13)                          $P = (1 - A' - rB')^{-1}W$

where $W$ is a column vector of wage costs paid by different industries per unit of their respective outputs.

Insertion in equation (2-13) of the numerical values of the flow coefficient matrix $A'$ as given in Table 2-3 and of capital coefficient matrix $B$ as given above and inverting the bracketed expression on the right-hand side yields an explicit solution of that equation for various values of the rate of return on capital, $r$. For instance,

$$\text{if } r = 10\%$$
$$p_1 = 1.55w + 0.26w_2$$
$$p_2 = 0.76w_1 + 1.34w_r$$

$$\text{if } r = 20\%$$
$$p_1 = 1.65w + 0.30w_r$$
$$p_2 = 0.87w + 1.45w_2$$

The magnitudes of all numerical parameters increase as the value of $r$ is raised from 10 to 20 percent. That means that, with given wage costs $w_1$ and $w_2$, a rise in the rate of return, that is, in the costs of capital, must obviously result in higher prices $p_1$ and $p_2$. With higher prices, the purchasing power of money wages (i.e., the real wages) must necessarily fall.

## III. Dynamic input-output analysis

The following set of linear difference equations represents dynamic input-output relationships employed in description and analysis of the process of economic growth.

$$(2\text{-}14) \qquad X(t) - AX(t) - B[X(t + 1) - X(t)] = Y(t)$$

The column vectors $X(t)$ and $X(t + 1)$ represent the output levels of different industries in time periods $t$ and $t + 1$, while the column vector $Y(t)$ represents the amounts of various goods and services delivered in year $t$ by these producing sectors to households and other final users. $A$ is the matrix of input coefficients referred to above, while $B$ is the matrix of capital coefficients described above.

The balance relationship described by equation (2-14) is based on the assumption that a good added to the capital stock in year $t$ is put to use in the year $t + 1$.

In a closed version of this dynamic system, the final demand sectors are treated as if they were absorbing, like ordinary industries, inputs originating in other sectors and producing outputs—for instance, labor services—that they, in turn, deliver to other sectors. The flow and the capital coefficients reflecting the structure of households, government, and other final demand sectors appear in a closed input-output model on the left-hand side of the dynamic balance equation, side by side with all other industries, so that the column vector $Y(t)$ becomes zero on the right-hand side, its contents having been transferred to the left-hand side.

By setting the determinant of the characteristic matrix $|1 - A - B|$ of the resulting homogeneous system of linear difference equations equal to zero, we can determine the values of its $n$ characteristic roots, $\lambda_{11}, \lambda_{21}, \ldots, \lambda_n$. By the so-called Frobenius theorem, the largest of these roots is necessarily simple and positive, and so are all elements of its characteristic vector.

The reciprocal of that root, $1/\lambda_{max}$, represents the rate at which the closed economy described by dynamic equations will expand, while the relative magnitudes of the elements of the characteristic vector corresponding to that root represent the relative levels of sectoral outputs (including the output of labor produced by households) that have to expand evenly from year to year.

The set of difference equations stating the price relationships corresponding to the physical relationships, described by equation (2-14), has to include, among other cost elements, interest payments on the stock of capital invested in each industry. The "real" rate of interest, that is, the money rate adjusted for the change in the general price level, turns out to be equal to $1/\lambda_{max}$, the growth rate of the economy.

The economy described in the following numerical example has the flow matrix shown in Table 2-2. The capital requirements of its three sectors are represented by the following matrix of capital coefficients:

$$B = \begin{bmatrix} 0.35 & 0.05 & 0.105 \\ 0.01 & 0.515 & 0.32 \\ 0 & 0 & 0 \end{bmatrix}$$

The right-hand column of coefficients describing the capital structure of a household refers to stocks of agricultural products normally held in family larders and textile products stored in linen closets.

Unlike agricultural and manufactured goods produced by the first two sectors, labor services supplied by the third cannot be stored and consequently cannot, according to the definitions used, be part of any capital structure. The bottom row of a $B$ matrix therefore contains only zeros, which means that the matrix $B$ is singular and cannot be inverted.

With only two industries contributing to capital formation, equation (2-14) can be transformed (by expressing the magnitude of the third variable in terms of the other two through the use of the third equation) into a system containing only two linear difference equations of the same general form. Its two roots are those of the original system. In the present example they are found to be 0.39252 and 24.981.

The corresponding eigenvectors of the original three-equation system are

$$\begin{bmatrix} 0.26388 \\ 0.1821 \\ 1.0 \end{bmatrix} \quad \text{and} \quad \begin{bmatrix} -0.041998 \\ 0.25007 \\ 1.00 \end{bmatrix}$$

The reciprocal of the larger of the two roots is $1/24.981 =$ 0.04003. That means that the economy as a whole, that is, all its three sectors, can expand at a rate of 4 percent per annum and that the relative level of their outputs will be proportional year after year to the relative magnitude of the three elements of a characteristic vector corresponding to that root.

The potential growth rate computed on the basis of the reciprocal of the much smaller second root would be much higher. However, since some of the elements of the corresponding characteristic vector have different signs, the output of some sectors would have to become negative with the passage of time, which of course is physically impossible.

Tests based on empirically observed sets of flow and capital coefficients have shown that in both the U.S. and the Japanese economies the relative levels of outputs of different sectors do not deviate very much from those computed on the basis of the corresponding closed dynamic models. Nevertheless, for the purposes of most practical applications, the closed version of the dynamic model has proved to be too deterministic and too rigid; the input-output analysis is usually conducted in terms of the open version of the dynamic model described by equation (2-14). The final bill of goods $Y(t)$ of successive years is treated in this case as given, that is, prescribed or projected on the basis of some exogenous information or assumption. Then the vector $X(0)$ describes the total output level of all producing sectors in the base year 0. The levels of output for subsequent years can be determined by a recursive computation based on rewriting equation (2-14) in the following form:

$$(2-15) \qquad X(1) = B^{-1}[(1 - A + B)X(0) - Y(0)]$$

The following simple example of an open dynamic input-output model is based on information contained in the coefficient matrices $A$ and $B$ used in the example of a closed model above. Since in the present case the vector of final demand is considered as given, the structural relation, if it exists at all, between the output and the input of households is considered to be unknown; only the feedback relationships between the agricultural and the manufacturing sectors have to be taken into account. Accordingly, what might be called the dynamic core of the system to be solved is reduced to only two equations. After insertion of the appropriately reduced matrices $A$ and $B$ into equation (2-15), starting with the given $X(0)$ and using in the successive rounds of computation the externally determined vectors of final demand, $Y(0)$, $Y(1)$ and so on, one can compute, step

## Table 2-5

Simplified example of solution of an open dynamic input-output model

| Year | Final demand Sector 1 | Final demand Sector 2 | Total output Sector 1 | Total output Sector 2 | Investment Sector 1 | Investment Sector 2 | Employment Sector 1 | Employment Sector 2 | Employment Sector 3 (Households) | Employment Total |
|------|------|------|------|------|------|------|------|------|------|------|
| 0 | 55 | 30 | 115 | 60 | 7.3 | 6.7 | 92 | 216 | 11 | 319 |
| 1 | 57.7 | 31.5 | 134 | 73 | 13.6 | 13.7 | 107 | 261 | 12 | 380 |
| 2 | 60.6 | 33.3 | 169 | 99 | 26.8 | 29.9 | 135 | 355 | 12 | 502 |

by step, the levels of output (and investment) of both industries for all the years. The corresponding employment levels are determined by a separate subsidiary computation using labor input coefficients taken from Table 2-2. Some results are shown in Table 2-5.

## IV. Technological change

Since the technological structure of each sector of the economy is represented by a column vector of input coefficients and the corresponding column vector of capital coefficients, technological change can be described concisely as a change in the magnitudes of the elements of these vectors. Introduction of new commodities or industries is represented through introduction of new and disappearance of old commodities (or industries) through elimination of old vectors from the structural matrix of the economy in question.

The choice between two (or more) alternative processes that might be available for production of a particular good or service must obviously be based on a comparison of the effects of a hypothetical shift from one technology to another. For instance, a shift from coal-generated to atomic energy would affect the cost of production, prices, and the level of output and input of goods directly or indirectly. To determine these effects, several input-output computations have to be carried out, each based on the introduction into the flow $(A)$ and into the capital $(B)$ matrix of the economy in question of coefficient vectors characterizing the alternative technologies available for the industries in question. In the case where the choice of appropriate technology can be based on maximizing or minimizing an explicitly defined function of some variable—such as the aggregate input requirements for labor or specific natural resources, investment requirements, or the cost of production of various goods (whose magnitudes can be determined by means of appropriate input-output computations)—it can be formalized and carried out with the help of an appropriate linear programming algorithm. George D. Dantzig, the inventor of the well-known Simplex method of linear programming, actually developed it first as a means of automating input-output computations involving sequential substitution of alternative column vectors into square input-output coefficient matrices.

## V. The scenario approach

Practical application of input-output analysis often takes the form of comparisons of the implications—described in terms of complete projected input-output tables—of several alternative scenarios, each based on a different set of assumptions concerning the level and composition of the final demand, changes in the magnitudes of input coefficients incorporated into various column vectors of the flow and capital coefficient matrices, or a combination of both.

Shortly before the end of World War II, President Franklin D. Roosevelt asked the U.S. Labor Department to assess the probable effect on the American economy of the impending transition from wartime to a peacetime footing. A static input-output model was constructed on the basis of a matrix of structural input coefficients derived from the 1939 input-output table of the American economy, the first such table compiled in the United States under government auspices. A comparison of the output and unemployment levels attained in all industries under war conditions, with the hypothetical output and employment level computed on the assumption that a vector of final demand representing normal civilian consumption would be substituted for the vector of final delivery dominated by military goods, provided a detailed and internally consistent answer to the question raised. To the great surprise of experts who predicted a slump in steel—conventionally considered to be a "war industry"—these input-output computations led to the conclusion that a substitution of a normal peacetime vector for the wartime vector of final demand would lead to a sharp rise in output and employment level in the steel sector. Subsequent development demonstrated that this conclusion was indeed correct.

Many, if not most, studies aimed at assessment of future energy demand and the effects of shift from oil to coal or to atomic power involved the use of supply and demand "elasticities" derived by means of simple or multiple correlation analyses applied to time series describing past changes in energy input, energy prices, and prices of other goods. The contribution of an input-output approach to a consideration of the energy problem consisted, on the other hand, in the construction of several alternative scenarios, each involving a different combination of input-output vectors describing the technical structures of various methods of producing and using energy.

Such computations have shown, for instance, that while alcohol distilled from grain does indeed improve the energy balance of Brazil, it would not do so in the United States. Taking into account the amounts of energy absorbed directly and indirectly in operating agricultural machinery and producing chemical fertilizer in the United States, one finds that more than one thermal unit would be used up to supply one unit in the form of alcohol. A similar computation based on the Brazilian input-output table yields an opposite result.

In this connection it must be pointed out again that such computations necessarily take into account the entire input-output structure of the economy in question, including also that of its foreign trade.

The first practical application of the input-output method to systematic study of materials flow was carried out at the end of World War II in the United States by Western Electric Company. Next to copper, lead was one of the principal materials used at that time to manufacture electric cable. Anticipating a rapid rise in demand for its own products, as well as the products of many other industries depending on supply of that material, the management of that company carried out an input-output projection of production and consumption a few years ahead and came to the conclusion that shortages were bound to develop. On the basis of that finding, Western Electric initiated a crash research program aimed at substituting lead with a suitable plastic material in cable manufacture.

A recent application of the input-output methodology to systematic study of materials use can be found in *The Future of Non-Fuel Minerals in the U.S. and World Economy* (see bibliography at the end of this chapter). It is based on a modified input-output model of the American economy imbedded into the previously constructed multiregional input-output model of the world economy. The core of the structural matrix consists of the official U.S. input matrix with the 5 of its 106 sectors which depict production of nonferrous minerals expanded to 36 sectors describing production and consumption of 26 nonfuel metallic and nonmetallic minerals. Mine output supplemented by product output resulting from other mining operations and reprocessing of scrap is described in the matrix of technical coefficients in great detail.

The system of 321 equations containing 328 variables describing the balance between the total supply including imports, and the total use including exports, of various goods, among them all nonferrous metals in different forms, as well as the generation and elimination of major pollutants and allocation of labor, is presented in a schematic form below.

The system is described by the following set of equations:

(2-16) $\quad (I - A_c) \cdot q_1^{(f)} \qquad\qquad\qquad\quad + I \cdot q_3^{(f)} \qquad\qquad = p_1^{(f)}$

(2-17) $\quad -B_c \cdot q_1^{(f)} + (I + C_c) \cdot q_2^{(f)} \qquad\quad + G_c \cdot q_4^{(f)} \qquad = p_2^{(f)}$

(2-18) $\quad L_c \cdot q_1^{(f)} \qquad\qquad\qquad - I \cdot q_3^{(f)} \qquad\qquad\qquad = p_3^{(f)}$

(2-19) $\quad M_c \cdot q_1^{(f)} + N_c \cdot q_2^{(f)} \qquad\qquad + H_c \cdot q_4^{(f)} \qquad = p_4^{(f)}$

(2-20) $\quad D_c \cdot q_1^{(f)} \qquad\qquad\qquad\qquad\qquad - I \cdot q_5^{(f)} = p_5^{(f)}$

Equation (2-16) states that the gross domestic output of each commodity plus imports minus intermediate consumption must satisfy final demand. Similarly, equation (2-17) states that the domestic output of minerals (own industry plus byproduct) plus competitive imports minus intermediate consumption must equal final demand for minerals. Equation (2-18) states that the level of imports for each commodity is equal to a specified fraction of domestic (own industry) output. Equation (2-19) states the same proposition for noncompetitive minerals (primary and scrap). Equation (2-20) states that the sum of each industry's value added, labor inputs, and emissions "output" equals the respective total for the economy as a whole. As explained previously, noncompetitive imports are goods used to satisfy intermediate or final demand for which there is no corresponding domestic producing sector.

A solution vector has the following form:

$$Q^f = \begin{cases} q_1^{(f)} = \text{a } 106 \times 1 \text{ vector of commodity output levels in time } r \\ q_2^{(f)} = \text{a } 36 \times 1 \text{ vector of mineral and scrap output levels in} \\ \qquad\quad \text{time } t \\ q_3^{(f)} = \text{a } 106 \times 1 \text{ vector of commodity imports levels in time } t \\ q_4^{(f)} = \text{a } 39 \times 1 \text{ vector of mineral and scrap import levels in} \\ \qquad\quad \text{time } t \\ q_5^{(f)} = \text{a } 34 \times 1 \text{ vector of value added, labor requirements,} \\ \qquad\quad \text{energy consumption, pollution emission and new scrap} \\ \qquad\quad \text{generation levels in time } t \end{cases}$$

and:

$$P^{(f)} = \begin{cases} \end{cases}$$

$p_1^{(f)}$ = a 106 × 1 vector of final demand components minus imports for 106 commodities valued in dollars for time $t$

$p_2^{(f)}$ = a 36 × 1 vector of final demand components minus imports for 36 mineral commodities in physical units for time $t$

$p_3^{(f)}$ = a 106 × 1 null vector

$p_4^{(f)}$ = a 39 × 1 vector with zeros everywhere except in rows 253, 254, 265, and 288, whose elements give final demand minus import levels for noncompetitive imports in time $t$

$p_5^{(f)}$ = a 34 × 1 null vector

The symbols used in equations (2-16) through (2-20) follow:

$A_c$     a commodity-by-commodity-matrix of input-output coefficients (106 × 106) whose elements $a_{ij}^{(c)}$ give dollar amounts of input $i$ required to produce one dollar's worth of output $j$ (valued in base year prices).

$0$     a null matrix or vector.

$I$     an identity matrix.

$-B_c$     an input-output coefficient matrix (36 × 106) whose elements $b_{ij}^{(c)}$ give the physical amount of mineral (primary or scrap) input $i$ required to produce one dollar's worth of output $j$ (only minerals produced in the United States are included in this submatrix).

$C_c$     a diagonal byproduct coefficients matrix (36 × 36) whose elements $c_{ij}^{(c)}$ give the physical amount of each mineral (primary or scrap) produced as a byproduct per physical unit of its own-industry output.

$G_c$     a step-diagonal matrix (36 × 40) whose nonzero elements $g_{ij}^{(c)} = 1$.

$L_c$     a diagonal import coefficient matrix (106 × 106) whose elements $l_{ij}^{(c)}$ give the dollar amount of imports per dollar's worth of $j$ $(i = j)$.

$M_c$     a matrix (39 × 106) whose only nonzero elements appear in IEA-USMIN rows 253, 254, 265, and 288; the elements of these four rows, $m_{ij}^{(c)}$, give the physical or dollar amount of noncompetitive import $i$ per dollar's worth of output $j(i = j)$.

$N_c$     a step-diagonal matrix (39 × 36) whose nonzero elements $n_{ij}^{(c)}$ give the physical amount of mineral (primary or scrap) $i$ imported per physical unit of mineral $j$'s own-industry output $(i = j)$.

$H_c$     a diagonal matrix (39 × 39) whose nonzero elements $h_{ij}^{(c)} = -1$, except in rows 253, 254, and 288, where $h_{ij}^{(c)} = 1$.

$D_c$     a matrix (34 × 106) whose elements $d_{ij}$ give the amounts in dollars or physical units of value added, labor, energy, pollution emissions, and new scrap associated with a dollar's worth of output of commodity $j$.

Such a system of equations was solved (to check its internal consistency) for the base year 1972 and for the years 1980, 1990, 2000, and 2030. Systematic projections of future changes in all sets of technological coefficients, particularly those reflecting efficient methods of extraction and refining and substitution between different materials were the most demanding part of that task. The estimates of future changes in the exports and imports (that enter into the system as vectors of exogenously determined variables) were obtained by incorporating the system into the multiregional input-output analysis of the world economy constructed for the United Nations several years earlier.

Alternative projections were computed, based on 11 different scenarios. Each of these represented a different combination of specific assumptions concerning the dependence of the U.S. economy on imports of nonferrous metals and future rates of technological change. Final conclusions were summarized in the form of separate observations on the present and expected future supply and demand for each nonferrous mineral on the domestic U.S. and international markets.

One of the most ambitious applications of the input-output approach was the construction of a multiregional, multisectoral, dynamic input-output model of the entire world economy referred to above. That model was employed in the preparation of long-run projections based on alternative scenarios of prospective developments of the economic relationship between the developed and less developed regions. It also provided the basis for long-run projections of the economic growth (or decline as the case may be) of the various regions under alternative assumptions concerning population growth, technical change—particularly in the field of agriculture and energy production—and in the uncertain supply of various natural resources.

## Selected bibliography for chapter 2

Carter, Anne P. *Structural Change in the American Economy.* Cambridge: Harvard University Press, 1970.

Davis, Craig H., and Everard M. Lofting. *Development of Interindustry Transactions Data on the Structure of United States Mining Industries for 1967 and a Comparison of Techniques for Updating Related Input-Output Coefficients.* Washington, D.C.: U.S. Department of the Interior, NTIS: PB 80-161425, April 30, 1979.

Leontief, W. "The Dynamic Inverse." In *Contributions to Input-Output Analysis*, edited by A.P. Carter and A. Brody, Amsterdam: North-Holland, 1970.

————. *Input-Output Economics.* New York: Oxford University Press, 1966.

————. *The Structure of the American Economy, 1919–39.* Reprinted by International Arts & Sciences Press (now M. E. Sharpe. Inc.), White Plains, N.Y., 1977.

Leontief, W., et al. *Studies in the Structure of the American Economy.* Reprinted by International Arts & Sciences Press (now M. E. Sharpe, Inc.), White Plains, N.Y., 1977.

Leontief, W., Anne Carter, and Peter Petri. *The Future of the World Economy.* New York: Oxford University Press, 1977.

Leontief, W., J. Koo, S. Nasar, and I. Sohn. *The Future of Non-Fuel Minerals in the U.S. and World Economy.* Lexington, Mass.: Lexington Books, D. C. Heath & Co., 1983.

# 3

## *An alternative to aggregation in input–output analysis and national accounts*

## ( 1 9 6 7 )

### I

The schematic uniformity of standard input-output computations accounts for certain practical advantages of that approach as well as for some of its peculiar limitations. One of the principal advantages of such uniformity is the opportunity it offers for using the matrix of technical coefficients, $A$, as a central storage bin for the basic factual information used again and again in various computations.

A comparison of the structural properties of two economies—or of the structural characteristics of the same economy at two different points of time—is reduced in this context to a comparison of two $A$ matrices. The only (and admittedly very serious) difficulty arising in any attempt to ascertain the differences and similarities between the magnitudes of individual technical coefficients—or of the whole rows, or entire columns of such coefficients—in two matrices is often caused by the incomparability of the sectoral breakdown in terms of which the two tables were originally compiled.

These differences might turn out to be of a merely terminological or classificatory kind. This means that, in principle at least, with full access to all the basic facts and figures, new matrices could be constructed that would describe the two essentially comparable economic structures in appropriately comparable terms.

The lack of perfect correspondence between the sectoral head-

From *The Review of Economics and Statistics* 49 (3), August 1967.
I want to express my thanks to the staff of the Harvard Economic Research Project and particularly to Brooks Byrd for the indispensable assistance in the preparation of the material presented in this paper. Frankly, the responsibility for the minor errors that might have crept into it rests with them.

ings of two input-output tables might, however, frequently reflect the presence in one of the two economies of some goods or services that are neither produced nor consumed in the other. In this instance, reclassification will not help. In the extreme, albeit most unlikely, case in which the two economies have no goods or services in common, the very thought of structural comparison would have to be given up.

More often, when all the justifiable preliminary realignments of the original classifications have been made, the two matrices will turn out to have some reasonably comparable sectors, while some of the other sectors contained in one of them will have no matching counterparts in the other. Even when such incomparability is known to be caused only by differences in the commodity and industry classifications used, the figures centered in those rows and columns must be treated as describing structures of incomparable kinds.

In current statistical practice, the solution of the difficulties described above is sought in aggregation. The difference between copper and nickel vanishes as soon as both are treated as "nonferrous metals," and both become indistinguishable from steel as soon as the qualifying specification "nonferrous" has been dropped too. The fact that comparability through aggregation is secured at the cost of analytical sharpness in the description of the underlying structural relationships is too well known to require explanation.

The method of double inversion described below permits us to reduce to a common denominator two input-output matrices that contain some comparable and also some incomparable sectors. In contrast to conventional aggregation, such analytical reduction is achieved without distortion of any of the basic structural relationships. The comparability of input-output tables attained through double inversion is limited in the sense that their respective structures are described only in terms of input-output relationships between goods and services of directly comparable kinds. It is, nevertheless, an overall comparability to the extent that all the structural characteristics of each of the two systems, including the magnitudes of the technical coefficients located in the "incomparable" rows and columns, are taken into account fully without omission or distortion.

## II

To facilitate the intuitive understanding of the transformation that leads to the construction of what might be called a reduced input-output matrix of a national economy, we will ask the reader to visualize a situation in which—for trading purposes—all industries of a country have been divided into two groups. The industries belonging to group I are identified as "contracting," and those in group II as "subcontracting" industries.

Each contracting (group I) industry covers its direct input requirements for the products of other group I industries by direct purchases, and each group II industry makes direct purchases from other group II industries. However, the products of group II industries delivered to group I industries are manufactured on the basis of special work contracts. Under such a contract, the group I industry placing an order with a group II industry provides the latter with the products of all group I industries (including its own), in amounts required to fill that particular order. To be able to do so, it purchases all these goods—from the group I industries that make them—on its own account. The relationship between a contracting (group I) and a subcontracting (group II) industry is thus analogous to the relationship between a customer who buys the cloth himself and the tailor who makes it up for him into a suit.

In determining the amounts of goods and services that he will have to purchase from his own and all the other group I industries, the procurement officer of each group I industry will have to add to the immediate input requirements of his own sector the amounts to be processed for it—under contract—by various group II industries. For all practical purposes, such augmented shopping lists now constitute the effective input vectors of all the group I industries.

The square array of $n_1$ such column vectors—each containing $n_1$ elements (some of which may, of course, be zero)—represents the reduced table of input coefficients that we seek. It describes the same system as the original table; however, it describes it only in terms of goods and services produced by the selected contracting industries included in group I.

The relationship between the two tables is similar to the relationship of an abbreviated timetable that lists only selected large stations to the complete, detailed timetable that also shows all the intermediate stops. The subdivision of all the sectors of an economy into groups I and II must, of course, depend on the specific purpose the consolidated system is intended to serve.

Using a reduced table for planning purposes, we can be sure that if the input-output flows among the group I industries shown in it are properly balanced, the balance between the outputs and inputs of all the group II industries omitted from it will also be secured.

In the process of consolidation, the allocation of so-called primary inputs will change as well. The new labor and capital coefficients of each group I industry must now reflect not only its own immediate labor and capital requirements but also the labor and capital requirements of all the group II industries from which it draws some of its supplies. It is as if, under the imaginary contractual arrangements described above, each group I industry had to provide the group II industries working for it, not only with the goods and services produced by any of the group I sectors, but also with all the capital and labor required by these group II industries to fulfill these contracts. Thus, the output levels of all the group I industries, as projected on the basis of a reduced input-output table (multiplied with the appropriate consolidated capital and labor coefficients), will account not only for the capital and labor requirements of these group I industries but also for those of all the group II industries without whose support these output levels could not have been attained.

## III

Not unlike conventional aggregation, the analytical procedure described below is aimed at a reduction of the number of sectors in terms of which the particular economic structure was originally described. It is, however, a "clean"—not an index number—operation. It does not involve introduction of weights or any other arbitrary constants.

Equation (3-1) describes—in conventional matrix notation—the relationships between the total output vector, $X$, of all the sectors of a particular economy and the corresponding final bill of goods, $Y$.

(3-1) $$(I - A)X = Y$$

In equation (3-2), both vectors are split into two parts: the column vectors $X_1$ and $Y_1$ represent the total outputs and the final deliveries of group I industries that produce the $n_1$ goods that will be retained in the reduced matrix, while $X_2$ and $Y_2$ represent the outputs and the final deliveries of all the other, (the $n_2$) goods produced by the group II industries that have to be eliminated.

(3-2) $$\left[ \begin{array}{c|c} (I - A_{11}) & -A_{12} \\ \hline -A_{21} & (I - A_{22}) \end{array} \right] \left[ \begin{array}{c} X_1 \\ X_2 \end{array} \right] = \left[ \begin{array}{c} Y_1 \\ Y_2 \end{array} \right]$$

The matrix $(I - A)$ on the left-hand side is partitioned, in conformity with the output vector into which it is multiplied. $A_{11}$ and $A_{22}$ are square matrices whose elements are technical coefficients that govern the internal flows between the sectors of the first and of the second groups, respectively, while $A_{12}$ and $A_{21}$ are rectangular (not necessarily square) matrices describing the direct requirements of industries of the second group for outputs of the first group, and vice versa.

Equation (3-3) is the solution of (3-2) for $X$ in terms of $Y$.

$$(3\text{-}3) \qquad \left[\frac{X_1}{X_2}\right] = \left[\begin{array}{c|c} B_{11} & B_{12} \\ \hline B_{21} & B_{22} \end{array}\right] \left[\frac{Y_1}{Y_2}\right]$$

Matrix $B$ is the *inverse* of $(I - A)$. It is partitioned in conformity with the partitioning of $(I - A)$ in equation (3-2). After the multiplication has been carried out on its right-hand side, equation (3-3) can be split in two:

$$(3\text{-}4) \qquad X_1 = B_{11}Y_1 + B_{12}Y_2$$
$$(3\text{-}5) \qquad X_2 = B_{21}Y_1 + B_{22}Y_2$$

Premultiplying both sides of (3-4) by $B_{11}^{-1}$, we have:

$$(3\text{-}6) \qquad B_{11}^{-1}X_1 = Y_1 + B_{11}^{-1}B_{12}Y_2$$

This equation can be interpreted as a reduced version of the original system (3-2). It describes the same structural relationships; however, it represents them only in terms of the goods and services produced by the $n_1$ industries assigned to group I. The variables contained in vector $X_2$—that is, the outputs of the $n_2$ industries assigned to group II—have been eliminated by means of two successive matrix inversions that led from (3-2) to (3-6).

Let a new structural matrix and a new final demand vector be defined by:

$$(3\text{-}7) \qquad A_{11}^\circ = I - B_{11}^{-1}$$
$$(3\text{-}8) \qquad Y_1^\circ = Y_1 + B_{11}^{-1}B_{12}Y_2$$

In this notation (3-6) can be rewritten as:

$$(3\text{-}9) \qquad (I - A_{11}^\circ)X_1 = Y_1^\circ$$

In perfect analogy with the original system (3-1), this equation describes the input-output relationships between the redefined vec-

tor of final deliveries, $Y_1^*$, and the corresponding vector of total outputs $X_1$.[1] Solved for $X_1$ in terms of $Y_1^*$, it yields:

$$(3\text{-}10) \qquad\qquad X_1 = (I - A_{11}^*)^{-1} Y_1^*$$

This equation is, of course, formally equivalent to (3-4). $A_{11}^*$ is the
structural matrix of the economy that was originally described by $A$.
However, the same structure is now described in terms of the $n_1$
group I industries alone. The first column of $A_{11}^*$ consists, for example, of $n_1$ technical coefficients, $a_{11}^*, a_{21}^*, \ldots, a_{n1}^*$, showing the number of units of each of these $n_1$ industries of group I required per
unit of the total output, $x_1$, of the first. Although not referring to
them explicitly, implicitly these coefficients reflect the input
requirements also of the other $n_2$ industries eliminated in the reduction process.

Let, for example, industry 1 produce "steel" and industry 2
"electric energy," both assigned to group I. In the reduced matrix
$A_{11}^*$, the coefficient $a_{21}^*$ thus represents the number of kilowatt-hours
(or a dollar's worth) of electricity required to produce a ton (or a
dollar's worth) of steel. This requirement is computed to cover not
only the direct deliveries of electricity from generating stations to
steel plants but also the indirect deliveries channeled through industries assigned to group II. If "iron mining" for instance, were considered as belonging to group II, the electricity used in extraction
and preparation of the iron ore that went into the production of one
ton (or a dollar's worth) of steel would also be included in the input
coefficient $a_{21}^*$, and so would electric power absorbed by the steel
industry via all other sectors assigned to group II.

In other words, the array of the input coefficients (with asterisks)
that make up the first column of matrix $A_{11}^*$ describes the combination of the products of industries included in group I with which the
economy in question would be capable of turning out a ton (or a
dollar's worth) of steel. Some of these inputs reach the steel industry
indirectly through industries assigned to group II.

The reduced structural matrix $A_{11}^*$ describes explicitly only the
input structure of the group I industries and this only in terms of
their own products. Implicitly, it reflects nevertheless the technological characteristics of all the other industries as well. The relationship between elements of the reduced and the original matrix is

---

[1] The symbol $X_1^*$ is not used because the reduced system has been derived in such a way
that $X_1 \equiv X_1^*$.

displayed clearly if $A_{11}^{\circ}$ is expressed directly in terms of the elements of the partitioned matrix $A$:[2]

$$(3\text{-}11) \qquad A_{11}^{\circ} = A_{11} + A_{12}(I - A_{22})^{-1}A_{21}$$

The well-known sufficient conditions for the ability of the given input-output system to maintain—without drawing on outside help—a positive level of final consumption, (that is, to possess a positive inverse $(I - A)^{-1}$, requires that none of the column (or row) totals of the technical coefficients in $A_{11}$ exceed one and at least one of these sum totals be less than one. This implies that the inverse $(I - A)^{-1}$ is nonnegative. All components of the second term on the right-hand side of (3-11) being either zero or positive, each element $a_{ij}^{\circ}$ of the consolidated structural matrix has to be either equal to or larger than the corresponding originally given input coefficient, $a_{ij}$.

The final deliveries on the right-hand side of the reduced system (3-6) are composed of two parts. Vector $Y_1$ is the demand for the products of the group I industries as it appears in the original system (3-2). Vector $B_{11}^{-1}B_{12}Y_2$ ($\equiv A_{12}(I - A_{22})^{-1}Y_2$) represents the final demand for the products of the second group of goods translated into the requirements for inputs of goods belonging to the first. In the special case in which the final users happen to demand directly only commodities and services of group I, while group II consists exclusively of intermediate goods, $Y_2$ vanishes and, save for the omission of its zero components, the final deliveries vector of the original system would enter without any change into the smaller, reduced system, too.

## IV

A primary input, such as labor, a natural resource, or—in a static system—a stock of some kind of capital goods, can be treated in the process of reduction as if it were a product of a separate industry included in group I.

[2]Since $B = (I - A)^{-1}$,

$$B(I - A) = I$$

In particular:

$$B_{11}(I - A_{11}) - B_{12}A_{21} = I$$
$$-B_{11}A_{12} + B_{12}(I - A_{22}) = 0$$

Eliminating $B_{12}$ and rearranging yields:

$$A_{11}^{\circ} = I - B_{11}^{-1} = A_{11} + A_{12}(I - A_{22})^{-1}A_{21}$$

The row assigned to each primary factor in the original matrix $A$ will contain the appropriate technical input coefficients: labor coefficients, capital coefficients, and so on. The columns corresponding to these rows will consist of zeros, since, in contrast to other goods and services, the output of a primary factor is not considered to be formally dependent on inputs originating in other industries.[3]

The labor, capital, and other primary factor coefficients appearing in the appropriate rows of matrix $A^*$ will never be smaller—and in most instances they will be larger—than the corresponding elements of the original matrix $A$. As all the other input coefficients in the reduced system, they cover not only the immediate requirements of each group I industry but also the labor and capital employed by group II industries (eliminated in the process of analytical reduction) from which that industry receives all its group II supplies.

## V

Any static input-output system implies the existence of linear relationships between the prices of all products and the "value added" in all the sectors per unit of their respective outputs.[4] While a reduction of a structural matrix eliminates some of the prices from the picture, it leaves the relationship between the remaining prices and the values added essentially intact.

Let $P$ be the price vector of the original system and $V$ the vector of values added per unit of output in its $n$ different sectors. The basic relationships between the two vectors,

$$(3\text{-}12) \qquad\qquad (I - A')P = V$$

can be solved for the unknown prices in terms of given values added:

$$(3\text{-}13) \qquad \begin{bmatrix} P_1 \\ P_2 \end{bmatrix} = \begin{bmatrix} B'_{11} & B'_{21} \\ B'_{12} & B'_{22} \end{bmatrix} \begin{bmatrix} V_1 \\ V_2 \end{bmatrix}$$

The primes above the $B$s indicate transposition, that is, permutation of rows and columns. The partitioning of the two vectors and of

---

[3]The matrix $(I - A)$ is nevertheless not singular: its main diagonal contains positive elements throughout.

[4]The "value added" in any industry can, in its turn, be described as a sum of the input coefficients of all factors multiplied by their respective prices augmented by the amount of positive or negative net surplus earned per unit of its output.

the structural matrix corresponds to a similar partitioning in (3-3) above. Solving for $P_1$ we have:

(3-14)                          $P_1 = B'_{11}V^\circ_1$, where
(3-15)                          $V^\circ_1 = V_1 + (B'_{11})^{-1}B'_{21}V_2$

The last equation shows that, analogous to the reduced final bill of goods $Y^\circ_1$ in (3-8), $V^\circ_1$ represents the augmented values-added vector of the group I industries. Each element of that augmented vector contains not only the value added—shown for each one of them in the original table—but also the value added in group II industries imputed through all the goods and services the particular group I sector receives from them. In view of (3-7), (3-14) can be rewritten as:

(3-16)                          $P_1 = (I - A^{\circ\prime})^{-1}V^\circ_1$

Inserting on the right-hand side the augmented values added in group I industries, we obtain on the left-hand side a set of prices identical with those that would have been derived from group I outputs from the original (unreduced) set of price equations (3-13) through (3-15).

# VI

A recently completed study of metalworking industries called for analysis of interdependence among the several branches of production belonging to this group and for an assessment of its position within the U.S. national economy as a whole. Of the 73 producing sectors in the 1958 input-output table,[5] 23 are making or transforming metals, 5 of them supply intermediate ferrous or nonferrous products, while the other 18 are engaged in the manufacture of basic materials and finished metal goods.

The immediate technical interdependence among the 23 metalworking sectors is reflected in the magnitude of the input coefficients located on the intersections of the 23 rows and the corresponding 23 columns in the large 73-sector table mentioned above.

The production of the nonmetal inputs absorbed by metalworking industries often requires the use of various metal products in its turn. The dependence of each metalworking sector upon all the others (taking into account such indirect requirements) is described by

[5]U.S. Department of Commerce, *Survey of Current Business* 44 (11), November 1964; and Anne P. Carter, "Changes in the Structure of the American Economy, 1974–1958, 1962," *Review of Economics and Statistics* XLIX, May 1967.

the augmented input coefficients entered in the 23 rows and columns of the reduced matrix that was obtained through analytical elimination of all 50 nonmetalworking sectors from the original table. The full interdependence among the 18 metalworking industries engaged in the manufacture of raw and finished metal products can be brought out through further reduction that also eliminates from the large table the five intermediate metalworking industries.

A row of labor coefficients and another of (total) capital coefficients were added at the outset to the original 73-sector matrix. After reduction, appropriately augmented labor and capital coefficients appeared in the last two rows of both reduced matrices as well.

In Table 3-1, the technical coefficients describing the inputs of various metal products required by the "motor vehicles and equipment" industry as they appear in the original 73-sector matrix are shown in the first column. The second column contains the corresponding augmented coefficients as they appear in the reduced matrix composed of the 23 metalworking sectors. The third column shows the 18 still more augmented coefficients as they appear in the "motor vehicles and equipment" column of a reduced matrix, from which the five basic metalworking industries were also eliminated. Appropriate labor and capital coefficients are entered at the bottom of all three columns.

# VII

Table 3-2 is an example of a reduced national input-output table. This complete but compact flow chart was derived from the official 1958 U.S. table[6] in two successive steps.

First, 34 of the 83 productive sectors of the original table were combined into eight groups. The resulting smaller 57-sector table contained these eight aggregated industries, the 49 sectors carried over from the original 83-order table, a corresponding column of final demand, and a value-added row.

This 57-sector table was reduced in a second step, through elimination of all 49 nonaggregated industries, to a compact 8-sector table. It should be noted that the figures shown in Table 3-2 are total flows, not input coefficients. They were obtained through multiplication of all elements of each column of the corresponding reduced

---

[6]U.S. Department of Commerce, *Survey of Current Business* 45 (9), September 1965.

**Table 3-1** Input coefficients describing the requirements of the motor vehicles and equipment industry for products from other U.S. metalworking industries[a] in 1958

| Sector number in the 73-sector matrix | Industry | original 73-sector matrix[b] | Input coefficients in the reduced 23-sector matrix[c] | reduced 18-sector matrix |
|---|---|---|---|---|
| 59 | Motor vehicles and equipment | 0.29757 | 0.29817 | 0.29991 |
| 37 | Primary iron and steel manufacturing | 0.08780 | 0.08874 | 0.10714 |
| 42 | Other fabricated metal products | 0.03603 | 0.03713 | |
| 41 | Screw machine products, bolts, nuts, etc., metal stamping | 0.03103 | 0.03137 | |
| 47 | General industrial and metalworking machinery and equipment | 0.02364 | 0.02456 | |
| 58 | Miscellaneous electrical machinery equipment and supplies | 0.01543 | 0.01557 | 0.01564 |
| 38 | Primary nonferrous metals manufacturing | 0.01144 | 0.01205 | 0.01871 |
| 56 | Radio, television, and communication equipment | 0.00523 | 0.00557 | 0.00576 |
| 62 | Professional, scientific, and control instruments and supplies | 0.00438 | 0.00460 | 0.00498 |
| 55 | Electric lighting and wiring equipment | 0.00420 | 0.00441 | 0.00475 |
| 43 | Engines and turbines | 0.00379 | 0.00402 | 0.00437 |
| 53 | Electrical industrial equipment | 0.00217 | 0.00236 | |
| 52 | Service industrial machinery, household appliances | 0.00129 | 0.00157 | 0.00208 |
| 44 | Farm machinery and equipment | 0.00105 | 0.00129 | 0.00144 |
| 40 | Heating, plumbing, and structural metal products | 0.00102 | 0.00147 | 0.00245 |
| 64 | Miscellaneous manufacturing | 0.00092 | 0.00201 | 0.00143 |
| 61 | Transportation equipment, miscellaneous | 0.00089 | 0.00123 | 0.00111 |
| 57 | Electronic components and accessories | 0.00079 | 0.00090 | 0.00094 |
| 45 | Construction, mining, oil field machinery and equipment | 0.00044 | 0.00062 | 0.00123 |
| 60 | Aircraft and parts | 0.00039 | 0.00086 | |
| 46 | Materials handling machinery and equipment | 0.00022 | 0.00027 | 0.00046 |
| 63 | Optical, ophthalmic, photographic equipment | 0.00005 | 0.00045 | 0.00053 |
| 51 | Office, computing, and accounting machines | 0.00000 | 0.00069 | 0.00079 |
| | Labor | 0.02645 | 0.04729 | 0.05614 |
| | Capital stock | 0.24313 | 0.47495 | 0.55890 |

[a]Units of measurement: for labor coefficients, man-years per $1000 of output; for all other coefficients, 1958 dollars per dollar of output.
[b]This matrix is based on the 1958 input-output table published by the Office of Business Economics, Department of Commerce. See Anne Carter, "Changes in the Structure of the American Economy," *Review of Economics and Statistics* XLIX, May 1967. The labor coefficients are based on Jack Alterman, "Inter-industry Employment Requirements," *Monthly Labor Review*, 88 (7), July 1965. The capital coefficients for manufacturing sectors were obtained from Robert Waddell, Philip Ritz, John DeWitt Norton, and Marshall K. Wood, *Capital Expansion Planning Factors, Manufacturing Industries* (Washington, D.C.: National Planning Association, April 1966). For nonmanufacturing sectors, the capital coefficients were compiled at the Harvard Economic Research Project.
[c]The sectors eliminated through the reduction procedure are those included in the 73-sector input-output table but not represented in this column of augmented coefficients.

**Table 3-2** Input-output table of the U.S. economy for the year 1958 reduced to 8 from 57 producing sectors[a]

| Column row | Industry | Food and Drugs (1) | House-wares (2) | Machinery (3) | Trans. Equip. & Consum. Appl. (4) | Construction (5) | Metals (6) | Energy (7) | Chemicals (8) | Final Demand | Gross Domestic Output |
|---|---|---|---|---|---|---|---|---|---|---|---|
| 1 | Food and drugs | 15,202 (12,468) | 547 (96) | 161 (11) | 353 (49) | 513 (17) | 165 (53) | 218 (62) | 386 (288) | 58,728 (55,320) | 76,272 |
| 2 | Textiles, clothing, and furnishings | 347 (155) | 12,815 (12,692) | 92 (37) | 821 (636) | 761 (524) | 171 (47) | 63 (8) | 61 (38) | 21,369 (20,033) | 36,500 |
| 3 | Machinery | 430 (28) | 215 (105) | 2,321 (2,186) | 2,061 (1,644) | 1,397 (748) | 819 (545) | 406 (141) | 200 (150) | 13,385 (11,293) | 21,233 |
| 4 | Transportation equipment and consumer appliances | 363 (29) | 158 (55) | 816 (691) | 11,791 (11,196) | 1,372 (753) | 485 (101) | 183 (29) | 53 (5) | 38,691 (32,670) | 53,912 |
| 5 | Construction | 1,158 (235) | 218 (18) | 115 (26) | 308 (109) | 48 (8) | 284 (131) | 1,541 (579) | 70 (6) | 65,117 (56,836) | 69,291 |
| 6 | Metals | 1,033 (46) | 475 (277) | 3,073 (2,631) | 6,038 (4,618) | 6,468 (3,650) | 7,959 (7,335) | 388 (110) | 479 (389) | 2,244 (−45) | 28,158 |
| 7 | Energy | 2,158 (783) | 652 (293) | 371 (226) | 805 (404) | 2,774 (1,536) | 1,704 (1,391) | 6,888 (6,236) | 1,127 (1,007) | 23,851 (17,702) | 40,330 |
| 8 | Chemicals | 1,956 (1,056) | 1,030 (218) | 201 (117) | 475 (115) | 1,218 (437) | 459 (283) | 713 (576) | 2,500 (2,351) | 3,218 (1,510) | 11,770 |
| | Value added | 53,625 (22,252) | 20,390 (12,844) | 14,083 (10,254) | 31,260 (20,677) | 54,308 (28,937) | 16,112 (10,509) | 29,930 (15,127) | 6,894 (4,674) | 178,912 | 405,515 |
| Total | | 76,272 | 36,500 | 21,233 | 53,912 | 69,291 | 28,158 | 40,330 | 11,770 | 405,515 | |
| | Labor | 8,182 (2,202) | 3,929 (2,808) | 1,820 (1,307) | 3,891 (2,467) | 8,581 (4,847) | 1,867 (1,155) | 1,755 (1,003) | 671 (403) | 26,430 | 57,146 |

[a]Derived from the 83-sector table published in "Transaction Table of the 1958 Input-Output Study and Revised Direct Requirements Data," *Survey of Current Business* 45 (9), September 1969. Each of the 8 sectors of the intermediate 57-sector table retained in this reduced table represents an aggregate of the following industries identified by the numbers they carry in the original 83-sector table:

(1) Food and drugs: 14, 15, 29; (2) textiles, clothing, furnishings: 16, 17, 18, 19, 34, 22, 23; (3) machinery (only final): 51, 44, 45, 46, 47, 48, 49, 50, 63; (4) transportation equipment and consumer appliances: 52, 54, 56, 59, 60, 61, 62; (5) construction: 11, 12; (6) metals: 37, 38; (7) energy: 31, 68; (8) chemicals: 27.
Corresponding entries in the unreduced 57-sector table appear in parentheses. The units are man-years in the labor row and millions of dollars in all other rows.

coefficient matrix by the given total output figure of the industry, the input structure of which that particular column describes.

Table 3-2 thus depicts the structure of the American economy in terms of flows of commodities and services among eight industrial sectors, a value-added row, and a column of final demand, both reduced in conformity with the rest of the table [see equation (3-8)]. Wages and salaries paid out by various sectors are, of course, included in the value-added row. In addition, a separate row of labor inputs, measured in man-years, was carried along through all computations. This row is reproduced separately at the bottom of the table.

In each cell of the table, below the number describing the appropriately augmented intersectoral transaction, another figure, enclosed in parentheses, is entered. This number represents the magnitude of the input—from the sector named on the left to the sector identified at the head of the column—as it appeared in the unreduced 57-sector table obtained at the end of the first step, that is, before the 49 unaggregated sectors were eliminated from the table in the second step.

In the final demand column, the larger entries represent the augmented deliveries to households, government, and other final users, while the entries in parentheses show the corresponding figures as they appeared in the 57-sector table. The first entry exceeds, in each instance, the figure in parentheses below by the amount of the particular type of goods that was absorbed in the production of those final deliveries that were eliminated from the original table. Values added in general—and labor inputs in particular—that were absorbed in this way appear now in the final demand.

# VIII

The idea that in the description of an economic system some processes and outputs can be reduced, that is, expressed in terms of others, goes back quite far into the history of economic thought. Adam Smith discussed at length the question of whether corn should be measured in labor units required to grow it or, on the contrary, labor measured in terms of corn that a worker needs to live. François Quesnay insisted that various branches of manufacturing should be represented in his tableau only by the amounts of rough materials that they transformed into finished products.

The notion of unproductive—as contrasted with productive—labor, whose product does not deserve to be included in the grand total of national product, was still propounded by Stuart Mill. The Marxist doctrine caused the Soviet official statistician, up until recently, to exclude transportation of persons and products of many service industries from national accounts, and, in the West, the output of governmental and other public services is still often treated in the same way.

In the latter case, the elimination of the output—as contrasted with the input—of the public sector from national accounts is justified, not so much by the distinction between productive and unproductive activities, but rather by the difficulty of measuring the output of "public administration," of "education," or of "national defense."

The number of goods and services that more and more detailed observation of various processes of production and consumption would permit us to distinguish is much greater than even an input-output matrix containing many thousands of rows and columns can possibly hold. For many purposes, that number might also be larger than we would need to carry from the first stage of the analytical procedure to the last. Aggregation, that is, summation of essentially heterogenous quantities, is one of the two devices that economists use to limit the number of variables and functional relationships in terms of which they describe what they observe. The other is reduction, that is, elimination of certian goods and processes. In this chapter, a systematic procedure has been presented that permits us to reduce the size of an input-output table through analytical elimination of any of its rows and columns. A less systematic, intuitive elimination of a much larger number of variables—considered to be secondary or intermediate—occurs, however, already during the collection of the primary statistical information. Thus, even a most detailed input-output table, as well as the national accounts constructed around it, can be said to present the actual economic system, not only in an aggregated but also in a reduced form.

# 4

## *Wages, profits, prices, and taxes*
### ( 1 9 4 7 )

Much has been said about wages, profits, and prices in recent months, and what has been said certainly does not represent the last word. The problem is so intricate, the number of factors involved so great, and their interrelationship so complex that personal judgment must of necessity constitute an important ingredient of any definite stand taken in the controversy.

To acknowledge the existence of serious gaps in our understanding does not mean, however, to profess complete ignorance. On the contrary, such an acknowledgment might help us to distinguish what we already know on the subject from what we have yet to learn. Nothing can contribute more to the development of sound judgment on a controversial issue than the delineation of an area of agreement, however narrow it may be. To present a few factual observations that may serve as a useful basis for exploration of the still debatable aspects of the wage-price problem is the principal purpose of this chapter.

Higher wages, bigger profits, and lower, or at least stable, prices are a happy combination which can easily win general acclaim. So long as and to the extent that technological progress, additional investment, and better management make possible a steadily increasing flow of commodities and services, the actual realization of such a program is entirely feasible. A steady rise in productivity has actually been responsible for the upward trend in the American standard of living, a trend that incidentally must be measured not

Reprinted with the permission of *Dun's Review*, June 1947, © 1947 by Dun & Bradstreet Publications Corporation.

only by the increasing per capita output and consumption of various goods and services but also by the steady reduction in the length of the normal average working week.

In considering the possibility of a 20 percent increase in wages and a similar increase in profits and agricultural income combined with a simultaneous reduction in prices—all of it taking place within a short span of 6, 12, or even 20 months—it is impossible to rely on the long but comparatively slow pull of general economic progress. Within the framework of a given technological structure and of a constant level of output, one can easily visualize wages, profits, and prices all moving up or down together; one can also conceive of a situation with profits rising and wages falling or vice versa; but, on the other hand, one cannot conceive of constant prices combined with falling wages and reduced profits.

The reason why some of these combinations seem to be natural and in a certain sense necessary while others appear improbable or even impossible in the short run must obviously be sought in the internal logic of the price-wage-profit relationships. The profit earned by an automobile manufacturer per unit of output equals the difference between the selling price of an automobile and its total unit costs. Given the actual amounts of all materials and services necessary in production of an average car, the unit costs can be computed by multiplying these amounts by the prices of the respective goods and services (including the overheads) and combining the results in a single figure. The labor input multiplied with the appropriate wage rates constitutes one of the major components of the unit costs. Since net profits after taxes fit better in the general scheme of the subsequent discussion, all business taxes, too, can be conveniently included as a separate item in unit costs.

Describing the same relationship from another angle, it can be said that the price of the finished product equals its unit costs, including the labor and the tax costs, augmented by the amount of unit profits.

## I. Cost-price structure

Passing from individual business enterprise to analysis of the whole economy, we observe that the prices entered in the cost account of the automobile manufacturer appear as revenue items in the sales accounts of steel producers, rubber manufacturers, tool makers, and scores of other suppliers. At the same time, the price of trucks sold by the automobile manufacturer will figure as a more or less important item in the unit cost computations of transportation companies, farmers, and many other businesses. Far from being independent of each other, the cost-price structures of all the separate industries are nothing but links in a vast network which embraces the whole national economy.

If prices of all commodities as well as all wage rates were prescribed by a universal price-fixing authority and business taxes, as they actually are, were fixed by appropriate authorities, the net profit or loss margins—as the case might be—would be automatically determined for each and every industry. An increase in any one price, such as the price of steel, would raise the profit margin of the steel industry but at the same time correspondingly reduce the profit margins of all steel-using industries.

If, instead of issuing price regulations, the same authority—banish the thought—had prescribed wage rates to be paid and profits to be earned per unit of output by each individual producer, the application of such a universal "cost plus" principle would amount to indirect price fixing, since one and only one system of prices can actually be compatible with a given wage and profit distribution. Had the prescribed wage rates in one particular industry been increased, for example, by 10 percent, a quite definite adjustment of all individual prices would be required to maintain the profit margins and the wage rates throughout all other industries at their original level.

Such examples demonstrate the existence of an indirect, complex, but nevertheless very real overall dependence among wage rates, profits earned, and taxes paid per unit of output in each of the many separate industries on the one hand and the prices of all different kinds of goods and services sold by these industries on the other. These necessary relationships reflect the fundamental nature of an economy based on a thoroughgoing division of labor. A rigidly planned economy could not escape the consequences of its operations any more than a free, competitive system.

Formulated in quite general terms, the proposition about the existence of such wage-profit-price relationships loses much of its operational significance. It might be true that a wage rise in the lumber industry—unless absorbed through compensating profit, wage, or tax reductions—will lead to some increase in the price of woolens, but unless one is able to restate this general assertion in at least approximate dollars-and-cents figures, it has the unreal quality of a sales display with price tags missing.

The four graphs appearing with this article show the results of a

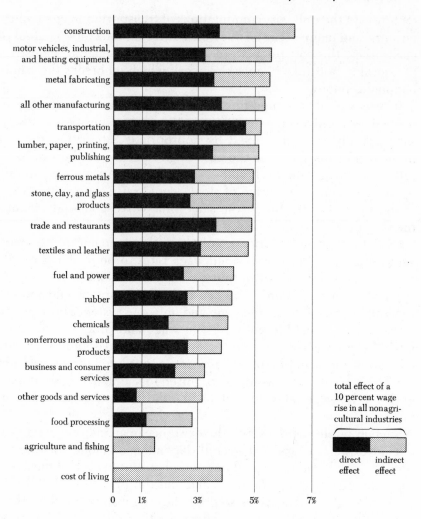

**Figure 4-1**

Price changes resulting from an assumed 10 percent wage rise in nonagricultural industries, computed on the basis of structural relationships prevailing in the American economy in 1939.

statistical study designed to translate the abstract argument into actual figures. The effect of an assumed general 10 percent wage rise in all nonagricultural industries is illustrated in Figure 4-1. Each bar reveals the impact of such a cost boost on the price of one of the 18 principal groups of commodities and services. The results of a flat 10 percent increase in all nonagricultural profit margins are represented in Figure 4-2.

What would happen to prices if the net farm income earned per unit of agricultural output were raised by 10 percent while all non-agricultural profits and wages as well as all business taxes were kept at their original level is shown in Figure 4-3. The price impact of a proportional 10 percent rise in all business taxes—computed on the assumption that none of it is taken out of the net profit or wages—is demonstrated in Figure 4-4.

The particular analytical technique used in arriving at these

**Figure 4-2**

Price changes resulting from an assumed 10 percent rise in profits and other nonwage incomes in nonagricultural industries, computed on the basis of structural relationships prevailing in the American economy in 1939.

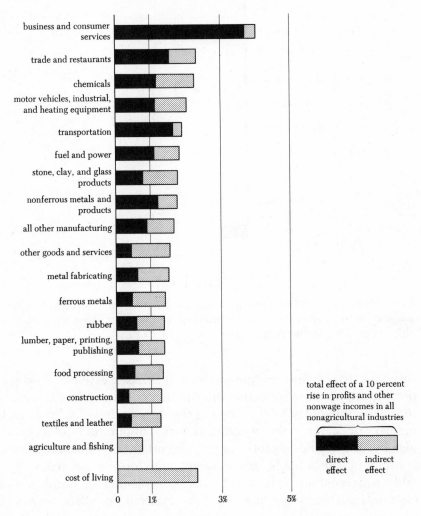

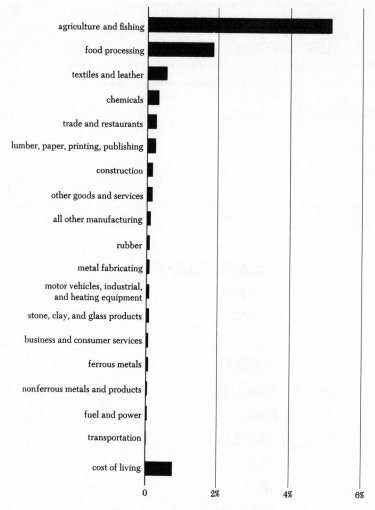

**Figure 4-3**

Price changes resulting from an assumed 10 percent rise in agricultural wage and nonwage income, computed on the basis of structural relationships prevailing in the American economy in 1939.

results is that of input-output analysis. It is based essentially on systematic exploitation of factual information contained in a large statistical double-entry table, showing the distribution of sales of each industry or sector of the economy in terms of purchases of its products by all the other sectors, namely the other individual industries, consumers' households, government, and foreign countries. The table thus contains information on the amounts of supplies and materials purchased by any one industry from the other sectors of the economy; it indicates also the amount of labor used as well as profits earned and taxes paid by each industry.

With this information in hand it becomes possible to trace through and evaluate in quantitative terms the direct and also the indirect results of any specific "primary change" such as an increase in the wage rate in one or several industries, a downward or upward adjustment of profit margins, or a change in taxes. The laborious and uncertain task of following through the resulting price adjustments

### Figure 4-4

Price changes resulting from an assumed 10 percent rise in business and excise taxes in all industries, computed on the basis of structural relationships prevailing in the American economy in 1939.

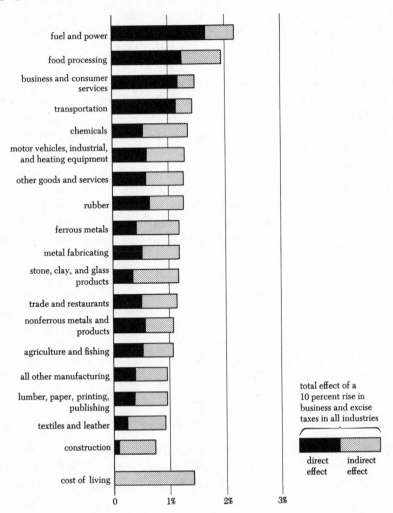

step by step can actually be avoided through the use of streamlined and much more efficient procedures of modern computational analysis.

The actual price effects of an assumed 10 percent wage rise could be predicted with accuracy only if we knew what effect such change would have on the net profit margins and the tax burden of all the individual industries. The controversy raised by the so-called Nathan Report—with its assumptions that even a 25 percent overall wage rise would actually be absorbed through corresponding all-around reductions in profits—can serve as ample illustration of this particular point. The chart dealing with a wage rise in nonagricultural industries (Figure 4-1) shows what would have happened to prices if wages had been increased by 10 percent while profit margins and taxes remained the same as before. In other words, the answer given here to our original question is a conditional one.

Only those who actually believe that neither profits nor tax reductions would absorb any substantial part of the increased wage costs can interpret it as a prediction. For others, it simply describes the probable results of an artificial experiment, an experiment that nevertheless might contribute to realistic understanding of the actual happenings and to a reasonable appraisal of various practical and impractical alternatives. The fact that construction costs prove to be more sensitive to a general rise in wages than any other of the 18 principal sectors of the economy may help, for example, to explain the difficulties encountered in solving the housing problem.

On the graph, the effects of the increase in each industry's own wage bill are shown separately from cost increases, which are indirect results of parallel wage increases in the other fields. The first component is usually more conspicuous than the second. The chart shows, however, that the latter in many instances actually contributes more to the total effect.

Profits constitute in general a much smaller element of the final price than wages. Thus, a 10 percent increase in all profit margins carries with it smaller price effects than a 10 percent wage rise. As should be expected, service industries lead the procession in the chart devoted to a profit rise in nonagricultural industries.

## II. Agriculture

The strategic position occupied by agriculture in our national economic policies justifies the separate treatment accorded to it in this analysis. The impact of a primary increase in agricultural income obtained through a 10 percent addition to the amount of net farm revenue, included in the price of all agricultural products, reaches other branches of the economy at a very uneven, steeply decreasing rate. No separation is made here between the direct and indirect components of the total effects for the simple reason that all of them, save in agricultural, are of the latter kind.

Under present-day conditions the 1939 tax figures have no other significance than that of a pleasant memory. The chart reflecting price changes arising out of tax increases is shown mainly for illustrative purposes. It indicates what would have happened in that year to the prices of various commodities and services if the combined amount of all business and excise taxes paid by each industry per unit of its output had been raised 10 percent and "passed forward" without reduction in either wage rates or net profit margins. It is worth noticing that under these conditions the prices of most categories of goods and services depend more upon the general tax level in all other branches of production than on taxes paid directly by the industry at their immediate origin.

Each of the four charts contains a bar labeled "cost of living." In a sense these bars tell us more about the effects of each of the four kinds of changes discussed above than does the rest of the graph. The cost of living bar in the wage rises chart measures the combined impact of all the separate price increases, shown on its left, on the purchasing power of an average consumer's dollar. Computed as a regular cost of living index, it represents the mean of the 18 price changes. Each of these changes is weighed in proportion to the importance of the particular item in the average consumer's budget.

A general, across-the-board 10 percent wage rise adds 3.92 percent to the cost of living. To interpret the significance of this figure one must remember that it is computed on the assumpton that profits, farm incomes, and taxes remain the same as before. This explains the 6.08 percent gain in real wages that workers under these circumstances would obtain through a 10 percent rise in their money wages. This gain actually represents a transfer of purchasing power from other groups of the population and from the government, who, facing higher prices with unchanged money income, must suffer a corresponding loss. The price system plays here the role of a silent but powerful redistributing agency.

Similar considerations explain how the 2.30 percent added to the cost of living through a 10 percent increase in nonagricultural profits leaves the receivers of this income with a 7.70 percent gain in real purchasing power. The real net gain that the farmer derives at the expense of the rest of the population, in consequence of a 10 percent boost in money income, amounts to approximately 9.28 percent. Under the 1939 conditions an additional 10 percent in business taxes—if not taken out of profits or wages—would have increased the real income of the government by 8.58 percent.

The leverage that any group of income receivers commands in the process of setting its own monetary claims against those of the rest of the community decreases as the share of this particular group in the total national income goes up, and vice versa. If wage rates, all profits in industry and agriculture, and all business taxes were simultaneously increased by 10 percent, the cost of living would go up by the combined amount of 8.38 percent, which leaves a meager real gain of 1.62 percent for each of the parties concerned.

Had the four types of income mentioned above comprised all the ultimate demands on the nation's annual net product, the resulting price rises would add up to exactly 10 percent, and the whole operation would leave workers, businesspeople, farmers, and the government just where they were before. The apparent windfall gain of 1.62 percent shown in the above computaton comes from noninclusion in the otherwise general inflation of all monetary incomes of various minor items, of which American payments for foreign imports are the largest. By having allowed the prices of imported commodities to escape the general upward trend, by assumption we have reduced the real purchasing power of foreign countries on the American market and increased at their expense the combined purchasing power of domestic income receivers.

The significance of the answer given here to some of the questions raised in the first part of this chapter must be judged in the light of the general observations made in its opening paragraphs. An unconditional answer to such questions as "What would happen to prices if wages were raised by 10 percent?" is, in the present state of our knowledge, clearly impossible. This does not mean, however, that we should not venture to make informed guesses. An informed guess is one that makes efficient use of available information and confines subjective judgment to those points that, for lack of such information, would otherwise remain unanswered. This discussion has purposefully been limited to those aspects of the wage-profit-price problem of which an economic analyst can give a reasonably reliable factual account.

# 5

## Domestic production and foreign trade: The American capital position reexamined

### ( 1 9 5 3 )

### I. The structural basis of international trade

Countries trade with each other because this enables them to participate in and profit from the international division of labor. Not unlike businesses and individuals, each area specializes in those lines of economic activity to which it happens to be best suited and then trades some of its own outputs for commodities and services in the production of which other countries have a comparative advantage. The word *comparative* is of particular significance in this connection.

The United States, for example, exports automobiles and imports newsprint. It does so because the quantity of Canadian paper we can obtain in exchange for, say, a million dollars' worth of American cars is larger than the additional amount of newsprint we would be able to produce at home if we withdrew the capital, labor, and other resources now absorbed in the manufacture of one million dollars' worth of automobiles and used it instead to increase the output of our domestic paper industry. Canada, for analogous but in a sense opposite reasons, finds it advantageous to obtain its automobiles from the United States in exchange for newsprint rather than to divert resources from their present employment in its paper industry into an increased domestic production of cars.

This essay appeared originally in *Proceedings of the American Philosophical Society*, vol. 97, no.4, September 1953.

This explanation of the international exchange of goods and services in terms of the comparative advantage of the alternative allocation of resources in each of the trading countries was originally developed in the writings of David Ricardo and other so-called classical economists of the late eighteenth and early nineteenth centuries. It still constitutes the basis of the modern theory of international trade. The theory of comparative costs—as many other economic theories—reigns, however, in the pages of college textbooks without actually governing the practice of empirical economic analysis.

Until recently, we had so little systematic knowledge of the productive structure of our own or of any other national economy that the application of such general theoretical principles to the analysis and explanation of actual foreign trade relationships has been practically out of the question. Most of what has been said on that subject consisted of reasonable common-sense conjectures or plausible examples, which—like the automobile and newsprint reference used above—serve well enough to illustrate the logic of the theoretical argument but had hardly any specific base in detailed facts and figures.[1]

A widely shared view on the nature of the trade between the United States and the rest of the world is derived from what appears to be a common-sense assumption that this country has a comparative advantage in the production of commodities that require for their manufacture large quantities of capital and relatively small amounts of labor. Our economic relationships with other countries are supposed to be based mainly on the export of such "capital-intensive" goods in exchange for foreign products that—if we were to make them at home—would require little capital but large quantities of American labor. Since the United States possesses a relatively large amount of capital—so goes this oft-repeated argument—and a comparatively small amount of labor, direct domestic production of such "labor-intensive" products would be uneconomical; we can much more advantageously obtain them from abroad in exchange for our capital-intensive products.

[1]As an example of the recent empirical studies in that field, see G. D. A. Macdougall, "British and American Export: A Study Suggested by the Theory of Comparative Costs," *Econ. Jour.* 61 (1): 697–724, 1951: also, G. D. A. Macdougall, "British and American Exports: A Study Suggested by the Theory of Comparative Costs," *Econ. Jour.* 62 (2): 487–522, 1952. A succinct discussion of the theoretical problems involved can be found in P. A. Samuelson, "International Trade and the Equalization of Factor Prices," *Econ. Jour.* 58: 163–184, 1948; and "International Factor Price Equalization Once Again," *Econ. Jour.* 59: 180–197, 1949.

Recent progress in the collection and systematic organization of detailed quantitative information on the structure of all the various branches of the American economy, accompanied by a parallel advance in the technique of large-scale numerical computation, now enables us to narrow the frustrating gap between theory and observation.[2]

This is the first preliminary progress report on a study designed to analyze the structural basis of trade relationships between the United States and the rest of the world.

## II. Direct and indirect input requirements

None of the basic factual information used here had to be collected especially for this particular inquiry. Both the statistical data and the analytical procedure employed constitute an integral part of the so-called input-output or interindustry research program jointly conducted by various agencies of the government and private institutions, including the Harvard Economic Research Project.

The factual information referred to above comprises many sets of figures of which the largest and in a sense the most important is organized in terms of a so-called input-output table.[3] This table describes the actual flow of commodities and services among all the different parts of the American economy. Specifically, it shows how each one of our manufacturing industries, each branch of agriculture, each kind of transportation and distribution—in short, each sector of the American economy—depends upon every other sector. A single column of an input-output table shows, for example, how many steel sheets, steel bars, and other steel products automobile manufacturers buy from the steel industry for every million dollars' worth of cars they produce; it also shows how many yards (or dollars' worth) they need of upholstery material, how much paint from the chemical industry, and so on. Similarly, the "steel industry" column of the same table describes the various kinds of inputs, such as coal, ore, and so on, which the steel industry must obtain from the other sectors of the economy in order to produce an additional million dollars' worth of its own output, which, of course, consists of various steel products. The table contains as

[2]For description of the so-called input-output approach to structural economic analysis, see Chapter 1 of this book.
[3]W. Duane Evans and Marvin Hoffenberg, "The Interindustry Relations Study for 1947, *Review of Economics and Statistics* 34: 97–142, 1952.

many columns as there are separate industries so that it presents each link connecting any two sections of the economy.

On the basis of the statistical information contained in an input-output table, one can determine the effect of any given increase or decrease in the level of output in any one sector of the economy upon the rate of production in all the other sectors.

Using the 1947 input-output structure of the American economy as the basis of such computations, one finds that to produce an additional million dollars' worth of automobiles the output of steel would have to increase by \$235,000 and the output of chemicals by

## Table 5-1

Capital and labor requirements for the final output of one million dollars' worth of motor vehicles

| Industry[a] | Output Requirements[b] | Requirements per Million Dollars of Output of Industry Listed on Left | | Requirements per Million Dollars of Final Output of Motor Vehicles | |
|---|---|---|---|---|---|
| | | Capital | Labor | Capital | Labor |
| 1 | 2 | 3 | 4 | 5 | 6 |
| | (thousands of dollars) | (thousands of dollars) | (man-years) | (thousands of dollars) | (man-years) |
| 26. motor vehicles (145) | 1,457.45[c] | 565.8 | 60.340 | 824.6 | 87.942 |
| 15. iron and steel | 235.14 | 1,026.3 | 77.777 | 241.3 | 18.288 |
| 19. other fabricated metal products | 118.25 | 713.5 | 95.335 | 84.5 | 11.273 |
| 16. nonferrous metals | 78.69 | 1,001.6 | 55.715 | 78.8 | 4.384 |
| 25. other electrical machinery | 75.50 | 551.1 | 102.638 | 41.6 | 7.749 |
| 22. other nonelectric machinery | 60.70 | 775.7 | 96.579 | 47.1 | 5.862 |
| 10. chemicals | 57.95 | 592.7 | 49.779 | 34.3 | 2.885 |
| 12. rubber products | 56.19 | 493.1 | 90.172 | 27.7 | 5.067 |
| 31. railroad transportation | 50.18 | 3,343.3 | 153.640 | 167.8 | 7.710 |
| 11. products of petroleum and coal | 46.85 | 1,397.2 | 29.843 | 65.5 | 1.398 |
| 4. textile mill products | 39.29 | 493.6 | 110.563 | 19.4 | 4.344 |
| 14. stone, clay, and glass products | 33.64 | 1,026.3 | 128.539 | 34.5 | 4.324 |
| 8. paper and allied products | 31.95 | 564.1 | 64.805 | 18.0 | 2.071 |
| 34. trade | 31.82 | 984.9 | 165.876 | 31.3 | 5.278 |
| 30. coal, gas, and electric power | 29.50 | 2,222.6 | 99.318 | 65.6 | 2.930 |
| 1. agriculture and fisheries | 27.53 | 2,524.4 | 82.025 | 69.5 | 2.258 |
| 21. metalworking machinery | 27.48 | 1,246.9 | 130.705 | 34.3 | 3.592 |
| 33. other transportation | 23.88 | 928.3 | 121.576 | 22.2 | 2.903 |
| 9. printing and publishing | 19.72 | 436.0 | 114.038 | 8.6 | 2.249 |
| 38. business services | 18.44 | 144.5 | 97.543 | 2.7 | 1.799 |
| 39. personal and repair services | 18.10 | 681.8 | 183.503 | 12.3 | 3.321 |
| 6. lumber and wood products | 15.98 | 537.9 | 141.540 | 8.6 | 2.262 |

[a]See footnote *b* for Table 5-2.
[b]The output required from each industry in order to produce one million dollars' worth of motor vehicles for export or domestic consumption. See W. Duane Evans and Marvin Hoffenberg, "The Interindustry Relations Study for 1947," *Review of Economics and Statistics* 34: Table 6, 1952.

$58,000, while raising the production of nonferrous metals by $79,000, of textiles by $39,000, and so on. Even the communication services—telephone and telegraph—would have to contribute indirectly to the production of a million dollars' worth of additional automobiles.

Column 2 in Table 5-1 shows the result of this particular computation. Without entering into the discussion of technical details, it may be sufficient to observe that the magnitude of every one of the entries depends upon all the input-output relationships among all the sectors of the economy and that the computation of each one of

| Industry[a] | Output Requirements[b] | Requirements per Million Dollars of Output of Industry Listed on Left | | Requirements per Million Dollars of Final Output of Motor Vehicles | |
|---|---|---|---|---|---|
| | | Capital | Labor | Capital | Labor |
| 1 | 2 | 3 | 4 | 5 | 6 |
| | (thousands of dollars) | (thousands of dollars) | (man-years) | (thousands of dollars) | (man-years) |
| 5. apparel | 13.74 | 262.2 | 108.795 | 3.6 | 1.495 |
| 29. miscellaneous manufacturing | 11.26 | 439.4 | 100.364 | 4.9 | 1.130 |
| 37. rental | 10.68 | 8,156.5 | 16.324 | 87.1 | .174 |
| 28. professional and scientific equipment | 10.35 | 841.8 | 133.129 | 8.7 | 1.378 |
| 2. food and kindred products | 9.98 | 361.9 | 43.143 | 3.6 | .431 |
| 36. finance and insurance | 9.83 | 28.2 | 92.242 | .3 | .907 |
| 35. communications | 6.21 | 4,645.4 | 163.097 | 28.8 | 1.013 |
| 44. eating and drinking places | 6.02 | 688.0 | 125.365 | 4.1 | .755 |
| 27. other transportation equipment | 5.11 | 759.0 | 122.419 | 3.9 | .626 |
| 13. leather and leather products | 5.06 | 264.0 | 109.629 | 1.3 | .555 |
| 23. motors and generators | 4.99 | 404.3 | 117.771 | 2.0 | .588 |
| 24. radios | 4.65 | 449.0 | 124.097 | 2.1 | .577 |
| 7. furniture and fixtures | 4.28 | 485.1 | 116.923 | 2.1 | .500 |
| 18. fabricated structural metal products | 3.79 | 441.9 | 83.300 | 1.7 | .316 |
| 20. agriculture, mining, and construction machinery | 3.65 | 838.6 | 87.794 | 3.1 | .320 |
| 17. plumbing and heating supplies | 2.67 | 509.9 | 99.388 | 1.4 | .265 |
| 40. medical, education, and nonprofit orgs. | 2.05 | 2,689.5 | 253.044 | 5.5 | .519 |
| 3. tobacco manufactures | .53 | 557.6 | 40.539 | .3 | .021 |
| 41. amusements | .10 | 1,082.9 | 166.899 | .1 | .017 |
| Total requirements in all industries per million dollars of final output of motor vehicles | | | | 2,104.8 | 201.476 |

[a]This figure includes the "back feed" within this industry, i.e., the automotive industry's purchases from itself, as well as the million dollars' worth of motor vehicles going to final consumers and the amounts needed by the various other industries to meet their output requirements. For detailed explantion of the technical point involved, see W. Duane Evans and Marvin Hoffenberg, 137 and 140.

these figures is equivalent to the solution of a system of as many simultaneous equations as there are distinct sectors in the economy.

The more minute the breakdown of industries in the basic input-output table, the more detailed the final results will be. The following analysis is based on a 200-industry breakdown consolidated in some of its stages—for purposes of computation and simplified presentation—into 50 sectors (38 of which trade their products directly on the international market).

## III.  Capital and labor inputs

The second and third sets of statistical data (columns 3 and 4, Table 5-1) show the direct capital and labor requirements of each industry. These figures are based on detailed information that tells us, for example, that to produce an additional million dollars' worth of finished cars, our automobile industry would have to invest in $175,000 worth of new buildings, $266,000 of additional machinery, and many other fixed items. It also would have to increase its inventories of raw materials and "goods in process" by $124,000. This adds up to $566,000, which represents the total additional capital (in 1947 prices) that would have to be invested in the American automobile industry if its capacity were raised so as to enable us to produce an additional million dollars' worth of cars per year.

But this is only one part of the total additional capital that would have to be invested in the American economy in order to enable it to produce—say, for export purposes—these additional automobiles. As we saw before, the input of steel into the automobile industry will have to increase by $235,000 and the input of textile by $39,000. This, of course, means additional investment in both the steel and textile industries. The magnitude of each of these capital requirements can be computed. To do so one must simply multiply the amount of capital each of these two industries requires per million dollars of its capacity by the additional demand for its product indirectly generated by the million-dollar rise in automobile output. The amounts of additional capital each one of the various sectors of the economy would need in order to enable the United States to increase its automobile export by one million dollars are listed in column 5 of Table 5-1. These add up to $2,105,000, which is the total amount of capital the United States economy of 1947 had to invest for every million dollars' worth of cars produced for export or final domestic use.

Like the tip of an iceberg visible above the surface of the water, the part invested in the automobile industry itself constitutes only a small portion of the total—26 percent to be exact; the rest is distributed among the other 42 productive sectors of the economy. Similar computations have been performed for each category of commodities and services we export or import (in competition with domestic output).

Labor is the other primary factor, the availability of which must obviously have a decisive role in establishing the pattern of specialization that determines the composition of our foreign trade. Not unlike capital, the man-years that go into the production of, say, one million dollars' worth of automobiles are partly absorbed by the automobile industry itself but are partly employed also by all other sectors of the economy. The computation of such direct and indirect labor requirements—as entered in columns 4 and 6—is quite analogous to the computation of the direct and indirect demand for capital (see columns 3 and 5, Table 5-1).

The summary of total quantities of capital and labor required for domestic production of each of the many types of commodities exported and imported by the United States is entered in columns 2 and 3 of Table 5-2. In this table most of the 38 large industry and commodity groups are broken down into their components, described in terms of the more detailed 200-industry input-output classification.

The figures entered in columns 2 and 3 were actually arrived at in two steps. First, the indirect capital and labor requirements generated by one million dollars' worth of demand for the product of each of the composite 38 sectors were computed. This computation (essentially a solution of corresponding systems of linear equations) was performed in terms of the consolidated 50-industry input-output table. Next, the *total* capital and labor requirements, respectively, of each *particular* commodity type within the sector were obtained by adding its *specific direct* requirements to the previously computed (in a sense, average) *indirect* requirements of the consolidated sector as a whole. Thus, the differences between the total capital and labor requirements of the industrial products belonging to the same consolidated sector result entirely from the difference in their *direct* requirements, since their *indirect* requirements are assumed to be the same.

The main reason for such a two-stage procedure is economic. If based throughout on the 200 × 200 input-output table, the computation of direct and indirect requirements would cost a thousand

**Table 5-2** Capital and labor requirments per million dollars of U.S. exports and import replacements[a]

| Industry[b] | Direct and Indirect Requirements per Million Dollars of Final Output | | Exports per Million Dollars of Total Exports[e] | Imports per Million Dollars of Total Imports[f] | Requirements per Million Dollars of Exports and Import Replacements of Average (1947) Composition | | | | Comparison of Export and Import Requirements[g] | |
| | Capital[c] | Labor[d] | | | Capital | | Labor | | Cap. | Lab. |
| | | | | | Exports | Import replace. | Exports | Import replace. | | |
| 1 | 2 | 3 | 4 | 5 | 6 | 7 | 8 | 9 | 10 | 11 |
| | *(millions of dollars)* | *(man-years)* | *(dollars/1,000,000)* | *(dollars/1,000,000)* | *(dollars)* | *(dollars)* | *(man-years)* | *(man-years)* | | |
| all industries | | | | | 2,550,780 | 3,091,339 | 182.313 | 170.004 | < | > |
| 1. agriculture and fisheries (1–10a) | 4.7120 | 158.710 | 100,987 | 257,526 | 475,851 | 1,213,463 | 16.028 | 40.872 | < | < |
| 2. food and kindred products | | | 105,701 | 98,045 | 3,119,593[b] | 3,349,589 | 159.847 | 183.508 | < | < |
|   meat packing and poultry (21) | 3.0158 | 149.032 | 17,568 | 7,189 | 52,982 | 21,681 | 2.618 | 1.071 | | |
|   processed dairy products (22) | 3.1334 | 165.081 | 15,217 | 2,429 | 47,681 | 7,611 | 2.512 | .401 | | |
|   canning, preserving, and freezing (23) | 3.2287 | 206.505 | 11,446 | 48,043 | 36,956 | 155,116 | 2.364 | 9.921 | | |
|   grain mill products (24) | 3.0375 | 146.371 | 45,928 | 1,522 | 139,506 | 4,623 | 6.723 | .223 | | |
|   bakery products (25) | 3.2447 | 221.331 | 468 | 32 | 1,519 | 104 | .104 | .007 | | |
|   miscellaneous food products (26) | 3.2610 | 175.271 | 10,553 | 8,825 | 34,413 | 28,778 | 1.850 | 1.547 | | |
|   sugar (27) | 4.1953 | 148.850 | 1,997 | 12,970 | 8,378 | 54,413 | .297 | 1.931 | | |
|   alcoholic beverages (28) | 3.2923 | 169.712 | 2,524 | 17,035 | 8,310 | 56,084 | .428 | 2.891 | | |
| 3. tobacco manufacturers (29) | 3.2887 | 173.472 | 13,245 | 21,439 | 43,559 | 70,506 | 2.298 | 3.719 | < | < |
| 4. textile mill products | | | 56,810 | 23,657 | 2,308,032 | 2,327,539 | 213.302 | 206.662 | < | > |
|   spinning, weaving, and dyeing (30) | 2.3114 | 215.250 | 53,758 | 9,796 | 124,256 | 22,643 | 11.571 | 2.109 | | |
|   special textile products (31) | 2.3420 | 201.558 | 684 | 8,922 | 1,602 | 20,895 | .138 | 1.798 | | |
|   jute, linen, cordage, and twine (32) | 2.3412 | 200.639 | 815 | 4,728 | 1,908 | 11,069 | .164 | .949 | | |
|   floor coverings (35a) | 2.1591 | 154.206 | 1,553 | 211 | 3,353 | 456 | .239 | .033 | | |
| 5. apparel | | | 21,129 | 36,029 | 1,661,527 | 2,213,875 | 233.802 | 207.139 | < | > |
|   canvas products (33) | 1.6106 | 237.848 | 174 | | 280 | 0 | .041 | 0 | | |
|   apparel except furs (34) | 1.6050 | 250.169 | 15,493 | 12,630 | 24,866 | 20,271 | 3.876 | 3.160 | | |
|   house furnishings, etc. (35b) | 1.6492 | 188.151 | 4,479 | 1,814 | 7,387 | 2,992 | .343 | .341 | | |
|   furs (hunting and trapping) (10b) | 2.6176 | 183.571 | 983 | 21,585 | 2,573 | 56,501 | .180 | 3.962 | | |
| 6. lumber and wood products | | | 10,223 | 31,787 | 1,560,785 | 1,617,910 | 242.003 | 231.636 | < | > |
|   logging (36) | 1.6383 | 188.365 | 378 | 9,149 | 619 | 14,989 | .071 | 1.723 | | |
|   sawmills, planning, and veneer mills (37) | 1.6383 | 251.604 | 7,153 | 20,435 | 11,719 | 33,479 | 1.800 | 5.142 | | |
|   plywood (38) | 1.3366 | 209.125 | 863 | 761 | 1,154 | 1,017 | .180 | .159 | | |
|   fabricated wood products (39) | 1.3465 | 226.188 | 1,217 | 632 | 1,639 | 851 | .275 | .143 | | |
|   wood containers and cooperage (40) | 1.3491 | 242.168 | 612 | 810 | 826 | 1,093 | .148 | .196 | | |

72

Table (rotated). Row labels at left; eight numeric data columns follow, with comparison-symbol marks (∧, ∨, ≥, ≤) shown between columns for certain group rows.

| Industry | 1 | 2 | 3 | 4 | 5 | 6 | 7 | 8 | rel |
|---|---|---|---|---|---|---|---|---|---|
| 7. furniture and fixtures (41–43) | 1.6821 | 233.687 | 2,075 | 437 | 3,490 | 735 | .485 | .102 | ∧ ∨ |
| 8. paper and allied products | | | 9,743 | 103,616 | 1,726,891 | 1,859,722 | 165.764 | 161.346 | |
|    pulp mills (44) | 1.8611 | 152.803 | 1,337 | 42,732 | 2,488 | 79,529 | .204 | 6.530 | |
|    paper and paper board mills (45) | 1.8611 | 167.325 | 4,401 | 60,447 | 8,191 | 112,498 | .736 | 10.114 | |
|    converted paper products (46) | 1.5346 | 169.389 | 4,005 | 437 | 6,146 | 671 | .678 | .074 | |
| 9. printing and publishing (47) | 1.3216 | 196.597 | 4,329 | 1,425 | 5,721 | 1,883 | .851 | .280 | |
| 10. chemicals | | | 49,153 | 105,398 | 2,337,851 | 2,390,120 | 167.681 | 147.602 | ∧ ∨ |
|    industrial inorganic chemicals (48) | 2.2968 | 171.293 | 7,303 | 9,748 | 17,669 | 22,389 | 1.318 | 1.670 | |
|    industrial organic chemicals (49) | 2.8055 | 161.081 | 3,082 | 4,340 | 20,489 | 12,176 | 1.176 | .699 | |
|    plastic materials (50) | 2.5614 | 159.740 | 342 | 97 | 7,894 | 249 | .492 | .015 | |
|    rubber (51) | 2.5208 | 141.238 | 1,739 | 55,751 | 862 | 140,537 | .048 | 7.874 | |
|    synthetic fiber (52) | 2.9200 | 212.841 | 342 | 2,720 | 5,078 | 7,942 | .370 | .579 | |
|    explosives (53) | 2.2814 | 197.963 | | 0 | 780 | 0 | .068 | 0 | |
|    drugs and medicines (54) | 2.1666 | 184.150 | 9,329 | 1,457 | 20,212 | 3,157 | 1.718 | .268 | |
|    soap and related products (55) | 2.1417 | 146.365 | 2,524 | 405 | 5,406 | 867 | .369 | .059 | |
|    paints and allied products (56) | 2.0430 | 152.411 | 3,663 | 340 | 7,484 | 695 | .558 | .052 | |
|    gum and wood chemicals (57) | 2.4267 | 184.907 | 2,140 | 3,854 | 5,193 | 9,353 | .396 | .713 | |
|    fertilizers (58) | 2.3700 | 180.631 | 450 | 356 | 1,067 | 844 | .081 | .064 | |
|    vegetable oils (59) | 2.0071 | 128.889 | 2,734 | 20,063 | 5,487 | 40,268 | .352 | 2.586 | |
|    animal oils (60) | 2.0062 | 136.738 | 1,079 | 2,672 | 2,165 | 5,361 | .148 | .356 | |
|    miscellaneous chemical industries (61) | 2.2467 | 170.497 | 6,733 | 3,595 | 15,127 | 8,077 | 1.148 | .613 | |
| 11a. crude petroleum and natural gas (17) | 3.2118 | 108.844 | 6,248 | 37,372 | 20,067 | 120,031 | .680 | 4.068 | |
| 11b. products of petroleum and coal | | | 34,566 | 21,730 | 2,600,946 | 2,674,929 | 94.110 | 93.465 | ∧ ∨ |
|    petroleum products (62) | 2.5514 | 94.011 | 32,881 | 19,658 | 83,893 | 50,155 | 3.091 | 1.848 | |
|    coke and products (63) | 3.8708 | 87.760 | 1,355 | 2,040 | 5,245 | 7,896 | .119 | .179 | |
|    paving and roofing material (64) | 2.3237 | 131.557 | 330 | 32 | 767 | 74 | .043 | .004 | |
| 12. rubber products | | | 10,199 | 389 | 1,817,051 | 1,801,799 | 194.823 | 205.636 | ∨ ≥ |
|    tires and inner tubes (65) | 1.8305 | 185.087 | 6,044 | 49 | 11,064 | 90 | 1.119 | .009 | |
|    miscellaneous rubber products (66) | 1.7975 | 208.989 | 4,155 | 340 | 7,469 | 611 | .868 | .071 | |
| 13. leather and leather products | | | 5,054 | 5,974 | 1,667,016 | 1,668,681 | 233.874 | 227.151 | ∧ ≤ |
|    tanning and finishing (67) | 1.6900 | 183.095 | 1,901 | 2,817 | 3,213 | 4,761 | .348 | .516 | |
|    other leather products (68) | 1.6395 | 271.302 | 749 | 1,360 | 1,228 | 2,230 | .203 | .369 | |
|    nonrubber footwear (69) | 1.6574 | 262.612 | 2,404 | 1,797 | 3,984 | 2,978 | .631 | .472 | |
| 14. stone, clay, and glass products | | | 12,788 | 27,560 | 1,961,425 | 2,345,091 | 192.211 | 177.794 | ∧ ∨ |
|    stone, sand, clay, and abrasives (18) | 2.5821 | 226.822 | 330 | 3,854 | 852 | 9,951 | .075 | .874 | |
|    sulphur (19) | 2.5821 | 139.703 | 1,385 | 0 | 3,576 | 0 | .193 | 0 | |
|    other nonmetallic minerals (20) | 2.5821 | 154.790 | 881 | 17,456 | 2,275 | 45,073 | .136 | 2.702 | |
|    glass (70) | 1.9293 | 199.932 | 1,043 | 1,295 | 8,526 | 2,498 | .883 | .259 | |
|    cement (71) | 2.4944 | 167.940 | 959 | 0 | 2,602 | 0 | .175 | 0 | |
|    structural clay products (72) | 1.7718 | 271.334 | 929 | 2,477 | 1,699 | 87 | .260 | .013 | |
|    pottery and related products (73) | 1.3682 | 261.934 | 246 | 65 | 1,271 | 3,389 | .243 | .649 | |
|    concrete and plaster products (74) | 1.6727 | 205.466 | 1,127 | 1,765 | 412 | 109 | .051 | .013 | |
|    abrasive products (75) | 1.4890 | 159.882 | 600 | 32 | 1,678 | 2,628 | .180 | .282 | |
|    asbestos products (76) | 1.4890 | 176.167 | | | 893 | 48 | .106 | .006 | |
|    other miscellaneous nonmetallic minerals (77) | 1.4948 | 179.324 | 869 | 567 | 1,299 | 848 | .156 | .102 | |

Table 5-2 (Cont.)

| Industry[b] | Direct and Indirect Requirements per Million Dollars of Final Output — Capital[c] | Labor[d] | Exports per Million Dollars of Total Exports[e] | Imports per Million Dollars of Total Imports[f] | Requirements per Million Dollars of Exports and Import Replacements of Average (1947) Composition — Capital, Exports | Capital, Import replace. | Labor, Exports | Labor, Import replace. | Comparison of Export and Import Requirements[g] — Cap. | Lab. |
| --- | --- | --- | --- | --- | --- | --- | --- | --- | --- | --- |
| 1 | 2 | 3 | 4 | 5 | 6 | 7 | 8 | 9 | 10 | 11 |
| 15a. iron ore mining (11) | 3.1683 | 212.434 | 552 | 7,675 | 1,749 | 24,317 | .117 | 1.630 | < | < |
| 15b. iron and steel | | | 37,732 | 4,695 | 2,724,880 | 2,655,654 | 181.305 | 151.438 | > | > |
|   blast furnaces (78) | 2.6394 | 142.525 | 396 | 3,676 | 1,045 | 9,702 | .056 | .524 | | |
|   steel works and rolling mills (79) | 2.7599 | 180.703 | 35,585 | 955 | 98,211 | 2,636 | 6.430 | .173 | | |
|   iron foundries (80) | 2.0344 | 232.540 | 672 | 32 | 1,367 | 65 | .156 | .007 | | |
|   steel foundries (81) | 2.0349 | 236.564 | 90 | 16 | | 33 | .021 | .004 | | |
|   iron and steel forgings (92) | 2.0311 | 179.672 | 989 | 16 | 2,009 | 33 | .178 | .003 | | |
| 16a. nonferrous metal mining | | | 468 | 47,154 | 4,402,991 | 4,372,254 | 286.325 | 281.885 | ≥ | ≥ |
|   copper mining (12) | 3.2280 | 197.862 | 0 | 5,263 | 0 | 16,989 | | 1.041 | | |
|   lead and zinc mining (13) | 2.6210 | 230.618 | 12 | 5,360 | 32 | 14,049 | .003 | 1.236 | | |
|   bauxite mining (14) | 2.6948 | 221.395 | 114 | 3,757 | 307 | 10,124 | .025 | .832 | | |
|   other nonferrous mining (15)[j] | 5.0347 | 310.689 | 342 | 32,774 | 1,722 | 165,007 | .106 | 10.183 | | |
| 16b. processing nonferrous metals | | | 9,516 | 57,759 | 2,402,427 | 2,445,386 | 149.222 | 127.461 | ≤ | > |
|   primary copper (82) | 2.4334 | 121.184 | 2,788 | 22,216 | 6,784 | 54,060 | .338 | 2.692 | | |
|   copper rolling and drawing (83) | 2.4348 | 155.831 | 1,565 | 49 | 3,811 | 119 | .244 | .008 | | |
|   primary lead (84) | 2.4340 | 120.806 | 40 | 6,720 | 73 | 16,357 | .004 | .812 | | |
|   primary zinc (85) | 2.4350 | 166.224 | 1,379 | 2,672 | 3,358 | 6,506 | .229 | .444 | | |
|   primary metals, n.e.c. (86) | 2.4348 | 131.553 | 396 | 18,913 | 964 | 46,049 | .052 | 2.488 | | |
|   nonferrous metal rolling, n.e.c. (87) | 2.4849 | 148.977 | 983 | 16 | 2,394 | 39 | .146 | .002 | | |
|   primary aluminum (88) | 3.2849 | 144.156 | 204 | 761 | 670 | 2,500 | .029 | .110 | | |
|   aluminum rolling and drawing (89) | 2.1816 | 177.628 | 1,769 | 0 | 3,859 | 0 | .314 | 0 | | |
|   secondary nonferrous metals (90) | 2.4355 | 125.398 | 282 | 6,396 | 687 | 15,578 | .035 | .802 | | |
|   nonferrous foundries (91) | 2.1821 | 244.406 | 120 | 16 | 262 | 35 | .029 | .004 | | |
| 17. plumbing and heating supplies | | | 3,202 | 49 | 2,048,157 | 2,046,700 | 211.118 | 204.647 | ≥ | > |
|   metal plumbing and vitreous fixtures (97) | 2.0510 | 223.913 | 1,085 | 0 | 2,225 | 0 | .243 | 0 | | |
|   heating equipment (98) | 2.0467 | 204.647 | 2,117 | 49 | 4,333 | 100 | .433 | .010 | | |
| 18. fabricated structural metal products | | | 4,053 | 179 | 1,748,187 | 1,796,648 | 182.087 | 178.771 | < | ≥ |
|   structural metal products (99) | 1.6954 | 183.767 | 2,518 | 49 | 4,269 | 83 | .463 | .009 | | |
|   boiler shop products (100a) | 1.8348 | 178.945 | 1,535 | 130 | 2,816 | 239 | .275 | .023 | | |
| 19. other fabricated metal products | | | 16,531 | 1,262 | 2,011,342 | 1,971,712 | 203.738 | 207.607 | ≥ | ≤ |
|   tin cans and other tinware (93) | 2.1458 | 174.998 | 791 | 32 | 1,697 | 69 | .138 | .006 | | |
|   cutlery (94) | 2.0414 | 241.579 | 1,229 | 178 | 2,509 | 363 | .297 | .043 | | |
|   tools and general hardware (95) | 2.0421 | 227.946 | 3,130 | 259 | 6,392 | 529 | .713 | .059 | | |
|   hardware, n.e.c. (96) | 2.0459 | 228.406 | 1,811 | 16 | 3,705 | 33 | .414 | .004 | | |

| Industry | | | | | | | |
|---|---|---|---|---|---|---|---|
| metal stampings (101) | 1.8530 | 202.075 | 2,075 | 453 | 3,845 | 839 | .419 | .092 |
| metal coating and engraving (102) | 2.0457 | 264.165 | | 0 | 0 | 0 | 0 | 0 |
| lighting fixtures (103) | 2.0419 | 195.244 | 2,140 | 16 | 4,370 | 33 | .418 | .003 |
| fabricated wire products (104) | 2.0401 | 169.167 | 3,286 | 49 | 6,704 | 100 | .556 | .008 |
| metal barrels, drums, etc. (105) | 2.0397 | 164.918 | 486 | 130 | 991 | 265 | .080 | .021 |
| tubes and foils (106) | 2.0399 | 206.580 | 282 | 32 | 575 | 65 | .058 | .007 |
| miscellaneous fabricated metal products (107) | 2.0406 | 190.366 | 258 | 65 | 527 | 133 | .049 | .012 |
| steel springs (108) | 2.0397 | 172.761 | 0 | 0 | 0 | 0 | 0 | 0 |
| nuts, bolts, and screw machine products (109) | 1.8550 | 216.333 | 1,043 | 32 | 1,935 | 59 | .226 | .007 |
| 20. agriculture, mining, and construction machinery | | | 34,518 | 5,667 | 2,063,252 | 2,115,952 | 193.059 | 202.400 |
| tractors (112a) | 2.1098 | 185.783 | 11,722 | 1,457 | 24,731 | 3,074 | 2.178 | .271 |
| farm equipment (113) | 2.1183 | 208.218 | 5,504 | 4,194 | 11,659 | 8,884 | 1.146 | .873 |
| construction and mining machinery (114) | 2.0541 | 188.271 | 12,081 | 16 | 24,816 | 33 | 2.275 | .003 |
| oil field machinery and tools (115) | 2.0541 | 204.419 | 5,211 | 0 | 10,704 | 0 | 1.065 | 0 |
| 21. metalworking machinery (116–117) | 2.1793 | 212.211 | 12,633 | 227 | 27,531 | 495 | 2.681 | .048 |
| 22. other nonelectric machinery | 1.6724 | 176.071 | 58,836 | 3,238 | 1,901,679 | 1,978,413 | 195.442 | 192.712 |
| fabricated pipe (100b) | 1.6334 | 234.085 | 1,409 | 0 | 0 | 0 | 0 | 0 |
| steam engines and turbines (110) | 1.6334 | 183.850 | 6,212 | 16 | 2,302 | 26 | .330 | .004 |
| internal combustion engines (111) | 1.8509 | 175.047 | 851 | 389 | 10,147 | 635 | 1.142 | .072 |
| industrial trucks (112b) | 2.1146 | 202.576 | 19,684 | 0 | 1,575 | 0 | .149 | .394 |
| special industrial machinery (118) | 1.8797 | 179.349 | 4,335 | 1,943 | 41,624 | 4,109 | 3.988 | 0 |
| pumps and compressors (119) | 1.8754 | 181.040 | 2,452 | 0 | 8,149 | 0 | .777 | 0 |
| elevators and conveyors (120) | 1.8744 | 182.857 | 396 | 0 | 4,599 | 0 | .444 | 0 |
| blowers and fans (121) | 1.8749 | 204.820 | 162 | 0 | 742 | 0 | .072 | 0 |
| power transmission equipment (122) | 1.8748 | 170.428 | 2,494 | 648 | 304 | 1,215 | .033 | .110 |
| industrial machinery, n.e.c. (123) | 1.8185 | 224.616 | 7,051 | 32 | 4,676 | 58 | .425 | .007 |
| commercial machines and equipment, n.e.c. (124) | 1.6074 | 169.170 | 6,697 | 0 | 12,822 | 0 | 1.584 | 0 |
| refrigeration equipment (125) | 2.2257 | 211.626 | 2,782 | 0 | 10,765 | 0 | 1.133 | 0 |
| valves and fittings (126) | 2.2110 | 233.258 | 1,457 | 32 | 6,192 | 71 | .589 | .007 |
| ball and roller bearings (127) | 2.2131 | 212.277 | 156 | 0 | 3,221 | 0 | .340 | 0 |
| machine shops (128) | 1.6404 | 170.386 | 2,698 | 178 | 345 | 292 | .033 | .030 |
| electrical appliances (135a) | 1.3747 | 202.568 | 4,383 | 97 | 4,426 | 133 | .460 | .020 |
| 23. motors and generators (131) | 1.5768 | 249.783 | 6,763 | 130 | 6,025 | 205 | .888 | .032 |
| 24. radios and related products (139) | | | 15,794 | 193 | 10,664 | | 1.689 | |
| 25. other electrical machinery | | | | | 1,767,716 | 1,771,503 | 218.121 | 202.073 |
| wiring devices and griphite products (129) | 1.7708 | 200.531 | 1,745 | 16 | 3,090 | 28 | .350 | .003 |
| measuring instruments (130) | 1.7690 | 297.422 | 971 | 0 | 1,718 | 0 | .289 | 0 |
| transformers (132) | 1.7678 | 226.812 | 726 | 32 | 1,283 | 57 | .165 | .007 |
| control apparatus (133) | 1.7763 | 297.568 | 947 | 0 | 1,682 | 0 | .282 | 0 |
| welding apparatus (134) | 1.7744 | 231.621 | 2,147 | 32 | 3,810 | 57 | .497 | .007 |
| heating appliances (135b) | 1.7695 | 154.318 | 576 | 16 | 1,019 | 28 | .089 | .002 |
| insulated wire and cable (136) | 1.7697 | 209.119 | 486 | 0 | 860 | 0 | .102 | 0 |
| engine electrical equipment (137) | 1.7742 | 276.505 | 923 | 16 | 1,638 | 28 | .255 | .004 |
| electric lamps (138) | 1.7748 | 224.339 | 714 | 16 | 1,267 | 28 | .160 | .004 |
| tubes (140) | 1.7713 | 204.589 | 971 | 0 | 1,720 | 0 | .199 | 0 |

## Table 5-2 (Cont.)

| Industry[b] | Direct and Indirect Requirements per Million Dollars of Final Output — Capital[c] | Labor[d] | Exports per Million Dollars of Total Exports[e] | Imports per Million Dollars of Total Imports[f] | Requirements per Million Dollars of Exports and Import Replacements of Average (1947) Composition — Capital: Exports | Capital: Import replace. | Labor: Exports | Labor: Import replace. | Comparison of Export and Import Requirements[g] — Cap. | Lab. |
|---|---|---|---|---|---|---|---|---|---|---|
| 1 | 2 | 3 | 4 | 5 | 6 | 7 | 8 | 9 | 10 | 11 |
| communication equipment (142) | 1.7731 | 214.419 | 1,679 | 0 | 2,977 | 0 | .360 | 0 | | |
| storage batteries (143) | 1.7717 | 183.887 | 1,289 | 49 | 2,284 | 87 | .237 | .009 | | |
| primary batteries (143) | 1.7181 | 179.511 | 1,163 | 0 | 1,998 | 0 | .209 | 0 | | |
| x-ray apparatus (144) | 1.7663 | 172.350 | 1,457 | 16 | 2,574 | 28 | .251 | .003 | | ≥ |
| 26. motor vehicles | | | 61,151 | 1,085 | 2,104,799 | 2,104,799 | 201.779 | 201.476 | = | |
| motor vehicles (145) | 2.1048 | 201.476 | 59,892 | 1,085 | 126,061 | 2,284 | 12.067 | .219 | | |
| truck trailers (146) | 2.1048 | 216.227 | 1,259 | 0 | 2,650 | 0 | .272 | 0 | | |
| automobile trailers (147) | 2.1048 | 210.641 | 0 | 0 | 0 | 0 | 0 | 0 | | |
| 27a. other transportation equipment | | | 20,236 | 1,247 | 1,678,459 | 1,528,148 | 189.761 | 169.206 | > | > |
| aircraft and parts (148) | 1.7328 | 235.024 | 7,525 | 130 | 13,039 | 225 | 1.769 | .031 | | |
| locomotives (150) | 1.6663 | 170.126 | 4,731 | 16 | 7,883 | 27 | .805 | .003 | | |
| railroad equipment (151) | 1.6663 | 158.126 | 6,433 | 0 | 10,719 | 0 | 1.017 | 0 | | |
| motorcycles and bicycles (152) | 1.5019 | 161.216 | 1,547 | 1,101 | 2,323 | 1,654 | .249 | .177 | | |
| 27b. ships and boats (149) | 2.1404 | 263.615 | 5,360 | 810 | 11,473 | 1,734 | 1.413 | .214 | | |
| 28a. professional and scientific equipment | | | 6,566 | 11,529 | 1,844,913 | 1,840,559 | 251.904 | 238.442 | ≥ | > |
| scientific instruments (153) | 1.8465 | 266.625 | 3,748 | 65 | 6,921 | 120 | .999 | .017 | | |
| medical and dental instruments and supplies (155) | 1.8437 | 229.939 | 2,039 | 97 | 3,759 | 179 | .469 | .022 | | |
| watches and clocks (156) | 1.8405 | 238.387 | 779 | 11,367 | 1,434 | 20,921 | .186 | 2.710 | | |
| 28b. optical, ophthalmic, and photo equipment (154) | 1.8465 | 311.213 | 4,707 | 680 | 8,692 | 1,256 | 1.465 | .212 | | |
| 29. miscellaneous manufacturing (157–163) | 1.4382 | 186.429 | 10,762 | 23,771 | 15,478 | 34,188 | 2.006 | 4.432 | | |
| 30. coal, gas, and electric power | | | 22,083 | 1,133 | 1,790,214 | 3,702,030 | 209.573 | 136.805 | < | > |
| coal mining (16) | 1.7821 | 209.883 | 22,011 | 259 | 39,226 | 462 | 4.620 | .054 | | |
| electric light and power (167) | 4.2709 | 115.066 | 72 | 874 | 308 | 3,733 | .008 | .101 | | |
| natural, manufactured, and mixed gas (168) | 2.2676 | 97.194 | 0 | 0 | 0 | 0 | 0 | 0 | | |
| 31. railroad transportation (169) | 3.9285 | 186.879 | 40,957 | 0 | 160,900 | 0 | 7.654 | 0 | | |
| 32. ocean transportation (172) | 2.6324 | 165.090 | 80,361 | 40,157 | 211,542 | 105,709 | 13.267 | 6.630 | | |

| 200-order industry | | | | | | | | sign |
|---|---|---|---|---|---|---|---|---|
| | | | | | | | | < > |
| 33. other transportation | | | | | | | | |
|   trucking (170) | 1.1152 | 152.922 | 20,068 | 2,007,843 | 2,364 | 2,151,946 | 165.238 | 150.592 |
|   warehousing and storage (171) | 3.9155 | 376.255 | 9,018 | 10,057 | 0 | 0 | 1.379 | 0 |
|   other water transportation (173) | 4.2776 | 119.141 | 1,529 | 5,987 | 696 | 2,977 | .575 | 0 |
|   air transportation (174) | 1.2650 | 163.866 | 3,933 | 16,824 | 1,668 | 2,110 | .469 | .083 |
|   pipeline transportation (175) | 1.8485 | 127.555 | 4,976 | 6,295 | | | .815 | .273 |
|   local and highway transportation (178) | 1.0436 | 173.106 | 612 | 1,131 | 0 | 0 | .078 | 0 |
| 34. trade | | | 62,302 | 1,417,208 | | | 185.452 | |
|   wholesale trade (176) | 1.4157 | 185.346 | 62,158 | 87,997 | 0 | 0 | 11.521 | 0 |
|   retail trade (177) | 2.0683 | 228.730 | 144 | 298 | 0 | 0 | .033 | 0 |
| 35. communications | | | 2,272 | 5,097,887 | | | 246.360 | |
|   telephone and telegraph (179) | 5.0979 | 246.360 | 2,272 | 11,582 | 0 | 0 | .560 | 0 |
|   radio broadcasting (186a) | .8310 | 57.460 | 0 | 0 | 0 | 0 | 0 | 0 |
| 36. banking, finance, and insurance (181) | .4699 | 134.774 | 8,106 | 3,809 | 16,516 | 7,761 | 1.092 | 2.226 |
| 37. business services[i] (186b–187) | 1.6345 | 240.990 | 156 | 255 | 0 | 0 | .038 | 0 |
| 38. amusement[i] (190) | 2.2801 | 237.204 | 7,687 | 17,527 | 0 | 0 | 1.823 | 0 |

aAll figures refer to 1947.
bThe composite industries are found in W. Duane Evans and Marvin Hoffenberg, "The Interindustry Relations Study for 1947," *Review of Economics and Statistics* 34: 97–142, 1952. The component industries are based on Bureau of Labor Statistics, Division of Interindustry Economics, *Interindustry Relations Study, 1947 Emergency Model Classification*, 1–25, 1952. In column 1, the numbers in parentheses correspond to this latter classification. These industries are indicated by a or b following the 200-order industry number. Their composition in terms of the Standard Industrial Classification is as follows:

| 200-order industry | SIC no. | | |
|---|---|---|---|
| 10a fisheries | 091 | 112a tractors | 3521 |
| 10b hunting and trapping | 0741 | 112b industrial trucks | 3565 |
| 35a floor coverings | 2274, 2295 | 135a electrical appliances | 3621 |
| 35b house furnishings, etc. | 2391–2399 | 135b heating appliances | 3581, 3583, 3584, 3589 |
| 100a boiler shop products | 3443 | 186a radio broadcasting | 771 |
| 100b fabricated pipe | 3592 | 186b advertising | 731 |

cThe derivation of these figures is given in the text. The basic data on the direct capital requirements (capital coefficients) of individual industries were computed by the Harvard Economic Research Project. For a general description of methods, see Wassily Leontief and members of the Harvard Economic Research Project, *Studies in the Structure of the American Economy* (New York: Oxford University Press, 1952), chapter 6.

dSee text for the derivation of these figures. The direct labor requirements (labor coefficients) were computed by the Harvard Economic Research Project from B.L.S. and census data.

eExport figures are based on Bureau of Labor Statistics, Division of Interindustry Economics, "Table I—Interindustry Flow of Goods and Services by Industry of Origin and Destination, Section 6," October 1952. Exports are valued at producers' value: transportation, insurance, and trade margins are charged separately as export items. The total value of exports in 1947 was $16,678.4 million; the actual value of the exports of each industry can be obtained by multiplying each item in column 4 by $16,678.4.

fImport figures are based on Bureau of Labor Statistics, *op. cit*, All import figures refer to competitive imports only. All competitive imports are valued at domestic port value, i.e., foreign port value plus transportation, insurance, etc., plus duties. The total value of competitive imports in 1947 was $6,175.7 million; column 5 times $6,175.7 gives the actual value of each type of competitive import.

gThe sign > indicates that the export requirement exceeds the corresponding requirements for import replacement; < shows the opposite. The signs ≥ and ≤ mark differences accounting to less than 2 percent of the larger of the two italicized figures.

hFor the meaning of the italicized figures, see text.

iThese two industries are numbered 38 and 41, respectively, elsewhere. They are numbered consecutively here because the intervening industries do not directly participate in international trade.

jBoth the capital and labor coefficients for "other nonferrous mining" (15) must be considered unreliable (too high), since they were based on output statistics that probably did not include operations performed under the authority of the Atomic Energy Commission.

dollars more. The errors caused by the shortcut are not likely to be of decisive importance, since the similarity of their structural relationship to the rest of the economy constituted the guiding principle in the aggregation of the individual industries into the larger sectors. Even more important is that any errors that do occur in these basic computations can have no biasing effect on the final results of our numerical analysis. The disregard of differences between the *indirect* capital and labor requirements of industries belonging to the same group has, furthermore, a theoretical reason, which will become clear in the course of the later argument.

## IV. Computation of export and of import replacement costs

Now we are ready to find out whether it is true that the United States exports commodities whose domestic production absorbs relatively large amounts of capital and little labor and imports foreign goods and services that—if we had produced them at home—would employ a great quantity of indigenous labor but a small amount of domestic capital.

Let us imagine a situation in which the United States wanted to reduce its dependence on foreign countries and, to achieve this end, decided to decrease both its imports and its exports by one million dollars each. Let us, in particular, examine the rather plausible case in which the reduction of exports is to be achieved by an equal proportional cut in each export commodity, so that after the reduction the percentage composition of exports remains unchanged. The same procedure can be applied to so-called competitive imports, imports of commodities that can be and are, at least in part, actually produced by domestic industries. The level of noncompetitive imports that conventionally are taken to comprise coffee, tea, jute (but not rubber, which can be commercially synthesized), and a few other, minor items, is assumed to remain at the same time unchanged. Such an exemption obviously has a good common-sense basis. Moreover, within the context of the present analysis, it also has the closely related reason that labor and capital requirements for the domestic production of, say, coffee, cannot be realistically assessed. For later reference, one might observe that hothouses and heating installations would in any case require inordinately large capital investment per million dollars' worth of competitively produced Florida or California coffee.

To replace a million dollars' worth of imports, we would have to raise the output of the corresponding U.S. industries. If competitive imports were, as has been assumed, cut proportionally all along the line, the domestic production of the specific goods involved would have to expand by the amounts equal to the reduction in the corresponding imports, that is, by the same proportional amounts. If, for example, newsprint constituted 20 percent of all competitive imports, and woolens were 10 percent, then in replacing the total of one million dollars' worth of competitive imports, the domestic output of newsprint would have to be increased by $200,000, and the production of woolens by $100,000.

Such domestic production for replacing imports would mean additional direct and indirect capital and labor requirements. These can be determined in the following way.

The large 200-industry input-output table of the American economy for the year 1947 shows the competitive imports for that year classified by the commodity groups into which they would fall if they had been produced by our domestic industries. Dividing each of these figures by the aggregate dollar value of all competitive imports gives us the amounts by which the domestic outputs of these goods and services would have to be increased if our economy proceeded to replace commodity by commodity an aggregate million dollars' worth of (proportionally reduced) competitive imports. Column 5 in Table 5-2 shows the composition of an average million dollars' worth of competitive imports. To compute the total amount of capital that would be required to produce domestically this particular collection of commodities, one has only to multiply each of these figures by the corresponding capital requirements listed in column 2 and then find the sum total of the resulting products. The products—one for each kind of the competitive imports—are entered in column 7.

An analogous computation yields the corresponding labor requirements. Column 9 shows the number of American man-years that, in combination with the capital entered in column 7, would have to be employed to replace the foreign goods and services listed in column 3 with similar goods produced domestically.[4]

[4]For the purposes of the present analysis, we were able to utilize the previously completed computation, which shows the effects of any given change in "final demand" on the levels of output of all American industries. (See Evans and Hoffenberg, ibid.) The results of these original computations must, however, be subjected to a quantitatively not very significant but in principle very important adjustment.

Common-sense reasoning as well as actual experience shows that whenever any one of the American industries expands or contracts, the level of its operation tends to increase (or to decrease) its demand for imported inputs in a way analogous to the increases (or decreases) in its requirements for materials and services of domestic origin. An increase

The quantities of capital and labor absorbed by the American economy per million dollars of its 1947 exports can be determined in exactly the same way. Column 4 in Table 5-2 shows the composition of an average million dollars' worth of U.S. exports. The quantities of capital and labor required to produce the indicated amount of each export—obtained by multiplying each figure in Column 4 by the corresponding figure in column 2 and 3—are entered in columns 6 and 8, respectively.

## V. Empirical findings and their interpretation

The principal findings of the quantitative factual analysis described above are summarized in the figures in Table 5-3. These figures show that an average million dollars' worth of our exports embodies

---

in the rate of domestic outputs will, therefore, in general lead to a rise in the volume of the dependent imports. The usual input-output computations thus present U.S. imports as depending on the level of final demand, which, in particular, implies that any rise in exports would necessarily require an increase in imports.

For the purposes of the present analysis, this conclusion should certainly be retained in respect to inputs that are unlikely to be replaced by a supply coming from domestic sources. Coffee, jute, tin, and a number of other raw materials can be safely included in this "noncompetitive" category. In evaluating the effect of increased exports on domestic capital requirements, it seems reasonable to assume that any additional indirect demand for the above type of goods that may arise will be satisfied by foreign sources. In other words, in contemplating any possible changes in the level and the composition of our exports and imports—as they would result from alternative patterns of American foreign economic policy—it is reasonable to assume that the volume of such *noncompetitive* imports will be, in the future as in the past, directly determined by structurally conditioned domestic requirements.

With the typical competitive imports—such as cars, most other highly manufactured products, and also some raw materials such as crude oil—the situation is entirely different. If the problem of comparative costs, that is, the question of possible alternative patterns of trade, is to have any meaning in respect to such commodities, one must explicitly consider stepped-up domestic production as being an alternative to imports, and vice versa. In this context, an increase in final demand and particularly an increase in export demand should not be assumed to result in an automatic rise in competitive imports. On the contrary, the domestic repercussion—for example, the change in domestic capital and labor requirements—of additional exports must first of all be computed on the assumption that any virtual demand for competitive importation that might arise will be satisfied entirely and only through expansion of domestic output. The possibility of increasing the imports of such competitive commodities has to be considered as a separate alternative. The capital saving effects of such imports are explicitly taken into account when one separately postulates the expected changes in the level of specific competitive imports and computes the repercussion of such imports on domestic capital requirements.

In a very open economy, such as the British, the difference between the domestic reactions computed first on the assumption of an automatically induced change in the level of competing imports and then without such induced changes might be quite large; in the case of the United States—the most self-sufficient of the modern western economies—such discrepancy will be quite small. It was still, however, taken into account in the present study.

## Table 5-3

Domestic capital and labor requirements per million dollars of
U.S. exports and of competitive import replacements (of
average 1947 composition)

|  | Exports | Import Replacements |
|---|---|---|
| Capital *(dollars in 1947 prices)* | 2,550,780 | 3,091,339 |
| Labor *(man-years)* | 182.313 | 170.004 |

considerably less capital and somewhat more labor[5] than would be
required to replace from domestic production an equivalent amount
of our competitive imports. America's participation in the international division of labor is based on its specialization on labor-intensive, rather than capital-intensive, lines of production. In other
words, this country resorts to foreign trade in order to economize
its capital and dispose of its surplus labor, rather than vice versa.
The widely held opinion that—as compared with the rest of the
world—the U.S. economy is characterized by a relative surplus of
capital and a relative shortage of labor proves to be wrong. As a matter of fact, the opposite is true.

What is the explanation of this somewhat unexpected result? The
conventional view of the position the United States occupies today
in the world economy is based—as has been previously explained—

[5]There exists a good reason to believe that the excess of the labor requirements per million dollars' worth of American exports over the labor requirements for the equivalent
amount of imports replacing output is actually larger than our computations show it to
be.

Part of the labor input entering in both of these figures consists of agricultural labor.
Agricultural employment figures are well known to be biased in the upward direction,
partly because many persons living on farms do not actually work on them and partly
because a very large portion of agricultural labor input is absorbed, one could nearly say
wasted, in marginal subsistence farming.

Since the agricultural employment contributes less to the labor requirement of our
exports than it does to the replacement requirements for our competitive imports, any
downward revision in that figure would tend to increase the difference between these
two figures.

The labor requirements shown in Table 5-3 are split between the agricultural and all
other labor as follows:

Agricultural and nonagricultural labor requirements per
million dollars of U.S. exports and of competitive import
replacements (of average 1947 composition)

|  | *Exports* | *Import Replacements* |
|---|---|---|
| Agricultural labor *(man-years)* | 22.436 | 40.934 |
| Nonagricultural *(man-years)* | 159.872 | 129.069 |
| Total | 182.308 | 170.003 |

first on an empirical observation and second on a factual assumption. The observation is that the United States possesses more productive capital per worker than any other country. This can hardly be disputed.

To reach the conclusion that this means that there exists a comparative surplus of capital and a scarcity of labor in this country, the conventional argument must combine the foregoing observation with the implicit assumption that the *relative* productivity of capital and labor—if compared industry by industry—is the same here and abroad. Concretely, this assertion means that if in the United States we can transform 10 pounds of yarn into a corresponding amount of finished cloth by using, say, one man-year and $2000 worth of machinery, and transform a barrel of oil into gasoline by using one man-year and $20,000 worth of equipment, the corresponding foreign industries can perform each of these two operations either with exactly identical inputs of capital and labor or—if this is not the case—at least with inputs differing in both (and all other) industries in the same proportion. So, for example, if in India one could weave 10 pounds of yarn by using two man-years and $4000 worth of machinery (instead of one man-year and $2000 as in the United States), the cracking of one barrel of oil could also be accomplished by using a double quantity of both factors, that is, two man-years and $40,000 worth of equipment.

Only on the basis of such an assumption will the comparative costs argument necessarily lead to the conclusion that a country possessing a large stock of capital and a relatively small number of workers will find it advantageous to specialize in industries that in terms of its own productive possibilities, require much capital and relatively little labor.

Let us, however, reject the simple but tenuous postulate of comparative technological parity and make the plausible alternative assumption that, in any combination with a given quantity of capital, one man-year of American labor is equivalent to, say, three man-years of foreign labor. Then, in comparing the relative amounts of capital and labor possessed by the United States and the rest of the world—a comparison used for the explanation of their respective specialization in capital- or labor-intensive industries, respectively—the total number of American workers must be multiplied by three, which would increase our 1947 labor force from 65 million to three times that number, or 195 million of "equivalent" foreign man-years. Spread thrice as thinly as the unadjusted figures suggest, the American capital supply per "equivalent worker" turns out to be comparatively smaller, rather than larger, than that of many other countries.

This, I submit, is the analytical explanation of the results of our empirical findings. In terms of the relative production possibilities here and abroad, the United States is rich in manpower and poor in capital. This country resorts to foreign trade to save its capital and to dispose of its relative surplus labor.

Our data obviously cannot explain why American labor is more productive than foreign labor. The problem of productivity is so intricate and has been so thoroughly discussed elsewhere that no casual remarks can possibly advance its solution. The following negative observation, however, has a direct bearing on the subject of the present analysis and on the possible interpretation of its principal findings.

The extent to which the high relative efficiency of American manpower causes this country to exchange goods that absorb relatively little capital for those that would require more capital if we chose to produce them at home *cannot* be caused simply by the large amount of capital American industry uses per employed worker.

The fact that workers are frequently replaced by machines cannot be denied. But such technological substitution, if profitable in the United States, would in general be profitable also in the corresponding industries abroad. The argument that the comparative shortage of capital might prevent the use of the same labor-saving technology by foreign countries would only hold if international trade, that is, the international division of labor, did not exist. Actually, it does take place, and if it were simply the problem of substituting capital for labor, foreign countries could and would imitate the American production practice industry by industry. At the same time their production would be concentrated on those commodities that, both there as well as in the United States, require relatively little capital and large amounts of labor. The United States would for similar reasons concentrate on capital-intensive industries, and the trade between it and the rest of the world would consist in an exchange of American capital-intensive against foreign labor-intensive goods.[6] Our empirical findings indicate that, in fact, the opposite is true.

[6]To clarify the internal logic of the argument leading to this assertion, let us consider—from the point of view of the world as a whole—the double problem of, first, allocating capital and labor among the various industries and, second, locating the various industries in specific countries endowed with different relative amounts of capital and labor.

If, in accordance with the conventional argument but in contradiction to the argument presented in this chapter, one considers the technological possibilities to be the same throughout the world—that is, if one assumes that with a given amount of capital and a

Thus, without denying that capital can be substituted for labor, we must still look for some other reason to explain the high productivity of labor in America as compared with the labor employed by similar industries abroad.

Entrepreneurship and superior organization have often been mentioned in this connection. In accepting this most plausible explanation, we must, however, make the following comment. Both of these, as well as such other factors as education or the general climate of our production-oriented soceity, certainly do make the American economy more efficient in the sense that it is able to achieve the same output of finished commodities and services with smaller inputs of capital and labor. There exists a definite statistical evidence that the man-hour and capital investments both measured per unit of output have been reduced in many of our industries through better utilization of equipment and more rational use of

---

given number of indigenous man-years every industry in England, in India, or anywhere else is able to produce an output equal to that which the corresponding American industry *could* achieve with the *same* amount of capital and an equal number of (American) man-years—that double task can be accomplished in the following two steps.

First, considering the total stock of capital and the combined supply of labor of all countries and taking into account the total world demand for various commodities and services, the proverbial "invisible hand" of competitive adjustment would determine—on the basis of the uniform technological possibilities of the world as a whole—the proper amounts of capital and labor that each industry would best use per, say, every million dollars' worth of its respective output. Barring certain special, unusual situations, this decision could and would be made without any regard to the actual distribution of the combined labor and capital resources of the world among the different countries. This distribution could be taken into account separately in the next step in which all the individual industries would be actually assigned to the separate countries. In accordance with the "comparative supply of factors" considerations described in the first section of this chapter, this second step will result in placing the industries requiring relatively large amounts of capital into the countries comparatively well supplied with that particular factor and in locating the labor-intensive lines of production in the areas having a comparatively larger supply of labor.

As a final result of such efficient "comparative costs" allocation, the capital-rich countries must specialize on the production and export of capital-intensive goods, while the labor-rich areas will produce and export labor-intensive commodities, while importing goods that, when produced at home, would absorb comparatively large amounts of capital and little labor.

It is particularly important to observe that under the assumption of technological parity the combination of capital and labor used in each industry—having been decided in the first stage of the two-stage allocation procedure described above—will necessarily be the same in all the countries. For example, any specific textile product requiring much capital and little labor when made in the United States would also require the same combination of these two factors if it had been produced in England, in India, or in any other country. Being short of capital, that is, of the factor that this product uses most, these other countries would, however, manufacture only relatively small amounts of that particular textile or even none at all.

labor.[7] To explain the comparative surplus of labor which our figures unmistakably reveal, we must, however, also infer that entrepreneurship, superior organization, and favorable environment must have increased—in comparison with other countries—the productivity of American labor much more than they have raised the efficiency of American capital.

From the point of view of sheer arithmetic, the American comparative capital shortage and labor surplus—as revealed in our figures—could, of course, be equally well explained if, instead of assuming that American man-years are more productive than foreign man-years, we took the labor productivity to be the same here and abroad but at the same time assumed the U.S. capital to be less productive than its dollar equivalent in foreign countries. Such an alternative explanation, implying an absolute inferiority of the American productive technology, hardly would pass the test of empirical scrutiny; it is plainly contradicted by the fact that an average American man-year receives a much higher remuneration than the man-year of labor employed in most other countries.

## VI. Empirical analysis of subsidiary relationships

Before directing our attention to the wider economic implications of these general conclusions, it is well to examine once more their empirical background.

Although computed on the basis of a rather detailed industrial classification, the amounts of capital and labor used in the production of American exports and those required for the replacement of competitive imports have been compared above only in terms of the overall averages. If the explanation that has been given to these quantitative findings is correct, similar relationships should also be discovered within separate commodity groups.

A visual presentation of the quantitative relationships revealed by the figures contained in the first four columns of Table 5-2 is given in Figure 5-1. Since we deal here with essentially four-dimensional phenomena, they cannot possibly be described in an ordinary two-dimensional graph. Each one of the black-white blocks on the graph must be visualized as standing on the flat surface of the paper, not unlike a diminutive skyscraper rising above the base map in a three-

[7]See Wassily Leontief, "Machines and Man," *Scientific American* 187: 150–60, 1952. A different point of view is presented in the detailed factual study by L. Rostas, *Comparative Productivity in British and American Industry* (Cambridge: Cambridge University Press, 1948).

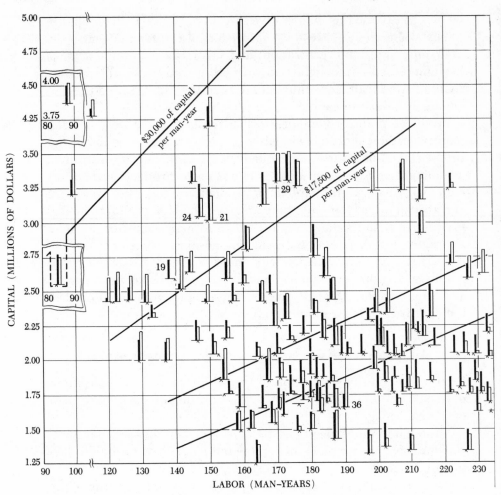

dimensional model of New York City. Each block represents a separate commodity type. Its position, or more exactly the position of its base, on the flat surface of the map reflects the capital-labor combination per million dollars of output required for its production in the United States, the capital requirement being measured upward along the scale marked along the left-hand side of the chart, and the labor requirements measured horizontally along the man-years scale entered along the bottom margin.

The length of the black strip in each block (in a truly three-dimensional figure it would be measured by its height above the capital-labor plane) represents the level of exports, and the white strip represents the imports of commodities of a particular kind.

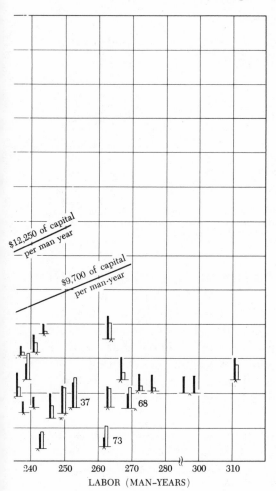

LABOR (MAN-YEARS)

### Figure 5-1

This graph displays the relationship between the differences in the quantities of capital and labor absorbed in the United States (directly and indirectly) in production of one million dollars' worth of various classes of goods and the comparative magnitude of the exports and imports of goods belonging in each class. The height of each black bar represents the total exports, and the height of its white twin represents the total inputs of one particular class of goods, while it position on the chart—as measured by the distance from the horizontal and the vertical coordinate, respectively—indicates the amount of capital and labor absorbed in production of one dollar's worth of that particular class of goods. Exports and imports are measured on a logarithmic scale, which reduces the contrast between the very tall and the very short bars.

To make it possible to distinguish at a glance the proportions in which capital and labor are combined in the U.S. production of the various commodities, slanting lines are entered on the chart showing the capital/labor ratios of $30,000 per man-year, $17,500 per man-year, and so on. The capital/labor ratios, that is, the slopes of these four lines, are chosen so as to include as nearly as possible one-fifth of the total U.S. foreign trade turnover (i.e., of exports per million dollars of total exports plus imports per million dollars of total imports, as listed in column 4 and column 5 of Table 5-2) into each of the resulting five radial segments in Figure 5-1.

One can clearly see that in the upper left-hand part of the map—in the sectors containing goods that require for their production

## Table 5-4

Exports and imports compared by sectors with different capital intensity

| Capital per Man-year (in dollars) | Trade Turnover[a] (in dollars) | Percentage of Turnover | |
|---|---|---|---|
| | | Exports | Imports |
| 1 | 2 | 3 | 4 |
| More than 30,000 | 411,103 | 27.39 | 72.61 |
| 30,000–17,750 | 394,465 | 47.90 | 52.10 |
| 17,750–12,250 | 372,425 | 48.31 | 51.69 |
| 12,250– 9,700 | 395,028 | 61.76 | 38.24 |
| Less than   9,700 | 393,869 | 69.62 | 30.38 |
| Aggregate | 1,966,890 | 50.82 | 49.18 |

[a]Turnover within the line segments is not exactly equal since they had to be summed for integral industries. Aggregate turnover differs from two million dollars due to rounding and omission of the "other nonferrous mineral mining" industry—see footnote *f*, Table 5-2.

larger amounts of capital and comparatively small quantities of labor—the white parts tend to be taller than the black parts of the same blocks. As one moves toward the lower right-hand corner, the black strips tend to become higher than the corresponding white strips; the tendency to export goods requiring much labor and little capital for their domestic production and to import those that demand much capital and little labor can in other words be as clearly discerned in this detailed picture as it is reflected in the overall averages presented above.[8]

The results of this visual examination are substantiated by the numerical compilation in Table 5-4. It shows that, as the capital/labor ratio goes down, exports make up an even larger and imports a smaller fraction of the corresponding foreign trade turnovers.

We have examined the overall choice that the American economy makes when it allocates its capital and labor to produce a million dollars' worth of the average combination of exportable goods instead of using them to replace an equivalent average combination of imports. Behind it are subsidiary choices based on differences in the labor and capital requirements of specific export and import goods belonging to the same commodity group and, because of that, directly competing with each other. The presence of direct com-

[8]The following 10 service industries are omitted from presentation in our figure: railroad transportation (31), trucking (170), warehousing and storage (171), pipeline transport (1975), local and highway transportation (178), wholesale trade (176), retail trade (177), banking, etc. (36), amusements (38), communications (35), and other water transportation (173). Being essentially nontransportable, the products of these industries cannot enter into any direct competition with imputed products of the same kind.

petitive relationships—or at least of more direct competitive relationships than those that exist among all commodities entering international trade—is of the essence for the existence of such separate subsidiary allocation problems. A proper isolation and detailed quantitative description of such "internally competitive" groups constitute the necessary prerequisites for their empirical analysis.

The study of this particular aspect of our primary data has not yet been completed.[9] A careful perusal of the composition of American exports and imports as listed in columns 4 and 5 of Table 5-2 enables us nevertheless to delineate a number of commodity groups that might reasonably, that is, on the basis of the general knowledge one has about them, qualify for preliminary analysis. As should be expected, they correspond rather closely to the 38 consolidated industries described above. Some of the latter, however, had to be broken down so as to separate important sets of obviously noncompeting operations such as the mining and final fabrication of metals; from some others, single noncompetitive components had to be eliminated. A large number of export and import goods (although all of these, of course, were included in the computation of the overall average capital and labor requirements) had to be omitted from the following analysis either because they did not fall into any definite competitive set or because they formed small sets containing only two or three items.

Most commodities were actually combined in "internally competing" groups, and each set was subjected separately to the same analysis that was previously applied to all exports and all competitive imports taken together. The average amount of capital and the average quantity of labor required to produce a million dollars' worth of exports falling within each such commodity group were computed; similar computations were performed for the corresponding sets of competitive—in this case, directly competitive—imports. In each instance the average was obtained by weighting the capital and labor requirements of an individual product (as listed in columns 2 and 3 of Table 5-2) in proportion to the value of the exports and imports of that particular product per million dollars of the exports and imports, respectively, for the group into which it belongs as a

[9]This study leads directly toward the problems involved in generalized formulation of interregional input-output theory. The distinction between typically "domestic" and the predominantly "international" commodities is as fundamental for such analysis as the lower-order distinction between "national" and "regional" commodities used in the study of the regional structure of the U.S. economy. (See Wassily Leontief, et al., *Studies in the Structure of the American Economy*, Chapters 4 and 5.)

whole. The results of these computations are entered in italics in columns 6, 7, 8, and 9, opposite the names of the groups listed on the left in column 1.

To facilitate the interpretation of these subsidiary computations, the results of the comparison of the capital and labor requirements for export and import replacement within each of the 26 distinct "internally competitive" groups are shown in the last two columns (columns 10 and 11) of Table 5-2. The sign > indicates that the export requirement exceeds the corresponding requirement for import replacement, < shows that the import replacement requirement is the larger of the two. To mark very small differences (amounting to less than 2 percent of the larger of the two figures), which should perhaps be interpreted as equalities, we used the signs ≥ and ≤.

The box scores in Tables 5-5 and 5-6 summarize the final results, showing the values of exports and competitive imports that fall within each of the distinct "comparative cost types" per million dollars of all exports and competitive imports, respectively. Only 63 percent of all exports and 59 percent of imports fell into specific competitive groups. The rest, which did not fit into any one of them, constitute a separate group. On the basis of its comparative labor and capital requirements for exports and import replacements, this residual group falls in the lower left box. It is represented by the figures in parentheses.

The examination of these figures shows that the direct competition between exports and imports belonging to the same commodity groups is dominated by our relative capital shortage and labor sur-

### Table 5-5

Exports                                    (*unit:* $1000)

Capital

| Labor | | < | ≤ ≥ | > | Total |
|---|---|---|---|---|---|
| | < | 106 | 45 | 0 | 150 |
| | ≤ ≥ | 63 | 78 | 0 | 141 |
| | > | 180 (+374) | 97 | 58 | 335 (+374) |
| | Total | 348 (+374) | 220 | 58 | |

### Table 5-6

Competitive imports   (*unit:* $1000)

Capital

| Labor | | < | ≤ ≥ | > | Total |
|---|---|---|---|---|---|
| | < | 98 | 6 | 0 | 104 |
| | ≤ ≥ | 3 | 50 | 0 | 53 |
| | > | 330 (+408) | 99 | 6 | 435 (+408) |
| | Total | 431 (+408) | 155 | 6 | |

plus, as is the overall average picture of American foreign trade which we have considered before. Goods of the type requiring comparatively more American man-years (but a smaller amount of capital) on the export side have a lion's share ($180,000 + $374,000) of our exports, while our competitive imports consist primarily of goods ($330,000 + $408,000) that, if they were produced at home, would absorb relatively large quantities of capital but smaller amounts of American labor. Disregarding the labor requirement entirely, we also see that commodities requiring for their production relatively small amounts of capital dominate our exports ($348,000 + $309,000) while the capital-intensive commodities— irrespective of their labor intensity—are preponderant among competitive imports ($431,000 + $408,000).

Invisible in all these tables but ever-present as a third factor, or rather as a whole additional set of factors determining this country's productive capacity and, in particular, its comparative advantage vis-à-vis the rest of the world, are the natural resources: agricultural land, forests, rivers, and rich mineral deposits. Absence of systematic quantitative information, similar to what has been collected, organized, and used in this chapter with respect to capital and labor, prevents us as yet from introducing this important element explicitly into this preliminary analysis.

However, indirect but clear signs of the influence of natural resources can easily be traced in the capital and labor input figures presented in Table 5-2 and depicted in Figure 5-1. This influence is revealed mostly in their deviation from the dominant pattern reflecting the comparative capital shortage and labor surplus of the American economy. Without embarking on a detailed but necessarily conjectural examination of such special cases, let me point to only a few of them as seen in Figure 5-1.

Near its lower right-hand corner we find a few entires in which, contrary to the general tendency prevailing in that part of the graph, the white part of the twin block is taller than its black part. Consulting Table 5-2, we find that these labor-intensive and capital-extensive industries showing such unusually weak position vis-à-vis competitive foreign imports comprise "sawmill" (37), "pottery" (73), and "leather products other than shoes" (68). All of them are based on natural materials in which the United States is obviously short as compared with the foreign countries. On the other side of the cluster among the capital-intensive and labor-extensive commodities of which we import as a rule more than we export, "sulphur" (19), "meat packing" (21), and "grain mill" (24) products show a considerable export surplus. The United States is apparently comparatively well situated with respect to the domestic supply of such specific mineral and agricultural natural resources as are required in the production of these particular goods.

Without the necessary additional information, any further pursuit of this line of reasoning is bound to become highly speculative. Conjecture about facts is intriguing but—at least in the field of economics—essentially futile in the long run. Since the facts pertaining to this particular subject are now being collected and organized, it might be well to refrain from further speculation, however tempting it may be.

## VII.  Some general implications

This study has been designed to ascertain the structural basis of U.S. trade with the rest of the world. We find that, contrary to widely held opinion, our exchange of domestically produced goods for competitive imports serves as a means to compensate for the comparative shortage of our domestic capital supply and a corresponding oversupply of American labor.

Without attempting a systematic exploration of the possible wide-reaching implications of these empirical findings, let me merely mention here a few questions whose answers might be seriously affected by the results of this preliminary investigation.

Foremost is the problem of the changing position of the United States in the natural resources—as compared with capital and labor—that dominated our early development and our trade relations with foreign countries up to about 1910. From the fact that at the present time capital appears to be comparatively more scarce than labor, one might surmise that this scarcity has dominated our entire economic development until now. This would mean that—in terms of a comparison with the rest of the world—our capital supply, while steadily growing, has still not caught up with the increase in our labor force, if the peculiarly high effectiveness of that labor force is taken into account. A larger supply of domestic capital, if not matched by a corresponding increase in domestic manpower, will in any case reduce rather than increase the comparative advantage in labor supply on which our present exchange of goods and services with foreign countries seems to be based. In other words, a more rapid rise in our average productive investment per worker would diminish rather than increase the advantage derived by the United States from its foreign trade. Only a spectacular additional increase in domestic capital stock could tip the balance of comparative advantage to the other side and thus bring about conditions that by common assumption are already supposed to exist, that is, a situation in which the United States would actually find it advantageous to use its foreign trade as a means to save American labor and to dispose of surplus American capital. In view of the determined effort of many so-called backward countries to increase their own capital stock, such tipping of the scale will take some time. On the other hand, the factors, whatever they may be, that are responsible for the peculiarly high relative productivity of American labor might soon become operative in other economies and thus accelerate the elimination of disparity between the effective comparative supply of capital and labor here and in foreign countries. This signifies, of course, a reduced incentive to the continued exchange of commodities and services between the United States and the rest of the world.

Since no discussion of foreign trade is considered to be well rounded without some mention of free trade and protection, I conclude with an observation on that timeless subject. An increase in the U.S. tariff must obviously reduce the volume of our competitive imports below what it otherwise would have been; by restricting the effective foreign demand for American goods, it would also bring about a corresponding cut in our exports. Since the exchange of goods and services with foreign countries serves as a means to relieve the pressure of our domestic labor surplus and our capital shortage, a partial closing of that valve will tend to increase such pressure. In other words, protectionist policies are bound to weaken the bargaining position of American labor and correspondingly strengthen that of the owners of capital.

# 6

## Factor proportions and the structure of American trade: Further theoretical and empirical analysis

### (1956)

### I

This is a second report on the progress of a continuing investigation into the structural basis of the trade relationships between the United States and the rest of the world. The first report, published in 1954,[1] elicited a number of critical comments.[2] Some of these are, I hope, at least partly answered by the results of the additional and more comprehensive analysis presented here. No reasonably conclusive replies to others can, however, be given without a much deeper and wider factual inquiry.

The classical theory of comparative costs, in its modernized version which explicitly allows for the existence of more than one scarce primary resource, makes up the formal background of the entire study.

For a full-fledged application of a general equilibrium approach

---

[1]"Domestic Production and Foreign Trade: The American Capital Position Re-Examined," *Proceedings of the American Philosophical Society* 97, September 1953. Also reprinted in *Economia Internazionale* VII, 1954.

[2]P. T. Ellsworth, "The Structure of American Foreign Trade: A New View Examined"; Boris Swerling, "Capital Shortage and Labor Surplus in the United States"—both published in *Review of Economics and Statistics* XXXVI, August 1954. Stefan Valavanis-Vail, "Leontief's Scarce Factor Paradox," *Journal of Political Economy* LXII, December 1954; Gustaaf F. Loeb, "A estrutura do comercio exterior da America do norte," *Revista Brasileira de Economia* 8, December 1954; David Granick, "The American Capital Position in Foreign Trade: A comment," *Southern Economic Journal* XXII, October 1955; Norman S. Buchanan, "Lines on the Leontief Paradox," *Economia Internazionale* VIII, 1955.

This chapter originally appeared in the *Review of Economics and Statistics*, Vol. 38, No. 4, 1956. This study was conducted as part of the research program of the Harvard Economic Research Project. Marie McCarthy and Charlotte Taskier, staff members of the project, were in charge of the statistical and computational work.

to the explanation of the level and composition of the trade between this country and the rest of the world, we would have to possess concrete quantitative information about (1) the endowment of each of the trading countries with the so-called primary factors of production, (2) the shapes of the production functions, that is, of the input-output relationships that govern in each country the transformation of these primary resources into various goods and services, and, last but not least, (3) preferences determining in each area the choice among alternative bundles of finished commodities it could actually attain through alternative combinations of domestic production and foreign trade.

Such wealth of data, of course, we do not yet possess. The information collected in the last 10 years within the framework of the systematic input-output studies of the American economy lays bare, however, at least one aspect of the hitherto almost entirely concealed structure—the part of it that can be seen when viewed from the side of one of the trading countries, the United States.

The formal setting of the problem can be elucidated by a schematic diagram such as Figure 6-1. It describes a situation involving two countries, two primary factors of production, and two commodities. Fixed amounts of the two factors of production are required per unit of output of each commodity. These amounts—referred to also as "technical coefficients"—are not assumed to be the same in both countries. As a matter of fact, the primary factors available and actually used in one of them might be entirely different from those employed in the other. The "final demand" functions are, however, taken to be identical in both areas, and by analogy with the production functions they are described in terms of a given fixed proportion between the amounts in which the two finished commodities are to be consumed. The similarity of the two demand functions is assumed only to simplify the graphic presentation. It is not essential to the basic argument.[3]

The upper right-hand quadrant of Figure 6-1 depicts the situation in country 1. The output of good $X$ is measured—from left to right—along the horizontal and the output of good $Y$ upward along the vertical axis. The straight line connecting points $y_a$ and $x_a$ describes all the alternative combinations of $X$ and $Y$ that could be produced if the entire amount of factor $A$ available in country I were used up in the production of these two commodities and if factor $B$

---

[3]An algebraic formulation of the model, generalized for any number of commodities and factors, is presented later in this chapter in Appendix 6-1.

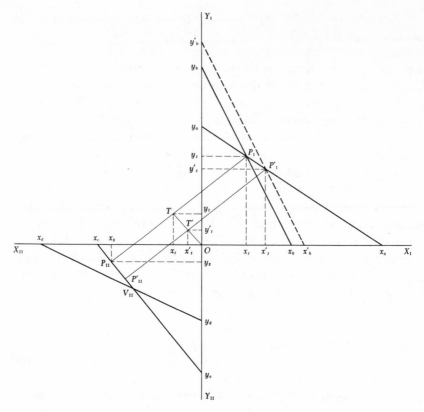

**Figure 6-1**

were available in unlimited supply. Analogously, the straight line
$y_b x_b$ contains all outputs of X and Y that would exhaust all the given
quantity of factor B, provided factor A were free. The combination
of these two limits, one imposed by the given quantity of A and the
other by the available amount of B, yields the broken convex line
$y_a P_1 x_b$ which delineates the effective productive capabilities of country I. The student of earlier literature will recognize it as the familiar
opportunity cost curve of commodity Y in terms of commodity X
and vice versa.

A similar construction in the lower left-hand quadrant describes
the productive capabilities of country II. Its output of good X is also
measured along the horizontal axis but in the opposite direction—
from right to left. The amount of good Y is represented by vertical
distances and is measured downward. The line $x_c y_c$ describes the
limits imposed on the productive capability of country II by the
available amount of the primary factor C, and line $x_d y_d$ shows the

limits imposed by the given supply of factor $D$; $x_c V_{II} y_d$ constitute thus the effective boundary of the overall productive capabilities of country II.

The total output of $X$ and $Y$ in both countries can now be easily measured. If point $P_I$ describes, for example, the output combination in country I and $P_{II}$ the corresponding combination in country II, the distance between points $x_2$ and $x_1$ represents the aggregate output of good $X$, and the stretch from $y_2$ to $y_1$ shows the corresponding total output of good $Y$.

The numerical ratio of the total output of $X$ to the total output of $Y$ can finally be identified as the slope of the line $P_{II}P_I$ connecting point $P_{II}$ with point $P_I$. Total production within the context of the argument equals total final consumption, and the slope of the production vector $P_{II}P_I$ (which could be also identified as the consumption vector) represents accordingly the relative amounts of $X$ and $Y$ consumed in both countries taken together. If that proportion is assumed to be structurally determined by the nature of their respective tastes and independent of the absolute level of consumption, the question of optimal utilization of the productive capacities of the two countries is reduced to the problem of fitting the longest possible production vector of the prescribed slope between the opportunity cost curves $x_c V_{II} y_d$ and $y_a P_I x_b$.

In the specific configuration of the productive capabilities described in Figure 6-1, $P_{II}P_I$ represents the longest production vector of the required slope that can thus be fitted; any other line parallel to it, spanning the distance between the two given opportunity cost curves, would obviously be shorter.

Now let us introduce a change in the data underlying the original situation by endowing country I with an additional amount of the primary factor $B$.

If both input coefficients describing the quantities of $B$ required to produce, respectively, a unit of $X$ and a unit of $Y$ remain the same, the overall productive capabilities of country I will rise. In the chart this increase will be reflected through an outward parallel displacement of the line $y_b x_b$. Let $y_b' x_b'$ be its new position; then $y_a P_I' X_b'$ will represent the new, expanded effective overall capacity of the economy.

Under these changed conditions $P_{II}' P_I'$ instead of $P_{II}P_I$ will be the best, that is, the longest, production vector of the prescribed slope attainable by the combined productive capacities of both countries. This means that in country I the output of $X$ will go from $x_1$ to $x_1'$ while the production of $Y$ will at the same time be reduced from $y_1$

to $y_1'$. An opposite shift from $X$ to $Y$ will take place in the output combination of country II.

To show what commodity and how much of it each of the two countries will trade for the product of the other, we must first explain the determination of the relative price of $X$ and $Y$, that is, of the ratio at which they will be exchanged when the most efficient production pattern has been established.

Note that the lower end of the optimal production vector $P_{II}P_I$ leans against one side of the opportunity cost curve of country II, while the other fits exactly in the corner, $P_I$, of the opportunity cost curve $y_a P_I x_b$ of country I. Such an asymmetrical position must necessarily result whenever one is attempting to fit the longest possible vector of a prescribed slope between two limits each composed of straight facets. A vector, both of whose ends abut upon the middle of such facets, can (if these do not happen to be parallel) always be lengthened through an upward or a downward shift. That shift must stop—and the optimal position of the vector will then have been reached—when either one of its two ends gets into a corner. Only in a very singular, and because of that exceptional, combination of structural conditions in the two countries would both ends of the vector hit such corner positions simultaneously. In all other cases the production vector, in its optimal position, will touch one of the opportunity cost curves between which it is stretched, not in a corner or at a point in which it touches the $X$ or $Y$ axis, but rather at a point located somewhere along one of its two facets.

In the figure the point of optimal output combination in country II, $P_{II}$, is located on the line $s_c y_c$ but not on $x_d y_d$. This signifies full utilization of the entire available supply of factor $C$ and only partial employment of factor $D$. It follows that in this case $D$ turns out to be a free good and $C$ that country's only scarce factor of production. As a matter of fact, the information on the available supply of factor $D$ and its required inputs for the production of $X$ and $Y$ in country II proves not to be required for the solution of our problem. The line $x_d y_d$, which represents on the graph all information pertaining to factor $D$, could be erased without affecting—within the given constellation of all the other structural conditions—the quantitative determination of the production, consumption, and trading of the two finished commodities between the two countries. Had factor $D$, however, not been available in country II, that area would obviously not be able to make for itself or supply abroad any commodities for the production of which that factor is required. This means that the availability or lack of some free resources can often explain the pres-

ence or absence of certain branches of industry or agriculture in a
particular area. At the same time the specific quantitative determination of the level of output of such industries—in case the factor
is available and the industries exist—would require neither any
knowledge of the total available supply of such a factor nor any
quantitative information concerning the specific requirements for
such factors by the industries concerned. Warm climate, water, certain types of soil and mineral deposits, possibly even the vague but
obviously important complex of human and social circumstances
defined as entrepreneurship—all of such factors and conditions
which are often available in some areas in great abundance but are
completely absent in many others—might occupy in the quantitative analysis of foreign trade a position similar to that of factor $D$ in
our simple diagram.

The relative prices of goods $X$ and $Y$ in country II must obviously
be equal to the ratio of the amounts of factor $C$ required to produce
these two commodities. On the graph, that ratio is represented by
the slope of the line $x_c y_c$; the steeper that slope, the higher the price
of $X$ must be in relation to the price of $Y$. Unlike the corner position
of $P_I$ in country I, the location of production point $P_{II}$ in country II
enables it to shift its primary resources out of the production of $X$
into that of $Y$ in response to every deviation of the relative prices of
the two commodities from their comparative real costs. That means
that the slope of lines $x_c y_c$ determines that price ratio not only for
country II but also for country I and the trade between the two. The
direction and the composition of that trade can now be ascertained.

Country I, having produced $x_1$ units of $X$ and $y_1$ units of $Y$, will
trade to country II $y_t$ units of $Y$ in exchange for $x_t$ units of $X$. In the
geometric language of our graph that transaction is described as a
move from point $O$ to point $T$ on the combined production vectors
of the two countries, $P_{II}P_I$. Line $OT$ is drawn parallel to $y_c x_c$, which
means that the exchange is transacted in accordance with the price
ratio determined before. The final consumption of $X$ by country I is
represented by the distance from $x_t$ to $x_1$ and its consumption of $Y$
by the distance between $y_t$ and $y_1$. Country II's consumption of $X$ is,
on the other hand, measured by the distance between $x_2$ and $x_t$ and
its consumption of $Y$ by the stretch from $y_2$ to $y_t$.

In short, the optimal production vector $P_{II}P_I$ is divided by the
point $T$ at its contact with the international trade vector $OT$ in two
parts, of which one, $TP_I$, represents the final demand (i.e., the consumption) vector of country I and the other, $TP_{II}$, the final demand
vector of country II.

The specific configuration of all these magnitudes can thus be explained in terms of the shapes of the production functions used, the supply of scarce factors, and the composition of the final demand in both countries. The effect of a change in any one of these structural determinants on the production and consumption of both commodities in each of the two countries and the trade relationships between them can, consequently, also be traced.

As has already been shown above, an increase in the supply of factor $B$ in country I will bring about a shift in the overall production vector to the new position $P'_{II}P'_{I}$. Now it can also be seen that that shift will be accompanied by a reduction in the length of the trade vector from $OT$ to $OT'$, that is, a shrinkage in the volume of international exchange.

An increase or a decrease in the supply of factor $C$ in country II, that is, an upward or downward parallel shift of line $x_c y_c$, would bring about a corresponding displacement of point $P_{II}$ without, however, producing any change in the position of the upper end, $P_{I}$, of the aggregate production vector $P_{I}P_{II}$ or in the length of the trade vector $OT$.

Without further elaboration or generalization of the conceptual approach exemplified by the two-dimensional graph, it can be seen that it simply represents a systematic linearization of the conventional neoclassical theory of international trade. All the familiar relationships and propositions that are usually described and derived in terms of more general continuous production and consumption functions appear here in the new garb of angular graphs and linear equations. Although in purely theoretical inquiry the fad for vectors, matrices, and the other paraphernalia of linear geometry and algebra does not seem to offer any tangible advantages over the derivatives and Lagrange multipliers of conventional calculus, for purposes of empirical analysis the restrictions imposed upon the formal properties of our system by the use of fixed consumption and production coefficients and linear equations seem to be quite appropriate. In the present instance, these restrictions introduce consistently into the conceptual framework of the theory of international trade the principle of linear approximation on which the following empirical analysis is essentially based.

A much more serious restriction than that resulting from recourse to linear approximation has been imposed on this study by the necessity to limit—at least at its present stage—the empirical investigation to the description of only one part of the total picture. It is as if we had observed the slopes and relative position of the curve on one side of our diagram, including the shape and length of the trade vector, but not on the other. In conventional partial supply-demand analysis an analogous situation arises whenver one is given, say, the shape of the supply curve and the point of its intersection with the demand curve without being otherwise informed about that demand curve's shape. All operational statements one can make in such a case in explanation of the observed quantities and prices must be based on partial conjecture or framed in conditional terms. Realizing that most of us prefer to make our own conjectures, I will now turn to facts.

## II

The winding course of a comprehensive empirical investigation is governed by a sequence of tactical decisions. Each one of these is based on the examination of intermediate results and also is critically dependent on the flow of primary data as well as the complexity and costs of various computational procedures.

The input-output matrix of the American economy for the year 1947, the corresponding sets of so-called capital and labor coefficients, and a detailed tabulation in dollar value terms of U.S. exports and imports—all of these different sets of figures organized and presented in terms of the same industrial classification—constitute the factual basis of our entire study. The immediate objective of the original inquiry was to determine the amounts of capital and labor required for the production in the United States of a million dollars' worth of two alternative composite commodities, one defined as the U.S. 1947 exports and the other as the U.S. 1947 competitive imports.

In simplified theoretical examples, such as that presented in Figure 6-1, the quantity of each primary factor absorbed in the production of any one of the traded goods is usually assumed to be immediately observable. In a real national economy—which can be concisely described only as a system of many interdependent activities or sectors—this obviously is not the case. The amount of capital or labor required for the production, say, of an additional million dollars' worth of automobiles for export or final domestic use can be determined only through the summation of as many separate capital and labor inputs as there are distinct sectors in the economy. Each industry, for example, participates at least indirectly in the production of automobiles and, consequently, contributes at least some part of its own capital and labor to the total quantities of these two factors used by the economic system as a whole for the production of that final output. The total, that is, direct and indirect, dependence of the output of each industry on the final demand for the products of any other industry is, in general, determined not only by the input-output structure of these two industries but also by those of all other sectors of the economy.

Without entering into the technical details of actual computations, let me simply observe that the original input-output table showing the direct input requirements of each industry for the products of other industries can be transformed into a new table called its inverse. The entries into this, also rectangular, array of figures indicate by how much the total output of each sector would be raised to satisfy the total, that is, direct and indirect, requirements corresponding to, say, one million dollars' worth of additional deliveries to final demand—of its own products or alternatively the products of any other sector.

Given the quantities of capital, labor, or any other factor employed by each industry per unit of its output,[4] these coefficients can be multiplied with the appropriate rows of the inverse. Thus, a new set of tables is obtained which show the additional amounts of these factors needed by each industry for the satisfaction of the direct and indirect demand for its output generated by each million dollars' worth of final deliveries of its own products and alternatively the products of all other sectors. A column-by-column summation of the entries in each of these tables yields the total quantities of the respective factor absorbed throughout the economy *as a whole* per million dollars' worth of final deliveries made by each of its productive sectors.[5]

After the requisite reclassification, the foreign trade statistics show how many dollars' worth of the final output of each industry were in fact exported per average million dollars' worth of aggregate 1947 exports. Since the total labor and capital inputs per dollars' worth of each kind of final output were previously determined, the total quantity of either factor absorbed in the production of a million dollars' worth of the composite commodity defined as "U.S. 1947 exports" is finally obtained as a weighted sum of the corresponding requirements of each of its many separate components.

The computation of the quantities of capital and labor directly and indirectly absorbed in the production of the composite commodity defined as "U.S. 1947 competitive imports" differs from the pro-

[4]See, in this chapter, Appendix 6-3, columns 1 and 2.
[5]See, in this chapter, Appendix 6-3, columns 3 and 4.

cedure just described only in its very last step. The average composition of one million dollars' worth of competitive imports—
instead of the corresponding structure of exports—determines the
weights used in the aggregation of the factor requirements first separately derived for each of the final outputs.

With its present technology and a given endowment of labor, capital, and natural resources, this country finds it advantageous to satisfy its entire demand for commodities such as coffee and other tropical products as well as certain minerals by imports from abroad.
These are identified for purposes of the present study as noncompetitive imports. The competitive imports comprise all other goods
that, although imported, are also produced in relatively substantial
quantities at home.

In an angular linearized system such as that represented in Figure
6-1, the distinction between the two would be quite clean and
sharp. If, for example, the slope of $P_I y_a$ were steeper instead of flatter than the slope of $V_{II} x_c$, the aggregate consumption vector $P_{II} P_I$
could have been lengthened by an upward shift. And the optimal
equilibrium position would only be attained when either the upper
end of that vector stops at point $y_a$ or its lower end stops at $x_c$,
depending on which of these two alternative positions is reached
first. In either case one of the countries would concentrate entirely
on the production of a single good. In terms of the given definition,
the import of the other good into that country would become noncompetitive. Had country I concentrated for this reason entirely on
the production of good $Y$, its actual input coefficient of factor $A$ in
the production of good $X$ could not have been observed, since such
production would actually not take place. Neither would the knowledge of the exact magnitude of that coefficient be required for the
explanation of the effect—on the observed situation—of small
changes in any of the basic data. A limited change in that particular
coefficient itself would have no repercussions whatsoever. Only if it
were to diminish to such an extent as to make the slope of $P_I y_a$ again
flatter than that of $P_{II} x_c$ would the trade vector be reshifted to its
original position. The analogy between these considerations and the
comments previously made on the explanatory role of the so-called
free factor is obvious. What we do not know about methods of production that are not actually used and resources that are not fully
employed cannot hurt our ability to explain the observed situation.

The allocation of scarce resources among various industries and
the structure of our foreign trade would hardly change if the actual
costs of cultivating coffee in the United States were cut, say, by 50

## Table 6-1

Domestic capital and labor requirements per million dollars of
U.S. exports and of competitive import replacement of average
1947 composition

|  | Exports | Competitive Imports |
|---|---|---|
| Capital *(in 1947 prices)* | 2,550,780 | 3,091,339 |
| Labor *(man-years)* | 182.313 | 170.004 |

or possibly even 80 percent. The question of distinction between
competitive and noncompetitive imports is closely related to the
larger and more important problem of natural resources, that is, primary factors other than capital and labor. This problem will be taken
up again later.

Some U.S. exports might be noncompetitive from the point of
view of the countries that purchase them. The level of our sales
abroad of such commodities would not, or rather would not directly,
depend on the comparative supply of capital and labor in the United
States, but instead on these other countries' rigidly determined
demand. The lack of proper quantitative information makes the
development of the full, two-sided general equilibrium analysis
required in this case not yet possible.

The numbers in Table 6-1 summarize the principal findings of the
original computation. In terms of the simple geometry of Figure 6-
1, these figures can be interpreted as follows. On the basis of the
relative quantities of capital required for their production, 1.21 (=
3,091/2,550) units of exports could be substituted in the output of
country I for each unit of competitive imports. In terms of comparative labor costs, the corresponding ratio is 0.93 (= 170/182) units
of exports for each unit of competitive imports. Since the first of
these two rates of substitution is larger than the second, the role of
capital in the American economy of 1947 corresponds to that of factor $B$ (in country I) in Figure 6-1 and the position of labor to that of
factor $A$. This means that an increase in the supply of capital would
tend to reduce, and alternatively a rise in the supply of labor would
tend to expand, the volume of our foreign trade.

This conclusion will obviously hold so long as the substitution rate
of exports for competitive imports expressed in terms of their comparative capital requirements is larger than the corresponding substitution rate based on the comparative labor costs, that is, so long
as the quotient 1.21/0.93 (=1.30) exceeds 1. One can determine

the magnitude of that quotient also by computing separately the capital-labor input ratios for exports and for competitive imports and then dividing the first by the second:

Exports, 2,550/182 = \$14,010 per man-year

Competitive imports, 3,091/170 = \$18,180 per man-year

$\alpha = 18,180/14,010 = 1.30$

For want of a commonly accepted term, the last number, $\alpha$, can be identified as an index of comparative capital-labor intensity in the production of competitive import and export goods.

The magnitude of this index depends only on the relative—not the absolute—amounts of capital and labor used per unit of each of these composite commodities. Thus, it is not affected by a change in the size of the respective units. Consequently, a variation in the relative price of the two types of products, that is, an increase or a fall in the amount of exports that have to be offered in exchange for a given quantity of competitive imports, cannot affect the magnitude and the significance of our index; so long, that is, as neither capital nor labor becomes free. So long as the trade vector $OT$ in Figure 6-1 remains steeper than the line $y_a x_a$ but less steep than $y_b x_b$, a change in its slope (i.e., a variation in the terms of trade) will not modify the basic proposition that an increase in the supply of factor $B$ in country I would reduce, and an increase in the supply of factor $A$ would raise, the volume of international trade.

Further analysis, to which we now turn, has strengthened and widened the factual basis of the original inquiry and refined— within the still very narrow limits set by the available empirical data—its theoretical design. I shall first describe one by one the principal changes in the bases of the data used and the analytical procedures employed in these more recent computations and then present the final numerical results.

## III

In the original analysis, although it was presented in terms of the 192-industry input-output classification, only the direct capital and labor inputs were accounted for in detail. The derivation of the indirect requirements was based on the inversion of a smaller, more aggregative, 50-sector matrix. The two largest of the present computations are based on the complete 192-industry inverse.

The set of input coefficients which makes up the standard struc-

tural matrix, the inverse of which was used in the original computation, reflected only the "current cost" flows among all the sectors
of the economy. The flows of buildings, machinery, and other durables each industry has to receive in order to maintain intact the
stocks of fixed capital on which its productive capacity depends are,
for purposes of short-run input-output analysis, always charged—as
part of the gross investment flow—directly to the final bill of goods.
This, however, is essentially a long-run problem, and in the longer
run the flow of goods and services required to maintain its fixed capital constitutes as much a part of the input structure of an industry
as the flow of fuel and various materials.

To adjust accordingly the basic matrix of the U.S. economy, it was
necessary to estimate the replacement and maintenance inputs of
each sector, specifying the industrial origin of all goods and services
of which they constitute a part. This was done through the multiplication of appropriate standard annual depreciation rates with the
"stock coefficients" showing the amount of every specific kind of
fixed capital used by each industry per unit of its capacity output. If
an industry employs $250 worth of electrical machinery per every
$1000 worth of its annual capacity output and the standard depre-
ciation rate applied to that specific type of equipment is 20 percent,
the estimated maintenance input coefficient describing the yearly
flow of electrical machinery required by that industry to maintain
its stock of that particular type of fixed capital would amount to $50
per unit of its yearly output.

The difference in the durability of various kinds of buildings,
equipment, and other goods that make up the capital stocks of all its
sectors are thus reflected not in the capital stock—but rather in the
flow—matrix of the economy. The less durable the particular
investment item is, the larger the replacement flow required per
unit of its stock.

The complete set of replacement coefficients, added term by term
to the original table of input coefficients, yields a complete description of the long-run input-output structure of the American economy. Since a full inversion of the new 200-by-200 matrix is very
expensive, the original inverse based on unadjusted figures was
instead corrected through a computational procedure involving
only a first- and selected second-order approximation.

The flows that serve to increase, rather than to maintain, the capital of an economy must, of course, be left out of account in static
comparative cost analysis. This does not mean, however, that such
analysis cannot be used consistently for the explanation of the for-

eign trade transactions of a growing, developing economy. Although, as time goes on, its total stock of capital increases, as a rule so does its labor force. The allocation of this stock at any given time between alternative productive uses must still be expected to follow the principle of comparative advantage. As a matter of fact, the higher its current rate of new investment, the greater will be the ability of an economy to adjust the specific commodity structure of its capital—particularly the composition of its stocks of buildings, equipment, and other durables—to the changing conditions of technology, the varying supply of other factors, and the shifting structure of demand, foreign as well as domestic. In a stationary economy, in contrast to a developing one, the mobility of capital is, on the other hand, strictly limited by the magnitude of the current replacement rates.

Only because and to the extent that such mobility does exist is it admissible to treat capital as a single homogeneous factor and to measure its aggregate amount by the combined dollar value of the stocks of many physically distinct commodities.

A similar problem arises in connection with the measurement of the other factor, labor. While in the original analysis it was described in terms of undifferentiated man-years, in certain phases of the subsequent inquiry a breakdown of labor inputs by major skill and occupational groups was introduced. The measurement of labor inputs in terms of wages paid reflects the same distinction, insofar as it amounts to weighting in the process of aggregation the man-years of each skill group by its respective average annual wage rate.

A further theoretical refinement introduced in the recent computations concerns the determination of the quantity of exports the United States must sell in the international market in order to secure an additional composite unit of competitive imports. In the original computation the labor and capital employed to produce one million dollars' worth of exports were assumed to be sufficient to provide—through exchange of their product for foreign goods—exactly one million dollars' worth of competitive imports. Such an assumption disregarded the fact that the production of either type of good in the United States requires, in addition to labor, capital, and other domestic factors, inputs falling into the category of noncompetitive imports. The latter by definition enter into the balance of foreign trade on the passive side, that is, they must be paid for by an equivalent quantity of exports.

This means that the amount of exports the United States would have to sell in order to obtain from abroad—instead of producing at home—a million dollars' worth of competitive imports might be either larger or smaller than "one million dollars' worth." On the one hand, some part of these additional exports will serve to pay for the noncompetitive imports directly and indirectly required for the production of the very same exports that pay for them. But the curtailment of the domestic output of competitively imported goods will eliminate those noncompetitive imports that were previously absorbed in their production.

Let $\Delta Y$ represent an increment in exports; $\Delta Z$ the corresponding increment in competitive imports; $D_1$ and $D_2$ the amounts of noncompetitive imports required (directly and indirectly) to produce in the United States one unit of exports and one unit of noncompetitive imports, respectively. If $P_y$, $P_z$, and $Q_1$, $Q_2$ represent the international prices of these four categories of goods, the balance of trade relationship that the two incremental changes must satisfy can be symbolically described by the following equation:

$$\Delta Y P_y = \Delta Z P_z + D_1 \Delta Y Q_1 - D_2 \Delta Z Q_2$$

Solved for $\Delta Y$ in terms of $\Delta Z$ and the six respective constants, this yields

$$\Delta Y = \frac{P_z - D_2 Q_2}{P_y - D_1 Q_1} \Delta Z$$

In actual empirical analysis each letter stands, of course, for a whole set of variables or constants, and the determination of the relationships between $\Delta Y$ and $\Delta Z$ involves solutions of a large set of simultaneous linear equations.[6]

In interpreting the meaning of the last formula, one must remember that for the purpose of input-output computations the physical units of all commodities have been defined so as to make all base-year (1947) prices equal 1 (million dollars). In computations related to other years or to hypothetical conditions in which the prices of the import and export goods different from those in which the original "per million dollars" units have been defined, the $P$s and $Q$s in the balance-of-trade equation must be interpreted as indices with the year 1947 used as a base. As the numerical results of our computations show, for an economy as self-sufficient as that of the United States, the balance-of-payment correction for noncompetitive imports is very small. It would be much larger for as open an economy as the British.

The distinction between competitive and noncompetitive imports can be viewed as the first step toward the extension of the empirical

[6]See Appendix 6-2 equation 6-14.

analysis of comparative costs to primary factors other than capital and labor. Theoretically this involves nothing more than a straight-forward generalization of the two factors—the two composite commodities' analysis presented above.[7] Absence of comprehensive statistical information concerning their supply and utilization makes an explicit inclusion of natural resources in our input-output computations, along with capital and labor, as yet impracticable. The deficiency in basic information can be remedied only through systematic fact-finding research. In the meantime, the effects of natural resources on the structure of U.S. foreign trade can be assessed only on the basis of partial information and indirect—and, because of that, admittedly tenuous—evidence.

We definitely know, for instance, that under present technical conditions this country does not allocate any of its available resources to the cultivation of coffee or to the mining of certain ores not found among our mineral deposits. We know enough about the potential input requirements of agricultural and mining output to be certain that even a very drastic change in the domestic supply of capital and labor would not lead to the establishment of these particular extractive industries at home. Insofar as such products can and actually are obtained in exchange for U.S. exports, the level of noncompetitive imports can be explained, as shown above, in terms of the requirements, for these foreign products, of established U.S. industries on the one hand and, on the other, by the demand of the same industries for domestic factors. Labor and capital are the two most important among these, but scarce domestic natural resources could also play a considerable role.

Nothing short of detailed factual inquiry and computations taking into account these other factors on a par with capital and labor can show conclusively how important they are in the determination of the pattern of U.S. foreign trade. In the meantime, the following tentative attempt has been made to obtain at least a preliminary answer to that question.

The actual supply of domestic natural resource either can be so great as to exceed the demand—in which case it would, of course, be free—or it might be short and thus impose an effective limit on the output of the extractive industry or industries that use it as a direct input. In the latter instance, if the products of these extractive industries—in contrast to the resource itself—are transportable, these products will probably be imported from abroad. Thus, the shortage of domestic mineral deposits is relieved through the use of

[7]See Appendix 6-1.

imported ores, and the limited supply of domestic pulpwood is alleviated through the purchase of foreign pulp. This means that, although they seem to compete with corresponding domestic outputs in our economy, such imports might play the same role as obviously noncompetitive imports, such as coffee, and consequently should be explained also in the same terms. For purposes of our computations this would simply mean shifting an additional group of raw and semifabricated imports from the list of competitive into that of noncompetitive commodities. In interpreting the results of such a computation (see computation D in Table 6-2) one must, however, keep in mind that the special theoretical assumptions on which it is based are very tenuous. The asymmetrical treatment of exports that should, but could not, be identified as—in the wider sense—noncompetitive from the point of view of the "other," that is, the buying, country is bound to make the result of such analysis greatly biased.

# IV

The principal numerical results of computations designed to determine the quantities of domestic capital and labor required to produce one million dollars' worth of U.S. exports or, alternatively, to replace an equivalent amount of competitive imports, are summarized in Table 6-2.

The basic matrix of input-output coefficients describing the mutual interdependence of its many individual productive sectors, as well as the sets of direct capital and labor coefficients showing the amounts of capital and labor employed in each one of them per unit of its respective output, used for all these computations reflects the internal structural characteristics of the American economy in 1947. For computations A and D, I have utilized in full the most detailed, that is, least aggregative, set of data corresponding to the 192-industry input-output classification. All other results were obtained on the basis of the more aggregative 50-by-50 input-output matrix; the direct—and contrasted with the indirect—labor and capital requirements of each one of the 192 distinct kinds of outputs are in this latter instance adjusted so as to incorporate the more detailed set of capital and labor coefficients. Only computations A and D take into account replacement costs, that is, the differences in durability of the specific kinds of fixed capital employed in various branches of the U.S. economy.

The composition of the two aggregative commodities, one defined

## Table 6-2

### Capital and labor requirements per million dollars of U.S. exports and competitive import replacements, 1947 and 1951, computed on the basis of 1947 structural relationships

(Figures in roman type are computed on the basis of the 1947 composition of U.S. exports and competitive imports; those in *italic type* are based on the corresponding composition for 1951.)

| Computation (1) | Capital and labor requirements cover employment in the following productive sectors (2) | Main conceptual differences (3) | Results show requirements per million dollars of (4) | Direct and indirect requirements of | | Capital requirements | Import ratio |
|---|---|---|---|---|---|---|---|
| | | | | Capital ($0000) (5a) | Labor (*man-years*)[a] (5b) | Labor requirements (6) | Export ratio (7) |
| A | 1–192 (all sectors) | The matrix, A, of input coefficients includes capital replacement.[b] | Competitive imports of all sectors | 224.39 | 164.28 | 1.3659 | |
| | | | | *–230.34* | *–167.81* | *–1.3726* | *1.1757* |
| | | | Exports of all sectors | 208.46 | 179.42 | 1.1618 | |
| | | | | (209.29)[c] | (180.14)[c] | (1.1618) | |
| | | | | (209.29)[c] | (180.14)[c] | (1.1618) | |
| | | | | *–225.68* | *–173.91* | *–1.2977* | |
| | | | | (*–233.23*)[c] | (*–179.72*)[c] | (*–1.2977*) | *–1.0577* |
| B | 1–192 (aggregated to 50 sectors) | The matrix, A, of input coefficients does not include capital replacement. Capital and labor coefficients are different from those used in all other computations.[d] | Competitive imports of all sectors | 309.13 | 170.00 | 1.8184 | |
| | | | | | | | 1.2996 |

111

# Table 6-2 (Cont.)

| Computation (1) | Capital and labor requirements cover employment in the following productive sectors (2) | Main conceptual differences (3) | Results show requirements per million dollars of (4) | Direct and indirect requirements of — Capital ($0000) (5a) | Direct and indirect requirements of — Labor (man-years)[a] (5b) | Capital requirements / Labor requirements (6) | Import ratio / Export ratio (7) |
|---|---|---|---|---|---|---|---|
| $C_1$ | 1–164 (all commodity-producing sectors) | The matrix of input coefficients does not include capital replacement.[d] | Exports of all sectors | 255.08 | 182.31 | 1.3992 | |
| | | | Competitive imports of all commodity-producing sectors | 220.78 (225.81)[e] | 158.89 (163.53)[e] | 1.3895 (1.3808)[e] | 1.2205 (1.2128)[e] |
| | | | | −230.59 | −162.46 | −1.4194 | −1.1112 |
| $C_2$ | 1–164 (all commodity-producing sectors) | As above in $C_1$. | Exports of all commodity-producing sectors | 197.89 | 173.82 | 1.1385 | |
| | | | | −214.10 | −167.61 | −1.2774 | |
| | | | Competitive imports of all sectors producing nonagricultural commodities | 198.98 (209.69)[e] | 168.19 (166.71)[e] | 1.1831 (1.2578)[e] | 1.1972 (1.2728)[e] |
| | | | | −210.98 | −161.43 | −1.3069 | −1.4098 |
| $C_3$ | 10–164 (all sectors producing nonagricultural commodities) | As above in $C_1$. | Exports of all sectors producing nonagricultural commodities | 178.24 | 180.37 | .9882 | |
| | | | | −166.63 | −179.76 | −.9270 | |
| | | | Competitive imports of all commodity-producing sectors | 143.35 | 123.89 | 1.1571 | |
| | | | | −175.10 | −134.02 | −1.3065 | |
| | | | Exports of all commodity-producing sectors | 115.87 | 148.70 | .7792 | 1.4850 |
| | | | | −153.86 | −136.73 | −1.1253 | −1.1610 |

| | | | | | | |
|---|---|---|---|---|---|---|
| $C_4$ | 10–164 (all sectors producing nonagricultural commodities) | As above in $C_1$. | | | | |
| | | Competitive imports of all sectors producing nonagricultural commodities | 178.00 / −186.82 | 157.44 / −150.51 | 1.1306 / −1.2412 | 1.2496 / **1.3410** |
| | | Exports of all sectors producing nonagricultural commodities | 150.15 / −156.22 | 165.94 / −168.77 | .9048 / −.9256 | |
| D | 1–192, excluding 1, 7 through 15, 17, 20, 23, 29, 36, 44, 59, 82, and 86 | As above in A. In addition, 19 resource industries were removed from the main body of the matrix and treated as noncompetitive imports | Competitive imports of all remaining sectors: 185.39 / −209.27 | 199.62 / −206.61 | .9287 / −1.0129 | .9171 / −.8813 |
| | | Exports of all remaining sectors | 227.47 / (201.60)ᶜ / −257.71 / (−221.89)ᶜ | 224.63 / (199.08)ᶜ / −224.23 / (−193.06)ᶜ | 1.0127 / (1.0127) / −1.1493 / (−1.1493) | |

ᵃLabor requirements in wage-dollars for 1947 only were obtained in computations $C_1$ and $C_2$:

Wage requirements per million dollars of

| | Exports | Import replacements |
|---|---|---|
| $C_1$ | 516,277 | 436,394 (452,581) |
| $C_2$ | 545,142 | 475,107 (468,770) |

For figures in parentheses, see footnote e below.

ᵇRequirements were computed on the basis of equations (6-11), Appendix 6-2, later in this chapter.

ᶜFigures in parentheses show requirements for exports per million dollars of competitive import replacements, i.e., requirements for the increase in exports accompanies an increase of $1,000,000 in competitive imports.

For computation A: An increase of $1,000,000 in 1947 competitive imports occasions an increase of $1,004,000 in exports, while an increase of $1,000,000 in 1951 competitive imports occasions an increase of $1,033,433 in exports. Computed from equation (6-14), Appendix 6-2.

For computation D: An increase of $1,000,000 in 1947 competitive imports occasions an increase of $886,267 in exports, while an increase of $1,000,000 in 1951 competitive imports occasions an increase of $861,010 in exports. Computed from equation (6-14), Appendix 6-2.

ᵈRequirements were computed on the basis of equation (6-12), Appendix 6-2.

ᵉFigures in parentheses pertain to import requirements computed with imports of raw cane sugar shifted from I.C. number 9 to I.C. number 27; data were not available for a similar computation for 1951.

as exports and the other as competitive imports, reflects the actual percentage breakdown of U.S. exports and imports, respectively, by products of the specific input-output industries. The distinction between the figures that are identified as being related to the year 1947 and those related to the year 1951 (in italic type) reflect only the difference in the material composition of U.S. exports and imports in these two years. All the internal structural relationships used in the computation of the capital and labor requirements for the production of exports and replacement of competitive imports for 1951 are based, as I have said above, entirely on 1947 internal structural relationships.

The use of the 1951 export and import weights is intended to test to what extent the general results of this analysis might be affected by the year-to-year changes in the composition of U.S. foreign trade. Had a complete 1951 input-output matrix, with corresponding sets of labor and capital coefficients, been available, it certainly would have served our purpose even better.

In computations, $C_1$, $C_2$, $C_3$, and $C_4$, both the exports and noncompetitive imports are defined so as to include the products of all branches of the economy other than the service industries. No figures on the exports and imports of the services of wholesale trade, transportation, banking, and so on, can be found in official foreign trade statistics. The input-output table for the year 1947 contains such information, but for the year 1951 one had to fall back on rather crude estimates. Thus it was deemed preferable to omit these categories entirely from most of the computations. Such an exclusion, incidentally, tends to reduce the computed capital requirements and to increase the labor requirements per unit of U.S. exports and has an opposite effect on the corresponding figures for the replacement of noncompetitive imports.

Agriculture, both as a producer of exports and competitive imports and as an employer of labor, presents a special problem. Fluctuations in yields here and abroad—not to speak of goverment intervention—affect foreign trade in farm products to such an extent that the amounts of agricultural commodities exported and imported in a single year can be expected to reflect long-run comparative cost conditions much less than in the case for any other type of good.

The fact that most direct labor used in U.S. agriculture is essentially self-employed makes all measures of agricultural employment highly speculative and the agricultural labor input coefficients less reliable than those of any other major industry. It was thus only natural to exclude agricultural labor requirements entirely from some of our computations. Although the agricultural capital coefficients are not open to the same kind of objections, serious (in my opinion unjustified) doubts have been raised concerning their validity. Hence, in computations $C_3$ and $C_4$, not only the agricultural labor inputs but the agricultural capital requirements as well are excluded from the final figures.

As explained before, the simple assumption that a million dollars' worth of U.S. exports can be exchanged on the international market for a million dollars' worth of competitive imports leaves out of account the unconditional domestic requirements for noncompetitive foreign imports. A more complete set of theoretical relationships which explicitly satisfies the balance-of-trade conditions (symbolically described in the formulas above) has been used for computations A and D. The table includes in both these cases two sets of capital and labor input figures for U.S. exports. One— enclosed in parentheses—represents the actual requirements per million dollars' worth of exports; the other shows the quantities of the two factors that would be absorbed in the production of that amount of competitive imports the United States would lose if it had reduced its exports by one million dollars. As the figures included in the footnotes to Table 6-2 show, in computation A, which is based on the regular, narrow, definition of noncompetitive imports, the balance-of-payment "correction" is, both in 1947 and 1951, so small as to be practically negligible. Because of that and also because this correction, as has been shown before, cannot affect the value of the $\alpha$ index, which finally reflects the comparative position of U.S. exports and competitive imports in respect to their relative requirements for capital and labor, all the other computations are based on a simpler formula which neglects the balance-of-payments implications of noncompetitive imports.

## V

After the elaborate analysis of the theoretical considerations that guided this inquiry and a systematic, although admittedly less detailed, presentation of its factual basis, I can abstain from an extended discussion of the final findings. They seem to support the principal conclusion of the original investigation. The United States exports commodities that, on the average, absorb in their production less capital and more domestic labor than would be required for the production, in this country, of those goods it apparently finds comparatively cheaper to import. Table 6-3 shows the breakdown of the total man-year inputs absorbed per million dollars of 1947

# Table 6-3

Labor requirements (by five levels of skill)[a] per million dollars of exports and competitive import replacements of all sectors, 1947

*Labor required for the exports and imports of*

| | All sectors (1–192) | | | | Agricultural sectors (1–9) | | | |
| | Exports | | Competitive import replacements | | Exports | | Competitive import replacements | |
| Level of skill | Man-years | Percent of total | Man-years | Percent of total | Man-years | Percent of total | Man-years | Percent of total |
|---|---|---|---|---|---|---|---|---|
| I. professional, etechnical, and managerial | 23,867 | 13.75 | 19,395 | 12.24 | 997 | 7.60 | 2,488 | 7.38 |
| II. clerical, sales and service | 38,307 | 22.07 | 26,954 | 17.00 | 1,432 | 10.92 | 3,326 | 9.86 |
| III. craftsmen and foremen | 26,298 | 15.15 | 18,696 | 11.79 | 609 | 4.64 | 1,542 | 4.57 |
| IV. operatives | 52,158 | 30.05 | 44,992 | 28.38 | 967 | 7.37 | 2,467 | 7.31 |
| V. laborers | 32,941 | 18.98 | 48,494 | 30.59 | 9,113 | 69.47 | 23,911 | 70.88 |
| Total | 173,571 | 100.00 | 138,531 | 100.00 | 13,118 | 100.00 | 33,734 | 100.00 |

*Labor required for the exports and imports of*

| | Mining and manufacturing sectors (10–164) | | | | Electricity, communications, and service sectors (167–192) | | | |
| | Exports | | Competitive import replacements | | Exports | | Competitive import replacements | |
| Level of skill | Man-years | Percent of total | Man-years | Percent of total | Man-years | Percent of total | Man-years | Percent of total |
|---|---|---|---|---|---|---|---|---|
| I. professional, technical, and managerial | 15,564 | 12.74 | 15,087 | 13.05 | 7,306 | 19.05 | 1,820 | 19.88 |
| II. clerical, sales and service | 24,883 | 20.38 | 20,498 | 17.72 | 11,992 | 31.28 | 3,130 | 34.19 |
| III. craftsmen and foremen | 20,938 | 17.15 | 16,397 | 14.18 | 4,751 | 12.39 | 757 | 8.27 |
| IV. operatives | 42,949 | 35.17 | 40,837 | 35.31 | 8,242 | 21.50 | 1,688 | 18.44 |
| V. laborers | 17,776 | 14.56 | 22,824 | 19.74 | 6,052 | 15.78 | 1,759 | 19.22 |
| Total | 122,110 | 100.00 | 115,643 | 100.00 | 38,343 | 100.00 | 9,154 | 100.00 |

[a]The breakdown of the labor coefficients by skill was developed by Dr. A. H. Conrad, staff member of the Harvard Economic Research Project, in connection with his investigation of the structure of the U.S. labor force.

exports and competitive import replacements by five skill and occupational categories. Furthermore, it shows how that employment was distributed among the three major subdivisions of the U.S. economy. As should have been expected, the relative excess of man-years incorporated in one million dollars' worth of U.S. exports over the quantity of labor absorbed in the production of an equivalent amount of domestic goods competing with foreign imports is definitely concentrated in the higher skills. The lowest, that is, unskilled, category taken by itself shows, as a matter of fact, a quite large surplus on the import side in terms of percentage.[8]

The role that scarce factors other than labor and capital play in the determination of the structure of U.S. foreign trade still has to be systematically explored. A comprehensive, two-sided explanation of our economic relationships with the rest of the world will not, of course, be possible before the internal economic structure of at least one of the most important of our trading partners has been studied as fully as that of our own.

My first article on structural determination of the composition of U.S. foreign trade contained a proposed explanation of the originally observed facts and also a tentative elaboration of some of its important implications. Now, after having described in detail the formal framework of the entire study and presented the results of further, more comprehensive empirical analysis, I shall not discuss again these other more speculative questions. New evidence seems to support, or at least not to contradict, the earlier conjecture that the very high productivity of American—as compared with foreign—labor plays a decisive role in the determination of the composition of those U.S. exports and imports that do not reflect directly the presence or absence in this country of certain natural resources. So long as one cannot yet present the full array of facts required to prove—or to refute—it, the reiteration of a controversial position would serve no useful purpose.

## Appendix 6-1

### Linearized model of interregional trade

*Notation*

Outputs of commodities 1, 2, . . . , $n$ in
    Country I: $x_1, x_2, \ldots, x_n$
    Country II: $y_1, y_2, \ldots, y_n$

[8]These findings confirm and possibly explain the findings of Irving B. Kravis.

Imports of commodities 1, 2, ... $n$, from country II to country I:

$t_1, t_2, \ldots, t_n$. Negative imports represent exports.

Prices of commodities 1, 2, ..., $n$ in both countries: $p_1, p_2, \ldots, p_n$.

Supply of (fully employed) primary factors in:

Country I: $F_1, F_2, \ldots, F_{m1}$

Country II: $G_1, G_2, \ldots, G_{m2}$

Each one of these $m_1 + m_2$ quantities might represent a different factor.

Prices of primary factors in:

Country I: $q_1, q_2, \ldots, q_{m1}$

Country II: $v_1, v_2, \ldots, v_{m2}$

Production coefficients:

Country I: $f_{ij}$ Country II: $g_{ij}$

Each coefficient represents the amount of factor $i$ required directly and indirectly for the production of one unit of commodity $j$. The $j$'s refer to the same commodities in both countries but the $i$'s not necessarily to the same factors.

Consumption coefficient, that is, the amounts of commodities 2, 3, ..., $n$ consumed per unit of commodity 1, in

Country I: $r_2, r_3, \ldots, r_n$

Country II: $u_2, u_3, \ldots, u_n$

*Equations*

Physical relations between the supply of factors and the quantities of outputs.

Country I:

(6-1)
$$f_{i1}x_1 + f_{i2}x_2 + \cdot \quad \cdot \quad \cdot + f_{in}x_n = F_i$$
$$i = 1, 2, \ldots, m_1$$

The number of equations must not exceed the number of unknowns.

(6-2)
$$m_1 \leq n$$

Country II:

(6-3)
$$g_{i1}y_1 + \cdots + g_{in}y_n = G_i$$

(6-4)
$$i = 1, 2, \ldots, m_2$$
$$m_2 \leq n$$

Cost-price relationships:

Country I:

(6-5)
$$f_{1i}q_1 + f_{2i}q_2 + \cdots + f_{m_1i}q_{m1} = p_i$$
$$i = 1, 2, \ldots, n$$

Country II:

(6-6)
$$g_{1i}v_1 + g_{2i}v_2 + \cdots + g_{m_2i}v_{m2} = p_i$$
$$i = 1, 2, \ldots, n$$

Considered together (6-5) and (6-6) constitute a system of $2n$ linear homogeneous equations of the first degree in $n + m_1 + m_2$ unknown absolute prices, and it can be solved for $n + m_1 + m_2 - 1$ relative prices only if $n + m_1 + m_2 - 1 = 2n$, that is,

(6-7) $$m_1 + m_2 = n + 1$$

Consumption equations:
  Country I:

(6-8) $$x_i + t_i = r_i(x_1 + t_1)$$
$$i = 2, 3, \ldots, n$$

where $x_i + t_i$, that is, the domestic output plus the imports (or minus the exports), represent the amount of the $i$th commodity available for consumption in country I.
  Country II:

(6-9) $$y_i - t_i = u_i(x_1 - t_1)$$
$$i = 2, 3, \ldots, n$$

The balance of trade equation:

(6-10) $$t_1 p_1 + t_2 p_2 + \cdots + t_n p_n = 0$$

The number of equations in the entire system:

| | |
|---|---|
| Set (6-1) | $m_1$ |
| Set (6-3) | $m_2$ |
| Set (6-5) | $n$ |
| Set (6-6) | $n$ |
| Set (6-8) | $n - 1$ |
| Set (6-9) | $n - 1$ |
| Set (6-10) | 1 |
| Total $m_1 + m_2 + 4n - 1$ equations | |

The number of unknowns in the entire system (if commodity 1 is chosen to serve as the numeraire, i.e., if $p_1 = 1$):

| | |
|---|---|
| Commodity prices $n - 1$ | |
| Factor prices | $m_1 + m_2$ |
| Outputs | $2n$ |
| Amounts traded | $n$ |
| Total | $m_1 + m_2 + 4n - 1$ unknowns |

In the simple system presented in Chart 1,

$$n = 2, m_1 = 2, m_2 = 2$$

## Appendix 6-2

Input-output computations for the determination of quantities of capital and labor required for the replacement of competitive imports and production of an equivalent amount of exports

*Notation*

$$x = \begin{bmatrix} x_1 \\ x_2 \\ \cdot \\ \cdot \\ \cdot \\ x_n \end{bmatrix}$$ is a column of outputs of the $n$ sectors of the economy.

$y$ is the value of total exports of all $n$ sectors in millions of dollars.
$z$ is the value of total competitive imports into all $n$ sectors in millions of dollars.

$$A = \begin{bmatrix} a_{11} & \cdots & a_{1n} \\ \cdot & & \cdot \\ \cdot & & \cdot \\ \cdot & & \cdot \\ a_{n1} & & a_{nn} \end{bmatrix}$$ is a square matrix of input coefficients; for all subscripts $i$ and $j$ $(i, j = 1, 2, \ldots, n)$, $a_{ij}$ is the amount of sector $i$'s product used by sector $j$ per unit of output of sector $j$ (physical unit = unit price, since a physical unit of any product is defined as a million dollars' worth of that product at base-year prices).

$d = [d_1 \, d_2, \ldots, d_n]$ is a row of noncompetitive-import input coefficients; for all subscripts $i(i = 1, 2, \ldots, n)$, $d_i$ represents the amount of noncompetitive imports into sector $i$ per unit of output of sector $i$.

$$b = \begin{bmatrix} b_1 \\ b_2 \\ \cdot \\ \cdot \\ \cdot \\ b_n \end{bmatrix}$$ is a column of export coefficients; for all $i$ $(i = 1, 2, \ldots, n)$, $b_i$ represents the amount of sector $i$'s exports per unit (i.e., per one million dollars) of total exports of all $n$ sectors.

$$c = \begin{bmatrix} c_1 \\ c_2 \\ \cdot \\ \cdot \\ \cdot \\ c_n \end{bmatrix}$$ is a column of competitive import coefficients; for all $i$ $(i = 1, 2, \ldots, n)$, $c_i$ is the amount of competitive imports into sector $i$ per unit (i.e., per one million of dollars) of total competitive imports into all sectors.

$$r = \begin{bmatrix} r_1 \\ r_2 \\ \cdot \\ \cdot \\ \cdot \\ r_n \end{bmatrix}$$ is a column of residual constants, each $r_i$ $(i = 1, 2, \ldots, n)$ representing that part of sector $i$'s output allocated directly to all final uses other than exports.

$r_d$ is that part of total noncompetitive imports allocated to final (as contrasted with productive) uses.

$k = [k_1 \; k_2, \ldots, k_n]$ is a row of capital coefficients.

### Balance equations

In matric notation, the balance equations of the system are:

$$(6\text{-}11) \qquad \left[\begin{array}{c|c} I - A & -b \\ \hline -d & 1 \end{array}\right] \left[\begin{array}{c} x \\ y \end{array}\right] + \left[\begin{array}{c} c \\ \hline -1 \end{array}\right] z = \left[\begin{array}{c} r \\ r_d \end{array}\right]$$

Each of the first $n$ equations of the system (6-11) states that the output of a sector $i$ plus competitive imports into that sector, that is, its total supply, is distributed to other sectors (including itself), to exports, and to the residual sector. The $(n + 1)$st, that is, the last, equation describes the balance-of-trade relationship; it states simply that total exports are equal to total competitive imports plus total noncompetitive imports. If the balance-of-trade equation is omitted, system (6-11) is reduced to

$$(6\text{-}12) \qquad [I - A][x] - [b]y + [c]z = [r]$$

### Computation of capital and labor requirements reduced to matrix operations

SYSTEM (6-11)

The computation of capital requirements per million dollars of competitive import replacements can be best presented as if it consisted of two stages.

First, the system (6-11) is solved for $\left[\begin{array}{c} x \\ y \end{array}\right]$ in terms of the other column

vectors, that is, the square matrix that appears on the left-hand side of that equation is inverted:

$$(6\text{-}11') \qquad \left[\begin{array}{c} x \\ y \end{array}\right] = \left[\begin{array}{c|c} I - A & -b \\ \hline -d & 1 \end{array}\right]^{-1} \left\{ - \left[\begin{array}{c} c \\ -1 \end{array}\right] x + \left[\begin{array}{c} r \\ r_d \end{array}\right] \right\}$$

Next, system (6-11') is premultiplied by the row of capital coefficients, $[k0]$:

$$(6\text{-}13) \qquad [k0] \left[\begin{array}{c} x \\ y \end{array}\right] = [k0] \left[\begin{array}{c|c} I - A & -b \\ -d & 1 \end{array}\right]^{-1} \left\{ - \left[\begin{array}{c} c \\ -1 \end{array}\right] z + \left[\begin{array}{c} r \\ r_d \end{array}\right] \right\}$$

The product,

$$[k0] \left[\begin{array}{c|c} I - A & -b \\ -d & 1 \end{array}\right]^{-1} \left[\begin{array}{c} c \\ \hline -1 \end{array}\right] = [K_n \; K_b] \left[\begin{array}{c} c \\ \hline -1 \end{array}\right]$$

in which $K_n$ is a row matrix and $K_b$ is a scalar, shows net capital requirements (direct and indirect) per million dollars of competitive import replacements. Note that the first $n$ elements of this product, that is, $[K_n] [c]$, before they have been added up, represent requirements of the $n$ sectors, while the final "foreign trade" term shows requirements for exports *per million dollars of competitive import replacements.* Requirements for exports per million dollars of total exports can be obtained easily from this. The last equation of system (6-11') is a statement of a linear relation between $y$ and $z$:

(6-14)                                      $y = \lambda z + \mu$

where $\lambda$ is the product of the last row of the inverse into the column

$$-\begin{bmatrix} c \\ -1 \end{bmatrix}$$

and $\mu$ is the product of the last row of the inverse into the column

$$\begin{bmatrix} r \\ r_d \end{bmatrix}$$

Hence, if $z$ increases by 1, $y$ increases by $\lambda$, and

$$\frac{\text{Requirements for exports per}}{\text{million dollars of exports}} = \frac{\substack{\text{Requirements for exports per} \\ \text{million dollars of competitive} \\ \text{imports}}}{\lambda}$$

SYSTEM (6-12)

This system differs from system (6-11) only to the extent that it does not contain the last, that is, the balance-of-payments, equation.

As with system (6-11), the first step of computation consists of the inversion of the matrix to obtain:

(6-12')                          $[x] = [I - A]^{-1}\{[b]y - [c]z + [r]\}$

Next, system (6-12') is premultiplied by the row $[k]$:

(6-13)                          $[k][x] = [k][I - A]^{-1}\{[b]y - [c]z + [r]\}$

The product $[k][I - a]^{-1}[b]$ gives capital requirements per million dollars of exports, and the product $[k][I - A]^{-1}[c]$ gives capital requirements per million dollars of competitive import replacements.

Labor requirements per million dollars of competitive import replacements and per million dollars of exports can, of course, be computed for either of the two systems by the same method as was used for capital requirements.

# Appendix 6-3

Industrial classification and some of the basic data used in the computation of labor and capital requirements per million dollars of exports and of competitive import replacements[a]

| 192 I-C No. | Direct labor coefficients[b] (man-years per $ million of output) (1) | Direct capital coefficient[c] ($ million per $ million of output) (2) | Total direct and indirect requirements per million dollars of final output[d] — Labor (man-years) (3) | Total direct and indirect requirements per million dollars of final output[d] — Capital ($0000) (4) | Exports per million dollars of total exports[e] (1947 dollars) — 1947 (5) | Exports per million dollars of total exports[e] (1947 dollars) — 1951 (6) | Competitive imports per million dollars of total competitive imports[e] (1947 dollars) — 1947 (7) | Competitive imports per million dollars of total competitive imports[e] (1947 dollars) — 1951 (8) |
|---|---|---|---|---|---|---|---|---|
| **Agriculture, fishing, hunting** | | | | | | | | |
| 1 meat animals and products | 82.60 | 1.6114 | 192.6 | 398.9 | 822 | 422 | 54747 | 58116 |
| 2 poultry and eggs | 82.60 | 1.6114 | 213.4 | 422.9 | 1277 | 941 | 793 | 542 |
| 3 farm diary products | 82.60 | 1.6114 | 164.0 | 343.6 | 72 | 32 | | |
| 4 food grains and feed crops | 82.60 | 1.6114 | 128.6 | 338.2 | 55515 | 91576 | 1102 | 19765 |
| 5 cotton | 82.60 | 1.6114 | 135.4 | 366.6 | 23605 | 67067 | 8097 | 4417 |
| 6 tobacco | 82.60 | 1.6114 | 105.7 | 263.1 | 5288 | 17784 | 32 | 86 |
| 7 oil-bearing crops | 82.60 | 1.6114 | 125.8 | 346.1 | 2668 | 7932 | 25812 | 16205 |
| 8 vegetables and fruits | 82.60 | 1.6114 | 125.6 | 226.0 | 9671 | 6557 | 23479 | 15823 |
| 9 all other agricultural products | 82.60 | 1.6114 | 120.4 | 232.3 | 2045 | 1416 | 138479 | 18896 |
| 10 fisheries, hunting, and trapping | 348.41 | 1.1274 | 392.0 | 150.7 | 1007 | 1007 | 26573 | |
| **Mining** | | | | | | | | |
| 11 iron ore mining | 105.90 | 1.4839 | 139.8 | 191.7 | | 1391 | 7675 | 10271 |
| 12 copper mining | 94.11 | 1.5511 | 139.8 | 191.7 | 552 | 8 | 5263 | 4092 |
| 13 lead and zinc mining | 126.87 | .9441 | 170.8 | 150.5 | 12 | 51 | 5360 | 7046 |
| 14 bauxite mining | 117.65 | 1.0179 | 150.5 | 144.4 | 114 | 77 | 3757 | 2763 |
| 15 other nonferrous mining | 222.37 | 3.3578 | 295.1 | 415.4 | 342 | 215 | 32774 | 21725 |
| 16 coal mining | 166.32 | .8091 | 197.6 | 115.0 | 22011 | 20002 | 259 | 234 |
| 17 crude petroleum and natural gas | 39.45 | 1.6005 | 54.8 | 179.8 | 6248 | 4529 | 37372 | 47517 |
| 18 stone, sand, clay, and abrasives | 151.67 | 1.5243 | 194.3 | 204.5 | 330 | 511 | 3854 | 10175 |
| 19 sulphur | 64.55 | 1.1061 | 76.4 | 132.2 | 1385 | 1693 | | |
| 20 other nonmetallic minerals | 79.64 | 1.5243 | 114.1 | 205.7 | 881 | 786 | 17456 | 11843 |
| **Manufacturing** | | | | | | | | |
| 21 meat packing and poultry | 24.54 | .0955 | 187.1 | 336.0 | 17568 | 12128 | 7189 | 34062 |
| 22 processed dairy products | 40.59 | .2131 | 174.0 | 266.9 | 15217 | 6799 | 2429 | 4840 |
| 23 canning, preserving, and freezing | 82.01 | .3084 | 202.0 | 183.8 | 11446 | 6722 | 48043 | 21985 |

## Appendix 6-3 (Cont.)

| 1921-C No. | Direct labor coefficients[b] (man-years per $ million of output) (1) | Direct capital coefficient[c] ($ million per $ million of output) (2) | Total direct and indirect requirements per million dollars of final output[d] — Labor (man-years) (3) | Capital ($0000) (4) | Exports per million dollars of total exports[e] (1947 dollars) 1947 (5) | 1951 (6) | Competitive imports per million dollars of total competitive imports[e] (1947 dollars) 1947 (7) | 1951 (8) |
|---|---|---|---|---|---|---|---|---|
| 24 grain mill products | 21.88 | .1172 | 130.1 | 232.0 | 45928 | 15832 | 1522 | 4079 |
| 25 bakery products | 96.84 | .3244 | 189.1 | 168.3 | 468 | 172 | 32 | 198 |
| 26 miscellaneous food products | 50.78 | .3407 | 145.7 | 180.0 | 10553 | 4653 | 8825 | 3904 |
| 27 sugar | 32.53 | .6063 | 160.1 | 274.3 | 1997 | 1030 | 12954 | 61553 |
| 28 alcoholic beverages | 45.22 | .3720 | 127.1 | 146.1 | 2524 | 1120 | 17035 | 21301 |
| 29 tobacco manufacturers | 40.54 | .1060 | 146.9 | 170.3 | 13245 | 3506 | 21439 | 12144 |
| 30 spinning, weaving, dyeing | 115.04 | .3113 | 207.9 | 181.3 | 53758 | 28966 | 9796 | 39187 |
| 31 special textile products | 101.35 | .3419 | 183.6 | 130.3 | 684 | 295 | 8922 | 7168 |
| 32 jute, linen, cordage, and twine | 100.43 | .3411 | 165.2 | 114.8 | 815 | 1049 | 4728 | 5512 |
| 33 canvas products | 103.70 | .1204 | 228.6 | 119.4 | 174 |  |  |  |
| 34 apparel | 116.02 | .1148 | 236.6 | 102.2 | 15493 | 7698 | 12695 | 11449 |
| 35 house furnishings and other nonapparel | 54.00 | .1590 | 191.9 | 144.5 | 6032 | 2677 | 2025 | 1540 |
| 36 logging | 94.67 | .5299 | 141.8 | 97.0 | 378 | 415 | 9149 | 7961 |
| 37 sawmills, planning, and veneer mills | 157.91 | .5299 | 235.6 | 124.3 | 7153 | 4650 | 20435 | 23317 |
| 38 plywood | 115.43 | .2282 | 202.0 | 95.6 | 863 | 46 | 761 | 1678 |
| 39 fabricated wood products | 132.49 | .2381 | 238.3 | 103.4 | 1217 | 818 | 632 | 1085 |
| 40 wood containers and cooperage | 148.47 | .2407 | 280.0 | 113.2 | 612 | 253 | 810 | 1313 |
| 41 wood furniture | 134.26 | .2160 | 242.9 | 105.9 | 797 | 408 | 421 | 969 |
| 42 metal furniture | 93.74 | .5374 | 203.0 | 156.2 | 1127 | 640 | 16 |  |
| 43 partitions, screens, shades, etc. | 107.95 | .2798 | 219.5 | 129.6 | 150 |  |  |  |
| 44 pulp mills | 51.22 | .6136 | 134.8 | 146.8 | 1337 | 3020 | 42732 | 34436 |
| 45 paper and board mills | 65.74 | .6136 | 147.0 | 155.4 | 4401 | 5706 | 60447 | 49342 |
| 46 converted paper products | 67.80 | .2871 | 160.0 | 132.8 | 4005 | 3419 | 437 | 1037 |
| 47 printing and publishing | 114.04 | .3940 | 178.7 | 104.1 | 4329 | 3921 | 1425 | 1830 |
| 48 industrial inorganic chemicals | 60.86 | .4279 | 144.8 | 163.9 | 7693 | 6419 | 9748 | 13792 |
| 49 industrial organic chemicals | 50.65 | .9366 | 140.2 | 224.9 | 7303 | 5809 | 4340 | 10599 |
| 50 plastic materials | 49.31 | .6925 | 154.9 | 217.2 | 3082 | 4009 | 97 | 227 |
| 51 synthetic rubber | 30.81 | .6519 | 111.8 | 212.4 | 342 | 454 | 55751 | 76136 |
| 52 synthetic fiber | 102.41 | 1.0511 | 165.5 | 184.3 | 1739 | 2532 | 2720 | 4868 |
| 53 explosive and fireworks | 87.53 | .4125 | 163.9 | 125.1 | 414 |  | 324 | 140 |
| 54 drugs and medicines | 73.72 | .2977 | 153.3 | 112.6 | 9329 | 19699 | 1457 | 1944 |
| 55 soap and related products | 35.93 | .2728 | 152.9 | 173.7 | 2524 | 3178 | 405 | 1072 |
| 56 paints and allied products | 41.98 | .1741 | 141.8 | 164.4 | 3663 | 3653 | 340 | 788 |
| 57 gum and wood chemicals | 74.48 | .5578 | 153.4 | 162.7 | 2140 | 2370 | 3854 | 379 |
| 58 fertilizers | 70.20 | .5011 | 177.6 | 198.2 | 450 | 603 | 356 | 796 |

124

| # | | | | | | | | | |
|---|---|---|---|---|---|---|---|---|---|
| 59 | vegetable oils | 18.46 | .1382 | 154.2 | 293.2 | 2734 | 14828 | 20063 | 18881 |
| 60 | animal oils | 26.31 | .1373 | 179.7 | 239.4 | 1079 | 7887 | 2672 | 4130 |
| 61 | misc. chemical industries | 60.07 | .3778 | 166.3 | 162.9 | 6733 | 9509 | 3595 | 1584 |
| 61 | petroleum products | 24.62 | .9401 | 78.0 | 243.7 | 32881 | 35810 | 19658 | 30332 |
| 63 | coke and products | 36.81 | 2.2595 | 199.3 | 419.2 | 1355 | 1730 | 2040 | 5157 |
| 64 | paving and roofing materials | 62.16 | .7124 | 154.1 | 203.1 | 330 | 248 | 32 | 54 |
| 65 | tires and inner tubes | 79.54 | .3487 | 180.9 | 156.3 | 6044 | 3044 | 49 | |
| 66 | misc. rubber products | 103.44 | .3157 | 187.5 | 122.7 | 4155 | 2658 | 340 | 1355 |
| 67 | leather tanning and fishing | 51.80 | .1359 | 79.7 | 44.3 | 1901 | 1133 | 2817 | 2749 |
| 68 | other leather products | 140.01 | .0854 | 209.8 | 67.4 | 1133 | 334 | 1360 | 1264 |
| 69 | footwear (excl. rubber) | 131.32 | .1033 | 215.7 | 63.3 | 749 | 912 | 1795 | 1197 |
| 70 | glass | 124.78 | .8715 | 190.4 | 157.5 | 2404 | 3213 | 1295 | 2917 |
| 71 | cement | 92.79 | 1.4366 | 162.4 | 233.8 | 4419 | 440 | 49 | 318 |
| 72 | structural clay products | 196.19 | .7140 | 254.3 | 141.8 | 1043 | 1322 | 2477 | 3041 |
| 73 | pottery and related products | 186.79 | .3104 | 234.2 | 81.5 | 959 | 879 | 65 | 307 |
| 74 | concrete and plaster products | 130.32 | .6149 | 227.7 | 178.4 | 929 | 228 | 1765 | 1745 |
| 75 | abrasive products | 84.73 | .4312 | 178.1 | 134.1 | 246 | 1369 | 32 | 189 |
| 76 | asbestos products | 101.02 | .4370 | 174.4 | 131.8 | 1127 | 760 | 567 | 3191 |
| 77 | other misc. nonmetallic minerals | 104.18 | .9550 | 182.1 | 146.2 | 600 | 1135 | 3676 | 9137 |
| 78 | blast furnaces | 25.62 | 1.0755 | 170.4 | 366.4 | 869 | 283 | 955 | 27053 |
| 79 | steel works and rolling mills | 73.89 | .3500 | 182.3 | 293.6 | 396 | 20738 | 32 | 80 |
| 80 | iron foundries | 126.00 | .3505 | 194.0 | 142.2 | 35585 | 696 | 16 | 38 |
| 81 | steel foundries | 130.03 | .7565 | 198.2 | 124.0 | 672 | 110 | 22216 | |
| 82 | primary copper | 17.44 | .7579 | 155.0 | 333.4 | 90 | 4553 | 49 | 22720 |
| 83 | copper rolling and drawing | 52.08 | .7571 | 161.5 | 283.2 | 2788 | 791 | 6720 | 2275 |
| 84 | primary lead | 17.06 | .7581 | 213.3 | 355.0 | 1565 | 31 | 2672 | 6952 |
| 85 | primary zinc | 62.48 | .7579 | 165.5 | 260.8 | 30 | 774 | 18913 | 15505 |
| 86 | primary metals, n.e.c. | 27.81 | .7580 | 232.8 | 374.9 | 1379 | 377 | 16 | 620 |
| 87 | nonferrous metal rolling, n.e.c. | 45.23 | 1.6080 | 164.6 | 280.0 | 396 | 703 | 761 | 4207 |
| 88 | primary aluminum | 40.41 | .5047 | 135.0 | 331.6 | 983 | 21 | | 1198 |
| 89 | aluminum rolling and drawing | 73.88 | .7586 | 161.9 | 243.8 | 204 | 560 | 6396 | 475 |
| 90 | secondary nonferrous metals | 21.65 | .5052 | 98.4 | 196.8 | 1769 | 83 | 16 | 14 |
| 91 | nonferrous foundries | 140.66 | .3467 | 210.0 | 158.6 | 282 | 11 | 16 | 100 |
| 92 | iron and steel forgings | 73.14 | .6395 | 178.4 | 191.9 | 120 | 528 | 32 | 20 |
| 93 | tin cans and other tin ware | 68.64 | .5351 | 192.3 | 245.9 | 989 | 730 | 32 | 646 |
| 94 | cutlery | 135.22 | .5358 | 201.1 | 121.7 | 791 | 365 | 178 | 490 |
| 95 | tools and general hardware | 121.59 | .5396 | 204.6 | 135.9 | 1229 | 1469 | 259 | 8 |
| 96 | hardware, n.e.c. | 122.05 | .5498 | 211.7 | 144.0 | 3130 | 942 | 16 | 45 |
| 97 | metal plumbing and vitreous fixtures | 114.32 | .5455 | 208.8 | 161.4 | 1811 | 727 | | |
| 98 | heating equipment | 94.05 | .2009 | 204.7 | 157.2 | 1085 | 1650 | 49 | |
| 99 | structural metal products | 84.59 | .5455 | 182.5 | 143.6 | 2117 | 4440 | 49 | |
| 100 | boiler shop prod. and pipe bending | 79.76 | .3403 | 189.2 | 160.5 | 2518 | 1824 | 130 | 319 |
| 101 | metal stampings | 95.72 | .3467 | 198.0 | 151.4 | 1535 | 1957 | 453 | 1036 |
| 102 | metal coating and engraving | 157.81 | .5394 | 208.1 | 124.8 | 2075 | 904 | | |
| 103 | lighting fixtures | 88.89 | .5356 | 197.2 | 151.1 | 2140 | 1279 | 16 | 46 |
| 104 | fabricated wire products | 62.81 | .5338 | 186.6 | 238.0 | 3286 | 805 | 49 | 1864 |
| 105 | metal barrels, drums, etc. | 58.56 | .5334 | 177.7 | 213.5 | 489 | 19 | 130 | |
| 106 | tubes and foils | 100.23 | .5336 | 212.1 | 203.0 | 282 | | 32 | 370 |

## Appendix 6-3 (Cont.)

| 192 I-C No. | Direct labor coefficients[b] (man-years per $ million of output) (1) | Direct capital coefficient[c] ($ million per $ million of output) (2) | Total direct and indirect requirements per million dollars of final output[d] — Labor (man-years) (3) | Capital ($0000) (4) | Exports per million dollars of total exports[e] (1947 dollars) 1947 (5) | 1951 (6) | Competitive imports per million dollars of total competitive imports[e] (1947 dollars) 1947 (7) | 1951 (8) |
|---|---|---|---|---|---|---|---|---|
| 107 misc. fabricated metal products | 84.01 | .5343 | 205.8 | 169.3 | 258 | 103 | 65 | |
| 108 steel springs | 66.41 | .5334 | 188.4 | 205.4 | | | | |
| 109 nuts, bolts, and screw machine products | 109.98 | .3487 | 195.4 | 144.9 | 1043 | 608 | 32 | 807 |
| 110 steam engines and turbines | 137.78 | .3013 | 242.4 | 119.3 | 1409 | 1431 | 16 | 206 |
| 111 internal combustion engines | 87.54 | .3013 | 203.6 | 125.7 | 6212 | 5759 | 389 | |
| 112 farm and industrial tractors | 78.74 | .5188 | 201.4 | 158.1 | 12573 | 17682 | 1457 | 8290 |
| 113 farm equipment | 101.18 | .5273 | 210.9 | 159.0 | 5504 | 7182 | 4194 | |
| 114 construction and mining machinery | 81.23 | .4631 | 192.4 | 141.1 | 12081 | 13523 | 16 | |
| 115 oil-field machinery and tools | 97.38 | .4631 | 185.8 | 134.8 | 5211 | 4230 | | |
| 116 machine tools and metalworking machinery | 128.24 | 1.0077 | 222.2 | 177.7 | 10972 | 8833 | 194 | 1521 |
| 117 cutting tools, jigs, and fixtures | 134.36 | .2333 | 210.5 | 91.0 | 1661 | 1338 | 32 | |
| 118 special industrial machinery | 106.27 | .7825 | 196.7 | 157.9 | 19684 | 20315 | 1943 | 4027 |
| 119 pumps and compressors | 83.04 | .5476 | 197.4 | 145.7 | 4335 | 3401 | | |
| 120 elevators and conveyors | 84.73 | .5433 | 177.8 | 136.4 | 2452 | 1176 | | |
| 121 blowers and fans | 86.55 | .5423 | 191.3 | 144.4 | 396 | 399 | | |
| 122 power transmission equipment | 108.51 | .5428 | 190.7 | 133.1 | 162 | 267 | | |
| 123 industrial machinery, n.e.c. | 74.12 | .5427 | 184.5 | 153.5 | 2494 | 971 | 648 | |
| 124 commercial machines and equipment, n.e.c. | 128.31 | .4864 | 200.1 | 111.1 | 7117 | 7985 | 32 | 733 |
| 125 refrigeration equipment | 72.86 | .2753 | 189.4 | 130.4 | 6697 | 7674 | | |
| 126 valves and fittings | 115.32 | .8936 | 206.2 | 179.9 | 2782 | 1809 | 32 | 410 |
| 127 ball and roller bearings | 136.95 | .3594 | 199.0 | 106.7 | 1457 | 1417 | | |
| 128 machine shops | 115.97 | .8810 | 197.0 | 168.5 | 156 | 37 | | |
| 129 wiring devices and graphite products | 95.10 | .3610 | 196.7 | 138.5 | 1745 | 2376 | 16 | 635 |
| 130 electrical measuring instruments | 118.91 | .3650 | 209.0 | 105.7 | 714 | 739 | 16 | |
| 131 motors and generators | 117.77 | .2008 | 211.6 | 138.2 | 4383 | 3919 | 97 | 1415 |
| 132 transformers | 99.16 | .3615 | 194.5 | 110.7 | 971 | 1163 | | |
| 133 electrical control apparatus | 111.84 | .3633 | 198.5 | 134.5 | 1679 | 1714 | 49 | |
| 134 electrical welding apparatus | 78.46 | .3619 | 203.4 | 131.6 | 1289 | 837 | 194 | |
| 135 electrical appliances | 74.08 | .3083 | 195.8 | 201.5 | 3861 | 3622 | 194 | 1828 |
| 136 insulated wire and cable | 66.92 | .3565 | 184.7 | | 1457 | | 16 | 47 |

| No. | Industry | | | | | | | | |
|---|---|---|---|---|---|---|---|---|---|
| 137 | engine electrical equipment | 191.99 | .3592 | 292.9 | 133.5 | 971 | 926 | 32 | 66 |
| 138 | electric lamps | 131.38 | .3580 | 203.0 | 107.0 | 726 | 701 | 130 | 123 |
| 139 | radio and related products | 124.10 | .2309 | 241.2 | 101.7 | 6763 | 5813 | | |
| 140 | tubes | 227.75 | .3646 | 289.0 | 114.6 | 947 | 1017 | 32 | |
| 141 | communication equipment | 126.19 | .3597 | 224.3 | 111.1 | 2147 | 1566 | 16 | |
| 142 | storage batteries | 48.89 | .3599 | 145.2 | 169.5 | 576 | 488 | | |
| 143 | primary batteries | 103.69 | .3644 | 173.4 | 128.1 | 486 | 911 | | |
| 144 | x-ray apparatus | 96.42 | .3877 | 167.9 | 93.9 | 923 | 434 | 16 | |
| 145 | motor vehicles | 60.25 | .3877 | 206.6 | 168.5 | 59892 | 64720 | 1085 | 4280 |
| 146 | truck trailers | 75.00 | .3877 | 195.6 | 150.7 | 1259 | 429 | | |
| 147 | automobile trailers | 69.41 | .4063 | 201.8 | 148.6 | 7525 | 1033 | 130 | 1054 |
| 148 | aircraft and parts | 142.44 | .8139 | 225.6 | 113.6 | 5360 | 64 | 810 | 115 |
| 149 | ships and boats | 171.03 | .3398 | 254.6 | 158.7 | 4731 | 2167 | 16 | |
| 150 | locomotives | 77.54 | .3398 | 225.0 | 146.6 | 6433 | 185 | | |
| 151 | railroad equipment | 65.54 | .1754 | 180.8 | 150.5 | 1547 | 1812 | 1101 | 980 |
| 152 | motorcycles and bicycles | 68.63 | .5819 | 176.3 | 106.5 | 3748 | 2323 | 65 | 9 |
| 153 | instruments, etc. | 132.03 | .5791 | 221.0 | 131.4 | | | | |
| 154 | optical, ophthalmic, and photo equipment | 176.62 | .5759 | 260.6 | 134.9 | 4707 | 4199 | 680 | 2907 |
| 155 | medical and dental instruments and supplies | 95.35 | .1871 | 208.0 | 164.4 | 2039 | 1857 | 97 | 534 |
| 156 | watches and clocks | 103.80 | .2666 | 212.7 | 143.4 | 779 | 638 | 11367 | 10324 |
| 157 | jewelry and silverware | 107.09 | .2666 | 180.2 | 114.3 | 1985 | 1093 | 14233 | 10582 |
| 158 | musical instruments and parts | 131.08 | .2666 | 215.2 | 85.4 | 432 | 203 | 1328 | 1708 |
| 159 | toys and sporting goods | 133.40 | .5570 | 220.1 | 103.4 | 1427 | 872 | 777 | 1328 |
| 160 | office supplies | 112.74 | .2666 | 177.2 | 84.9 | 2812 | 1640 | 340 | 156 |
| 161 | plastic products | 86.93 | .1489 | 168.0 | 144.5 | 1055 | 611 | 49 | 109 |
| 162 | cork products | 71.43 | .2666 | 142.8 | 99.4 | 204 | 234 | 453 | 469 |
| 163 | motion picture production | 81.66 | 3.2979 | 120.1 | 49.5 | | | | |
| 164 | misc. manufactured products | 88.20 | 1.2946 | 203.2 | 120.9 | 2710 | 1388 | 6202 | 8757 |
| | Public utilities and transportation | | | | | | | | |
| 167 | electric light and power | 71.50 | 3.3391 | 122.5 | 412.5 | 72 | 104 | | |
| 168 | natural, mfd, and mixed gas | 53.63 | .4344 | 97.2 | 234.1 | 40957 | 50601 | 874 | 722 |
| 169 | railroads | 153.64 | 3.2347 | 203.5 | 388.0 | 9018 | 11143 | | |
| 170 | trucking | 106.31 | 1.9027 | 162.9 | 111.1 | 1529 | 1889 | | |
| 171 | warehousing and storage | 329.64 | 3.5968 | 404.6 | 405.2 | 80361 | 79540 | 40157 | 38821 |
| | trade and services | | | | | | | | |
| 172 | overseas transportation | 107.47 | 1.1677 | 178.1 | 263.6 | 3933 | 4860 | 696 | 497 |
| 173 | other water transportation | 72.52 | .5840 | 193.7 | 503.5 | 4976 | 7409 | 1668 | 4050 |
| 174 | air transportation | 117.25 | 1.2366 | 177.4 | 130.3 | 612 | 1334 | | |
| 175 | pipeline transportation | 80.94 | .3628 | 106.5 | 153.6 | | | | |
| 176 | wholesale trade | 139.22 | 4.3293 | 173.8 | 106.8 | 62158 | 76806 | | |
| 177 | retail trade | 182.60 | .6538 | 225.0 | 208.8 | 144 | 178 | | |
| 178 | local and highway transportation | 126.49 | .0286 | 165.4 | 86.3 | | | | |
| 179 | telephone and telegraph | 120.42 | 1.5443 | 274.4 | 475.8 | 2272 | 2741 | | |
| 180 | eating and drinking places | 125.37 | | 215.8 | 200.0 | | | | |
| 181 | banking, finance, and insurance | 93.85 | | 132.1 | 38.9 | 8106 | 10017 | | |
| 182 | hotels | 258.81 | | 316.0 | 263.4 | | | 16516 | 6711 |

# Appendix 6-3 (Cont.)

| 192 I-C No. | Direct labor coefficients[b] (man-years per $ million of output) (1) | Direct capital coefficient[c] ($ million per $ million of output) (2) | Total direct and indirect requirements per million dollars of final output[d] | | Exports per million dollars of total exports[e] (1947 dollars) | | Competitive imports per million dollars of total competitive imports[e] (1947 dollars) | |
|---|---|---|---|---|---|---|---|---|
| | | | Labor (man-years) (3) | Capital ($0000) (4) | 1947 (5) | 1951 (6) | 1947 (7) | 1951 (8) |
| 183 real estate and rentals | 16.32 | 8.1587 | 48.7 | 876.3 | | | | |
| 184 laundries and dry cleaning | 256.99 | .9791 | 309.6 | 174.7 | | | | |
| 185 other personal services | 167.44 | .1074 | 235.7 | 132.6 | | | | |
| 186 advertising, incl. radio and television | 31.52 | .0624 | 164.9 | 98.9 | 156 | 193 | | |
| 187 business services | 233.33 | .1074 | 267.4 | 58.3 | | | | |
| 188 automobile repair services and garages | 173.07 | | 266.5 | 127.9 | | | | |
| 189 other repair services | 133.10 | | 213.4 | 81.3 | | | | |
| 190 motion picture and other amusements | 166.90 | 1.0737 | 224.3 | 211.9 | 7687 | 11854 | | |
| 191 medical, dental, and other professional services | 155.54 | 1.0182 | 191.0 | 161.8 | | | | |
| 192 nonprofit institutions | 331.67 | 3.6344 | 367.0 | 421.5 | | | | |
| Total | | | 35914.0 | 34717.2 | 1,000,000 | 1,000,000 | 1,000,000 | 1,000,000 |

[a]For data used for computation B, see Wassily Leontief, "Domestic Productiioon and Foreign Trade: The American Capital Position Reexamined," reprinted from *Proceedings of the American Philosophical Society* 97, September 1953; the above data were used for all other computations.
[b]Labor coefficients were computed at the Harvard Economic Research Project, under the direction of Alfred H. Conrad.
[c]Capital coefficients were computed at the Harvard Economic Research Project, by a group headed by James M. Henderson.
[d]The inverse matrix used was based on the sum of the matrix $D_2$ of 1947 dollar transactions (which does not include capital replacement flows) and a capital replacement flow matrix obtained at the Harvard Economic Research Project, this inverse was estimated by Marie McCarthy.
[e]Export and import figures for 1947 are based on Bureau of Labor Statistics, Division of Interindustry Economics, *Table I—Interindustry Flows of Goods and Services by Industry of Origin and Destination*, Section 6, October 1952. Export and import figures for 1951 are based on U.S. Department of Commerce, Foreign Trade Division of the Bureau of the Census, *Summary of Foreign Commerce of the United States, January–December 1951*.

# 7

# *Multiregional input-output analysis*

## ( 1 9 6 3 )

## I. A system of multiregional relations

In multiregional input-output analysis the economic system is described not only in terms of interdependent industries, but also in terms of several interrelated regions. The output of each region is defined as a combination of outputs of economic activities carried on within its geographic boundaries; its input accordingly comprises the direct inputs of these industries and the goods and services absorbed directly by the final demand sectors of that region.

The economic interdependence between two regions is the interdependence between the industries located within their respective boundaries. It is direct to the extent to which commodities and services produced in one region are absorbed by the industries or the final demand sectors of the other; it is indirect (from the regional point of view) to the extent to which the connection between such inputs and outputs is established through industries located in some other regions.

The movement of commodities or services from one region to another obviously reflects the existence of a direct input-output relationship between the industries—or an industry and the final demand sector—located within their respective boundaries. Indirect regional interdependence gives rise to what is commonly called triangular or multilateral trading patterns.

---

Written in collaboration with Alan Strout. From *Structural Inter-dependence and Economic Development*, Tibor Barna (ed.). Reprinted by permission of Macmillan & Company, Ltd., and St. Martin's Press, Inc.

The multiregional input-output scheme described below is not intended to provide a systematic theoretical description of the many factors and relationships that ultimately determine the pattern of a multiregional economic system; it is designed rather as a rough and ready working tool capable of making effective use of the limited amount of factual information with which, even in statistically advanced countries, economists have to work. It is for this reason that, after having experimented with linear programming models, we now avoid explicit use of the cost minimization or revenue maximization principle in the basic formulation of the multiregional scheme. As in the case of ordinary input-output analysis, the opportunities for formal choice between alternative production (and interregional shipments) patterns can be introduced later, step by step, as better factual information becomes available.

The peculiar theoretical problem of multiregional input-output analysis stems from the simple fact that identical goods can be, and actually are, produced and consumed in different regions. The regional origin of the particular batch of a given kind of good absorbed by its users in one particular region is as irrelevant to them as the ultimate regional destinations their outputs are to producers. It is as if the producers of a specific commodity or service located in one particular region had merged their output in a single regional supply pool, and the users of that commodity or service located in a given region had ordered and received it through a regional demand pool. All interregional movements of a particular commodity or service within a multiregional economy can thus be visualized as shipments from regional supply to regional demand pools of that good. In accordance with that overall point of view, the general equilibrium system described below consists of a set of regional interindustrial input-output systems of conventional design linked together in—or rather fitted into—a separately constructed system of interregional relationships.

## The system of equations

We will describe the regional input-output systems first. Let $X_{i.og}$ represent the total internal input (i.e., production + imports − exports) of good $i$ in region $g$, $X_{j.go}$ the output of good $j$ in region $g$, and $Y_{ig}$ the final demand for good $i$ in region $g$. The following equation describes, for any region $g$, the balance between the total internal input and output of good $i$, the output of all other goods and the internal final regional demand for good $i$:

(7-1)     $X_{i.og} = \sum\limits_{j=1}^{n} [a_{ij.g}X_{j.go}] + Y_{i.g}$     $(i = 1, 2, \ldots, n)$

$(g = 1, 2, \ldots, m)$

The constants $a_{ij.g}$ are the familiar technical input coefficients describing the amount of good $i$ required to produce one unit of good $j$ in region $g$.

If the $mn$ final demands are considered as given, the $mn$ equations of system (7-1) contain $2mn$ unknowns: $mn$ regional outputs and $mn$ regional internal inputs. The interdependence between the outputs and inputs of the different regions is described below.

In an isolated multiregional economy subdivided into $m$ separate regions, the interregional flows of each good $i$ must satisfy $2m$ balance equations of the following kind:

(7-2)     $X_{i.go} = \sum\limits_{h=1}^{m} X_{i.gh}$     $(i = 1, 2, \ldots, n)$

$(g = 1, 2, \ldots, m)$

(7-3)     $X_{i.oh} = \sum\limits_{g=1}^{m} X_{i.gh}$     $(h = 1, 2, \ldots, m)$

The variable $X_{i.go}$ represents here, as before, the supply pool of good $i$ in region $g$, $X_{i.oh}$ the demand pool of good $i$ in region $h$, and $X_{i.gh}$ the total shipment of good $i$ from the supply pool in region $g$ to its demand pool in region $h$.

A multiregional economy trading with the world outside can be formally transformed into an isolated system by the simple device of treating the "outside world" as its additional internal region. An alternative, well-known device for closing an open multiregional system with respect to foreign trade is the inclusion of goods exported by each region into the region's final bill of goods; imports must, of course, be entered on the right-hand side of (7-1) with a minus sign.

Summing each of these two sets of equations over all regions, we see that the aggregate supply of good $i$ for the isolated multiregional economy as a whole equals the aggregate demand for that good:

(7-4)     $\sum\limits_{g=1}^{m}{}'\sum\limits_{h=1}^{m} X_{i.gh} = \sum\limits_{g=1}^{m} X_{i.go} = \sum\limits_{h=1}^{m} X_{i.oh} = X_{i.oo}$     $(i = 1, 2, \ldots, n)$

The structural equations that we propose to use in explaining the magnitude of all interregional flows of any commodity or service $i$ are of the following general form:

(7-5) $\qquad X_{i.gh} = \dfrac{X_{i.go}X_{i.oh}}{X_{i.oo}} Q_{i.gh} \qquad \begin{array}{l} (i = 1, 2, \ldots, n) \\ (g = 1, 2, \ldots, m) \\ (g \neq h)(h = 1, 2, \ldots, m) \end{array}$

The flow of the particular good $i$ from region $g$ to any *other* region $h$ is assumed to be directly proportional to its total output in region $g$ and to its total input in region $h$, and inversely proportional to the aggregate amount of commodity $i$,

$$ X_{i.oo}\left( = \sum_{g=1}^{m} X_{i.go} = \sum_{h=1}^{m} X_{i.oh} \right) $$

produced and consumed in all the regions of the economy as a whole. The coefficients $Q_{i.gh}$ are empirical constants; their signifi-cance and determination will be discussed in sections II and III below.

The multiplicative form in which the total output of good $i$ in the exporting regions and its total input in the importing regions enter into (7-5) permits us to characterize it as a special type of *gravity* or *potential model*. It implies that there can be no flow from region $g$ to region $h$ if either one of those two magnitudes is equal to zero. The introduction of the aggregate output of good $i$ into the denom-inator implies that, if that aggregate output—as well as output $X_{i.go}$ in region $g$ and total input $X_{i.oh}$ in region $h$—doubles, the flow of that good from region $g$ to region $h$ will double too.

If neither $X_{i.go}$ or $X_{i.oh}$ nor $X_{i.ho}$ or $X_{i.og}$ is equal to zero, and if the coefficients $Q_{i.gh}$ and $Q_{i.hg}$ are positive, both $X_{i.gh}$ and $X_{i.hg}$ will be pos-itive too; that is, good $i$ will be shipped between regions $g$ and $h$ simultaneously in both directions. In an ideal system in which both regions are defined as locational points, in which good $i$ is consid-ered to be perfectly homogeneous and all shipments are assumed to result from strictly rational decisions based on perfect information, cross-shipments, of course, could not occur. In actual empirical analysis, however, good $i$ will as a rule be defined as an aggregate of several similar but not strictly identical items, while regions $g$ and $h$ will often represent more or less extended areas, so that the average distance (or the average unit costs of transportation) between them would necessarily conceal the actual diversity of commodity flows connecting many distinct pairs of sending and receiving points. Under such circumstances cross-shipments should be expected, and actually are observed, nearly everywhere. Moreover, the interre-gional commodity flow ideally should represent rates of flows at one specific point of time. In fact, they usually refer to an interval of time as long as an entire year. Such aggregation over time is liable to show cross-hauling where there are shipments in opposite directions in different months.

Thus, the ability of equations (7-5) to allow for the existence of simultaneous flows of the same good $i$ between two regions in opposite directions should be considered as a desirable characteristic, not a flaw. In those instances, however, in which the actual conditions approach the ideal and cross-shipments do not occur or are so small that they can be interpreted as being accidental, we can, by setting the appropriate coefficient $Q_{i.gh}$ equal to zero, exclude the possibilities of the appearance of one of the two opposite flows (see section II below).

Substituting from (7-5) into (7-2), we obtain:

$$
(7\text{-}6) \qquad X_{i.go} = \frac{X_{i.go} \sum_{r=1}^{m} [X_{i.or} Q_{i.gr}]}{X_{i.oo}} + X_{i.gg} \qquad \begin{matrix} (Q_{i.gg} = 0) \\ (g = 1, 2, \ldots, m) \\ (i = 1, 2, \ldots, n) \end{matrix}
$$

The term $X_{i.gg}$, the internally absorbed part of the output of region $g$, appears on the right-hand side because equations (7-5) pertain only to interregional flows. The subsidiary condition $Q_{i.gg} = 0$ reduces to zero the term $X_{i.og} Q_{i.gg}$.

A substitution from (7-5) into (7-3) yields:

$$
(7\text{-}7) \qquad X_{i.oh} = \frac{X_{i.oh} \sum_{r=1}^{m} [X_{i.ro} Q_{i.rh}]}{X_{i.oo}} + X_{i.hh} \qquad \begin{matrix} (Q_{i.hh} = 0) \\ (h = 1, 2, \ldots, m) \\ (i = 1, 2, \ldots, n) \end{matrix}
$$

The multiregional system is now formally complete. It contains $3mn$ equations and an equal number of unknowns (the final demand for each good in every region being considered as given). There are $mn$ equations in set (7-1), which constitutes the intraregional part of the system, and $2mn$ equations in its interregional part represented by sets (7-6) and (7-7). The unknown variables are the $mn$ outputs $X_{i.go}$ and the $mn$ total inputs $X_{i.oh}$ of each of $n$ goods in each of $m$ regions, and also the $mn$ $X_{i.gg}$'s, which represent the internally absorbed parts of the outputs of each good in each region. The last group of variables appears explicitly only in the interregional equations (7-6) and (7-7).

## Toward a numerical solution

As a first step toward a numerical solution of the system described above, the $mn$ variables $X_{i.gg}$ (or $X_{i.hh}$) can be eliminated and the number of equations that have to be treated simultaneously reduced from $3mn$ to $2mn$.

By substituting $g$ for $h$, rewrite (7-7) in the notation used in (7-6):

$$(7\text{-}7a) \qquad X_{i.og} = \frac{X_{i.og} \sum_{r=1}^{m} [X_{i.ro} Q_{i.rg}]}{X_{i.oo}} + X_{i.gg} \qquad \begin{array}{l} (Q_{i.gg} = 0) \\ (g = 1, 2, \ldots, m) \\ (i = 1, 2, \ldots, n) \end{array}$$

From (7-6) and (7-7a), we have:

$$(7\text{-}8) \qquad X_{i.go}X_{i.oo} - X_{i.go} \sum_{r=1}^{m} [X_{i.or}Q_{i.gr}] = X_{i.og}X_{i.oo} - X_{i.og} \sum_{r=1}^{m} [X_{i.ro}Q_{i.rg}]$$

$$(Q_{i.gg} = 0)$$
$$(i = 1, 2, \ldots, n)$$
$$(g = 1, 2, \ldots, m)$$

Equation (7-4) can be transcribed as,

$$(7\text{-}4a) \qquad \sum_{g=1}^{m} X_{i.og} = \sum_{g=1}^{m} X_{i.go} (\equiv X_{i.oo}) \qquad \begin{array}{l} (i = 1, 2, \ldots, n) \\ (g = 1, 2, \ldots, m) \end{array}$$

Now let $\sum_{g=1}^{m} X_{i.og}$ be substituted for $X_{i.oo}$ on the left-hand side of (7-8) and $\sum_{g=1}^{m} X_{i.go}$ on its right-hand side; and let the constants $Q_{i.gr}$ be replaced by new constants $L_{i.gr}$ defined as

$$(7\text{-}9) \qquad L_{i.gr} = 1 - Q_{i.gr} \qquad (L_{i.gg} = 1) \qquad \begin{array}{l} (i = 1, 2, \ldots, n) \\ (g = 1, 2, \ldots, m) \\ (r = 1, 2, \ldots, m) \end{array}$$

Thus, we arrive at the following new set of interregional equations:

$$(7\text{-}10) \qquad X_{i.go} \sum_{r=1}^{m} [X_{i.or} L_{i.gr}] = X_{i.og} \sum_{r=1}^{m} [X_{i.ro} L_{i.rg}] \qquad \begin{array}{l} (L_{i.gg} = 1) \\ (i = 1, 2, \ldots, n) \\ (g = 1, 2, \ldots, m) \end{array}$$

This set contains $mn$ equations and $2mn$ variables $X_{i.og}$ and $X_{i.go}$ (the $X_{i.gg}$'s having been eliminated). However, $n$ of these equations are redundant—one in each set of $m$ describing the interdependence among all the regional outputs and inputs of one particular good $i$. To demonstrate this, let us form a new equation by summing over regions $g$, the left-hand and the right-hand sides of such a subgroup of equations (7-10) corresponding to any one particular commodity $i$:

(7-11)
$$\sum_{g=1}^{m}\sum_{r=1}^{m} [X_{i.go}X_{i.or}L_{i.gr}] = \sum_{g=1}^{m}\sum_{r=1}^{m} [X_{i.og}X_{i.ro}L_{i.rg}]$$

This is, in fact, an identity: by interchanging the subscripts $g$ and $r$ on the right-hand side (which leaves the double sum essentially unchanged) one can show it to be identical with the expression on the left-hand side. It follows that any one of the $m$ equations, which have been added together to form (7-11), can be derived from the other $m - 1$ and consequently could be omitted.

From the set (7-10) as a whole we can, for example, omit the $n$ equations identified by the subscript $g = m$. This reduces the number of (independent) equations in that set to $mn - n$. On the other hand, the $n$ balance equations (7-4a)—which were redundant so long as (7-6) and (7-7) were not yet combined into (7-7a)—must now be considered as imposing additional constraints on our system and, consequently, must be included in it.

Thus, after elimination of the $mn$ unknowns $X_{i.gg}$, the multiregional system in its new compressed form comprises $mn$ regional input-output equations (7-1), $mn - n$ structural interregional equations of set (7-10), and $n$ interregional balance equations (7-4a), a total of $2mn$ equations. The $mn$ total regional outputs $X_{i.go}$ and the $mn$ total regional inputs $X_{i.og}$ make up the corresponding set of $2mn$ unknowns.

With the $mn$ final demands $Y_{i.g}$—for $n$ different goods in $m$ different regions—considered as given, a general solution of this system can show, for example, what effect a change in any one $Y_{i.g}$ would have on the total output and the total input of each good in every region. Having computed the magnitudes of all the $X_{i.go}$'s and $X_{i.og}$'s, we can insert them in (7-6) and (7-7a) to determine the values of $X_{i.gg}$ for any $i$ and $g$; the magnitudes of all the interregional flows, $X_{i.gh}$ ($g \neq h$), can be similarly derived from the basic set of structural interregional equations (7-5).

The conventional input-output equations of set (7-1), as well as the interregional balance equations (7-4a), are linear. The interregional structural equations (7-10) are nonlinear; for purposes of numerical computation they can, however, be linearized by means of a first-order approximation.

Let the value of each variable be split into two parts, its base-year magnitude and a deviation of its actual magnitude from that base-year value. The system can be solved for the deviations of all dependent variables from their base-year magnitudes, on the assumption that the base-year magnitudes are known and that the deviations of the regional final demands $Y_{i.g}$ from their base-year magnitudes are given.

Below we will use a bar to identify the magnitude of each variable in the base year and, up to the end of this section, the increment sign $\Delta$ to mark the deviations of all variables from their respective base-year values.

To obtain a linear approximation of (7-10), we substitute in it $(\overline{X}_{i.go} + \Delta X_{i.go})$ for $X_{i.go}$ and $(\overline{X}_{i.og} + \Delta X_{i.og})$ for $X_{i.og}$. In the resulting expression all terms containing a product of two barred letters will cancel out, because equation (7-10) holds for the base year, and all the products of two deviations of variables can be dropped because they represent second-order terms. Thus, the first-order approximation of (7-10) takes the form of the following set of linear relationships:

$$(7\text{-}12) \quad \sum_{r=1}^{m} [\Delta X_{i.or} M_{i.gr}] - \sum_{r=1}^{m} [\Delta X_{i.ro} N_{i.rg}] = 0 \quad (i = 1, 2, \ldots, n)$$

$$(g = 1, 2, \ldots, m - 1)$$

The new constants are introduced to simplify the form of these equations; they can be computed from the previously used constants and the base-year values of the regional inputs and outputs:[1]

$$(7\text{-}13) \qquad M_{i.gr} = \begin{cases} \overline{X}_{i.go} L_{i.gr} & \text{(if } r \neq g) \\[2ex] \overline{X}_{i.go} - \sum_{q=1}^{m} [\overline{X}_{i.qo} L_{i.qg}] & \text{(if } r = g) \end{cases}$$

$$N_{i.rg} = \begin{cases} \overline{X}_{i.og} L_{i.rg} & \text{(if } r \neq g) \\[2ex] \overline{X}_{i.og} - \sum_{q=1}^{m} [\overline{X}_{i.oq} L_{i.gq}] & \text{(if } r = g) \end{cases}$$

In passing from (7-10) to (7-12), we have dropped the $n$ equations

---

[1] In terms of the constants appearing in basic structural equations (7-5),

$$M_{i.gr} = \begin{cases} \overline{X}_{i.go}(1 - Q_{i.gr}) & \text{(if } r \neq g) \\[2ex] \overline{X}_{i.go} - \overline{X}_{i.oo} + \sum_{q=1}^{m} [\overline{X}_{i.qo} Q_{i.gg}] & \text{(if } r = g) \end{cases}$$

$$(7\text{-}13\text{b}) \qquad N_{i.rg} = \begin{cases} \overline{X}_{i.og}(1 - Q_{i.rg}) & \text{(if } r \neq g) \\[2ex] \overline{X}_{i.og} - \overline{X}_{i.oo} + \sum_{q=1}^{m} [\overline{X}_{i.oq} Q_{i.gq}] & \text{(if } r = g) \end{cases}$$

$$(Q_{i.gg} = 0)$$

with the subscript $q = m$ because, as demonstrated above, they can be considered redundant.

Equations (7-1), (7-4a), and (7-12) constitute a complete linear system which enables us to determine the dependence of changes in total outputs and total inputs of all goods in all regional subdivisions of a multiregional economy on given changes in the regional vectors of final demand. The corresponding changes in all intraregional flows $\Delta X_{i.gg}$ and interregional flows $\Delta X_{i.gh}$ can, of course, be determined by inserting the previously computed values of $\Delta X_{i.go}$ and $\Delta X_{i.oh}$ into equations (7-5) and (7-6), or (7-7a).

The magnitude of the errors resulting from the linearization of the nonlinear interregional relationships can be assessed through insertion of the computed $\Delta X_{i.go}$'s and $\Delta X_{i.og}$'s into the original system (7-10). The differences between the left-hand and right-hand terms of each equation will indicate how close an approximation has actually been attained. Since all these quadratic equations are homogeneous of the first degree, the errors caused by the linear approximation would be nil (for any given $i$) if all the computed increments $\Delta X_{i.go}$ and $\Delta X_{i.og}$ happened to be strictly proportional to the base-year levels $\overline{X}_{i.go}$ and $\overline{X}_{i.og}$ of the corresponding variable, that is, if $\Delta X_{i.go}/\overline{X}_{i.go} = \Delta X_{i.og}/\overline{X}_{i.og} = \lambda$ for all $g$'s where $\lambda$ is some constant. This means that the linearization error depends not on the absolute but only on the relative magnitude of incremental changes of these variables.

In case the first-order approximation, by which equation (7-12) has been derived from the nonlinear set (7-8), proves to be insufficient, a higher degree of approximation could most likely be attained through an iterative procedure in which the total value of the variables obtained in one round of computations is used to determine their base values for the next round.[2]

---

[2]A purely linear multiregional system is obtained if, instead of deriving its interregional part from structural equation (7-5), one substitutes for it the following set of analogous relationships between variables describing each region's external trade:

$$(7-5') \qquad X_{i.gh} = \frac{Z_{i.go}Z_{i.oh}Q_{i.gh}}{Z_{i.oo}} \quad (g \neq h) \qquad \begin{array}{l} (i = 1, 2, \ldots, n) \\ (g = 1, 2, \ldots, m) \\ (h = 1, 2, \ldots, m) \end{array}$$

Where $Z_{i.go}$ and $Z_{i.oh}$ represent respectively the gross exports of good $i$ from region $g$ and the gross imports of that good into region $h$:

$$Z_{i.go} = X_{i.go} - X_{i.gg}$$
$$Z_{i.oh} = X_{i.oh} - X_{i.hh}$$

From (7-4) it also follows that,

$$(7-4') \qquad \sum_{r=1}^{m} Z_{i.or} = \sum_{r=1}^{m} Z_{i.ro} = X_{i.oo} - \sum_{r=1}^{m} X_{i.rr}$$

## II. The interregional coefficients

Having presented the analytical basis of the entire system and its overall design, we turn now to discussion of the constants $Q_{i.gh}$ appearing in (7-5) and all interregional equations derived from it. The three subscripts attached indicate to each of them that equations describing a system with $n$ goods and $m$ regions will contain $nm^2$ such constants. They can be best visualized arranged in $n$ square matrices. Each of these matrices contains the constants characterizing the structure of the interregional flows of one particular good and has $m$ rows and columns, the row number $g$ indicating the origin and the column number $h$ the destination of the specific interregional flow characterized by the particular $Q_{i.gh}$. Since they all refer to the same good, the coefficients contained in each such matrix will naturally have the same $i$ subscript.

Equations (7-5), (7-6), and (7-7), which make up the basis of the interregional part of our system, can also be conveniently subdivided into $n$ groups, each group containing $m^2$ equations from set (7-5), $m$ equations from set (7-6), and $m$ equations from set (7-7), all pertaining to one particular good $i$. All variables in each one of such subsets of interregional equations must carry the same subscript $i$ as will the constants $Q_{i.gh}$ that will appear in these equations; these constants will accordingly belong to one of the distinct coefficient matrices mentioned above.

In the analysis that follows we will be concerned with one such single group of equations describing the structure and the balance of the interregional flows of one particular good, say steel or electrical machinery. To simplify notation in the formulas presented in this section, the subscript $i$ under all variables and constants is omitted; for example, instead of $X_{i.gh}$ we write $X_{gh}$. In determining the numerical magnitudes of various parameters, we will interpret the observed magnitude of all the different flows as if they represented the base-year value of the corresponding variables.

In case the available base-year statistics comprise information not only on regional output and inputs $\overline{X}_{go}$ and $\overline{X}_{og}$ but also on interre-

---

When the values of $X_{i.gh}$ as defined by (7-5′) are substituted in (7-2) and (7-3), the interregional balance equations, corresponding to the nonlinear equations (7-6) and (7-7) above, turn out to be of a linear form:

$$(7-6') \qquad \sum_{r=1}^{m} Z_{i.or} = \sum_{r=1}^{m} [Z_{i.or}Q_{i.gr}] \quad (Q_{i.gg} = 0) \qquad \begin{array}{l} (i = 1, 2, \ldots, n) \\ (g = 1, 2, \ldots, m) \end{array}$$

$$(7-7') \qquad \sum_{r=1}^{m} Z_{i.ro} = \sum_{r=1}^{m} [Z_{i.ro}Q_{i.rh}] \quad (Q_{i.hh} = 0) \qquad \begin{array}{l} (i = 1, 2, \ldots, n) \\ (g = 1, 2, \ldots, m) \end{array}$$

gional flows $\overline{X}_{gh}$ ($g \neq h$), a direct estimate of any constants $Q_{gh}$ can be obtained through insertion of the base-year values of the appropriate variables in the corresponding equation (7-5).[3] This procedure is analogous to that which is conventionally used to derive the matrix of the technical coefficients $a_{ij}$ from an input-output table compiled for some base year. In section III below, this method of deriving the magnitude of interregional constants from complete base-year information will be referred to as the *single-point estimate.*

Systematic statistical information on the interregional flows of many, if not most, goods and services is, however, unavailable in many countries. To overcome this major obstacle to the practical application of the multiregional input-output system presented in section I above, an analytical procedure is described in this section which makes it possible to apply that system even in those instances for which no base-year information on interregional flows is available. The constants $Q_{gh}$ can in this case be estimated indirectly from the base-year magnitudes of total regional inputs and outputs; supplemental information on interregional distances or, more generally; on unit transportation costs can also be utilized in these indirect estimates of the structural parameters.

For the purpose of the following analysis, each of the constants $Q_{gh}$ will be described in terms of four subsidiary parameters appearing on the right-hand side of (7-14):

$$(7\text{-}14) \qquad Q_{gh} = (C_g + K_h)d_{gh}\delta_{gh} \quad (g = 1, 2, \ldots, m)$$
$$(h = 1, 2, \ldots, m)$$

Equation (7-5) can accordingly be rewritten as:

$$(7\text{-}5a) \qquad X_{gh} = \frac{X_{go}X_{oh}(C_g + K_h)d_{gh}\delta_{gh}}{X_{oo}} \quad (g \neq h)$$
$$(g = 1, 2, \ldots, m)$$
$$(h = 1, 2, \ldots, m)$$

For the time being, let $\delta_{gh}$ be assumed to be equal to 1. (We shall see that the only other value assigned to this parameter will be zero.)

The constant $d_{gh}$ is intended to be a measure of the inverse of the

---

[3]This observation and all that follow apply to cases in which the number of interrelated regions is greater than three. With only three regions—if the three total regional exports, $X_{go} - X_{gg}$, and the three total regional imports, $X_{oh} - X_{hh}$, are given—the magnitudes of all six possible interregional flows $X_{gh}$ ($g, h = 1, 2, 3$) can be derived immediately, without recourse to any structural equations, from the six balance equations (7-2) and (7-3). In case of only two interrelated regions, even the total exports and the total imports of each cannot be considered as exogenously given, since from (7-2) and (7-3) it follows that $X_{10} = X_{12} = X_{02}$ and $X_{20} = X_{21} = X_{01}$.

per-unit transportation costs that would be incurred in moving the good in question from region $g$ to region $h$. For lack of better information, it might, for example, represent the *reciprocal* of the distance between these two regions; however, in general, $d_{gh}$ is not necessarily equal to $d_{hg}$.

The constants $C_g$ and $K_h$ are parameters characterizing in a summary way the relative position of region $g$ vis-à-vis all other regions as a supplier, and of region $h$ as a user, of good $i$. The introduction of these essentially summary parameters emphasizes the fundamental difference between this system and the analytically more explicit and empirically more demanding linear programming models.

The $C_g$'s and $K_h$'s cannot be observed; they can only be computed indirectly. In partial analysis—in an analysis that does not take into account the interregional balance equations (7-6) and (7-7)—these parameters can be derived statistically through the application of the least squares or some other conventional curve-fitting procedure (see section III below). Within the framework of a consistent interregional equilibrium system, of which (7-6) and (7-7) constitute a part, the values of $C_g$ and $K_h$ can also be determined through solutions of a set of simultaneous linear equations involving the use of factual information concerning the magnitudes of total output $\overline{X}_{go}$, inputs $\overline{X}_{oh}$, and the internal use of the domestic production $\overline{X}_{hh}$ of the particular good in each region in a given base year.

Let us rewrite equations (7-6) and (7-7) describing all $Q_{gh}$'s in terms of the four new parameters and substituting for all the regional inputs and outputs their observed base-year values:

$$(7\text{-}6a) \quad \overline{X}_{go} \sum_{r=1}^{m} [\overline{X}_{or}(C_g + K_r)d_{gr}\delta_{gr}] = (\overline{X}_{go} - \overline{X}_{gg})\overline{X}_{oo} \qquad (\delta_{gg} = 0)$$

$$(g = 1, 2, \ldots, m)$$

$$(7\text{-}7b) \quad \overline{X}_{oh} \sum_{r=1}^{m} [\overline{X}_{ro}(C_r + K_h)d_{rh}\delta_{rh}] = (\overline{X}_{oh} - \overline{X}_{hh})\overline{X}_{oo} \qquad (\delta_{hh} = 0)$$

$$(h = 1, 2, \ldots, m)$$

The magnitudes of all the $X$'s can now be considered as given, as well as the magnitudes of the transportation costs or distances $(d_{gh})$. The subsidiary conditions $\delta_{gg} = 0$ and $\delta_{hh} = 0$ correspond to the subsidiary conditions $Q_{gg} = 0$ and $Q_{hh} = 0$ in the original equations (7-6) and (7-7); for all other subscripts, $\delta_{gh}$ can still be assumed to equal 1.

Combined together, (7-6a) and (7-7b) can be viewed as representing a system of $2m$ simultaneous linear equations with $2m$ variables: the unknown parameters $C_g$ and $K_h$. Since the observed base-year values of the regional outputs and inputs necessarily satisfy the overall relationship (7-4), one of the $2m$ balance equations in system (7-6a) and (7-7b) is redundant. In other words, a set of variables that can satisfy any $2m - 1$ of these equations will necessarily satisfy the last equation too. This means that one (any one) of these equations must be dropped, and only if the value of one of the unknowns is arbitrarily fixed can the remaining $2m - 1$ equations be solved for all the other $C_g$'s and $K_h$'s.

Examining the structural equations (7-5a), we can, moreover, see that if some particular set of $C_g$'s and $K_h$'s, say $C_g^0$ and $K_h^0$, can satisfy them, the set $C_g^0 + \alpha$, $K_h^0 - \alpha$ (where $\alpha$ is an arbitrary constant) will satisfy them too. This means that if structural relationships of that form do actually hold, $2m - 1$ and not $2m$ of these parameters could determine uniquely the magnitudes of all the interregional flows. Thus, before solving the linear system (7-6a)–(7-7b), we must not only eliminate one of its component equations but also fix arbitrarily the value of one of the $2m$ unknown $C_g$'s or $K_h$'s. We will drop the first equation (corresponding to $h = 1$) in (7-7b) and set $K_1 = 0$.

For computational purposes, it is convenient to consider not the parameters $C_g$ and $K_h$ but rather the products $\overline{X}_{go}C_g$ and $\overline{X}_{oh}K_h$ as our unknowns. For the same reason, the units in which all $\overline{X}_{go}$'s and $X_{oh}$'s are measured can be redefined so as to make the total base-year output $\overline{X}_{oo}(= \sum_g \overline{X}_{go} = \sum_h \overline{X}_{oh})$ of good $i$ in the entire system equal to 1.

The structure of the resulting system of $2m - 1$ linear relationships can best be shown by writing it as a matrix equation form. The variables in (7-15) are written out in the form of a horizontal vector on the top. To each one of them there corresponds a column of constants in the square matrix below. The constants from the right-hand side of all equations make up the vertical column vector to the right.

The system can be solved and the base-year values of the constants $C_g$ and $K_h$ (for $g, h = 1, 2, \ldots, m$) determined through inversion of the square matrix on the left-hand side.

## The problem of cross-hauling

The fact that within a given network of interregional shipments the flow from some particular region $g$ to some region $h$ equals zero has a significance fundamentally different from the observation that region $h$ imports from one region a small, from another a larger, and from some other a still larger positive amount. A zero flow is most

(7-15)

$$
\begin{bmatrix}
\dfrac{\sum\limits_r \bar{X}_{r0}d_{r2}\delta_{r2}}{\bar{X}_{02}} & 0 & \cdots & 0 & \vline & d_{12}\delta_{12} & 0 & d_{32}\delta_{32} & \cdots & d_{m2}\delta_{m2} \\[2ex]
0 & \dfrac{\sum\limits_r \bar{X}_{r0}d_{r3}\delta_{r3}}{\bar{X}_{03}} & \cdots & 0 & \vline & d_{13}\delta_{13} & d_{23}\delta_{23} & 0 & \cdots & d_{m3}\delta_{m3} \\[2ex]
0 & 0 & \cdots & \dfrac{\sum\limits_r \bar{X}_{r0}d_{rm}\delta_{rm}}{\bar{X}_{0m}} & \vline & d_{1m}\delta_{1m} & d_{2m}\delta_{2m} & d_{3m}\delta_{3m} & \cdots & 0 \\[2ex]
\hline
d_{12}\delta_{12} & d_{13}\delta_{13} & \cdots & d_{1m}\delta_{1m} & \vline & \dfrac{\sum\limits_r \bar{X}_{0r}d_{1r}\delta_{1r}}{\bar{X}_{10}} & 0 & 0 & \cdots & 0 \\[2ex]
0 & d_{23}\delta_{23} & \cdots & d_{2m}\delta_{2m} & \vline & 0 & \dfrac{\sum\limits_r \bar{X}_{0r}d_{2r}\delta_{2r}}{\bar{X}_{20}} & 0 & \cdots & 0 \\[2ex]
d_{32}\delta_{32} & 0 & \cdots & d_{3m}\delta_{3m} & \vline & 0 & 0 & \dfrac{\sum\limits_r \bar{X}_{0r}d_{3r}\delta_{3r}}{\bar{X}_{30}} & \cdots & 0 \\[2ex]
d_{m2}\delta_{m2} & d_{m3}\delta_{m3} & \cdots & 0 & \vline & 0 & 0 & 0 & \cdots & \dfrac{\sum\limits_r \bar{X}_{0r}d_{mr}\delta_{mr}}{\bar{X}_{m0}}
\end{bmatrix}
=
\begin{bmatrix}
1 - \dfrac{\bar{X}_{22}}{\bar{X}_{02}} \\[2ex]
1 - \dfrac{\bar{X}_{33}}{\bar{X}_{03}} \\[2ex]
\vdots \\[1ex]
1 - \dfrac{\bar{X}_{mm}}{\bar{X}_{0m}} \\[2ex]
\hline
1 - \dfrac{\bar{X}_{11}}{\bar{X}_{10}} \\[2ex]
1 - \dfrac{\bar{X}_{22}}{\bar{X}_{20}} \\[2ex]
1 - \dfrac{\bar{X}_{33}}{\bar{X}_{30}} \\[2ex]
\vdots \\[1ex]
1 - \dfrac{\bar{X}_{mm}}{\bar{X}_{m0}}
\end{bmatrix}
$$

with column headings $\bar{X}_{02}K_2,\ \bar{X}_{03}K_3,\ \ldots,\ \bar{X}_{0m}K_m \mid \bar{X}_{10}C_1,\ \bar{X}_{20}C_2,\ \bar{X}_{30}C_3,\ \ldots,\ \bar{X}_{m0}C_m$

likely to reflect a fairly persistent disadvantage of that particular delivery route as compared with other delivery routes that compete with it. Such disadvantage will, more often than not, continue to exist—that is, the shipment from the particular region $g$ to the particular $h$ will remain zero—even after some relatively small shifts in the magnitudes of the regional pools of demand and of supply in these two or in some other regions would bring about corresponding readjustments in the magnitudes of all nonzero (i.e., positive) flows throughout the entire system. It takes a larger change in the magnitudes of the $X_{go}$'s and the $X_{oh}$'s to start new flows where they did not exist before, or to eliminate entirely some of the existing interregional flows, than to increase or to reduce the levels of previously existing flows.

The reader familiar with the principles of linear programming and with its conventional application to transportation problems will recognize that a change affecting only the (positive) magnitudes of the existing flows means an adjustment of the "solution" without, however, any shift in the original "base," while the introduction of new, or discontinuation of the existing, flows signifies a more radical adjustment involving a change of base.

In equations (7-6a) and (7-7b), the subsidiary conditions $\delta_{i.hh} = 0$ and $\delta_{i.gg} = 0$ serve as a convenient device for eliminating the corresponding terms under the summation signs; all other $\delta_{i.gh}$'s have been, so to say, completely neutralized by the preliminary assumption that $\delta_{i.gh} = 1$, if $g \neq h$.

As long as all $\delta_{i.gh}$'s are assumed to equal 1 when $g \neq h$, the empirical application of the multiregional system described above would be based on factual information of two kinds: (1) the base-year magnitudes of the regional supply-and-demand pools $\overline{X}_{i.go}$, $\overline{X}_{i.oh}$, and $\overline{X}_{i.gg}$, and (2) the distances—or some other measures of the relative costs of transporting each good $i$—from each region $g$ to every other region $h$. This latter information is incorporated into the interregional equations through the magnitudes assigned to the coefficient $d_{i.gh}$.

By setting the appropriate $\delta_{i.gh}$'s equal to zero even when $g \neq h$, we introduce in the empirical basis of our computations a third significant and—what is particularly important—easily secured type of factual information: (3) the knowledge that, for essentially logistic reasons, good $i$ is not being shipped at all from a particular region $g$ to another particular region $h$. Large changes in the other factors can, of course, modify even a relatively stable logistic pattern. However, such changes must be very great indeed before, for example, even a single ton of bricks will be shipped, in the United States, from Illinois to Texas.

The mathematical structure of our system is such that its solution would, in general, contain at least some shipments of each good from every region to every other region—that is, as long as the corresponding $\delta_{gh}$'s are not explicitly assumed to be equal to zero. Thus, whenever the available information indicates that the good in question is not actually being shipped from one particular region to another—and most likely will not be shipped in the future either—the appropriate $\delta_{gh}$ can be put equal to zero in the structural equation (7-5a) in all the balance equations derived from it, and consequently also in the structural matrix (7-15). This will affect, of course, the numerical values of all the constants $C_g$ and $K_h$ computed through inversion of that matrix.

In section I above, while discussing the problem of cross-hauling, we observed that in an aggregate multiregional system nominally identical—and even actually identical—goods can be expected to be moving between two regions simultaneously in opposite directions. This does not mean, however, that in such a system all goods must necessarily be traded in both directions between all regions. Even in setting up an aggregate system, we often know—for reasons that do not need to be explained in detail—that a particular good $i$ can be expected to flow from region $g$ to region $h$ but not from region $h$ to region $g$. The simple device of setting the appropriate $\delta_{i.gh} = 1$ but the corresponding $\delta_{i.hg} = 0$ will automatically incorporate that important kind of factual information in our system of equations.

## Computing procedures

The method of determining for each good $i$ the numerical values of the interregional constants $C_{i.g}$ and $K_{i.h}$ described above is in principle similar to the procedure used in computing the technical coefficients $a_{ij}$ from a given interindustrial input-output matrix. In both instances we obtain a single-point estimate from a given set of base-year figures.

The computation of the interregional parameters does not require knowledge of the actual base-year interregional flows $\overline{X}_{i.gh}$. Once the magnitudes of the $C_{i.g}$'s and $K_{i.h}$'s have been computed, however, they can be inserted—together with the externally determined parameters $d_{i.gh}$ and $\delta_{i.gh}$ and with the base-year magnitudes of the total regional inputs and outputs $\overline{X}_{i.go}$, $\overline{X}_{i.oh}$, and $\overline{X}_{i.gg}$—in (7-5), which will then yield the "theoretical" magnitude of the corresponding interregional flows $X_{i.gh}$.

If the actual base-year magnitudes of the interregional flows happen to be known, they can be compared with the corresponding indirectly computed theoretical values. Such comparison, as shown in section III, permits us to test the goodness of fit of at least some of the interregional equations. On the other hand, instead of being used for testing purposes, such additional information can be directly incorporated into the analytical system, thus strengthening its empirical base. As indicated above, if the actual magnitudes of the flow $X_{i.gh}$ from region $g$ to region $h$ happens to be known, all four figures can be inserted respectively on the right-hand and left-hand sides of (7-5). The magnitude of the corresponding coefficient $Q_{i.gh}$ can then be determined from that equation directly. This still leaves open the possibilities of using the method described at the beginning of this section to determine the coefficients pertaining to all those interregional flows on which no base-year information is available. To do so, it will only be necessary to remove in equations (7-5) and (7-6) the terms containing the directly computed $Q_{i.gh}$'s from under the summation sign and place them separately along with $X_{i.gg}$ and $X_{i.hh}$.

In addition to those described above, other procedures could obviously be used to determine the magnitude of the interregional coefficients $C_{i.g}$ and $K_{i.h}$.

While presented as a device for conditional projection, the multiregional input-output system put forth here can also serve as an instrument of regional, or rather multiregional, economic planning. Not only can the magnitudes of final regional demand be prescribed rather than projected, but the values of some of the interregional parameters can be prescribed too. If, for example, commodity $i$ is to be produced in region $g$—in which it has not been manufactured before—the corresponding column of technical input coefficients must be included in that region's internal structural matrix. In case the new industry is intended to serve only the internal demand of region $g$ itself, the parameters $\delta_{i.gh}$ for that particular $g$ and all $h$'s should be set equal to zero; if, on the other hand, exports to some other region are planned, the corresponding $\delta_{i.gh}$ should be set equal to 1. In either case, the completed multiregional computation will reveal the effects—on the outputs and inputs of each good in every region—of the proposed introduction of the new industry $i$ in region $g$.

The complexity of all kinds of theoretical schemes that can be effectively used in practical empirical analysis is, as a rule, strictly limited by the nature and the amount of factual information available. The multiregional input-output system presented above has been designed as an "economy model" that can be used for projection or planning with a bare minimum of statistical data. As additional information becomes available, it also will supply a flexible but at the same time internally consistent general equilibrium framework into which one can build in more powerful tools of partial analysis, such as linear programming.

## III. Empirical solutions

As a first step toward the empirical implementation of the multiregional input-output system described above, a few experimental computations were performed to test its interregional part. Four different estimating methods were used, called the *exact solution*, the *simple solution*, the *least squares procedure*, and the *point estimate procedure*.

In the exact solution, the values of the structural parameters $C_g$ and $K_h$ are determined through solutions of the set (7-15) of simultaneous linear equations as described in section II above. Information on the magnitudes of the actually observed interregional shipments enter into these computations only to the extent that it helps us to decide which of the subsidiary constants $\delta_{gh}$ should be set equal to zero and which equal to 1.

Inserted into (7-5), together with other exogenously determined parameters $d_{gh}$, $C_g$'s and $K_h$'s permit us to derive the values of the corresponding interregional flows. The discrepancies between these computed and the corresponding actual magnitudes of the interregional flows provide a basis for measuring the effectiveness of the estimating procedure.

This method of estimating interregional flows yields total estimated exports and imports for each region, which correspond exactly to the (observed) regional output, input, and internal consumption figures ($\overline{X}_{go}$, $\overline{X}_{og}$, and $\overline{X}_{gg}$) used in deriving the values of the parameters $C_g$ and $K_g$ inserted on the right-hand side of equation (7-5). Thus, the resulting estimates can be said to be entirely consistent with the primary information incorporated into them, at least in the base year.

The simple solution is what its name indicates. Instead of containing $m^2$ overall—and many more subsidiary—constants as does (7-5a), the structural equations used in this case contain only one constant (for each good) besides the $\delta_{i.gh}$'s:

(7-16)
$$X_{gh} = \frac{X_{go}X_{oh}}{X_{oo}} b\delta_{gh} \quad (g \neq h)$$
$$(g = 1, 2, \ldots, m)$$
$$(h = 1, 2, \ldots, m)$$

The constant $b$ is computed from the observed base-year magnitudes of all total regional outputs and inputs $X_{go}$ and $X_{oh}$:

(7-17)
$$b = \frac{\overline{X}_{oo} - \sum\limits_{r=1}^{m} \overline{X}_{rr}}{\sum\limits_{g=1}^{m} \sum\limits_{h=1}^{m} \dfrac{\overline{X}_{go}\overline{X}_{oh}\delta_{gh}}{\overline{X}_{oo}}} \quad (\delta_{gh} = 0 \text{ when } g = h)$$

With $b$, the exogenously determined $\delta_{gh}$'s and the observed regional outputs inserted on its right-hand side, equations (7-16) yield the estimates of all the interregional flows $X_{gh}$.

The method by which the magnitude of the constant $b$ is determined guarantees that the grand total of the estimated flows of good $i$ between all regions will equal the actually observed total of all regional exports or imports, $\overline{X}_{oo} = \sum\limits_{r=1}^{m}\overline{X}_{rr}$. However, unlike in the case of the exact solution, the estimated total exports and total imports of each region—obtained through summation of the appropriate (estimated) interregional flows—will differ in the case of the simple solution from the actually observed $\overline{X}_{go}$'s and $\overline{X}_{oh}$'s. Because of that, the simple solution may be said to yield an internally inconsistent estimate of unknown interregional flows even for the base year. Whatever predictive power the simple solution has is due to the nonlinear expression $X_{go}X_{oh}/X_{oo}$ on the right-hand side of equation (7-16), which it incidentally shares with the basic structural relationship (7-5).

Each of the two procedures described above enables us to estimate the interregional flows $X_{gh}$ in some particular year without recourse to information on the actual magnitude of such flows in that or any other year. In both instances we only need to know the total regional outputs $\overline{X}_{go}$, inputs $\overline{X}_{og}$, and intraregional flows $\overline{X}_{gg}$ of the year for which the estimate is being made.

The least squares method, on the other hand, represents a direct application of the conventional statistical curve-fitting procedure to the structural equation (7-5a). In addition to information concerning the values of the external parameters $d_{gh}$ and $\delta_{gh}$ and the observed base-year levels of all the regional outputs and inputs $\overline{X}_{go}$ and $\overline{X}_{oh}$ employed in the exact solution, this procedure also requires base-year information on the actual magnitudes of all the interregional flows $\overline{X}_{gh}$.

Let a new auxiliary variable $\overline{X}_{gh}^{\circ}$ be defined by:

(7-18)     $\overline{X}_{gh}^{\circ} = \dfrac{\overline{X}_{go}\overline{X}_{oh}}{\overline{X}_{oo}} \, d_{gh}\delta_{gh},$     $(\delta_{gh} = 0$ when $g = h)$

$(g = 1, 2, \ldots, m)$

$(h = 1, 2, \ldots, m)$

The difference $u_{gh}$ between the observed interregional flow $X_{gh}$ and the corresponding flow computed theoretically on the basis of the structural function (7-5a) is then described by:

(7-19)     $u_{gh} = \overline{X}_{gh}^{\circ}(C_g + K_h) - \overline{X}_{gh}$   $(g \neq h)$

The sum of the squares of all the $u_{gh}$—let it be called $S$—can accordingly be described by:

(7-20)   $S = \displaystyle\sum_{g}\sum_{h} u_{gh}^2 = \sum_{g=1}^{m}\sum_{h=1}^{m} [\overline{X}_{gh}^{\circ}(C_g + K_h) - \overline{X}_{gh}]^2$   $(g \neq h)$

To minimize this sum, equate to zero its partial derivative in respect to each $C_g$ and $K_h$:

(7-21)   $\dfrac{\delta S}{\delta C_g} = 2\displaystyle\sum_{h=1}^{m} [C_g\overline{X}_{gh}^{\circ 2} + K_h\overline{X}_{gh}^{\circ 2} - \overline{X}_{gh}\overline{X}_{gh}^{\circ}] = 0 \; (g = 1, 2, \ldots, m)$

(7-22)   $\dfrac{\delta S}{\delta K_h} = 2\displaystyle\sum_{g=1}^{m} [K_h\overline{X}_{gh}^{\circ 2} + C_g\overline{X}_{gh}^{\circ 2} - \overline{X}_{gh}\overline{X}_{gh}^{\circ}] = 0 \; (h = 1, 2, \ldots, m)$

Since the sum totals of the observed regional inputs and outputs, from which $\overline{X}_{gh}^{\circ}$ has been computed, balance each other for the system as a whole, one of these $2m$ "normal" equations is redundant, and one of the unknown $2m$ parameters, say $K_1$, can be set equal to zero. All the other $C_g$'s and $K_h$'s can be computed through solution of the system of $2m - 1$ simultaneous equations made up of sets (7-21) and (7-22) with, say, the first equation in (7-21) struck out.

The theoretical estimates of all the interregional flows can be finally determined from (7-5a). In contrast to the exact model, the least squares method does not involve the assumption that total imports and total exports of the good in question as estimated for each region must necessarily equal the observed values. The imposition of such additional conditions would make the number of estimating equations equal to the number of available observations and thus transform the least squares into the exact model. Since, in fact, the estimated regional exports and imports will in this case differ from the actual, this estimate is internally inconsistent in the same sense in which the estimate based on the simple solution was said to be internally inconsistent.

Similarly to the least squares method, the point estimate procedure requires complete base-year information on interregional flows. Since such direct derivation of the magnitudes of all parameters $Q_{gh}$ involves the use of as many degrees of freedom as there are such flows, it obviously precludes the possibility of any discrepancy appearing between the estimated and the observed figures in the base-year itself. This is the reason why the point estimate procedure was not used in computations related to a single year.

## Errors of estimation

The errors of estimation entered in the tables given below are computed from the absolute differences (i.e., differences regardless of sign) between the actual and the estimated magnitudes of the variable considered in each particular instance. Thus, for interregional flows, the *weighted average percentage error* is computed as follows:

$$(7\text{-}23) \quad D(X_{gh}) = \frac{\displaystyle\sum_{g=1}^{m}\sum_{h=1}^{m}\left[\frac{|X_{gh}-\overline{X}_{gh}|}{\overline{X}_{gh}}\overline{X}_{gh}\right]}{\displaystyle\sum_{g=1}^{m}\sum_{h=1}^{m}\overline{X}_{gh}} = \frac{\displaystyle\sum_{g=1}^{m}\sum_{h=1}^{m}[|X_{gh}-\overline{X}_{gh}|]}{\overline{X}_{oo}-\displaystyle\sum_{r=1}^{m}\overline{X}_{rr}}$$

$$(g \neq h)$$

The corresponding formulas for the total regional exports and total regional imports are:

$$(7\text{-}24) \quad D(X_{go}) = \frac{\displaystyle\sum_{g=1}^{m}\left|\sum_{h=1}^{m}\left[\frac{X_{gh}-\overline{X}_{gh}}{\overline{X}_{gh}}\overline{X}_{gh}\right]\right|}{\displaystyle\sum_{g=1}^{m}\sum_{h=1}^{m}\overline{X}_{gh}} = \frac{\displaystyle\sum_{g=1}^{m}\left|\sum_{h=1}^{m}[X_{gh}-\overline{X}_{gh}]\right|}{\overline{X}_{oo}-\displaystyle\sum_{r=1}^{m}\overline{X}_{rr}}$$

$$(g \neq h)$$

$$(7\text{-}25) \quad D(X_{oh}) = \frac{\displaystyle\sum_{h=1}^{m}\left|\sum_{g=1}^{m}\left[\frac{X_{gh}-\overline{X}_{gh}}{\overline{X}_{gh}}\overline{X}_{gh}\right]\right|}{\displaystyle\sum_{g=1}^{m}\sum_{h=1}^{m}\overline{X}_{gh}} = \frac{\displaystyle\sum_{h=1}^{m}\left|\sum_{g=1}^{m}[X_{gh}-\overline{X}_{gh}]\right|}{\overline{X}_{oo}-\displaystyle\sum_{r=1}^{m}\overline{X}_{rr}}$$

$$(g \neq h)$$

Absolute errors are used in these formulas rather than their squares in order to avoid an undue sensitivity of the index to differences in the sizes of the individual regions. If a large area, for example, is split in two, the sum total of the absolute deviations between the actual and the predicted in-and-out flows of the two subareas will be of the same general order of magnitude as the corresponding differences previously computed for the combined region as a whole; the sum total of their squares would be much smaller than the sum total of the squared deviations computed for the larger region as a whole. Thus, an average of the absolute deviations can be expected to be less dependent on the size distribution of the economic regions than a corresponding average of their squares.

## The results

Empirical implementation of an analytical model is a slow, laborious process, particularly when the model is as complex as the interregional system described above. In presenting the results of the computations, we only intend to show what kind of known, partly known, and unknown data are involved in this type of analysis and what their orders of magnitude are.

Table 7-1 describes the results of the base-year analysis of interregional flows of four goods: bituminous coal and lignite, portland cement, soybean oil, and steel shapes (i.e., iron and steel ingots, billets, blooms, slabs, etc.). The regional breakdowns are rather rough: for coal the continental United States is subdivided into 13 regions, for the other three goods into only 9 regions.

A comparison of columns 3 and 4 of Table 7-1 shows that, of the two estimating procedures that do not require information on the actual interregional flows, the exact solution yields better estimates of these flows than the simple solution. The least squares procedure, which requires for its application full knowledge of the base-year interregional flows, gives an even closer fit, but when utilized for a base-year estimate it does not actually yield an estimate of unknown flows but simply smooths out their observed distribution.

Since the estimated total exports and total imports of each region are obtained through summation of the corresponding interregional flows, the errors shown in part B of the table are smaller both for the simple solution and the least squares method. The exact solution, when it is applied to the estimation of base-year interregional flows, permits no discrepancy between the actual and the indirectly computed totals; hence column 3 in Table 7-1B contains only zeros.

Table 7-2 shows the errors of estimation characterizing the prediction, by various methods, of interregional steel shape movements in 1950, 1952, and 1958. Structural parameters in every case were computed from 1954 (base-year) information.

In addition to the three methods of estimation whose results are shown in Table 7-1, a fourth method based on the direct, single-point estimate of parameter $Q_{gh}$ was used for the non-base-year predictions in Table 7-2. For the exact, simple, and least squares methods of estimation, figures in the 1954 (base-year) column of Table

### Table 7-1

Weighted average errors for base-year estimates, by
commodity and method of estimation[a]

A. INTERREGIONAL FLOWS ($X_{gh}$; $g \neq h$)

| Commodity (1) | No. of Nonzero Flows (2) | Weighted Average Percentage Errors[b] | | |
|---|---|---|---|---|
| | | Exact Solution (3) | Simple Solution (4) | Least Squares Procedure (5) |
| bituminous coal and lignite | 25 | 27 | 55 | 21 |
| portland cement | 17[c] | 51 | 94 | 37 |
| soybean oil | 22 | 42 | 51 | 35 |
| steel shapes | 17 | 14 | 39 | 8 |

B. TOTAL EXPORTS FROM OR IMPORTS TO A REGION

| Commodity (1) | No. of Regions with Exports or Imports (2) | Weighted Average Percentage Errors[d] | | |
|---|---|---|---|---|
| | | Exact Solution (3) | Simple Solution (4) | Least Squares Procedure (5) |
| Exports $\left( \sum_{h=1}^{m} X_{gh}; g \neq h \right)$ | | | | |
| bituminous coal and lignite | 8 | 0 | 15 | 8 |
| portland cement | 8[c] | 0 | 40 | 15 |
| soybean oil | 6 | 0 | 8 | 8 |
| steel shapes | 6 | 0 | 11 | 6 |
| Imports $\left( \sum_{g=1}^{m} X_{gh}; g \neq h \right)$ | | | | |
| bituminous coal and lignite | 12 | 0 | 32 | 5 |
| portland cement | 8[c] | 0 | 64 | 23 |
| soybean oil | 8 | 0 | 13 | 13 |
| steel shapes | 8 | 0 | 22 | 2 |

[a]For commodity description, regional classification, data sources, etc., see Tables 7-5, 7-6, and section IV. Detailed estimates for an illustrative commodity, steel shapes, are shown in Table 7-7.
[b]Computed using equation (7-23).
[c]A 2 percent near-zero flow criterion was employed in identifying nonzero cement movements. For details, see Table 7-5 and section IV.
[d]Computed using equations (7-24) and (7-25).

7-2 are taken directly from Table 7-1; for the point estimate method, the base-year interregional flows satisfying structural equations (7-5) must obviously be identical to the observed; that is, the base-year "errors" will equal zero, and zeros are therefore shown in Table 7-2 for the point estimate model in 1954.

## Table 7-2

Weighted average errors of estimation,[a] steel shapes, base-year (1954)
parameters applied to estimates for 1950, 1952, 1958 (in percentages)

| | | Year | | |
| Solution method<br>(1) | 1950<br>(2) | 1952<br>(3) | 1954[b]<br>(4) | 1958<br>(5) |
| --- | --- | --- | --- | --- |
| A. *Interregional movements* $(X_{gh};\ g \neq h)$ | | | | |
|     exact solution | 50 | 43 | 14 | 47 |
|     least squares solution | 54 | 46 | 8 | 51 |
|     simple model | 36 | 25 | 39 | 69 |
|     point estimate model | 54 | 47 | 0 | 71 |
| B. *Total exports from a region* $\left( \sum_{h=1}^{m} X_{gh};\ g \neq h \right)$ | | | | |
|     exact solution | 34 | 26 | 0 | 20 |
|     least squares solution | 40 | 32 | 6 | 21 |
|     simple model | 29 | 22 | 11 | 31 |
|     point estimate model | 37 | 30 | 0 | 36 |
| C. *Total imports to a region* $\left( \sum_{g=1}^{m} X_{gh};\ g \neq h \right)$ | | | | |
|     exact solution | 23 | 18 | 0 | 32 |
|     least squares solution | 24 | 19 | 2 | 35 |
|     simple model | 25 | 20 | 22 | 51 |
|     point estimate model | 22 | 19 | 0 | 44 |

[a]Computed using equations (7-23)–(7-25). Data sources, etc., are the same as for Table 7-4.
[b]1954 values for all but point estimate model are taken from Table 7-1. Base-year errors for the point
estimate model are zero by definition.

In years other than 1954, Table 7-2 indicates that the simple
model performed best in two of the three years studied. The exact
model gave best results in the third year (1958) and was superior to
both the least squares and the point estimate methods in all three
non-base years. The exact solution also performed better than any
of the others in predicting total regional imports in two of the three
non-base years. The least squares and point estimate procedures,
both requiring more detailed base-year information, had the highest
weighted average errors of prediction of interregional movements.

Table 7-3 gives volume of base-year movements, in terms of both
tons and ton-miles, for the four commodity groups. Inter- and
intraregional movements have been differentiated. Average distances moved have been computed by dividing ton-miles by tons.

Table 7-4 presents volume-of-movement data for all observed
region-to-region movements of steel shapes in the years covered by
Table 7-2. Each region-to-region flow is described in terms of tons
shipped and of average mileage per ton; this latter figure was

obtained by dividing the total number of ton-miles moved from the specific region of origin to the specified region of destination by the corresponding tonnage figure. An examination of these figures calls attention to the following two problems that are likely to play a considerable role in further work on empirical application of our multiregional input-output scheme.

The large variations in the average number of miles that an average ton of steel had to travel between the same two regions in different years brings up the question of regional aggregation. The largest of all the tonnages transported between two regions was shipped from the Middle Atlantic (MA) to the East North Central (ENC) states; the second largest moved in the opposite direction. The distance, that is, the average mileage, traveled from the first to the second region in 1954 is only half as long as that from the second

## Table 7-3

Volume of observed base-year shipments, all commodity groups tested[a]

| Commodity (1) | Location of Shipments (2) | Tons Shipped (000's) (3) | Shortline Ton-Miles (millions) (4) | Average Distance Moved[b] (miles) (5) |
|---|---|---|---|---|
| portland cement | interregional | 64.5 | 18.8 | 292 |
| | intraregional | 219.4 | 26.1 | 119 |
| | total | 283.8 | 44.9 | 158 |
| steel shapes | interregional | 21.0 | 3.5 | 168 |
| | intraregional | 50.0 | 3.9 | 78 |
| | total | 70.9 | 7.5 | 105 |
| soybean oil | interregional | 8.6 | 5.9 | 688 |
| | intraregional | 3.0 | 0.5 | 162 |
| | total | 11.6 | 6.4 | 554 |
| bituminous coal and lignite[c] | interregional | 66.0 | 20.3 | 307 |
| | intraregional | 98.6 | 17.5 | 177 |
| | total | 164.6 | 37.7 | 229 |

[a]For data sources, regional classification, etc., see Tables 7-5, 7-6, section IV, and footnote [c], below. Volume figures based on Interstate Commerce Commission rail shipments have been inflated for sample coverage.
[b]Except for coal, the distances have been computed by dividing reported ton-miles by reported tons shipped. In the case of coal where ton-mile figures were not available, approximate straight-line distances were first measured between each producing region and each consuming state and then used to estimate the ton-miles for each reported movement from producing region to consuming state. The sums of these estimated ton-miles are shown in column 4, and average distances in column 5 have been computed using the total ton-miles shown.
[c]Commodity coverage and regional classification for bituminous coal are not the same as used elsewhere in this chapter. Coverage, although based upon the same data source as listed in section IV, is limited to industrial use only. Reported shipments have been reclassified into the same nine regions used for the other three commodity groups shown, and the interregional–intraregional breakdown is therefore comparable in all four commodity groups.

## Table 7-4

Volume and average distances moved, railroad shipments of steel shapes, by originating and terminating regions, 1950, 1952, 1954, and 1958[a]

| Regions[b] | | 1950 | | 1952 | | 1954 | | 1958 | |
|---|---|---|---|---|---|---|---|---|---|
| From (1) | To | Average Miles (2) | Tons (000's) (3) | Average Miles (4) | Tons (000's) (5) | Average Miles (6) | Tons (000's) (7) | Average Miles (8) | Tons (000's) (9) |
| **A. INTERREGIONAL RAILROAD SHIPMENTS** | | | | | | | | | |
| NE | MA | 255 | 51 | 255 | 39 | 255 | 40 | 377 | 18 |
| MA | NE | 438 | 179 | 460 | 117 | 459 | 120 | 283 | 189 |
| MA | ENC | 200 | 2122 | 261 | 1561 | 186 | 641 | 188 | 391 |
| MA | SA | 140 | 1049 | 195 | 833 | 175 | 44 | 153 | 68 |
| ENC | NE | 669 | 47 | 668 | 42 | 658 | 20 | 727 | 15 |
| ENC | MA | 142 | 1316 | 162 | 1227 | 79 | 718 | 113 | 488 |
| ENC | WNC | 307 | 43 | 357 | 94 | 377 | 43 | 325 | 36 |
| ENC | SA | 286 | 117 | 441 | 232 | 60 | 326 | 45 | 199 |
| ENC | ESC | 242 | 18 | 630 | 23 | 506 | 4 | 176 | 76 |
| ENC | WSC | 1080 | 39 | 1157 | 32 | 1076 | 2 | 655 | 7 |
| ENC | Pac. | 2094 | 5 | 2487 | 42 | 2115 | 3 | 2219 | 17 |
| SA | NE | 353 | 25 | 383 | 18 | 318 | 35 | 292 | 13 |
| SA | MA | 210 | 155 | 131 | 112 | 177 | 57 | 108 | 36 |
| ESC | ENC | 213 | 93 | 176 | 33 | 285 | 14 | 357 | 27 |
| ESC | SA | | 0 | | 0 | 259 | 5 | | 0 |
| ESC | WSC | | 0 | 321 | 21 | 441 | 7 | 469 | 34 |
| Pac. | WSC | | 0 | | 0 | 813 | 18 | | 0 |
| other[c] | | 1330 | 165 | 1274 | 242 | | 0 | 771 | 40 |
| total interregional | | 232 | 5425 | 320 | 4668 | 169 | 2096 | 211 | 1655 |
| (index 1954 = 100) | | (137) | (259) | (189) | (223) | (100) | (100) | (125) | (79) |
| **B. INTRAREGIONAL RAILROAD SHIPMENTS** | | | | | | | | | |
| NE | NE | 48 | 65 | 82 | 51 | 64 | 67 | 96 | 49 |
| MA | MA | 60 | 2551 | 69 | 2976 | 67 | 1832 | 83 | 1736 |
| ENC | ENC | 99 | 5405 | 106 | 4418 | 79 | 2988 | 70 | 3202 |
| SA | SA | 11 | 5 | 12 | 10 | 446 | 11 | 16 | 29 |
| ESC | ESC | | 0 | 220 | 30 | 204 | 21 | 94 | 9 |
| WSC | WSC | | 0 | | 0 | 265 | 32 | | 0 |
| Pac. | Pac. | 70 | 51 | 166 | 91 | 264 | 46 | 97 | 56 |
| WNC | WNC | | 0 | | 0 | | 0 | 250 | 5 |
| Mt. | Mt. | | 0 | 589 | 33 | | 0 | | 0 |
| total intraregional | | 86 | 8077 | 94 | 7609 | 78 | 4998 | 75 | 5088 |
| (index 1954 = 100) | | (110) | (162) | (121) | (152) | (100) | (100) | (96) | (102) |
| total shipments | | 145 | 13502 | 180 | 12277 | 105 | | 109 | 6742 |
| (index 1954 = 100) | | (138) | (190) | (171) | (173) | | | (104) | (95) |

[a]*Source:* U.S. Interstate Commerce Commission, "Carload Waybill Statistics; State-to-State Distribution of Manufactures and Miscellaneous and Forwarder (C.L.) Traffic and Revenue," various years. All average miles shown are computed by dividing reported shortline ton-miles by reported short tons moved. Tonnage figures shown have been inflated to represent total Class I railroad shipments. Individual tonnages may not add up to totals shown because of rounding.
[b]For regional designations and descriptions, see Table 7-6B.
[c]Includes all interregional shipments reported as zero in the base year (1954).

to the first. Moreover, the distance—from ENC to MA—fell between 1952 and 1954 by more than 50 percent. The grossly aggregative definition of trading regions is obviously responsible for all this. There is good reason to believe that it is also responsible, at least in part, for the high errors of estimation registered in Tables 7-1 and 7-2.

Can this phenomenon be accounted for within the framework of the multiregional input-output system presented above, or will its explanation require a change in the general form of some of the basic structural equations? Much further empirical and analytical work will be required before even a tentative answer to such a question can be found. Its theoretical implications lead directly to the important problem of the homogeneity or nonhomogeneity of the system. In their present form, both the linear equations describing input-output relationships within each region and the nonlinear relationships that describe the interdependence of the different regions are homogeneous (of the first degree). That means that a proportional change in the magnitude of all the independent variables of the system, that is, the final demands $Y_{i,g}$ for all $n$ goods in all the $m$ regions, would be accompanied by an equal proportional change in all regional outputs and inputs and in all interregional flows. In particular, all intraregional and interregional flows will in this case fall and rise exactly in the same proportions. The disproportionality of the cyclical fluctuation reflected in Table 7-4 could be explained on the basis of the present homogeneous system only in terms of uneven, that is, disproportional, fluctuations in the components of the final bill of goods.

If, on the other hand, all elements of the final bill of goods do in fact move strictly in the same proportion, only replacement of at least some of the homogeneous equations in our system with corresponding nonhomogeneous relationships would make it possible to explain the disproportional fluctuation observed in Table 7-4. In linear approximation this would require introduction in these equations of free-standing constant terms. Before resorting to this rather radical solution, it might be advisable to explore the empirical and analytical implications of the first possibility.

## IV. Sources and organization of data used in the empirical computations

In the United States, regional production and consumption as well as interregional shipment figures are available in reasonably complete form for only one commodity—bituminous coal (including lignite)—and the post–World War II years for which we have data are 1946 and the coal-year 1945–46.[4] Major movements of coal by rail and water are included in these figures as shown in Table 7-5. Coverage of truck movements is limited, but the omissions are small in the aggregate. An important omission from the data is railroad consumption of coal, an amount equal to about one-third of domestic production in the years covered. Most overseas exports have also been excluded. We have no information on actual distances moved, but we do have estimates made by James Henderson of unit coal transportation costs in the year 1947.[5] (The distance estimates shown in Table 7-3 are only rough approximations.) Henderson, in preparing his estimates, excluded movements of both railroad fuel and bituminous coal used for coke manufacture.

Movements of bituminous and lignite coal from producing district to consuming state for the coal year 1945–46 have been aggregated to a total of 13 regions (see Table 7-6A). Total movements originating in a region, including shipments terminating within the region, have been termed regional production ($X_{go}$). Total movements terminating in a region, including shipments originating within the region, have been termed regional consumption ($X_{oh}$). Not included in any of the figures are coal for bunker fuel or railroad fuel, coal used at coal mines, coal exported, certain amounts of coal shipped by truck, and a moderately large number of shipments whose destination is unknown. Total exclusions amount to about 40 percent of production.

For the transportation cost term $d_{gh}$, the reciprocals of Henderson's 1947 interregional unit transportation costs are used. The only complicating factor is the need to aggregate Henderson's regions 2 and 3 to give a 13-region arrangement consistent with that derived from the Bureau of Mines' coal movement data.

Of the possible $m^2 - m$ or 156 interregional flows, actual movements were reported for 55 cases in 1945–46. These included 30 relatively small movements, each of which amounted to less than 2½ percent of both the originating region's total output and the consuming region's total consumption. In the aggregate, these 30 flows totaled 1,184,000 short tons, or 0.6 percent of total interregional movements. These small, near-zero flows were excluded from fur-

[4]U.S. Bureau of Mines, "Bituminous Coal Distribution," Mineral Market Report, M.M.S. no. 1497 (coal year 1945–46) and no. 1592 (1946).

[5]James M. Henderson, The Efficiency of the Coal Industry (Cambridge: Harvard University Press, 1958), Table A-4, pp. 130–131.

# Table 7-5

| | | Coverage | |
| | | | |
| Commodity Name<br>(1) | Type of Sample<br>(2) | Percent of<br>Domestic<br>Production<br>(3) | Year<br>(4) |
|---|---|---|---|
| bituminous coal and lignite | monthly dock operators' reports and producers' reports from mines with average daily production of 50 tons or more per day | 59.8 | April 1945–March 1946 |
| cement, natural and portland (I.C.C. no. 633) | 1 percent I.C.C. railroad waybill sample | 53.9 | 1954 |
| soybean oil (I.C.C. no. 515) | 1 percent I.C.C. railroad waybill sample | 89.7 | 1954 |
| steel ingots, billets, blooms, slabs, etc. (I.C.C. nos. 575, 577) | 1 percent I.C.C. railroad waybill sample | 39.5[a] | 1950<br>1952<br>1954<br>1958 |

B. INTERREGIONAL MOVEMENTS OBSERVED

| | | | Number of observations (excluding intraregional) | | | |
| Commodity<br>(1) | Year<br>(2) | No. of<br>Regions<br>($m$)<br>(3) | Maximum<br>Possible<br>($m^2 - m$)<br>(4) | Zero<br>Flows<br>(5) | Near-Zero<br>Flows<br>(6) | Non-Zero<br>Flows<br>(7) |
|---|---|---|---|---|---|---|
| coal | 1945–46 | 13 | 156 | 101 | 30 | 25 |
| cement | 1954 | 9 | 72 | 41 | 17[b]<br>14[c] | 14<br>17 |
| soybean oil | 1954 | 9 | 72 | 50 | 0 | 22 |
| steel shapes | 1950 | 9 | 72 | 52 | 0 | 20 |
| | 1952 | 9 | 72 | 46 | 0 | 26 |
| | 1954 | 9 | 72 | 55 | 0 | 17 |
| | 1958 | 9 | 72 | 48 | 0 | 24 |

[a]In 1954.

[b]Includes all movements equal to or less than 2½ percent of both the exporting region's total production and the importing region's total consumption. (This was the criterion used to identify near-zero flows for all other commodity groups.)

[c]Includes all movements equal to or less than 2.0 percent of both the exporting region's total production and the importing region's total consumption.

# Table 7-6

| Regional Designation | | States Included |
|---|---|---|
| This Study | Henderson[a] | |
| 1 | 1 | Pennsylvania, Maryland[b] |
| 2 | 2, 3 | West Virginia,[b] Virginia,[b] Kentucky,[b] District of Columbia |
| 3 | 4 | Alabama,[b] Tennessee,[b] Georgia,[b] North Carolina, South Carolina, Florida, Mississippi, Louisiana |
| 4 | 5 | Ohio[b] |
| 5 | 6 | Illinois,[b] Indiana,[b] Michigan[b] |
| 6 | 7 | Iowa,[b] Missouri,[b] Kansas,[b] Arkansas,[b] Oklahoma,[b] Texas[b] |
| 7 | 8 | North Dakota,[b] South Dakota,[b] Nebraska |
| 8 | 9 | Montana,[b] Wyoming,[b] Utah,[b] Idaho |
| 9 | 10 | Colorado,[b] New Mexico,[b] Arizona,[b] California, Nevada |
| 10 | 11 | Washington,[b] Oregon[b] |
| 11 | 12 | Maine, Vermont, New Hampshire, Rhode Island, Connecticut, Massachusetts |
| 12 | 13 | New York, New Jersey, Delaware |
| 13 | 14 | Minnesota, Wisconsin |

B. REGIONAL CLASSIFICATION[c] USED FOR CEMENT, SOYBEAN OIL, AND STEEL SHAPES

| Regions | States Included |
|---|---|
| 1. New England (NE) | Maine, New Hampshire, Vermont, Rhode Island, Massachusetts, Connecticut |
| 2. Middle Atlantic (MA) | New York, New Jersey, Pennsylvania |
| 3. East North Central (ENC) | Ohio, Indiana, Illinois, Michigan, Wisconsin |
| 4. West North Central (WNC) | Minnesota, Iowa, Missouri, North Dakota, South Dakota, Nebraska, Kansas |
| 5. South Atlantic (SA) | Delaware, Maryland, District of Columbia, Virginia, West Virginia, North Carolina, South Carolina, Georgia, Florida |
| 6. East South Central (ESC) | Kentucky, Tennessee, Alabama, Mississippi |
| 7. West South Central (WSC) | Arkansas, Louisiana, Oklahoma, Texas |
| 8. Mountain (Mt.) | Montana, Idaho, Wyoming, Colorado, New Mexico, Arizona, Utah, Nevada |
| 9. Pacific (Pac.) | Washington, California, Oregon |

[a]James M. Henderson, Table 11, p. 44.
[b]States that produced bituminous coal or lignite in 1945. See U.S. Bureau of Mines, *Minerals Yearbook*, 1946, pp. 326–339.
[c]*Census of Manufactures*, 1954, Volume I, Industry Statistics, Department of Commerce, Bureau of the Census.

ther computations, leaving a total of 25 off-diagonal, nonzero flows with which to test the interregional trade models.

Although bituminous coal is the only commodity for which reasonably complete information is available on the interregional movement, the transportation patterns of other commodities transported largely by rail may be examined using the U.S. Interstate Commerce Commission's annual 1 percent waybill sample analysis.[6] To obtain this sample, the I.C.C. uses copies of one out of every 100 waybills issued by railroads during the course of a year. These waybills are coded by commodity classification, quantity shipped, short-line distance between the two points involved, and transportation revenue. The waybill sample is aggregated to show state-to-state movements by commodity classification. It is this body of data that forms the basis for most of our current knowledge of U.S. freight movements and costs of transportation. The sampling error in cases in which the number of individual shipments observed between two particular regions is very small—say, between one and four—is bound to be quite large.

From this body of data for 1954 we selected a moderately high-value-per-ton, homogeneous commodity group (soybean oil); a low-value-per-ton, homogeneous commodity group (hydraulic cement); and a moderately low-value-per-ton, moderately homogeneous group (steel ingots, billets, blooms, bars, rods, and slabs). The steel shipments in the year 1954 represented about 40 percent of all interplant shipments (after inflating for sample coverage but without allowing for possible sample bias arising from the issuance of two or more waybills for a single movement of freight). Soybean oil and cement railroad shipments in 1954 represented about 90 and 54 percent, respectively, of total domestic shipments. As in the case of coal, each region's production and consumption were set equal to total shipments originating or terminating within the region. What bias this may introduce into our calculations has not yet been investigated; whatever bias exists will, of course, decrease as total railroad shipments originating or terminating within the region approach total shipments made by all means of transportation.

As transportation cost constants $d_{gh}$, we used for these last three commodity groups the reciprocals of weighted average rail dis-

---

[6]U.S. Interstate Commerce Commission, Bureau of Transport Economics and Statistics, "Carload Waybill Statistics: State-to-State Distribution of Manufactures and Miscellaneous and Forwarder (C.L.) Traffic and Revenue," Statement SS-6, each year since 1947. Excluded from the published data is information on shipments originating or terminating in Canada and Mexico and on shipments originating in states with less than three shippers.

tances between two regions. (For steel shapes these average rail distances are shown in column 6 of Table 7-4.) Weights used in computing regional average distances were actual sample tons shipped of the particular commodity group. The regional grouping consisted of the nine regions standard for U.S. Census data. (See Table 7-7B.)

Of the $m^2 - m$, or 72, interregional flows that were possible for each of the three commodity groups, 1954 sample data showed only 22 flows for soybean oil, 17 flows for steel shapes, and 31 flows for cement. On a near-zero criterion of 2½ percent of an exporting region's production and an importing region's consumption, none of

## Table 7-7

Estimated parameters and estimated and calculated values of interregional trade in steel shapes, 1954[a]

*(steel quantities in thousands of short tons)*

| Direction of Shipment[b] | | Value of $(C_g + K_h)$ | | Actual Shipments ($X_{gh}$) | Calculated Shipments ($X_{gh}$) | | Difference ($M_{gh}$) | |
|---|---|---|---|---|---|---|---|---|
| From (g) | To (h) | Exact Solution | Least Squares | | Exact Solution | Least Squares | Exact Solution | Least Squares |
| | (1) | (2) | (3) | (4) | (5) | (6) | (7) | (8) |
| NE | NE | (not estimated) | | 67.4 | n.a. | n.a. | n.a. | n.a. |
| NE | MA | 252 | 253 | 39.5 | 39.5 | 39.5 | 0 | 0 |
| MA | NE | 424 | 326 | 119.6 | 83.2 | 63.8 | −36.4 | −55.8 |
| MA | MA | (not estimated) | | 1831.9 | n.a. | n.a. | n.a. | n.a. |
| MA | ENC | 87 | 88 | 641.1 | 632.5 | 641.1 | −8.6 | 0 |
| MA | SA | 109 | 70 | 43.9 | 88.9 | 57.3 | 45.0 | 13.4 |
| ENC | NE | 392 | 343 | 20.1 | 83.4 | 72.9 | 63.3 | 52.8 |
| ENC | MA | 36 | 37 | 718.5 | 691.6 | 718.5 | −26.9 | 0 |
| ENC | ENC | (not estimated) | | 2987.8 | n.a. | n.a. | n.a. | n.a. |
| ENC | WNC | 652 | 652 | 42.6 | 42.6 | 42.6 | 0 | 0 |
| ENC | SA | 76 | 87 | 326.1 | 282.8 | 323.2 | −43.3 | −2.9 |
| ENC | ESC | 123 | 123 | 3.5 | 3.5 | 3.5 | 0 | 0 |
| ENC | WSC | 280 | 72 | 2.1 | 9.0 | 2.3 | 6.9 | 0.2 |
| ENC | Pac. | 253 | 253 | 3.4 | 3.4 | 3.4 | 0 | 0 |
| WNC | WNC | (not estimated) | | 0 | n.a. | n.a. | n.a. | n.a. |
| SA | NE | 741 | 574 | 35.1 | 8.2 | 6.4 | −26.9 | −28.7 |
| SA | MA | 385 | 269 | 57.1 | 84.0 | 58.6 | 26.9 | 1.5 |
| SA | SA | (not estimated) | | 11.2 | n.a. | n.a. | n.a. | n.a. |
| ESC | ENC | 266 | 170 | 14.1 | 22.7 | 14.5 | 8.6 | 0.4 |
| ESC | SA | 287 | 152 | 4.6 | 2.9 | 1.5 | −1.7 | −3.1 |
| ESC | ESC | (not estimated | | 21.4 | n.a. | n.a. | n.a. | n.a. |
| ESC | WSC | 492 | 137 | 7.3 | 0.4 | 0.1 | −6.9 | −7.2 |
| WSC | WSC | (not estimated) | | 32.2 | n.a. | n.a. | n.a. | n.a. |
| Mt. | Mt. | (not estimated) | | 0 | n.a. | n.a. | n.a. | n.a. |
| Pac. | WSC | 27156 | 26690 | 17.8 | 17.8 | 17.5 | 0 | −0.3 |
| Pac. | Pac. | (not estimated) | | 45.8 | n.a. | n.a. | n.a. | n.a. |
| | Total | | | 7094.1 | 2096.4 | 2066.7 | 0 | −29.7 |

[a]Excludes all zero flows.
[b]For regional identification and description, see Table 7-6B.
*Source:* Column (2)     Values obtained from solving equation set (7-15).
         (3)     Values obtained from solving equation sets (7-21), (7-22).
         (4)     Same as Table 7-4, column 7.
         (5), (6)  Calculated by inserting $C_g + K_h$ values from columns (2) and (3) into equation (7-5a).
         (7), (8)  Equals column (5) or (6) minus column (4).

the soybean oil or steel shapes movements falls into the near-zero category. This was not true for cement, where 17 of the 31 observed flows could be classed as near zero. For cement, this reduced the number of observed movements to the point where the least squares model became overdetermined; that is, the system of equations (7-21) and (7-22) contained more parameters than were needed to estimate the observed movements. It later became desirable in the case of cement, therefore, to reduce the near-zero flow rejection criterion from 2½ percent to 2 percent. This added three more interregional movements to the list of observed flows and permitted a solution to be found for the least squares model. (Alternatively, it would have been possible to reduce the number of solution equations by 1.) The effect of these three additional flows on the exact solution model was to decrease the calculated goodness of fit slightly.

Finally, in order to test the applicability of base-year parameters to interregional movements in a second year, railroad shipments of steel shapes were compiled by regions for the years 1950, 1952, and 1958. Parameters ($C$'s + $K$'s) are calculated from the 17 interregional movements observed in 1954, which served as the base year. These parameters are shown in Table 7-7, along with the calculated 1954 shipments derived from their use in equation (7-5a). These 1954 parameters were then used to estimate the same 17 movements in each of the other three years. In each of these three years it turned out that there were interregional flows that had not been observed in 1954 (and for which, therefore, the estimated flow in the second year had been automatically set equal to zero). These are the "other" interregional flows shown in Table 7-4. There were also a few zero flows in these other years between regions that had been observed to trade with one another in 1954. (These interyear differences may very likely arise from the 1 percent coverage of the I.C.C. sample. In evaluating a model's goodness of fit in these other years, however, we have assumed that this type of estimating error arises entirely from our initial assumption that a zero flow in the base year implies absence of shipments in all other years.)

# 8

## *The structure of development*

### (1963)

### I

Estimates of gross national product, total consumption, income per capita, rate of investment, and similar indices of economic activity are now compiled and published by practically all countries. Such figures give quantitative expression to the otherwise plainly apparent fact that some countries are rich and others are poor. When they have been plotted over the recent past, they indicate that the gap between the rich and the poor has been widening. These statistics do not of themselves suggest any ready explanation of the difference in overall performance among the national economies. Nor do they point to any practical ways to narrow the gap.

The earth's resources are ample for the needs of the present world population and even for a much larger one. It is true that the distribution of resources is uneven. It is also true that the poor countries do not make full use of the resources they have. They raise less food per acre and per man-hour, and they realize little of the value of their mineral wealth above the price of the ore or the crude oil at the dockside. Described in these terms the disparities in the well-being of nations are nowadays summed up in the somewhat more useful observation that they reflect differences in degree of "development."

For the understanding that must precede any constructive action, it is necessary to penetrate below the surface of global statistics and such round terms as *development*. Each economic system—even that of an underdeveloped country—has a complicated internal

1963 by Scientific American, Inc.

structure. Its performance is determined by the mutual relations of its differentiated component parts, just as the motion of the hands of a clock is governed by the gears inside. Over the past 25 years the internal economic gearwork of a large number of countries has been described with increasing clarity and precision by a technique known as interindustry analysis, or input-output analysis. Because the results improve as more fine-grained statistics are fed into it, the technique has demonstrated its effectiveness largely in the study of more highly developed economic systems.

## II

The data of input-output analysis are the flows of goods and services inside the economy that underlie the summary statistics by which economic activity is conventionally measured. Displayed in the input-output table, the pattern of transactions between industries and other major sectors of the system shows that the more developed the economy, the more its internal structure resembles that of other developed economies. Moreover, from one economy to the next the ratios between these internal transactions and the external total activity of the system—true gear ratios in the sense that they are determined largely by technology—turn out to be relatively constant.

Recent advances in input-output analysis and in the bookkeeping of underdeveloped countries have made it possible to apply the technique to a number of these economies. Their input-output tables show that in addition to being smaller and poorer they have internal structures that are different, because they are incomplete, compared with the developed economies. From such comparative studies a fundamental analytical approach to the structure of economic development is now emerging.

Construction of a national input-output table is a major statistical enterprise. By now tables for some 40 countries have been prepared. Some countries (among the underdeveloped countries: Israel, Egypt, Spain, and Argentina) have published comprehensive, detailed, and quite accurate tables. Others, having just entered the field, have not yet advanced beyond rather sketchy compilations of limited accuracy. The growing literature in this field, however, testifies to the fact that, with the practical know-how gained in the preparation of the first experimental table, the second- and third-generation tables become invested with the elaboration and professional finish required for an effective scientific instrument.

The input-output table is not merely a device for displaying or storing information; it is above all an analytical tool. Depending on the purpose at hand and the availability of reliable information, the economy can be broken down into any number of industries or sectors. The table for the U.S. economy as of 1947, prepared by the Bureau of Labor Statistics of the U.S. Department of Labor, has 450 sectors. For purposes of this demonstration, an economy can be broken down into two industrial sectors: agriculture and manufactures. (See Table 8-1.) In the table for such a simple model economy the numbers in the horizontal row labeled "agriculture" show that this sector, in the course of delivering 55 units of output as end products to "final demand" and 20 units as raw materials (for example, cotton) to "manufactures," delivers 25 units of its own output (for example, feed grains) to itself. "Final demand" can here be taken as including the goods and services consigned to investment and export as well as to current consumption in the households of the

## Table 8-1

Input-output table (*top*) and input-coefficient matrix (*bottom*) show "internal" transactions between productive sectors of simple model economy in relation to "final demand" and "total output" of each sector. The table displays outputs from each sector in the corresponding horizontal row, inputs to each sector in the vertical column. In the matrix the columns display the ratio of each input to a sector and the total output of the sector.

|  | Input | | | |
|  | Sector 1: Argiculture | Sector 2: Manufactures | Final Demand | Total Output |
| --- | --- | --- | --- | --- |
| Sector 1: Agriculture | 25 | 20 | 55 | 100 units |
| Sector 2: Manufactures | 14 | 6 | 30 | 50 units |
| Household Services | 80 | 180 | 40 | 300 units |

|  | Input/Output Coefficients | |
|  | Sector 1: Agriculture | Sector 2: Manufactures |
| --- | --- | --- |
| Sector 1: Agriculture | 0.25 | 0.40 |
| Sector 2: Manufactures | 0.14 | 0.12 |
| Household Services | 0.80 | 3.60 |

economy. The total output of 100 units from the agricultural sector therefore satisfies both the "direct" final demand for its end products and the "indirect" demand for its intermediate products. On the input side the numbers in the column labeled "agriculture" show that in order to produce 100 units of total output this sector absorbs not only 25 units of its own product but also 14 units of input (for example, implements) from "manufactures" and 80 units—of labor, capital, and other prime factors—from the sector called, by convention, "household services."

## III

The great virtue of input-output analysis is that it surfaces the indirect internal transactions of an economic system and brings them into the reckonings of economic theory. Within each sector there is a relatively invariable connection between the inputs it draws from other sectors and its contribution to the total output of the economy. This holds for an underdeveloped economy, where the input from "household services" necessary to produce 100 units of agricultural output might represent a full 80 man-years of labor, as well as for a highly developed country where this input would reflect a larger component of capital and is likely to be offset by inputs of fertilizers, insecticides, and the like from the industrial sectors. In fact, for use as an analytical tool, the input-output table must be recast into a matrix showing the input ratios, or coefficients, characteristic of each sector. The input-output table for the model economy, recast into such a matrix, shows that 0.25 unit of agricultural output, 0.14 unit of manufactures, and 0.80 unit of prime factors from "household services" are required to produce one unit of total output from the agricultural sector. (See Table 8-1.)

Each sector or industry thus has its own "cooking recipe." The recipe is determined in the main by technology; in a real economy it changes slowly over the periods of time usually involved in economic forecasting and planning. The input-coefficient matrix can be derived, as it is in the present demonstration, from the interindustry transactions for a given year or from engineering data or from a combination of these and other sources of information. For any bill of final demand, the matrix makes it possible to compute the inputs each industry must absorb from all other industries in the course of fulfilling the final demand for its output and meeting the indirect demand for that output generated by the final demands of the industries to which it in turn supplies inputs. The computation involves the iterative solution of a set of simultaneous linear equations. Since the number of equations increases with the number of sectors, the computing of a table sufficiently detailed to yield significant information is a task for machines.

It was the labor of computation that prompted the first systematic studies of the structural characteristics of an economy as they are displayed in an input-output table. During the late 1940s Marshall K. Wood, George D. Dantzig, and their associates in Project SCOOP of the U.S. Air Force undertook to rearrange the rows and columns in a table of the U.S. economy in such a way as to minimize the computation required to yield numerical solutions. Such rearrangement brought into sharper relief the interindustry and intersectoral transactions that tie industries and sectors together in the subunits of the total structure of the ecomomy. As more and more countries have begun to compile tables, comparative studies of their structural characteristics have begun to appear.

## IV

Dependence and independence, hierarchy and circularity (or multiregional interdependence) are the four basic concepts of structural analysis. The definition and practical significance of each of these ideas can be demonstrated visually by schematic model tables in which dark gray squares rather than numbers signify the presence or absence of interindustry transactions. (See Figure 8-1.) In the first of these tables a square appears in every one of the 225 boxes formed by the intersection of the 15 numbered rows and columns of the industrial sectors. Each industry in such a system is dependent on all the others; it supplies inputs to all other sectors and draws inputs from all of them. Translated into mathematical language, this means that each of the 15 variables representing the output of each of the sectors figures directly in each of the input-output equations. In the operation of this economy any increase in the output delivered by any one sector to final demand (represented by the light gray square at the right-hand end of the row) would require an increase in the inputs to this sector (reading down the column) from all other sectors without exception. Hence a single increase in direct demand can set up a whole chain of indirect demands, ultimately increasing the total output of every sector in the system.

A more likely and natural system is represented by the model in which some boxes are empty. The industry in whose column one of these empty boxes appears draws no input (or perhaps an insignificant input) from the industry whose row it intersects at this point.

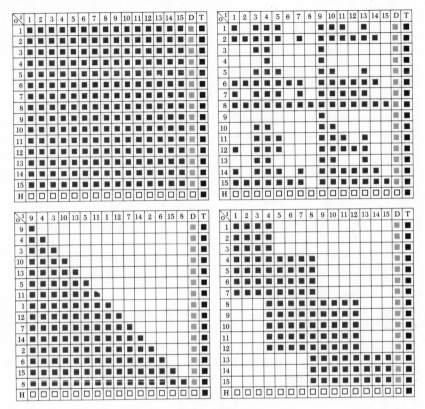

**Figure 8-1**

Internal structures of model economies are revealed by input-output tables. Dark gray squares signify inputs from the sector in a given horizontal row to sectors in vertical columns intersected by the row; light gray squares, the input from each sector to "final demand" (*D*); black squares, the total output (*T*) of each sector; open squares, the inputs of prime factors from "household services" (*H*). The table at the upper left shows a completely "interdependent" economy; the table at the upper right shows a random pattern of interindustry transactions. The latter table appears at the lower left with sectors rearranged (note sequence of sector "call numbers"); this "triangulation" of the table reveals a hierarchical pattern of interindustry transactions. The "block triangular" model at the lower right shows interdependence on industries within blocks, as in the first model, and hierarchical relation between blocks, as in the third.

If the corresponding box formed by the reverse combination of column and row is empty, then these two sectors can be described as being independent of each other. Where intersectoral dependence is indicated by a square in this table, however, one such square may trigger a whole chain of indirect demands, finally involving both members of an apparently independent pair of sectors.

Such relations become clearer in the model in which all the squares fall below the diagonal running from the upper left corner to the lower right corner of the matrix. Actually this "triangular" system was constructed by rearrangement of the rows and columns of the "natural" system described above, as is indicated by the sequence in which the call numbers of the sectors now appear. The highly structured hierarchical relation among the different sectors was obscured in the first random display—an accidental effect, perhaps, of the sequence in which the census bureau of this imaginary economy assigned call numbers to the sectors. In the rearranged table it can be plainly seen that sector 9, now in the far left column, absorbs inputs from all the other sectors but delivers its entire output directly to final demand. Sector 8, now in the far right column, requires for its operation, in addition to a portion of its own output, only labor, capital, and other prime factors from "household services"; on the other hand, this sector delivers inputs to all other sectors as well as to final demand.

In the hierarchical order of an economy with a strictly triangular matrix, the sectors above and below the horizontal row of any given sector bear quite different relations to that sector. Those below are its suppliers; any increase in final demand for its product generates indirect demands that cascade down the diagonal slope of the matrix and leave the sectors above unaffected. The sectors above, however, are its customers; an increase in final demand for the output of any one of them generates indirect demand for the output of the sector in question. An economist charged with the task of computing the indirect effects of an increase in final demand for the output of this sector would need to know, therefore, only the input coefficients for sectors below it. If the economist wants to compute the indirect effects on this sector of demand originating elsewhere, he or she needs to work only with the input coefficients for this sector and the sectors above it. In the case of the fourth "block triangular" model, the economist would find that relations between sectors within each block are similar to the mutual interdependence that ties together all the sectors in the first of these model systems, whereas the relations between the blocks ("multiregional interdependence") are analogous to those between the sectors in the triangular model.

# V

The convenience of the economist and the computing machine does not, of course, constitute the sole or the most significant purpose served by such rearrangement of an input-output table. The triangulation of the table serves also to expose the internal structure of the interindustry transactions. These define groups and blocks of more closely related industries. The forecaster is likely to find that he or she must reckon with the fortunes of all the industries within a group in order to plot the future course of one of them. The planner may discover that the effort to promote the growth of an industry in one block requires the prior development of industries in another block and may trigger the development of industries in still another block.

The triangulation of a real input-output table—that is, the discovery of its peculiar structural properties—is a challenging task. It is complicated by the fact that one must take into account not only the distinction between zero and nonzero entries but also the often more important difference between their actual numerical magnitudes. The degree to which triangulation reveals significant structural details depends also on the fineness of the sectoral breakdown. A single entry in a highly aggregated table may conceal the solid block of a triangular matrix or a narrow strip of finer intersectoral relations. Lack of sufficiently detailed information about the internal structure of groups and blocks of industries may impose severe limitations on attempts to explain the behavior of the economic system as a whole.

The larger and the more advanced an economy is, the more complete and articulated is its structure. The United States and Western Europe, respectively, produce about a third and a quarter of the world's total output of goods and services. It is not surprising, therefore, to discover that their input-output tables yield the same triangulation. Discounting the larger overall size of the U.S. economy, the similarity between the two sets of intersectoral relations comes vividly to the fore when the triangulated input-output tables of the two systems are superposed on each other. (See Figure 8-2.) Between them they contain—with some well-known but minor exceptions—a complete array of economic activities of all possible kinds.

# VI

Each of the industries in this combined table has its own peculiar input requirements, characteristic of that industry not only in the United States and in Europe but also wherever it happens to be in operation. The recipe for satisfying the appetite of a blast furnace,

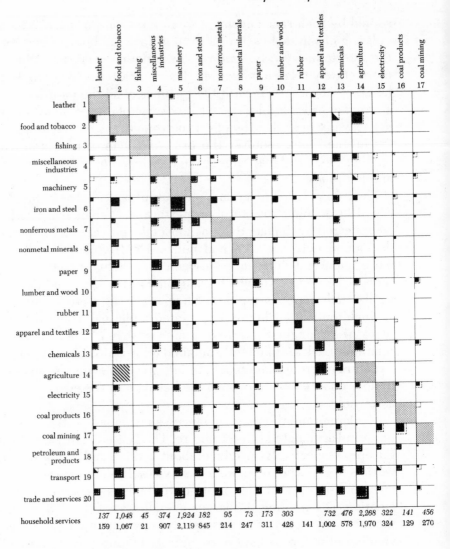

a cement kiln, or a thermoelectric power station will be the same in India or Peru as it is, say, in Italy or California. In a sense the input-coefficient matrix derived from the U.S.–European input-output table represents a complete cookbook of modern technology. It constitutes, without doubt, the structure of a fully developed economy insofar as development has proceeded anywhere today.

An underdeveloped economy can now be defined as underdeveloped to the extent that it lacks the working parts of this system. This lack can be explained in narrowly economic terms as resulting from the amount and distribution of productively invested capital, in

| petroleum and products | transport | trade and services | O.E.E.C. Europe: West German Federal Republic (not including West Berlin), Austria, Belgium, Denmark, France, Greece, Ireland, Iceland, Italy, Luxembourg, Norway, Netherlands, Portugal, United Kingdom, Sweden, Switzerland, Turkey | |
|---|---|---|---|---|
| 18 | 19 | 20 | FINAL DEMAND | TOTAL OUTPUT |
| | | | 233 | 243 |
| | | | 251 | 269 |
| | | | 2,973 | 3,328 |
| | | | 2,848 | 3,233 |
| | | | 36 | 58 |
| | | | 13 | 30 |
| | | | 506 | 897 |
| | | | 740 | 1,286 |
| | | | 2,612 | 2,813 |
| | | | 3,030 | 3,370 |
| | | | 90 | 583 |
| | | | 542 | 1,304 |
| | | | −39 | 211 |
| | | | 58 | 342 |
| | | | 107 | 152 |
| | | | 264 | 385 |
| | | | 43 | 312 |
| | | | 98 | 461 |
| | | | 320 | 496 |
| | | | 433 | 581 |
| | | | 145 | 273 |
| | | | 1,124 | 1,244 |
| | | | 1,331 | 1,527 |
| | | | 326 | 836 |
| | | | 430 | 1,073 |
| | | | 629 | 2,947 |
| | | | 1,002 | 2,938 |
| | | | 143 | 440 |
| | | | 181 | 408 |
| | | | 154 | 373 |
| | | | 116 | 244 |
| | | | 101 | 572 |
| | | | 109 | 304 |
| | | | −60 | 146 |
| | | | 358 | 648 |
| | | | 673 | 1,206 |
| | | | 1,397 | 2,070 |
| | | | 3,631 | 4,305 |
| | | | 8,713 | 10,237 |
| 43 | 886 | 3,982 | U.S. (1947) O.E.E.C. EUROPE (1953) | |
| 538 | 1,664 | 9,126 | (all units = 10 million dollars) | |

**Figure 8-2**

Developed economies of the United States (black squares and roman numbers) and of Western Europe (open squares and italic numbers) show great similarity in structure when their input-output tables are "triangulated" in the same order and superposed. Areas of black and open squares overlapping are proportioned to the volume of interindustry transactions, scaling from the largest black square at row 6, column 5. The diagonal-lined square at row 14, column 2, indicates transactions too large for this scale. "Intraindustry" transactions, along the diagonal, are not shown. The two negative figures in Western European final demand indicate that imports of the commodities in question exceed domestic deliveries to final demand.

social terms as a reflection of the composition and efficiency of the labor force, or in geographical terms as the result of the country's endowment with natural resources. This last element deserves special mention, because much has been said in recent years about the possibility of designing custom-made technologies to meet the special conditions prevailing in certain underdeveloped countries. Celso Furtado, in his article "The Development of Brazil (*Scientific American*, September 1963), mentions the scarcity of coal in that country and speaks of the need for a new technology to reduce the iron in the abundant local ores. Leaving aside the intrinsic merit of such proposals, the fact is that the choice of alternative technologies hardly exists. The process of development consists essentially in the installation and building of an approximation of the system embodied in the advanced economies of the United States and Western Europe and, more recently, of the Soviet Union—with due allowance for limitations imposed by the local mix of resources and the availability of technology to exploit them.

In the absence of such complete development a country can consume goods without producing them because it can import them. It must pay for its imports, however, by producing other goods for export instead of for domestic consumption. Two countries can thus display identical, or at least very similar, patterns of domestic final demand and yet have very different patterns of production. The smaller and the less developed a country is, the more it can be expected to exploit its productive capacity independently of its immediate needs and to bridge the gap between production and consumption by means of foreign trade. Consequently, the full diagnosis of the ills of an underdeveloped country—as well as the formulation of a realistic development plan—requires a detailed quantitative analysis of the dependence of all the domestic industries not only on the configuration of final domestic demand but also on the composition of the country's foreign trade.

Of all developing countries, Israel possesses the most detailed and complete statistics necessary for an analysis of this kind. An input-output table prepared from data compiled by Michael Bruno of the Bank of Israel and triangulated according to the U.S.-Europe plan appears in Table 8-2. In this table final demand is broken down into three components: domestic final demand (including investment as well as consumption), exports, and imports. The import figures are printed in italic because they are negative figures with respect to the country's foreign trade account and because they must be subtracted from the sum total of domestic final demand, exports, and the deliveries of the commodity in question to other industrial sectors (indirect demand) in order for one to arrive at the figures for total output at the end of each row.

Israel's heavy dependence on imports becomes apparent on inspection of the table. In five sectors ("ships, aircraft," "machinery," "basic metals," "industrial crops," and "mining") it can be seen that the country's imports exceed domestic output by large margins. In five other sectors ("grains, fodder," "forestry," "motor vehicles," "electrical appliances," and "paper and products") imports are equal to more than 50 percent of domestic production. Imports exceed domestic final demand plus exports in six sectors ("grains, fodder," "basic metals," "paper and products," "basic chemicals," "industrial crops," and "mining"); this is because the indirect demand for imports of the commodities in question exceeds final demand. Most of these imports, in other words, are distributed as inputs to other industries along the row in which they are entered.

Perhaps the most useful way to see how Israel—or any other underdeveloped country—stands today is to construct a model of the economy as it would appear if it enjoyed self-sufficiency, that is, to determine the structure of production Israel would have to achieve in order to maintain its present actual consumption and investment entirely from domestic output and without recourse to foreign trade. Such a model will show, among other things, how far Israel falls short of possessing a fully articulated modern industrial economy, in which sectors it is weakest, and in which sectors it can push its development most fruitfully. See Table 8-2.[1]

The first step in the construction of such a model is to prefabricate the sector "modules" from which it is to be built. This means to compute from the input-coefficient matrix of the economy the inputs that are required—directly and indirectly—to enable each sector to deliver an additional unit of output to domestic final demand. Direct demand for IL1000 (Israeli pounds) of "basic chemicals," for example, generates indirect demand for inputs from 34 to 42 sectors into which the Israeli economy is broken down in the matrix—including an input of products worth IL266 from "basic chemicals" itself. (See Figure 8-3.) Similarly, direct demand for IL1000 of output from the "fish, meat, dairy products" sector calls for the input of IL725 of "livestock" and IL292 of "grains, fodder," along with numerous inputs of smaller value from other sectors. It should be noted that the direct demand for "basic chemicals" generates an indirect demand of IL5 on the "fish, meat, dairy products" sector and, reciprocally, that the direct demand for "fish, meat, dairy products" sets up an indirect demand for IL70 of "basic chem-

---

[1]The underdeveloped economy of Israel is displayed (in Table 8-2) in our input-output table with sectors triangulated as in the U.S.-Europe tables earlier. The 42 industrial sectors reveal the structure of the economy in finer detail, and final demand is shown in three columns: domestic final demand, exports, and imports. Import figures in italics are subtracted from the sum of inputs to industrial sectors, final demand, and exports to give total domestic outputs; imports exceed 50 percent of domestic output in many sectors. Israel's principal exports are from diamond polishing and citrus sectors. Upper sectors in the table deliver most of their output to final demand; lower sectors deliver most of their output as inputs to the other industrial sectors, thus satisfying final demand indirectly.

Column legend (rotated headers, columns 1–10):

1. housing: public and private
2. construction: industrial and agricultural
3. construction: services and transportation
4. diamond polishing
5. apparel
6. leather and products
7. canning, beverages, sweets, tobacco
8. vegetables, fruits
9. poultry, eggs
10. flour mills, bakery products

| | 1 | 2 | 3 | 4 | 5 | 6 | 7 | 8 | 9 | 10 |
|---|---|---|---|---|---|---|---|---|---|---|
| housing: public and private 1 | | | | | | | | | | |
| construction: industrial and agricultural 2 | | | | | | | | | | |
| construction: services and transportation 3 | | | | | | | | | | |
| diamond polishing 4 | | | | 532 | | | | | | |
| apparel 5 | | | | | 15.355 | 61 | 48 | 1,140 | | 325 |
| leather and products 6 | 1 | | | | 36 | 208 | 18,321 | 3 | | 11 |
| canning, beverages, sweets, tobacco 7 | | | | 1 | 2 | 19 | 21,056 | | | 4,392 |
| vegetables, fruits 8 | | | | | | | 13,536 | 1,582 | | 96 |
| poultry, eggs 9 | | | | | | | 24 | 2,986 | 8.707 | 483 |
| flour mills, bakery products 10 | | | | | | | 1,877 | | 19,065 | 35,803 |
| fish, meat, dairy products 11 | | | | 8 | 2.019 | 5,911 | 3,749 | | 965 | 1,399 |
| cement, glass, ceramics 12 | 44,689 | 17,987 | 14,275 | 67 | | 25 | 1,358 | | | 18 |
| ships, aircraft 13 | | | | | | | | | | |
| motor vehicles 14 | 248 | 889 | 830 | | | | | 1,231 | | |
| miscellaneous industries 15 | 173 | | 13 | | 914 | 67 | 6 | | | |
| machinery 16 | | | | 7 | 192 | 62 | 287 | 478 | | 404 |
| electrical appliances 17 | 4,921 | 2,336 | 1,306 | | 2 | | | | 14 | |
| metal products 18 | 11,168 | 12.556 | 5,000 | 18 | 54 | 588 | 3,448 | | 621 | 143 |
| basic metals 19 | 13,811 | 5,797 | 7,749 | 100 | 14 | | 555 | | | 30 |
| printing, publishing 20 | | | 1 | | 40 | | 928 | | | 27 |
| paper and products 21 | 152 | 1 | 36 | 2 | 542 | 246 | 3,002 | 324 | 467 | 618 |
| carpentry, joinery 22 | 23,133 | 2,570 | 6,974 | | 201 | | | | | |
| wood products 23 | 1,674 | 962 | 1,753 | | 14 | 328 | 370 | 1,304 | 294 | 4 |
| rubber and plastic products 24 | 63 | 5 | 1 | | 339 | 183 | 218 | 17 | | 19 |
| spinning, weaving, dyeing 25 | | | | | 81,578 | 1,554 | 16 | 4 | | 8 |
| basic chemicals 26 | 5,383 | 628 | 977 | 9 | 75 | 1,752 | 2,445 | 7,439 | 5,331 | 866 |
| livestock (excluding poultry) 27 | | | | | | 24 | 413 | 7,532 | | 32 |
| grains, fodder 28 | | | | | | | 1,965 | 4,058 | 24,309 | 46,081 |
| citrus fruits 29 | | | | | | | 2,405 | | | 6 |
| forestry and reclamation 30 | 1,780 | 1,227 | 213 | | 261 | 24 | 3,781 | 3,656 | | 71 |
| industrial crops 31 | | | | | | 763 | 11,880 | | | 334 |
| electricity 32 | | | | 192 | 465 | 210 | 2,572 | | 102 | 1,764 |
| oil, soap 33 | 803 | | 86 | | 29 | 148 | 612 | | 11,679 | 3,252 |
| petroleum 34 | 784 | 440 | 899 | | 128 | 67 | 1,365 | 558 | | 1,259 |
| mining 35 | 6,999 | 1,166 | 4,822 | 45,814 | 6 | 37 | 367 | 169 | | 231 |
| water 36 | 38 | 6 | 13 | | 14 | 15 | 322 | 8,752 | 32 | 128 |
| bus and taxi services 37 | | | | | | | | | | |
| railways and trucks 38 | 19,118 | 6,466 | 9,085 | 13 | 984 | 173 | 927 | 3,248 | 2,691 | 4,139 |
| shipping and air transport 39 | | | | | | | | | | |
| communication services 40 | 405 | 264 | 102 | 1,063 | 280 | 252 | 573 | 268 | 1,257 | 2,758 |
| trade 41 | 6,670 | 2,491 | 2,018 | 9 | 1,283 | 1,237 | 4,630 | 919 | 4,718 | 1,527 |
| services and overhead expenses 42 | 18.979 | 5,889 | 10,699 | 1,167 | 7,481 | 4,763 | 11,905 | 600 | 400 | 10,375 |
| household services | 156,238 | 55,457 | 60,746 | 19,954 | 92,206 | 44,060 | 56,045 | 103,531 | 74,139 | 20,781 |

## Table 8-2

Underdeveloped economy of Israel *(Israeli pounds)*

174

| fish, meat, dairy products | cement, glass, ceramics | ships, aircraft | motor vehicles | miscellaneous industries | machinery | electrical appliances | metal products | basic metals | printing, publishing | paper and products | carpentry, joinery | wood products |
|---|---|---|---|---|---|---|---|---|---|---|---|---|
| 11 | 12 | 13 | 14 | 15 | 16 | 17 | 18 | 19 | 20 | 21 | 22 | 23 |
|  |  |  |  | 31 | 152 |  | 77 |  |  |  |  |  |
| 68 | 40 | 9 | 31 | 27 | 2 | 13 | 230 | 2 | 16 | 10 | 407 | 11 |
| 1 | 2 | 2 | 20 | 174 | 51 | 1 | 7 | 1 | 6 | 1 |  | 1 |
| 2,624 | 6 |  | 13 | 80 | 4 | 22 |  |  | 17 | 153 | 40 | 64 |
| 346 |  |  |  |  |  |  |  |  |  |  |  |  |
| 2,126 |  |  |  |  |  |  |  |  |  |  |  |  |
| 201 |  |  |  |  |  |  |  |  |  | 1 |  |  |
| 8,189 | 20 |  |  | 7 | 12 |  |  |  |  |  | 1 | 32 |
| 860 | 10,561 | 3 | 661 | 481 | 78 | 610 | 449 | 644 | 11 | 69 | 167 | 27 |
|  |  | 1,056 |  |  |  |  |  |  |  |  |  |  |
|  | 400 | 1 | 23,161 | 51 | 232 | 71 | 2,776 | 13 |  |  | 8 | 1 |
| 4 | 40 |  | 25 | 1,435 | 153 | 171 | 628 | 185 | 119 | 47 | 1 |  |
| 240 | 1,182 | 715 | 2,089 | 27 | 7.359 | 705 | 2,182 | 452 | 100 | 79 | 168 | 169 |
|  | 123 | 119 | 305 | 254 | 1.381 | 8,046 | 576 | 482 |  |  |  | 5 |
| 841 | 1,946 | 192 | 1,629 | 627 | 5.593 | 3,208 | 19,017 | 1,007 | 5 | 115 | 3,689 | 523 |
| 132 | 2,048 | 422 | 4,158 | 2,256 | 6.505 | 4,459 | 28,039 | 13.158 | 157 | 28 | 2,162 | 148 |
| 118 | 6 |  | 27 | 11 | 5 | 35 | 1 |  | 21,054 | 177 | 1 | 1 |
| 853 | 2,010 | 49 | 402 | 1,313 | 28 | 389 | 431 | 85 | 8,950 | 12,098 | 1 | 34 |
|  | 93 |  | 6 |  |  | 102 | 509 |  |  |  | 9,843 | 100 |
| 129 | 66 | 33 | 142 | 582 | 329 | 604 | 544 | 2 | 27 | 33 | 7,461 | 4,876 |
| 19 | 126 | 43 | 700 | 380 | 181 | 1,261 | 618 | 67 | 17 | 33 | 1,278 | 15 |
| 5 | 49 | 28 | 614 | 355 | 45 | 128 | 39 | 8 | 413 | 316 | 3,334 | 1 |
| 298 | 1,592 | 138 | 913 | 883 | 981 | 1,490 | 3,090 | 610 | 995 | 1,330 | 1,016 | 1,062 |
| 95,745 |  |  | 77 |  |  |  |  |  |  |  | 2 | 12 |
| 5 |  |  | 14 |  |  | 42 | 16 |  |  |  |  |  |
| 123 |  |  |  |  |  |  |  |  |  |  |  |  |
| 25 | 300 | 182 | 239 | 525 | 81 | 85 | 780 | 1 | 8 | 35 | 9,210 | 11,712 |
| 514 |  |  |  |  |  |  | 222 |  |  |  |  |  |
| 650 | 3,262 | 117 | 594 | 135 | 346 | 306 | 1,320 | 487 | 327 | 679 | 307 | 493 |
| 11,559 |  |  | 36 | 11 | 2 | 27 | 41 | 105 | 54 | 72 | 7 | 13 |
| 415 | 4,530 | 108 | 201 | 97 | 117 | 137 | 688 | 658 | 51 | 411 | 46 | 430 |
| 52 | 5,833 |  | 194 | 62 | 8 | 75 | 197 | 2,083 | 3 | 127 |  |  |
| 110 | 173 |  | 6 | 7 | 1 |  | 60 |  | 1 | 90 | 2 | 3 |
| 336 | 5,579 | 59 | 586 | 182 | 389 | 407 | 1,182 | 683 | 282 | 494 | 591 | 418 |
| 125 | 608 | 40 | 615 | 131 | 448 | 308 | 1,434 | 710 | 89 | 568 | 561 | 572 |
| 756 | 1.811 | 165 | 2,107 | 995 | 1,237 | 1,500 | 4,105 | 1,211 | 2,139 | 1,115 | 2,136 | 1,043 |
| 1,787 | 7,667 | 933 | 4,830 | 3,337 | 3,341 | 4,567 | 8,460 | 1,486 | 8,150 | 3,370 | 7,163 | 3,131 |
| 14,859 | 56,330 | 7,424 | 33,173 | 16,914 | 26,191 | 24,375 | 64,943 | 15,179 | 33,134 | 13,493 | 51,082 | 13,911 |

| | | rubber and plastic products 24 | spinning, weaving, dyeing 25 | basic chemicals 26 | livestock (excluding poultry) 27 | grains, fodder 28 | citrus fruits 29 | forestry and reclamation 30 | industrial crops 31 | electricity 32 | oil, soap 33 |
|---|---|---|---|---|---|---|---|---|---|---|---|
| housing: public and private | 1 | | | | | | | | | | |
| construction: industrial and agricultural | 2 | | | | | | | | | | |
| construction: services and transportation | 3 | | | | | | | | | | |
| diamond polishing | 4 | | | | | | | | | | |
| apparel | 5 | 20 | 967 | 58 | | 295 | | | | 62 | 78 |
| leather and products | 6 | 59 | 25 | 1 | | 3 | 5 | | | | 1 |
| canning, beverages, sweets, tobacco | 7 | | 70 | 967 | 1,101 | | | | | | 43 |
| vegetables, fruits | 8 | | | | 600 | | | | | | 392 |
| poultry, eggs | 9 | | | | | | 814 | | | | |
| flour mills, bakery products | 10 | | 1 | 891 | 4,684 | | | | | | |
| fish, meat, dairy products | 11 | 18 | 33 | 237 | 96 | | | | | | |
| cement, glass, ceramics | 12 | 23 | 26 | 601 | | | | | | 37 | 144 |
| ships, aircraft | 13 | | | | | | | | | | |
| motor vehicles | 14 | | | | 384 | 3,553 | 1,292 | 2,024 | 331 | 105 | |
| miscellaneous industries | 15 | 30 | 62 | 55 | | | | | | 20 | 4 |
| machinery | 16 | 157 | 581 | 34 | 149 | 1,376 | 500 | 757 | 123 | | 219 |
| electrical appliances | 17 | 9 | 24 | 1 | | | | | | 206 | 1 |
| metal products | 18 | 683 | 52 | 1,373 | 407 | 1 | 416 | 2,513 | | 596 | 103 |
| basic metals | 19 | 82 | 210 | 114 | | | | 5,161 | | 53 | 5 |
| printing, publishing | 20 | 33 | 20 | 72 | | | | | | 7 | 42 |
| paper and products | 21 | 219 | 418 | 806 | | | 2,607 | | | 5 | 388 |
| carpentry, joinery | 22 | | | | | | | | | | 1 |
| wood products | 23 | 26 | 106 | 102 | 61 | | 11,464 | 1,038 | | 284 | 31 |
| rubber and plastic products | 24 | 2,279 | 131 | 554 | 3 | 38 | 15 | 47 | 7 | 20 | 5 |
| spinning, weaving, dyeing | 25 | 6,201 | 67,571 | 452 | 56 | | | | 796 | 2 | 1 |
| basic chemicals | 26 | 7,125 | 4,000 | 15,560 | 997 | 9,633 | 5,642 | 56 | 2,066 | 235 | 3,152 |
| livestock (excluding poultry) | 27 | | 1,758 | 14 | 4,498 | | 2,632 | | | | |
| grains, fodder | 28 | | | 23 | 59,682 | 9,225 | | | 1,490 | | |
| citrus fruits | 29 | | | | | | | | | | |
| forestry and reclamation | 30 | 4,114 | 76 | 728 | | | 694 | 396 | 800 | 4 | 46 |
| industrial crops | 31 | 7 | 15,622 | | | | | | 705 | | 29,877 |
| electricity | 32 | 1,062 | 2,264 | 2,344 | | | | | | | 447 |
| oil, soap | 33 | 38 | 310 | 2,549 | 8,852 | | | | | | 3,223 |
| petroleum | 34 | 348 | 676 | 3,208 | 112 | 1,358 | 508 | 1,495 | 112 | 15,815 | 189 |
| mining | 35 | 311 | 28 | 6,611 | | | | | 85 | 1 | 82 |
| water | 36 | 8 | 141 | 210 | 7,106 | 8,622 | 8,591 | 2,124 | 3,926 | | 96 |
| bus and taxi services | 37 | | | | | | | | | | |
| railways and trucks | 38 | 307 | 591 | 2,237 | 6,041 | 5,652 | 2,522 | 585 | 830 | 1,623 | 863 |
| shipping and air transport | 39 | | | | | | | | | | |
| communication services | 40 | 502 | 766 | 916 | 365 | 107 | 359 | 25 | 20 | 24 | 1,247 |
| trade | 41 | 681 | 816 | 3,558 | 1,492 | 973 | 590 | 888 | 177 | 1,190 | 3,233 |
| services and overhead expenses | 42 | 4,426 | 10,099 | 7,590 | 2,200 | 1,100 | 400 | 1,900 | 100 | 7,968 | 3,896 |
| household services | | 22,500 | 58,098 | 27,268 | 78,827 | 44,433 | 78,537 | 29,603 | 19,826 | 34,919 | 14,278 |

Table 8-2 (Cont.)

176

| petroleum | mining | water | bus and taxi services | railways and trucks | shipping and air transport | communication services | trade | services and overhead expenses | domestic final demand | exports | imports | total output |
|---|---|---|---|---|---|---|---|---|---|---|---|---|
| 34 | 35 | 36 | 37 | 38 | 39 | 40 | 41 | 42 | | | | |
| | | | | | | | | 4.700 | 312.530 | | | 317,230 |
| | | | | | | | | | 117,137 | | | 117,137 |
| | | | | | | | | | 127,598 | | | 127,598 |
| | | | | | | | | 26 | 68.755 | | *581* | 68,992 |
| 1 | 162 | | 342 | 58 | 233 | 517 | 1,303 | 15 | 170,828 | 15,178 | *2,440* | 205.473 |
| | 5 | | 140 | | | 3 | 3 | | 59,147 | 2,513 | *649* | 80,103 |
| | 139 | | | | 4 | 2 | | 1,848 | 121,472 | 20,886 | *22,337* | 152,688 |
| | | | | | | | | | 130,240 | 4,668 | *1,661* | 149,799 |
| | | | | | | | | | 122,500 | 17,174 | *23* | 154,791 |
| | | | | | | | | 183 | 78,186 | 4,513 | *8,021* | 137,384 |
| | 5 | | | | | | | 424 | 143.036 | 21.097 | *43,143* | 144,115 |
| 45 | 257 | 122 | 2 | | 24 | 6 | 2,781 | 783 | 6,616 | 5,533 | *3,637* | 106,403 |
| | | | | 2.466 | | | | 47 | 42,516 | 931 | *35,178* | 11,838 |
| 20 | 39 | 212 | 8,293 | 19,366 | | | | 6,173 | 48,458 | 4,536 | *47,261* | 77,437 |
| 3 | 28 | 35 | 39 | 7 | 2 | 10 | 25 | 3,287 | 27,525 | 5,679 | *9,382* | 31,410 |
| 376 | 753 | 440 | 66 | 4 | | 518 | | 8,945 | 97,877 | 1,375 | *75,813* | 55,334 |
| 6 | 276 | 222 | 359 | 829 | | 210 | | 8,728 | 61,895 | 1,150 | *40,732* | 53,054 |
| 271 | 331 | 518 | 10 | 199 | 220 | 89 | 2,561 | 3,536 | 74,391 | 4,857 | *22,372* | 142,743 |
| 778 | 750 | 111 | 47 | 63 | 13 | 51 | | 733 | 2,247 | 753 | *63,563* | 39,336 |
| | | 221 | | 10 | 1 | | 622 | 23,810 | 28,789 | 2,431 | *2,365* | 76,125 |
| 3 | 53 | 19 | 11 | | 4 | 18 | 8,003 | 3,217 | 3,568 | 1,969 | *18,397* | 34,944 |
| | | 1 | | | | | | | 57,130 | 52 | *31* | 100,684 |
| | 7 | | 1 | 71 | 4 | | 3,461 | 22 | 1,799 | 7,906 | *9,106* | 38,808 |
| 6 | 31 | 53 | 2,625 | 5,529 | | 14 | 2,366 | 3,697 | 11,424 | 18,205 | *1,364* | 51,268 |
| | 4 | 15 | 20 | 5 | 153 | 16 | 49 | 7 | 13,604 | 12,853 | *24,758* | 165,542 |
| 1,115 | 664 | 149 | | 7 | 114 | 70 | 3 | 646 | 18,955 | 8,024 | *38,381* | 79,135 |
| | | | | | | | | | 72,030 | 558 | *7,614* | 177,713 |
| | | | | | | | | | 4,803 | 8,326 | *72,974* | 87,065 |
| | | | | | | | | | 28,366 | 86,390 | | 117,290 |
| | 162 | 17 | | | 1 | 27 | | 1 | 43,515 | 355 | *36,119* | 49,016 |
| | | | | | | | | | 3,736 | 6,505 | *39,509* | 30,656 |
| | 1,197 | 21,106 | 47 | 45 | 21 | 632 | | 3,994 | 17,138 | | *1,511* | 63,114 |
| 6 | 53 | 1 | | | 2 | | | 2,414 | 23,580 | 1,766 | *9,243* | 62,087 |
| 928 | 1,285 | 771 | 5,348 | 9,598 | 2,513 | 599 | | 6,782 | 19,659 | 1,786 | *20,517* | 65,963 |
| 47,799 | 434 | 107 | | | | 5 | | 4 | 3,312 | 13,290 | *108,987* | 31,327 |
| 128 | 235 | | 4 | 8 | | 41 | 59 | | 1,254 | 7,611 | *2* | 49,935 |
| | | | | | | | | 30,878 | 77,122 | | | 108,000 |
| 126 | 881 | 1,638 | 865 | 4,463 | 361 | 5,401 | 385 | 63,884 | 42,827 | 7,321 | | 207,435 |
| | | | | 14,573 | | | | 13,917 | 22,755 | 92,149 | *22,604* | 120,790 |
| 5,406 | 49 | 21 | 367 | 176 | 444 | 2,728 | 150 | 29,171 | 18,907 | 10,160 | *2,671* | 82,670 |
| 37 | 485 | 344 | 3,199 | 5,648 | 867 | 179 | 21,078 | 6,396 | 385,961 | 9,521 | *770* | 492,367 |
| 1,901 | 5,171 | 5,082 | 6,066 | 14,029 | 55,885 | 5,381 | 59,796 | 200,029 | 464,062 | 75,840 | *192,601* | 870,800 |
| 7,008 | 17,871 | 18,951 | 79,928 | 147,400 | 42,768 | 66,130 | 389,781 | 441,273 | | | | |

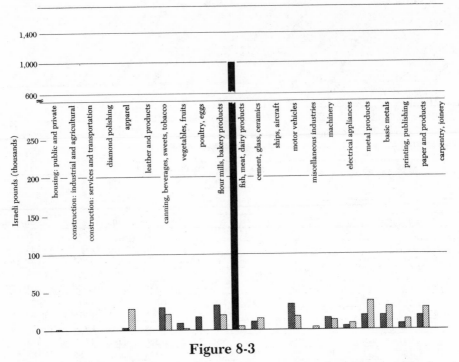

**Figure 8-3**

Indirect demand generated in the Israeli economy by direct or final
demand for IL1000 worth of products from "basic chemicals" (horizontal-
lined bar) and "fish, meat, dairy products" (black bar) sectors is shown
here. Inputs from other industries to these sectors (shown as diagonal-lined
and stippled bars, respectively) needed to satisfy indirect demand were
computed from input coefficients for these sectors. Reference to Table 8-
2, the Israeli input-output table, shows that many of these inputs ("grains,

icals." In these computations it is not necessary to distinguish
between imports and domestic production, because the coefficients
remain constant whether the inputs are imported or produced at
home. With the computations run for all sectors it is possible to
determine the total outputs required of the entire economy in order
to allow each domestic industry to satisfy the domestic final demand
for its products.

## VII

The final demand to be met from within the Israeli economy is displayed as a series of blocks running across the top of Figure 8-4. As
in the input-output table (Table 8-2), the country's exports are

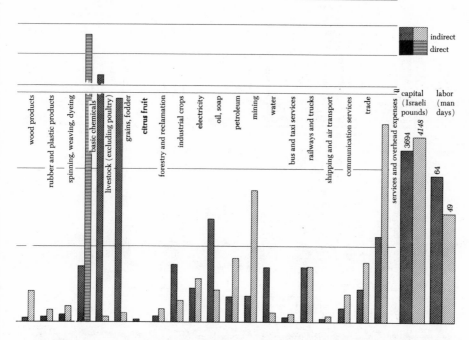

fodder" particularly) are drawn from imports. Note that direct demand on each sector generates indirect demand for its own products. Similar input-coefficient "modules" constructed for all sectors of the economy make it possible to compute the total output required to satisfy the direct and indirect demand generated by any given level of final demand or by any given volume of exports or by import-replacing outputs from domestic industries, as shown in "skyline" tables of the Israeli economy and other economies (Figures 8-4 and 8-5).

added (as extensions) to the tops of the blocks; the imports, represented by blocks of hatched lines, are subtracted. This presentation shows vividly how much the Israeli economy depends on imports, with blocks of hatched lines cutting deep into the gray blocks and even descending below them in the six sectors where the imports required to satisfy indirect demands exceed final demand.

The Israeli economy in the hypothetical state of self-sufficiency is represented by the row of blocks of equal height that runs across Figure 8-4. Although they represent sectors of greatly different magnitude, all the blocks in this chart are of equal height because the vertical scale represents percent of self-sufficiency, and the monetary dimensions of the sectors are shown on the horizontal scale. The area of each block thus represents the total output

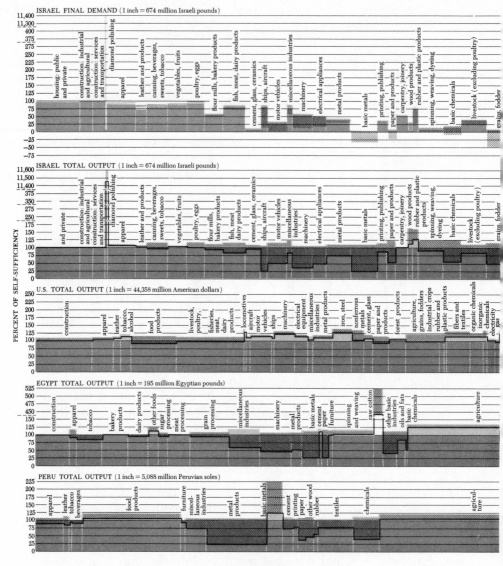

## Figure 8-4

Developed and underdeveloped economies are contrasted in these skyline tables of the United States and of Israel, Egypt, and Peru. Total output required for self-sufficiency is indicated by height of shaded blocks (see key at right). Horizontal scales give monetary dimension of each sector; vertical scales, percent of self-sufficiency. Heavy line shows actual total output of.

180

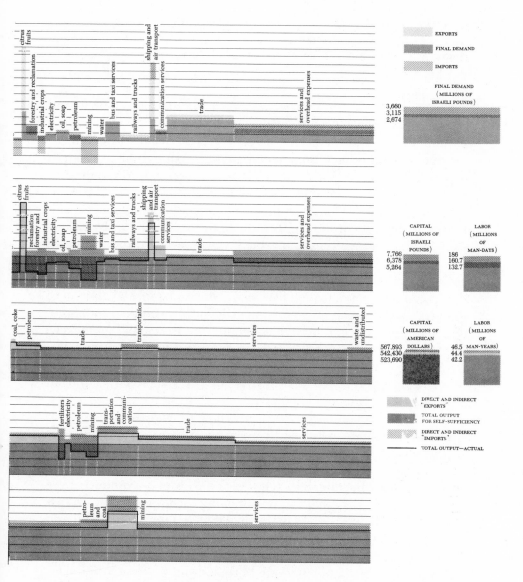

each economy; underdeveloped economies fall short of self-sufficiency. The final demand profile for Israel at top shows the volume of domestic demand (consumption and investment), exports and imports, to be satisfied directly and indirectly by outputs shown in the row below. Graphs at far right show Israeli foreign trade deficit and capital and labor components of domestic output and foreign trade.

required of that sector in order to satisfy the direct and indirect demands of the Israeli economy at self-sufficiency. The percentage that is allocated directly to final demand in each case is indicated by the height of the corresponding final demand block in the row of blocks above.

As a matter of fact, with the combination of labor, capital, and natural resources available to it in 1956, the year on which these hypothetical computations are based, the Israeli economy could not possibly have produced sufficient amounts of all the different kinds of goods and services that directly or indirectly were required to maintain the actual consumption and investment levels of the economy in that year. Domestic final demand was nonetheless maintained at those levels through recourse to foreign trade. By raising some outputs above the requirements of domestic direct and indirect demand, the country produced exportable surpluses. In other sectors imports filled the gap between domestic output and the total direct and indirect demand of the economy. In Israel and elsewhere imports filled the gap between domestic output and the total direct and indirect demand of the economy. In Israel and elsewhere imports serve to economize resources that happen to be comparatively scarce, whereas exports provide a way to put to good use other resources that would otherwise be less effectively employed or perhaps not employed at all.

The crucial relation between foreign trade and the structure of the Israeli economy can best be assessed in two steps. To the tops of the blocks of the hypothetical self-sufficient system are added lighter blocks; these represent the direct and indirect demand that would have to be met by each sector in order to produce from domestic resources, and without drawing on imports, the exports shown by the lighter blocks in the final demand row above. As might be expected, some sectors are called on to increase their outputs even though none or scarcely any of this output goes directly into exports. The substantial increase in the output of "grains, fodder," for example, would be accounted for, in part at least, by the indirect demand set up by exports of "fish, meat, dairy products," in accordance with the input coefficient shown in Figure 8-3.


# VIII

The next step takes account of the effect of imports. The effect is analogous to that of exports, but it works in the opposite direction.

An import of IL1000 worth of "basic chemicals," for example, not only eliminates directly the demand for an equal amount of "basic chemicals" from the domestic industry but also, as shown in Figure 8-3, reduces the indirect demand for the products of 33 other industries and "basic chemicals" as well. From the input coefficients for all sectors, hatched blocks are now constructed to represent the amount of each kind of goods that would be required, directly and indirectly, to produce in Israel the bill of imports shown in the final demand row at the top of the chart. These theoretical import-replacing outputs are subtracted from the total height of the blocks in the self-sufficiency row. The lowered and irregular skyline thereby established shows the actual output of the Israeli economy from sector to sector as a percentage of the level of output that would give the country self-sufficiency.

The fact that so few sectors of the Israeli economy rise above the self-sufficiency horizon and that so many fall below it is explained to a great extent by the relatively large amount of foreign aid received by the country. In addition to offsetting the export-import deficit, such aid also permits the country to substitute capital indirectly for labor. As the bar graph at the right-hand end of the chart of the hypothetical self-sufficient Israeli economy shows, the attainment of actual self-sufficiency would require a larger outlay of labor than of capital.

These considerations undoubtedly also apply to resources, although lack of sufficiently detailed information at present makes it impossible to establish the precise relation between domestic resources and the structure of the Israeli (or any other) economy. In connection with resources it should be remarked that no economy can be completely self-sufficient. As employed in the present analysis, self-sufficiency should be taken to mean the state of development at which nonreplaceable imports are covered by the exports needed to pay for them. The skyline in the chart indicates that the Israeli economy still falls well below self-sufficiency thus defined. Foreign aid makes it possible, however, for Israel to maintain not only a much higher level of domestic consumption than it could have achieved otherwise but also a much higher rate of investment and growth toward mature development.

The same chart presents analogous skylines for the U.S. economy and for the underdeveloped economies of Egypt and Peru. Comparison of one of these countries to another must be qualified because of the differences in the way their statisticians have aggregated the various industries of each country into sectors. The sectors are arrayed, however, in each profile in the same sequence in which they should and—let us hope—will eventually appear on a triangulated input-output table of the economic system of the entire world.

## IX

In common with Israel, it can be seen, Egypt and Peru present jagged total output profiles, with many sectors falling short of the self-sufficiency line. The U.S. profile, in contrast, is flat and averages out somewhat above self-sufficiency. This is a reflection of the country's mature developments, its favorable balance of trade, and the additional outflow of foreign aid-in-kind. The chart also demonstrates, incidentally, that the celebrated unfavorable balance of payments and the worrisome weakness of the dollar are the result of paper transactions.

Each of the underdeveloped countries specializes in the massive export of a few agricultural and mineral commodities and depends on imports for the supply of a broad spectrum of manufactured goods. (The diamond-polishing industry of Israel is worth special mention; established in that country by refugees from Nazism, it serves a comparatively minuscule domestic final demand and earns significant foreign credits to cover imports.) The U.S. economy, on the other hand, exports a great diversity of manufactured goods and imports a few agricultural and mineral commodities. An underdeveloped economy is consequently the mirror image of an advanced economy.

Comparison of the four national economic structures reveals a striking hierarchy based on the ratio of agriculture to total economic activity. The agricultural and food sectors of the United States, although they far outproduce those of the other countries, constitute only about 15 percent of the country's total output. Israel comes next, with about 24 percent of its total activity in agriculture, then Egypt with 36 percent and Peru with 40 percent. This may serve as a fair index of their different degrees of development.

The skylines of the three underdeveloped countries, instead of displaying random ups and downs, are characterized by gradual transitions from clearly defined high plateaus to well-formed valleys. This is no accident; the sectors that approach one another in height represent groups of industries closely related by their inter-industry transactions. In the Israeli profile, for example, there are

obvious connections in the three-step order of the "metal products," "electrical appliances," and "machinery" sectors, which are
stated more explicitly at the intersections of their rows and columns
in the input-output table.

Economic systems tend naturally to combine the international
division of labor with the minimization of transportation costs. The
latter costs can be kept down if an industry is located or developed
in close proximity to the largest direct customers for its outputs or
the suppliers of its inputs. Quite independently of transportation
costs, however, a growing economy derives a considerable,
although less measurable, advantage from developing whole fami-
lies of structurally related industries rather than isolated industries
that depend on foreign trade for supplies and markets. The incessant
process of technological change derives strong stimulus from inti-
mate contact between sellers and buyers, between the maker and
the potential user of a new process or product. As an economy
passes from one phase of its development to another, "block reac-
tion" will cause low blocks to grow tall, whereas blocks that now
protrude above the skyline will gradually lose their domineering
stature.

Developmental evolution along these lines is illustrated by the
comparison of the actual profile of the Peruvian economy for 1955
with the hypothetical profile of that economy for 1965; this projection is based on the projections of the United Nations Economic
Commission for Latin America. (See Figure 8-5.) The upward shift
of the self-sufficiency horizon reflects a large increase in the overall
level of final domestic demand. This upward shift is accompanied by
a horizontal displacement of the sectors from left to right that
reflects the faster growth of the industrial sectors in relation to that
of the agricultural sectors. Dependence on imports is diminished,
although the same commodities continue to account for the bulk of
the country's imports. Agriculture, basic metals, and the extractive
industries continue to provide, directly and indirectly, the exportable surpluses. As the result of rapid industrial growth, however, the
profile shows that Peru will cease to be an exporter of petroleum
and coal and will become, for a while at least, an importer of these
fuels.

Input-output analysis thus makes it possible to project changes in
the structure of a developing economy in terms of the underlying
composition of domestic consumption and investment, exports and
imports. The predetermined coefficients of inputs required directly
and indirectly to deliver each type of goods and services to final

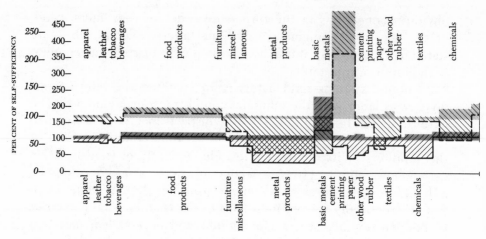

**Figure 8-5**

Development of Peru projected as of 1965 by UN Economic Commission
for Latin America is compared with the actual state of the economy as of
1955. Monetary value of the outputs of sectors is indicated by the horizontal scale. Overall increase of 73 percent in total gross output satisfying
domestic demand lifts the self-sufficiency line to the higher level indicated
by the scale in italics at left. Output required by direct and indirect demand
of exports is added above the line and represented by light gray blocks;
output similarly required to replace imports is represented by hatched

demand provide modules that can be combined in many different
ways to draft internally consistent blueprints for the future. The
mere existence of an elaborate projection will not, of course, bring
about economic growth. Much political acumen and drive, much

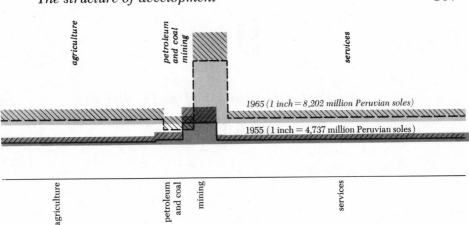

agriculture | petroleum and coal mining | services

1965 (1 inch = 8,202 million Peruvian soles)

1955 (1 inch = 4,737 million Peruvian soles)

agriculture | petroleum and coal | mining | services

blocks and is subtracted from new totals for each sector. The heavy broken line at the base of these export blocks shows domestic output projected for 1965. The corresponding picture for 1955 is shown in black and dark gray profile below. The sectors in the skyline for 1965 shows a general shift from left to right, reflecting larger expansion of output from industrial sectors. The agricultural and extractive sectors continue to generate the principal exports, and the country's dependence on imports is reduced. Industrial expansion requires a substantial increase in fuel consumption and imports of fuels exported in 1955.

sweat and tears go into the actual realization even of the best-conceived developmental plan. Progress, however, will be faster along a road well mapped in advance, and the cost of progress in terms of labor, capital, and human sacrifice will be considerably less.

# 9

## *The economic effects of disarmament*

### ( 1 9 6 1 )

### I

The federal government of the United States has been spending somewhat more than $40 billion per year on the maintenance of the military establishment and the procurement of arms. These outlays have absorbed about 10 percent of the gross national product, and they have exceeded by several billion dollars the combined net annual investment in manufacturing, service industries, transportation, and agriculture. The negotiation of disarmament would eventually raise the possibility of a substantial cut in the military budget. Economists, market analysts, and the makers of fiscal policy in government and business have therefore begun to consider how the economy might otherwise employ the labor, the plant, and the physical resources that now serve—directly and indirectly—the demands of the military establishment.

An increase in personal consumption, expansion of educational and medical services and facilities, acceleration of the rate of investment in domestic economic growth, enlargement of economic aid to underdeveloped countries—these are only a few of the many kinds of demand that would lay competing claims on the productive capacity made available by disarmament. There would be no problem if the goods that are listed in the typical procurement order from the U.S. Air Force missile base at Cape Canaveral also made up the shopping list of the average homemaker. It would be merely a question of maintaining the total level of demand during the transition period. But swords do not serve readily as plowshares. In fact, the military shopping list is very different from the bills of goods

Marvin Hoffenberg is coauthor of this paper.

presented by the various categories of civilian demand, and these in turn differ greatly from one another. So even if the total level of expenditures were maintained, the shift from military to nonmilitary budgets must be expected to increase the demand for the products of some industries and reduce the demand for the products of others. Furthermore, how the sales and employment figures of various industries will respond to the shifts depends upon the proportion in which each type of civilian demand, with its characteristic bill of goods, shares in the increase in total civilian demand.

The composition of the total civilian demand could possibly inhibit the overall increase in nonmilitary expenditures and so hold the country's economic activity at a lower level following a cut in the military budget. If most of the money saved were spent on highway construction, for example, a bottleneck would quickly develop in the supply of cement; meanwhile the electronics industry, which contributes much to military output but relatively little (directly or indirectly) to road building, would remain idle. On the other hand, if funds were allocated to a more balanced pattern of demand, they would secure more nearly full employment of the available human and physical resources. In the long run, of course, any mismatch between the productive capacities of individual industries and the changed pattern of demand would be rectified by reallocation of capital and labor. But such adjustment, as is well known, is quite painful and could take many months or even several years. The loss of time would represent an irredeemable loss of real income to individual citizens and to the nation as a whole.

## II

What is needed in order to anticipate and forestall such losses is a picture of the dependence of various industries on military demand, plus the bill of goods of each one of the more important kinds of private and public nonmilitary demand that are likely to increase when military demand is reduced. The present study is a pilot effort to develop this information and show how it can be applied to forecasting the consequences of the transfer of expenditures from military to civilian purchases. Our research was supported in part by the Research Program on Economic Adjustments to Disarmament of the Center for Research in Conflict Resolution at the University of Michigan. The study does not attempt to predict how much the various kinds of civilian purchase might expend, any more than it tries to predict the actual magnitude of military cuts. The eight tables presented here, however, make it possible to analyze the consequences of such shifts from military to civilian expenditures as can be predicted. They should be of considerable help in spelling out the concrete quantitative implications of the alternative fiscal measures that the government may have to take if and when disarmament becomes a fact. They should also enable business analysts to derive specific estimates of the demand for any particular goods or services or of the employment in a given industry from their own overall projections of public and private expenditure.

These tables embody insights afforded by input-output analysis. This technique is used today in many countries by governments and private businesses to chart the state of the national economy and to appraise the implications of specific economic actions that might affect its course. It anchors forecasting in the relatively stable fine structure of the economy and develops the important indirect relationships among the interdependent elements in the system.

In the highly integrated U.S. economy, for example, many industries deliver a large part or even all of their output not to final users but to other industries; in other words, a part or all of their output serves the needs of final users indirectly rather than directly. This does not make their dependence on the level and the structure of final demand any weaker, but it does make it more difficult to measure. In order to determine how much the demand for crude sulfur would diminish if the army cut its purchases of trucks by $1 million, one must determine how much crude sulfur the chemical industry needs to make $1 million worth of sulfuric acid, how much sulfuric acid is used in the finishing of $1 million worth of steel sheet, and how much steel sheet goes into $1 million worth of trucks. This is only one of several such linked chains connecting the output of crude sulfur to the final sales of automobiles. The input-output table of a national economy incorporates just this kind of information. The table (more properly a deck of punched cards or a magnetic tape) of interindustry relationships shows how much of the product of every other industry each industry requires to make one unit of its output. It also shows the distribution of the output of each industry to every other industry and to the various categories of final demand.

### III

As can be imagined, the preparation of such a table represents a major fact-finding and analytical task. The last complete, detailed input-output table of the United States was constructed for the year 1947. A trial check shows, however, that the structural relationships shown for that year still yield a reasonably good description of interindustry relationships in 1958. In the tables presented here the description of the interindustry relations, that is, the input-output matrix itself, has been omitted in order to bring into relief the less obvious but crucially important structural relationships between the industries and the various kinds of demand they serve. In other words, our tables show the end product of analytical computations, not the raw statistical material that went into them.

The industries have been aggregated in 20 or 58 production sectors. The horizonal rows in each case show the outputs of each sector as they are distributed to various categories of civilian and military demand. The categories of demand approximate those in which the gross national product is commonly stated, and the columns under each demand heading show the input of each production sector to that category in demand.

The first seven tables constitute the set of tools for working out the repercussions of an assumed step in disarmament and the accompanying transfer of expenditures to other categories of demand. The eighth table shows the answers yielded by such analysis in one particular, typical case.

The basic economic data for the year 1958 are presented in the first pair of tables. The figures in Table 9-1 are those in which the workings of the econmy are commonly stated; they show only the direct purchases from each industry by each type of demand. For technical and statistical reasons the industry-by-industry outputs are stated in 1947 dollars; the figures in the columns therefore do not add up to the totals in 1958 dollars in the bottom row. Conceptually it is best to regard these 1947 figures as standing for physical quantities measured, not in tons, yards, or bushels, but rather in units defined as the amounts of the respective goods that could be purchased for $1 million at the prices prevailing in 1947.

Table 9-2 gives effect to the interindustry transactions and thus shows the true total dependence of each industry on each type of demand. At the end of each row is shown the total 1958 output of the industry in question. The entries to the left of it show by how much the total output would have been diminished if the direct purchases in that category of demand (Table 9-1) had been reduced to zero. Thus, the entries in the "military" services column show that complete elimination of the military budget would have reduced the demand for "food and kindred products" by $1,513 million, for

## Table 9-1

Direct purchases by demand category *(millions of 1947 dollars)*

|  | | personal consumption | business investment | residential construction | public services construction | maintenance construction | exports (except military) | exports to India (except food) | government (nonmilitary) | military |
|---|---|---|---|---|---|---|---|---|---|---|
| food and kindred products | 1 | 38.396 | | | | | 3,199 | [5] | 169 | 536 |
| apparel and textile-mill products | 2 | 14,532 | 20 | | | | 1,167 | [11] | 109 | 143 |
| leather products | 3 | 2,038 | 14 | | | | 45 | | 20 | 24 |
| paper and allied products | 4 | 597 | | | | | 184 | [1] | 104 | |
| chemicals and allied products | 5 | 3,879 | 49 | | | | 1,114 | [16] | 412 | 85 |
| fuel and power | 6 | 10,943 | | | | | 536 | [4] | 556 | 991 |
| rubber and rubber products | 7 | 782 | | | | | 153 | [2] | 23 | 6 |
| lumber and wood products | 8 | 2.555 | 526 | | | | 108 | [1] | 66 | 19 |
| nonmetallic minerals and products | 9 | 316 | 20 | | | | 91 | [2] | 17 | |
| primary metals | 10 | 21 | | | | | 473 | | 4 | |
| fabricated metal products | 11 | 1,109 | 186 | | | | 330 | [1] | 57 | 106 |
| machinery (except electrical) | 12 | 968 | 5,957 | | | | 1,651 | [23] | 288 | 166 |
| electrical machinery | 13 | 3,160 | 2,150 | | | | 464 | [6] | 74 | 915 |
| transportation equipment and ordnance | 14 | 5,574 | 2,863 | | | | 962 | [22] | 352 | 9,478 |
| instruments and allied products | 15 | 389 | 265 | | | | 122 | [2] | 19 | 22 |
| miscellaneous manufacturing industries | 16 | 2,088 | 96 | | | | 91 | | 97 | |
| transportation | 17 | 7,714 | 341 | | | | 1,844 | [35] | 705 | 730 |
| trade | 18 | 37,242 | 2,161 | | | | 812 | [15] | 40 | 78 |
| service and finance | 19 | 90,025 | | | | | 882 | [2] | 11,029 | 705 |
| construction | 20 | | | 16,844 | 12,082 | 5,956 | 10,429 | | | 967 |
| unallocated and waste products | 21 | | | | | | 390 | [7] | | 742 |
| *expenditures (millions of 1958 dollars)* | | −292,956 | −46,102 | −18,893 | −7,770 | −17,713 | −22,576 | [−189] | −37,184 | −41,585 |

PRODUCTION BY SECTOR

"apparel" by $575 million, and so on. These figures are considerably larger than the figures in the corresponding boxes in Table 9-1. The reason for this is that the direct purchase figures show only the goods delivered to the military establishment, while the figures in Table 9-2 show the indirect as well as direct military demand and include the goods and services that must be delivered to other industries that need these inputs in order to produce, in their turn, the goods and services demanded by the final military users. Thus, as Table 9-1 shows, the rubber industry delivered in 1958 only $6 million worth of its goods to the military establishment; Table 9-2 shows, however, that a much larger part of its total output, $244 million, depended upon military demand. All told, the $41.6 billion ($16.7 billion in 1947 dollars) of direct purchases for military purposes in 1958 generated a total of some $86 billion ($34.5 billion in 1947 dollars) of direct and indirect military demand in the economy as a whole.

In the next pair of tables the relationships developed in Table 9-2 are restated in a form that begins to make them useful for purposes of analysis. It now becomes possible to deal with the question of how the sales and employment of various industries would be affected by a cut in military demand and a corresponding increase in one or another category of civilian demand. Table 9-3 shows the quantity of goods and services each industry has to produce in order to enable the economy as a whole to satisfy $1 million worth of direct purchases in any one category of demand. With these figures it is possible to estimate the total output of each industry that would be developed under any set of assumptions about the magnitude of

### Table 9-2

Direct and indirect demand by demand category *(millions of 1947 dollars)*

| PRODUCTION BY SECTOR | | personal consumption | business investment | residential construction | public services construction | maintenance construction | exports (except military) | government (nonmilitary) | military | total output |
|---|---|---|---|---|---|---|---|---|---|---|
| food and kindred products | 1 | 86,166 | 754 | 462 | 70 | 351 | 5,766 | 1,362 | 1,513 | 96,444 |
| apparel and textile-mill products | 2 | 26,557 | 640 | 248 | 51 | 139 | 1,986 | 387 | 575 | 30,582 |
| leather products | 3 | 3,314 | 117 | 23 | 8 | 19 | 113 | 77 | 116 | 3,786 |
| paper and allied products | 4 | 7,333 | 926 | 408 | 133 | 380 | 793 | 542 | 788 | 11,303 |
| chemicals and allied products | 5 | 10,208 | 1,047 | 380 | 126 | 853 | 1,960 | 1,183 | 877 | 16,634 |
| fuel and power | 6 | 26,530 | 1,969 | 557 | 553 | 623 | 1,846 | 1,533 | 2,633 | 36,243 |
| rubber and rubber products | 7 | 2,727 | 588 | 85 | 65 | 74 | 388 | 163 | 244 | 4,333 |
| lumber and wood products | 8 | 4,918 | 2,309 | 2,446 | 120 | 883 | 340 | 198 | 451 | 11,665 |
| nonmetallic minerals and products | 9 | 1,940 | 1,776 | 1,150 | 711 | 756 | 305 | 150 | 337 | 7,123 |
| primary metals | 10 | 8,138 | 7,393 | 1,092 | 651 | 1,434 | 2,445 | 695 | 3,384 | 25,230 |
| fabricated metal products | 11 | 5,988 | 4,462 | 1,147 | 428 | 1,438 | 945 | 382 | 1,281 | 16,071 |
| machinery (except electrical) | 12 | 3,635 | 7,947 | 205 | 190 | 204 | 2,237 | 537 | 823 | 15,780 |
| electrical machinery | 13 | 5,757 | 4,128 | 343 | 121 | 407 | 852 | 245 | 3,110 | 14,962 |
| transportation equipment and ordnance | 14 | 10,421 | 4,090 | 145 | 139 | 131 | 1,443 | 640 | 10,609 | 27,617 |
| instruments and allied products | 15 | 786 | 377 | 23 | 37 | 22 | 160 | 61 | 370 | 1,835 |
| miscellaneous manufacturing industries | 16 | 3,403 | 235 | 35 | 14 | 36 | 166 | 218 | 119 | 4,225 |
| transportation | 17 | 15,147 | 2,261 | 951 | 512 | 675 | 2,658 | 1,418 | 1,486 | 25,108 |
| trade | 18 | 44,420 | 4,168 | 1,489 | 254 | 1,334 | 1,350 | 537 | 735 | 54,287 |
| service and finance | 19 | 118,402 | 3,196 | 1,350 | 913 | 893 | 2,410 | 12,204 | 1,886 | 141,254 |
| construction | 20 | | 16,844 | 12,082 | 5,956 | 10,429 | | | 967 | 46,278 |
| unallocated and waste products | 21 | 9,583 | 2,172 | 490 | 190 | 433 | 1,270 | 1,143 | 2,144 | 17,426 |

## Table 9-3

Direct and indirect demand per $1 million direct purchases by demand category *(1947 dollars)*

PRODUCTION BY SECTOR

| | | personal consumption | business investment | residential construction | public services construction | maintenance construction | exports (except military) | exports to India (except food) | government (nonmilitary) | military |
|---|---|---|---|---|---|---|---|---|---|---|
| food and kindred products | 1 | 294,127 | 16,362 | 24,459 | 9,022 | 19,839 | 255,386 | [98,413] | 36,623 | 36,374 |
| apparel and textile-mill products | 2 | 90,653 | 13,880 | 13,100 | 6,525 | 7,842 | 87,987 | [99,471] | 10,400 | 13,825 |
| leather products | 3 | 11.312 | 2,534 | 1,196 | 991 | 1,084 | 5,014 | [3,704] | 2,063 | 2,777 |
| paper and allied products | 4 | 25 032 | 20,095 | 21,596 | 17,156 | 21,425 | 35,108 | [40,741] | 14,565 | 18,959 |
| chemicals and allied products | 5 | 34,844 | 22,704 | 20,119 | 16,255 | 48,168 | 86,818 | [134,392] | 31,823 | 21,087 |
| fuel and power | 6 | 90,560 | 42,703 | 29,477 | 71,145 | 35,194 | 81,773 | [94,709] | 41,219 | 63,309 |
| rubber and rubber products | 7 | 9 309 | 12,750 | 4,473 | 8,314 | 4,189 | 17,178 | [25,926] | 4,384 | 5,858 |
| lumber and wood products | 8 | 16,788 | 50,093 | 129,461 | 15,405 | 49,822 | 15,038 | [19,577] | 5,333 | 10,850 |
| nonmetallic minerals and products | 9 | 6,621 | 38,512 | 60,880 | 91,441 | 42,675 | 13,488 | [23,810] | 4,026 | 8,092 |
| primary metals | 10 | 27.778 | 160,366 | 57,794 | 83,745 | 80,929 | 108,279 | [119,577] | 18,694 | 81,373 |
| fabricated metal products | 11 | 20,439 | 96,788 | 60,705 | 55,045 | 81,189 | 41,867 | [46,561] | 10,284 | 30,812 |
| machinery (except electrical) | 12 | 12,409 | 172,381 | 10,872 | 24,466 | 11,540 | 99,101 | [164,021] | 14,439 | 19,788 |
| electrical machinery | 13 | 19,652 | 89,534 | 18,139 | 15,611 | 22,972 | 37,726 | [61,905] | 6,581 | 74,779 |
| transportation equipment and ordnance | 14 | 35,572 | 88,705 | 7,691 | 17,851 | 7,396 | 63,895 | [158,730] | 17,206 | 255,126 |
| instruments and allied products | 15 | 2,680 | 8,184 | 1,228 | 4,736 | 1,225 | 7,074 | [13,228] | 1,638 | 8,890 |
| miscellaneous manufacturing industries | 16 | 11.615 | 5,095 | 1,826 | 1,828 | 2,044 | 7,340 | [4,233] | 5,860 | 2,869 |
| transportation | 17 | 51,703 | 49,041 | 50,336 | 65,933 | 38,108 | 117,736 | [233,333] | 38,129 | 35,729 |
| trade | 18 | 151,627 | 90,410 | 78,802 | 32,716 | 75,295 | 59,816 | [106,878] | 14,439 | 17,667 |
| service and finance | 19 | 404,164 | 69,329 | 71,466 | 117,542 | 50,421 | 106,728 | [91,005] | 328,208 | 45,348 |
| construction | 20 | | 365,364 | 639,496 | 766,538 | 588,777 | | | | 23.254 |
| unallocated and waste products | 21 | 32,711 | 47,113 | 25,925 | 24,402 | 24,462 | 56,272 | [89,947] | 30,739 | 51,567 |

expenditures in the various demand categories. In other words, the figures are useful for economic forecasting in general, quite apart from the question of disarmament. All of the figures in the main body of Table 9-2 can be synthesized, for example, by multiplying each one of the 1958 expenditure totals in Table 9-1 by the entries in the corresponding columns of Table 9-3.

In Table 9-4 the output figures of Table 9-3 are translated into figures that show the volume of employment, industry by industry, engaged directly and indirectly in satisfying $100 million worth of direct purchases in each category of demand. This table may therefore be used along with Table 9-3 in estimating the detailed consequences of one or another change in the total pattern of demand. One simply multiplies the figures in each column by the assumed or given total expenditure in that demand category and thereby determines the level of employment in each industry that corresponds to that volume of expenditure. Again, as in the case of Table 9-3, the actual 1958 employment figures can be synthesized by performing these multiplications with the 1958 expenditure totals given in Table 9-1.

For the specific purpose of conjuring with the effects of a transfer of expenditures from the military to the various categories of civilian demand, Tables 9-5 and 9-6 provide a way to shortcut the task of computation. These tables show the net effect the sales (or employment) of each industry that would result from the transfer of $1 mil-

### Table 9-4

Total employment per $100 million direct purchases by demand category
*(1985 man-years)*

| | | personal consumption | business investment | residential construction | public services construction | maintenance construction | exports (except military) | exports to India (except food) | government (nonmilitary) | military |
|---|---|---|---|---|---|---|---|---|---|---|
| food and kindred products | 1 | 498 | 21 | 28 | | 20 | 374 | [128] | 56 | 53 |
| apparel and textile-mill products | 2 | 658 | 80 | 72 | 35 | 41 | 502 | [560] | 66 | 86 |
| leather products | 3 | 107 | 24 | 11 | 9 | 10 | 47 | [34] | 19 | 27 |
| paper and allied products | 4 | 121 | 97 | 104 | 85 | 105 | 170 | [197] | 71 | 91 |
| chemicals and allied products | 5 | 180 | 128 | 94 | 85 | 211 | 481 | [660] | 168 | 128 |
| fuel and power | 6 | 359 | 163 | 114 | 236 | 127 | 283 | [318] | 172 | 220 |
| rubber and rubber products | 7 | 54 | 74 | 27 | 49 | 24 | 100 | [151] | 26 | 34 |
| lumber and wood products | 8 | 141 | 421 | 1,084 | 126 | 420 | 126 | [164] | 45 | 92 |
| nonmetallic minerals and products | 9 | 60 | 348 | 548 | 828 | 385 | 123 | [217] | 36 | 73 |
| primary metals | 10 | 133 | 782 | 262 | 435 | 380 | 496 | [599] | 88 | 364 |
| fabricated metal products | 11 | 160 | 695 | 387 | 386 | 500 | 333 | [392] | 90 | 258 |
| machinery (except electrical) | 12 | 97 | 1,379 | 85 | 175 | 88 | 755 | [1,301] | 108 | 169 |
| electrical machinery | 13 | 145 | 781 | 110 | 91 | 153 | 313 | [513] | 51 | 662 |
| transportation equipment and ordnance | 14 | 156 | 466 | 38 | 73 | 36 | 370 | [991] | 78 | 2,467 |
| instruments and allied products | 15 | 36 | 110 | 17 | 63 | 16 | 94 | [177] | 22 | 119 |
| miscellaneous manufacturing industries | 16 | 103 | 45 | 16 | 14 | 17 | 65 | [37] | 52 | 25 |
| transportation | 17 | 518 | 488 | 506 | 669 | 380 | 764 | [1,523] | 383 | 322 |
| trade | 18 | 2,674 | 1,600 | 1,369 | 616 | 1,297 | 1,060 | [1,900] | 258 | 322 |
| service and finance | 19 | 3,715 | 705 | 665 | 856 | 391 | 937 | [883] | 9,296 | 584 |
| construction | 20 | | 2,091 | 3,658 | 4,396 | 3,364 | | | | 134 |
| employees in business establishments | | 9,915 | 10,499 | 9,193 | 9,228 | 7,965 | 7,394 | [10,746] | 11,086 | 6,230 |
| households | | 870 | | | | | | | | |
| government: civilian | | | | | | | | | 9,649 | 1,977 |
| armed forces | | | | | | | | | | 6,329 |
| total employees | | 10,785 | 10,499 | 9,193 | 9,228 | 7,965 | 7,394 | [10,746] | 20,734 | 14,536 |

EMPLOYMENT BY SECTOR

## Table 9-5

Production by sector after reallocation of $1 million direct military purchases *(thousands of 1947 dollars)*

| | | exports to India (except food) | exports (except military) | business investment | personal consumption | public services construction | residential construction | maintenance construction | government (nonmilitary) | military |
|---|---|---|---|---|---|---|---|---|---|---|
| transportation equipment and ordnance | 14 | −96 | −191 | −166 | −220 | −237 | −247 | −248 | −238 | 255 |
| instruments and allied products | 15 | 4 | −2 | −1 | −6 | −4 | −8 | −8 | −7 | 9 |
| electrical machinery | 13 | −13 | −37 | 15 | −55 | −59 | −57 | −52 | −68 | 75 |
| food and kindred products | 1 | 62 | 219 | −20 | 258 | −27 | −12 | −17 | | 36 |
| leather products | 3 | 1 | 2 | | 9 | −2 | −2 | −2 | −1 | 3 |
| apparel and textile-mill products | 2 | 85 | 74 | | 77 | −7 | −1 | −6 | −3 | 14 |
| machinery (except electrical) | 12 | 144 | 79 | 153 | −7 | 5 | −9 | −8 | −5 | 20 |
| fuel and power | 6 | 31 | 18 | −21 | 27 | 8 | −34 | −28 | −22 | 63 |
| primary metals | 10 | 38 | 27 | 79 | −54 | 2 | −24 | | −63 | 81 |
| miscellaneous manufacturing industries | 16 | 1 | 4 | 2 | 9 | −1 | −1 | −1 | 3 | 3 |
| rubber and rubber products | 7 | 20 | 11 | 7 | 3 | 2 | −1 | −2 | −1 | 6 |
| nonmetallic minerals and products | 9 | 16 | 5 | 30 | −1 | 83 | 53 | 35 | −4 | 8 |
| fabricated metal products | 11 | 16 | 11 | 66 | −10 | 24 | 30 | 50 | −21 | 31 |
| chemicals and allied products | 5 | 113 | 66 | 2 | 14 | −5 | −1 | 27 | 11 | 21 |
| paper and allied products | 4 | 22 | 16 | 1 | 6 | −2 | 3 | 3 | −4 | 19 |
| lumber and wood products | 8 | 9 | 4 | 39 | 6 | 5 | 119 | 39 | −6 | 11 |
| transportation | 17 | 198 | 82 | 13 | 16 | 30 | 15 | 2 | 2 | 36 |
| trade | 18 | 89 | 42 | 73 | 134 | 15 | 61 | 58 | −3 | 18 |
| service and finance | 19 | 46 | 61 | 24 | 359 | 72 | 26 | 5 | 283 | 45 |
| construction | 20 | −23 | −23 | 342 | −23 | 743 | 616 | 566 | −23 | 23 |

(PRODUCTION BY SECTOR)

lion (or $100 million) from the "military" column to each of the other demand columns. The order of columns and rows has been arranged in these tables so as to segregate the italic figures—the negative changes in output and demand—above the diagonal falling from left to right. (The roman figures—the positive changes in output and demand—fall correspondingly below the diagonal.) The tables bring out clearly the pronounced differences in the responses of the various industries and the equally pronounced differences in the capacity of the various types of civilian demand to absorb the goods and services now serving final military demand.

The "transportation equipment and ordnance" industry emerges in the italic figures at the tops of these tables as the one that depends most heavily upon military demand. This group of industries includes the aircraft, motor vehicle, shipbuilding, and railway equipment industries along with ordnance proper. It is followed in the hierarchy of dependence upon military demand by "instruments and related products" and "electrical machinery." On the other hand, in the lower rows of the table, the roman figures opposite the "transportation," "trade," and "service and finance" industries show that their outputs are bound to increase whichever type of civilian demand lays claim to the resources that are released from military needs.

The reader will note that the industries appear in a slightly different order in the two tables, suggesting that an increase in output could be accompanied in some cases by a decrease in employment. This apparent inconsistency is a consequence of the necessarily

## Table 9-6

Employment by sector after reallocation of $100 million direct military purchases *(1958 man-years)*

EMPLOYMENT BY SECTOR

| | | exports to India (except food) | exports (except military) | business investment | personal consumption | public services construction | residential construction | maintenance construction | government (nonmilitary) |
|---|---|---|---|---|---|---|---|---|---|
| transportation equipment and ordnance | 14 | *-1,476* | *-2,097* | *-2,001* | *-2,311* | *-2,394* | *-2,429* | *-2,431* | *-2,389* |
| instruments and allied products | 15 | 57 | -25 | -9 | -83 | -56 | -102 | -103 | -97 |
| electrical machinery | 13 | *-149* | *-349* | 119 | -517 | -571 | -552 | -509 | *-611* |
| apparel and textile-mill products | 2 | 473 | 416 | -6 | 572 | -51 | -14 | -45 | -20 |
| leather products | 3 | 8 | 20 | -3 | 80 | -18 | -16 | -17 | -8 |
| fuel and power | 6 | 98 | 63 | -57 | 139 | 16 | -106 | -93 | -48 |
| machinery (except electrical) | 12 | 1,132 | 586 | 1,210 | -72 | 6 | -84 | -81 | -61 |
| food and kindred products | 1 | 75 | 321 | -32 | 445 | -53 | -25 | -33 | 3 |
| miscellaneous manufacturing industries | 16 | 12 | 40 | 20 | 78 | -11 | -9 | -8 | 27 |
| rubber and rubber products | 7 | 117 | 66 | 40 | 20 | 15 | -7 | -10 | -8 |
| primary metals | 10 | 235 | 132 | 418 | -231 | 71 | -102 | 16 | -276 |
| chemicals and allied products | 5 | 532 | 353 | | 52 | -43 | -34 | 83 | 40 |
| nonmetallic minerals and products | 9 | 144 | 50 | 275 | -13 | 755 | 475 | 312 | -37 |
| fabricated metal products | 11 | 143 | 75 | 437 | -98 | 128 | 129 | 242 | -168 |
| paper and allied products | 4 | 106 | 79 | 6 | 30 | -6 | 13 | 14 | -20 |
| lumber and wood products | 8 | 72 | 34 | 329 | 49 | 34 | 992 | 328 | -47 |
| trade | 18 | 1,578 | 738 | 1,278 | 2,352 | 294 | 1,047 | 975 | -64 |
| service and finance | 19 | 247 | 353 | 121 | 3,131 | 272 | 81 | -193 | 8,712 |
| transportation | 17 | 1,147 | 442 | 166 | 196 | 347 | 184 | 58 | 61 |
| construction | 20 | *-134* | *-134* | 1,957 | *-134* | 4,262 | 3,524 | 3,230 | *-134* |
| net increase in business employment | | 4,516 | 1,163 | 4,268 | 3,685 | 2,997 | 2,963 | 1,735 | 4,855 |
| total negative change | | *-1,625* | *-2,471* | *-2,108* | *-3,325* | *-3,203* | *-3,480* | *-3,523* | *-3,854* |
| total negative change (from Table 9-7) | | *-2,897* | *-3,117* | *-2,768* | *-3,610* | *-3,724* | *-3,746* | *-3,911* | *-4,114* |

## Table 9-7

Employment after reallocation of $100 million military purchases to each of eight other demand categories *(1958 man-years)*

| | exports (except military) | exports to India (except food) | business investment | personal consumption | public services construction | maintenance construction | residential construction | government (nonmilitary) |
|---|---|---|---|---|---|---|---|---|
| aircraft and parts 14 | -1,653.5 | -1,544.7 | -1,652.9 | -1,703.8 | -1,707.1 | -1,707.1 | -1,707.1 | -1,705.0 |
| ordnance 14 | -341.7 | -341.7 | -341.7 | -341.7 | -341.7 | -341.7 | -341.7 | -341.7 |
| ships and boats 14 | -275.1 | -267.6 | -271.0 | -338.5 | -349.1 | -343.6 | -343.0 | -343.9 |
| radio 13 | -408.3 | -352.6 | -238.9 | -433.3 | -497.3 | -466.8 | -497.3 | -482.8 |
| aluminum 10 | -7.6 | -9.9 | -4.0 | -25.1 | -21.7 | -12.2 | -20.4 | -26.4 |
| instruments 15 | -24.3 | 58.3 | -9.1 | -82.7 | -55.5 | -102.2 | -101.7 | -96.8 |
| apparel 2 | -5.0 | -23.1 | -24.3 | 390.6 | -27.1 | -27.1 | -27.1 | -.2 |
| copper 10 | 8.0 | -7.9 | 12.0 | -30.8 | -19.2 | -12.0 | -12.0 | -32.9 |
| plastics 5 | 51.8 | 14.4 | -4.7 | -17.1 | -27.7 | -19.3 | -26.4 | -34.6 |
| overseas transportation (water) 17 | 103.3 | 228.0 | -9.7 | -6.6 | -9.7 | -10.0 | -10.2 | -7.5 |
| other transportation 17 | -33.8 | -9.7 | -64.3 | 73.7 | -44.0 | -66.9 | -64.4 | 50.5 |
| electric light and power 6 | -14.8 | -2.1 | -11.2 | 72.2 | -21.8 | -29.9 | -23.9 | 23.1 |
| professional and services 19 | -219.6 | -189.9 | -10.3 | 1,011.0 | -185.1 | -246.5 | -26.1 | 8,555.7 |
| motors, generators 13 | .6 | 60.2 | 61.0 | -67.2 | -62.3 | -66.5 | -68.9 | -76.2 |
| other nonferrous metals 10 | 4.4 | 18.8 | 16.9 | -31.6 | -25.3 | -13.3 | -22.7 | -38.0 |
| metal stamping 11 | 1.9 | 55.4 | 18.9 | -51.2 | -66.8 | -64.1 | -68.5 | -67.9 |
| machine tools 12 | 66.3 | 337.3 | 150.0 | -37.3 | -37.6 | -43.0 | -91.5 | -86.8 |
| petroleum 6 | 1.4 | 63.2 | 75.9 | -4.5 | 3.7 | -74.2 | -91.5 | -86.8 |
| power transmission equipment 12 | 24.5 | 77.5 | 31.3 | -8.3 | -3.6 | -13.7 | -14.2 | -12.5 |
| engines and turbines 12 | 83.5 | 108.3 | 50.4 | -10.8 | -9.8 | -13.7 | -14.0 | -6.7 |
| metal containers 11 | 16.3 | 11.0 | -2.0 | 7.2 | -5.6 | -3.0 | -6.2 | -7.2 |
| electrical equipment (n.e.c.) 13 | 50.2 | 94.6 | 222.3 | -9.1 | -14.0 | -8.3 | -6.3 | -17.5 |
| industrial machinery 12 | 116.6 | 162.6 | 531.9 | -29.9 | -33.2 | -26.5 | -25.3 | -29.5 |
| leather and leather products 3 | 20.7 | 6.9 | -2.6 | 80.0 | -17.7 | -16.5 | -15.6 | -7.6 |
| livestock, poultry 1 | 42.1 | 27.6 | -14.1 | 113.8 | -19.5 | -12.1 | -15.3 | -1.2 |
| railway equipment 14 | 47.7 | 440.2 | 33.1 | -5.8 | -3.0 | -6.0 | -5.7 | -3.2 |
| iron and steel forging 10 | 12.2 | 82.0 | 63.8 | -56.8 | 36.7 | -38.4 | -38.5 | -63.6 |
| cutlery, tools 11 | 25.9 | 28.8 | 56.5 | -41.0 | -7.8 | -5.8 | 17.2 | -54.1 |
| medical supplies 5 | 62.6 | 142.0 | -9.0 | 23.5 | -10.1 | -8.8 | -9.5 | 22.0 |
| food products 1 | 218.7 | 5.5 | -21.8 | 271.0 | -30.2 | -24.6 | -24.9 | 3.7 |
| insulated wire and cable 13 | 1.8 | 45.6 | 71.1 | -29.0 | -9.5 | 28.7 | 13.5 | -33.7 |
| iron and steel 10 | 115.3 | 152.2 | 329.7 | -86.3 | 100.7 | 92.1 | -8.7 | -114.7 |
| organic chemicals 5 | 90.2 | 117.2 | | 9.3 | -8.7 | 3.8 | -8.2 | -4.4 |
| rubber and rubber products 7 | 66.0 | 116.6 | 40.4 | 20.4 | 14.8 | -9.8 | -7.1 | -8.3 |
| plumbing fixtures 11 | 5.8 | -4.1 | 28.2 | 1.6 | -3.8 | 149.4 | 95.4 | -9.6 |
| miscellaneous manufacturing industries 16 | 39.5 | 11.9 | 20.1 | 77.8 | -11.0 | -8.3 | -9.3 | 27.2 |
| textile mill 2 | 421.0 | 497.1 | 17.8 | 181.1 | -24.5 | -18.0 | 13.3 | -19.9 |
| grain and feed crops 1 | 9.6 | 1.7 | -.3 | 5.0 | -1.0 | .1 | .1 | -.2 |
| paper and allied products 4 | 79.0 | 106.0 | 6.8 | 30.6 | -5.7 | 14.4 | 13.7 | -19.9 |
| inorganic chemicals 5 | 63.8 | 60.2 | .3 | 7.1 | -4.4 | 2.5 | -3.5 | 62.8 |

## Table 9-7 (Cont.)

| | | exports (except military) | exports to India (except food) | business investment | personal consumption | public services construction | maintenance construction | residential construction | government (nonmilitary) |
|---|---|---|---|---|---|---|---|---|---|
| fabricated metals | 11 | 25.4 | 43.6 | 335.6 | -14.6 | 212.3 | 165.3 | 91.2 | -29.5 |
| nonmetallic minerals | 9 | 49.8 | 144.0 | 274.8 | -12.9 | 754.6 | 312.1 | 475.5 | -36.6 |
| business services | 19 | 200.0 | 389.7 | 50.0 | 465.2 | 197.4 | -18.0 | -3.7 | 14.1 |
| motor vehicles | 14 | 125.9 | 247.5 | 231.6 | 78.8 | 7.3 | -33.0 | -31.4 | 5.3 |
| farm, building, mining machinery | 12 | 198.6 | 242.0 | 347.0 | -.8 | 76.2 | 5.6 | -2.8 | 27.7 |
| miscellaneous chemicals | 5 | 84.0 | 198.5 | 13.0 | 28.9 | 7.6 | 104.2 | 13.6 | -5.9 |
| lumber, wood products | 8 | 33.9 | 71.9 | 328.9 | 49.2 | 34.2 | 328.1 | 991.6 | -47.0 |
| pumps, compressors | 12 | 96.6 | 204.5 | 99.6 | 15.2 | 13.9 | 10.3 | 15.3 | -.7 |
| electrical appliances | 13 | 5.9 | 3.2 | 3.1 | 20.8 | 12.0 | 3.4 | 6.1 | -1.5 |
| trade | 18 | 737.9 | 1,577.5 | 1,277.0 | 2,351.6 | 294.0 | 974.9 | 1,046.2 | -64.9 |
| tobacco, alcoholic beverages | 1 | 50.3 | 40.4 | 3.9 | 55.4 | -2.4 | 3.8 | 14.5 | .3 |
| railroads, trucking | 17 | 373.5 | 983.4 | 240.8 | 129.0 | 401.4 | 135.4 | 258.6 | 18.7 |
| coal and coke | 6 | 73.0 | 30.4 | 25.5 | 28.2 | 27.5 | 9.3 | 6.2 | 14.5 |
| gas utilities | 6 | 2.9 | 6.0 | 4.2 | 42.4 | 5.6 | 1.3 | 2.5 | 1.3 |
| auto and other repairs | 19 | 15.0 | 19.7 | 39.0 | 83.4 | 177.2 | 44.4 | 37.2 | 14.1 |
| banking, finance | 19 | 138.9 | 79.7 | 42.4 | 714.6 | 82.3 | 27.2 | 73.3 | 30.2 |
| restaurants, hotels, amusements | 19 | 218.4 | | | 856.3 | | | | 97.6 |
| construction | 20 | -133.7 | -133.7 | 1,957.1 | -133.7 | 4,262.7 | 3,229.9 | 3,524.2 | -133.7 |
| business employment: increase | | 4,280.7 | 7,413.1 | 7,036.0 | 7,294.9 | 6,722.1 | 5,646.2 | 6,709.2 | 8,968.8 |
| decrease | | -3,117.4 | -2,897.0 | -2,767.8 | -3,610.4 | -3,724.5 | -3,910.9 | -3,746.0 | -4,113.9 |
| net change | | 1,163.3 | 4,516.1 | 4,268.2 | 3,684.5 | 2,997.6 | 1,735.3 | 2,963.2 | 4,854.9 |
| total employment: increase | | 4,280.7 | 7,413.1 | 7,036.0 | 8,165.3 | 6,722.1 | 5,646.2 | 6,709.2 | 16,641.0 |
| decrease | | -11,423.2 | -11,202.8 | -11,073.6 | -11,916.2 | -12,030.3 | -12,216.7 | -12,051.8 | -10,443.0 |
| net change | | -7,142.5 | -3,789.7 | -4,037.6 | -3,750.9 | -5,308.2 | -6,570.5 | -5,342.6 | 6,198.0 |

gross "product mix" involved in summarizing the industrial economy in only 20 sectors; it reflects the fact that the principal increases in output are coming in these cases from industries having a lower ratio of labor to output. Since employment is necessarily foremost among the concerns in any econmic forecast, the industry-by-industry employment figures are shown in the fine detail of a 58-industry breakdown in Table 9-7.

What would be the effect on employment of a 20 percent, or $8 billion, cut in a $40 billion military budget if this cut were accompanied by an equal increase in nonmilitary expenditures? Taking the simple case of the transfer of the entire expenditure to one or another category of civilian demand, one need only multiply the figures in the chosen category in Table 9-7 by 80. Thus, on the unlikely assumption that the entire expenditure is moved into the "government" column (which comprises all governmental demand except for military and construction activities of the government), as many as 329,000 jobs held in private business establishments would be eliminated, and this would be offset by the creation of 717,000 new jobs in other private industries. The equally unlikely shift of demand to "exports" to foreign countries would cause far less strain as measured in turnover of the labor force (only 249,000 jobs would be lost and 342,000 new jobs created). As this result suggests, exports draw upon much the same industries as the military, though for different products. The column "exports to India," which appears in all the tables except 9-2 and 9-8, makes it possible to perform similar computations with the quite different bill of goods that would be involved in a substantial increase in economic aid to underdeveloped countries.

Table 9-8 shows the effects upon employment in the 58 industries that follow from a more reasonable assumption. The projected $8 billion cut in the military budget is here transferred pro rata to the various categories of civilian demand, leaving their relative magnitudes unchanged. As can be seen, a total of 253,815 jobs would be eliminated in 19 industries, and a total of 541,855 new jobs would be created in the other 39 industries—a net gain of 288,040 jobs. For purposes of comparison, it may be observed that during the recession of 1957 and 1958, employment fell in 54 and expanded in only 4 of the 58 industries; the combined loss of jobs amounted at that time to 1,411,000 man-years and the gain to only 7,000.

The net increases in "business employment" indicated in the transfer of expenditures from military to civilian demand are important, for it is likely that disarmament would be accompanied by the release of large numbers of civilian and uniformed personnel of the Department of Defense. If the cuts in personnel were directly proportional to the cut in the budget, then each $100-million cut would be accompanied by the release of 1,977 civilian and 6,329 uniformed workers. Not one of the net increases in total business employment computed in Tables 9-7 and 9-8 would be adequate to absorb entirely this addition to rolls of job seekers. The tables provide the means, however, for trying out sets of assumptions different from the simple ones demonstrated here.

# IV

The analytical methods employed in this study can obviously be used to answer many further questions. How would the industrial

# Table 9-8

Employment after reallocation of $8 billion military purchases to other demand categories *(thousands of 1958 man-years)*

| | change in employment | percent change in employment |
|---|---|---|
| ordnance 14 | -27,336.0 | -19.24 |
| aircraft and parts 14 | -135,600.0 | -17.90 |
| ships and boats 14 | -26,320.8 | -10.99 |
| radio 13 | -33,036.8 | -6.07 |
| aluminum 10 | -1,707.2 | -2.82 |
| instruments 15 | -5,944.0 | -2.42 |
| copper 10 | -2,022.4 | -2.36 |
| motors, generators 13 | -4,086.4 | -2.04 |
| iron and steel forging 10 | -3,050.4 | -1.31 |
| other nonferrous metals 10 | -1,920.0 | -1.31 |
| metal stamping 11 | -3,526.4 | -1.06 |
| plastics 5 | -1,152.8 | -.70 |
| cutlery, tools 11 | -1,924.0 | -.70 |
| insulated wire and cable 13 | -1,035.2 | -.61 |
| machine tools 12 | -1,055.2 | -.47 |
| petroleum 6 | -1,988.8 | -.38 |
| power transmission equipment 12 | -258.4 | -.29 |
| overseas transportation (water) 17 | -139.2 | -.27 |
| iron and steel 10 | -1,711.2 | -.26 |
| engines and turbines 12 | 38.4 | .04 |
| paper and allied products 4 | 1,945.6 | .36 |
| metal containers 11 | 344.0 | .44 |
| organic chemicals 5 | 800.8 | .46 |
| other transportation 17 | 3,064.8 | .60 |
| rubber and rubber products 7 | 1,592.0 | .63 |
| railroads, trucking 17 | 12,338.4 | .67 |
| electrical equipment (n.e.c.) 13 | 1,388.0 | .67 |
| electric light and power 6 | 3,609.6 | .73 |
| inorganic chemicals 5 | 1,048.0 | .74 |
| industrial machinery 12 | 2,915.2 | .74 |
| fabricated metals 11 | 3,062.4 | .78 |
| nonmetallic minerals 9 | 5,231.2 | .81 |
| coal and coke 6 | 2,186.4 | .92 |

# Table 9-8 (Cont.)

| | change in employment | percent change in employment |
|---|---:|---:|
| plumbing fixtures 11 | 1,073.6 | .93 |
| miscellaneous chemicals 5 | 2,328.0 | .94 |
| lumber, wood products 8 | 9,634.4 | .98 |
| business services 19 | 26,111.2 | 1.00 |
| motor vehicles 14 | 6,437.6 | 1.01 |
| leather and leather products 3 | 4,108.0 | 1.15 |
| medical supplies 5 | 1,694.4 | 1.17 |
| miscellaneous manufacturing industries 16 | 4,548.0 | 1.21 |
| textile mill 2 | 11,252.0 | 1.24 |
| pumps, compressors 12 | 2,124.8 | 1.26 |
| construction 20 | 36,086.4 | 1.36 |
| livestock, poultry 1 | 5,940.8 | 1.40 |
| grain and feed crops 1 | 297.6 | 1.40 |
| electrical appliances 13 | 1,187.2 | 1.44 |
| farm, building, mining machinery 12 | 3,953.6 | 1.44 |
| professional and services 19 | 108,730.4 | 1.46 |
| gas utilities 6 | 2,317.6 | 1.47 |
| trade 18 | 144,533.6 | 1.51 |
| auto and other repairs 19 | 5,402.4 | 1.51 |
| food products 1 | 14,848.0 | 1.53 |
| apparel 2 | 20,199.2 | 1.61 |
| banking, finance 19 | 39,332.0 | 1.66 |
| tobacco, alcoholic beverages 1 | 3,225.6 | 1.69 |
| restaurants, hotels, amusements 19 | 46,824.8 | 1.81 |
| railway equipment 14 | 99.2 | 1.95 |
| business employment: increase | 541,855.2 | 1.42 |
| decrease | −253,815.2 | −6.85 |
| net change | 288,040.0 | .69 |
| total employment: increase | 639,376.5 | 1.41 |
| decrease | −760,135.2 | −11.99 |
| net change | −120,758.7 | −.22 |

impact of disarmament be felt in various parts of the country? What would be the magnitude—and the effect on other industries—of the short-run production bottlenecks that could prevent some industries from supplying the additional output called for by changes in the composition of demand? How would the creation of the additional productive capacities required to meet such increased demand affect the level of output in industries supplying the requisite capital goods?

In making use of the material presented here and in formulating additional questions, it is most important to keep in mind the fact that military expenditures constitute only one factor affecting the state of the U.S. economy. Since a substantial portion of the economic resources now serving military needs could be used to increase private or public investment, the question of the economic implications of disarmament necessarily leads to the more general problem of economic development and growth. Insofar as foreign trade and, in particular, foreign aid enter into the picture, the effects of reduced military expenditures would have to be traced beyond the borders of our own national economy. This means that the present study does not pretend to answer all the questions and suggests the nature of the fact-finding labor that is required if major economic changes are to be subjected to concrete, quantitative analysis.

# 10

## The economic impact—industrial and regional—of an arms cut

### ( 1 9 6 5 )

## I. The problem and its analytical formulation

The object of the computations described in this chapter was to determine what effect a hypothetical reduction in military demand accompanied by a compensating increase in nonmilitary demand would have on the industrial composition and regional distribution of employment in the continental United States. By compensation is meant the maintenance of the total level of employment in the economy.

In a paper published in 1961,[1] input-output analysis was used to estimate the effect of such a change in the structure of final demand on the industrial distribution of the labor force for the country as a whole. The present study carries that inquiry one step further. The impact of the hypothetical shift from military to civilian demand is projected here not only in interindustrial but also in interregional terms. Specifically, the territory of the continental United States has been subdivided into 19 distinct regions, and the shift in the industrial composition of output and employment was assessed for each one of them.

Had we attempted to study each region separately and then simply add the results to arrive at corresponding aggregates for the country as a whole, the total national output figures and the corresponding total input figures for each distinct category of goods and services could not have been expected to match. In other words, the

---

[1]Wassily Leontief and Marvin Hoffenberg, "The Economic Effect of Disarmament," *Scientific American*, April 1961. Included as Chapter 9 in this volume.
Alison Morgan, Karen Polenske, David Simpson, and Edward Tower are coauthors of this chapter.

results of such isolated regional studies would not comprise a consistent picture of the national economy as a whole. The simple scheme of multiregional analysis on which the present computations are based provides for simultaneous balancing of all input-output flows from the point of view of each individual region, as well as for the U.S. economy as a whole.

For some goods—let them be called *local*—a balance between production and consumption tends to be established separately within each region; for other goods—let them be identified as *national*—such a balance typically is achieved only for the country as a whole. Within each region the output of a national good might exceed or fall short of its total input, the deficit or surplus being evened out by exports to or imports from other regions. Retail trade and auto repair services are characteristically local industries, while coal mining and aircraft manufacturing are typically national. The difference between the two obviously should be explained in terms of the relative mobility or transportability of their output.

To separate national industries from local, all sectors were arranged in order of the increasing magnitude of interregional, as compared with intraregional, trade of their respective products. Then, an admittedly somewhat arbitrary cut was made across that array, setting apart the local industries, serving mainly users located within the region in which production occurs, from the national industries, supplying the entire national or even international market, whose products typically are being shipped for this reason in comparatively large amounts across regional lines.[2]

The multiregional input-output computation itself can be visualized best as being performed in three distinct, successive rounds. The first consists of a conventional input-output calculation designed to determine the direct and indirect effects of the given shift from military to nonmilitary final demands on the total output of all—local as well as of national—goods for the country as a whole. The regional distribution of these total figures is determined in the second and third rounds. All basic information on the input structure of each local or national industry used again and again throughout these computations stems from the same large input-output table of the American economy. This common source of structural data ensures the internal consistency of all the final results.

[2]The concluding observations at the end of this chapter describe a possible refinement of this approach which introduces a graduated distinction between national, regional, and subregional industries and goods.

For national industries the regional apportionment of the increase or the reduction in the total U.S. output is based in each instance on a simple but, in the first approximation, well-justified assumption of a uniform percentage change. For example, if the first-stage computation indicates that as a result of curtailed military purchases and a simultaneous expansion of deliveries serving various types of final civilian demand, the total U.S. output of electronic equipment will fall by 5 percent, then in the second stage that aggregate cut is allocated among the different regions on the assumption of an equal 5 percent cut applied across the board. That presupposes, of course, knowledge of the actual output and employment levels maintained by the national industries in each region before the shift occurs.

The third and last step determines the geographic distribution of changes in the level of activities of local industries producing goods for which the balance between supply and demand tends to be maintained within each region with relatively limited recourse to interregional trade. The input requirements that must be covered in each region by the output of its local industries comprise (1) deliveries to final military and civilian users located in the same region, (2) input requirements of the national industries operating in it, and (3) the input requirements of the local industries themselves.

Thus, the calculation of regional outputs of local industries requires not only a knowledge of final demand for the United States as a whole but also a breakdown of military and nonmilitary final demand by regions. While changes in the level of final deliveries of steel, chemicals, and other national goods need be specified only for the country as a whole, the given shifts in military procurement and civilian purchases of electric power, gas and water, office supplies, and other local goods have to be specified separately for each region before the analysis of their regional impact can begin. The amounts of local goods absorbed in each particular region by national industries operating in it can be ascertained easily by applying appropriate sets of technical input coefficients to the regional output figures derived for all national industries in the previous, second round of computations.

The regional output levels of local industries, finally, can be derived through separate input-output computations in which the deliveries of local goods to final users located in each region and to national industries operating within it play the role of a given bill of goods.

In this last stage of multiregional analysis, households are treated as one of the local industries—the largest one, in fact. The output of

that industry consists of labor services of various types. In contrast
to previous computations of this kind, for reasons of practical convenience the quantities of labor services are measured in this study
not in man-years but rather in terms of the total wage and salary
payments received for them (in 1958 rates of pay).

The inputs of the "households" sector are consumer goods purchased by it. Its input structure, like the input structure of any other
industry, can be described accordingly by an array of consumption
coefficients, each of which represents the amount of one particular
type of good absorbed by the "households" sector per unit of its
own output, that is, per dollar of salaries and wages received by it.

That means, of course, that in the third stage of the multiregional
input-output computations, the given regional bill of goods is redefined so as to include all military and nonmilitary governmental purchases and private investment expenditures, but not the private consumption expenditures. Since "households" are treated at this stage
of the computations as one of the local industries, all goods absorbed
by them appear, not as final deliveries, but rather as components of
that part of all output of each sector that serves indirect demand.

The internal consistency of the entire procedure is demonstrated
by the fact that, if separated from deliveries to other local and all
the national industries and summed for the country as a whole, these
regional inputs into "households" will match exactly the private
consumption column of the final bill of goods introduced into the
computations in its very first stage.

That bill of goods itself, of course, must reflect the anticipated effect
of a hypothetical reduction of military and a corresponding increase
in civilian expenditures. For purposes of the present analysis, such
a shift has been assumed to have occurred in the year 1958, which
at the present time is the latest year for which a detailed input-output table of the U.S. economy has been compiled. The final bill of
goods is represented by three components: military purchases, private household consumption, and nonhousehold civilian final
demand.[3] The latter demand "contains" nonmilitary deliveries to

[3]Morris R. Goldman, Martin L. Marimont, and Beatrice N. Vaccara, "The Interindustry
Structure of the United States: A Report on the 1958 Input-Output Study," *Survey of
Current Business* (Washington, D.C.: U.S. Department of Commerce, November 1964) A
detailed description of the definitions and composition of the final demand vectors used
in this study is given in section IV. The vectors only include estimates of final purchases
from endogenous industries; for example, the military vector does *not* include purchases
from new construction since this is exogenous in this study. Thus, the sum of the elements
included in the vectors does not represent all final demand. See footnotes to Table 10-5,
this volume.

the federal state, and local governments; private and public gross investment; and net exports.

The hypothetical cut in military expenditures is visualized to take the form of a 20 percent across-the-board reduction in each kind of military purchase. With the total 1958 defense expenditure included in the military vector amounting to $31.3 billion, that means reducing it by $6.3 billion to $25.0 billion. The compensating rise in nonmilitary demand was assumed, on the other hand, to be represented by a proportional across-the-board increase in all kinds of nonmilitary final deliveries. Its total magnitude is chosen deliberately with the view of maintaining the total level of employment, or rather the combined wage and salary bill of all industries, at its original—that is, the actually observed—1958 level.

Had the military shopping list contained the same goods and in the same proportions as the civilian, each million dollars' worth of additional nonmilitary demand could reemploy the same number of hands and heads—commanding the same amount of wages and salaries—as would have been released by each million dollars' worth of military budget cut. However, the military product mix is very different from the civilian. A comparison of the results of two auxiliary input-output computations has shown that in 1958 the total wages and salaries paid for all the labor engaged directly and indirectly in production of $1 million worth of goods and services combined in the proportion demanded by the military are some 21 percent larger than wages and salaries paid for labor imputs required for production of $1 million worth of outputs delivered in amounts reflecting the average product mix of all nonmilitary final users.

Thus, it would take $7.6 billion of additional civilian demand to compensate the cancellation of $6.3 billion worth of military spending. Nonmilitary final demands as defined for this study amounted in 1958 to $418.0 billion. Stated in percentage terms, the shift in the economic impact as described below combines a 20 percent cut in military purchases with a 1.8 percent increase in the amount of goods and services absorbed by each of the two categories of final civilian users.

With the total labor input and wage bill remaining constant, a 1.8 percent increase in the amount of all goods and services allocated to private consumption can be described as a proportional increase in all consumption coefficients. Accordingly, the column of technical coefficients used in the last stage of the multiregional input-output computations to describe the input requirements of "households" was obtained by raising by 1.8 percent the consumption coefficients derived from the 1958 U.S. input-output table.

A translation of the theoretical scheme described above into concise mathematical language is presented below. A reader not interested in details of computational procedure can skip this and proceed directly to the summary of the principal conclusions of this study.

## II. Mathematical formulation of a linear multiregional input-output system[4]

### Notation

The multiregional economy described below consists of $n$ national and $(l - 1)$ local industries. When "households" is treated as an endogenous sector, the total number of local sectors is $l$. The locational distribution of all inputs and outputs is specified in terms of $r$ distinct regions.

The quantities of all goods, including the labor services, are measured in physical units defined in each instance as the amount purchasable for \$1 at 1958 prices.

Capital letters are used to designate rectangular and square matrices, lower-case italic letters describe column and row vectors, and Greek letters define scalar magnitudes, except matrix dimensions, which are in parentheses.

$A =$      square, $(n + l - 1)$ by $(n + l - 1)$ matrix of input coefficients of all national and local industries, excluding "Households"

$A^\circ =$ 

$$\left[\begin{array}{c|c} A^\circ_{NN} & A^\circ_{NL} \\ \hline A^\circ_{LN} & A^\circ_{LL} \end{array}\right]$$

augmented square, $(n + l)$ by $(n + l)$ matrix of input coefficients of all sectors including "households," partitioned into the following

$A^\circ_{NN} =$      square, $n$ by $n$, submatrix of input coefficients describing flows from national to national industries

$A^\circ_{NL} =$      rectangular, $n$ by $l$, submatrix of input coefficients describing flows from national to local sectors, including "households"

$A^\circ_{LN} =$      rectangular, $l$ by $n$, submatrix of input coefficients describing flows from local industries, including "households," to national industries.

---

[4]The first—materially different but formally similar to the present—version of the system was presented in Wassily Leontief (ed.), *Studies in the Structure of the American Economy* (New York: Oxford University Press, 1953), Chapter 4.

$A_{LL}^\circ =$     square, $l$ by $l$, submatrix of input coefficients describing flows from local to local industries, including "households"

$w' =$     row vector of $n + l - 1$ labor input coefficients of all national and local industries, excluding "households"

$c_0^\circ =$     column vector of the original $n + l$ consumption coefficients, that is, the input coefficients of "households," including the coefficient describing inputs from "households" to "households"

$c_1^\circ =$     column vector of $n + l$ consumption coefficients, including the input from "households" to "households," adjusted to the change in the level of living that has resulted from the shift in final demand

$x =$     column vector of $n + l - 1$ total outputs of national and local industries, excluding "households"

$x^\circ = \begin{bmatrix} x_N \\ \hline x_L^\circ \end{bmatrix} =$     column vector of $n + l$ total outputs of all sectors partitioned into:
$x_N$ column vector of $n$ total outputs of national industries
$x_L^\circ$ column vector of $l$ total outputs of local industries, including "households"

$\hat{X}_N =$     diagonal matrix with the total outputs of national industries entered on its principal diagonal in the same order in which they are shown in $x_N$

$m, h, q =$     three column vectors of $n + l - 1$ quantities, measured in 1958 dollars, of national and local goods, excluding labor, representing, respectively, the military, the household, and the nonhousehold civilian components of the original, total final bill of goods

$m^\circ, q^\circ =$     two column vectors of $n + l$ quantities of military and non-household civilian final demand, including labor

$v_M, v_H, v_Q =$     three amounts of labor directly entering, respectively, into the military, the household, and the nonhousehold civilian demand components of the original, total final bill of goods

$\hat{M}_L^\circ, \hat{Q}_L^\circ =$     two diagonal, $l$ by $l$, matrices of quantities of local goods, including labor, representing, respectively, the military and the nonhousehold civilian component of the original, total final bill of goods

$X_N^R =$     rectangular, $n$ by $r$, matrix, each column of which shows the output levels of all national industries in one particular region

$P_N =$     rectangular, $n$ by $r$, matrix, each column of which shows what fractions of the total output of each of the national industries are produced in one particular region

$D_M^\circ, D_Q^\circ =$     rectangular, $l$ by $r$, matrices, the columns of which represent, respectively, proportions of the total military and of nonhousehold civilian final demand for the products of dif-

ferent local industries, including "households," absorbed in
one particular region

$\alpha =$     the ratio of the magnitude of each element of total final military demand after the shift from military to nonmilitary
expenditure to its magnitude before the shift

$\beta =$     the ratio of the magnitude of each element of the household
and of the nonhousehold civilian components of total final
demand after the shift from military to nommilitary expenditures to its magnitude before the shift

## Derivation or computational formulas

Basic relationship between the total final bill of goods—comprising
deliveries to household, nonhousehold civilian, and military final
demand—and the total outputs of the national and local industries,
excluding "households":

$$(10\text{-}1) \qquad x = (I - A)^{-1}(h + q + m)$$

Corresponding relationship between the original, total level of
employment and the combined labor inputs indirectly absorbed by
all national and local industries plus those directly entering final
demand:

$$(10\text{-}2) \qquad v = w'x + v_H + v_Q + v_M$$

Relationship between the new final bill of goods and the new total
level of employment that—by assumption—equals the original
level of employment:

$$(10\text{-}3) \qquad v = w'(I - A)^{-1}[\beta(h + q) + \alpha m] + \alpha v_M + \beta(v_H + v_Q)$$

Solution of equation (10-3) for $\beta$, with all other magnitudes
appearing on its right-hand side considered as given:

$$(10\text{-}4) \qquad \beta = \frac{v - \alpha[w'(I - A)^{-1}m + v_M]}{w'(I - A)^{-1}(h + q) + v_H + v_Q}$$

Derivation of the new vector of the input coefficients of the
"households" sector through adjustment of the original vector to
the shift in the level of living:

$$(10\text{-}5) \qquad c_1^\circ = c_0^\circ \beta$$

Derivation of the new[5] total output levels of national and local
industries, including "households":

$$(10\text{-}6) \qquad x^\circ = (I - A^\circ)^{-1}(\beta q^\circ + \alpha m^\circ)$$

[5]Strictly speaking, a subscript should be used to distinguish old and new outputs.

Derivation of the new regional outputs of national industries from their new total outputs:

$$(10\text{-}7) \qquad X_N^R = \hat{X}_N P_N$$

Derivation of the new regional outputs of local industries, including "households":

$$(10\text{-}8) \qquad X_L^{\circ R} = (I - A_{LL}^{\circ})^{-1}[A_{LN}^{\circ} \cdot X_N^R + (\beta \hat{Q}_L^{\circ} \cdot \hat{D}_Q^{\circ} + \alpha \hat{M}_L^{\circ} \hat{D}_M^{\circ})]$$

The sum of the last two terms is a rectangular, $l$ by $r$, matrix, each column of which represents the new combined military and non-household civilian final demand for the products of local industries—including "households"—in one particular region. The multiplication of $\beta \hat{Q}_L^{\circ}$ by $\hat{D}_Q^{\circ}$ and $\alpha \hat{M}_L$ by $\hat{D}_{ML}^{\circ}$ are analogous to that performed on the right-hand side of equation (10-7); it involves application of given sets of regional distribution coefficients to previously obtained total figures of final military and nonhousehold civilian deliveries of each kind of local good. Any other method of determining the amounts of local goods absorbed by military and nonhousehold civilian final demand in each region would be equally acceptable, provided the regional figures add up to the corresponding elements of the diagonal matrix $(\beta \hat{Q}_L^{\circ} + \alpha \hat{M}_L^{\circ})$, that is, provided the sum of all regional deliveries of each local good equals the corresponding total amount of military and nonhousehold civilian deliveries for the country as a whole.

One of the $l$ rows of the rectangular matrix $X_L^{\circ R}$ on the left-hand side of equation (10-8) describes the new regional outputs of the "households" sector, that is, the level of employment attained in each region after the hypothetical shift in the relative magnitude of the military and of the nonmilitary components of final demand.

The formulas presented above describe the computations of regional output and employment figures after the shift from military to nonmilitary expenditures. If the proportionality factors $\alpha$ and $\beta$ are set equal to 1, the formulas describe the state of the economy and, in particular, the level and regional distribution of output and employment before the shift.

## III. Summary of the principal findings

When the numerical conclusions presented are based on a straightforward application of a systematically developed theoretical scheme, the results need little additional explanation. In the present instance most of the explaining was done when the procedure was described by which the primary factual information fed into an analytical machine is transformed into final figures describing the results of the entire computation. They appear in the form of tables which describe in great detail changes in the interindustrial and the interregional distribution of output and employment that would be brought about by a hypothetical 20 percent reduction in the military bill of goods, combined with a compensating proportional increase in the nonmilitary components of the final bill of goods. This nonmilitary demand comprises consumption by private households, total investment (which includes new construction), and nonmilitary governmental expenditures.

A detailed explanation of sources and methods used to obtain the basic matrix of input-output coefficients of all national and local industries, to ascertain the actual composition of the military and nonmilitary vectors of the U.S. final bill of goods for the year 1958, and, last but not least, to determine the regional distribution of the outputs of national industries and of the final military and nonmilitary demand for locally produced goods will be found in section IV of this chapter.

The number of industries in terms of which the productive apparatus of the American economy is described is 58, and the number of regions into which the territory of the continental United States was subdivided for purposes of this description is 19; thus, the total number of output and employment figures resulting from this multiregional input-output computation could exceed 1000. In fact, since not all industries are present in all regions, the detailed tables reproduced at the end of this chapter contain a certain number of empty cells.

Since the hypothetical shift in the composition of final demand was balanced so as to leave the overall level of employment for the country as a whole the same as it was before, its economic impact takes the form of shifts in the labor force among different industries and among different regions.

The magnitudes of changes in output and employment that we are about to examine are—when expressed in relative terms—at most on the order of a few percentage points up or a few percentage points down; in most instances they are even smaller. Considering, however, that an unemployment rate of 5.5 percent commonly is interpreted as a sign of serious malfunctioning of our economic system and that an eventual reduction of that figure to 4 percent has been recognized as one of the major goals of national economic policies, even a change of one-half of 1 percent in employment level in

## Table 10-1

Percentage changes[a] in output and employment[b] by industries, after a compensated[c] 20 percent cut in armament expenditures[d]

| Sector Numbers[e] | Industry | Percentage Change (%) |
|---|---|---|
| 36N | aircraft | −16.05 |
| 40N | ordnance | −15.42 |
| 41N | research and development | −13.26 |
| 34N | electronics equipment | − 5.40 |
| 29N | nonferrous metals | − 2.21 |
| 38N | instruments | − 1.59 |
| 32N | electrical apparatus | − 0.92 |
| 37N | other transportation equipment | − 0.23 |
| 28N | iron and steel | − 0.04 |
| 31N | nonelectrical machinery | − 0.03 |
| 18N | chemicals | 0.15 |
| 13L | maintenance construction | 0.20 |
| 24N | rubber, plastics | 0.30 |
| 33N | appliances, lighting | 0.34 |
| 22N | oil fields | 0.38 |
| 23N | petroleum products | 0.45 |
| 3L | transportation | 0.48 |
| 21N | paint | 0.48 |
| 30N | fabricated metals | 0.54 |
| 11N | miscellaneous fabricated textiles | 0.54 |
| 19N | plastics, synthetics | 0.59 |
| 26N | glass | 0.81 |
| 16N | paper | 0.83 |
| 17N | paperboard containers | 0.93 |
| 9N | miscellaneous textiles, rugs | 0.97 |
| 14L | government enterprises | 0.98 |
| 5N | coal mining | 0.98 |
| 13N | wood containers | 1.05 |
| 27N | stone and clay | 1.10 |
| 1L | printing, publishing | 1.12 |
| 10L | business services | 1.14 |
| 8N | fabrics, yarn | 1.19 |
| 15N | office furniture | 1.19 |
| 20N | drugs | 1.21 |
| 35N | motor vehicles | 1.21 |
| 39N | miscellaneous manufacturing | 1.23 |
| 2L | electricity, gas, water | 1.24 |
| 12N | lumber, wood products | 1.26 |
| 5L | communications | 1.26 |
| 14N | household furniture | 1.27 |
| 12L | medical, educational services | 1.31 |
| 3N | forestry, fisheries | 1.33 |
| 4L | trade | 1.40 |
| 6L | finance, insurance | 1.48 |
| 9L | auto repair services | 1.48 |
| 8L | personal services | 1.56 |

## Table 10.1 (Cont.)

| Sector Numbers[e] | Industry | Percentage Change (%) |
|---|---|---|
| 25N | leather | 1.57 |
| 7L | real estate, rentals | 1.57 |
| 2N | other agriculture | 1.65 |
| 11L | amusements | 1.66 |
| 10N | apparel | 1.66 |
| 6N | food and kindred products | 1.66 |
| 1N | livestock | 1.67 |
| 7N | tobacco | 1.76 |
| 17L | households[f] | 1.81 |
| 4N | agricultural services | 2.14 |

[a]Each figure represents the change in output and employment in each industry as a percentage of total output and employment in that industry before the arms cut.
[b]Employment and its regional distribution are measured in each industry by labor earnings.
[c]Compensation is assumed to consist of a uniform proportional increase in all components of nonmilitary final demand sufficiently large to maintain the aggregate employment in all sectors (consequently in all regions) taken together unchanged.
[d]Source of data: Tables 10-9 and 10-10.
[e]Note that the two local sectors that are dummy industries have been omitted from this ranking. N refers to national industry number, L to local industry number.
[f]Note that this percentage reflects the 1.81 percent increase in all consumption coefficients. It represents the change in employment of employees in households such as domestic help or baby sitters.

one region or another must be taken to represent a noteworthy shift. The percentages to be examined may not meet that degree of accuracy, but they should indicate the direction of change in regional employment levels.

Table 10-1 describes the impact of a postulated demilitarization of the final demand in terms of individual industries. The percentage figures show that of the 56 sectors listed,[6] only 10 will experience a reduction in total output and employment; "aircraft," "ordnance," and, significantly, "research and development" will take large cuts of over 13 percent, while "electronic equipment," "nonferrous metals," and "instruments" will drop between 1.59 and 5.40 percent. Among the 4 other industries registering losses rather than gains is "iron and steel," which, with its token 0.04 percent cut, barely maintains the traditional standing as an armament industry. Positive changes, on the other hand, are distributed more evenly and among a much larger number of industries.

Food products and other soft consumer goods and services gain

[6]Two local dummy sectors, 15L "office supplies" and 16L "business travel and entertainment," are not included in this tabulation.

most, and basic industries such as "chemicals," "petroleum products," and "paper" gain least, with "printing and publishing," "motor vehicles," and other branches of processing showing intermediate gains a few points above and below 1 percent. The skewness of the entire distribution, specifically the bunched negative and widespread positive shifts, reflect, of course, the contrast between the specialized nature of military demand and the broad product mix of the civilian demand.

The regional projection of the economic impact of disarmament is summarized in Table 10-2. As can be seen from the percentage entries, in 10 of the 19 regions employment can be expected to contract, while in the other 9 it will expand. The largest loss, $-1.85$ percent, will be experienced in California, and the biggest gain, $+1.54$ percent, will be in the midwestern region comprising Minnesota and the two Dakotas.

Neither the shift from one industry to another nor the move from

## Table 10-2

Percentage change in output and employment by region after a compensated 20 percent cut in armament expenditures

| Region Number | Region | Total Net Change (%) (1) | Total Gross Increase (%) (2) | Total Gross Decrease (%) (3) |
|---|---|---|---|---|
| 19 | California | $-1.85$ | 0.54 | 2.39 |
| 16 | Colorado, New Mexico | $-1.40$ | 0.67 | 2.07 |
| 17 | Arizona, Nevada, Utah | $-1.35$ | 0.69 | 2.04 |
| 9 | Maryland, Virginia, Delaware, W. Virginia, D.C. | $-1.36$ | 0.66 | 2.02 |
| 14 | Texas | $-1.00$ | 0.73 | 1.73 |
| 18 | Oregon, Washington | $-0.81$ | 0.91 | 1.72 |
| 12 | Mississippi, Alabama | $-0.73$ | 0.89 | 1.62 |
| 8 | Georgia, North and South Carolina | $-0.57$ | 1.02 | 1.59 |
| 10 | Florida | $-0.43$ | 1.12 | 1.55 |
| 1 | New England | $-0.06$ | 1.05 | 1.11 |
| 13 | Arkansas, Louisiana, Oklahoma | 0.21 | 1.26 | 1.05 |
| 7 | Kansas, Iowa, Nebraska, Missouri | 0.44 | 1.46 | 1.02 |
| 11 | Kentucky, Tennessee | 0.37 | 1.31 | 0.94 |
| 2 | New York | 0.66 | 1.44 | 0.78 |
| 3 | New Jersey, Pennsylvania | 0.53 | 1.26 | 0.73 |
| 15 | Idaho, Montana, Wyoming | 1.28 | 1.83 | 0.55 |
| 4 | Michigan, Ohio | 0.89 | 1.43 | 0.54 |
| 5 | Indiana, Illinois, Wisconsin | 0.93 | 1.46 | 0.53 |
| 6 | Minnesota, North and South Dakota | 1.54 | 1.96 | 0.42 |
|   | Total United States | — | 1.16 | 1.16 |

one region to another, considered separately, measures the total magnitude of readjustments that will be required of the members of each regional labor force. Such a measure must take both into account simultaneously. What is needed is a figure that shows what proportion of all men and women initially employed in all the different industries operating in a given region will lose their jobs and will have to look for new jobs in a different industry in the same region or in another region; in the latter case, the jobs they find in another region might or might not be in the same industry in which they worked before.

The figures entered in column 3 of Table 10-2 accordingly show what proportion of all wage and salary earners will receive discharge notices and will have to look for new jobs. To emphasize the importance of these figures, the sequence in which the 19 regions are listed on the table reflects the order of decreasing magnitude of these "gross displacement" rates.

California is again at the head of the procession with the highest rate of 2.39 percent, and Minnesota with North and South Dakota ranks lowest with only 0.42 percent. A comparison of entries in column 1 with those in column 3 reveals that one region can experience a larger expansion in the total level of employment than another but at the same time be subject to a greater stress as measured by the gross displacement figure. According to the computations the New York region, for example, would expand its total employed labor force by 0.66 percent while the corresponding figure for the Kentucky and Tennessee region is 0.37 percent. At the same time, 0.78 percent of the original job holders in New York would have to change their jobs as against 0.94 percent in Kentucky and Tennessee.

Employment agencies might be interested in the total number of new jobs created in a particular region, that is, in the sum total of the increases in employment figures of the industries expected to expand in that region. Expressed as percentages of total labor force initially employed in the region, these "gross job gains" figures are entered in column 2. Strictly speaking, they do not present us with any new information since by definition they can be obtained simply by adding pairwise the corresponding entries in column 1 and column 3.

The regional impacts of disarmament as summarized in Table 10-2 are described graphically in Figure 10-1. Each set of bars depicts the impact of the same hypothetical shift from military to nonmilitary demand on the employment situation in one of the 19 regions.

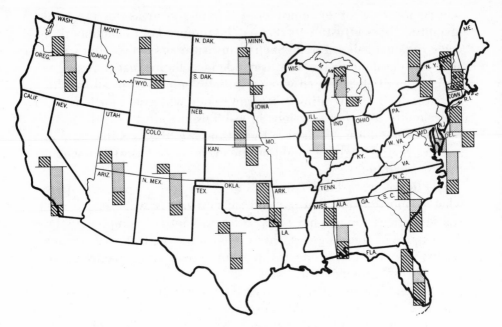

**Figure 10-1**

Percentage change in output and employment resulting from a hypothetical 20 percent reduction in military spending and a compensating rise in
civilian final demand. (Bars extending above the baseline represent
increases; those extending below the baseline represent decreases. The
stippled portions of the bars represent the net increase or decrease.)

The total length of the bar extended downward from the horizontal
baseline measures the gross job loss (described in column 3 in Table
10-2). The total length of a bar extended upward represents the corresponding gross gain in jobs (described in column 2 of Table 10-
2). The solidly shaded section of the longer of the two bars shows
the difference between their lengths; in other words, it measures
the change in the total level of employment in a particular region.
That change is negative when the solid bar extends below the horizontal line, and it is positive when it is above.

The geographic picture confirms the well-known fact that most of
the resources serving final military demand directly or indirectly
come from the western, southwestern, and southeastern regions,
while the Midwest, the Great Lakes region, and the North Atlantic
and New England states depend to a large extent on civilian
demand. A cut in military expenditures, accompanied by an expansion of the nonmilitary bill of goods, thus will create more serious

readjustment problems in the first than in the second group of regions.

## IV. Data and methods of computation

The basic concern of this study was to determine the regional, combined with the industrial, effects of a reduction in armaments. Table 10-3 toward the end of this chapter gives the industrial classification used. The aggregation of states into 19 regions was chosen to make the data collection and the computations of manageable size while maintaining sufficient detail to detect regional differences.

The $A$ matrix consisted of a domestic-base, 1958 80-order interindustry coefficient matrix made available by the Office of Business Economics in November 1964 and aggregated to 60 sectors at the Harvard Economic Research Project.[7] New construction coefficients were removed from the endogenous sectors to form a final demand column. Row distributions of final demand were used to derive the final demand columns other than new construction and military.[8]

The next step was to estimate vector $m$ of military final demands shown later in this chapter in Table 10-5. Since more specific data for the military final demand vector were unobtainable at the time this study was begun, the estimates for military final demand were developed working with adjusted control totals[9] given for various sectors in the military prime contracts[10] and with the 1958 federal government vector itself. The military final demand vector was made so that military purchases from any industry did not exceed federal government spending for products of that industry. Whenever a degree of arbitrariness entered into the determination of components of military final demand, the estimate was biased toward the metal industries.

[7]The 60-sector classification is given in Table 10-3, distinguishing between national and local industries. A column of import coefficients also was obtained from the Department of Commerce for use in the calculations.

[8]The row distributions are given in "The Interindustry Structure of the United States," *Survey of Current Business*, November 1964, Table I, p. 21. The calculation of household final demand is designated as vector $h$, while the final demands of the federal government (other than military), state and local government, net inventory change, gross private capital formation, competitive imports, exports, and new construction are referred to as a group called nonhousehold civilian vector $q$. Refer to footnotes for Table 10-5.

[9]The fiscal year was adjusted to a calendar year base; also, "actions of less than $10,000" were distributed proportionally over prime military contract figures. These adjusted figures were used as control totals in determining how much military spending there was within groups of industries.

[10]*Military Prime Contract Awards and Subcontract Payments,* Office of the Secretary of Defense, (July 1962–June 1963), Tables 6 and 7.

# Table 10-3, Part I

## Industrial classification scheme

| National Industry | Office of Business Economics 80-Order Sector[a] | National Industries |
|---|---|---|
| 1N | 1 | livestock |
| 2N | 2 | other agriculture |
| 3N | 3 | forestry and fisheries |
| 4N | 4 | agriculture services |
| 5N | 7 | coal mining |
| 6N | 14 | food |
| 7N | 15 | tobacco |
| 8N | 16 | fabrics, yarn |
| 9N | 17 | rugs, miscellaneous textiles |
| 10N | 18 | apparel |
| 11N | 19 | miscellaneous fabricated textile products |
| 12N | 20 | lumber and wood products |
| 13N | 21 | wooden containers |
| 14N | 22 | household furniture |
| 15N | 23 | office furniture |
| 16N | 24 | paper |
| 17N | 25 | paperboard containers |
| 18N | 10, 27 | chemicals |
| 19N | 28 | plastics, synthetics |
| 20N | 29 | drugs |
| 21N | 30 | paint |
| 22N | 8 | oil fields |
| 23N | 31 | petroleum products |
| 24N | 32 | rubber |
| 25N | 33, 34 | leather |
| 26N | 35 | glass |
| 27N | 9, 36 | stone and clay |
| 28N | 5, 37 | iron and steel |
| 29N | 6, 38 | nonferrous metals |
| 30N | 39–42 | fabricated metals |
| 31N | 43–52 | nonelectrical machinery |
| 32N | 53, 58 | electrical apparatus |
| 33N | 54, 55 | appliances and lighting equipment |
| 34N | 56, 57 | communications and electronic equipment |
| 35N | 59 | motor vehicles |
| 36N | 60 | aircraft |
| 37N | 61 | other transportation equipment |
| 38N | 62, 63 | instruments |
| 39N | 64 | miscellaneous manufacturing |
| 40N | 13 | ordnance |
| 41N | 74 | research and development |

[a]Classification for Office of Business Economics 80-order sector is taken from "The Interindustry Structure of the United States," *Survey of Current Business*, November 1964.

220

## Table 10-3, Part II

### Industrial classification scheme

| Local Industry | Office of Business Economics 80-Order Sector[a] | Local Industries |
|---|---|---|
| 1L | 26 | printing and publishing |
| 2L | 68 | electricity, gas, water |
| 3L | 65 | transportation, warehousing |
| 4L | 69 | trade |
| 5L | 66, 67 | communications |
| 6L | 70 | finance, insurance |
| 7L | 71 | real estate and rentals |
| 8L | 72 | personal and repair services, hotels |
| 9L | 75 | auto repair services |
| 10L | 73 | business services |
| 11L | 76 | amusements |
| 12L | 77 | medical and educational services |
| 13L | 12 | maintenance construction |
| 14L | 78, 79 | government enterprises |
| 15L | 82 | office supplies |
| 16L | 81 | business travel, entertainment |
| 17L | | households |

[a]Classification for Office of Business Economics 80-order sector is taken from "The Interindustry Structure of the United States," *Survey of Current Business*, November 1964.

All sectors with zero federal government final demand were assigned zero military final demand.[11] In the case of "aircraft" (36N) and "ordnance" (40N), the entire federal government final demand was put in the military final demand vector. For the remaining sectors, each item in military prime contracts that served as a control total for military purchases from a particular group of industries was distributed in the proportion the sectors were to one another in the total federal government bill of goods, or in the proportion that the Department of Defense payrolls were to other federal government payrolls.[12]

The three vectors of final demand are shown in Tables 10-4 and

[11]These include "livestock" (1N), "coal mining," (5N), "tobacco" (7N), "oil fields" (22N), "finance" (6L). "Forestry and fisheries" (3N) and "lumber" (12N) had negative federal government final demands but were assigned zero military final demand since it appeared that the military would not provide inputs to these industries. "Crops" (2N) also was assigned zero military final demand since the large entry for this sector in the total federal government vector represented operations of the Commodity Credit Corporation. Since sectors 1N, 2N, and 3N now had zero elements in the military vector, "agricultural services" (4N) also was assumed to have zero military final demand.

[12]When it could be assumed that military and nonmilitary expenditures would parallel closely the number of workers in each sector.

# Table 10-4, Part I

Consumption and labor coefficients for national industries

| National Industry | Consumption Coefficient[a] | Labor Coefficient[b] |
|---|---|---|
| 1N  livestock | .0065 | .3050° |
| 2N  other agriculture | .0076 | .2926 |
| 3N  forestry and fisheries | .0009 | .3437° |
| 4N  agricultural services | | .3115° |
| 5N  coal mining | .0008 | .4405 |
| 6N  food | .1423 | .1562 |
| 7N  tobacco | .0133 | .0691 |
| 8N  fabrics, yarn | .0022 | .2221 |
| 9N  rugs, miscellaneous textiles | .0024 | .2252 |
| 10N  apparel | .0347 | .3441 |
| 11N  miscellaneous fabricated textile products | .0035 | .2266 |
| 12N  lumber and wood products | .0005 | .3211 |
| 13N  wooden containers | | .3358 |
| 14N  household furniture | .0075 | .3511 |
| 15N  office furniture | .0004 | .4101 |
| 16N  paper | .0027 | .2609 |
| 17N  paperboard containers | .0001 | .2928 |
| 18N  chemicals | .0007 | .2484 |
| 19N  plastics, synthetics | .0000 | .2270 |
| 20N  drugs | .0116 | .2043 |
| 21N  paint | .0001 | .2427 |
| 22N  oil fields | | .2122 |
| 23N  petroleum products | .0226 | .1142 |
| 24N  rubber | .0040 | .3142 |
| 25N  leather | .0081 | .3648 |
| 26N  glass | .0004 | .4028 |
| 27N  stone and clay | .0007 | .3454 |
| 28N  iron and steel | .0001 | .3128 |
| 29N  nonferrous metals | .0000 | .2300 |
| 30N  fabricated metals | .0022 | .3490 |
| 31N  nonelectrical machinery | .0015 | .3902 |
| 32N  electrical apparatus | .0009 | .3877 |
| 33N  appliances and lighting equipment | .0086 | .2903 |
| 34N  communications and electronic equipment | .0047 | .3699 |
| 35N  motor vehicles | .0286 | .1865 |
| 36N  aircraft | .0001 | .4136°° |
| 37N  other transportation equipment | .0023 | .3868 |
| 38N  instruments | .0025 | .3928 |
| 39N  miscellaneous manufacturing | .0079 | .3447 |
| 40N  ordnance | .0005 | .2972°° |
| 41N  research and development | | .0568 |

## Table 10-4, Part II

Consumption and labor coefficients for local industries

|  | Local Industry | Consumption Coefficient[a] | Labor Coefficient[b] |
|---|---|---|---|
| 1L | printing and publishing | .0076 | .4624 |
| 2L | electricity, gas, water | .0251 | .1979 |
| 3L | transportation, warehousing | .0262 | .5181 |
| 4L | trade | .1900 | .6152 |
| 5L | communications | .0134 | .4315 |
| 6L | finance, insurance | .0365 | .4891 |
| 7L | real estate and rentals | .1242 | .0516 |
| 8L | personal and repair services, hotels | .0294 | .6003 |
| 9L | auto repair services | .0136 | .1966 |
| 10L | business services | .0058 | .3975 |
| 11L | amusements | .0102 | .3590 |
| 12L | medical and educational services | .0634 | .6131° |
| 13L | maintenance construction |  | .3049 |
| 14L | government enterprises | .0029 | .4488°° |
| 15L | office supplies |  |  |
| 16L | business travel, entertainment |  |  |
| 17L | households | .0108 | .0108° |

[a]Column vector of personal consumption expenditure coefficients which became endogenous for the last part of computations.

Consumption coefficients obtained from row distribution of final demands: "The Interindustry Structure of the United States," *Survey of Current Business*, November 1964, Table I, p. 21.

[b]Row vector of labor input coefficients after adjusting for interest and dividends. Those marked with ° were not adjusted for interest and dividends. Those marked °° had special calculations made for interest and dividends.

Labor coefficients: sources used to obtain uninflated coefficients are given in Table 10-12.

10-5.[13] The next step, represented earlier as equation (10-3), was to establish the control total, $v$, the aggregate level of direct and indirect labor earnings in 1958, which was to remain constant throughout the computations. This total included direct earnings in household, military, and nonhousehold civilian final demand categories, as well as the direct and indirect earnings received from the endogenous sectors. Earnings were defined to include wages and salaries and income of unincorporated enterprises, with a fixed markup of 20 percent in all but a few sectors to account for consumer expenditures by those with incomes from sources other than employment. Such an even markup does not affect the role of earnings as a measure of labor input.

Since $v$ was to remain constant, the drop in total labor earnings caused by the decrease in military spending had to be offset by an increase in the other components of final demand which would pro-

[13]"Housholds" was separated from the other final demands because in the later calculations this sector would become endogenous.

# Table 10-5, Part I

Final demands for national industries

| | National Industry | Military[a] ($ millions) | Nonhousehold Civilian ($ millions)[b] |
|---|---|---|---|
| 1N | livestock | | 396.4 |
| 2N | other agriculture | | 3170.3 |
| 3N | forestry and fisheries | | − 393.0 |
| 4N | agricultural services | | |
| 5N | coal mining | | 367.0 |
| 6N | food | 132.2 | 389.9 |
| 7N | tobacco | | 383.7 |
| 8N | fabrics, yarn | 54.3 | −147.7 |
| 9N | rugs, miscellaneous textiles | 5.0 | − 259.4 |
| 10N | apparel | 42.8 | 66.4 |
| 11N | miscellaneous fabricated textile products | 103.7 | 10.6 |
| 12N | lumber and wood products | | 2919.5 |
| 13N | wooden containers | 1.2 | − 11.3 |
| 14N | household furniture | 17.7 | 493.3 |
| 15N | office furniture | 15.1 | 1161.4 |
| 16N | paper | 43.6 | − 378.5 |
| 17N | paperboard containers | 2.1 | 15.6 |
| 18N | chemicals | 294.0 | 1353.3 |
| 19N | plastics, synthetics | 2.8 | 256.8 |
| 20N | drugs | 90.4 | 559.1 |
| 21N | paint | 1.7 | 218.6 |
| 22N | oil fields | | −1208.0 |
| 23N | petroleum | 664.9 | 1222.5 |
| 24N | rubber | 78.8 | 621.2 |
| 25N | leather | 21.7 | 51.2 |
| 26N | glass | 1.9 | 86.5 |
| 27N | stone and clay | 15.2 | 4618.4 |
| 28N | iron and steel | 46.8 | 1950.4 |
| 29N | nonferrous metals | 213.6 | 237.0 |
| 30N | fabricated metals | 89.5 | 7396.6 |
| 31N | nonelectrical machinery | 421.9 | 12975.5 |
| 32N | electrical apparatus | 224.8 | 2314.3 |
| 33N | appliances and lighting equipment | 33.7 | 1253.0 |
| 34N | communications and electronic equipment | 1363.8 | 1532.0 |
| 35N | motor vehicles | 122.8 | 3920.0 |
| 36N | aircraft | 6488.4 | 589.7 |
| 37N | other transportation equipment | 264.1 | 1776.6 |
| 38N | instruments | 277.2 | 1478.0 |
| 39N | miscellaneous manufacturing | 22.6 | 449.2 |
| 40N | ordnance | 2263.0 | 100.0 |
| 41N | research and development | 3643.7 | 1496.3 |

## Table 10-5, Part II

### Final demand for local industries

| Local Industry | Military[a] ($ millions) | Nonhousehold Civilian[b] ($ millions) |
|---|---|---|
| 1L  printing and publishing | 52.5 | 282.2 |
| 2L  electricity, gas, water | 50.8 | 933.9 |
| 3L  transportation, warehousing | 1037.7 | 5414.7 |
| 4L  trade | 493.2 | 11129.8 |
| 5L  communications | 27.1 | 947.3 |
| 6L  finance, insurance | | 689.2 |
| 7L  real estate and rentals | 18.2 | 2043.9 |
| 8L  personal and repair services, hotels | 35.8 | 291.9 |
| 9L  auto repair services | 18.6 | 448.6 |
| 10L  business services | 82.4 | 3749.5 |
| 11L  amusements | 2.5 | 251.6 |
| 12L  medical and educational services | 95.1 | 391.3 |
| 13L  maintenance construction | 936.5 | 349.4 |
| 14L  government enterprises | 101.4 | 218.6 |
| 15L  office supplies | 43.2 | 172.0 |
| 16L  business travel, entertainment | | 62.1 |
| 17L  households | 11198.0 | 47695.0 |
| Total all industries (national and local) | 31258.0 | 131647.8 |

[a]When this study was begun, specific data were not available for the military final demand vector; therefore, the dollar amounts are estimates developed from adjusted control totals given for various sectors in *Military Prime Contract Awards and Subcontract Payments* (Office of the Secretary of Defense, July 1962–June 1963), Tables 6 and 7. The vector only includes estimates of final purchases from industries defined as endogenous for this study. Purchases by the military on prime contracts differ from military purchases defined by the Office of Business Economics. Some of these differences are explained in *Hearings Before the Subcommittee on Defense Procurement of the Joint Economic Committee*, Congress of the United States, June 12, 1961, "Progress Made by the Department of Defense in Reducing the Impact of Military Procurement on the Economy," p. 141, and in the source cited above, p. 48.

[b]Row distributions of final demand were used to derive the final demand columns other than new construction and military. "The Interindustry Structure of the United States . . . ," *Survey of Current Business*, November 1964, Table 1, p. 21. Only the percentage distributions were released by the Office of Business Economics at the time this chapter was written. The vector presented above includes new construction but excludes military and household final demands. The vector also includes only final purchases from the 57 industries defined as endogenous for this study.

duce a compensating increase in labor earnings. The postulated value for $\alpha$ was 0.8; then, using equation (10-4), $\beta$ was determined to be approximately 1.02.[14] Earlier, the output and labor earnings generated by the three components of final demand were calculated to determine what the requirements actually were in 1958 (referred to as "before the shift"); now, the new requirements associated with the new final demands (referred to as "after the shift") were esti-

[14]Therefore, a reduction of 20 percent in military expenditures was compensated by an approximate 2 percent increase in the household and nonhousehold civilian components of final demand.

mated. The next step was to calculate the regional distribution of labor earnings both before and after the shift.

By including "households" as an endogenous sector in the subsequent computations, the repercussion effect of household incomes and expenditures on the rest of the industries could be taken into account. Matrix $A^*$ had to be constructed separately for the base year 1958 and for the situation after the level of living was increased by 1.81 percent as part of the compensation for the arms cut. In both cases it was formed by adding a row of labor coefficients and a column of consumption coefficients.

The labor coefficients were obtained by dividing wages and salaries plus income of unincorporated enterprises, inflated by 20 percent, for each industry by output in that industry.[15] The column of consumption coefficients for 1958 was obtained by dividing the deliveries from each industry to "households" ($h$) by the total amount of labor earnings for the country as a whole ($v$).[16] The elements of this column of consumption coefficients were multiplied by 1.81 to obtain the adjusted column. The new diagonal element of the labor coefficient row and the consumption coefficient column was obtained by dividing direct earnings in "households" ($v_H$), by the figure $v$.

Then, the two new $A^*$ matrices—one matrix containing the original consumption coefficients, the other the adjusted consumption coefficients—were partitioned into four submatrices by dividing all industries into two categories: national and local.[17] In the classification used, there were 41 national industries and 17 Local industries, including "households."[18]

The regional distribution of the output of national industries, $X_N^R$, was obtained by directly allocating the share of national output to a region in proportion to that region's share in the productive capacity of a particular industry.[19] The change in labor earnings by region

[15]See Table 10-4, column 2. Sources for labor earnings are given in Table 10-12.

[16]See Table 10-4, column 1. Consumption coefficients after the shift can be obtained by multiplying each element of this column by 101.8 percent.

[17]The division was based upon the data given in Charts 17 and 19, pp. 144 and 146 of Wassily Leontief (ed.), *Studies in the Structure of the American Economy*, showing the proportion of the output of different industries that is consumed within a region and that which is exported for two types of regions: states and census divisions; a diagram of the partition is shown in section II.

[18]See Table 10-3. Since "business travel and entertainment" and the "office supplies" sectors are dummy sectors, their assignment to local industries is arbitrary.

[19]The sources for the $P_N$ matrix, the distribution factors for national industries, are given in Table 10-13. The actual distribution factors used are shown in Table 10-7.

for national industries was determined by subtracting the regional distribution of outputs before the shift from the distribution of outputs after the shift and multiplying by the labor coefficients.[20]

The first step in establishing the level of output of each local industry in each region was to distribute the final demand for local industries by regions. Military demand was distributed according to Department of Defense payrolls in each region. Nonhousehold civilian final demand was subdivided into its seven component bills of goods, each one was distributed according to a factor representing the importance of that final demand in a particular region, and the seven resulting matrices were added.[21]

Then, the output in each local industry in each region was obtained by inserting the appropriate matrices and vectors on the right-hand side of equation (10-8). Outputs of local industries before the shift were subtracted from the outputs after the shift, and the result was multiplied by the labor coefficients to give the change in labor earnings in local industries.[22] The total change in labor earnings by regions, finally, was obtained by adding the change occurring in local industries in a region to that occurring in national industries and to that originating within the military and nonhousehold civilian sectors of the economy.[23]

## V.  Concluding observations on further research

The same analytical scheme that permitted us to assess the economic implications of a hypothetical step toward disarmament, implemented by the same body of factual data, also can be used for evaluating the probable effect of specific measures of economic policies intended to mitigate the stresses of the transitional period. Such measures are usually designed to modify directly or indirectly the level, the composition, and the regional distribution of the new civilian bill of goods. To assess their effect on the interindustrial and interregional distribution of outputs and employment, it will be necessary only to repeat the sequence of computations described above with these readjusted versions of the final bill of goods. Whenever

[20]See Table 10-9, which includes the change in dollar terms and in percentage terms. Only one column is needed to represent the percentage changes for national industries, since total U.S. demand for the industry's product determines the output within a particular region.
[21]The sources for the $D_O$ and $D_M$ matrices, the distribution factors for local industries, are given in Table 10-14. Table 10-6 contains the regionally distributed final demands.
[22]See Table 10-10 for dollar changes and for percentage changes in local industries.
[23]See Table 10-11.

information on specific military budget cuts becomes available, this information can replace the hypothetical assumption of the proportional 20 percent cut in military spending and the compensating 2 percent increase in civilian purchases.

The following two refinements can be introduced into the procedure described above without changing the analytical basis of the general approach. The admittedly rigid assumption that whenever the total output of a national good goes up or down it increases or decreases in the same proportion in all regions can be relaxed. After completion of the three-stage computation described above, the new regional distribution of consumption of each national good can be determined and then compared with the old. Some regions will turn out to be increasing their relative shares at the expense of the others. Accordingly, the geographic distribution of the output can be expected to be affected by this, at least to some extent. If the demand for steel were to contract in a western region but to expand in the eastern regions, the share of the latter in the total output of steel might be expected to increase somewhat and the share of the western mills to fall. To take account of this, a second round of multiregional input-output computations can be undertaken in which the set of the regional distribution coefficients applied to each of the national industries would be revised in light of the numerical results of the first round.

The second refinement of the original procedure consists in breaking down the regions into subregions.[24] The region, for example, that in the present computation includes Illinois, Indiana, and Wisconsin, can be subdivided into two parts, one comprising Illinois and Indiana and the other consisting of Wisconsin. The percentage figures describing the participation of these three states in the total production of each national good would have to be split into two separate figures. The outputs of the industries originally classified as local can be treated in two different ways. The regional outputs of some local goods might balance the demand not only for the three states together but also separately in each of the two subregions. That might be true of automobile repair services and retail trade. Other local goods, while not moving in sufficiently large amounts across the borders of the three-state region, still might be traded freely between its two parts. For such goods the distribution of the total regional output between the two subregions might be described better by a set of constant subregional coefficients. On the

[24]See Wassily Leontief (ed.), *Studies in the Structure of the American Economy*, Chapter 4.

lower subregional level, these empirically determined coefficients would play a role analogous to that assigned to regional coefficients in determining the interregional distribution of the total output of each national good. Without elaborating the technical details of such a complicated analytical scheme involving not one but several layers of regional breakdowns, it suffices to observe that while the successive rounds of such computations can be introduced one by one without modifying the results of the higher rounds, the overall results always will be internally consistent at every stage.

Finally, an entirely different nonlinear, multiregional input-output scheme was proposed in 1963.[25] It is being tested now in the United States, in Latin America, and also in Europe. All of these interregional input-output schemes require detailed regional information, which is not always available.

Thus, highest priority should be assigned to improvement of the basic data. For statistics collected on a national level, a systematic regional breakdown becomes more and more important. On the other hand, most data collected by local and state organizations— often in connection with various programs of regional economic development—are limited in their usefulness because of lack of comparability with other regional and national statistics. This needs to be remedied by agreement on and compliance with certain common classifications and standards.

[25]Tibor Barna, *Structural Interdependence and Economic Development* (London: Macmillan, 1963) Chapter 7; Wassily Leontief and Alan Strout, "Multiregional Input-Output Analysis," included as Chapter 11 in the first edition of this book (1966).

## Table 10-6, Part I

### Military final demand for outputs

|  |  | 1<br>NEW<br>ENGLAND | 2<br>NEW<br>YORK | 3<br>NEW JER.<br>PENNSYL. | 4<br>MICH.<br>OHIO | 5<br>INDIANA<br>ILLINOIS<br>WISC. | 6<br>MINN.<br>SO. DAK.<br>NO. DAK. | 7<br>IOWA<br>MO., NEB.<br>KANSAS | 8<br>GEORGIA<br>NO. CAR.<br>SO. CAR. |
|---|---|---|---|---|---|---|---|---|---|
| printing, publishing | 1 | 3. | 2. | 4. | 2. | 2. | 0. | 2. | 5. |
| electricity, gas, water | 2 | 3. | 2. | 3. | 2. | 2. | 0. | 2. | 5. |
| transportation, warehsng | 3 | 53. | 44. | 71. | 38. | 44. | 8. | 44. | 97. |
| trade | 4 | 25. | 21. | 34. | 18. | 21. | 4. | 21. | 46. |
| communications | 5 | 1. | 1. | 2. | 1. | 1. | 0. | 1. | 3. |
| finance, insurance | 6 | 0. | 0. | 0. | 0. | 0. | 0. | 0. | 0. |
| real estate, rentals | 7 | 1. | 1. | 1. | 1. | 1. | 0. | 1. | 2. |
| repair services, hotels | 8 | 2. | 2. | 2. | 1. | 2. | 0. | 2. | 3. |
| auto repair services | 9 | 1. | 1. | 1. | 1. | 1. | 0. | 1. | 2. |
| business services | 10 | 4. | 4. | 6. | 3. | 3. | 1. | 4. | 8. |
| amusements | 11 | 0. | 0. | 0. | 0. | 0. | 0. | 0. | 0. |
| medical, educ. services | 12 | 5. | 4. | 7. | 4. | 4. | 1. | 4. | 9. |
| maintenance construction | 13 | 48. | 40. | 64. | 35. | 40. | 7. | 40. | 88. |
| government enterprises | 14 | 5. | 4. | 7. | 4. | 4. | 1. | 4. | 10. |
| office supplies | 15 | 2. | 2. | 3. | 2. | 2. | 0. | 2. | 4. |
| business travel | 16 | 0. | 0. | 0. | 0. | 0. | 0. | 0. | 0. |
| households | 17 | 571 | 477. | 769. | 413. | 474. | 86. | 478. | 1052. |
| region total | | 724. | 605. | 974. | 523. | 600. | 109. | 606. | 1333. |

## Table 10-6, Part II

### Nonhousehold civilian demand for

|  |  | 1<br>NEW<br>ENGLAND | 2<br>NEW<br>YORK | 3<br>NEW JER.<br>PENNSYL. | 4<br>MICH.<br>OHIO | 5<br>INDIANA<br>ILLINOIS<br>WISC. | 6<br>MINN.<br>SO. DAK.<br>NO. DAK. | 7<br>IOWA<br>MO., NEB.<br>KANSAS | 8<br>GEORGIA<br>NO. CAR.<br>SO. CAR. |
|---|---|---|---|---|---|---|---|---|---|
| printing, publishing | 1 | 23. | 48. | 32. | 31. | 39. | 9. | 20. | 19. |
| electricity, gas, water | 2 | 60. | 109. | 86. | 89. | 96. | 25. | 53. | 44. |
| transportation, warehsng | 3 | 390. | 816. | 705. | 583. | 682. | 133. | 360. | 390. |
| trade | 4 | 710. | 1187. | 1296. | 1263. | 1464. | 242. | 577. | 518. |
| communications | 5 | 59. | 98. | 105. | 105. | 117. | 19. | 48. | 42. |
| finance, insurance | 6 | 41. | 80. | 66. | 69. | 79. | 18. | 34. | 25. |
| real estate, rentals | 7 | 121. | 182. | 243. | 245. | 273. | 38. | 99. | 92. |
| repair services, hotels | 8 | 21. | 33. | 28. | 26. | 28. | 8. | 18. | 17. |
| auto repair services | 9 | 28. | 51. | 43. | 42. | 49. | 11. | 24. | 19. |
| business services | 10 | 227. | 452. | 357. | 356. | 421. | 94. | 190. | 142. |
| amusements | 11 | 9. | 52. | 14. | 18. | 19. | 8. | 8. | 4. |
| medical, educ. services | 12 | 33. | 56. | 47. | 46. | 49. | 12. | 29. | 34. |
| maintenance construction | 13 | 301. | 516. | 427. | 426. | 440. | 112. | 266. | 321. |
| government enterprises | 14 | 24. | 35. | 30. | 26. | 29. | 8. | 20. | 27. |
| office supplies | 15 | 15. | 24. | 21. | 20. | 21. | 5. | 13. | 15. |
| business travel | 16 | 2. | 3. | 3. | 3. | 7. | 2. | 3. | 1. |
| households | 17 | 3954. | 6401. | 5721. | 5316. | 5887. | 1406. | 3398. | 3859. |
| region total | | 6017. | 10143. | 9224. | 8664. | 9699. | 2144. | 5161. | 5568. |

# Table 10-6, Part I (Cont.)

## of local industries ($ millions)

| 9 VA., W.VA. MARYLAND D.C., DEL. | 10 FLORIDA | 11 TENNESSEE KENTUCKY | 12 ALA. MISS. | 13 OKLA. LA., ARK. | 14 TEXAS | 15 MONTANA WYOMING IDAHO | 16 COLO. N. MEX. | 17 ARIZONA NEVADA UTAH | 18 OREGON WASH. | 19 CALIF. | 20 U.S. TOTAL |
|---|---|---|---|---|---|---|---|---|---|---|---|
| 7. | 2. | 2. | 2. | 2. | 5. | 0. | 2. | 1. | 2. | 8. | 52. |
| 7. | 2. | 2. | 2. | 2. | 4. | 0. | 2. | 1. | 2. | 7. | 51. |
| 140. | 37. | 33. | 41. | 43. | 92. | 6. | 33. | 27. | 36. | 149. | 1038. |
| 67. | 18. | 16. | 19. | 21. | 44. | 3. | 16. | 13. | 17. | 71. | 493. |
| 4. | 1. | 1. | 1. | 1. | 2. | 0. | 1. | 1. | 1. | 4. | 27. |
| 0. | 0. | 0. | 0. | 0. | 0. | 0. | 0. | 0. | 0. | 0. | 0. |
| 2. | 1. | 1. | 1. | 1. | 2. | 0. | 1. | 0. | 1. | 3. | 18. |
| 5. | 1. | 1. | 1. | 1. | 3. | 0. | 1. | 1. | 1. | 5. | 36. |
| 3. | 1. | 1. | 1. | 1. | 2. | 0. | 1. | 0. | 1. | 3. | 19. |
| 11. | 3. | 3. | 3. | 3. | 7. | 0. | 3. | 2. | 3. | 12. | 82. |
| 0. | 0. | 0. | 0. | 0. | 0. | 0. | 0. | 0. | 0. | 0. | 2. |
| 13. | 3. | 3. | 4. | 4. | 8. | 1. | 3. | 2. | 3. | 14. | 95. |
| 126. | 34. | 30. | 37. | 39. | 83. | 6. | 30. | 24. | 32. | 135. | 936. |
| 14. | 4. | 3. | 4. | 4. | 9. | 1. | 3. | 3. | 3. | 15. | 101. |
| 6. | 2. | 1. | 2. | 2. | 4. | 0. | 1. | 1. | 1. | 6. | 43. |
| 0. | ·0. | 0. | 0. | 0. | 0. | 0. | 0. | 0. | 0. | 0. | 0. |
| 1512. | 404. | 353. | 439. | 466. | 991. | 67. | 361. | 288. | 385. | 1613. | 11198. |
| 1916. | 512. | 447. | 557. | 591. | 1257. | 85. | 457. | 365. | 488. | 2044. | 14193. |

# Table 10-6, Part II (Cont.)

## outputs of local industries ($ millions)

| 9 VA., W.VA. MARYLAND D.C., DEL. | 10 FLORIDA | 11 TENNESSEE KENTUCKY | 12 ALA. MISS. | 13 OKLA. LA., ARK. | 14 TEXAS | 15 MONTANA WYOMING IDAHO | 16 COLO. N. MEX. | 17 ARIZONA NEVADA UTAH | 18 OREGON WASH. | 19 CALIF. | 20 U.S. TOTAL |
|---|---|---|---|---|---|---|---|---|---|---|---|
| 32. | 10. | 10. | 9. | 13. | 20. | 3. | 7. | 6. | 11. | 46. | 388. |
| 102. | 29. | 28. | 22. | 38. | 50. | 11. | 21. | 18. | 33. | 125. | 1039. |
| 607. | 230. | 188. | 170. | 288. | 461. | 58. | 153. | 130. | 236. | 914. | 7494. |
| 754. | 323. | 300. | 255. | 393. | 669. | 104. | 190. | 182. | 362. | 1329. | 12118. |
| 78. | 22. | 27. | 22. | 33. | 54. | 8. | 14. | 13. | 31. | 106. | 1003. |
| 37. | 22. | 16. | 12. | 23. | 31. | 8. | 13. | 12. | 20. | 84. | 689. |
| 126. | 42. | 58. | 49. | 69. | 121. | 15. | 24. | 22. | 64. | 198. | 2082. |
| 53. | 10. | 11. | 8. | 13. | 18. | 4. | 8. | 6. | 12. | 44. | 366. |
| 44. | 16. | 12. | 10. | 17. | 23. | 5. | 10. | 9. | 15. | 60. | 487. |
| 290. | 128. | 91. | 71. | 132. | 179. | 43. | 77. | 72. | 116. | 482. | 3920. |
| 12. | 6. | 4. | 1. | 4. | 6. | 1. | 4. | 12. | 4. | 77. | 257. |
| 48. | 17. | 16. | 15. | 22. | 34. | 5. | 13. | 11. | 19. | 75. | 582. |
| 445. | 154. | 149. | 144. | 201. | 323. | 48. | 120. | 101. | 177. | 697. | 5368. |
| 55. | 12. | 13. | 12. | 16. | 27. | 4. | 11. | 9. | 14. | 52. | 422. |
| 24. | 8. | 7. | 7. | 10. | 15. | 2. | 6. | 5. | 8. | 33. | 259. |
| 3. | 5. | 1. | 1. | 3. | 3. | 2. | 2. | 3. | 2. | 11. | 62. |
| 6778. | 2204. | 1908. | 1778. | 2597. | 4077. | 668. | 1610. | 1386. | 2247. | 9009. | 70202. |
| 9489. | 3239. | 2840. | 2586. | 3872. | 6112. | 989. | 2282. | 1998. | 3370. | 13341. | 106739. |

# Table 10-7

## Distribution factors and total

| | | 1 | 2 | 3 | 4 | 5 | 6 | 7 | 8 |
|---|---|---|---|---|---|---|---|---|---|
| | | | | | | INDIANA | MINN. | IOWA | GEORGIA |
| | | NEW | NEW | NEW JER. | MICH. | ILLINOIS | SO. DAK. | MO., NEB. | NO. CAR. |
| | | ENGLAND | YORK | PENNSYL. | OHIO | WISC. | NO. DAK. | KANSAS | SO. CAR. |
| | | | | FRACTION OF TOTAL INDUSTRY OUTPUT | | | | | |
| livestock | 1 | 0.027 | 0.032 | 0.041 | 0.054 | 0.158 | 0.092 | 0.217 | 0.043 |
| other agriculture | 2 | 0.016 | 0.016 | 0.021 | 0.046 | 0.087 | 0.069 | 0.134 | 0.087 |
| forestry, fisheries | 3 | 0.182 | 0.023 | 0.030 | 0.010 | 0.008 | 0.005 | 0.001 | 0.053 |
| agricultural services | 4 | 0.083 | 0.097 | 0.099 | 0.088 | 0.069 | 0.030 | 0.050 | 0.039 |
| coal mining | 5 | 0.001 | 0. | 0.279 | 0.054 | 0.089 | 0. | 0.010 | 0. |
| food, kindred products | 6 | 0.047 | 0.095 | 0.107 | 0.092 | 0.154 | 0.039 | 0.098 | 0.036 |
| tobacco | 7 | 0.008 | 0.006 | 0.152 | 0.016 | 0.001 | 0. | 0. | 0.390 |
| fabrics, yarn | 8 | 0.177 | 0.037 | 0.104 | 0.004 | 0.006 | 0.001 | 0.000 | 0.538 |
| misc. textiles, rugs | 9 | 0.207 | 0.084 | 0.201 | 0.073 | 0.081 | 0.005 | 0.008 | 0.189 |
| apparel | 10 | 0.070 | 0.325 | 0.190 | 0.022 | 0.051 | 0.007 | 0.027 | 0.103 |
| misc. fabric textile prdt | 11 | 0.076 | 0.279 | 0.149 | 0.109 | 0.080 | 0.012 | 0.036 | 0.068 |
| lumber, wood products | 12 | 0.049 | 0.032 | 0.028 | 0.036 | 0.070 | 0.016 | 0.023 | 0.077 |
| wooden containers | 13 | 0.069 | 0.037 | 0.061 | 0.070 | 0.102 | 0.013 | 0.022 | 0.116 |
| household furniture | 14 | 0.060 | 0.096 | 0.089 | 0.077 | 0.163 | 0.008 | 0.026 | 0.148 |
| office furniture | 15 | 0.040 | 0.161 | 0.104 | 0.229 | 0.162 | 0.010 | 0.043 | 0.035 |
| paper | 16 | 0.145 | 0.101 | 0.102 | 0.117 | 0.136 | 0.025 | 0.018 | 0.065 |
| paperboard containers | 17 | 0.087 | 0.143 | 0.159 | 0.128 | 0.166 | 0.013 | 0.049 | 0.050 |
| chemicals | 18 | 0.026 | 0.068 | 0.156 | 0.128 | 0.075 | 0.005 | 0.046 | 0.041 |
| plastics, synthetics | 19 | 0.050 | 0.047 | 0.139 | 0.088 | 0.021 | 0.006 | 0.009 | 0.097 |
| drugs | 20 | 0.048 | 0.171 | 0.237 | 0.112 | 0.214 | 0.010 | 0.054 | 0.028 |
| paints | 21 | 0.036 | 0.072 | 0.216 | 0.174 | 0.189 | 0.013 | 0.053 | 0.026 |
| oil fields | 22 | 0. | 0.004 | 0.014 | 0.017 | 0.027 | 0.005 | 0.041 | 0. |
| petroleum products | 23 | 0.012 | 0.017 | 0.159 | 0.062 | 0.140 | 0.007 | 0.039 | 0.004 |
| rubber, misc. plastics | 24 | 0.164 | 0.066 | 0.121 | 0.286 | 0.140 | 0.005 | 0.029 | 0.009 |
| leather | 25 | 0.325 | 0.172 | 0.126 | 0.046 | 0.121 | 0. | 0.087 | 0.012 |
| glass | 26 | 0.009 | 0.149 | 0.233 | 0.174 | 0.139 | 0. | 0.002 | 0.037 |
| stone and clay | 27 | 0.055 | 0.062 | 0.148 | 0.142 | 0.129 | 0.022 | 0.067 | 0.036 |
| iron and steel | 28 | 0.025 | 0.052 | 0.265 | 0.221 | 0.197 | 0.019 | 0.014 | 0.004 |
| non ferrous metals | 29 | 0.108 | 0.080 | 0.154 | 0.136 | 0.140 | 0.009 | 0.016 | 0.006 |
| fabricated metals | 30 | 0.084 | 0.080 | 0.162 | 0.190 | 0.196 | 0.012 | 0.039 | 0.011 |
| non electrical machinery | 31 | 0.106 | 0.105 | 0.127 | 0.229 | 0.220 | 0.007 | 0.045 | 0.012 |
| electrical apparatus | 32 | 0.084 | 0.118 | 0.183 | 0.180 | 0.242 | 0.011 | 0.041 | 0.014 |
| appliances, lighting eqpt. | 33 | 0.091 | 0.083 | 0.128 | 0.221 | 0.244 | 0.012 | 0.041 | 0.003 |
| electronics equipment | 34 | 0.110 | 0.153 | 0.216 | 0.036 | 0.252 | 0.006 | 0.023 | 0.022 |
| motor vehicles | 35 | 0.009 | 0.060 | 0.060 | 0.569 | 0.157 | 0.004 | 0.037 | 0.017 |
| aircraft | 36 | 0.082 | 0.076 | 0.049 | 0.098 | 0.049 | 0.005 | 0.089 | 0.019 |
| other transpt. equipment | 37 | 0.132 | 0.061 | 0.161 | 0.069 | 0.119 | 0.008 | 0.020 | 0.009 |
| instruments | 38 | 0.128 | 0.320 | 0.174 | 0.061 | 0.147 | 0.043 | 0.015 | 0.003 |
| misc. manufacturing | 39 | 0.181 | 0.228 | 0.142 | 0.106 | 0.129 | 0.007 | 0.037 | 0.042 |
| ordnance | 40 | 0.075 | 0.150 | 0.033 | 0.062 | 0.038 | 0.026 | 0.042 | 0.007 |
| research and development | 41 | 0.052 | 0.108 | 0.059 | 0.031 | 0.121 | 0.017 | 0.011 | 0.007 |

# Table 10-7 (Cont.)

## outputs of national industries

| 9 A., W.VA. MARYLAND D.C., DEL. | 10 FLORIDA | 11 TENNESSEE KENTUCKY | 12 ALA. MISS. | 13 OKLA. LA., ARK. | 14 TEXAS | 15 MONTANA WYOMING IDAHO | 16 COLO. N. MEX. | 17 ARIZONA NEVADA UTAH | 18 OREGON WASH. | 19 CALIF. | 20 TOTAL U.S. OUTPUTS b $ MIL. |
|---|---|---|---|---|---|---|---|---|---|---|---|
| | | | | FRACTION OF TOTAL INDUSTRY OUTPUT | | | | | | | |
| 0.032 | 0.010 | 0.030 | 0.029 | 0.037 | 0.048 | 0.029 | 0.025 | 0.018 | 0.021 | 0.056 | 26026.576 |
| 0.023 | 0.035 | 0.033 | 0.033 | 0.062 | 0.102 | 0.031 | 0.022 | 0.022 | 0.040 | 0.123 | 22983.756 |
| 0.121 | 0.084 | 0.004 | 0.034 | 0.066 | 0.090 | 0.004 | 0.001 | 0.001 | 0.120 | 0.166 | 1140.311 |
| 0.052 | 0.037 | 0.024 | 0.018 | 0.035 | 0.030 | 0.006 | 0.014 | 0.016 | 0.025 | 0.188 | 1547.279 |
| 0.365 | 0. | 0.132 | 0.036 | 0.006 | 0. | 0.003 | 0.010 | 0.016 | 0.001 | 0. | 2741.108 |
| 0.043 | 0.017 | 0.032 | 0.015 | 0.029 | 0.038 | 0.007 | 0.012 | 0.009 | 0.027 | 0.102 | 63693.906 |
| 0.190 | 0.073 | 0.159 | 0.005 | 0. | 0. | 0. | 0. | 0. | 0. | 0.000 | 5921.980 |
| 0.048 | 0. | 0.019 | 0.050 | 0.003 | 0.009 | 0. | 0. | 0. | 0.003 | 0.001 | 10595.784 |
| 0.056 | 0.001 | 0.020 | 0.024 | 0.006 | 0.007 | 0. | 0. | 0. | 0. | 0.036 | 2180.782 |
| 0.040 | 0.005 | 0.046 | 0.031 | 0.010 | 0.021 | 0. | 0.001 | 0.002 | 0.005 | 0.043 | 14219.708 |
| 0.034 | 0.006 | 0.020 | 0.015 | 0.008 | 0.023 | 0. | 0.002 | 0.002 | 0.015 | 0.067 | 2288.032 |
| 0.041 | 0.016 | 0.030 | 0.046 | 0.053 | 0.023 | 0.043 | 0.008 | 0.009 | 0.275 | 0.124 | 7884.100 |
| 0.065 | 0.046 | 0.085 | 0.068 | 0.031 | 0.034 | 0. | 0.003 | 0. | 0.056 | 0.122 | 442.306 |
| 0.061 | 0.020 | 0.055 | 0.024 | 0.026 | 0.024 | 0. | 0.003 | 0.004 | 0.018 | 0.099 | 3271.536 |
| 0.045 | 0.011 | 0.008 | 0.004 | 0.009 | 0.032 | 0.001 | 0.007 | 0.004 | 0.009 | 0.086 | 1496.222 |
| 0.035 | 0.028 | 0.019 | 0.046 | 0.050 | 0.020 | 0. | 0.001 | 0. | 0.057 | 0.033 | 9478.669 |
| 0.042 | 0.012 | 0.016 | 0.003 | 0.022 | 0.015 | 0. | 0.003 | 0.001 | 0.014 | 0.077 | 3626.548 |
| 0.109 | 0.014 | 0.066 | 0.015 | 0.054 | 0.105 | 0.003 | 0.014 | 0.001 | 0.038 | 0.035 | 12049.209 |
| 0.234 | 0.052 | 0.181 | 0. | 0.016 | 0.048 | 0. | 0. | 0. | 0. | 0.012 | 4216.304 |
| 0.035 | 0.002 | 0.011 | 0.004 | 0.000 | 0.010 | 0. | 0.001 | 0. | 0.001 | 0.061 | 6605.578 |
| 0.023 | 0.008 | 0.033 | 0.004 | 0.005 | 0.032 | 0. | 0.006 | 0. | 0.009 | 0.100 | 1866.465 |
| 0.011 | 0.000 | 0.010 | 0.015 | 0.262 | 0.421 | 0.029 | 0.048 | 0.007 | 0.001 | 0.089 | 9611.329 |
| 0.010 | 0.003 | 0.006 | 0.003 | 0.127 | 0.250 | 0.020 | 0.008 | 0.006 | 0.010 | 0.118 | 17268.340 |
| 0.033 | 0.001 | 0.014 | 0.019 | 0.008 | 0.013 | 0. | 0.019 | 0.001 | 0. | 0.072 | 6810.759 |
| 0.027 | 0.002 | 0.034 | 0. | 0.008 | 0.008 | 0.000 | 0.008 | 0.000 | 0.002 | 0.020 | 3967.797 |
| 0.113 | 0.017 | 0.012 | 0.012 | 0.017 | 0.014 | 0. | 0. | 0. | 0.019 | 0.052 | 2136.530 |
| 0.054 | 0.025 | 0.033 | 0.019 | 0.036 | 0.039 | 0.003 | 0.014 | 0.015 | 0.016 | 0.087 | 8825.600 |
| 0.066 | 0.000 | 0.013 | 0.041 | 0.002 | 0.018 | 0.001 | 0.012 | 0.011 | 0.005 | 0.035 | 19860.596 |
| 0.044 | 0.004 | 0.002 | 0.002 | 0.026 | 0.027 | 0.039 | 0.026 | 0.080 | 0.039 | 0.060 | 10171.033 |
| 0.030 | 0.011 | 0.023 | 0.013 | 0.015 | 0.025 | 0.001 | 0.004 | 0.004 | 0.012 | 0.087 | 19904.552 |
| 0.014 | 0.002 | 0.014 | 0.004 | 0.009 | 0.026 | 0.001 | 0.004 | 0.004 | 0.007 | 0.064 | 23872.903 |
| 0.020 | 0.005 | 0.005 | 0.003 | 0.003 | 0.006 | 0. | 0.004 | 0.000 | 0.008 | 0.073 | 6560.784 |
| 0.019 | 0.001 | 0.076 | 0.006 | 0.004 | 0.001 | 0. | 0.000 | 0. | 0.004 | 0.066 | 5893.912 |
| 0.034 | 0.005 | 0.009 | 0.005 | 0.004 | 0.015 | 0. | 0.001 | 0.007 | 0.001 | 0.102 | 8507.819 |
| 0.017 | 0.001 | 0.009 | 0.004 | 0.002 | 0.010 | 0. | 0.001 | 0.000 | 0.004 | 0.040 | 22732.506 |
| 0.035 | 0.002 | 0.001 | 0.013 | 0.011 | 0.065 | 0. | 0.002 | 0.009 | 0.083 | 0.311 | 12646.511 |
| 0.136 | 0.026 | 0.009 | 0.067 | 0.034 | 0.033 | 0.001 | 0.001 | 0.001 | 0.041 | 0.073 | 3721.171 |
| 0.013 | 0.002 | 0.008 | 0.000 | 0.004 | 0.013 | 0. | 0.002 | 0.002 | 0.002 | 0.065 | 4988.633 |
| 0.003 | 0.006 | 0.014 | 0.010 | 0.010 | 0.004 | 0.001 | 0.013 | 0.005 | 0.008 | 0.053 | 5291.864 |
| 0.044 | 0.018 | 0.013 | 0.001 | 0. | 0.014 | 0. | 0.051 | 0.023 | 0. | 0.405 | 4641.848 |
| 0.164 | 0.014 | 0.062 | 0.012 | 0.010 | 0.020 | 0.002 | 0.026 | 0.002 | 0.007 | 0.277 | 5301.661 |

[a] In all tables an entry of zero followed only by a decimal point indicates the cell is empty. An entry consisting of zeros with no blank space indicates the cell contains a figure of negligible size.

[b] These gross domestic output figures were estimated before the 1958 transactions matrix was released by the Office of Business Economics and are expected to vary somewhat from the OBE output figures.

## Table 10-8

### Direct labor earnings before change by region *($ millions)*

| | Region | Military direct labor earnings[a] (1) | Civilian nonhousehold direct labor earnings (2) | Household direct labor earnings[b] (3) |
|---|---|---|---|---|
| 1 | New England | 571. | 2812. | 225. |
| 2 | New York | 477. | 5447. | 332. |
| 3 | New Jersey, Pennsylvania | 769. | 4184. | 385. |
| 4 | Michigan, Ohio | 413. | 4491. | 399. |
| 5 | Indiana, Illinois, Wisconsin | 474. | 4940. | 432. |
| 6 | Minnesota, North and South Dakota | 86. | 1234. | 78. |
| 7 | Kansas, Iowa, Nebraska, Missouri | 478. | 2441. | 197. |
| 8 | Georgia, North and South Carolina | 1052. | 1756. | 162. |
| 9 | Maryland, Virginia, Delaware, W. Virginia, D.C. | 1512. | 3754. | 203. |
| 10 | Florida | 404. | 1397. | 62. |
| 11 | Kentucky, Tennessee | 353. | 1202. | 91. |
| 12 | Mississippi, Alabama | 439. | 899. | 69. |
| 13 | Arkansas, Louisiana, Oklahoma | 466. | 1665. | 108. |
| 14 | Texas | 991. | 2094. | 168. |
| 15 | Idaho, Montana, Wyoming | 67. | 534. | 30. |

## Table 10-9, Part I

| | | 1 NEW ENGLAND | 2 NEW YORK | 3 NEW JER. PENNSYL. | 4 MICH. OHIO | 5 INDIANA ILLINOIS WISC. | 6 MINN. NO. DAK. SO. DAK. | 7 IOWA KANSAS MO., NEB. | 8 GEORGIA SO. CAR. NO. CAR. | 9 VA., W.VA D.C., DEL. MARYLAN |
|---|---|---|---|---|---|---|---|---|---|---|
| livestock | 1 | 3.6 | 4.3 | 5.5 | 7.2 | 21.0 | 12.2 | 28.8 | 5.8 | 4.2 |
| other agriculture | 2 | 1.8 | 1.8 | 2.4 | 5.1 | 9.7 | 7.6 | 14.9 | 9.6 | 2.6 |
| forestry, fisheries | 3 | 0.9 | 0.1 | 0.2 | 0.1 | 0.0 | 0.0 | 0.0 | 0.3 | 0.6 |
| agricultural services | 4 | 0.9 | 1.0 | 1.0 | 0.9 | 0.7 | 0.3 | 0.5 | 0.4 | 0.5 |
| coal mining | 5 | 0.0 | 0. | 3.3 | 0.6 | 1.1 | 0. | 0.1 | 0. | 4.3 |
| food, kindred products | 6 | 7.8 | 15.7 | 17.8 | 15.2 | 25.5 | 6.5 | 16.2 | 5.9 | 7.2 |
| tobacco | 7 | 0.1 | 0.0 | 1.1 | 0.1 | 0.0 | 0. | 0. | 2.8 | 1.4 |
| fabrics, yarn | 8 | 5.0 | 1.0 | 2.9 | 0.1 | 0.2 | 0.0 | 0.0 | 15.1 | 1.3 |
| misc. textiles, rugs | 9 | 1.0 | 0.4 | 1.0 | 0.4 | 0.4 | 0.0 | 0.0 | 0.9 | 0.3 |
| apparel | 10 | 5.7 | 26.5 | 15.4 | 1.8 | 4.2 | 0.5 | 2.2 | 8.4 | 3.3 |
| misc. fabric textile prdt | 11 | 0.2 | 0.8 | 0.4 | 0.3 | 0.2 | 0.0 | 0.1 | 0.2 | 0.1 |
| lumber, wood products | 12 | 1.5 | 1.0 | 0.9 | 1.1 | 2.2 | 0.5 | 0.7 | 2.4 | 1.3 |
| wooden containers | 13 | 0.1 | 0.1 | 0.1 | 0.1 | 0.2 | 0.0 | 0.0 | 0.2 | 0.1 |
| household furniture | 14 | 0.9 | 1.4 | 1.3 | 1.1 | 2.4 | 0.1 | 0.4 | 2.2 | 0.9 |
| office furniture | 15 | 0.3 | 1.2 | 0.8 | 1.7 | 1.2 | 0.1 | 0.3 | 0.3 | 0.3 |
| paper | 16 | 3.0 | 2.1 | 2.1 | 2.4 | 2.8 | 0.5 | 0.4 | 1.3 | 0.7 |
| paperboard containers | 17 | 0.9 | 1.4 | 1.6 | 1.3 | 1.6 | 0.1 | 0.5 | 0.5 | 0.4 |
| chemicals | 18 | 0.1 | 0.3 | 0.7 | 0.6 | 0.3 | 0.0 | 0.2 | 0.2 | 0.5 |
| plastics, synthetics | 19 | 0.3 | 0.3 | 0.8 | 0.5 | 0.1 | 0.0 | 0.1 | 0.5 | 1.3 |
| drugs | 20 | 0.8 | 2.8 | 3.9 | 1.8 | 3.5 | 0.2 | 0.9 | 0.5 | 0.6 |
| paints | 21 | 0.1 | 0.2 | 0.5 | 0.4 | 0.4 | 0.0 | 0.1 | 0.1 | 0.1 |
| oil fields | 22 | 0. | 0.0 | 0.1 | 0.1 | 0.2 | 0.0 | 0.3 | 0. | 0.1 |
| petroleum products | 23 | 0.1 | 0.2 | 1.4 | 0.5 | 1.2 | 0.1 | 0.3 | 0.0 | 0.1 |
| rubber, misc. plastics | 24 | 1.1 | 0.4 | 0.8 | 1.9 | 0.9 | 0.0 | 0.2 | 0.1 | 0.2 |
| leather | 25 | 7.4 | 3.9 | 2.9 | 1.1 | 2.7 | 0. | 2.0 | 0.3 | 0.6 |
| glass | 26 | 0.1 | 1.0 | 1.6 | 1.2 | 1.0 | 0. | 0.0 | 0.3 | 0.8 |
| stone and clay | 27 | 1.8 | 2.1 | 4.9 | 4.7 | 4.3 | 0.7 | 2.3 | 1.2 | 1.8 |
| iron and steel | 28 | −0.1 | −0.1 | −0.7 | −0.6 | −0.5 | −0.1 | −0.0 | −0.0 | −0.2 |
| non-ferrous metals | 29 | −5.6 | −4.1 | −7.9 | −7.0 | −7.2 | −0.5 | −0.8 | −0.3 | −2.3 |
| fabricated metals | 30 | 3.2 | 3.0 | 6.1 | 7.1 | 7.4 | 0.5 | 1.5 | 0.4 | 1.1 |
| non-electrical machinery | 31 | −0.3 | −0.3 | −0.3 | −0.6 | −0.6 | −0.0 | −0.1 | −0.0 | −0.0 |
| electrical apparatus | 32 | −2.0 | −2.8 | −4.3 | −4.2 | −5.7 | −0.3 | −1.0 | −0.3 | −0.5 |
| appliances, lighting eqpt. | 33 | 0.5 | 0.5 | 0.7 | 1.3 | 1.4 | 0.1 | 0.2 | 0.0 | 0.1 |
| electronics equipment | 34 | −18.6 | −26.0 | −36.7 | −6.1 | −42.9 | −1.0 | −4.0 | −3.8 | −5.7 |
| motor vehicles | 35 | 0.5 | 3.1 | 3.1 | 29.2 | 8.1 | 0.2 | 1.9 | 0.8 | 0.9 |
| aircraft | 36 | −68.7 | −64.2 | −41.5 | −82.0 | −40.9 | −4.1 | −74.5 | −16.2 | −29.5 |
| other transpt. equipment | 37 | −0.4 | −0.2 | −0.5 | −0.2 | −0.4 | −0.0 | −0.1 | −0.0 | −0.5 |
| instruments | 38 | −4.0 | −10.0 | −5.4 | −1.9 | −4.6 | −1.3 | −0.5 | −0.1 | −0.4 |
| misc. manufacturing | 39 | 4.1 | 5.1 | 3.2 | 2.4 | 2.9 | 0.2 | 0.8 | 0.9 | 0.1 |
| ordnance | 40 | −16.0 | −31.9 | −7.0 | −13.1 | −8.1 | −5.5 | −8.9 | −1.4 | −9.3 |
| research and development | 41 | −2.1 | −4.3 | −2.4 | −1.3 | −4.8 | −0.7 | −0.4 | −0.3 | −6.5 |
| net increase | | −64.2 | −62.3 | −18.5 | −24.7 | −7.9 | 17.3 | −14.3 | 39.1 | −17.0 |
| gross increase | | 53.5 | 81.6 | 88.3 | 92.4 | 107.8 | 30.7 | 76.0 | 61.5 | 37.8 |
| gross decrease | | 117.7 | 143.9 | 106.8 | 117.0 | 115.8 | 13.4 | 90.3 | 22.5 | 54.8 |

# Table 10-8 (Cont.)

### Direct labor earnings before change by region *($ millions)*

| Region | Military direct labor earnings[a] (1) | Civilian nonhousehold direct labor earnings (2) | Household direct labor earnings[b] (3) |
|---|---|---|---|
| 16 Colorado, New Mexico | 361. | 888. | 48. |
| 17 Arizona, Nevada, Utah | 288. | 809. | 42. |
| 18 Oregon, Washington | 385. | 1477. | 94. |
| 19 California | 1613. | 5783. | 345. |
| Total United States | 11198. | 47807. | 3472. |

[a]Military direct labor earnings include earnings of both civilian and military employees of the Department of Defense. See Table 10-14.
[b]Households were included as a local industry rather than as a separate final demand category.

# Table 10-9, Part I (Cont.)

### Change in labor earnings in national industries by regions *($ millions)*

| 10 FLORIDA | 11 TENNESSEE KENTUCKY | 12 ALA. MISS. | 13 OKLA. LA., ARK | 14 TEXAS | 15 MONTANA WYOMING IDAHO | 16 COLO. N. MEX. | 17 ARIZONA NEVADA UTAH | 18 OREGON WASH. | 19 CALIF. | 20 U.S. NET INCREASE | 21 U.S. GROSS INCREASE | 22 U.S. GROSS DECREASE |
|---|---|---|---|---|---|---|---|---|---|---|---|---|
| 1.3 | 3.9 | 3.8 | 4.9 | 6.4 | 3.9 | 3.3 | 2.3 | 2.8 | 7.5 | 132.8 | 132.8 | 0. |
| 3.9 | 3.7 | 3.7 | 6.9 | 11.3 | 3.5 | 2.4 | 2.4 | 4.4 | 13.6 | 111.2 | 111.2 | 0. |
| 0.4 | 0.0 | 0.2 | 0.3 | 0.5 | 0.0 | 0.0 | 0.0 | 0.6 | 0.9 | 5.2 | 5.2 | 0. |
| 0.4 | 0.2 | 0.2 | 0.4 | 0.3 | 0.1 | 0.1 | 0.2 | 0.3 | 1.9 | 10.3 | 10.3 | 0. |
| 0. | 1.6 | 0.4 | 0.1 | 0. | 0.0 | 0.1 | 0.2 | 0.0 | 0. | 11.8 | 11.8 | 0. |
| 2.9 | 5.2 | 2.4 | 4.8 | 6.4 | 1.1 | 2.1 | 1.4 | 4.5 | 16.9 | 165.6 | 165.6 | 0. |
| 0.5 | 1.1 | 0.0 | 0. | 0. | 0. | 0. | 0. | 0. | 0.0 | 7.2 | 7.2 | 0. |
| 0. | 0.5 | 1.4 | 0.1 | 0.2 | 0. | 0. | 0. | 0.1 | 0.0 | 28.0 | 28.0 | 0. |
| 0.0 | 0.1 | 0.1 | 0.0 | 0.0 | 0. | 0. | 0. | 0. | 0.2 | 4.8 | 4.8 | 0. |
| 0.4 | 3.7 | 2.5 | 0.8 | 1.7 | 0. | 0.1 | 0.2 | 0.4 | 3.5 | 81.3 | 81.3 | 0. |
| 0.0 | 0.1 | 0.0 | 0.0 | 0.1 | 0. | 0.0 | 0.0 | 0.0 | 0.2 | 2.8 | 2.8 | 0. |
| 0.5 | 1.0 | 1.5 | 1.7 | 0.7 | 1.4 | 0.3 | 0.3 | 8.8 | 4.0 | 31.9 | 31.9 | 0. |
| 0.1 | 0.1 | 0.1 | 0.0 | 0.1 | 0. | 0.0 | 0. | 0.1 | 0.2 | 1.6 | 1.6 | 0. |
| 0.3 | 0.8 | 0.4 | 0.4 | 0.3 | 0. | 0.0 | 0.1 | 0.3 | 1.4 | 14.6 | 14.6 | 0. |
| 0.1 | 0.1 | 0.0 | 0.1 . | 0.2 | 0.0 | 0.1 | 0.0 | 0.1 | 0.6 | 7.3 | 7.3 | 0. |
| 0.6 | 0.4 | 0.9 | 1.0 | 0.4 | 0. | 0.0 | 0. | 1.2 | 0.7 | 20.4 | 20.4 | 0. |
| 0.1 | 0.2 | 0.0 | 0.2 | 0.1 | 0. | 0.0 | 0.0 | 0.1 | 0.8 | 9.8 | 9.8 | 0. |
| 0.1 | 0.3 | 0.1 | 0.2 | 0.5 | 0.0 | 0.1 | 0.0 | 0.2 | 0.2 | 4.6 | 4.6 | 0. |
| 0.3 | 1.0 | 0. | 0.1 | 0.3 | 0. | 0. | 0. | 0. | 0.1 | 5.7 | 5.7 | 0. |
| 0.0 | 0.2 | 0.1 | 0.0 | 0.2 | 0. | 0.0 | .0. | 0.0 | 1.0 | 16.3 | 16.3 | 0. |
| 0.0 | 0.1 | 0.0 | 0.0 | 0.1 | 0. | 0.0 | 0. | 0.0 | 0.2 | 2.2 | 2.2 | 0. |
| 0.0 | 0.1 | 0.1 | 2.1 | 3.3 | 0.2 | 0.4 | 0.1 | 0.0 | 0.7 | 7.8 | 7.8 | 0. |
| 0.0 | 0.1 | 0.1 | 1.1 | 2.2 | 0.2 | 0.1 | 0.1 | 0.1 | 1.0 | 8.8 | 8.8 | 0. |
| 0.0 | 0.1 | 0.1 | 0.1 | 0.1 | 0. | 0.1 | 0.0 | 0. | 0.5 | 6.5 | 6.5 | 0. |
| 0.1 | 0.8 | 0. | 0.2 | 0.2 | 0.0 | 0.2 | 0.0 | 0.0 | 0.4 | 22.7 | 22.7 | 0. |
| 0.1 | 0.1 | 0.1 | 0.1 | 0.1 | 0. | 0. | 0. | 0.1 | 0.4 | 7.0 | 7.0 | 0. |
| 0.8 | 1.1 | 0.7 | 1.2 | 1.3 | 0.1 | 0.5 | 0.5 | 0.5 | 2.9 | 33.5 | 33.5 | 0. |
| 0.2 | −0.0 | −0.1 | −0.0 | −0.0 | −0.0 | −0.0 | −0.0 | −0.0 | −0.1 | −2.7 | 0. | 2.7 |
| 0.2 | −0.1 | −0.1 | −1.4 | −1.4 | −2.0 | −1.3 | −4.1 | −2.0 | −3.1 | −51.7 | 0. | 51.7 |
| 0.4 | 0.9 | 0.5 | 0.6 | 0.9 | 0.0 | 0.2 | 0.2 | 0.4 | 3.3 | 37.5 | 37.5 | 0. |
| 0.0 | −0.0 | −0.0 | −0.0 | −0.1 | −0.0 | −0.0 | −0.0 | −0.0 | −0.2 | −2.8 | 0. | 2.8 |
| 0.1 | −0.1 | −0.1 | −0.1 | −0.1 | 0. | −0.1 | −0.0 | −0.2 | −1.7 | −23.4 | 0. | 23.4 |
| 0.8 | 0.4 | 0.0 | 0.0 | 0.0 | 0. | 0.0 | 0. | 0.0 | 0.4 | 5.8 | 5.8 | 0. |
| 0.8 | −1.5 | −0.9 | −0.7 | −2.5 | 0. | −0.1 | −1.2 | −0.2 | −17.4 | −170.0 | 0. | 170.0 |
| 0.0 | 0.5 | 0.2 | 0.1 | 0.5 | 0. | 0.0 | 0.0 | 0.2 | 2.1 | 51.4 | 51.4 | 0. |
| 1.8 | −1.2 | −10.8 | −9.2 | −54.6 | 0. | −1.8 | −7.8 | −70.0 | −260.9 | −839.6 | 0. | 839.6 |
| 0.1 | −0.0 | −0.2 | −0.1 | −0.1 | −0.0 | −0.0 | −0.0 | −0.1 | −0.2 | −3.3 | 0. | 3.3 |
| 0.1 | −0.3 | −0.0 | −0.1 | −0.4 | 0. | −0.0 | −0.1 | −0.1 | −2.0 | −31.1 | 0. | 31.1 |
| 0.1 | 0.3 | 0.2 | 0.2 | 0.1 | 0.0 | 0.3 | 0.1 | 0.2 | 1.2 | 22.4 | 22.4 | 0. |
| 3.8 | −2.7 | −0.1 | 0. | −3.0 | 0. | −10.9 | −5.0 | 0. | −86.1 | −212.7 | 0. | 212.7 |
| 0.6 | −2.5 | −0.5 | −0.4 | −0.8 | −0.1 | −1.0 | −0.1 | −0.3 | −11.1 | −39.9 | 0. | 39.9 |
| 6.1 | 20.2 | 6.9 | 15.8 | −24.6 | 8.5 | −4.9 | −10.2 | −47.4 | −316.2 | −498.3 | 879.0 | 1377.3 |
| 3.5 | 28.6 | 19.8 | 27.8 | 38.5 | 10.6 | 10.4 | 8.0 | 25.5 | 66.6 | 879.0 | 879.0 | 0. |
| 7.4 | 8.4 | 12.9 | 12.0 | 63.0 | 2.1 | 15.3 | 18.3 | 72.9 | 382.8 | 1377.3 | 0. | 1377.3 |

## Table 10-9, Part II

### Change in labor earnings in national industries[a]

| National Industry | | Labor Earnings (% change) |
|---|---|---|
| 1 | livestock | 1.67 |
| 2 | other agriculture | 1.65 |
| 3 | forestry and fisheries | 1.33 |
| 4 | agricultural services | 2.14 |
| 5 | coal mining | 0.98 |
| 6 | food | 1.66 |
| 7 | tobacco | 1.76 |
| 8 | fabrics, yarn | 1.19 |
| 9 | rugs, miscellaneous textiles | 0.97 |
| 10 | apparel | 1.66 |
| 11 | miscellaneous fabricated textile products | 0.54 |
| 12 | lumber and wood products | 1.26 |
| 13 | wooden containers | 1.05 |
| 14 | household furniture | 1.27 |
| 15 | office furniture | 1.19 |
| 16 | paper | 0.83 |
| 17 | paperboard containers | 0.93 |
| 18 | chemicals | 0.15 |
| 19 | plastics, synthetics | 0.59 |
| 20 | drugs | 1.21 |
| 21 | paint | 0.48 |
| 22 | oil fields | 0.38 |

## Table 10-10, Part I

### Change in labor earnings in local industries ($ millions)

| | | 1 NEW ENGLAND | 2 NEW YORK | 3 NEW JER. PENNSYL. | 4 MICH. OHIO | 5 INDIANA ILLINOIS WISC. | 6 MINN. SO. DAK. NO. DAK. | 7 IOWA MO., NEB. KANSAS | 8 GEORGIA NO. CAR. SO. CAR. | 9 VA., W.V MARYLA D.C., DEI |
|---|---|---|---|---|---|---|---|---|---|---|
| printing, publishing | 1 | 3.9 | 9.0 | 9.5 | 11.9 | 12.9 | 3.0 | 5.0 | 2.1 | 0.2 |
| electricity, gas, water | 2 | 2.9 | 6.5 | 7.2 | 8.7 | 9.6 | 2.2 | 3.7 | 1.8 | 0.6 |
| transportation, warehsng | 3 | 4.6 | 19.0 | 17.6 | 25.0 | 28.0 | 6.8 | 9.2 | −2.2 | −10.0 |
| trade | 4 | 49.2 | 107.5 | 117.4 | 143.5 | 157.8 | 35.7 | 59.7 | 26.2 | 7.6 |
| communications | 5 | 3.6 | 8.0 | 8.9 | 10.8 | 11.9 | 2.7 | 4.4 | 2.2 | 0.8 |
| finance, insurance | 6 | 11.4 | 24.4 | 26.9 | 32.3 | 35.8 | 8.3 | 14.0 | 6.8 | 2.5 |
| real estate, rentals | 7 | 3.0 | 6.3 | 7.0 | 8.4 | 9.3 | 2.2 | 3.7 | 1.7 | 0.6 |
| repair services, hotels | 8 | 7.0 | 15.2 | 16.6 | 20.2 | 22.0 | 4.9 | 8.2 | 3.6 | 1.3 |
| auto repair services | 9 | 1.4 | 3.0 | 3.2 | 3.9 | 4.4 | 1.0 | 1.7 | 0.7 | 0.2 |
| business services | 10 | 6.0 | 13.4 | 14.5 | 17.8 | 19.0 | 4.4 | 8.1 | 4.7 | 2.5 |
| amusements | 11 | 2.0 | 4.6 | 4.7 | 5.7 | 6.2 | 1.4 | 2.3 | 1.0 | 0.4 |
| medical, educ. services | 12 | 11.8 | 25.6 | 30.2 | 38.7 | 38.8 | 9.2 | 16.0 | 6.3 | −5.5 |
| maintenance construction | 13 | 0.9 | 6.1 | 4.5 | 8.3 | 9.0 | 2.5 | 2.5 | −2.9 | −6.4 |
| government enterprises | 14 | 2.3 | 6.0 | 6.2 | 8.1 | 8.8 | 2.1 | 3.1 | 0.8 | −0.6 |
| office supplies | 15 | 0. | 0. | 0. | 0. | 0. | 0. | 0. | 0. | 0. |
| business travel | 16 | 0. | 0. | 0. | 0. | 0. | 0. | 0. | 0. | 0. |
| households | 17 | 3.9 | 8.2 | 9.0 | 10.8 | 11.9 | 2.6 | 4.4 | 2.0 | 0.8 |
| net increase | | 113.9 | 262.9 | 283.5 | 354.3 | 385.5 | 89.0 | 146.1 | 54.7 | −4.9 |
| gross increase | | 113.9 | 262.9 | 283.5 | 354.3 | 385.5 | 89.0 | 146.1 | 59.8 | 17.6 |
| gross decrease | | 0. | 0. | 0. | 0. | 0. | 0. | 0. | 5.1 | 22.5 |

## Table 10-9, Part II (Cont.)

### Change in labor earnings in national industries[a]

| National Industry | | Labor Earnings (% change) |
|---|---|---|
| 23 | petroleum products | 0.45 |
| 24 | rubber | 0.30 |
| 25 | leather | 1.57 |
| 26 | glass | 0.81 |
| 27 | stone and clay | 1.10 |
| 28 | iron and steel | −0.04 |
| 29 | nonferrous metals | −2.21 |
| 30 | fabricated metals | 0.54 |
| 31 | nonelectrical machinery | −0.03 |
| 32 | electrical apparatus | −0.92 |
| 33 | appliances and lighting equipment | 0.34 |
| 34 | communications and electronic equipment | −5.40 |
| 35 | motor vehicles | 1.21 |
| 36 | aircraft | −16.05 |
| 37 | other transportation equipment | −0.23 |
| 38 | instruments | −1.59 |
| 39 | miscellaneous manufacturing | 1.23 |
| 40 | ordnance | −15.42 |
| 41 | research and development | −13.26 |

[a]These figures are valid for the national industries on the regional as well as on the national level. This is because demand for the output of a national industry, no matter where it is located, is a function only of the total U.S. demand for its output; thus, the percentage change in output (equal to the percentage change in employment) of that industry in each region will be identical.

## Table 10-10, Part I (Cont.)

| 10 | 11 | 12 | 13 | 14 | 15 | 16 | 17 | 18 | 19 | 20 | 21 | 22 |
|---|---|---|---|---|---|---|---|---|---|---|---|---|
| | TENNESSEE | ALA. | OKLA. | | MONTANA WYOMING | COLO. | ARIZONA | OREGON | | U.S. NET | U.S. GROSS | U.S. GROSS |
| FLORIDA | KENTUCKY | MISS. | LA., ARK | TEXAS | IDAHO | N. MEX. | NEVADA UTAH | WASH. | CALIF. | INCREASE | INCREASE | DECREASE |
| 1.0 | 2.1 | 0.6 | 2.3 | 1.1 | 1.0 | −0.0 | 0.0 | 1.0 | −1.6 | 65.2 | 66.8 | 1.6 |
| 0.7 | 1.7 | 0.6 | 1.9 | 1.0 | 0.8 | 0.1 | 0.0 | 0.6 | −1.1 | 49.6 | 50.7 | 1.1 |
| −0.4 | 2.8 | −1.5 | 2.9 | −3.7 | 2.0 | −2.5 | −2.0 | 0.2 | −14.6 | 81.4 | 118.2 | 36.8 |
| 1.6 | 26.4 | 9.5 | 28.8 | 17.1 | 12.6 | 1.6 | 1.7 | 12.4 | −9.4 | 816.8 | 826.2 | 9.4 |
| 1.0 | 2.1 | 0.8 | 2.3 | 1.3 | 1.0 | 0.1 | 0.1 | 0.8 | −1.6 | 61.4 | 63.0 | 1.6 |
| 2.8 | 6.2 | 2.4 | 7.0 | 4.6 | 3.0 | 0.6 | 0.5 | 2.9 | −1.9 | 190.5 | 192.4 | 1.9 |
| 0.7 | 1.6 | 0.6 | 1.9 | 1.3 | 0.8 | 0.2 | 0.2 | 0.8 | −0.2 | 50.1 | 50.3 | 0.2 |
| 1.5 | 3.7 | 1.3 | 4.0 | 2.2 | 1.8 | 0.2 | 0.2 | 1.7 | −1.8 | 113.9 | 115.7 | 1.8 |
| 0.3 | 0.7 | 0.3 | 0.8 | 0.5 | 0.4 | 0.1 | 0.1 | 0.4 | −0.0 | 22.9 | 22.9 | 0.0 |
| 2.1 | 3.6 | 1.4 | 4.1 | 3.3 | 1.6 | 0.5 | 0.5 | 2.0 | 1.1 | 110.6 | 110.6 | 0. |
| 0.5 | 1.0 | 0.4 | 1.2 | 0.7 | 0.5 | 0.1 | 0.2 | 0.5 | 0.2 | 33.6 | 33.6 | 0. |
| 2.2 | 4.4 | 1.9 | 7.4 | 3.3 | 3.4 | −0.7 | 0.3 | 2.8 | −14.9 | 181.2 | 202.2 | 21.1 |
| −0.9 | 0.3 | −1.3 | 0.2 | −3.0 | 0.7 | −1.4 | −1.1 | −0.6 | −6.9 | 10.3 | 34.9 | 24.6 |
| 0.4 | 1.3 | 0.2 | 1.4 | 0.2 | 0.7 | −0.2 | −0.2 | 0.3 | −2.4 | 38.7 | 42.0 | 3.4 |
| 0. | 0. | 0. | 0. | 0. | 0. | 0. | 0. | 0. | 0. | 0. | 0. | 0. |
| 0. | 0. | 0. | 0. | 0. | 0. | 0. | 0. | 0. | 0. | 0. | 0. | 0. |
| 0.8 | 2.0 | 0.7 | 2.2 | 1.3 | 0.9 | 0.2 | 0.2 | 0.9 | −0.3 | 62.7 | 63.0 | 0.3 |
| 24.5 | 60.0 | 18.0 | 68.2 | 31.2 | 31.2 | −1.2 | 0.8 | 26.7 | −55.5 | 1888.7 | 1992.6 | 103.8 |
| 25.7 | 60.0 | 20.8 | 68.2 | 37.9 | 31.2 | 3.6 | 4.1 | 27.3 | 1.3 | 1888.7 | 1992.6 | 0. |
| 1.3 | 0. | 2.7 | 0. | 6.7 | 0. | 4.9 | 3.3 | 0.6 | 56.8 | 0. | 0. | 103.8 |

## Table 10-10, Part II

Percentage change in labor

| | | 1<br>NEW<br>ENGLAND | 2<br>NEW<br>YORK | 3<br>NEW JER.<br>PENNSYL. | 4<br>MICH.<br>OHIO | 5<br>INDIANA<br>ILLINOIS<br>WISC. | 6<br>MINN.<br>SO. DAK.<br>NO. DAK. | 7<br>IOWA<br>MO., NEB.<br>KANSAS | 8<br>GEORGIA<br>NO. CAR.<br>SO. CAR. | 9<br>VA., W.VA.<br>MARYLAND<br>D.C., DEL. |
|---|---|---|---|---|---|---|---|---|---|---|
| printing, publishing | 1 | 1.0 | 1.6 | 1.5 | 1.8 | 1.8 | 2.3 | 1.5 | 0.8 | 0.1 |
| electricity, gas, water | 2 | 1.2 | 1.8 | 1.5 | 1.8 | 1.9 | 2.6 | 1.7 | 1.0 | 0.3 |
| transportation, warehsng | 3 | 0.5 | 1.2 | 0.9 | 1.3 | 1.3 | 1.8 | 1.0 | −0.3 | −1.0 |
| trade | 4 | 1.3 | 1.9 | 1.8 | 2.1 | 2.1 | 2.7 | 1.8 | 1.0 | 0.2 |
| communications | 5 | 1.1 | 1.7 | 1.6 | 1.9 | 1.9 | 2.5 | 1.6 | 1.0 | 0.3 |
| finance, insurance | 6 | 1.4 | 2.0 | 1.9 | 2.2 | 2.2 | 2.8 | 1.9 | 1.1 | 0.3 |
| real estate, rentals | 7 | 1.5 | 2.2 | 2.0 | 2.4 | 2.4 | 2.9 | 2.0 | 1.2 | 0.4 |
| repair services, hotels | 8 | 1.5 | 2.2 | 2.0 | 2.4 | 2.4 | 3.1 | 2.0 | 1.1 | 0.3 |
| auto repair services | 9 | 1.4 | 2.1 | 1.9 | 2.3 | 2.3 | 2.7 | 1.9 | 1.0 | 0.3 |
| business services | 10 | 1.0 | 1.4 | 1.3 | 1.6 | 1.5 | 2.0 | 1.5 | 1.0 | 0.5 |
| amusements | 11 | 1.6 | 2.2 | 2.2 | 2.5 | 2.5 | 3.1 | 2.1 | 1.2 | 0.3 |
| medical, educ. services | 12 | 1.3 | 1.9 | 2.0 | 2.5 | 2.3 | 2.9 | 2.0 | 1.0 | −0.6 |
| maintenance construction | 13 | 0.3 | 1.3 | 0.9 | 1.5 | 1.5 | 1.9 | 0.8 | −1.2 | −2.1 |
| government enterprises | 14 | 0.9 | 1.6 | 1.4 | 1.8 | 1.8 | 2.4 | 1.4 | 0.4 | −0.3 |
| office supplies | 15 | 0. | 0. | 0. | 0. | 0. | 0. | 0. | 0. | 0. |
| business travel | 16 | 0. | 0. | 0. | 0. | 0. | 0. | 0. | 0. | 0. |
| households | 17 | 1.7 | 2.5 | 2.3 | 2.7 | 2.7 | 3.4 | 2.2 | 1.2 | 0.4 |
| net increase | | 1.2 | 1.8 | 1.7 | 2.0 | 2.0 | 2.6 | 1.7 | 0.8 | −0.1 |
| gross increase | | 1.2 | 1.8 | 1.7 | 2.0 | 2.0 | 2.6 | 1.7 | 0.8 | 0.2 |
| gross decrease | | 0. | 0. | 0. | 0. | 0. | 0. | 0. | 0.1 | 0.3 |

## Table 10-11

### Total change in labor earnings by region ($ million)

| Region | Military Direct Labor Earnings (1) | Nonhousehold Civilian Direct Labor Earnings (2) | Total[a] Gross Decrease (3) | Total[b] Gross Increase (4) | Total Net Increase (col. 4– col 3) (5) |
|---|---|---|---|---|---|
| 1 New England | − 114.20 | 50.66 | 231.9 | 218.1 | − 13.8 |
| 2 New York | − 95.43 | 98.14 | 239.3 | 442.6 | 203.3 |
| 3 New Jersey, Pennsylvania | − 153.70 | 75.39 | 260.5 | 447.2 | 186.7 |
| 4 Michigan, Ohio | − 82.53 | 80.92 | 199.5 | 527.6 | 328.1 |
| 5 Indiana, Illinois, Wisconsin | − 94.71 | 89.01 | 210.5 | 582.3 | 371.8 |
| 6 Minnesota, North and South Dakota | − 17.18 | 22.23 | 30.6 | 141.9 | 111.3 |
| 7 Kansas, Iowa, Nebraska, Missouri | − 95.70 | 43.99 | 186.0 | 266.1 | 80.1 |
| 8 Georgia, North and South Carolina | − 210.32 | 31.63 | 237.9 | 152.9 | − 85.0 |
| 9 Maryland, Virginia, W. Virginia, Delaware, D.C. | − 302.37 | 67.73 | 379.7 | 123.0 | −256.7 |
| 10 Florida | − 80.78 | 25.17 | 89.5 | 64.4 | − 25.1 |
| 11 Kentucky, Tennessee | − 70.59 | 21.66 | 79.0 | 110.3 | 31.3 |
| 12 Mississippi, Alabama | − 87.81 | 16.21 | 103.4 | 56.8 | − 46.6 |
| 13 Arkansas, Louisiana, Oklahoma | − 93.19 | 29.99 | 105.2 | 126.0 | 20.8 |
| 14 Texas | − 198.27 | 37.73 | 268.0 | 114.1 | −153.9 |
| 15 Idaho, Montana, Wyoming | − 13.37 | 9.62 | 15.5 | 51.4 | 35.9 |
| 16 Colorado, New Mexico | − 72.18 | 15.99 | 92.4 | 30.0 | − 62.4 |
| 17 Arizona, Nevada, Utah | − 57.63 | 14.59 | 79.2 | 26.7 | − 52.5 |
| 18 Oregon, Washington | − 77.02 | 26.61 | 150.5 | 79.4 | − 71.1 |
| 19 California | − 322.59 | 104.19 | 762.2 | 172.1 | −590.1 |
| Total United States[c] | −2239.58 | 861.36 | 3727.0 | 3727.0 | |

[a]Column 1, plus gross decrease in national and local industries, Tables 10-7 and 10-8.
[b]Column 2, plus gross increase in national and local industries, Tables 10-7 and 10-8.
[c]Totals may not add because of rounding.

# Table 10-10, Part II (Cont.)

earnings for local industries by region

| 10 FLORIDA | 11 TENNESSEE KENTUCKY | 12 ALA. MISS. | 13 OKLA. LA., ARK | 14 TEXAS | 15 MONTANA WYOMING IDAHO | 16 COLO. N. MEX. | 17 ARIZONA NEVADA UTAH | 18 OREGON WASH. | 19 CALIF. | 20 U.S. NET INCREASE | 21 U.S. GROSS INCREASE | 22 U.S. GROSS DECREASE |
|---|---|---|---|---|---|---|---|---|---|---|---|---|
| 0.9 | 1.4 | 0.6 | 1.3 | 0.4 | 2.1 | −0.0 | 0.1 | 0.6 | −0.3 | 1.1 | 1.1 | 0.0 |
| 1.1 | 1.6 | 0.8 | 1.4 | 0.5 | 2.2 | 0.2 | 0.0 | 0.6 | −0.3 | 1.2 | 1.3 | 0.0 |
| −0.1 | 0.6 | −0.4 | 0.5 | −0.4 | 1.4 | −1.1 | −1.0 | 0.0 | −0.9 | 0.5 | 0.7 | 0.2 |
| 1.1 | 1.7 | 0.8 | 1.6 | 0.6 | 2.5 | 0.2 | 0.2 | 0.8 | −0.2 | 1.4 | 1.4 | 0.0 |
| 1.1 | 1.6 | 0.8 | 1.5 | 0.6 | 2.4 | 0.2 | 0.2 | 0.6 | −0.3 | 1.3 | 1.3 | 0.0 |
| 1.2 | 1.8 | 1.0 | 1.7 | 0.7 | 2.5 | 0.3 | 0.3 | 0.8 | −0.2 | 1.5 | 1.5 | 0.0 |
| 1.3 | 1.9 | 1.0 | 1.6 | 0.7 | 2.5 | 0.4 | 0.4 | 0.9 | −0.1 | 1.6 | 1.6 | 0.0 |
| 1.2 | 1.9 | 0.9 | 1.8 | 0.6 | 2.9 | 0.2 | 0.2 | 0.9 | −0.3 | 1.6 | 1.6 | 0.0 |
| 1.1 | 1.8 | 0.8 | 1.6 | 0.6 | 2.5 | 0.3 | 0.3 | 0.9 | −0.0 | 1.5 | 1.5 | 0.0 |
| 1.2 | 1.4 | 0.9 | 1.3 | 0.7 | 1.9 | 0.4 | 0.5 | 0.9 | 0.1 | 1.1 | 1.1 | 0. |
| 1.3 | 2.0 | 1.0 | 1.9 | 0.7 | 2.9 | 0.3 | 0.6 | 0.9 | 0.1 | 1.7 | 1.7 | 0. |
| 0.9 | 1.2 | 0.7 | 1.7 | 0.5 | 2.9 | −0.4 | 0.2 | 0.8 | −1.0 | 1.3 | 1.5 | 0.2 |
| −0.9 | 0.2 | −1.1 | 0.1 | −1.1 | 1.4 | −1.7 | −1.5 | −0.4 | −1.3 | 0.2 | 0.7 | 0.5 |
| 0.5 | 1.3 | 0.3 | 1.1 | 0.1 | 2.0 | −0.4 | −0.4 | 0.3 | −0.6 | 1.0 | 1.1 | 0.1 |
| 0. | 0. | 0. | 0. | 0. | 0. | 0. | 0. | 0. | 0. | 0. | 0. | 0. |
| 0. | 0. | 0. | 0. | 0. | 0. | 0. | 0. | 0. | 0. | 0. | 0. | 0. |
| 1.4 | 2.2 | 1.1 | 2.0 | 0.8 | 3.1 | 0.4 | 0.4 | 1.0 | −0.1 | 1.8 | 1.8 | 0.0 |
| 0.9 | 1.5 | 0.6 | 1.4 | 0.4 | 2.3 | −0.1 | 0.0 | 0.6 | −0.4 | 1.2 | 1.3 | 0.1 |
| 0.9 | 1.5 | 0.7 | 1.4 | 0.5 | 2.3 | 0.2 | 0.2 | 0.7 | 0.0 | 1.2 | 1.3 | 0. |
| 0.0 | 0. | 0.1 | 0. | 0.1 | 0. | 0.2 | 0.2 | 0.0 | 0.4 | 0. | 0. | 0.1 |

# Table 10-12

Source references for labor earnings

| Sector | Industry | Procedure | Source |
|---|---|---|---|
| 1, 2 | livestock, other agriculture | estimates of net income of farmers | U.S. Dept. of Agriculture, *Agriculture Statistics*, 1961. |
| 3, 4 | forestry, agricultural services | wages and salaries of employees | U.S. Dept. of Commerce, *Survey of Current Business*, July 1961. |
| 5–41 | manufacturing sectors | wages and salaries of payroll workers, salaries of administrative workers, and income of unincorporated business were summed | U.S. Dept. of Commerce, *Census of Manufactures*, 1958, and *Survey of Current Business*,[a] July 1961. |
| all local sectors 1–16 | trade and service sectors | same as for manufacturing | U.S. Dept. of Commerce, *Census of Business and Selected Services*, 1958; Bureau of Employment Security, *Employment and Wages*, 1958; U.S. Dept. of Commerce, *Survey of Current Business*,[a] July 1961. |

[a]When the *Survey of Current Business* statistics were not detailed enough, the income of unincorporated business was distributed among the 60-order sectors according to information given in Internal Revenue Service, *Corporation Income Tax Returns*, July 1958–June 1959.

## Table 10-13

### Source references for national industry output distribution factors

| Sector | Industry | Factor | Source |
|---|---|---|---|
| 1, 2 | livestock, other agriculture | Cash receipts from farm marketings | U.S. Dept. of Commerce, *Statistical Abstract of United States*, 1959, Table 832. |
| 3 | forestry, fisheries | An index composed of value of catch and volume of raw timber cut | Same as above, Tables 919, 947. |
| 4 | agricultural services | Wages and salaries of employees | Bureau of Employment Security, *Employment and Wages*, 1958. |
| 5–40 | manufacturing sectors | Wages and salaries of employees | U.S. Dept. of Commerce, *Census of Manufactures*, 1958. |
| 41 | research and development | Payrolls | U.S. Dept. of Commerce, *Census of Selected Services*, 1958. |

## Table 10-14

### Source references for local industry distribution factors

| Final Demand Category | Factors Used to Distribute Aggregate Local Outputs | Sources |
|---|---|---|
| exports and net inventory change | Regional distribution of labor earnings in each local industry | Real estate: U.S. Dept. of Commerce, *Statistical Abstract of U.S.*, 1961, Table 1067. Finance: *Statistical Abstract of U.S.*, 1960, Table 619. Others: U.S. Dept. of Commerce, *Census of Selected Services*, or Bureau of Employment Security, *Employment and Wages*, 1958. |
| imports | Regional distribution of total wages and salaries in all industries within a region | U.S. Dept. of Commerce, *Survey of Current Business*, August 1961, Tables 4–27 line 2. |
| gross private capital formation | Expenditures on new plants and equipment | U.S. Dept. of Commerce, *Statistical Abstract of U.S.*, 1961, Table 1097, p. 795. |
| construction | Wages in contract construction | Bureau of Employment Security, *Employment and Wages*, 1958. |
| state and local government | Wages and salaries of state and local government employees | U.S. Dept. of Commerce, *Survey of Current Business*, August 1961, Table 4–27, lines 28, 29, 30. |
| federal government | Wages and salaries of federal employees, except Department of Defense | Same as above. |
| military | Payrolls and allowances (only FY 1959 was available) | U.S. Congress, Joint Economic Committee, "Background Material on Economic Aspects of Military Procurement and Supplies," Subcommittee on Defense, March 1963, Table 3, p. 4. |

# 11

# *Environmental repercussions and the economic structure: An input-output approach*

# ( 1 9 7 0 )

## I

Pollution is a byproduct of regular economic activities. In each of its many forms it is related in a measurable way to some particular consumption or production process. The quantity of carbon monoxide released in the air, for example, bears a definite relationship to the amount of fuel burned by various types of automotive engines; the discharge of polluted water into streams and lakes is linked directly to the level of output of the steel, the paper, the textile, and all the other water-using industries, and its amount depends, in each instance, on the technological characteristics of the particular industry.

Input-output analysis describes and explains the level of output of each sector of a given national economy in terms of its relationships to the corresponding levels of activities in all the other sectors. In its more complicated multiregional and dynamic versions, the input-output approach permits us to explain the spatial distribution of output and consumption of various goods and services and of their growth or decline—as the case may be—over time.

Frequently unnoticed and too often disregarded, undesirable byproducts (as well as certain valuable but unpaid-for natural

This paper was presented in Tokyo in March 1970 at the International Symposium on Environmental Disruption in the Modern World, held under the auspices of the International Social Science Council, Standing Committee on Environmental Disruption. Published in *The Review of Economics and Statistics* 52, 3 (August 1970).

Peter Petri and Ed Wolff, both members of the research staff of the Harvard Economic Research Project, programmed and carried out the computations described in this chapter. For their invaluable assistance I owe my sincerest thanks.

inputs) are linked directly to the network of physical relationships that govern the day-to-day operations of our economic system. The technical interdependence between the levels of desirable and undesirable outputs can be described in terms of structural coefficients similar to those used to trace the structural interdependence among all the regular branches of production and consumption. As a matter of fact, it can be described and analyzed as an integral part of that network.

It is the purpose of this chapter, first, to explain how such "externalities" can be incorporated into the conventional input-output picture of a national economy and, second, to demonstrate that—once this has been done—conventional input-output computations can yield concrete replies to some of the fundamental factual questions that should be asked and answered before a practical solution can be found to problems raised by the undesirable environmental effects of modern technology and uncontrolled economic growth.

## II

Proceeding on the assumption that the basic conceptual framework of a static input-output analysis is familiar to the reader, I will link up the following exposition to the numerical examples and elementary equations presented in Chapter 7 of the first edition of this book (New York: Oxford University Press, 1966).

Consider a simple economy consisting of two producing sectors, agriculture and manufacture, and households. Each one of the two industries absorbs some of its annual output itself, supplies some to the other industry, and delivers the rest to final consumers—in this case represented by the households. These intersectoral flows can be conveniently entered in an input-output table. (See Table 11-1, for example.) The magnitude of the total outputs of the two industries and of the two different kinds of inputs absorbed in each of them depends on (1) the amounts of agricultural and manufactured goods that had to be delivered to the final consumers, the households, and (2) the input requirements of the two industries determined by their specific technological structures. In this particular instance agriculture is assumed to require $0.25$ ($= {}^{25}\!/_{100}$) units of agricultural and $0.14$ ($= {}^{14}\!/_{100}$) units of manufactured inputs to produce a bushel of wheat, while the manufacturing sector needs $0.40$ ($= {}^{20}\!/_{50}$) units of agricultural and $0.12$ ($= {}^{6}\!/_{50}$) units of manufactured product to make a yard of cloth.

The "cooking recipes" of the two producing sectors can also be

### Table 11-1

Input-output table of a national economy *(in physical units)*

| from | Sector 1 Agriculture | Sector 2 Manufacture | Final Demand Households | Total Output |
|---|---|---|---|---|
| Sector 1 Agriculture | 25 | 20 | 55 | 100 bushels of wheat |
| Sector 2 Manufacture | 14 | 6 | 30 | 50 yards of cloth |

presented in a compact tabular form. (See Table 11-2.) This is the structural matrix of the economy. The numbers entered in the first column are the technical input coefficients of the agriculture sector, and those shown in the second are the input coefficients of the manufacture sector.

### III

The technical coefficients determine how large the total annual outputs of agricultural and of manufactured goods must be if they are to satisfy not only the given direct demand (for each of the two kinds of goods) by the final users, the households, but also the intermediate demand depending in its turn on the total level of output in each of the two productive sectors.

These somewhat circular relationships are described concisely by the following two equations:

$$X_1 - 0.25X_1 - 0.40X_2 = Y_1$$
$$X_2 - 0.12X_2 - 0.14X_1 = Y_2$$

Or, in a rearranged form,

(11-1)
$$0.75X_1 - 0.40X_2 = Y_1$$
$$-0.14X_1 + 0.88X_2 = Y_2$$

### Table 11-2

Input requirements per unit of output

| from | Sector 1 Agriculture | Sector 2 Manufacture |
|---|---|---|
| Sector 1 Agriculture | 0.25 | 0.40 |
| Sector 2 Manufacture | 0.14 | 0.12 |

$X_1$ and $X_2$ represent the unknown total outputs of agricultural and manufactured commodities, respectively; $Y_1$ and $Y_2$ are the given amounts of agricultural and manufactured products to be delivered to the final consumers.

These two linear equations with two unknowns can obviously be solved for $X_1$ and $X_2$ in terms of any given $Y_1$ and $Y_2$.

Their general solution can be written in the form of the following two equations:

(11-2) $$X_1 = 1.457Y_1 + 0.662Y_2$$
$$X_2 = 0.232Y_1 + 1.242Y_2$$

By inserting on the right-hand side the given magnitudes of $Y_1$ and $Y_2$, we can compute the magnitudes of $X_1$ and $X_2$. In the particular case described in Table 11-1, $Y_1 = 55$ and $Y_2 = 30$. Performing the necessary multiplications and additions, one finds the corresponding magnitudes of $X_1$ and $X_2$ to be, indeed, equal to the total outputs of agricultural (100 bushels) and manufactured (50 yards) goods, as shown in Table 11-1.

The matrix, that is, the square set table of numbers appearing on the right-hand side of (11-2),

(11-3) $$\begin{bmatrix} 1.457 & 0.662 \\ 0.232 & 1.242 \end{bmatrix}$$

is called the "inverse" of matrix

(11-4) $$\begin{bmatrix} 0.75 & -0.40 \\ -0.14 & 0.88 \end{bmatrix}$$

describing the set constants appearing on the left-hand side of the original equations in (11-1).

Any change in the technology of either manufacture or agriculture, that is, in any one of the four input coefficients entered in Table 11-2, would entail a corresponding change in the structural matrix (11-4) and, consequently, in its inverse (11-3). Even if the final demand for agricultural ($Y_1$) and manufactured ($Y_2$) goods remained the same, their total outputs, $X_1$ and $X_2$, would have to change if the balance between the total outputs and inputs of both kinds of goods were to be maintained. On the other hand, if the level of the final demands $Y_1$ and $Y_2$ had changed, but the technology remained the same, the corresponding changes in the total outputs $X_1$ and $X_2$ could be determined from the same general solution (11-2).

In dealing with real economic problems one, of course, takes into account simultaneously the effect both of technological changes and of anticipated shifts in the levels of final deliveries. The structural matrices used in such computations contain not two but several hundred sectors, but the analytical approach remains the same. In order to keep the following verbal argument and the numerical examples illustrating it quite simple, pollution produced directly by households and other final users is not considered in it. A concise description of the way in which pollution generated by the final demand sectors can be introduced—along with pollution originating in the producing sectors—into the quantitative description and numerical solution of the input-output system is relegated to the mathematical appendix at the end of this chapter.

## IV

As has been said before, pollution and other undesirable—or desirable—external effects of productive or consumptive activities should for all practical purposes be considered part of the economic system.

The quantitative dependence of each kind of external output (or input) on the level of one or more conventional economic activities to which it is known to be related must be described by an appropriate technical coefficient, and all these coefficients have to be incorporated into the structural matrix of the economy in question.

Let it be assumed, for example, that the technology employed by the manufacture sector leads to a release into the air of 0.20 grams of a solid pollutant per yard of cloth produced by it, while agricultural technology adds 0.50 grams per unit (i.e., each bushel of wheat) of its total output.

Using $\overline{X}_3$ to represent the yet unknown total quantity of this external output, we can add to the two original equations of output system (11-1) a third,

(11-5)
$$0.75X_1 - 0.40X_2 \qquad = Y_1$$
$$-0.14X_1 + 0.88X_2 \qquad = Y_2$$
$$0.50X_1 + 0.20X_2 - \overline{X}_3 = 0$$

In the last equation the first term describes the amount of pollution produced by agriculture as depending on that sector's total output, $X_1$, while the second represents, in the same way, the pollution originating in manufacture as a function of $X_2$. The equation as a whole simply states that $\overline{X}_3$, the total amount of that particular type pollution generated by the economic system as a whole, equals the sum total of the amounts produced by all its separate sectors.

Given the final demands $Y_1$ and $Y_2$ for agricultural and manufactured products, this set of three equations can be solved not only for their total outputs $X_1$ and $X_2$ but also for the unknown total output $\overline{X}_3$ of the undesirable pollutant.

The coefficients of the left-hand side of augmented input-output system (11-5) form the matrix,

$$
(11\text{-}5a) \qquad \begin{Bmatrix} 0.75 & -0.40 & 0 \\ -0.14 & 0.88 & 0 \\ 0.50 & 0.20 & -1 \end{Bmatrix}
$$

A general solution of system (11-5) would be similar in its form to the general solution (11-2) of system (11-1) but it would consist of three rather than two equations and the inverse of the structural matrix (11-4) appearing on the right-hand side would have three rows and columns.

Instead of inverting the enlarged structural matrix, one can obtain the same result in two steps. First, use the inverse (11-4) of the original smaller matrix to derive, from the two-equation system (11-2), the outputs of agricultural $(X_1)$ and manufactured $(X_2)$ goods required to satisfy any given combination of final demands $Y_1$ and $Y_2$. Second, determine the corresponding "output" of pollutants, $\overline{X}_3$, by entering the values of $X_1$ and $X_2$ thus obtained in the last equation of set (11-5).

Let $Y_1 = 55$ and $Y_2 = 30$; these are the levels of the final demand for agricultural and manufactured products as shown on the input-output Table 11-1. Inserting these numbers on the right-hand side of (11-5), we find—using the general solution (11-2) of the first two equations—that $X_1 = 100$ and $X_2 = 50$. As should have been expected, they are identical with the corresponding total output figures in Table 11-1. Using the third equation in (11-5), we find $X_3 = 60$. This is the total amount of the pollutant generated by both industries.

By performing a similar computation for $Y_1 = 55$ and $Y_2 = 0$, and then for $Y_1 = 0$ and $Y_2 = 30$, we could find out that 42.62 of these 60 grams of pollution are associated with agricultural and manufactured activities contributing directly and indirectly to the delivery to households of 55 bushels of wheat, while the remaining 17.38 grams can be imputed to productive activities contributing directly and indirectly to final delivery of 30 yards of cloth.

Had the final demand for cloth fallen from 30 yards to 15, the amount of pollution traceable in it would be reduced from 17.38 to 8.69 grams.

## V

Before proceeding with further analytical exploration, it seems appropriate to introduce in Table 11-3 the pollution flows explicitly in the original Table 11-1.

The entry at the bottom of the final column in Table 11-3 indicates that agriculture produced 50 grams of pollutant and 0.50 grams per bushel of wheat. Multiplying the pollutant-output coefficient of the manufacturing sector with its total output we find that it has contributed 10 to the grand total of 60 grams of pollution.

Conventional economic statistics concern themselves with production and consumption of goods and services that are supposed to have some positive market value in our competitive private enterprise economy. This explains why the production and consumption of DDT are, for example, entered in conventional input-output tables while the production and consumption of carbon monoxide generated by internal combustion engines are not. Since private and public bookkeeping, which constitutes the ultimate source of the most conventional economic statistics, does not concern itself with such "nonmarket" transactions, their magnitude has to be estimated indirectly through detailed analysis of the underlying technical relationships.

Problems of costing and of pricing are bound to arise, however, as soon as we move beyond explaining and measuring pollution toward doing something about it.

## VI

A conventional national or regional input-output table contains a value-added row. It shows in dollar figures the wages, depreciation

### Table 11-3

Input-output table of the national economy with pollutants included
*(in physical units)*

| into<br>from | Sector 1<br>Agriculture | Sector 2<br>Manufacture | Households | Total Output |
|---|---|---|---|---|
| Sector 1<br>Agriculture | 25 | 20 | 55 | 100 bushels<br>of wheat |
| Sector 2<br>Manufacture | 14 | 6 | 30 | 50 yards<br>of cloth |
| Sector 3<br>Air pollution | 50 | 10 | | 60 grams of<br>pollutant |

charges, profits, taxes, and other costs incurred by each producing
sector in addition to payments for inputs purchased from other producing sectors. Most of that value added represents the cost of
labor, capital, and other so-called primary factors of production and
depends on the physical amounts of such inputs and their prices.
The wage bill of an industry equals, for example, the total number
of man-years times the wage rate per man-year.

In Table 11-4 the original national input-output table is extended
to include the labor input or total employment row.

The "cooking recipes" as shown in Table 11-2 can be accordingly
extended to include the labor input coefficients of both industries
expressed in man-hours as well as in money units.

In section III of this chapter it was shown how the general solution
of the original input-output system (11-2) can be used to determine
the total outputs of agricultural and manufactured products ($X_1$ and
$X_2$) required to satisfy any given combination of deliveries of these
goods ($Y_1$ and $Y_2$) to final households. The corresponding total labor
inputs can be derived by multiplying the appropriate labor coefficients ($l_1$ and $l_2$) with each sector's total output. The sum of both
products yields the labor input $L$ of the economy as a whole.

$$(11\text{-}6) \qquad\qquad L = l_1X_1 + l_2X_2$$

Assuming a wage rate of $1 per hour, we find the payment for
primary inputs per unit of the total output to be $0.80 in agriculture
and $3.60 in manufacture. (See Table 11-5.) That implies that the
prices of one bushel of wheat ($p_1$) and of a yard of cloth ($p_2$) must be
just high enough to permit agriculture to yield a value added of $v_1$
(= 0.80) and manufacture $v_2$ (= 3.60) per unit of their respective

**Table 11-4**

Input-output table with labor inputs included *(in physical and in money units)*

| from | into Sector 1 Agriculture | Sector 2 Manufacture | Households | Total Output |
|---|---|---|---|---|
| Sector 1 Agriculture | 25 | 20 | 55 | 100 bushels of wheat |
| Sector 2 Manufacture | 14 | 6 | 30 | 50 yards of cloth |
| Labor inputs (value added) | 80 ($80) | 180 ($180) | | 260 man-years ($260) |

## Table 11-5

Input requirements per unit of output *(including labor or value added)*

| from | into | Sector 1 Agriculture | Sector 2 Manufacture |
|---|---|---|---|
| Sector 1 Agriculture | | 0.25 | 0.40 |
| Sector 2 Manufacture | | 0.14 | 0.12 |
| Primary input labor in man-hours (at \$1 per hour) | | 0.80 (\$0.80) | 3.60 (\$3.60) |

outputs after having paid for all the other inputs specified by their respective "cooking recipes."

$$p_1 - 0.25p_1 - 0.14p_2 = v_1$$
$$p_2 - 0.12p_2 - 0.40p_1 = v_2$$

Or in a rearranged form,

(11-7)
$$0.75p_1 - 0.14p_2 = v_1$$
$$-0.40p_1 + 0.88p_2 = v_2$$

The general solution of these two equations, permitting one to compute $p_1$ and $p_2$ from any given combination of values added, $v_1$ and $v_2$, is

(11-8)
$$p_1 = 1.457v_1 + 0.232v_2$$
$$p_2 = 0.662v_1 + 1.242v_2$$

With $v_1 = \$0.80$ and $v_2 = \$3.60$, we have $p_1 = \$2.00$ and $p_2 = \$5.00$. Multiplying the physical quantities of wheat and cloth entered in the first and second rows of Table 11-4 with appropriate prices, we can transform it into a familiar input-output table in which all transactions are shown in dollars.

## VII

Within the framework of the open input-output system described above, any reduction or increase in the output level of pollutants can be traced to changes in the final demand for specific goods and services, changes in the technical structure of one or more sectors of the economy, or some combination of the two.

Economists cannot devise new technology, but, as has been demonstrated above, they can explain or even anticipate the effect of any given technological change on the output of pollutants (as well as of all the other goods and services). They can determine the effects of such a change on sectoral and, consequently, also the total demand for the primary factor of production. With given values-added coefficients they can, moreover, estimate the effect of such a change on prices of various goods and services.

After the explanations given above, a single example should suffice to show how any of these questions can be formulated and answered in input-output terms.

Consider the simple two-sector economy whose original state and structure were described in Tables 11-3, 11-4, 11-5, and 11-6. Assume that a process has been introduced permitting elimination (or prevention) of pollution and that the input requirements of that process amount to 2 man-years of labor (or \$2.00 of value added) and 0.20 yards of cloth per gram of pollutant prevented from being discharged—either by agriculture or manufacture—into the air.

Combined with the previously introduced sets of technical coefficients, this additional information yields the following complex structural matrix of the national economy.

The input-output balance of the entire economy can be described by the following set of four equations.

$$(11\text{-}9) \qquad 0.75X_1 - 0.40X_2 = Y_1 \text{ (wheat)}$$
$$-0.14X_1 + 0.88X_2 - 0.20X_3 = Y_2 \text{ (cotton cloth)}$$
$$0.50X_1 + 0.20X_2 - X_3 = Y_3 \text{ (pollutant)}$$
$$-0.80X_1 - 3.60X_2 - 2.00X_3 + L = Y_4 \text{ (labor)}$$

Variables:

$X_1$ = total output of agricultural products
$X_2$ = total output of manufactured products
$X_3$ = total amount of eliminated pollutant
$L$ = employment
$Y_1$ = final demand for agricultural products
$Y_2$ = final demand for manufactured products
$Y_3$ = total uneliminated amount of pollutant
$Y_4$ = total amount of labor employed by households and other final demand sectors[1]

Instead of describing complete elimination of all pollution, the

---

[1] In all numerical examples presented in this chapter, $Y_4$ is assumed to be equal to zero.

## Table 11-6

Structural matrix of a national economy with pollution output and antipollution input coefficients included

| Inputs and Pollutants' Output | Output Sectors | | |
|---|---|---|---|
| | Sector 1 Agriculture | Sector 2 Manufacture | Elimination of Pollutant |
| Sector 1 Agriculture | 0.25 | 0.40 | 0 |
| Sector 2 Manufacture | 0.14 | 0.12 | 0.20 |
| Pollutant (output) | 0.50 | 0.20 | |
| Labor | 0.80 | 3.60 | 2.00 |
| (value added) | ($0.80) | ($3.60) | ($2.00) |

third equation contains on its right-hand side $Y_3$, the amount of uneliminated pollutant. Unlike all other elements of the given vector of final deliveries, it is not "demanded" but, rather, tolerated.[2]

The general solution of that system for the unknown $X$'s in terms of any given set of $Y$'s is written out in full below.

$$(11\text{-}10) \quad X_1 = 1.573Y_1 + 0.749Y_2 - 0.149Y_3 + 0.000Y_4 \text{ Agriculture}$$
$$X_2 = 0.449Y_1 + 1.404Y_2 - 0.280Y_3 + 0.000Y_4 \text{ Manufacture}$$
$$X_3 = 0.876Y_1 + 0.655Y_2 - 1.131Y_3 + 0.000Y_4 \text{ Pollutant}$$
$$L = 4.628Y_1 + 6.965Y_2 - 3.393Y_3 + 1.000Y_4 \text{ Labor}$$

The square set of coefficients (each multiplied with the appropriate $Y$) on the right-hand side of (11-10) is the inverse of the matrix of constants appearing on the left-hand side of (11-9). The inversion was, of course, performed on a computer.

The first equation shows that each additional bushel of agricultural product delivered to final consumers (i.e., households) would require (directly and indirectly) an increase of the total output of the agricultural sector $(X_1)$ by 1.573 bushels, while the final delivery of an additional yard of cloth would imply a rise of total agricultural outputs by 0.749 bushels.

The next term in the same equation measures the (direct and indirect) relationship between the total output of agricultural products

[2]In (11-6), which describes a system that generates pollution but does not contain any activity combating it, the variable $X_3$ stands for the total amount of uneliminated pollution that is in system (11-8) represented by $Y_3$.

$(X_1)$ and the "delivery" to final users of $Y_3$ grams of uneliminated pollutants.

The constant $-0.149$ associated with it in this final equation indiciates that a reduction in the total amount of pollutant delivered to final consumers by 1 gram would require an increase of agricultural output by 0.149 bushels.

Tracing down the column of coefficients associated with $Y_3$ in the second, third, and fourth equations, we can see what effect a reduction in the amount of pollutant delivered to the final users would have on the total output levels of all other industries. Manufacture would have to produce an additional 0.280 yards of cloth. Sector 3, the antipollution industry itself, would be required to eliminate 1.131 grams of pollutant to make possible the reduction of its final delivery by 1 gram, the reason for this being that economic activities required (directly and indirectly) for elimination of pollution do, in fact, generate some of it themselves.

The coefficients of the first two terms on the right-hand side of the third equation show how the level of operation of the antipollution industry $(X_3)$ would have to vary with changes in the amounts of agricultural and manufactured goods purchased by final consumers, if the amount of uneliminated pollutant $(Y_3)$ were kept constant. The last equation shows that the total, that is, direct and indirect, labor input required to reduce $Y_3$ by 1 gram amounts to 3.393 man-years. This can be compared with 4.628 man-years required for delivery to the final users of an additional bushel of wheat and 6.965 man-years needed to let them have one more yard of cloth.

Starting with the assumption that households, the final users, consume 55 bushels of wheat and 30 yards of cloth and also are ready to tolerate 30 grams of uneliminated pollution, the general solution (11-10) was used to determine the physical magnitudes of the intersectoral input-output flows shown in Table 11-7. The entries in the third row show that the agricultural and manufactured sectors generate 63.93 (= 52.25 + 11.68) grams of pollution, of which 33.93 are eliminated by the antipollution industry and the remaining 30 are delivered to households.

## VIII

The dollar figures entered in parentheses in Table 11-7 are based on prices whose derivation is explained below.

The original equation, system (10-7), describing the price-cost relationships within the agricultural and manufacturing sectors, has now to be expanded through inclusion of a third equation stating

## Table 11-7

Input-output table of the national economy (surplus pollution eliminated by the antipollution industry)

| Inputs and Pollutants Output | Output Sectors Sector 1 Agriculture | Sector 2 Manufacture | Antipollution | Final Deliveries to Households | Totals |
|---|---|---|---|---|---|
| Sector 1 Agriculture (bushels) | 26.12 ($52.24) | 23.37 ($46.74) | 0 | 55 ($110.00) | 104.50 ($208.99) |
| Sector 2 Manufacture (yards) | 14.63 ($73.15) | 7.01 ($35.05) | 6.79 ($33.94) | 30 ($150.00) | 58.43 ($292.13) |
| Pollutant (grams) | 52.25 | 11.68 | −33.93 | 30 ($101.80 paid for elimination of 33.93 grams of pollutant) | |
| Labor (man-years) | 83.60 ($83.60) | 210.34 ($210.34) | 67.86 ($67.86) | 0 | 361.80 ($361.80) |
| Column Totals | $208.99 | $292.13 | $101.80 | $361.80 | |

$p_1 = \$2.00$, $p_2 = \$5.00$, $p_3 = \$3.00$, $p_l = \$1.00$ (wage rate).

that the price of eliminating 1 gram of pollution (i.e., $p_3$) should be just high enough to cover—after payment for inputs purchased from other industries has been met—the value added, $v_3$, that is, the payments to labor and other primary factors employed directly by the antipollution industry.

$$p_1 - 0.25p_1 - 0.14p_2 = v_1$$
$$p_2 - 0.12p_2 - 0.40p_1 = v_2$$
$$p_3 \qquad\quad - 0.20p_2 = v_3$$

or in rearranged form,

(11-11)
$$0.75p_1 - 0.14p_2 \qquad\quad = v_1$$
$$-0.40p_1 + 0.88p_2 \qquad\quad = v_2$$
$$- 0.20p_2 + p_3 = v_3$$

The general solution of these equations—analogous to (11-8)—is

(11-12)
$$p_1 = 1.457v_1 + 0.232v_2$$
$$p_2 = 0.662v_1 + 1.242v_2$$
$$p_3 = 0.132v_1 + 0.248v_2 + v_3$$

Assuming, as before, $v_1 = 0.80$, $v_2 = 3.60$, and $v_3 = 2.00$, we find

$$p_1 = \$2.00$$
$$p_2 = \$5.00$$
$$p_3 = \$3.00$$

The price (= cost per unit) of eliminating pollution turns out to be $3.00 per gram. The prices of agricultural and manufactured products remain the same as they were before.

Putting corresponding dollar values on all the physical transactions shown in the input-output Table 11-7, we find that the labor employed by the three sectors adds up to $361.80. The wheat and cloth delivered to final consumers cost $260.00. The remaining $101.80 of the value added earned by the households will just suffice to pay the price, that is, to defray the costs of eliminating 33.93 of the total 63.93 grams of pollution generated by the system. These payments could be made directly or they might be collected in the form of taxes imposed on the households and used by the government to cover the costs of the privately or publicly operated antipollution industry.

The price system would be different if through voluntary action or to obey a special law each industry undertook to eliminate, at its own expense, all or at least some specified fraction of the pollution generated by it. The added costs would, of course, be included in the price of its marketable product.

Let, for example, the agricultural and manufacturing sectors bear the costs of eliminating 50 percent of the pollution that under prevailing technical conditions would be generated by each one of them. They may either engage in antipollution operations on their own account or pay an appropriately prorated tax.

In either case the first two equations in (11-11) have to be modified by inclusion of additional terms: the outlay for eliminating 0.25 grams and 0.10 grams of pollutant per unit of agricultural and industrial output, respectively.

(11-13)  
$$0.75p_1 - 0.14p_2 - 0.25p_3 = v_1$$
$$-0.40p_1 + 0.88p_2 - 0.10p_3 = v_2$$
$$- 0.20p_2 + p_3 = v_3$$

The "inversion" of the modified matrix of structural coefficients appearing on the left-hand side yields the following general solution of the price system:

(11-14)
$$p_1 = 1.511v_1 + 0.334v_2 + 0.411v_3$$
$$p_2 = 0.703v_1 + 1.318v_2 + 0.308v_3$$
$$p_3 = 0.141v_1 + 0.264v_2 + 1.062v_3$$

With values added in all three sectors remaining the same as they were before (i.e., $v_1 =$ \$.80, $v_2 =$ \$3.60, $v_3 =$ \$2.60), these new sets of prices are as follows:

$$p_1 = \$3.234$$
$$p_2 = \$5.923$$
$$p_3 = \$3.185$$

When purchasing a bushel of wheat or a yard of cloth, the purchaser now pays for elimination of some of the pollution generated in production of that good. The prices are now higher than they were before. From the point of view of households, the final consumers, the relationship between real costs and real benefits remains the same nevertheless; having paid for some antipollution activities indirectly, they will have to spend less on them directly.

## IX

The final table, Table 11-8, shows the flows of goods and services among all the sectors of the national economy analyzed above. The structural characteristics of the system—presented in the form of a complete set of technical input-output coefficients—were assumed to be given; so was the vector of final demand, that is, quantities of products of each industry delivered to households (and other final users) as well as the uneliminated amount of pollutant that, for one reason or another, they are prepared to tolerate. Each industry is assumed to be responsible for elimination of 50 percent of the pollution that would have been generated in the absence of such countermeasures. The households defray—directly or through tax contributions—the cost of reducing the net output of pollution still further to the amount that they do in fact accept.

On the basis of this structural information we can compute the outputs and the inputs of all sectors of the economy, including the antipollution industries, corresponding to any given bill of final demand. With information on value added, that is, the income paid out by each sector per unit of its total output, we can furthermore determine the prices of all outputs, the total income received by the final consumer, and the breakdown of total expenditures by types of goods consumed.

## Table 11-8

Input-output table of a national economy with pollution-related activities presented separately

| | Agriculture | | | Manufacture | | | Antipollution | Final Deliveries to Households | National Totals |
|---|---|---|---|---|---|---|---|---|---|
| | Wheat | Antipollution | Total | Cloth | Antipollution | Total | | | |
| Agriculture | 26.12 ($84.47) | 0 | 26.12 ($84.47) | 23.37 ($75.58) | 0 | 23.37 ($75.58) | 0 | 55 ($177.87) | 105.50 ($337.96) |
| Manufacture | 14.63 ($86.65) | 5.23 ($30.98) | 19.86 ($117.63) | 7.01 ($41.52) | 1.17 ($6.93) | 8.18 ($48.45) | .39 ($2.33) | 30 ($177.69) | 58.43 ($346.07) |
| Pollutant | 52.25 | −26.13 | 26.12 | 11.69 | −5.85 | 5.84 | −1.97 | 30 ($6.26 paid for elimination of 1.97 grams of pollutant) | |
| Labor (value added) | 83.60 ($83.60) | 52.26 ($52.26) | 135.86 ($135.86) | 210.34 ($210.34) | 11.70 ($11.70) | 222.04 ($222.04) | 3.93 ($3.93) | | 361.80 |
| Total costs | ($254.72) | ($83.24) | ($337.96) | ($327.44) | ($18.63) | ($346.07) | ($6.26) | ($361.80) | ($361.80) |

$p_1 = \$3.23, p_2 = \$5.92, p_3 = \$3.19$
$v_1 = \$0.80, v_2 = \$3.60, v_3 = \$2.00$

The 30 grams of pollutant entered in the bill of final demand are delivered free of charge. The $6.26 entered in the same box represents the costs of that part of antipollution activities that were covered by households directly rather than through payment of higher prices for agricultural and manufactured goods.

The input requirements of antipollution activities paid for by the agricultural and manufacturing sectors and all the other input requirements are shown separately and then combined in the total input columns. The figures entered in the pollution row show accordingly the amount of pollution that would be generated by the principal production process, the amount eliminatd (entered with a minus sign), and finally the amount actually released by the industry in question. The amount (1.97 grams) eliminated by antipollution activities not controlled by other sectors is entered in a separate column that shows also the corresponding inputs.

From a purely formal point of view, the only difference between Table 11-7 and Table 11-8 is that in the former all input requirements of agriculture and manufacture and the amount of pollutant released by each of them are shown in a single column, while in the latter the productive and antipollution activities are also described separately. If such subdivision proves to be impossible and if, furthermore, no separate antipollution industry can be identified, we have to rely on the still simpler analytical approach that led up to the construction of Table 11-3.

# X

Once appropriate sets of technical input and output coefficients have been compiled, generation and elimination of all the various kinds of pollutants can be analyzed as what they actually are—integral parts of the economic process.

Studies of regional and multiregional systems, multisectoral projections of economic growth, and, in particular, the effects of anticipated technological changes, along with all other special types of input-output analysis, can thus be extended to cover the production and elimination of pollution as well.

The compilation and organization of additional quantitative information required for such extension could be accelerated by systematic utilization of practical experience gained by public and private research organizations already actively engaged in compilation of various types of input-output tables.

# Mathematical appendix

## *Notation—static-open input-output system with pollution-related activities built in*

### *Commodities and services*

$$1, 2, 3, \ldots, i, \ldots m, m + 1, m + 2, \ldots, g, \ldots, k, \ldots, n$$
$$\underbrace{\qquad\qquad\qquad}_{\text{useful goods}} \qquad\qquad \underbrace{\qquad\qquad\qquad}_{\text{pollutants}}$$

### *Technical coefficients*

$a_{ij}$ = input of good $i$ per unit of output of good $j$ (produced by sector $j$)

$a_{ig}$ = input of good $i$ per unit of eliminated pollutant $g$ (eliminated by sector $g$)

$a_{gi}$ = output of pollutant $g$ per unit of output of good $i$ (produced by sector $i$)

$a_{gk}$ = output of pollutant $g$ per unit of eliminated pollutant $k$ (eliminated by sector $k$)

$r_{gi}, r_{gk}$ = proportion of pollutant $g$ generated by industry $i$ or $k$ eliminated at the expense of that industry

### *Variables*

$x_i$ = total output of good $i$

$x_g$ = total amount of pollutant $g$ eliminated

$y_i$ = final delivery of good $i$ (to households)

$y_g$ = final delivery of pollutant $g$ (to households)

$p_1$ = price of good

$p_g$ = the "price" of eliminating one unit of pollutant $g$

$v_i$ = value added in industry $i$ per unit of good $i$ produced by it

$v_g$ = value added in antipollution sector $g$ per unit of pollutant $g$ eliminated by it

### *Vectors and matrices*

$$A_{11} = [a_{ij}] \quad i, j = 1, 2, 3, \ldots, m$$
$$A_{21} = [a_{gi}] \quad i = 1, 2, 3, \ldots, m$$
$$A_{12} = [a_{ig}] \quad g = m + 1, m + 2, m + 3, \ldots$$
$$A_{22} = [a_{gk}] \quad g, k = m + 1, m + 2, m + 3, .$$
$$Q_{21} = [q_{gi}] \quad i = 1, 2, \ldots, m$$
$$\qquad\qquad\qquad g = m + 1, m + 2, \ldots, n$$
$$Q_{22} = [q_{gk}] \quad g, k = m + 1, m + 2, \ldots n$$

where $q_{gi} = r_{gi}a_{gi}$

$\qquad q_{gk} = r_{gk}a_{gk}$

$$X_1 = \begin{Bmatrix} x_1 \\ x_2 \\ \cdot \\ \cdot \\ \cdot \\ x_m \end{Bmatrix} \qquad Y_1 = \begin{Bmatrix} y_1 \\ y_2 \\ \cdot \\ \cdot \\ \cdot \\ y_m \end{Bmatrix} \qquad V_1 = \begin{Bmatrix} v_1 \\ v_2 \\ \cdot \\ \cdot \\ \cdot \\ v_m \end{Bmatrix}$$

$$X_2 = \begin{Bmatrix} x_{m+1} \\ x_{m+2} \\ \cdot \\ \cdot \\ \cdot \\ x_n \end{Bmatrix} \qquad Y_2 = \begin{Bmatrix} y_{m+1} \\ y_{m+2} \\ \cdot \\ \cdot \\ \cdot \\ y_n \end{Bmatrix} \qquad V_2 = \begin{Bmatrix} v_{m+1} \\ v_{m+2} \\ \cdot \\ \cdot \\ \cdot \\ v_n \end{Bmatrix}$$

*Physical input-output balance*

(11-15)
$$\begin{bmatrix} I - A_{11} & -A_{12} \\ A_{21} & -I + A_{22} \end{bmatrix} \begin{bmatrix} X_1 \\ X_2 \end{bmatrix} = \begin{bmatrix} Y_1 \\ Y_2 \end{bmatrix}$$

(11-16)
$$\begin{bmatrix} X_1 \\ X_2 \end{bmatrix} = \begin{bmatrix} I - A_{11} & -A_{12} \\ A_{21} & -I + A_{22} \end{bmatrix}^{-1} \begin{bmatrix} Y_1 \\ Y_2 \end{bmatrix}$$

*Input-output balance between prices and values added*

(11-17)
$$\begin{bmatrix} I - A'_{11} & -Q'_{21} \\ -A'_{12} & I - Q'_{22} \end{bmatrix} \begin{bmatrix} P_1 \\ P_2 \end{bmatrix} = \begin{bmatrix} V_1 \\ V_2 \end{bmatrix}$$

(11-18)
$$\begin{bmatrix} P_1 \\ P_2 \end{bmatrix} = \begin{bmatrix} I - A'_{11} & -Q'_{21} \\ -A'_{12} & I - Q'_{22} \end{bmatrix}^{-1} \begin{bmatrix} V_1 \\ V_2 \end{bmatrix}$$

# Supplementary notation and equations accounting for pollution generated directly by final consumption

## Technical coefficients

$a_{gy,\,(i)}$ = output of pollutant generated by consumption of one unit of commodity $i$ delivered to final demand

## Variables

$y_g^\circ$ = sum total of pollutant $g$ "delivered" from all industries to and generated within the final demand sector

$x_g^\circ$ = total gross output of pollutant $g$ generated by all industries and in the final demand sector

$$A_y = \begin{Bmatrix} a_{m+1,\,y(1)} & a_{m+1,\,y(1)} & \cdots & a_{m+1,\,y(m)} \\ a_{m+2,\,y(2)} & a_{m+2,\,y(2)} & \cdots & a_{m+2,\,y(m)} \\ \cdot & \cdot & & \\ \cdot & \cdot & & \\ \cdot & \cdot & & \\ a_n y_1 & a_n y_2 & \cdots & a_n\, y_m \end{Bmatrix}$$

$$Y_2^* = \left\{ \begin{array}{c} y^*_{m+1} \\ y^*_{m+2} \\ \cdot \\ \cdot \\ \cdot \\ y_n^* \end{array} \right\} \qquad x_g^* = \left\{ \begin{array}{c} x^*_{m+1} \\ x^*_{m+2} \\ \cdot \\ \cdot \\ \cdot \\ x_n^* \end{array} \right\}$$

In case some pollution is generated within the final demand sector itself, the vector $Y_2$ appearing on the right-hand side of (11-15) and (11-16) has to be replaced by vector $Y_2 - Y_2^*$, where

(11-19) $$Y_2^* = A_y Y_1$$

The price and value added equations (11-17) and (11-18) do not have to be modified.

Total gross output of pollutants generated by all industries and the final demand sector does not enter explicitly in any of the equations presented above; it can, however, be computed on the basis of the following equation:

(11-20) $$X^* = [A_{21} \vdots A_{22}] \left[ \begin{array}{c} X_1 \\ \cdots \\ X_2 \end{array} \right] + Y_2^*$$

# 12

## National income, economic structure, and environmental externalities

### (1973)

### I. National income as a welfare index

The per capita net national income used as a measure of the level of welfare is a typical index number. The computation of an index number involves application of some well-defined but essentially arbitrary conventional procedures to direct or indirect measurements of observed, or at least in principle observable, phenomena.

The conventional interpretation of net national income valued in some constant prices can be conveniently rationalized in terms of the ad hoc assumption that preferences of a representative average consumer can be described by a social utility function or a fixed set of well-behaving social indifference curves.

At this point observed or at least observable facts come in. The bundle of goods actually consumed by a representative individual has been obviously preferred—so goes the argument—to all the other alternative bundles that were accessible to that consumer.

Under the special conditions of a market economy, the set of all alternative bundles accessible to a representative consumer is uniquely determined by (1) the amounts of various goods that he or she has actually consumed and (2) the relative prices of these goods. The relative prices represent the marginal opportunity costs of each good in terms of every other good as seen from the point of their actual or potential consumer.

This factual information, combined with the before-mentioned ad

From M. Moss (ed.), *The Measurement of Economic and Social Performance*, Studies in Income and Wealth, vol. 38 (New York: National Bureau of Economic Research, 1973), pp. 565–76.

hoc assumption concerning the existence of a well-behaved set of collective indifference lines, permits us to identify *some* of the bundles of goods that the representative consumer apparently judges to be *less desirable* than the particular bundle that he or she actually chose to use.

This analytical proposition constitutes the basic, not to say the sole, theoretical justification for interpreting the *differences* in per capita net national income—valued in fixed prices—as an index of changes in the level of average per capita welfare attained by a particular society in different years.

Goods acquired through means other than purchases at given prices on a free market can still be taken into account in computation of the conventional welfare index provided their opportunity costs—as perceived by the representative consumer—can be ascertained in some other way.

Much of the work aimed at inclusion of various nonmarketable components into the measure of national income is centered on devising plausible methods of determining the imputed prices or more generally the opportunity costs of such goods.

In the light of what has been said above, the inclusion of pollutants and other kinds of environmental repercussions of economic activities in the measurement of the per capita national income as a welfare index requires answers to two sets of questions. One concerns the establishment of acceptable conventions pertaining to the inclusion of environmental repercussions in the conceptual framework of an all-embracing social utility function and a corresponding set of representative indifference curves. The other pertains to the actual physical description and measurement of the generation and elimination of pollutants by the economic system and the empirical determination of their opportunity costs in terms of ordinary goods and of each other.

The answer that one can give to these questions is critically influenced by the typically external nature of most environmental repercussions of economic activities and also by the fact that, because of that, measures aimed at abatement of their undesirable effects must in most instances be promulgated by the government.

Speaking in this context of collective indifference lines or preferences of a representative individual, one must interpret such preference—at least so far as the environmental effects of economic activities are concerned—as being revealed not through private but rather through collective choice reflected in specific actions of the government.

Moreover, in case the conjectured opportunity costs reflected in the level of antipollution actions actually observed differ from the true opportunity costs, it is the former rather than the latter that would have to provide the base for proper weighting of pollution components to be included in a revised, more comprehensive national income index.

Who would pretend to know what opportunity costs (if any) are being taken into account in the design of antipollution measures now actually being carried out in the United States?

Many economists when touching upon problems of social valuation abandon the difficult revealed preference criteria in favor of a strictly axiomatic approach.

That solves the problem of welfare measurement as simply as Columbus solved his problem with the egg. One chooses ad hoc a social utility function which for some ethical or mathematical reason is appealing, inserts into it the levels of consumption of ordinary goods and net output of pollutants as they actually are, and then compares the index of welfare thus attained with the highest number of points that could be reached if the society were to move to the optimal point along the empirically given opportunity costs frontier.

Who can decide, however, what social utility function one should finally choose? Certainly not the economists in their professional capacity!

## II. Enlarged input-output table, structural coefficients, and intersectoral dependence

Figure 12-1 presents a schematic outline of an expanded input-output table that traces not only the intersectoral flows of ordinary commodities and services but also the generation and elimination of pollutants. The conventional classification of economic activities and goods is accordingly expanded to include the names of various pollutants and activities aimed at their elimination.

### Notes to Figure 12-1

(1,1) This square represents inputs of (ordinary) goods into industries. Most of these goods are produced by industries listed on the left, but some might originate as the "byproduct" in pollution-eliminating activities. See (1,3).

(1,2) In this square are inputs of ordinary goods into various pollution-elim-

| | Industries 1 | Pollution-eliminating Activities 2 | Final Demand Sector 3 | | Totals 4 |
|---|---|---|---|---|---|
| Industries 1 | (1,1) Inputs of goods into industries (+)  $[a_{ij}]$ | (1,2) Inputs of goods into pollution-eliminating activities (+)  Outputs of goods by pollution-eliminating activities (−)  $[a_{ig}]$ | (1,3A) Delivery of goods to final demand sector (+) | (1,3B) (Empty) | (1,4) Total outputs of goods excluding the amounts generated by the pollution-eliminating activities |
| Pollutants 2 | (2,1) Outputs of pollutants by industries (+)  $[a_{gi}]$ | (2,2) Elimination of pollutants by pollution-eliminating activities (−)  Outputs of pollutants by pollution-eliminating activities (+)  $[a_{gk}]$ | (2,3A) Outputs of pollutants by final demand sector (connected with the consumption of goods) (+)  $[c_{gi}]$ | (2,3B) Outputs of pollutants by the final demand sector (connected with the consumption of primary factors) (+)  $[c_{gf}]$ | (2,4) *Net outputs of pollutants* (+) |
| Primary Inputs 3 | (3,1) Inputs of primary factors into industries (+)  $[v_{fi}]$ | (3,2) Inputs of primary factors into pollution-eliminating activities (+)  $[v_{fg}]$ | (3,3A) (Empty) | (3,3B) Delivery of primary factors to final demand sector (+) | (3,4) Total inputs of primary factors (+) |

**Figure 12-1**

Interindustrial flows expanded to include the generation and elimination of pollutants

inating activities and outputs of ordinary goods (entered with a negative sign) generated as byproducts of pollution-eliminating activities. Reprocessed materials, for example, are entered here.

(1,3A) Goods delivered to the final demand sector are entered along the main diagonal of this square. See (3,3B).

(1,4) These totals do not include amounts of ordinary goods (as their byproducts) originating in the pollution-eliminating activities and thus represent the activity levels of ordinary industries.

(2,1) Each row shows the amounts of one particular pollutant generated by industries listed at the heads of different columns. In otherwords, pollutants are treated here the way byproducts are treated in ordinary input-output tables.

(2,2) Along each row are entered—as negative numbers—the amounts of one particular pollutant eliminated by activities named at the heads of different columns. The amounts of a pollutant generated, as is often the case, in the process of elimination of some other pollutants are entered along its appropriate row as positive numbers.

(2,3A), (2,3B) For purely descriptive purposes, the total amounts of various pollutants generated in the final demand sector can be presented in a single column. For purposes of structural analyses, however, these totals should be distributed among as many separate columns as there are different inputs, that is, industrial product inputs and primary factor inputs, absorbed by the final demand sector. In the process of final consumption each of these inputs is liable to generate its own "column" of pollutants. The inputs of ordinary goods into the final demand sector are entered in rows along the main diagonal of the square formed by (1,2) and (2,2) considered together. It sounds rather complicated, but that is the price one has to pay for orderly bookkeeping.

(2,4) Each figure in this column is obtained by subtracting the sum of all negative entries from the sum of all positive entries appearing to the left along the entire length of the row. These are the undesirable *net* outputs of various pollutants delivered by the economic system to the final users alongside the desirable ordinary goods and primary factors entered in (1,3A) and (3,3B). Together they make up the final results of economic activities upon which the welfare of the society supposedly depends.

(3,1), (3,2), (3,3B), (3,4) These contain a single row of aggregated value-added figures or several rows of physical or dollar figures, depending on the amount of detail one wants to present.

The entries are organized in such a way as to have each column contain inputs and outputs controlled by the same autonomous set of structural relationships (i.e., by the same "cooking recipe"). The figure is subdivided into rows and corresponding column strips. Each strip can be thought of as containing many rows of figures not shown in this schematic presentation. Each of the rectangular intersections on a row and a column can be conveniently identified by two numbers.

All entries can be interpreted as representing physical quantities measured in appropriate physical units or indices of physical amounts. All dollar figures appearing in the figure can be interpreted as such indices (with a defined or undefined base). Hence, the usual column sums are pointedly omitted.

## III. Structural relationship and opportunity costs

The figures entered in each one of the separate columns of the first three vertical strips of the enlarged flow table can be interpreted as representing the inputs absorbed and outputs generated by one particular process carried on side by side with many other structurally

different processes within the framework of the given economic
system.

Assuming that the structure of each such process can be described
in terms of a linear or at least linearized "cooking recipe," the actual
level of each output and each input as entered in the flow table can
be interpreted as a product of two numbers: a technical coefficient
and a number describing the level at which the process that absorbs
that particular input or generates that particular output actually
operates.

The levels of operation of ordinary industries are usually measured in terms of their principal output, while the level of operation
of a pollution-eliminating activity can be conveniently described by
the number of units of the specific pollutant that it eliminates. The
levels of consumption activities that might generate pollution are
described by the number of units of a particular good or primary
factor delivered to the final demand sector.

The structural matrix of the economy—corresponding to the
enlarged flow table described above—can be written in the partitioned form of Figure 12-2. The elements of each submatrix are
technical input or output coefficients; they are defined concisely in
the mathematical appendix at the end of this chapter.

While the input coefficients of ordinary goods can usually be
derived from the observed flows, information on the magnitude of
the structural coefficient describing the generation and elimination
of pollutants in most instances has to be obtained directly from technological sources. Combined with appropriate figures of the outputs
of all pollution-generating activities, these coefficients provide a
basis for estimation of the pollution flows.

In many, not to say in most, instances pollution is being combated
not through the operation of separate elimination processes but
rather through the use of less polluting alternative techniques for
production of ordinary goods. To incorporate such additional information, the structural matrix would have to describe the input structure of some industrial sectors and possibly even some final demand
sectors in terms of several alternative columns of input and output
coefficients. The corresponding flow tables would and actually do
already in many instances show for some sectors two or more columns of input-output flows.

Without explaining in detail the mathematical formulation and
solution of the system of input-output equations involved,[1] it suffices

[1]See this chapter's mathematical appendix. See also Chapter 11 and Chapter 13 in this
volume.

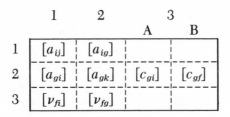

**Figure 12-2**

here to say that on the basis of the information contained in an enlarged structural matrix of a given economy it would be possible to compute (and some such computations have already been made) the total factor inputs (measured in physical amounts or more or less aggregated value-added dollars) required directly and indirectly (1) to deliver to final users one additional unit of any particular good while keeping the deliveries of all the other goods and the net outputs of all pollutants constant and (2) to reduce by one unit the *net* output of any particular pollutant while keeping constant the net outputs of all the other pollutants and final deliveries of all goods.

This means that factual information contained in an enlarged structural matrix of a particular economy would permit us to compute in a rough and ready fashion the opportunity costs of an additional unit of any good and of an eliminated unit of the net output of each pollutant. The basic matrix of structural coefficients that governs the physical flows presented on the enlarged input-output table determines also a corresponding set of price-cost relationships.

The elimination of pollutants originating in various sectors can be paid for either directly by the final users or by the producing sectors in which they are being generated. In the latter case the cost of doing so will obviously be included in the price of the finished product. I have explained elsewhere how these institutionally determined parameters can be introduced in standard input-output formulation of balanced price-cost equations.[2]

If the prices are expected to reflect the true opportunity costs of various goods (including the "products" of pollution-eliminating activities) to final users, they must cover the costs of eliminating all additional pollution generated in the process of their production. Otherwise, in purchasing a useful good the consumer would

[2]Ibid.

receive, probably unwittingly, an additional delivery of undesirable pollutants. Hence, the system of prices to be used for purposes of welfare decisions should be computed on the assumption that each industry and each pollution-eliminating process bears the full cost of eliminating all pollutants generated by it. This, of course, does not imply that the actual institutional arrangement and consequently the actual pricing should necessarily be governed by the same principle, especially since the distributional effect of such "pure" opportunity cost pricing might turn out to be undesirable.

Once the prices of all outputs (including those of all antipollution activities) have been determined, all entries in the expanded tables of interindustrial flows can be valued in dollars. Marginal totals can be entered not only at the end of each row but also at the bottom of each column. The outputs of all pollutants will be represented by negative dollar figures, the amounts of pollutants eliminated by positive dollar figures. In particular, the net outputs of pollutants delivered to final users (2,4) will add up to a negative figure. It can be interpreted as representing the upper limit of the amount that would have to be spent (but in fact was not spent) for this particular purpose if the final users decide to eliminate all pollution actually delivered to them.

## Mathematical appendix

### The numbering of goods, pollutants, and primary factors

$1, 2, \ldots, i, \ldots, j, \ldots, n$                                     $n$ goods

$n + 1, n + 2, \ldots, g, \ldots, k, \ldots, n + m$         $m$ pollutants

$n + m + 1, n + m + 2, \ldots, f, \ldots, n + m + h$   $h$ primary factors

### Technical coefficients

$a_{ij}$ = input of good $i$ per unit of output of good $j$ (produced by industry $j$)

$a_{ig}$ = if $> 0$, input of good $i$ per unit of eliminated pollutant $g$; if $< 0$, output of good $i$ per unit of eliminated pollutant $g$

$a_{gi}$ = if $> 0$, output of pollutant $g$ per unit of output of good $i$ (produced by industry $i$); if $< 0$, input (productive use) of pollutant $g$ per unit of output of good $i$ (produced by industry $i$)

$a_{gk}$ = output of pollutant $g$ per unit of eliminated pollutant $k$

$c_{gi}$ = output of pollutant $g$ generated in the final demand sector in the process of consuming one unit of good $i$

$c_{gf}$ = output of pollutant $g$ generated in the final demand sector in the process of consuming one unit of the primary factor $f$

$v_{fi}$ = input of factor $f$ per unit output of good $i$ (produced by industry $i$)

$v_{fg}$ = input of factor $f$ per unit of eliminated pollutant $g$

$v_i$ = value added paid out by industry $i$ per unit of its output

$v_g$ = value added paid out by the pollution-eliminating sector $g$ per unit of pollution eliminated

## Vectors of technical coefficients

$$[a_{ij}], [a_{ig}], \text{ etc.}$$

## Variables

$x_i$ = total output of good $i$ by industry $i$

$x_g$ = total amount of pollutant $g$ eliminated by pollutant-eliminating activity $g$

$x_f$ = total amount of factor $f$ used in all sectors

$y_i$ = total amount of good $i$ delivered to final demand

$y_g$ = net output of pollutant (delivered to final demand)

$y_f$ = total amount of factor $f$ delivered to final demand

$p_i$ = price of one unit of good produced by industry $i$

$p_g$ = price of eliminating one unit of pollution $g$ by sector $g$

## Vectors of variables

$$
X_1 = \begin{bmatrix} x_1 \\ x_2 \\ \cdot \\ \cdot \\ \cdot \\ x_i \\ \cdot \\ \cdot \\ \cdot \\ x_j \\ \cdot \\ \cdot \\ \cdot \\ x_n \end{bmatrix}
\quad
X_2 = \begin{bmatrix} x_{n+1} \\ x_{n+2} \\ \cdot \\ \cdot \\ \cdot \\ x_g \\ \cdot \\ \cdot \\ \cdot \\ x_k \\ x_{n+m} \end{bmatrix}
\quad
X_3 = \begin{bmatrix} x_{n+m+1} \\ x_{n+m+2} \\ \cdot \\ \cdot \\ \cdot \\ x_f \\ \cdot \\ \cdot \\ \cdot \\ x_{n+m+h} \end{bmatrix}
$$

$$Y_1 \begin{bmatrix} y_1 \\ y_2 \\ \cdot \\ \cdot \\ \cdot \\ y_i \\ \cdot \\ \cdot \\ y_j \\ \cdot \\ \cdot \\ \cdot \\ y_n \end{bmatrix} \qquad Y_2 = \begin{bmatrix} y_{n+1} \\ y_{n+2} \\ \cdot \\ \cdot \\ \cdot \\ y_g \\ \cdot \\ \cdot \\ y_k \\ \cdot \\ \cdot \\ \cdot \\ y_{n+m} \end{bmatrix} \qquad Y_3 = \begin{bmatrix} y_{n+m+1} \\ y_{n+m+2} \\ \cdot \\ \cdot \\ \cdot \\ y_f \\ \cdot \\ \cdot \\ y_{n+m+h} \end{bmatrix}$$

$$V_1 = \begin{bmatrix} v_1 \\ v_2 \\ \cdot \\ \cdot \\ v_i \\ \cdot \\ \cdot \\ v_j \\ \cdot \\ \cdot \\ \cdot \\ v_n \end{bmatrix} \quad V_2 = \begin{bmatrix} v_{n+1} \\ v_{n+2} \\ \cdot \\ \cdot \\ v_g \\ \cdot \\ \cdot \\ v_k \\ \cdot \\ \cdot \\ \cdot \\ v_{n+m} \end{bmatrix} \quad P_1 = \begin{bmatrix} p_1 \\ p_2 \\ \cdot \\ \cdot \\ p_i \\ \cdot \\ \cdot \\ p_j \\ \cdot \\ \cdot \\ \cdot \\ p_n \end{bmatrix} \quad P_2 = \begin{bmatrix} p_{n+1} \\ p_{n+2} \\ \cdot \\ \cdot \\ p_g \\ \cdot \\ \cdot \\ p_k \\ \cdot \\ \cdot \\ \cdot \\ p_{n+m} \end{bmatrix}$$

## Balance equations

Each of the following matrix equations describes the balance between the outputs and the inputs entered in one of the three row strips of the enlarged input-output table.

(12-1)  Goods $[I - a_{ij}]X_1 - [a_{ig}]X_2 \qquad\qquad = Y_2$

Pollutants $- [a_{gi}]X_1 + [I - a_{gk}]X_2 = [c_{gi}]Y_1 - Y_2 + [c_{gf}]Y_3$

Factors $- [v_{fi}]X_1 - [v_{fg}]X_2 + X_3 \quad = \qquad\qquad Y_3$

The general solution of that system for the unknown $x$'s in terms of given $y$'s is

(12-2)

$$
\begin{bmatrix} X_1 \\ \hline X_2 \\ \hline X_3 \end{bmatrix}
$$

$$
= \begin{bmatrix} [I - a_{ij}] & -[a_{ig}] & 0 \\ \hline -[a_{gi}] & [I - a_{gk}] & 0 \\ \hline -[v_{fi}] & -[v_{fg}] & [I] \end{bmatrix}^{-1}
\begin{bmatrix} Y_1 \\ \hline [c_{gi}]Y_1 - Y_g + [c_{gf}]Y_3 \\ \hline Y_3 \end{bmatrix}
$$

Separating the effects of the three kinds of outputs delivered to the final demand sector and expressing the relationship (12-2) in incremental terms,

(12-3)

$$
\begin{bmatrix} \Delta X_1 \\ \hline \Delta X_2 \\ \hline \Delta X_3 \end{bmatrix}
= \begin{bmatrix} & & \\ & M & \\ & & \end{bmatrix}^{-1}
\begin{bmatrix} \Delta Y_1 \\ \hline [c_{gi}]\,\Delta Y_1 \\ \hline 0 \end{bmatrix}
$$

$$
+ \begin{bmatrix} & & \\ & M & \\ & & \end{bmatrix}^{-1}
\begin{bmatrix} 0 \\ \hline -\Delta Y_2 \\ \hline 0 \end{bmatrix}
+ \begin{bmatrix} & & \\ & M & \\ & & \end{bmatrix}^{-1}
\begin{bmatrix} 0 \\ \hline [c_{gf}]\,\Delta Y_3 \\ \hline \Delta Y_3 \end{bmatrix}
$$

The inverse of the enlarged structural matrix of the economy appearing on the right-hand side is the same that appears in (12-2) above.

The first and third terms on the right-hand side describe the effect—on the output of goods ($\Delta X_1$), the level of antipollution activities ($\Delta X_2$), and total factor inputs ($\Delta X_3$)—of a given change in the final demand for goods ($\Delta Y_1$) and, respectively, final demand for primary factors ($\Delta Y_2$). These effects are computed on the assumption that the level of pollution-eliminating activities will be adjusted in such a way as to leave the net delivery of pollutants to final users unchanged (i.e., $\Delta Y_2 = 0$).

The second right-hand term shows what it would take—in total outputs of goods and total primary factor inputs—to *reduce* the delivery of (uneliminated) pollution to final users by the amount $\Delta Y_2$ while holding the deliveries of goods and factor services constant ($\Delta Y_1 = 0$, $\Delta Y_3 = 0$).

For purposes of price-cost computations, all primary factor flows entered along the second row-strip of the expanded input-output table can be valued in dollars and consolidated into a single row of value-added figures. Accordingly, the two coefficient matrices $-[v_{fi}]$ and $[v_{fg}]$ can be reduced to row vectors $V_1$ and $V_2$ of value-added coefficients.

If each industry and each antipollution activity were to pay—and include in the price of its product—the costs of eliminating all pollution directly generated by it,[3] the balance between revenues and outlays in all goods-producing and pollution-eliminating sectors could be described by the following matrix equations:

(12-4)          Goods                    $[I - a'_{ij}]P_1 - [a'_{gi}]P_2 = V_1$

            Pollutant elimination $[a'_{ig}]P_1 + [I - a'_{gk}]P_2 = V_2$

The general solution of that system for unknown $p$'s in terms of given $v$'s is

(12-5)
$$
\begin{bmatrix} P_1 \\ \hline P_2 \end{bmatrix} = \begin{bmatrix} [I - a'_{ij}] & -[a'_{gi}] \\ \hline -[a'_{ig}] & [I - a'_{gk}] \end{bmatrix}^{-1} \begin{bmatrix} V_1 \\ \hline V_2 \end{bmatrix}
$$

---

[3]For price computations based on different assumptions, see Chapter 13.

# 13

## Air pollution and the economic structure: Empirical results of input-output computations

### ( 1 9 7 2 )

### I

Generation and elimination of various pollutants, in principle at least, lends itself as easily to systematic description and analysis within the framework of a conventional input-output system as production and consumption of all ordinary industrial products and services. Pollutants are byproducts of industries already described in detail in a conventional input-output table. Economic activities that would mitigate the environmental disruption that accompanies industrial operations can also be incorporated into an appropriately expanded input-output system.

The formal organization of such an extended input-output system has been described in a paper prepared for the Symposium on Environmental Disruption held under UNESCO sponsorship in Tokyo in March 1970.[1] Primary data that are being collected both in the United States and, we are told, in Japan should eventually permit that system's full empirical implementation.

The structural coefficient matrix of a national economy extended to cover not only production and (productive) consumption of ordinary goods but also generation and elimination of pollutants can be presented in the partitioned form shown in Figure 13-1. The con-

---

[1]"Environmental Repercussions and the Economic Structure: An Input-Output Approach," in Shigeto Tsuru, ed., *A Challenge to Social Scientists* (Tokyo: Asahi, 1970), pp. 114–34. Reprinted in *Review of Economics and Statistics*, vol. LII, no. 3, August 1970, pp. 262–71.

Daniel Ford is coauthor of this chapter. A. Brody and A. P. Carter, eds., *Input-Output Techniques*. © 1972. North-Holland Publishing Company.

$$
\begin{array}{|c|c|}
\hline
A_{11} & A_{12} \\
\hline
A_{21} & A_{22} \\
\hline
v_1\,v_2\ \cdots\ v_m & v_{m+1}\ \cdots\ v_n \\
\hline
\end{array}
\equiv
\begin{array}{|cccc|ccc|}
\hline
a_{11}\,a_{12} & \cdots & a_{1m} & & a_{1\,m+1} & \cdots & a_{1n} \\
a_{21}a_{22} & \cdots & a_{2m} & & a_{2\,m+1} & \cdots & a_{2n} \\
\vdots & & \vdots & & \vdots & & \vdots \\
a_{m1}\,a_{m2} & \cdots & a_{mm} & & a_{m\,m+1} & \cdots & a_{mn} \\
\hline
a_{m+11}\,a_{m+12} & \cdots & a_{m+1\,m} & & a_{m+1\,m+1} & \cdots & a_{m+1\,n} \\
a_{m+21} & & \vdots & & \vdots & & \vdots \\
\vdots & & & & & & \\
a_{n1}\,a_{n2} & \cdots & a_{nm} & & a_{n\,m+1} & \cdots & a_{nn} \\
\hline
v_1\,v_2 & \cdots & v_m & & v_{m+1} & \cdots & v_n \\
\hline
\end{array}
$$

**Figure 13-1**

tents of the matrices $A_{11}$, $A_{21}$, $A_{12}$, and $A_{22}$ are described on the right-hand side. The various types of coefficients are defined as follows:

$a_{ij}$ = input of good $i$ per unit of output of good $j$ (produced by sector $j$); $i, j = 1, 2, 3, \ldots, m$

$a_{ig}$ = input of good $i$ per unit of eliminated pollutant $g$ (eliminated by sector $g$)

$a_{gi}$ = output of pollutant $g$ per unit of output of good $i$ (produced by sector $i$)

$\left.\begin{array}{l} \\ \\ \\ \\ \\ \end{array}\right\}$ $i = 1, 2, 3, \ldots, m$
$g = m + 1, m + 2, m + 3, \ldots, n$

$a_{gk}$ = output of pollutant $g$ per unit of eliminated pollutant $k$ (eliminated by sector $k$); $g, k = m + 1, m + 2, m + 3, \ldots, n$

Therefore, $A_{11}$ is the usual matrix of interindustry coefficients, $A_{21}$ is the matrix of direct pollution output coefficients, $A_{12}$ is the input structure coefficients of specific antipollution activities, and $A_{22}$ is the pollution output coefficient matrix for the antipollution activities.

Finally, $v_1, v_2, \ldots, v_m$ represent the value added in each industry per unit of output produced by it, and $v_{m+1}, v_{m+2}, \ldots v_n$ represent the value added in each antipollution sector per unit of pollutant eliminated by it.

Substances described as pollutants can sometimes be and often actually are utilized as inputs in the production of useful goods. (Trash, for example, can be used as a fuel and nitrogen and phosphorus as raw material in production of fertilizers.) The corresponding input coefficients must be accordingly entered in matrix $A_{21}$, but with a negative rather than a positive sign. In case a particular pollutant happens to be both generated and used as an input by the same industry, the difference between corresponding output and input coefficients has to be entered in matrix $A_{21}$ with appropriate sign.

In the description of a pollution-eliminating activity, the coefficients entered into the corresponding columns of matrices $A_{12}$ and $A_{22}$ describe all inputs and outputs per unit of eliminated pollutant. Entries in the $A_{22}$ matrix can represent the tradeoff between the level of output of different pollutants, permitting determination, for example, of the tons of particulates emitted into the atmosphere per ton of solid waste eliminated by municipal waste incineration plants. In case a given antipollution activity itself happens to generate the same pollutant, it is important to note whether the amount eliminated is measured in gross or net terms.

In fact, only matrices $A_{11}$ and $A_{21}$ were actually available. And, instead of a value-added row for separate antipollution activities, only increments to the value-added coefficients of regular activities for elimination of four pollutants (particulates, sulfur oxides, hydrocarbons, and carbon monoxide) taken together were available.

The data presented in Tables 13-1 through 13-7 are represented in terms of the notation of the partitioned matrix of structural coefficients. In some cases, matrices were transposed for presentational convenience.

# II

As a beginning step in the empirical implementation of an input-output model with environmental dimensions, we present a preliminary report on the dependence of five types of air pollution—particulates, sulfur oxides, hydrocarbons, carbon monoxide, and nitrogen oxides—on the input-output structure of the American economy and the observed past and anticipated future changes in that structure from the year 1958 over the years 1963 and 1967, toward 1980. The results of these computations are summarized in seven tables.

The basic input-output data for the year 1963 are those compiled and published by the office of Business Economics (U.S. Department of Commerce). The projected matrix of 1980 technical coefficients and the corresponding 1980 final demand vector used in this study were originally developed for the Interagency Growth Project.[2]

---

[2]See Appendix 13-2.

The original 370-sector tables were aggregated into 90-sector tables in which the 30 sectors from which most of the atmospheric pollution comes are described in a relatively detailed breakdown, while the remaining 60 are shown in broader groupings.[3] This is one version of the $A_{11}$ matrix used in our computations. Another version is based on the 83-sector matrix published in the OBE for the year 1958 and later projected to 1980.

The additional information which permits us to incorporate the five special pollutant output rows into the conventional input-output table, consists of five sets of pollution-output coefficients. The (regular) outputs of all industries are expressed in 1963 prices for the year 1967, but for the years 1958 and 1980 they are expressed in 1958 prices. The pollution coefficients, describing the thousands of tons of particular pollutants emitted by each industry per million dollars' worth of its total output, are based on primary information collected for the year 1967. However, when used in conjunction with the 1958, 1963, or 1980 input-output tables, they were adjusted to the appropriate price base.

The five sets of pollution-output coefficients that make up matrix $A_{21}$ used in our computations are shown in Table 13-1. As explained in Appendix 13-2, these technical coefficients were derived from sampling estimates that in many instances cannot be considered to be truly representative. Hence the results of our computations based on these data will have to be revised as more accurate estimates for the basic pollution-output coefficients become available.

Pollution produced by privately used passenger cars is omitted in the emission data and all following computations since so much work has already been done in this area. However, the pollution generated by other automotive transportation sources is included. Residential space-heating emissions are accounted for in the coefficient for the real estate and rental industry, as explained in Appendix 13-2.

As is well known, the inverse $(I - A)^{-1}$ of $(I - A)$, where $A$ represents the structural (input coefficients) matrix of a given economy, describes the total, that is, direct and indirect, effect of a \$1 million worth increase in the final demand for the products of any given industry on the total output of this and every other industry. The amounts of each one of the five different kinds of pollutants generated in connection with the increase in level of all outputs contributing directly or indirectly to delivery to final users of \$1 million

[3]See Appendix 13-1.

## Table 13-1

Direct 1967 air pollution output coefficients (thousands of tons emitted into the atmosphere per million dollars of output, output of each industry measured in 1963 prices)

| 90-order industry | (1) Part. | (2) SO$_x$ | (3) HC | (4) CO | (5) NO$_x$ |
|---|---|---|---|---|---|
| 1 Water and sanitary services | 0.24270 | 0.0 | 0.28760 | 0.56080 | 0.14380 |
| 2 Electric utilities | 0.27100 | 0.73250 | 0.0 | 0.0 | 0.17090 |
| 3 Plup mills | 0.14020 | 0.0 | 0.0 | 0.0 | 0.0 |
| 4 Iron and steel foundries | 0.05070 | 0.0 | 0.0 | 0.75830 | 0.0 |
| 5 Primary steel | 0.06670 | 0.0 | 0.0 | 0.0 | 0.0 |
| 6 Primary nonferrous metals | 0.01750 | 0.71070 | 0.0 | 0.0 | 0.0 |
| 7 Industrial chemicals | 0.00330 | 0.04200 | 0.0 | 0.0 | 0.0 |
| 8 Fertilizers | 0.00760 | 0.0 | 0.0 | 0.0 | 0.0 |
| 9 Petroleum refining | 0.00420 | 0.09210 | 0.04090 | 0.08770 | 0.0 |
| 10 Paving mixtures | 0.99810 | 0.0 | 0.0 | 0.0 | 0.0 |
| 11 Cement, hydraulic | 0.72290 | 0.0 | 0.0 | 0.0 | 0.0 |
| 12 Lime | 2.16350 | 0.0 | 0.0 | 0.0 | 0.0 |
| 13 Coal mining | 0.05170 | 0.0 | 0.0 | 0.0 | 0.0 |
| 14 Wholesale trade | 0.0 | 0.0 | 0.01940 | 0.0 | 0.0 |
| 15 Grain milling | 0.12620 | 0.0 | 0.0 | 0.0 | 0.0 |
| 16 Paints and allied products | 0.0 | 0.0 | 0.00170 | 0.0 | 0.0 |
| 17 Secondary nonferrous metals | 0.04360 | 0.0 | 0.0 | 0.0 | 0.0 |
| 18 Livestock and livestock products | 0.0 | 0.00910 | 0.0 | 0.0 | 0.0 |
| 19 Other agricultural products | 0.0 | 0.05160 | 0.0 | 0.0 | 0.0 |
| 20 Forestry and fishery products | 0.0 | 0.02680 | 0.0 | 0.0 | 0.0 |
| 21 Agricultural, forestry, and fishery services | 0.0 | 0.0 | 0.0 | 0.0 | 0.0 |
| 22 Iron and ferroalloy ores mining | 0.0 | 0.0 | 0.0 | 0.0 | 0.0 |
| 23 Nonferrous metal ores mining | 0.0 | 0.0 | 0.0 | 0.0 | 0.0 |
| 24 Crude petroleum and natural gas | 0.0 | 0.00860 | 0.0 | 0.0 | 0.0 |
| 25 Stone and clay mining and quarrying | 0.0 | 0.02460 | 0.0 | 0.0 | 0.0 |
| 26 Chemical and fertilizer mineral mining | 0.0 | 0.0 | 0.0 | 0.0 | 0.0 |
| 27 New construction | 0.0 | 0.01510 | 0.0 | 0.0 | 0.0 |
| 28 Maintenance and repair construction | 0.0 | 0.00870 | 0.0 | 0.0 | 0.0 |
| 29 Ordnance and accessories | 0.0 | 0.0 | 0.0 | 0.0 | 0.0 |
| 30 Food and kindred products | 0.0 | 0.00430 | 0.0 | 0.0 | 0.0 |
| 31 Tobacco manufactures | 0.0 | 0.0 | 0.0 | 0.0 | 0.0 |
| 32 Fabrics, yarn, and thread mills | 0.0 | 0.0 | 0.0 | 0.0 | 0.0 |
| 33 Textile goods and floor coverings | 0.0 | 0.0 | 0.0 | 0.0 | 0.0 |
| 34 Apparel | 0.0 | 0.0 | 0.0 | 0.0 | 0.0 |
| 35 Miscellaneous fabricated textile products | 0.0 | 0.0 | 0.0 | 0.0 | 0.0 |
| 36 Lumber and wood products | 0.0 | 0.00690 | 0.0 | 0.0 | 0.0 |
| 37 Wooden containers | 0.0 | 0.0 | 0.0 | 0.0 | 0.0 |
| 38 Household furniture | 0.0 | 0.0 | 0.0 | 0.0 | 0.0 |
| 39 Other furniture and fixtures | 0.0 | 0.0 | 0.0 | 0.0 | 0.0 |

## Table 13-1 (Cont.)

Direct 1967 air pollution output coefficients (thousands of tons emitted into the atmosphere per million dollars of output, output of each industry measured in 1963 prices)

| 90-order industry | (1)<br>Part. | (2)<br>$SO_x$ | (3)<br>HC | (4)<br>CO | (5)<br>$NO_x$ |
|---|---|---|---|---|---|
| 40 Paper and allied products | 0.03630 | 0.01210 | 0.0 | 0.0 | 0.0 |
| 41 Paperboard containers and boxes | 0.0 | 0.01150 | 0.0 | 0.0 | 0.0 |
| 42 Printing and publishing | 0.0 | 0.00330 | 0.0 | 0.0 | 0.0 |
| 43 Agricultural and miscellaneous chemicals | 0.0 | 0.03950 | 0.0 | 0.0 | 0.0 |
| 44 Plastics and synthetic materials | 0.0 | 0.22400 | 0.0 | 0.0 | 0.0 |
| 45 Drugs, cleaning and toilet preparations | 0.0 | 0.00870 | 0.0 | 0.0 | 0.0 |
| 46 Asphalt felts and coatings | 0.0 | 0.19920 | 0.0 | 0.0 | 0.0 |
| 47 Rubber and plastic products | 0.0 | 0.00460 | 0.0 | 0.0 | 0.0 |
| 48 Leather tanning, products | 0.0 | 0.0 | 0.0 | 0.0 | 0.0 |
| 49 Footwear and other leather products | 0.0 | 0.0 | 0.0 | 0.0 | 0.0 |
| 50 Glass and glass products | 0.0 | 0.0 | 0.0 | 0.0 | 0.0 |
| 51 Stone and clay products | 0.0 | 0.01300 | 0.0 | 0.0 | 0.0 |
| 52 Iron and steel forgings | 0.0 | 0.0 | 0.0 | 0.0 | 0.0 |
| 53 Miscellaneous nonferrous metals | 0.0 | 0.0 | 0.0 | 0.0 | 0.0 |
| 54 Metal containers | 0.0 | 0.0 | 0.0 | 0.0 | 0.0 |
| 55 Heating, plumbing, and fabricated structural metal products | 0.0 | 0.00590 | 0.0 | 0.0 | 0.0 |
| 56 Screws and metal stampings | 0.0 | 0.0 | 0.0 | 0.0 | 0.0 |
| 57 Other fabricated metal products | 0.0 | 0.00600 | 0.0 | 0.0 | 0.0 |
| 58 Engines and turbines | 0.0 | 0.0 | 0.0 | 0.0 | 0.0 |
| 59 Farm machinery and equipment | 0.0 | 0.0 | 0.0 | 0.0 | 0.0 |
| 60 Construction, mining, and oil field equipment | 0.0 | 0.0 | 0.0 | 0.0 | |
| 61 Materials handling machinery and equipment | 0.0 | 0.0 | 0.0 | 0.0 | 0.0 |
| 62 Metalworking machinery and equipment | 0.0 | 0.0 | 0.0 | 0.0 | 0.0 |
| 63 Special industrial machinery and equipment | 0.0 | 0.0 | 0.0 | 0.0 | 0.0 |
| 64 General industrial machinery and equipment | 0.0 | 0.01000 | 0.0 | 0.0 | 0.0 |
| 65 Machine shop products | 0.0 | 0.0 | 0.0 | 0.0 | 0.0 |
| 66 Office, computing, and accounting machines | 0.0 | 0.0 | 0.0 | 0.0 | 0.0 |
| 67 Service industry machines | 0.0 | 0.0 | 0.0 | 0.0 | 0.0 |
| 68 Electric industrial equipment and apparatus | 0.0 | 0.00820 | 0.0 | 0.0 | 0.0 |
| 69 Household appliances | 0.0 | 0.0 | 0.0 | 0.0 | 0.0 |
| 70 Electric lighting and wiring equipment | 0.0 | 0.01750 | 0.0 | 0.0 | 0.0 |
| 71 Radio, TV, and communications equipment | 0.0 | 0.00450 | 0.0 | 0.0 | 0.0 |
| 72 Electronic components and accessories | 0.0 | 0.0 | 0.0 | 0.0 | 0.0 |

Table 13-1 (Cont.)

Direct 1967 air pollution output coefficients (thousands of tons emitted into the atmosphere per million dollars of output, output of each industry measured in 1963 prices)

| 90-order industry | (1) Part. | (2) $SO_x$ | (3) HC | (4) CO | (5) $NO_x$ |
|---|---|---|---|---|---|
| 73 Electrical machinery equipment and supplies | 0.0 | 0.0 | 0.0 | 0.0 | 0.0 |
| 74 Motor vehicles and equipment | 0.0 | 0.00130 | 0.0 | 0.0 | 0.0 |
| 75 Aircraft and parts | 0.0 | 0.00550 | 0.0 | 0.0 | 0.0 |
| 76 Other transportation equipment | 0.0 | 0.0 | 0.0 | 0.0 | 0.0 |
| 77 Scientific and controlling instruments | 0.0 | 0.0 | 0.0 | 0.0 | 0.0 |
| 78 Optical, ophthalmic, and photographic equipment | 0.0 | 0.0 | 0.0 | 0.0 | 0.0 |
| 79 Miscellaneous manufacturing | 0.0 | 0.0 | 0.0 | 0.0 | 0.0 |
| 80 Railroad transportation | 0.01350 | 0.00670 | 0.02020 | 0.00670 | 0.02700 |
| 81 Bus transportation | 0.0 | 0.0 | 0.0 | 0.0 | 0.03000 |
| 82 Truck transportation | 0.01070 | 0.00350 | 0.01420 | 0.00700 | 0.01450 |
| 83 Air transportation | 0.0 | 0.0 | 0.03590 | 0.28710 | 0.0 |
| 84 Water transportation | 0.02430 | 0.07290 | 0.02430 | 0.07290 | 0.04860 |
| 85 Miscellaneous transportation | 0.0 | 0.0 | 0.0 | 0.0 | 0.0 |
| 86 Communications | 0.0 | 0.00760 | 0.0 | 0.0 | 0.0 |
| 87 Gas utilities | 0.0 | 0.0 | 0.0 | 0.0 | 0.0 |
| 88 Retail trade | 0.0 | 0.00770 | 0.0 | 0.0 | 0.0 |
| 89 Finance and insurance | 0.0 | 0.00340 | 0.0 | 0.0 | 0.0 |
| 90 General services | 0.00200 | 0.00960 | 0.0 | 0.0 | 0.00580 |

worth of each particular kind of good are represented accordingly by the matrix product $A_{21} (I - A_{11})^{-1}$. The results of such a computation are shown in Table 13-2.

Examining the entries in column 3 of Table 13-2, we see, for example, that the additional output of sulphur oxide generated under the given technical conditions by all industries contributing to the delivery to final users of an additional million dollars' worth of household furniture (industry 38) amounts to 31.1 tons. The total final demand for furniture amounted in the year 1963 to $3267 million (in 1963 prices). Multiplying 31.1 by 3267, we find that in that year that particular type of demand was responsible for the generation of 101,607 tons of sulfur oxides. Similar computations were performed for each of the five pollutants and for all components of final demand split into personal consumption expenditures, private investment expenditures, government expenditures, and so on. In matrix notation the complete set of such multiplications can be described as follows: $A_{21} (I - A_{11})^{-1} Y_k$, where $Y_k$ is the column vector of deliveries to final consumers of one particular kind.

The results of computations showing the total amounts of each

## Table 13-2

Direct and indirect air pollution coefficients (thousands of tons of emissions directly and indirectly generated per million 1963 dollars of each industry's sales to final demand

| | 90-order industry | (1) Part. | (2) SO$_x$ | (3) HC | (4) CO | (5) NO$_x$ |
|---|---|---|---|---|---|---|
| 1 | Water and sanitary services | 0.25469 | 0.03201 | 0.29040 | 0.57295 | 0.15299 |
| 2 | Electric utilities | 0.29552 | 0.78882 | 0.00305 | 0.01145 | 0.18516 |
| 3 | Pulp mills | 0.17734 | 0.04018 | 0.00976 | 0.03223 | 0.00946 |
| 4 | Iron and steel foundries | 0.08349 | 0.04669 | 0.00454 | 0.97239 | 0.00844 |
| 5 | Primary steel | 0.08937 | 0.03717 | 0.00319 | 0.16390 | 0.00657 |
| 6 | Primary nonferrous metals | 0.05861 | 1.03858 | 0.00488 | 0.02333 | 0.01358 |
| 7 | Industrial chemicals | 0.02476 | 0.10642 | 0.00767 | 0.04537 | 0.00808 |
| 8 | Fertilizers | 0.02827 | 0.05721 | 0.00665 | 0.02565 | 0.00939 |
| 9 | Petroleum refining | 0.01391 | 0.12767 | 0.04676 | 0.10858 | 0.00576 |
| 10 | Paving mixtures | 1.03489 | 0.06245 | 0.01726 | 0.04029 | 0.00841 |
| 11 | Cement, hydraulic | 0.75159 | 0.05489 | 0.00369 | 0.01147 | 0.01384 |
| 12 | Lime | 2.19173 | 0.04357 | 0.00439 | 0.01458 | 0.01055 |
| 13 | Coal mining | 0.07540 | 0.03400 | 0.00255 | 0.03164 | 0.00763 |
| 14 | Wholesale trade | 0.00664 | 0.01593 | 0.02227 | 0.00996 | 0.00393 |
| 15 | Grain milling | 0.15993 | 0.04487 | 0.00644 | 0.01781 | 0.00685 |
| 16 | Paints and products | 0.01539 | 0.05498 | 0.00812 | 0.04567 | 0.00555 |
| 17 | Secondary nonferrous metals | 0.05917 | 0.12761 | 0.00632 | 0.01320 | 0.00894 |
| 18 | Livestock | 0.02988 | 0.05518 | 0.00481 | 0.01302 | 0.00491 |
| 19 | Other agricultural products | 0.01024 | 0.07768 | 0.00526 | 0.01608 | 0.00457 |
| 20 | Forestry and fishery products | 0.00683 | 0.04856 | 0.00296 | 0.01748 | 0.00209 |
| 21 | Agricultural, forestry, and fishery services | 0.01613 | 0.04693 | 0.00436 | 0.02697 | 0.00419 |
| 22 | Iron and ferroalloy ores mining | 0.01697 | 0.03603 | 0.00379 | 0.04038 | 0.00908 |
| 23 | Nonferrous metal ores mining | 0.01833 | 0.04101 | 0.00356 | 0.04364 | 0.00913 |
| 24 | Crude petroleum and natural gas | 0.00748 | 0.02718 | 0.00164 | 0.01098 | 0.00460 |
| 25 | Stone and clay mining and quarrying | 0.04940 | 0.06149 | 0.00404 | 0.02930 | 0.00773 |
| 26 | Chemical and fertilizer mineral mining | 0.01736 | 0.03764 | 0.00481 | 0.03926 | 0.00923 |
| 27 | New construction | 0.02914 | 0.05157 | 0.00426 | 0.06876 | 0.00501 |
| 28 | Maintenance and repair construction | 0.02292 | 0.03596 | 0.00361 | 0.03515 | 0.00389 |
| 29 | Ordnance and accessories | 0.01008 | 0.04089 | 0.00210 | 0.03711 | 0.00365 |
| 30 | Food and kindred products | 0.02086 | 0.03991 | 0.00454 | 0.02286 | 0.00523 |
| 31 | Tobacco manufactures | 0.00530 | 0.02226 | 0.00186 | 0.00757 | 0.00244 |
| 32 | Fabrics, yarn, and thread mills | 0.01347 | 0.04412 | 0.00450 | 0.01303 | 0.00619 |
| 33 | Textile goods and floor coverings | 0.01523 | 0.04246 | 0.00516 | 0.01464 | 0.00617 |
| 34 | Apparel | 0.00830 | 0.02481 | 0.00330 | 0.00879 | 0.00413 |
| 35 | Miscellaneous fabricated textile products | 0.01157 | 0.03285 | 0.00443 | 0.01216 | 0.00529 |
| 36 | Lumber and wood products | 0.00960 | 0.03735 | 0.00331 | 0.02130 | 0.00478 |
| 37 | Wooden containers | 0.01763 | 0.03329 | 0.00436 | 0.10791 | 0.00695 |
| 38 | Household furniture | 0.01175 | 0.03114 | 0.00360 | 0.04602 | 0.00497 |
| 39 | Other furniture and fixtures | 0.01755 | 0.03101 | 0.00333 | 0.11608 | 0.00495 |
| 40 | Paper and allied products | 0.07393 | 0.04918 | 0.00578 | 0.01803 | 0.00786 |
| 41 | Paperboard containers and boxes | 0.03564 | 0.04523 | 0.00454 | 0.01643 | 0.00618 |

Table 13-2 (Cont.)

| 90-order industry | (1) Part. | (2) SO$_x$ | (3) HC | (4) CO | (5) NO$_x$ |
|---|---|---|---|---|---|
| 42 Printing and publishing | 0.01844 | 0.02659 | 0.00281 | 0.00919 | 0.00477 |
| 43 Agricultural and miscellaneous chemicals | 0.01756 | 0.08927 | 0.00607 | 0.03104 | 0.00610 |
| 44 Plastics and synthetic materials | 0.01978 | 0.07647 | 0.00583 | 0.02458 | 0.00636 |
| 45 Drugs, cleaning and toilet preparations | 0.01228 | 0.03897 | 0.00361 | 0.02369 | 0.00515 |
| 46 Asphalt felts and coatings | 0.03783 | 0.25003 | 0.01318 | 0.04204 | 0.00708 |
| 47 Rubber and plastic products | 0.01307 | 0.04128 | 0.00365 | 0.01947 | 0.00543 |
| 48 Leather tanning, products | 0.01828 | 0.03426 | 0.00469 | 0.01565 | 0.00569 |
| 49 Footwear and other leather products | 0.00976 | 0.02244 | 0.00311 | 0.01315 | 0.00407 |
| 50 Glass and glass products | 0.01670 | 0.02926 | 0.00318 | 0.01418 | 0.00559 |
| 51 Stone and clay products | 0.09510 | 0.04766 | 0.00447 | 0.02948 | 0.00721 |
| 52 Iron and steel forgings | 0.03768 | 0.06668 | 0.00365 | 0.34144 | 0.00702 |
| 53 Miscellaneous nonferrous metals | 0.03022 | 0.37882 | 0.00416 | 0.02870 | 0.00918 |
| 54 Metal containers | 0.03987 | 0.03635 | 0.00397 | 0.40669 | 0.00625 |
| 55 Heating, plumbing, and fabricated structural metal products | 0.02972 | 0.06886 | 0.00351 | 0.25642 | 0.00583 |
| 56 Screws and metal stampings | 0.02652 | 0.04928 | 0.00315 | 0.22478 | 0.00544 |
| 57 Other fabricated metal products | 0.02576 | 0.07516 | 0.00321 | 0.17625 | 0.00563 |
| 58 Engines and turbines | 0.01818 | 0.04633 | 0.00289 | 0.07850 | 0.00442 |
| 59 Farm machinery and equipment | 0.02195 | 0.03384 | 0.00352 | 0.14846 | 0.00499 |
| 60 Construction, mining, and oil field equipment | 0.02191 | 0.03379 | 0.00297 | 0.12781 | 0.00474 |
| 61 Materials handling machinery and equipment | 0.01895 | 0.03536 | 0.00312 | 0.12470 | 0.00455 |
| 62 Metalworking machinery and equipment | 0.01754 | 0.03685 | 0.00253 | 0.09101 | 0.00429 |
| 63 Special industrial machinery and equipment | 0.01782 | 0.03876 | 0.00298 | 0.10166 | 0.00449 |
| 64 General industrial machinery and equipment | 0.01930 | 0.05384 | 0.00287 | 0.10932 | 0.00453 |
| 65 Machine shop products | 0.01736 | 0.04104 | 0.00239 | 0.08549 | 0.00461 |
| 66 Office, computing, and accounting machines | 0.00805 | 0.02261 | 0.00187 | 0.03249 | 0.00297 |
| 67 Service industry machines | 0.01857 | 0.05161 | 0.00352 | 0.10305 | 0.00484 |
| 68 Electric industrial equipment and apparatus | 0.01632 | 0.06227 | 0.00297 | 0.08174 | 0.00465 |
| 69 Household appliances | 0.01923 | 0.05010 | 0.00355 | 0.10927 | 0.00535 |
| 70 Electric lighting and wiring equipment | 0.01766 | 0.07978 | 0.00359 | 0.08936 | 0.00495 |
| 71 Radio, TV, and communications equipment | 0.00844 | 0.03395 | 0.00230 | 0.02909 | 0.00344 |
| 72 Electronic components and accessories | 0.01275 | 0.04270 | 0.00289 | 0.03952 | 0.00459 |
| 73 Electrical machinery equipment and supplies | 0.01582 | 0.10205 | 0.00318 | 0.04978 | 0.00493 |
| 74 Motor vehicles and equipment | 0.01934 | 0.03802 | 0.00322 | 0.12062 | 0.00487 |

## Table 13-2 (Cont.)

Direct and indirect air pollution coefficients (thousands of tons of emissions directly and indirectly generated per million 1963 dollars of each industry's sales to final demand

| 90-order industry | (1) Part. | (2) SO$_x$ | (3) HC | (4) CO | (5) NO$_x$ |
|---|---|---|---|---|---|
| 75 Aircraft and parts | 0.01047 | 0.04527 | 0.00240 | 0.03943 | 0.00392 |
| 76 Other transportation equipment | 0.02174 | 0.04081 | 0.00330 | 0.13526 | 0.00503 |
| 77 Scientific and controlling instruments | 0.01196 | 0.03842 | 0.00272 | 0.05067 | 0.00422 |
| 78 Optical and photographic equipment | 0.01013 | 0.03407 | 0.00247 | 0.02408 | 0.00361 |
| 79 Miscellaneous manufacturing | 0.01403 | 0.03927 | 0.00329 | 0.04858 | 0.00470 |
| 80 Railroad transportation | 0.02156 | 0.02219 | 0.02473 | 0.02844 | 0.03115 |
| 81 Bus transportation | 0.00609 | 0.02154 | 0.00461 | 0.01226 | 0.03467 |
| 82 Truck transportation | 0.01650 | 0.01952 | 0.01919 | 0.01653 | 0.01927 |
| 83 Air transportation | 0.00496 | 0.02171 | 0.04306 | 0.31263 | 0.00287 |
| 84 Water transportation | 0.03508 | 0.10337 | 0.03272 | 0.10373 | 0.06085 |
| 85 Miscellaneous transportation | 0.00882 | 0.02206 | 0.00197 | 0.00644 | 0.00521 |
| 86 Communications | 0.00482 | 0.01981 | 0.00125 | 0.00429 | 0.00307 |
| 87 Gas utilities | 0.00515 | 0.01420 | 0.00148 | 0.01093 | 0.00311 |
| 88 Retail trade | 0.00843 | 0.02797 | 0.00182 | 0.00523 | 0.00527 |
| 89 Finance and insurance | 0.00897 | 0.02513 | 0.00210 | 0.00605 | 0.00604 |
| 90 General services | 0.01090 | 0.02941 | 0.00269 | 0.01268 | 0.01038 |

## Table 13-3

Air pollution content of the 11 1963 final demand vectors (air pollution directly and indirectly generated by industry to produce each vector of final demand per total final demand in that vector, thousands of tons per million dollars of final demand)

| Final Demand Vector | (1) Part. | (2) SO$ix$ | (3) HC | (4) CO | (5) NO$_x$ |
|---|---|---|---|---|---|
| 1 | −0.032 | −0.101 | −0.009 | −0.094 | −0.010 |
| 2 | 0.019 | 0.045 | 0.007 | 0.025 | 0.011 |
| 3 | 0.023 | 0.046 | 0.004 | 0.075 | 0.005 |
| 4 | 0.023 | 0.052 | 0.007 | 0.070 | 0.006 |
| 5 | 0.023 | 0.065 | 0.010 | 0.071 | 0.011 |
| 6 | 0.017 | 0.052 | 0.005 | 0.049 | 0.008 |
| 7 | 0.014 | 0.026 | 0.005 | 0.049 | 0.003 |
| 8 | 0.043 | 0.089 | 0.009 | 0.062 | 0.019 |
| 9 | 0.020 | 0.056 | 0.001 | 0.028 | 0.069 |
| 10 | 0.026 | 0.058 | 0.009 | 0.055 | 0.011 |
| 11 | 0.028 | 0.051 | 0.003 | 0.053 | 0.008 |

1. Competitive imports. 2. Personal consumption expenditures. 3. Gross private fixed capital formation. 4. Net inventory change. 5. Net exports. 6. Federal government purchases, defense. 7. Federal government purchases, other. 8. State and local government purchases, education. 9. State and local government purchases, health, welfare, and sanitation. 10. State and local government purchases, safety. 11. State and local government purchases, other.

kind of pollutant ascribable to a million dollars' worth of each of the 11 distinct kinds of final demand are reproduced in Table 13-3.

The same analytical approach was used to arrive at a *conditional* estimate of the level of atmospheric pollution generated by the projected 1980 aggregate final demand. The anticipated 1980 matrix of production coefficients and the projected changes in the level and the composition of final demand were borrowed for the purposes of this computation from the forementioned Interagency Growth Project report. Our projection derives its conditional character from the fact that, instead of attempting to construct new sets of anticipated 1980 technical pollution-output coefficients, we used in these computations the 1967 coefficients described above. The resulting estimate of the total amounts of the four kinds of pollutants that could be expected to be generated in the year 1980 by each of the 23 principal air-polluting industries is shown in Table 13-4.

### Table 13-4

Projection of industrial air pollution to 1980 (in thousands of tons, assuming no change in the 1967 pollution characteristics of each industry's technology)

| 83-order OBE industry | (1) Part. | (2) $SO_x$ | (3) HC | (4) CO | (5) $NO_x$ |
|---|---|---|---|---|---|
| 7 Coal mining | 246.0 | 0.0 | 0.0 | 0.0 | 0.0 |
| 14 Food | 2086.0 | 483.0 | 0.0 | 0.0 | 0.0 |
| 24 Paper | 1314.0 | 283.0 | 0.0 | 0.0 | 0.0 |
| 27 Chemicals | 151.0 | 1692.0 | 0.0 | 0.0 | 0.0 |
| 30 Paint | 0.0 | 0.0 | 8.0 | 0.0 | 0.0 |
| 31 Petroleum refinery | 1045.0 | 3555.0 | 1502.0 | 3225.0 | 0.0 |
| 36 Stone and clay | 2599.0 | 201.0 | 0.0 | 0.0 | 0.0 |
| 37 Iron and steel | 2336.0 | 0.0 | 0.0 | 4375.0 | 0.0 |
| 38 Nonferrous metals | 257.0 | 6901.0 | 0.0 | 0.0 | 0.0 |
| 65 Transportation | 774.0 | 646.0 | 1420.0 | 3886.0 | 1548.0 |
| 68 Utilities | 12335.0 | 29163.0 | 1943.0 | 3792.0 | 7780.0 |
| 69 Wholesale and retail trade | 0.0 | 1147.0 | 1929.0 | 0.0 | 0.0 |
| 71 Real estate | 315.0 | 1555.0 | 0.0 | 0.0 | 925.0 |
| 72 Hotels | 53.0 | 262.0 | 0.0 | 0.0 | 156.0 |
| 73 Business services | 149.0 | 735.0 | 0.0 | 0.0 | 438.0 |
| 75 Auto repair | 35.0 | 172.0 | 0.0 | 0.0 | 102.0 |
| 76 Amusements | 22.0 | 108.0 | 0.0 | 0.0 | 64.0 |
| 77 Institutions | 120.0 | 592.0 | 0.0 | 0.0 | 352.0 |
| 78 Federal enterprises | 20.0 | 99.0 | 0.0 | 0.0 | 59.0 |
| 79 State enterprises | 26.0 | 131.0 | 0.0 | 0.0 | 78.0 |
| 81 Business travel | 24.0 | 118.0 | 0.0 | 0.0 | 70.0 |
| 82 Office supplies | 9.0 | 45.0 | 0.0 | 0.0 | 27.0 |
| 83 Scrap | 2.0 | 12.0 | 0.0 | 0.0 | 7.0 |
| Total | 23919.0 | 47898.0 | 6803.0 | 15278.0 | 11607.0 |

Grand total: 105506

As time goes on, the total amount of pollution emitted is affected by (1) the increase in the aggregate level of final demand and (2) changes in the distribution of this aggregate demand among different goods, as well as (3) changes in industrial technology, as reflected in a changing *A* matrix. To display separately the effects of (2) and (3) on the output of pollution, two subsidiary computations were performed, the results of which are shown on Tables 13-5 and 13-6.

Table 13-5 shows how much pollution emitted by various industries would increase or decrease if we held the 1958 *A* matrix and 1958 aggregate level of final demand constant and changed only the commodity composition of 1958 final demand from its 1958 to its projected 1980 structure. Table 13-6 shows how much pollution

## Table 13-5

Change in pollution resulting from changing final demand from 1958 to 1980 structure with unchanged 1958 technological coefficients (in thousands of tons)

| 83-order OBE industry | (1) Part. | (2) $SO_x$ | (3) HC | (4) CO | (5) $NO_x$ |
|---|---|---|---|---|---|
| 7  Coal mining | −9.0 | 0.0 | 0.0 | 0.0 | 0.0 |
| 14 Food | −268.0 | −62.0 | 0.0 | 0.0 | 0.0 |
| 24 Paper | 63.0 | 14.0 | 0.0 | 0.0 | 0.0 |
| 27 Chemicals | 5.0 | 53.0 | 0.0 | 0.0 | 0.0 |
| 30 Paint | 0.0 | 0.0 | 0.0 | 0.0 | 0.0 |
| 31 Petroleum refinery | −44.0 | −149.0 | −63.0 | −135.0 | 0.0 |
| 36 Stone and clay | −47.0 | −4.0 | 0.0 | 0.0 | 0.0 |
| 37 Iron and steel | 114.0 | 0.0 | 0.0 | 214.0 | 0.0 |
| 38 Nonferrous metals | 9.0 | 233.0 | 0.0 | 0.0 | 0.0 |
| 65 Transportation | 4.0 | 4.0 | 8.0 | 21.0 | 8.0 |
| 68 Utilities | 244.0 | 577.0 | 38.0 | 75.0 | 154.0 |
| 69 Wholesale and retail trade | 0.0 | 1.0 | 2.0 | 0.0 | 0.0 |
| 71 Real estate | 20.0 | 98.0 | 0.0 | 0.0 | 58.0 |
| 72 Hotels | 0.0 | 1.0 | 0.0 | 0.0 | 0.0 |
| 73 Business services | 2.0 | 8.0 | 0.0 | 0.0 | 4.0 |
| 75 Auto repair | −1.0 | −5.0 | 0.0 | 0.0 | −3.0 |
| 76 Amusements | −1.0 | −7.0 | 0.0 | 0.0 | −4.0 |
| 77 Institutions | 7.0 | 37.0 | 0.0 | 0.0 | 22.0 |
| 78 Federal enterprises | 1.0 | 3.0 | 0.0 | 0.0 | 2.0 |
| 79 State enterprises | 1.0 | 5.0 | 0.0 | 0.0 | 3.0 |
| 81 Business travel | 1.0 | 4.0 | 0.0 | 0.0 | 2.0 |
| 82 Office supplies | 1.0 | 3.0 | 0.0 | 0.0 | 2.0 |
| 83 Scrap | 2.0 | 9.0 | 0.0 | 0.0 | 5.0 |
| Total: absolute | 103.0 | 821.0 | −15.0 | 175.0 | 254.0 |
| Total: percent change | +1.2 | +5.6 | −0.01 | +2.7 | +7.3 |

Grand total: absolute = 1,337,000 tons
Grand total: percent = +3.7

## Table 13-6

Change in pollution resulting from changing (from 1958 to 1980) technological coefficients with a fixed 1958 bill of goods (in thousands of tons)

| 83-order OBE industry | (1) Part. | (2) SO$_x$ | (3) HC | (4) CO | (5) NO$_x$ |
|---|---|---|---|---|---|
| 7 Coal mining | −53.0 | 0.0 | 0.0 | 0.0 | 0.0 |
| 14 Food | 4.0 | 1.0 | 0.0 | 0.0 | 0.0 |
| 24 Paper | −35.0 | −8.0 | 0.0 | 0.0 | 0.0 |
| 27 Chemicals | 12.0 | 129.0 | 0.0 | 0.0 | 0.0 |
| 30 Paint | 0.0 | 0.0 | 0.0 | 0.0 | 0.0 |
| 31 Petroleum refining | −61.0 | −208.0 | −88.0 | −189.0 | 0.0 |
| 36 Stone and clay | −17.0 | −1.0 | 0.0 | 0.0 | 0.0 |
| 37 Iron and steel | −370.0 | 0.0 | 0.0 | −692.0 | 0.0 |
| 38 Nonferrous metals | 6.0 | 173.0 | 0.0 | 0.0 | 0.0 |
| 65 Transportation | −34.0 | −28.0 | −62.0 | −169.0 | −67.0 |
| 68 Utilities | 1259.0 | 2977.0 | 198.0 | 387.0 | 794.0 |
| 69 Wholesale and retail trade | 0.0 | 24.0 | 40.0 | 0.0 | 0.0 |
| 71 Real estate | −5.0 | −22.0 | 0.0 | 0.0 | −13.0 |
| 72 Hotels | 0.0 | −2.0 | 0.0 | 0.0 | −1.0 |
| 73 Business services | 13.0 | 66.0 | 0.0 | 0.0 | 39.0 |
| 75 Auto repair | 1.0 | 5.0 | 0.0 | 0.0 | 3.0 |
| 76 Amusements | 0.0 | 2.0 | 0.0 | 0.0 | 1.0 |
| 77 Institutions | 0.0 | 1.0 | 0.0 | 0.0 | 1.0 |
| 78 Federal enterprises | 0.0 | 0.0 | 0.0 | 0.0 | 0.0 |
| 79 State enterprises | 1.0 | 5.0 | 0.0 | 0.0 | 3.0 |
| 81 Business travel | −3.0 | −14.0 | 0.0 | 0.0 | −8.0 |
| 82 Office supplies | 1.0 | 3.0 | 0.0 | 0.0 | 2.0 |
| 83 Scrap | −3.0 | −16.0 | 0.0 | 0.0 | −10.0 |
| Total: absolute change | 717.0 | 3086.0 | 88.0 | −663.0 | 743.0 |
| Total: percent change | +8.4 | +21.0 | +3.4 | −11.2 | +21.4 |

Grand total: absolute = 3,971,000 tons
Grand total: percent = +11.1

emitted by various industries would increase or decrease if we held 1958 final demand constant and changed the $A$ matrix from its 1958 to its projected 1980 technological structure. In mathematical notation, the figures entered on Tables 13-4, 13-5, and 13-6 represent results of the following matrix operations:

Table 13-4 $\quad A_{21}^{67}(I - A_{11}^{80})^{-1}Y^{80}$

Table 13-5 $\quad A_{21}^{67}(I - A_{11}^{58})^{-1}Y^{80(58)} - A_{21}^{67}(I - A^{58})^{-1}Y^{58}$

Table 13-6 $\quad A_{21}^{67}(I - A^{80})^{-1}Y^{58} - A_{21}^{67}(I - A^{58})Y^{58}$

The simple superscript indicates the year for which data for a given vector or matrix were compiled, while $Y^{80(58)}$ represents a hypothetical column vector of final demand. That hypothetical vector was constructed by reducing all elements of the projected 1980 bill of goods so that they will add up to the actual 1958 level of final demand (GNP), in symbols $(\Sigma_i Y_i^{58}/\Sigma_i Y_i^{80})(Y^{80})$.

The analytical paper referred to in footnote 1 of this chapter contains a theoretical description of computations taking explicitly into consideration actual or potential processes aimed at prevention or elimination of pollution. Empirical implementation of this type of analysis requires detailed knowledge of the input structure of such antipollution or nonpolluting processes. Such information is, in particular, indispensable for all kinds of cost and price computations related to a choice of appropriate levels of antipollution activities.

Although we expect such data to be compiled soon, they were not available at the time this paper was completed. The most we were able to secure were rather crude estimates of the wage and interest costs of certain typical pollution control processes. Neglecting, because of lack of requisite information, the costs of all the other inputs required for the operation of such processes, we undertook to estimate the price effects of several specific antipollution measures that are now being discussed in the United States. The results are shown in Table 13-7.

The calculations are based on the following system of standard static value-added price equations:

$$P^k = V^k(I - A^{63})^{-1}$$
$$V^k = (v_1^{63}, v_2^{63}, v_3^{63}, \ldots, v_m^{63}) + (v_1^k, v_2^k, v_3^k, \ldots, v_m^k)$$

where $v_i^k$ represents the increment to value-added coefficient of industry $i$ resulting from the use of pollution control strategy $k$.

With the matrix $A_{11}$ of structural input coefficients of all the producing sectors of the economy considered as given, the price of each type of output can be computed as a function of the value added (per unit of their respective outputs) given for all the industries. The actual 1963 value-addeds were augmented in each instance by the additional wage-and-interest cost that would have to be incurred if the particular kind of antipollution measure were actually put into effect.

All prices listed in these tables exceed, of course, the actual 1963 prices of the same outputs, which for purposes of the computations were standardized at the uniform level of $1 per appropriately defined physical unit.

Column 1 of Table 13-7 shows what industrial prices would be if the 20 industries mainly responsible for the generation of particulates, sulfur oxides, hydrocarbons, and carbon monoxide actually complied with the standards of the Clean Air Act of 1967. The excess above 1963 unit prices signifies the percentage increase in

# Table 13-7

Price effects of four hypothetical air pollution control strategies
(1963 price = $1.00000)

| 90-order industry | (1) | (2) | (3) | (4) |
|---|---|---|---|---|
| 1  Water and sanitary services | 1.02650 | 1.00056 | 1.00079 | 1.02322 |
| 1  Electric utilities | 1.07318 | 1.02704 | 1.03810 | 1.02894 |
| 3  Pulp mills | 1.00702 | 1.00059 | 1.00083 | 1.03222 |
| 4  Iron and steel foundries | 1.03507 | 1.00072 | 1.00101 | 1.02918 |
| 5  Primary steel | 1.02186 | 1.00063 | 1.00089 | 1.01473 |
| 6  Primary nonferrous metals | 1.16824 | 1.00151 | 1.00213 | 1.03405 |
| 7  Industrial chemicals | 1.00651 | 1.00080 | 1.00112 | 1.10286 |
| 8  Fertilizers | 1.00825 | 1.00077 | 1.00108 | 1.04666 |
| 9  Petroleum refining | 1.00222 | 1.00043 | 1.00061 | 1.08260 |
| 10  Paving mixtures | 1.09398 | 1.00062 | 1.00087 | 1.26881[a] |
| 11  Cement, hydraulic | 1.01279 | 1.00156 | 1.00220 | 1.03571 |
| 12  Lime | 1.00801 | 1.00102 | 1.00144 | 1.03760 |
| 13  Coal mining | 1.00504 | 1.00088 | 1.00124 | 1.06103 |
| 14  Wholesale trade | 1.00131 | 1.00028 | 1.00039 | 1.02087 |
| 15  Grain milling | 1.00387 | 1.00040 | 1.00057 | 1.02941 |
| 16  Paints and allied products | 1.00530 | 1.00044 | 1.00062 | 1.07422 |
| 17  Secondary nonferrous metals | 1.03043 | 1.00051 | 1.00072 | 1.01920 |
| 18  Livestock and livestock products | 1.00181 | 1.00032 | 1.00045 | 1.03400 |
| 19  Other agricultural products | 1.00162 | 1.00027 | 1.00038 | 1.04884 |
| 20  Forestry and fishery products | 1.00134 | 1.00014 | 1.00019 | 1.03093 |
| 21  Agricultural, forestry, and fishery services | 1.00252 | 1.00027 | 1.00038 | 1.02936 |
| 22  Iron and ferroalloy ores mining | 1.00403 | 1.00084 | 1.00118 | 1.02361 |
| 23  Nonferrous metal ores mining | 1.00477 | 1.00101 | 1.00142 | 1.01841 |
| 24  Crude petroleum and natural gas | 1.00158 | 1.00035 | 1.00049 | 1.01201 |
| 25  Stone and clay mining and quarrying | 1.00466 | 1.00084 | 1.00118 | 1.03062 |
| 26  Chemical and fertilizer mineral mining | 1.00440 | 1.00091 | 1.00128 | 1.01935 |
| 27  New construction | 1.00601 | 1.00035 | 1.00050 | 1.02478 |
| 28  Maintenance and repair construction | 1.00429 | 1.00029 | 1.00041 | 1.02148 |
| 29  Ordnance and accessories | 1.00622 | 1.00033 | 1.00046 | 1.01053 |
| 30  Food and kindred products | 1.00211 | 1.00034 | 1.00049 | 1.02364 |
| 31  Tobacco manufactures | 1.00086 | 1.00015 | 1.00021 | 1.01359 |
| 32  Fabrics, yarn, and thread mills | 1.00248 | 1.00058 | 1.00082 | 1.02891 |
| 33  Textile goods and floor coverings | 1.00248 | 1.00052 | 1.00074 | 1.02997 |
| 34  Apparel | 1.00161 | 1.00037 | 1.00052 | 1.01589 |
| 35  Miscellaneous fabricated textile products | 1.00214 | 1.00047 | 1.00066 | 1.02090 |
| 36  Lumber and wood products | 1.00226 | 1.00039 | 1.00055 | 1.01935 |
| 37  Wooden containers | 1.00547 | 1.00054 | 1.00076 | 1.01800 |
| 38  Household furniture | 1.00393 | 1.00040 | 1.00056 | 1.01577 |
| 39  Other furniture and fixtures | 1.00645 | 1.00041 | 1.00058 | 1.01517 |
| 40  Paper and allied products | 1.00412 | 1.00063 | 1.00089 | 1.02831 |
| 41  Paperboard containers and boxes | 1.00293 | 1.00047 | 1.00066 | 1.02460 |
| 42  Printing and publishing | 1.00178 | 1.00035 | 1.00049 | 1.01449 |
| 43  Agricultural and miscellaneous chemicals | 1.00347 | 1.00049 | 1.00070 | 1.06416 |
| 44  Plastics and synthetic materials | 1.00359 | 1.00056 | 1.00079 | 1.06220 |
| 45  Drugs, cleaning and toilet preparations | 1.00235 | 1.00034 | 1.00048 | 1.02619 |
| 46  Asphalt felts and coatings | 1.00380 | 1.00053 | 1.00074 | 1.18910[a] |
| 47  Rubber and plastic products | 1.00274 | 1.00049 | 1.00070 | 1.02419 |
| 48  Leather tanning, products | 1.00210 | 1.00045 | 1.00064 | 1.02379 |
| 49  Footwear and other leather products | 1.00175 | 1.00033 | 1.00047 | 1.01346 |

Table 13-7 (Cont.)
Price effects of four hypothetical air pollution control strategies
(1963 price = $1.00000)

| 90-order industry | (1) | (2) | (3) | (4) |
|---|---|---|---|---|
| 50 Glass and glass products | 1.00266 | 1.00053 | 1.00075 | 1.01585 |
| 51 Stone and clay products | 1.00431 | 1.00061 | 1.00086 | 1.02466 |
| 52 Iron and steel forgings | 1.01914 | 1.00067 | 1.00095 | 1.02397 |
| 53 Miscellaneous nonferrous metals | 1.06066 | 1.00094 | 1.00132 | 1.02128 |
| 54 Metal containers | 1.01636 | 1.00051 | 1.00071 | 1.02047 |
| 55 Heating, plumbing, and fabricated structural metal products | 1.01632 | 1.00050 | 1.00071 | 1.01769 |
| 56 Screws and metal stampings | 1.01311 | 1.00048 | 1.00068 | 1.01688 |
| 57 Other fabricated metal products | 1.01490 | 1.00052 | 1.00073 | 1.01754 |
| 58 Engines and turbines | 1.00901 | 1.00040 | 1.00057 | 1.01486 |
| 59 Farm machinery and equipment | 1.00869 | 1.00041 | 1.00057 | 1.01521 |
| 60 Construction, mining, and oil field equipment | 1.00845 | 1.00043 | 1.00060 | 1.01318 |
| 61 Materials handling machinery and equipment | 1.00817 | 1.00039 | 1.00055 | 1.01507 |
| 62 Metalworking macinery and equipment | 1.00756 | 1.00040 | 1.00056 | 1.01318 |
| 63 Special industrial machinery and equipment | 1.00808 | 1.00039 | 1.00055 | 1.01721 |
| 64 General industrial machinery and equipment | 1.00918 | 1.00041 | 1.00058 | 1.01581 |
| 65 Machine shop products | 1.00816 | 1.00043 | 1.00061 | 1.01109 |
| 66 Office, computing, and accounting machines | 1.00349 | 1.00025 | 1.00035 | 1.00859 |
| 67 Service industry machines | 1.00981 | 1.00042 | 1.00059 | 1.01537 |
| 68 Electric industrial equipment and apparatus | 1.00956 | 1.00043 | 1.00060 | 1.01586 |
| 69 Household appliances | 1.00937 | 1.00045 | 1.00063 | 1.01569 |
| 70 Electric lighting and wiring equipment | 1.01080 | 1.00044 | 1.00062 | 1.02275 |
| 71 Radio, TV, and communications equipment | 1.00426 | 1.00030 | 1.00042 | 1.00977 |
| 72 Electronic components and accessories | 1.00619 | 1.00042 | 1.00060 | 1.01329 |
| 73 Electrical machinery equipment and supplies | 1.01634 | 1.00046 | 1.00065 | 1.01446 |
| 74 Motor vehicles and equipment | 1.00825 | 1.00040 | 1.00056 | 1.01327 |
| 75 Aircraft and parts | 1.00616 | 1.00035 | 1.00050 | 1.01153 |
| 76 Other transportation equipment | 1.00940 | 1.00043 | 1.00061 | 1.01515 |
| 77 Scientific and controlling instruments | 1.00608 | 1.00035 | 1.00049 | 1.01204 |
| 78 Optical and photographic equipment | 1.00429 | 1.00030 | 1.00042 | 1.01465 |
| 79 Miscellaneous manufacturing | 1.00558 | 1.00039 | 1.00055 | 1.01697 |
| 80 Railroad transportation | 1.00177 | 1.00018 | 1.00025 | 1.03504 |
| 81 Bus transportation | 1.00123 | 1.00028 | 1.00039 | 1.06305 |
| 82 Truck transportation | 1.00092 | 1.00022 | 1.00031 | 1.04333 |
| 83 Air transportation | 1.00109 | 1.00019 | 1.00026 | 1.09771 |
| 84 Water transportation | 1.00162 | 1.00021 | 1.00030 | 1.04180 |
| 85 Miscellaneous transportation | 1.00190 | 1.00058 | 1.00081 | 1.01720 |
| 86 Communications | 1.00103 | 1.00028 | 1.00039 | 1.00827 |
| 87 Gas utilities | 1.00106 | 1.00020 | 1.00028 | 1.01115 |
| 88 Retail trade | 1.00169 | 1.00053 | 1.00075 | 1.01158 |
| 89 Finance and insurance | 1.00172 | 1.00052 | 1.00074 | 1.00767 |
| 90 General services | 1.00171 | 1.00038 | 1.00053 | 1.01340 |

[a]Computer prices are not realistic for these sectors because they use large quantities of petroleum products as raw materials rather than as fuels.

each industry's price accompanying this pollution abatement program. As is explained in Appendix 13-2, the cost for control devices in each of the 20 industries was based on engineers' selections of the most economical available control technique for pollutants in those industries.

Column 2 shows what the prices of all goods and services would be if all electric utilities substituted low-sulfur coal and low-sulfur oil for the high-sulfur fuels they use now. The computation is based on actual 1970 price differentials between high-sulfur and low-sulfur fuels. The corresponding increase in fuel costs (per unit of output) was interpreted as an increase in the value added ($v_2^k$) paid out by electric utilities per unit of their output. This explains why the price increase in the products of petroleum refining (industry 9) as shown in column 2 of Table 13-7 is so small. (In fact, most low-sulfur oil used in the United States has to be imported.) To the extent to which the premium paid for high-grade fuel would actually rise if demand for it increases, the numerical results of our computation underestimate the probable price effect of the postulated fuel switching.

Since when shifting to less polluting fuels the electric utilities tend to replace not only high-sulfur oil but also high-sulfur coal by low-sulfur oil, we separately computed and show in column 3 how this would lead to somewhat greater cost and price increases.

Finally, the entries in column 4 show how prices would be altered if the fuel-switching policy were extended from the electric power industry to cover space heating—both domestic and commercial—as well as all other industrial combustion, with low-sulfur coal and oil replacing all high-sulfur fuel. Naturally, the price effects of this extended case of fuel switching are more pronounced than those shown in columns 2 and 3.

The industrial pollution abatement costs included in the price computations reported in Table 13-7 do not take into account the fact that processes used to control one kind of pollutant often generate other kinds of pollutants. As explained earlier, information was not available on the values of coefficients in matrices $A_{12}$ and $A_{22}$; coefficients in these two matrices were assumed in the price computations to be equal to zero. We suspect that this assumption results in a general underestimation of the repercussions on the industrial price structure of pollution abatement measures.

Further advance in this empirical inquiry will depend on the availability of reasonably complete information on the input structure of special abatement processes and of new production techniques—for example, nuclear electric power generation—that could be adopted by industries presently bearing major responsibility for atmospheric pollution.

Water pollution and its control can, of course, be analyzed witin the same theoretical framework.

Once appropriate sets of pollution output and abatement coefficients have been compiled, a more detailed and differentiated study of environmental repercussions can be undertaken within the framework of multiregional, regional, and metropolitan input-output systems that have already been implemented in recent years.

From a purely formal point of view the system can be easily extended to cover the relationship between the (net) output of pollutants on the one hand, and public health and corresponding demand for health care on the other hand. But, here again, the real advance of knowledge and of understanding will depend, not primarily on the flight of the model builder's theoretical fantasy, but on the progress of systematic fact-finding efforts.

## Appendix 13-1

Producing sectors in the 90-order A-matrix and corresponding OBE 370-order sector numbers

1 Water and sanitary services (68.03)
2 Electric utilities (68.01)
3 Pulp mills (24.01)
4 Iron and steel foundries (37.02)
5 Primary steel (37.01)
6 Primary nonferrous metals (38.01–0.04)
7 Industrial chemicals (27.01)
8 Fertilizers (27.02)
9 Petroleum refining (31.01)
10 Paving mixtures (31.02)
11 Cement, hydraulic (36.01)
12 Lime (36.13)
13 Coal mining (7.00)
14 Wholesale trade (69.01)

16 Paints and allied products (30.00)
17 Secondary nonferrous metals (38.06)
18 Livestock and livestock products (1.00)

19 Other agricultural products (2.00)
20 Forestry and fishery products (3.00)
21 Agricultural, forestry, and fishery services (4.00)
22 Iron and ferroalloy ores mining (5.00)
23 Nonferrous metal ores mining (6.00)
24 Crude petroleum and natural gas (8.00)
25 Stone and clay mining and quarrying (9.00)
26 Chemical and fertilizer mineral mining (10.00)
27 New construction (11.00)
28 Maintenance and repair construction (12.00)
29 Ordnance and accesories (13.00)
30 Food and kindred products (14.01–14.13, 14.18–14.32)

31 Tobacco manufactures (15.00)

32 Fabrics, yarn, and thread mills (16.00)

33 Textile goods and floor coverings (17.00)

34 Apparel (18.00)

35 Miscellaneous fabricated textile products (19.00)

36 Lumber and wood products (20.00)

37 Wooden containers (21.00)

38 Household furniture (22.00)

39 Other furniture and fixtures (23.00)

40 Paper and allied products (24.02–24.07)

41 Paperboard containers and boxes (25.00)

42 Printing and publishing (26.00)

43 Agricultural and miscellaneous chemicals (27.03–27.04)

44 Plastics and synthetic materials (28.00)

45 Drugs, cleaning and toilet preparations (29.00)

46 Asphalt felts and coatings (31.03)

47 Rubber and plastic products (32.00)

48 Leather tanning, products (33.00)

49 Footwear and other leather products (34.00)

50 Glass and glass products (35.00)

51 Stone and clay products (36.02–36.12, 36.14–36.22)

52 Iron and steel forgings (37.03–37.04)

53 Miscellaneous nonferrous metals (38.05, 38.07–38.14)

54 Metal containers (39.00)

55 Heating, plumbing, and fabricated structural metal products (40.00)

56 Screws and metal stampings (41.00)

57 Other fabricated metal products (42.00)

58 Engines and turbines (43.00)

59 Farm machinery and equipment (44.00)

60 Construction, mining, and oil field equipment (45.00)

61 Materials handling machinery and equipment (46.00)

62 Metalworking machinery and equipment (47.00)

63 Special industrial machinery and equipment (48.00)

64 General industrial machinery and equipment (49.00)

65 Machine shop products (50.00)

66 Office computing, and accounting machines (51.00)

67 Service industry machines (52.00)

68 Electric industrial equipment and apparatus (53.00)

69 Household appliances (54.00)

70 Electric lighting and wiring equipment (55.00)

71 Radio, TV, and communication equipment (56.00)

72 Electronic components and accessories (57.00)

73 Electrical machinery equipment and supplies (58.00)

74 Motor vehicles and equipment (59.00)

75 Aircraft and parts (60.00)

76 Other transportation equipment (61.00)

77 Scientific and controlling instruments (62.00)

78 Optical and photographic equipment (63.00)

79 Miscellaneous manufacturing (64.00)

80 Railroad transportation (65.01)

81 Bus transportation (65.02)

82 Truck transportation (65.03)

83 Air transportation (65.05)

84  Water transportation (65.04)       87  Gas utilities (68.02)
85  Miscellaneous    transportation    88  Retail trade (69.02)
    (65.06–65.07)                       89  Finance and insurance (70.00)
86  Communications         (66.00–     90  General services (71.00–83.00)
    67.00)


# Appendix 13-2

EMISSION DATA

The basic sources of industry-by-industry emission data for particulates, sulfur oxides, hydrocarbons, and carbon monoxide was M. E. Fogel, et al., *Comprehensive Economic Cost Study of Air Pollution Control Costs for Selected Industries and Selected Regions,* final report R-OU-455 to the National Air Pollution Control Administration, Research Triangle Institute, February 1970. Data on nitrogen oxides was obtained from National Air Pollution Control Administration, *Nationwide Inventory of Air Pollutant Emissions 1968,* August 1970. The Research Triangle Institute emission estimates were based on application of emission factors—largely from R. L. Duprey, *Compilation of Air Pollutant Emission Factors,* National Center for Air Pollution Control, 1968. These emission factors were applied to estimates for flue-gas volumes in process manufacturing sectors and stationary combustion sources. Emissions estimated for specific SIC sectors were divided by the output in 1967 in 1963 prices of the most detailed sector in the OBE 370-order matrix containing that SIC industry. More aggregate figures, such as emissions from industrial boilers, were allocated to industries on the basis of their proportion of total fuel use of the fuels associated with specific pollutants. Pollutants generated by household space heating were assigned to industry 90, the industry that contains the payments of apartment dwellers to real estate companies together with the imputed rental value of owned-occupied dwellings. Pollution generated by automobiles used in private households is not included in the emission data.

The emission data were incorporated into an *A* matrix aggregated to 90-order from the OBE 370-order 1963 matrix. The emission coefficients were also deflated and aggregated to the OBE 83-order classification for computations with the 1958 and 1980 matrices.

INPUT-OUTPUT MATRICES AND FINAL DEMANDS

Computation of direct and indirect pollution coefficients, the pollution content of final demand, and price changes accompanying four pollution control strategies use a 90-order input-output matrix and set of final demand column vectors that were aggregated from the 370-order official U.S. matrix for 1963 as published by the U.S. Department of Commerce in *Input-Output Structure of the U.S. Economy: 1963, Volume 1—Detailed Transactions,* Washington, D.C., 1969. Before aggregation, the matrix was adjusted to domestic base by subtracting competitive imports and margins from the endogenous flows and correspondingly adjusting final demand.

Computations for Tables 13-4 through 13-6 use the 83-order OBE 1958 matrix as published in the September 1965 *Survey of Current Business* and adjusted to domestic base, and the official 1980 projected *A* matrix of the Interagency Growth Project as published in the U.S. Department of Labor, Bureau of Labor Statistics, Patterns of U.S. Economic Growth, B.L.S. Bulletin 1672, 1970. The 1958 and 1980 matrices are in 1958 dollars. The 1980 final demand vector is that of the "basic" 4 percent unemployment B.L.S. model.

## Cost of control estimates

Research Triangle Institute, cited above, estimated an annual cost of control for selected industries to meet the standards of the Clean Air Act of 1967 in 100 metropolitan areas. These figures, scaled by the ratio of national emissions in those industries to emissions in those industries in the 100 metropolitan areas, were used in price computation shown in column 1 of Table 13-7. The other price computations on the ramifications of fuel switching rest on estimated price differentials for fossil fuels of different sulfur content. The price differentials, a 30 percent premium for low-sulfur coal and a 100% premium for low-sulfur oil, were assumed on the basis of consultation with utility company executives; data contained in "The Economy, Energy, and the Environment," a background study prepared by the Legislative Reference Service, Library of Congress, for the Joint Economic Committee, September 1, 1970, p. 105; Ernst and Ernst, *The Fuel of Fifty Cities*, Report to the National Air Pollution Control Administration, November 1968; and the Boston Edison Company, "Alternative Plans—Low Sulfur Fuel Utilization," September 29, 1970, Appendix C.

# 14

## *The dynamic inverse*

### ( 1 9 7 0 )

### I

The purpose of this chapter is to introduce the notion of the dynamic inverse, which could play a role in the empirical study of economic change analogous to the role played in static input-output analysis by the inverse of the flow coefficient matrix.

First, I shall describe the open dynamic input-output system in terms of a simple set of linear equations. Next, I shall present a general solution of that system, that is, the inverse of its structural matrix. Each element of this inverse represents the combined direct and indirect inputs required from the row industry to permit an additional output of $1 million by the column industry. While in a static inverse such effects can be described by a single number, within the framework of dynamic analysis they have to be presented in a time series: as soon as capacity expansion and the corresponding investment processes are introduced explicitly into the system, the inputs contributing directly or indirectly to the delivery of a certain final output in a given year must also be dated. These come out of the computer as a sequence of numbers stretched back in time. The last sections of this chapter are devoted to a brief discussion of the corresponding dynamic price system.[1]

[1]Basic concepts, the industry classification system, and the sources of data used in the study are presented in Appendices 14-2, 14-3, and 14-4.

From A. P. Carter and A. Brody (eds.), *Contributions to Input-Output Analysis* (Amsterdam: North-Holland Publishing, 1970), pp. 17–46.

In preparation of this chapter the author was assisted by Brookes Byrd, Richard Berner, and Peter Petri.

# II

Let the column vector $x$ represent the $n$ sectoral outputs, $_tX_1$, $_tx_2$, ..., $_tX_n$, produced in year $t$, and $c$ the corresponding column vector, $_tc_1$, $_tc_2$, ..., $_tc_n$, of deliveries to final demand. This final demand does *not* include the annual additions to the stock of fixed and working capital (inventories) used by the $n$ productive sectors mentioned above. The structural characteristics of the economy are described by $A_t$, the square $(n \times n)$ matrix of technical flow coefficients that specifies the direct current input requirements of all industries, and $B_t$, the corresponding square matrix of capital coefficients. Capital goods produced in year $t$ are assumed to be installed and put into operation in the next year, $t + 1$.

The direct interdependence between the outputs of all the sectors of a given national economy in two successive years can be described by the following familiar balance equation:

$$(14\text{-}1) \qquad x_t - A_t x_t - B_{t+1}(x_{t+1} - x_t) = c_t$$

The second term on the left-hand side represents the current input requirements of all $n$ industries in year $t$; the third represents the investment requirements, that is, additions to productive stock that would permit all industries to expand their capacity outputs from the year $t$ to the next year, $t + 1$, from $x_t$ to $x_{t+1}$. The time subscripts attached to both structural matrices provide the possibility of using different sets of flow and capital coefficients for different years, thus incorporating technological change into the dynamic system. It should be noted that the time subscript attached to matrix $B_{t+1}$ identifies, not the year in which the particular capital goods are produced, but rather the year in which they are first put to use. Equation (14-1) can be rewritten as:

$$(14\text{-}2) \qquad G_t x_t - B_{t+1} x_{t+1} = c_t$$

Where $G_t = (1 - A_t + B_{t+1})$. A set of interlocked balance equations of this type describing the development of the given economy over a period of $m + 1$ years can be combined to form a system of $m + 1$ linear equations:

$$(14\text{-}3) \quad \begin{bmatrix} G_{-m} - B_{-m+1} & & & & \\ & G_{-m+1} - B_{-m+2} & & & \\ & & \cdot & \cdot & \\ & & \cdot & \cdot & \\ & & \cdot & \cdot & \\ & & G_{-2} - B_{-1} & \\ & & & G_{-1} - B_0 & \\ & & & & G_0 \end{bmatrix} \begin{bmatrix} x_{-m} \\ x_{-m+1} \\ \cdot \\ \cdot \\ \cdot \\ x_{-2} \\ x_{-1} \\ x_0 \end{bmatrix} = \begin{bmatrix} c_{-m} \\ c_{-m+1} \\ \cdot \\ \cdot \\ \cdot \\ c_{-2} \\ c_{-1} \\ c_0 \end{bmatrix}$$

## III

The solution of this system determines the sequence of annual total sectoral outputs that would enable the economy to yield the sequence of final annual deliveries described by the array of column vectors entered on the right-hand side. Starting with the last equation, substituting its solution into the equation next to the last and thus proceeding stepwise to the first, we arrive at the following solution of system (14-3) for the unknown $x$'s in terms of a given set of the $c$'s.

(14-4)

$$
\begin{bmatrix} x_{-m} \\ \cdot \\ \cdot \\ \cdot \\ x_{-2} \\ x_{-1} \\ x_0 \end{bmatrix} = \begin{bmatrix} G_{-m}^{-1} \ldots R_{-m} \ldots R_{-3}R_{-2}G_{-1}^{-1} & R_{-m} \ldots R_{-3}R_{-2}R_{-1}G_0^{-1} \\ & \cdot & \cdot \\ & \cdot & \cdot \\ & \cdot & \cdot \\ & R_{-2}G_{-1}^{-1} & R_{-2}R_{-1}G_0^{-1} \\ & G_{-1}^{-1} & R_{-1}G_0^{-1} \\ & & G_0^{-1} \end{bmatrix} \begin{bmatrix} c_{-m} \\ \cdot \\ \cdot \\ \cdot \\ c_{-2} \\ c_{-1} \\ c_0 \end{bmatrix}
$$

where $R_t = G_t^{-1}B_{t+1} = (1 - A_t + B_t^{+1})^{-1}B_{t+1}$.

The square matrix on the right-hand side of equation (14-4) is the inverse of the structural matrix that appears on the left-hand side of equation (14-3). Every element of this inverse is itself a square matrix.

The wedge-shaped column on the right describes the direct and indirect input requirements generated by the delivery to final demand of one unit (or $1 million worth) of the products of any one of the $n$ industries in the year 0. These requirements are distributed backward over time. Matrix $G_0^{-1}$ shows the input requirements that must be filled in year 0, that is, the same year in which the final deliveries are made; as in a static inverse each column of $G_0^{-1}$ identifies the industry making the delivery to final demand, and each row identifies the industry supplying the specific input. The preceding term, $R_{-1}G_0^{-1}$, specifies the requirements that have to be filled in the preceding year $-1$; $R_{-2}R_{-1}G_0^{-1}$ specifies those to be filled in the year $-2$; and so on. The longest term, $R_{-m}, \ldots R_{-2}R_{-1}G_0^{-1}$, describes the increments in the outputs of all industries in the year $-m$, that is, the inputs that have to be provided $m$ years before an additional batch of goods can be delivered to final users. Each term of equation (14-4) located above the diagonal can be computed by multiplying the term located below it by an appropriate transformation matrix, $R_{-t}$.

## IV

In the absence of any technical change the time subscript can be eliminated from all the structural constants. The elements of each column can in this case be described in receding order by the same simple geometric series:

$$(14\text{-}5) \qquad G^{-1}, RG^{-1}, R^2G^{-1}, \ldots, R^tG^{-1}, \ldots, R^mG^{-1}$$

It is well known that as the exponent $t$ becomes sufficiently large, the ratio between the magnitude of all the similarly located elements of $R^t$ and $R^{t+1}$ asymptotically approaches the same constant, equal to the real part of the dominant characteristic root of $R$. If $\mu$ is the dominant root, the $R^{t+1} \to \mathbf{R}(\mu)R^t$ as $t \to \infty$, where $\mathbf{R}(\mu)$ denotes the real part of the root $\mu$. If $\mu$ is real, positive, and less than 1, the increments to outputs required to deliver any given combination of additional goods to final demand in the final year 0— traced back a sufficiently large number of years—will become smaller and smaller, and will finally become infinitely small.[2]

Thus, for all practical purposes, the chains of inputs stretching backward from the year in which the delivery to final users is actually made can, in case of such convergence, be treated as if they were of finite length. The same will be true even if the technical structure of the economy changes from year to year, that is, when the $R$ matrices retain their time subscripts. The series of required inputs converges backward in this case, too, although not necessarily as smoothly as it does without technological change.

The distribution of such required inputs over time, however, varies greatly among industries. Some of the input series even dip below the zero line at their forward ends. This is the well-known effect of the so-called acceleration principle. As soon as the additional goods demanded directly or indirectly by the final users have been produced, the stocks of capital goods employed in making them will be released. The balance equation (14-1) is set up in such a way as to indicate negative investment, that is, disinvestment, in case $x_{t+1} < x_t$. In fact, such potentially idle capacity will usually be absorbed by the direct or indirect input requirements generated by increases in final deliveries scheduled for the next and subsequent

---

[2]A mathematical analysis of the convergence properties of the dynamic inverse is presented in Appendix 14-1.

years. As will be shown below, these must be entered into dynamic input-output accounting in the form of separate but overlapping chains. So long as, in a given year, the sum total of positive incremental output requirements exceeds the sum total of the negative, the output of that sector will increase.

One of the analytically and operationally most useful properties of open input-output systems is the linear additivity of their solutions with respect to any changes in final demand. Each element of the final bill of goods generates a separate chain of direct and indirect input requirements. The total requirements generated by any given vector of final demand are thus represented by the sum of such chains, each corresponding to one particular component of that vector.

This remains true even if some of the separable sets have negative elements, provided the others contain corresponding positive elements large enough to yield a positive or, at least, a nonnegative sum total. In static input-output computations, competitive imports are treated, for example, as generating negative (direct and indirect) input requirements, which are subtracted from the corresponding input requirements generated by the positive (or at least nonnegative) sum total. Strictly speaking, this already constitutes a departure from true separability: if that total turns out, for some particular output, to be negative, the entire result is invalidated. A new computation has to be undertaken with the imports previously treated as competitive now shifted into the noncompetitive category. The treatment of the direct and indirect effects of one part of the final bill of goods turns out, in this case, to be dependent on the magnitude of the—admittedly separately computed—requirements generated by all the other components of that vector. This introduces into the analytical picture cross-dependencies typical of nonlinear systems.

The use of the dynamic inverse brings the obvious advantages of separability and additivity into the empirical analysis of economic change. The presence of negative elements in many of the separate input chains (describing the time sequence of the direct—but mostly indirect—input requirements generated by each individual element of a given time-phased final bill of goods) imposes obvious limits on the strict use of the additivity assumption. Consistent, that is, feasible sequences of total input requirements can be determined on the basis of a given dynamic inverse only for those time-phased bills of goods that generate larger positive than negative output requirements for the products of each industry in each period of time.

A time-phased vector of final demand—premultiplied by a given dynamic inverse—may arithmetically yield negative total direct and indirect output requirements for some goods in some periods of time. If so, at least some of the balance equations in system (14-3) do not represent the real world. As everyone who has dealt with this kind of system knows, the problem arises because equation (14-3) assumes full-capacity utilization in all the sectors all the time. By applying, for example, the simplex method routine of linear programming we could find a number of feasible production programs capable of delivering such a time-phased switching in and switching out of productive capacities and possibly the planned stockpiling of current outputs.

The operation of an economic process of such a discontinuous kind would be much more difficult to understand and to explain than that of a system whose change can be described in terms of continuous and additive components. In other words, a system with a diverging dynamic inverse that contains negative elements, whose magnitude grows as one goes back in time, could be programmed; however, the actual existence of such an economy would be very difficult to imagine. The explanation of the convergence of the actually observed dynamic inverse of the American economy that I will now describe should possibly be sought in the gradual substitution of new for the old columns of $A$ and $B$ coefficients, characterizing long-run technological change.

# V

An open dynamic input-output system was constructed and its inverse computed on the basis of two sets of $A$ and $B$ matrices, one describing the structural properties of the American economy in the year 1947, the other in the year 1958. A third system was formed and inverted on the assumption that the shift from the 1947 to the 1958 technology occurred gradually over the intervening years. In all three instances the dynamic inverse turned out to be well behaved: all time series of which it consists converged backward toward zero.

The same sectoral breakdown is used for both years. It contains 52 endogenous industries and a final bill of goods subdivided into household consumption (durables and nondurables) and government consumption. An alternative treatment of private consumption separates final deliveries to households into deliveries of nondurables and of the estimated replacement requirements for consumers' durables. The rest of the latter is charged to a special household investment account, controlled by an appropriate vector of capital coefficients.

Labor requirements were computed on the basis of sectoral labor input coefficients, and total capital requirements for each sector were determined through summation of all elements of the appropriate column of the $B$ matrix.

All inputs and outputs were measured both for 1947 and 1958 in 1958 prices. In other words, the units in terms of which the numerical computations were performed and their results presented should be interpreted as amounts of the respective commodities and services purchasable for one dollar at 1958 prices.

The entire computation absorbed about an hour's time on the IBM 7094 computer. The program included automatic plotting of the resulting time series by the machine. A selection of such plots is presented in the eight figures that I will now discuss.

Figure 14-1 illustrates the typical variety of shapes encountered among the time series, each of which constitutes a single element of the dynamic inverse. Each of the four curves represents the time-phased amount of the product of one of the four different industries that were contributing directly or indirectly to supplying (in year 0) final users with one additional unit of the output of the machinery industry. Two of the inputs—"metals" and "rubber and plastic products"—are primary materials; their input curves ascend gradually but steadily from the beginning to the end. The demand for primary metals is much larger and anticipates the final delivery in significant amounts by some eight years. The first significant demand for rubber and plastic products is registered in the year $-3$.

The corresponding input requirements for transportation equipment and lumber, on the other hand, show a dip below the zero line in the years preceding the delivery of the final product. As explained above, this is typical of goods playing an important part in the process of capital accumulation.

Figure 14-2 supplements Figure 14-1 by showing the amounts of labor and of capital, that is, of investment goods, absorbed by *all industries* in the process of filling the direct and indirect input requirements for the delivery to final users (in year 0) of $1 million worth of the product of the machinery industry. The smoothness of the gradual rise does, of course, in both instances result from the mutual cancellation of irregularities in the employment and investment requirements of the many different individual industries com-

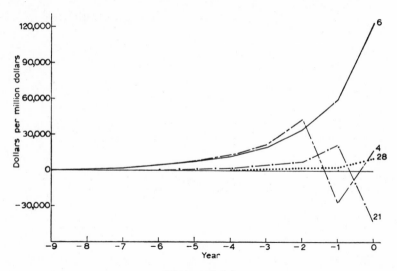

**Figure 14-1**

Elements of the dynamic inverse showing the direct and indirect effects of
a $1 million increase in the final demand for the products of industry 3,
machinery products, in year 0, on the outputs of industries 4, 6, 21, and
28 in this and the preceding year. *Key:*— - — - —, transportation equipment and consumer appliances (4); _____, metals (6); · — · — · —,
lumber and products, excluding containers (21); · · · · · · ·, rubber and
plastic products (28).


**Figure 14-2**

Time series of total direct and indirect labor and capital inputs required to
deliver $1 million worth of the products of industry 3, machinery products,
to final demand in year 0 (the left scale refers to labor, the right scale to
capital). *Key:* _____, labor; - - - - - - - - - - - - -, capital.

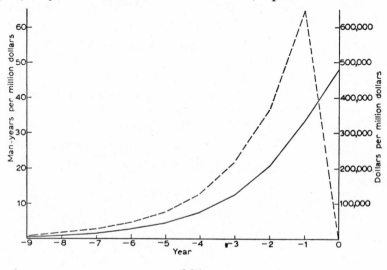

301

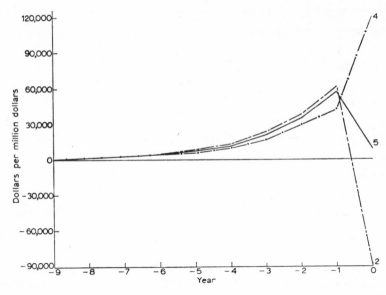

**Figure 14-3**

Elements of the dynamic inverse showing the alternative direct and indirect effects on the output of industry 6, metals, of $1 million worth of deliveries to final demand for the products of industries 2, 4, and 5 in year 0. *Key:* · — · —, transportation equipment and consumer appliances (4); — · — · —, textiles, clothing, furnishings (2); ————, construction (5).

bined in each of these two totals. The one-year time lag between the installation of new capacities and the delivery of additional outputs explains the last year's drop in the investment curve.

The differences among the reactions of the same industry to various kinds of final deliveries are shown in Figure 14-3. Metals behave as a typical raw material in their contribution to the production of transportation equipment—that is, mainly automobiles—delivered to final users; they react, however, as a typical investment good in response to an increase in the final demand for textiles. An intermediate pattern of behavior marks the contribution of the metals sector to the satisfaction of the final demand for the output of the construction industry.

A similar difference can be seen in Figure 14-4 between the shapes of two time series, both tracing the requirements for products of the metal sector, one reflecting an additional $1 million worth of government demand and the other anticipating a delivery of $1 million worth of goods and services demanded by households. The first curve reaches its crest one year before the final delivery can actually be made and stays above the zero line in the last; the second starts to fall off a year earlier and plunges below the zero line at the end. As should have been expected, the intermediate product mixture of the combined total demand yields an intermediate time profile weighted in favor of households.

The time series of total labor inputs contributing to the two principal components of final demand, as shown in Figure 14-5, are similar in shape to those shown in Figure 14-4. The same is true of the corresponding total capital requirements shown in Figure 14-6.

The three sets of curves in Figure 14-7 demonstrate how the dynamic inverse can reveal the effects of specified technical change on the dynamic properties of a given economic system. Each part of the chart presents the same element of the dynamic inverse in three alternative versions.

All three curves at the top represent the time-phased increase in the output of chemicals contributing directly and indirectly to the

## Figure 14-4

Elements of the dynamic inverse showing the alternative direct and indirect effects on the output of industry 6, metals, of $1 million worth of increases in the household, government, and total final demand in year 0. *Key:* _____, household final demand (61); — · — · —, government final demand (63); · — · — · —, total final demand (64).

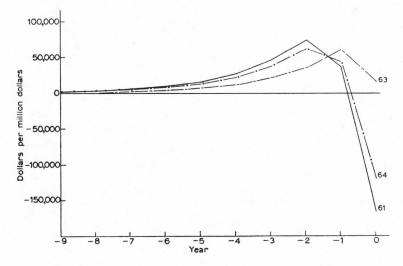

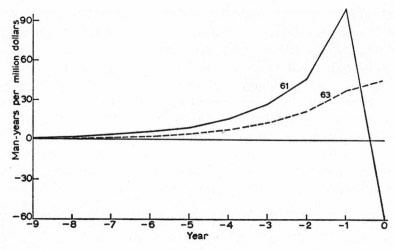

**Figure 14-5**

Time series of alternative direct and indirect labor inputs required to deliver $1 million worth of increases in the government and household final demand vectors in year 0. *Key:* _____, household final demand (61); - - - - - - - - - - -, government final demand (63).


**Figure 14-6**

Time series of alternative direct and indirect capital inputs required to deliver $1 million worth of increases in the government and household final demand vectors in year 0. *Key:* _____, household final demand (61); - - - - - - - - - - -, governmental final demand (63).

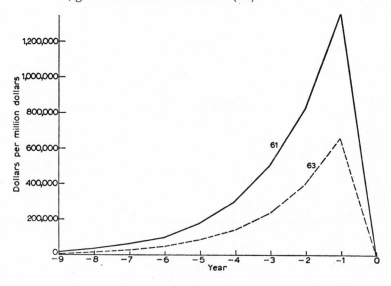

304

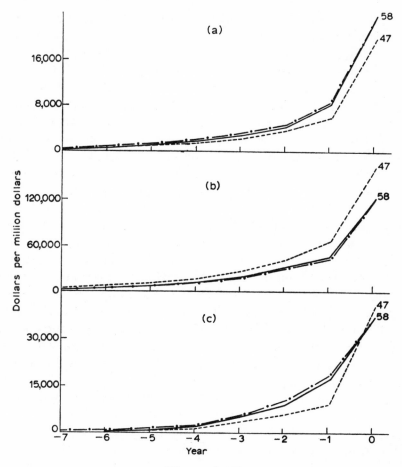

**Figure 14-7**

Effects of technological change on the elements of the dynamic inverse. (*a*) Time series of direct and indirect requirements for chemicals (8) to deliver $1 million worth of food and drugs (1) in year 0, computed on the basis of flow and capital coefficients representing the technologies of: - - - - - - - - - - - -, 1947; · — · —, 1958; _____, shifting year by year from 1947 to 1958. (*b*) Time series of direct and indirect requirements for metals (6) to deliver $1 million worth of transportation equipment (4) in year 0, computed on the basis of flow and capital coefficients representing the technologies of: - - - - - - - - - - - -, 1947; · — · —, 1958; _____, shifting year by year from 1947 to 1958. (*c*) Time series of direct and indirect requirements for chemicals (8) to deliver $1 million worth of nonferrous mining products (16) in year 0, computed on the basis of flow and capital coefficients representing the technologies of: - - - - - - - - - - - -, 1947; · — · —, 1958; _____, shifting year by year from 1947 to 1958.

delivery of an additional \$1 million worth of food and drug products to final demand in the year 0. The first is computed on the basis of $A_{1947}$ and $B_{1947}$, that is, of the flow and capital coefficients characterizing the input structures of the 52 producing sectors of the American economy in the year 1947, the second on the basis of $A_{1958}$ and $B_{1958}$, that is, of 1958 technology. The third inverse was computed—in accordance with equation (14-4)—from a sequence of 11 different pairs of dated $A$ and $B$ matrices tracing the gradual shift from the 1947 technology to the 1958 technology. On the left this curve coincides with the first, but in the terminal year it catches up with the second.

The three sets of curves demonstrate how differently the same overall change can affect various elements of the same dynamic inverse. The combined effects of the many technical shifts reflected in the difference between the magnitude of the flow and the capital coefficients describing the input structures of the 52 sectors of the American economy in 1947 and 1958 led to an upward shift in the time series of chemical inputs required for delivery to final users of \$1 million worth of food and drugs. The three curves in the middle part of the chart indicate that the same combination of structural changes reduced the inputs of metals contributing to the final delivery of consumers' appliances.

The contribution of chemicals to nonferrous metals mining shown on the bottom was affected by the same structural shifts in a more complicated way: the input requirements dropped in the last year of the series, that is, the year of the final delivery, but they rose in all the previous years.

## VI

The dynamic input-output system described above—not unlike the static input-output system—can be of little help in derivation of the golden rules of economic growth or in formulation of any other purely theoretical generalizations. It is too loosely jointed, too flexible for serving such an ambitious purpose. The dynamic inverse is primarily a storehouse of systematically organized factual information. This information is presented in a form particularly suitable for analytical description of intertemporal relations. The individual elements of the inverse can be spun into longer strands, each attached to a given time sequence of final deliveries. These strands can be woven into a broad fabric of intersectoral and intertemporal relationships which make up the analytical picture of economic growth.

Figure 14-8 illustrates graphically the structure of one such sim-ple strand describing—or explaining, if you will—the increase in the level of output of primary metals called for by a delivery to final users of $1 million worth of nondurable consumers' goods (and of proportionally increased services of durable consumers' goods) per year over a period of 17 years. The first delivery to final users is made in the year 0, the last in the year +16.

Each of the partly superimposed curves represents the sequence of inputs required for delivery of an additional $1 million worth of consumers' goods to households. The year of final delivery is indi-cated by the position of the forward end of the curve. While the first delivery is due in the year 0, the first incremental input of nonne-gligible size must be made in year −8. From then on, a new input sequence has to be started every year over a period of 17 years; the entire series of required total annual inputs—traced by the heavy black line on the chart—spans an interval of 25 years. The typical hump at the beginning reflects the buildup of the required addi-tional capital stocks; the falling off at the end indicates, on the other hand, a reduction of these stocks, a gradual liquidation that sets in many years before the last delivery to households of an additional $1 million worth of consumers' goods.

The flat portion of the curve marks what might be called the

## Figure 14-8

Direct and indirect effects on the output of industry 6, metals, of annual increases of $1 million, continued over a 17-year period (years 0 through +16), in the household final demand vector (61). *Key:* - - - - - - - -, effects of an increase in demand for a single year; _____, combined effects of all increases in annual demands.

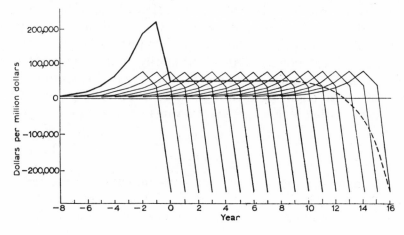

period of stationary reproduction, during which only current annual input requirements, including capital replacements, have to be covered. With the $A$ and $B$ matrices invariant and the vector of final deliveries $c$ constant over a sufficiently long period of time, the corresponding time-phased output vector $x$ can—according to (14-5)—be determined as follows:

(14-6) $$x = (1 + R + R^2 + \cdots + R^m)G^{-1}c$$

If the series on the right-hand side converges,

$$x \to (1 - R)^{-1}G^{-1}c = [G(1 - G^{-1}B)]^{-1}c = (G - B)^{-1}c = (1 - A)^{-1}c$$

as $m \to \infty$.

Under stationary conditions governing the flat portion of the cumulative curve in Figure 14-8, the dependence of sectoral outputs on final demand is controlled by the static inverse $(1 - A)^{-1}$.

Information anticipating the level of final demand eight years hence would, in this particular case, suffice for a reasonably accurate assessment of direct and indirect input needs. The degree of foresight required depends, of course, on the profile of the elements of the inverse from which the total input curve has to be built up. So long as the total final demand continues to rise from year to year, no liquidation of productive stock is likely to be called for. In the summation of the overlapping series of direct and indirect effects of successive changes in final deliveries, the positive elements of the dynamic inverse will tend to dominate its few negative components.

In recent contributions to the pure theory of economic growth, the problem of so-called terminal conditions has attracted much attention. According to the evidence presented above, the time horizon on which we could base our plans or make our projections should vary from sector to sector. The time shape of the elements of the dynamic inverse that governs direct and indirect requirements for the products of one particular industry might be such that its output in a given year depends primarily on the composition and level of the final demand vector of the same year. For another industry that shape might be such that the level of its output in a given year reflects final deliveries, say, four or five years later.

## VII

The balance equation (14-1), and consequently also the formulas describing the dynamic inverse derived from it, are based on the assumption of a uniform one-period ("one-year") time lag between the installation of additional stocks of capital goods and the increase in the flow of output resulting from their first use. The same time unit enters into the definition of all the elements of the capital coefficient matrix $B$ ("stock per unit of *annual* output"). In fact, the time lags between the installation and initial full utilization of incremental capacities in various productive sectors of the U.S. economy—defined in terms of the degree of aggregation used in this study—seem to be around one year or somewhat shorter.

A change in the absolute magnitude of the time unit used in describing an actual economic system in terms of equations (14-1) would signify a corresponding real change in the length of all the lags. If, despite that change, the real capital requirements of all the sectors remain the same, the capital coefficients described by matrix $B$ have to be "translated" into the new time unit. Thus, if the time lag is reduced from one year to half a year, all elements of $B$ have to be multiplied by 2.

The effect of such a shift on the dominant characteristic root of the system and, consequently, on its convergence are analyzed in Appendix 14-1. Changes in the time lags and in the magnitudes of the $B$ coefficients tend to offset each other. The three curves entered in Figure 14-9 show how the time sequence of labor inputs required to increase total deliveries to final demand by $1 million is affected if the basic structural investment lag is cut from one year to six or four months. The horizontal axis of the graph is in natural years.

## VIII

In static input-output analysis, the inverse of the structural matrix of a particular economy postmultiplied by a given column vector of final demand yields the vector of corresponding total sectoral outputs. The transpose of the same inverse when postmultiplied by a given vector of values added (wage, profit, tax, and other final payments disbursed by each industry per unit of its total physical output) yields the corresponding vector of equilibrium prices, that is, of prices at which the total outlay (including the values added) of each sector would equal its aggregate receipts. In dynamic input-output analysis, the transpose of the dynamic inverse determines the relationship between the time-phased vectors of values added in each of the producing sectors and the set of equilibrium prices that would balance the total outlays and the total receipts of each producing sector over time.

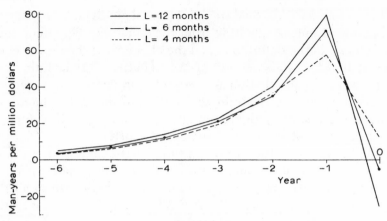

**Figure 14-9**

Direct and indirect labor inputs required to deliver an additional $1 million worth of goods to total final demand in year 0, assuming investment lags of 12 months, 6 months, and 4 months.

Let $p_t$ represent a column vector, ${}_t p_1$, ${}_t p_2$, . . . , ${}_t p_n$, of the prices of goods and services sold and purchased by various sectors in year $t$, and $v_t$ a column vector, ${}_t v_1$, ${}_t v_2$, . . . , ${}_t v_n$, of the values added in each sector per unit of its output in year $t$. Value added can be best defined residually as all current outlays of a producing sector other than payments for inputs purchased from the same or from other industries.

Equation (14-7) below states that in any year $t$ the prices of all goods represented by the vector on the left-hand side must equal their unit costs as represented by the terms appearing on the right-hand side. The product of the transpose of the flow coefficient matrix $A'$ and the price vector $p_t$ represents the costs of current inputs purchased by each productive sector from itself and from other industries. The elements of the value-added (column) vector $v_t$ comprise wages, rents, taxes, and profits paid out or charged per unit of its output by the respective industries in year $t$.

The two terms enclosed in square brackets describe the unit cost or gains conventionally booked through the capital account. For purposes of proper cost accounting, the stocks of capital goods are assumed to be acquired by each sector, in accordance with technological requirements, one year before the delivery of the output they produce and then sold off together with that output; in fact, the sale will, in most cases, be purely nominal since the sector disposing of the capital goods will repurchase them again and again.

Both transactions, of course, are supposed to be made at prices prevailing in the time period during which they take place. The value of capital stock purchased in the year $t - 1$ is multiplied by $1 + r_{t-1}$; $r_{t-1}$ represents the annual money rate of interest prevailing in that year. As has been observed before, the stocks of capital released from production of outputs delivered in year $t$ are employed at once to produce goods that will be delivered in the following year $t + 1$. The $A$ and $B$ matrices on the right-hand side are dated to reflect the process of technical change.

$$(14\text{-}7) \qquad P_t = A'_t p_t + [(1 + r_{t-1})\, B'_t p_{t-1} - B'_{t+1} p_t] + v_t$$

Equation (14-7) can be rewritten as

$$(14\text{-}8) \qquad G'_t p_t - \alpha_{t-1} B'_t p_{t-1} = v_t$$

where

$$G'_t = (1 - A'_t + B'_{t\,+1}) \text{ and } \alpha_t = 1 + r_t$$

Assigning the values $-m, -m + 1, -m + 2, \ldots, -2, -1, 0$, to the time subscript $t$, we can construct a system of interlocked equations analogous to (14-3). The structural matrix on the left-hand side of that new system would resemble the transpose of the structural matrix appearing in (14-3), with the difference that each $B_t$ is multiplied by a corresponding scalar $\alpha_{t-1}$.

The solution of that system for the unknown price vector $p_0$ in terms of the value-added vectors of the same and all the previous years $v_0, v_{-1}, v_{-2}, \ldots$, and of the corresponding "force of interest" factors $\alpha_0, \alpha_{-1}, \alpha_{-2}, \ldots$, has the form:

$$(14\text{-}9) \quad p_0 = (G_0^{-1})' v_0 + (R_{-1} G_0^{-1})'\, \alpha_{-1} v_{-1} + (R_{-2} R_{-1} G_0^{-1})'\, \alpha_{-2} \alpha_{-1} v_{-2}$$
$$+, \ldots, + (R_{-m}, \ldots, R_{-2} R_{-1} G_0^{-1})'\, \alpha_{-m}, \ldots, \alpha_{-2} \alpha_{-1} v_{-m}$$
$$+ (R_{-m}, \ldots, R_{-2} R_{-1} G_0^{-1})'\, \alpha_{-m}, \ldots, \alpha_{-2} \alpha_{-1} B'_{-m} p_{-(m+1)}$$

The bracketed matrix products on the right-hand side of the first line are identical with the elements of the last column of the dynamic inverse appearing on the right-hand side of (14-4). These coefficients, however, enter into (14-9) in their transposed form. Since the series $R_{-1}, R_{-2} R_{-1}, R_{-3} R_{-2} R_{-1}, \ldots$, converges toward 0, the last term on the right-hand side—containing the price vector $p_{-(m+1)}$—can be disregarded provided that the sequence is extended back over a sufficient number of years.

The price vector of any given year has thus been shown to depend on the value-added vectors of that and all preceding years. This dependence is governed by the transpose of the same dynamic inverse that determines the dated sequence of input requirements generated in the corresponding physical system by a given time-phased bill of goods. For example, in the absence of technical change and on the assumption that both the rate of interest and the value-added vectors remain constant over time, equation (14-9) is reduced to

$$(14\text{-}10) \quad p_0 \rightarrow [G^{-1}]' \, [1 + R'\alpha + (R')^2\alpha^2 + (R')^3\alpha^3 \cdots (R')^t\alpha^t]v$$

As $t \rightarrow \infty$.

After $t$ becomes sufficiently large, the ratio between two successive terms of the exponential series on the right-hand side tends to equal $\mu_1\alpha$, where $\mu_1$ is the dominant characteristic root of $R'$. The series will converge and thus yield a finite price vector $p$ only if $\mu_1\alpha < 1$ or, since $\alpha = 1 + r$, if $r < (1 - \mu_1/\mu_1)$. The conclusion that, under certain conditions, the characteristic root of the matrix of an open dynamic input-output system imposes an upper limit on the rate of interest was presented many years ago by Michio Morishima.[3]

Figure 14-10 shows how the price of the bundle[4] of consumers' goods delivered to final users in 1958 depends on the annual values added per unit of the metal industry's output. The solid curve, based on the unrealistic assumption that the rate of interest through the entire 11-year period was equal to 0 (i.e., $\alpha = 1$), is identical with the corresponding solid curve in Figure 14-4. The dip below the zero line in the last year reflects negative costs, that is, the revenue that would have been secured from the liquidation of capital stock purchased in the previous year. The positive expenditure on capital goods reflected in the other points of the same curve will, in most cases, offset this negative amount.

The other two curves were drawn on the assumption that interest rates of 10 and 25 percent, respectively, prevailed over the entire interval. They show how a rise in the interest rate increases the dependence of present prices on past values added (and, consequently, also on past prices).

Much of this should have a familiar ring. The "productive advances" of Francois Quesnay, the process of expanded reproduction of Karl Marx, and the "roundabout production" of Böhm-Bawerk all contain the basic theoretical notions incorporated in the derivation of the dynamic inverse. But while these great economists had

---

[3]Michio Morishima, *Equilibrium, Stability, and Growth* (London: Oxford University Press, 1964).

[4]A "final demand bundle" consists of goods, weighted according to 1958 consumption patterns, costing $1 in 1958 prices.

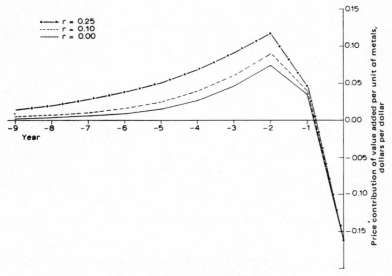

**Figure 14-10**

Portion of the price of a 1958 final demand bundle, directly and indirectly attributable to value added paid by the metal industry in year $t$.

to content themselves with verbal description and deductive reasoning, we can measure and we can compute. Therein lies the real difference between the past and the present state of economics.

## Appendix 14-1

To analyze the convergence properties of the series

$$(14\text{-}11) \quad R_{-1}, R_{-2}R_{-1}, R_{-3}R_{-2}R_{-1}, \ldots, R_{-t}, \ldots, R_{-3}R_{-2}R_{-1})^{-1}B_{t+1}$$
$$R_t = (1 - A_t + B_{t+1})^{-1}B_{t+2}$$

we can first consider the case in which

$$A_t = A \text{ and } B_t = B, \text{ for all } t\text{'s and, consequently,}$$
$$R_t = R \text{ for all } t\text{'s}$$

In this case, series (14-11) is transformed into the geometric series.

$$(14\text{-}12) \qquad\qquad R, R^2, R^3, \ldots, R^t$$
$$(14\text{-}13) \qquad\qquad R = (1 - A + B)^{-1}B$$
$$(14\text{-}14) \qquad (1 - A + B) = (1 - A)\,[1 + (1 - A)^{-1}B]$$
$$(14\text{-}15) \quad (1 - A + B)^{-1}B = [1 + (1 - A)^{-1}B]^{-1}\,(1 - A)^{-1}B$$
$$= (1 + U)^{-1}U$$

where $U = (1 - A)^{-1}B$.

Since $(1 - A)^{-1} > 0$, and $B \geq 0$ and is irreducible, therefore $U > 0$.

(14-16)                    $[(1 + U)^{-1}U]^{-1}(1 + U) = (1 + U^{-1})$

Consequently,

(14-17)                                    $R = (1 + U^{-1})^{-1}$

Let $\lambda_i$ ($i = 1, 2, 3, \ldots, n$) represent the $n$ roots of the square, nonsingular, and indecomposable matrix $U$. Since $U > 0$, it has—according to the well-known theorem of Frobenius—a positive dominant simple root. Moreover, this root, and only this root, has associated with it a positive eigenvector. Let $\lambda_1$ be this root.

For real $\lambda_i$ the corresponding roots of $U^{-1}$ and of $1 + U^{-1}$ are $1/\lambda_i$ and $1 + (1/\lambda l_i)$, respectively. Thus, according to equation (14-17), the roots of $R$ are

(14-18)          $\mu_i = \dfrac{\lambda_i}{1 + \lambda_i}$ and, in particular, $\mu_1 = \dfrac{\lambda_1}{1 + \lambda_1}$

From $\lambda_1 > 0$, it follows that $0 < \mu_1 < 1$, which means that $R$ always has a simple positive root $\mu_1$ smaller than 1, associated with a positive eigenvector.

Figure 14-11 depicts the relationship between $\mu_i$ and $\lambda_i$ for all real $\lambda_i$. If some of these subdominant roots are smaller than $-0.5$, the corresponding $\mu_i$ will be greater than 1 in absolute value. The eigenvectors associated with them will have elements of different signs.[5]

This implies that series $R^1, R^2, R^3, \ldots$, could be divergent. Depending on whether the dominant root is real or complex and whether its real part is positive or negative, the elements of the corresponding dynamic inverse would, in this case, diverge—as one moves back in time—expanding without limit either monotonically in the positive or negative direction or fluctuating with increasing amplitude between the positive and negative domain.

If $R_t$ changes with $t$ but does so with infinite lower and upper limits, say, $\underline{R}$ and $\overline{R}$, its higher terms will lie between the corresponding higher terms of the series $\underline{R}^1, \underline{R}^2, \ldots$, and $\overline{R}^1, \overline{R}^2$.

The convergence properties of the dynamic inverse depend on the time unit in terms of which the capital coefficients that enter into matrix $B$ are defined. In the basic balance equation (14-1), that unit also represents the

---

[5]The analysis holds for complex roots with the following modification:

$$\text{Let } \lambda_i = a + b_i.$$

Then, the real part of the corresponding $\mu_i$ becomes

$$\mathbf{R}(\mu_i) = \frac{a(a + 1) + b^2}{(a + 1)^2 + b^2}$$

To guarantee convergence, we must have $(a^2 + 1.5a) > -(b^2 + 0.5)$. If $b = 0$, these formulas reduce to the simpler form stated in the text.

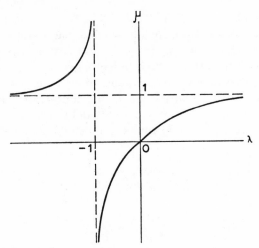

**Figure 14-11**

Schematic graph of relationship between $\mu$ and $\lambda$.

lag, that is, the difference between the time when additional stocks of capital goods, or inventories of current inputs, are accumulated and the time when they can be put to use.

Let $t$ be a given time interval described in original units and $t^\circ$ the same time interval measured in different units. If $\alpha$ is the ratio of the length of the first to that of the second unit,

$$(14\text{-}19) \qquad\qquad t^\circ = \alpha t$$

If, for example, $t$ describes a given stretch of time in years and $t^\circ$ measures it in months, then $\alpha = 12$.

The technical flow coefficients have no time dimensions; hence the elements of matrix $A$ will remain the same after the time unit—and consequently the lag built into equation (14-11)—has been changed from a year to, say, a month. But all the capital coefficients, that is, the elements of matrix $B$, will become 12 times larger. Continuing to use an asterisk to mark the values of matrices and their roots after the change of the time unit, we have

$$(14\text{-}20) \qquad\qquad B^\circ = B\alpha$$
$$U^\circ = U\alpha \text{ and } 1 + U^{\circ -1} = 1 + U^{-1}/\alpha$$

It follows that

$$\lambda_i^\circ = \lambda_i \alpha$$

and, in accordance with (13-18)

$$(14\text{-}21) \qquad\qquad \mu_i^\circ = \frac{\lambda_i/\alpha}{1 + \lambda_i/\alpha}$$

The relationship between $\mu_i^\circ$ and $\lambda_i/\alpha$ is thus the same as that between $\mu_i$ and $\lambda_i$, explained above. Inspecting it, we find that if root $\mu_1$ happens to be dominant its dominance will not be affected by any change in the time unit and the lag. If, on the other hand, some other root $\mu_i$ were dominant and, consequently, the system were divergent, an increase in $\alpha$, that is, a shortening of the lag, if sufficiently large, could shift any negative magnitude $\lambda_i/\alpha$ into the interval between $-0.5$ and $0$ and thus make $\mu_i^\circ$ dominant. A lengthening of the lag could, of course, have the opposite effect.

## Appendix 14-2

CONCEPTS

I. *A* matrix

The *A* matrix includes current flow coefficients and replacement coefficients. It is on a domestic output base.

II. *B* matrix

The *B* matrix is made up of the capital stock coefficients for all industries. Residential construction is included in the real estate and rental industry. The capital coefficients are capacity based.

III. Labor row

The labor row consists of man-years per $1000 of output.

IV. Total capital row

This row is simply the column sums of the *B* matrix.

V. Alternative bills of goods

A. Household nondurable goods including replacement of durable

This vector of final demand includes current purchases of nondurable goods and replacement of durable goods by households. It also contains a capital coefficient column, consisting of the stock of consumer durables (the stock of residential construction is in the real estate and rental column). The labor entry into this vector is domestic help.

B. Household goods, durable and nondurable

This vector of final demand contains current purchases of durable and nondurable goods by households.

C. Government

The government vector of final demand consists of purchases by federal, state, and local governments.

D. Total final demand

Final demand includes expenditures by households (durable and nondurable goods); federal, state, and local governments; exports; and competitive imports. It excludes the gross private capital formation and net inventory change vectors.

All items are in 1958 prices.

DATA FOR 1947 THROUGH 1958

Information regarding capital and technical coefficients is usually unavailable on a year-by-year basis. Since the dynamic model with technological change requires such data for, say, a dozen consecutive years, and since data may exist for no more than three years in this interval, most of the information has to be derived through interpolation. For most coefficients, exponential interpolation is used to approximate a constant rate of growth. When one of the terminal year coefficients is zero, the exponential method becomes impractical, and the program approximates with a linear technique.

Suppose $a(47)$ and $a(58)$ represent corresponding elements of two terminal year matrices. Then,

if $a(47) > 0$ and $a(58) > 0$ exponential interpolation is used,

if $a(47) = 0$ and $a(58) > 0$ linear interpolation is used,

if $a(47) > 0$ and $a(58) = 0$ linear interpolation is used, and

if $a(47) = 0$ and $a(58) = 0$ linear interpolation is used.

## Appendix 14-3

### 59-order classification

| Number | Name | Corresponding 83-order sectors |
|---|---|---|
| 1 | Food and drugs | 14, 15, 29 |
| 2 | Textiles, clothing, furnishings | 16, 17, 18, 19, 34, 22, 23 |
| 3 | Machinery (just final) | 51, 44, 45, 46, 47, 48, 49, 50, 63 |
| 4 | Transportation equipment and consumer appliances | 52, 54, 56, 59, 60, 61, 62 |
| 5 | Construction | 11, 12 |
| 6 | Metals | 37, 38 |
| 7 | Energy | 7, 31, 68 |
| 8 | Chemicals | 27 |
| 9 | ——— | — |
| 10 | ——— | — |
| 11 | Livestock | 1 |
| 12 | Crops | 2 |
| 13 | Forestry | 3 |
| 14 | Agricultural services | 4 |
| 15 | Iron ore mining | 5 |
| 16 | Nonferrous ore mining | 6 |
| 17 | Petroleum mining | 8 |
| 18 | Stone and clay mining | 9 |
| 19 | Chemical mining | 10 |
| 20 | ——— | — |
| 21 | Lumber and products, excluding containers | 20 |
| 22 | Wooden containers | 21 |
| 23 | Paper products and containers | 24, 25 |

| Number | Name | Corresponding 83-order sectors |
|---|---|---|
| 24 ——— | | — |
| 25 | Printing and publishing | 26 |
| 26 | Plastics and synthetics | 28 |
| 27 | Paint and allied products | 30 |
| 28 | Rubber and plastic products | 32 |
| 29 | Leather tanning | 33 |
| 30 | Glass and glass products | 35 |
| 31 | Stone and clay products | 36 |
| 32 | Metal containers | 39 |
| 33 | Heating, plumbing, structural metals | 40 |
| 34 | Stampings, screw machine products | 41 |
| 35 | Hardware, plating, valves, wire products | 42 |
| 36 | Engines and turbines | 43 |
| 37 | Electric apparatus and motors | 53 |
| 38 | Electric lighting and wiring equipment | 55 |
| 39 | Electronic components | 57 |
| 40 | Batteries, x-ray and engine electrical equipment | 58 |
| 41 | Miscellaneous manufacturing | 64 |
| 42 | Transportation and warehousing | 65 |
| 43 | Communications, excluding radio and TV | 66 |
| 44 | Radio and TV broadcasting | 67 |
| 45 | Trade | 69 |
| 46 | Finance and insurance | 70 |
| 47 | Real estate and rental | 71 |
| 48 | Hotels, personal, and repair services | 72 |
| 49 | Business services | 73 |
| 50 | Research and development | 74 |
| 51 | Automobile repair services | 75 |
| 52 | Amusements and recreation | 76 |
| 53 | Medical and educational institutions | 77 |
| 54 ——— | | — |
| 55 ——— | | — |
| 56 | Noncompetitive imports | 80 |
| 57 | Entertainment and business travel | 81 |
| 58 ——— | | — |
| 59 | Scrap and byproducts | 83 |
| 60 | Total labor row | |
| 61 | Household nondurables, including replacement of durables column | |
| 62 | Household durables and nondurables column | Alternative |
| 63 | Government final demand column | bills of |
| 64 | Total final demand, excluding gross private capital formation and net inventory change, column | goods |
| 65 | Total capital row | |

## Appendix 14-4

### Sources of data

1958   A matrix, current flow coefficients
       This matrix is based on the 1958 input-output table published by the
       Office of Business Economics, Department of Commerce. See A. P.
       Carter, "Changes in the Structure of the American Economy, 1947–
       1958, 1962," *Review of Economics and Statistics* XLIX (May 1967).

1958   A matrix, replacement coefficients
       This matrix was developed at the Harvard Economic Research Pro-
       ject, based on 1958 capital coefficients and U.S. Treasury Depart-
       ment, Internal Revenue Service, *Depreciation Guidelines and Rules*,
       Publication No. 456 (Washington, D.C.: U.S. Government Printing
       Office, 1964).

1958   B matrix, capital coefficients
       The capital coefficients for manufacturing sectors were obtained
       from Robert Waddell, Philip Ritz, John DeWitt Norton, and Marshall
       K. Wood, *Capital Expansion Planning Factors, Manufacturing Indus-
       tries*, (Washington, D.C.: National Planning Association, April
       1966). For nonmanufacturing sectors, the capital coefficients were
       compiled at the Harvard Economic Research Project by Samuel A.
       Rea Jr. and others in 1966 and 1967.

1958   Labor coefficients
       The labor coefficients are based on Jack Alterman, "Interindustry
       Employment Requirements," *Monthly Labor Review* 88, 7 (July
       1965).

1958   Final demand vectors
       The final demand vectors are based on the 1958 input-output table
       published by the Office of Business Economics, Department of Com-
       merce, and on Raymond W. Goldsmith, *The National Wealth of the
       United States in the Postwar Period*, (Princeton, N.J.: National Bureau
       of Economic Research, 1962).

1947   A matrix, current flow coefficients
       This matrix is based on the Bureau of Labor Statistics 450-order
       input-output table for 1947, which was obtained by the Harvard
       Economic Research Project on cards (Deck A) from the Bureau of
       Labor Statistics along with mimeographed documentation for indi-
       vidual sectors. It is published at a 50-order level and is described in
       W. D. Evans and M. Hoffenberg," The Interindustry Relations Study
       for 1947," *Review of Economics and Statistics* XXXIV (May 1952).
       Adjustments have been made to the 1947 matrix in order to make it
       comparable with the 1958 matrix. See A. P. Carter, cited above.
       Further work in this area is currently being done by Beatrice Vac-
       cara and others at the Office of Business Economics and by the Har-
       vard Economic Research Project.

1947  *A* matrix, replacement coefficients

This matrix was developed at the Harvard Economic Research Project, based on the 1947 capital coefficients and U.S. Treasury Department, cited above.

1947  *B* matrix, capital coefficients

The 1947 capital coefficients are based on James M. Henderson et al. "Estimates of the Capital Structure of American Industries, 1947," (Harvard Economic Research Project, June 1953), and Robert N. Grosse, *Capital Requirements for the Expansion of Industrial Capacity*, Vol. 1, Part 1 (Washington, D.C.: Executive Office of the President, Bureau of the Budget, Office of Statistical Standards, November 1953). Further revisions were made to the coefficients by Alan Strout and others in 1958–1962. Additional adjustments to make the 1947 capital coefficients comparable with the 1947 were made by Samuel A. Rea Jr. and others (1966–1967) at the Harvard Economic Research Project.

1947  Labor coefficients

Same source as 1958 labor coefficients.

1947  Final demand vectors

The final demand vectors are based on the Bureau of Labor Statistics 450-order input-output table and on Raymond W. Goldsmith, cited above.

# 15

## Structure of the world economy: Outline of a simple input-output formulation

### ( 1 9 7 4 )

### I

The world economy, like the economy of a single country, can be visualized as a system of interdependent processes. Each process, be it the manufacture of steel, the education of youth, or the running of a family household, generates certain outputs and absorbs a specific combination of inputs. Direct interdependence between two processes arises whenever the output of one becomes an input of the other: coal, the output of the coal mining industry, is an input of the electric power generating sector. The chemical industry uses coal not only directly as a raw material but also indirectly in the form of electrical power. A network of such links constitutes a system of elements that depend upon each other directly, indirectly, or both.

The state of a particular economic system can be conveniently described in the form of a two-way input-output table showing the flows of goods and services among its different sectors, and to and from processes or entities ("value added" and "final demand") viewed as falling outside the conventional borders of an input-output system. As the scope of the inquiry expands, new rows and columns are added to the table, and some of the external inflows and outflows become internalized. Increasing the number of rows and

Nobel Memorial Lecture. ©The Nobel Foundation, 1974. Published in *The Swedish Journal of Economics*, Vol. 76, 1974.

The author is indebted to Peter Petri for setting up and performing all the computations whose results are presented in this lecture, and to D. Terry Jenkins for preparing the graphs and providing editorial assistance.

columns that describe an economic system also permits a more detailed description of economic activities commonly described in highly aggregative terms.

Major efforts are presently under way to construct a data base for a systematic input-output study not of a single national economy but of the world economy viewed as a system composed of many inter-related parts. This global study, as described in the official document, is aimed at

> helping Member States of the United Nations make their 1975 review of world progress in accelerating development and attacking mass poverty and unemployment. First, by studying the results that prospective environmental issues and policies would probably have for world development in the absence of changes in national and international development policies, and secondly, by studying the effects of possible alternative policies to promote development while at the same time preserving and improving the environment. By thus indicating alternative future paths which the world economy might follow, the study would help the world community to make decisions regarding future development and environmental policies in as rational a manner as possible.[1]

Preliminary plans provide for a description of the world economy in terms of 28 groups of countries, with about 45 productive sectors for each group. Environmental conditions will be described in terms of 30 principal pollutants, the use of nonagricultural natural resources in terms of some 40 different minerals and fuels.

## II

The subject of this chapter is the elucidation of a particular input-output view of the world economy. This formulation should provide a framework for assembling and organizing the mass of factual data needed to describe the world economy. Such a system is essential for a concrete understanding of the structure of the world economy as well as for a systematic mapping of the alternative paths along which it could move in the future.

Let us consider a world economy consisting of (1) a *developed* and (2) a *less developed* region. Let us further divide the economy of each region into three productive sectors: an *extraction industry*, producing raw materials; *all other production*, supplying conven-

[1]Quoted from "Brief Outline of the United Nations Study on the Impact of Prospective Environmental Issues and Policies on the International Development Strategy," April 1973.

## Table 15-1

### World economy in 1970 *(billions of 1970 dollars)*

DEVELOPED COUNTRIES

|  | Extraction industry | Other production | Abatement industry | Final demand | | Total output |
|---|---|---|---|---|---|---|
|  |  |  |  | Domestic | Trade |  |
| Extraction industry | 0 | 76 | 0 | 2 | −15 | 63 |
| Other production | 21 | 1809 | 21 | 2414 | 19 | 4284 |
| Pollution | 5 | 62 | −63 | 60 | 0 | 64 |
| Employment | 18 | 1372 | 20 | 287 | 0 | |
| Other value added | 21 | 996 | 22 | 0 | 0 | |

LESS DEVELOPED COUNTRIES

|  | Extraction industry | Other production | Abatement industry | Final demand | | Total output |
|---|---|---|---|---|---|---|
|  |  |  |  | Domestic | Trade |  |
| Extraction industry | 0 | 8 | 0 | 2 | 15 | 25 |
| Other production | 7 | 197 | 0 | 388 | −19 | 573 |
| Pollution | 2 | 8 | 0 | 11 | 0 | 21 |
| Employment | 9 | 149 | 0 | 99 | 0 | |
| Other value added | 8 | 220 | 0 | 0 | 0 | |

tional goods and services; and a *pollution abatement industry*. In addition to these three sectors, there is also a consumption sector specified for each region. The function of the abatement industry is to eliminate pollutants generated by the productive sectors, consumers, and the abatement industry itself.

The two input-output tables displayed as Table 15-1 describe the intersectoral flows of goods and services within the developed and the less developed economies. The flow of natural resources from the less developed to the developed countries as well as the opposite flow of other goods from the developed to the less developed countries are entered in both tables, positively for the exporting region and negatively for the importing region.

In each of the two tables the entries at the far right in the first and second rows represent the total domestic outputs of the extraction industry and of other production, respectively.

Each positive number along the third (pollution) row shows the physical amount of pollutant generated by the activity named at the head of the column in which that number appears. The negative quantity shown at the intersection of the third column and the third row represents the amount of pollutant eliminated by abatement activities. Inputs such as power, chemicals, and so on, purchased by the abatement industry from other sectors and value added paid out by that industry are entered as positive amounts in the same third column. The difference between the total amount of pollution generated in all sectors and the amount eliminated by the abatement sector is represented by the *net* emission figure, the entry at the far right in the third row. Finally, labor inputs used in each sector and payments made to other income-receiving agents are shown in the bottom two rows.

The numbers in these two tables are, strictly speaking, fictitious. But their general order of magnitude reflects crude, preliminary estimates of intersectoral flows within and between the developed and less developed regions during the 1960s.[2]

For analytical purposes, the outputs and inputs of the extraction industry and other production, as well as the amounts of pollutants generated and abated, can be interpreted as quantities measured in the appropriate physical units (pounds, yards, kilowatts, etc.). The same is true of the services of some of the so-called primary factors; labor inputs, for example, are entered in the second to last row of each table. A similar physical measurement of the other components of value added, even if it were possible in principle, is impossible given the present state of knowledge. In pure or, should I say, speculative economic theory, we can overcome this kind of difficulty by introducing some convenient albeit unrealistic assumptions. But a theoretical formulation designed to permit empirical analysis has to account for the fact that at least some components of value added cannot be interpreted as payments for measurable physical inputs but must be treated as purely monetary magnitudes.

### III

The flows described in the two input-output tables are interdependent. They have to satisfy three distinct sets of constraints. First,

[2]All quantities are measured in billions of dollars "in current prices"; pollutants are "priced" in terms of average "per unit" abatement costs.

within each production or consumption process there exists a technological relationship between the level of output and the required
quantities of various inputs. For example, if we divide each figure
in the first column of the first section of Table 15-1 (the inputs of
the extraction industry) by the total output of that sector (the last
figure in the first row), we find that to produce one unit of its output
this sector absorbed 0.3372 units of the output of other production,
used 0.2867 units of labor services, and spent 0.3332 dollars for
other value added. Moreover, for each unit of useful output the
extraction industries generated 0.0859 units of pollution. Other sets
of input-output coefficients describe the technical structure of every
sector of production and consumption in both groups of countries.

While statistical input-output tables continue to serve as the principal source of information on the input requirements or "cooking
recipes" of various industries, increasingly we find economists using
engineering data as a supplemental source. Complete structural
matrices of the two groups of countries used in our example are
shown in Table 15-2.

The second set of constraints that has to be satisfied by every viable system requires that the total (physical) amounts of outputs and
inputs of each type of good must be in balance; that is, total supply
must equal total demand. In the case of a pollutant, *net* emission
must equal the total amount generated by all sectors less the amount
eliminated by the abatement process.

For example, the balance between the total output and the com-

## Table 15-2

### Technical and consumption coefficients[a]

*Developed countries*

$$A_1 = \begin{bmatrix} .0 & .0178 & .0 \\ .3372 & .4223 & .3298 \\ .0859 & .0144 & .0118 \end{bmatrix} \qquad C_1 = \begin{bmatrix} .0007 \\ .8834 \\ .0218 \end{bmatrix}$$

$$l_1 = [.2867 \quad .3203 \quad .3161]$$
$$r_1 = [.3332 \quad .2324 \quad .3482]$$

$$l_1^c = [.1050]$$
$$r_1 = [.0 \quad ]$$

*Less developed countries*

$$A_2 = \begin{bmatrix} .0 & .0141 & .0 \\ .2934 & .3437 & .3298 \\ .0859 & .0144 & .0118 \end{bmatrix} \qquad C_2 = \begin{bmatrix} .0037 \\ .7943 \\ .0218 \end{bmatrix}$$

$$l_2 = [.3729 \quad .2597 \quad .3161]$$
$$r_2 = [.3337 \quad .3825 \quad .3541]$$

$$l_2^c = [.2020]$$
$$r_2 = [.0 \quad ]$$

[a]The coefficients in these tables do not sum to unity because the pollution generated by industry and
by final demand is only partially abated in the developed countries and is not abated at all in the less
developed countries.

bined inputs of extracted raw materials can be described by the following equation:

(15-1)

$$(1 - a_{11})x_1 - a_{12}x_2 \qquad - a_{13}x_3 \qquad - c_1y \qquad - T_1 \qquad = 0$$

(net output    (amount        (amount        (amount        (amount
of extrac-     delivered      delivered      delivered      exported)
tion in-       to other       to the         to final
dustry)        production)    abatement      users)
                              industry)

The equation describing the balance between generation, abatement, and net emission of pollution reads as follows:

(15-2)

$$-a_{31}x_1 - a_{32}x_2 \quad + \quad (1 - a_{33})x_3 \quad - \quad c_3y \qquad + \quad E \qquad = 0$$

(gross amount     (amount        (gross amount     (net amount
of pollution      abated by      generated by      emitted into
generated by      abatement      consumers         the environ-
sectors 1 and 2)  activities)    and govern-       ment)
                                 ment)

The total outputs of the extraction industry and of other production, respectively, are represented by $x_1$ and $x_2$; $x_3$ represents the level of activity of the abatement sector; $y$ is the sum total of values added, that is, gross national income. The "technical coefficient" $a_{ij}$ represents the number of units of the product of sector $i$ absorbed (or generated in the case of pollution) by sector $j$ in producing one unit of its output; $c_j$ is a "consumption coefficient" describing the number of units of the output of sector $j$ consumed (or generated in the case of pollution) per unit of total value added, that is, per unit of gross national income.

Table 15-3 displays the complete set of linear equations describing the physical balances between outputs and inputs of all sectors in both countries in terms of compact matrix notation. The last of these equations—written below in its explicit form—describes the flows of exports and imports that link the developed and the less developed areas into a single world economy.

(15-3)                        $B = T_2p_2 - T_1p_1$

The balance of trade $B$, that is, the difference between the monetary value of the two opposite trade flows, depends not only on the quantities $T_1$ and $T_2$ of traded goods but also on their prices, $p_1$ and $p_2$. The higher the price a country receives for its exports, or the lower the price it pays for its imports, the better are its "terms of trade."

## Table 15-3

### Physical subsystem

| Equation number | Variable $_1X_1\ _1X_2\ _1X_3$ | $L_1$ | $Y_1$ | $E_1$ | $_2X_1\ _2X_2\ _2X_3$ | $L_2$ | $Y_2$ | $E_2$ | $T_1$ | $T_2$ | $B$ | |
|---|---|---|---|---|---|---|---|---|---|---|---|---|
| 1.1 | | | | | | | | | 1 | | | |
| 1.2 | $I - A_1$ | | | | | | | | | $-1$ | | |
| 1.3 | | | | 1 | | | | | | | | |
| 1.4 | $l_1$ | | $-1$ | $l_1^c$ | | | | | | | | |
| 1.5 | | | | | | | | $-1$ | | | | $= [0]$ |
| 1.6 | | | | | $I - A_2$ | $-C_2$ | | | | 1 | | |
| 1.7 | | | | | | | | 1 | | | | |
| 1.8 | | | | | $I_2$ | | $-1$ | $l_2^c$ | | | | |
| 1.9 | | | | | | | | | $p_1$ | $-p_2$ | 1 | |

### Price subsystem

| Equation number | Variable $_1p_1\ _1p_2$ | $_1p_3$ | $w_1$ | $_1r_1\ _1r_2\ _1r_3$ | $_2p_1\ _2p_2$ | $_2p_3$ | $w_2$ | $_2r_1\ _2r_2\ _2r_3$ | |
|---|---|---|---|---|---|---|---|---|---|
| 2.1 | | $-_1q_1 \cdot {_1a_{31}}$ | | | | | | | |
| 2.2 | $I - A_1'$ | $-_1q_2 \cdot {_1a_{32}}$ | $-l_1'$ | $-I$ | | | | | |
| 2.3 | | $1 - {_1q_3} \cdot {_1a_{33}}$ | | | | | | | |
| 2.4 | | | | | | $-_2q_1 \cdot {_2a_{31}}$ | | | $= [0]$ |
| 2.5 | | | | | $I - A_1'$ | $-_2q_2 \cdot {_2a_{32}}$ | $-l_2'$ | $-I$ | |
| 2.6 | | | | | | $1 - {_2q_3} \cdot {_2a_{33}}$ | | | |
| 2.7 | 1 | 8 | | | $-1$ | | | | |
| 2.8 | $-1$ | | | | 1 | | | | |

The last of the three sets of relationships describes the interdependence of the prices of all goods and services and the values added paid out, per unit of output, by each industry. For example, a typical equation in this set states that the price at which the extraction sector sells one unit of its output equals the average outlay incurred in producing it. This includes the costs (i.e., quantities × prices) of inputs purchased from other sectors, wages paid, and all other value added:

$$(15\text{-}4) \quad p_1 - a_{11}p_1 - a_{21}p_2 - q_1 a_{31}p_3 - l_1 w - r_1 = 0$$

(15-4) price of output — cost of material inputs — cost of pollution abatement — cost of labor inputs — other value added

The technical coefficients ($a_{ij}$ and $l_i$) appearing in this equation are the same as those appearing in the structural matrices of Table 14-2. The abatement ratios $q_i$ represent the fraction of the gross pollution emission of industry $i$ that is eliminated (at that industry's expense)[3] by the abatement industry.

In this example, the system of physical balances contains 9 equations with 15 variables, while the price-values-added system has 8 equations with 14 variables. But these 14 variables are reduced to 12 and the number of equations to 6 if one assumes from the outset that the internationally traded products of the extraction industry and other production have the same price in the developed and the less developed countries. Equations 2.7 and 2.8 in Table 15-3, worked out explicitly, read:

$$(15\text{-}5) \qquad {}_1p_1 = {}_2p_1(\equiv p_1) \text{ and } {}_1p_2 = {}_2p_2(\equiv p_2)$$

The combination of both systems viewed as a whole contains 29 unknowns but only 17 equations. Thus, to arrive at a unique solution, we have to fix the values of 12 variables on the basis of some outside information; that is, their values have to be determined exogenously.

Two types of quantitative information are required for the solution of this system. First, some data are used in the form of appropriate structural coefficients. Other kinds of factual information are introduced by assigning specific numerical values to appropriate "exogenous" variables.

In view of the uneven quality of data that will constitute the empirical basis of the present inquiry, it would be a tactical mistake to pour all the factual information we possess into the rigid mold of a single, all-embracing, inflexible explanatory scheme. The decision of which variables should be treated as dependent and which should be fixed exogenously is essentially a tactical one. The theoretical formulation is a weapon; in deciding how to use it we must take into account the nature of the particular empirical terrain.

To assess the influence of factors considered external to our theoretical description of the world economy, we earmark six physical and five value-added variables as "exogenous." Tables 15-4 and 15-5 show which variables are endogenous and assign values to all exogenous variables. These assumptions permit us to project changes in

---

[3]This formulation is based on the assumption that the pollution generated by a particular sector is being eliminated at its own expense. In case the abatement cost is being paid by the government out of its tax revenues, the price equations have to be modified accordingly. See Chapters 11 and 12 in this volume.

## Table 15-4

### Physical system assumptions

| Variables | | Developed countries | | | Less developed countries | | |
|---|---|---|---|---|---|---|---|
| | | Case I | Case II | Case III | Case I | Case II | Case III |
| Extraction output $X_1$ | | Capacity limited to 150% of 1970 levels | | | Endogenous | | |
| Other production $X_2$ | | Endogenous | | | Capacity grows 6.4% per annum between 1970 and 2000 | | |
| Abatement output $X_3$ | | Endogenous | | | 0 | Endogenous | |
| Employment | $L$ | Increase proportional to population increase | | | Endogenous | | |
| Final demand | $Y$ | Endogenous | | | | | |
| Net pollution emission | $E$ | Limited to current levels assuming 1970 standards | | | Endogenous | Limited to twice 1970 levels | |
| Net trade in extractive goods | $T_1$ | Endogenous | | | | | |
| Net trade in other goods | $T_2$ | | | | | | |
| Trade balance | $B$ | A deficit for less developed countries amounting to 1% of developed countries' income, reflecting capital flows and aid | | | | | |
| Technical coefficients | $A$ | Unchanged from 1970 | Twice 1970 levels for extraction industry | Unchanged from 1970 | | | |
| Labor coefficients | $I$ | ½ 1970 levels due to increased productivity | ⅔ 1970 levels for extraction industry | ½ 1970 levels due to increased productivity | | | |
| Consumption coefficients | $C$ | Unchanged from 1970 | | | | | |
| Extraction goods price | $P_1$ | Obtained from solution of price system | | | | | |
| Other goods price | $P_2$ | | | | | | |

our simple world economy from a state representative of the present ("1970") to three alternative hypothetical states about 30 years hence ("2000 I," "2000 II," and "2000 III").

Total labor input in developed countries, $L_1$, is exogenous; under full or nearly full employment, its magnitude depends on demo-

**Table 15-5**

Price system assumptions

| Variables | | Developed countries | | | Less developed countries | | |
|---|---|---|---|---|---|---|---|
| | | Case I | Case II | Case III | Case I | Case II | Case III |
| Extraction goods price | $P_1$ | Endogenous | | | Endogenous | | |
| Other goods price | $P_2$ | | | | | | |
| Abatement price | $P_3$ | | | | | | |
| Wage rate | $w$ | Kept at 1970 level (index = 1.0) | | | Endogenous | | |
| Other value added in other production | $r_1$ $r_2$ | Kept at 1970 levels (index = 1.0) | | | Kept at 1970 level (index = 1.0) | | |
| Other value added in abatement | $r_3$ | | | | | | |
| Technical coefficients | $A$ | Unchanged from 1970 | | Twice 1970 levels for extraction industry | Unchanged from 1970 | | |
| Labor coefficients | $l$ | ½ 1970 levels due to increased productivity | | ½ 1970 levels for extraction industry | ½ 1970 levels due to increased productivity | | |
| Abatement coefficients | $q$ | $q_1 = q_2 = q_3 = x_3/(x_3 + E)$, that is, all abatement coefficients of a given country are set to a value that reduces net pollution to the exogenously specified level $E$ | | | | | |

330

graphic and cultural factors not accounted for within our formal theoretical system. Substantial endemic unemployment in the less developed countries makes it advisable to consider the level of total employment as depending on the level of output—that is, to treat $L_2$ as endogenous.

The output of the extraction industry in the developed countries is restricted by the limited availability of natural resources. We account for this limitation by making $_1x_1$ exogenous. In the less developed countries, where natural resources are still plentiful, the output of the extraction industry, $_2x_1$, depends partly on a small domestic market but primarily on the import requirements of developed countries. Thus, $_2x_1$ can be treated as a dependent variable.

The situation is reversed in the case of other production. In developed countries the output of manufactured goods normally adjusts to the level of final demand, making $_1x_2$ a dependent variable. Yet in the less developed countries the output of other production, $_1x_2$, is restricted by external factors such as weak infrastructure and limited capital. In this case rising domestic inputs usually stimulate a growing demand for imports. Hence, $_2x_2$ is treated as independent and $T_1$ and $T_2$ as dependent variables.

In the price-value-added system of equations, all money wages and other value-added payments in the developed countries ($w$, $r_1$, $r_2$, and $r_3$) are exogenously determined. This means that the prices of all three products can be derived endogenously. In less developed countries the situation seems to be different: since the prices of commodities produced by extraction and other production are determined by the cost of their production (including the exogenous valued added) in the developed countries, the value added that can be paid out by the two sectors producing these goods in the less developed countries, $_2r_1$ and $_2r_2$, simply reflect the difference between a given price and the production costs.

Raw materials are, as a rule, relatively more abundant and more cheaply extracted in less developed countries; thus, the value added earned by extraction industries in less developed countries can be expected to be relatively high. David Ricardo speaks in this connection of "mining rents." On the other hand, technical input coefficients or, more properly, costs in other production of the less developed countries can be expected to be higher than in developed countries. Because of this, the value added earned per unit of output in that sector tends to be relatively low.

Since a principal purpose of the aforementioned United Nations project is a "realistic evaluation of the effects of alternative types of environmental policies on the economic prospects of less developed countries," net pollution emissions $E_1$ and $E_2$ are treated as exogenously determined in two of our projections.

Assigning specific numerical magnitudes to all exogenously determined variables permits effective use of a variety of external data in arriving at a unique numerical solution of the formal input-output system. As the empirical inquiry advances, exogenous variables can be internalized through introduction of additional equations.

The most important but also the most demanding step in implementing an empirical input-output system is the determination of values of hundreds or even thousands of structural coefficients. The relevant methodologies are so varied and specialized that I abstain from discussing them in this general context.

## IV

As has been explained above, three different sets of factual assumptions provided the basis for the three alternative projections of the state of one simple world economy for the year "1970" to the year "2000." Tables 15-4 and 15-5 contain their full specification, while the results of the computations are summarized in three pairs of input-output tables presented in Appendix 15-1 at the end of this chapter.

The bar charts displayed in Figures 15-1 and 15-2 facilitate a systematic examination of these findings. The width of each bar represents the relative size of the corresponding economic activity measured in base-year dollars. The length of each bar indicates the percentage increase or decrease in the level of each activity as the world economy passes from one state to another. Exogenous variables are identified by asterisks.

The long bars in the uppermost rows of these economic profiles indicate an upsurge in output and total consumption and a downward movement of prices, a "great leap forward" from 1970 to 2000. Case I is a projection that critically depends on two assumptions. First, the employed labor force in developed countries will increase with population growth. Second, labor productivity in both regions (the reciprocal of the labor coefficient) will be three times as high in 2000 as in 1970, with all other input coefficients remaining the same. Strict enforcement of standards contained in the United States Clean Air Act of 1967 (as amended in 1970) will bring about a sharp drop in unabated emissions in the developed areas, while in less developed countries the absence of any abatement

## PHYSICAL SYSTEM CHANGES

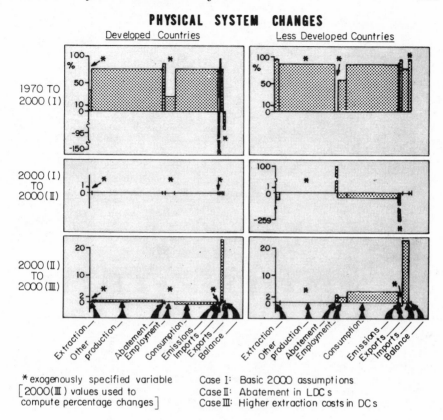

Developed Countries      Less Developed Countries

*exogenously specified variable
[2000(Ⅲ) values used to
compute percentage changes]

Case I: Basic 2000 assumptions
Case Ⅱ: Abatement in LDC s
Case Ⅲ: Higher extraction costs in DC s

**Figure 15-1**

activity will force the pollution level up. International trade will expand faster than domestic economic activities. Prices (measured in wage units) will decline, while the value added in less developed countries will rise in the extraction industry but fall in other production.

How would the future economic picture change if strict antipollution standards were also observed in less developed countries? The answer is presented in the second rows of bar graphs in Figures 15-1 and 15-2. In the developed countries there will be practically no change. In less developed countries the inauguration of abatement activities aimed at limiting pollution to twice its 1970 level would bring about expanded employment while requiring some sacrifices in consumption. Value added would fall sharply in the extraction industry and somewhat less in other production.

How would the situation thus attained be affected by a significant

## PRICE SYSTEM CHANGES

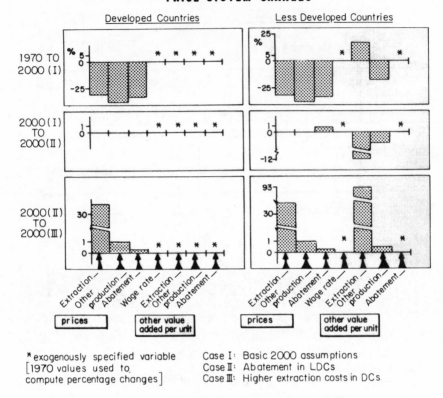

* exogenously specified variable
[1970 values used to
compute percentage changes]

Case I: Basic 2000 assumptions
Case II: Abatement in LDCs
Case III: Higher extraction costs in DCs

**Figure 15-2**

increase in the operating costs of the extraction industry in the developed countries? The bottom rows of profiles in Figures 15-1 and 15-2 show how the conditions in both regions of the world economy would be affected if the productivity of labor in the extraction industry of developed countries rose only 1.5 rather than 3 times between 1970 and 2000 while the amounts of other extraction inputs doubled per unit of output. The output of other production in the developed countries would register a slight increase and the level of consumption a slight decrease. Consumption in the less developed countries would experience a substantial increase. The mechanism responsible for such a redistribution of income between the developed and the less developed countries involves a steep increase in the price of extraction goods compared to other prices, a corresponding rise in value added (rents yielded by the extraction industry of the less developed countries), and, finally, a substantial increase in imports accompanied by slight reduction of exports from these countries, both reflecting a marked improvement in their "terms of trade."

I refrain from drawing any factual conclusion from the economic projections presented above. The computer received fictitious inputs and necessarily issued fictitious outputs. All theories tend to shape the facts they try to explain; any theory may thus turn into a procrustean bed. Our proposed theoretical formulation is designed to protect investigators from this danger; it does not permit them to draw any special or general conclusions before they complete the always difficult and seldom glamorous task of ascertaining the necessary facts.

## Appendix 15-1

Projected world economy in 2000 (Case I) *(billions of 1970 dollars)*

DEVELOPED COUNTRIES

|  | Extraction industry | Other production | Abatement industry | Final demand | | Total output |
|---|---|---|---|---|---|---|
|  |  |  |  | Domestic | Trade |  |
| Extraction industry | 0 | 316 | 0 | 8 | −226 | 98 |
| Other production | 33 | 7502 | 160 | 9713 | 357 | 17765 |
| Pollution | 8 | 256 | −479 | 240 | 0 | 25 |
| Employment | 9 | 1897 | 51 | 379 | 0 | |
| Other value added | 33 | 4129 | 169 | 0 | 0 | |

LESS DEVELOPED COUNTRIES

|  | Extraction industry | Other production | Abatement industry | Final demand | | Total output |
|---|---|---|---|---|---|---|
|  |  |  |  | Domestic | Trade |  |
| Extraction | 0 | 52 | 0 | 12 | 226 | 290 |
| Other production | 85 | 1254 | 36 | 2632 | −357 | 3650 |
| Pollution | 25 | 53 | −108 | 72 | 0 | 42 |
| Employment | 36 | 316 | 12 | 223 | 0 | |
| Other value added | 100 | 1118 | 39 | 0 | 0 | |

## Projected world economy in 2000 (Case II) *(billions of 1970 dollars)*
### DEVELOPED COUNTRIES

|  | Extraction industry | Other production | Abatement industry | Final demand Domestic | Trade | Total output |
|---|---|---|---|---|---|---|
| Extraction industry | 0 | 316 | 0 | 8 | −226 | 98 |
| Other production | 33 | 7502 | 160 | 9713 | 357 | 17765 |
| Pollution | 8 | 256 | −479 | 240 | 0 | 25 |
| Employment | 9 | 1897 | 51 | 379 | 0 | |
| Other value added | 33 | 4129 | 169 | 0 | 0 | |

### LESS DEVELOPED COUNTRIES

|  | Extraction industry | Other production | Abatement industry | Final demand Domestic | Trade | Total output |
|---|---|---|---|---|---|---|
| Extraction industry | 0 | 52 | 0 | 12 | 226 | 290 |
| Other production | 85 | 1255 | 0 | 2668 | −357 | 3650 |
| Pollution | 25 | 53 | 0 | 73 | 0 | 151 |
| Employment | 36 | 316 | 0 | 226 | 0 | |
| Other value added | 112 | 1143 | 0 | 0 | 0 | |

## Projected world economy in 2000 (Case III) *(billions of 1970 dollars)*
### DEVELOPED COUNTRIES

|  | Extraction industry | Other production | Abatement industry | Final demand Domestic | Trade | Total output |
|---|---|---|---|---|---|---|
| Extraction industry | 0 | 315 | 0 | 8 | −225 | 98 |
| Other production | 66 | 7472 | 159 | 9678 | 461 | 17836 |
| Pollution | 8 | 255 | −477 | 239 | 0 | 25 |
| Employment | 19 | 1890 | 51 | 378 | 0 | |
| Other value added | 33 | 4112 | 168 | 0 | 0 | |

## Projected world economy in 2000 (Case III) *(billions of 1970 dollars)*
### LESS DEVELOPED COUNTRIES

|  | Extraction industry | Other production | Abatement industry | Final demand Domestic | Final demand Trade | Total output |
|---|---|---|---|---|---|---|
| Extraction industry | 0 | 51 | 0 | 13 | 225 | 289 |
| Other production | 85 | 1254 | 37 | 2735 | −461 | 3650 |
| Pollution | 25 | 53 | −111 | 75 | 0 | 42 |
| Employment | 36 | 316 | 12 | 232 | 0 | |
| Other value added | 189 | 1125 | 40 | 0 | 0 | |

# 16

## Population growth and economic development: Illustrative projections

### (1979)

The summary of the papers presented at the World Population Conference held in Bucharest in 1975 expresses on behalf of the Secretary General of the United Nations the hope that "models of the economy reflect both important aspects of the process of socio-economic development and the impact of population growth on various sectors of the economy. . . . Even if such models cannot make successful predictions, they may (if they are well formulated and if adequate data are available) help in the assessment of alternative consequences of the rate of population growth in specific development contexts."[1]

The construction of a global economic model of the world economy began under the sponsorship of the United Nations a year before the publication of the above lines. The immediate purpose of that study was to assess the conditions under which the "income gap" between developing and developed countries could be reduced by the year 2000 to one half of what it was in 1970. A study, *The Future of the World Economy,* based on that model, completed in 1976, and published in 1977,[2] concluded that while no insurmountable physical and environmental barriers exist to the

[1]"The Population Debate," Papers of the World Population Conference, Bucharest, 1974, UN Document 54/ESA/SER. A/57 (New York: United Nations, 1975).

[2]Wassily Leontief, Ann P. Carter, and Peter Petri, *The Future of the World Economy* (New York: Oxford University Press, 1977).

Reprinted with permission of the Population Council from *Population and Development Review* 5 1 (March 1979): 1–27.

This paper was written in collaboration with Faye Duchin and Ira Sohn. It was first presented at the meeting of the International Union for the Scientific Study of Population in Helsinki, September 1978.

accelerated development of the developing regions during the remainder of the twentieth century, such development would require far-reaching internal social, political, and institutional changes and significant changes in the world economic order.

The structure of the model used in the study permits taking into account the demographic factor. However, in formulating different scenarios as a basis for computation of alternative patterns of future economic growth of the developing and the developed countries, the possibility of investigating the effects of alternative assumptions concerning the prospective population trends was explored only to a very limited extent. The aim here is to extend the previous analysis in this direction. Specifically, the question addressed is: How will faster (slower) population growth in developing and developed regions affect economic growth in these regions themselves and how will it affect economic growth in other groups of regions?

## I. The Global Model

Using 1970 as the base year and projecting through 1980 and 1990 to the year 2000, the global model displays various possible inter-relationships between environmental and other economic policies. Input-output analysis, an econometric technique that attempts to take account of the interdependence of various sectors of the economy in the empirical analysis of production and consumption, is used to describe the complex and highly differentiated structure of the producing and consuming sectors of various regions and, ultimately, of the world economy. Schematically, the world economy is reduced primarily to a set of $N$ linear equations in $N + M$ variables. The fact that the system contains more variables than equations provides for flexibility. A unique particular solution can be obtained by fixing the values of $M$ of these variables selected in accordance with the assumptions underlying the specific question whose answer that particular solution is intended to represent.

Despite its global scope, the model contains and displays a great amount of detail. The world is divided into 15 regions that fall into three main groups:[3] the developed regions—North America, Eastern Europe, Western Europe (high and medium income), the Soviet Union, Japan, Oceania, South Africa—characterized by advanced, not to say completed, industrialization and relatively high average per capita income; the developing regions—the Middle East, Ven-

[3]For detailed tabulation of the individual countries included in each of the 15 regions, see ibid., Technical Appendix I.

ezuela, some Andean countries, and some parts of tropical and northern Africa—rich in natural resources; and the developing countries with few resources.

The system of 2625 simultaneous equations contained in the model provides a concise description of the structural relationships that govern the intersectoral relationships within and between the 15 different regions. Each region is described in terms of 45 sectors of economic activity. In agriculture, four subsectors are analyzed: livestock products, grains, high-protein crops, and roots. With respect to mineral resources, emphasis is on copper, bauxite, nickel, zinc, lead, iron ore, petroleum, natural gas, and coal. Manufacturing activities are divided into 22 sectors, including food processing, primary metals, textiles, fertilizer, and various types of machinery and equipment. Utilities and construction, trade and services, transportation, and communication are treated separately. The model also describes emissions of major pollutants and types of pollution-abatement activity.

Each of the 15 regions is treated separately. The balancing of exports and imports of internationally traded goods, as well as of each type of international financial transaction such as investing (lending), borrowing, and granting developmental assistance, is described in terms of some 40 international trading pools, one for each class of traded goods and for each type of financial transaction.

The state of technology used in each of the 45 sectors of a particular region at any given time is represented by a set of input coefficients describing the amounts of products of other sectors required to produce a unit of output in the given sector; the physical capital requirements are described by corresponding sets of capital coefficients. Anticipated changes in these structural coefficients, that is, technological change, can be projected separately for each sector in each region. For every developing region, the procedure for introducing such changes in the model is a gradual, step-by-step introduction of input and capital coefficients already used in the more developed regions, the pace being controlled by the increase in the given region's average per capita income. For the developed regions, the changes in the technical coefficients and the consumption coefficients describing the structure of final consumers' demand are projected by conventional methods. For instance, as the per capita income in a particular region goes up from 1970 to 1980, 1990, and 2000, the fraction of it that is spent on food, as incorporated in our projections, is gradually falling, while expenditures on transportation or on housing are rising. Consumption of goods is a function of per capita income. Prices of internationally traded goods are set to cover full costs in North America and are taken as given elsewhere.

In *The Future of the World Economy*, these structural relationships were used to make two different types of projections designed to provide answers to two different kinds of questions.

Scenario X prescribed per capita income targets to be attained in each of the developing and developed regions by 1980, 1990, and 2000. The purpose of the computations based on several variations of this scenario was to find out what adjustments in the present patterns of economic growth would be required to reduce the income gap between the developed and the developing countries from the 1970 ratio of 12:1 to a ratio of 7:1 by the year 2000. The results detailed the levels of sectoral outputs, consumption, and investment in each of the 15 regions as well as the magnitudes of international commodity flows and corresponding financial transactions that would have to be realized in order to achieve such an ambitious objective.

Scenario A, instead of incorporating a set of externally prescribed income targets, was designed to project the future actual (rather than desirable) levels of income in all regions along with the corresponding magnitudes of all the other endogenously determined variables. This essentially conservative scenario assumed that all future international transactions—interregional capital movements, credit, and developmental assistance—would be governed by the same structural relationships that have controlled them in recent years.

While computations based on variants of scenario X throw light on the nature and magnitude of shifts in international economic relationships that could permit the attainment of ambitious developmental goals associated with the notion of a "new economic order," the set of projections based on scenario A provides a deeper insight into the complex interaction of economic forces that shape the development of the world economy at the present time. Hence the decision was made to base the new computations aimed at assessing the potential influence of alternative population trends on future economic growth on scenarios of the A type.

## II. Treatment of Population Variables in the Model

In our input-output computations, population figures are treated as given, or exogenously determined, magnitudes. This means that, although the model as formulated permits us to assess the potential effect of population change on different aspects of economic growth, it does not enable us to account for the effect of economic change on population growth.

Formally, nothing would be easier than to "generalize" or "close" the system by including in it additional structural equations purporting to describe, say, the influence of rising per capita income or changes in occupational structure on the birth and death rates and, consequently, on the population growth in each region. A numerical solution of such an enlarged system could be obtained at small additional cost.

It was decided, however, not to include in the present version of the model relationships purporting to explain the rates of population growth because of the uncertainty surrounding present understanding of these relationships.

The methodological procedure employed consists in broadening the spectrum of alternative scenarios to incorporate various combinations of assumptions concerning future rates of population growth, with the specific purpose of gaining a better insight into the role that this demographic factor can be expected to play in shaping the future economic relationships between the developed and the developing countries.

The relation between population size and the overall level of economic activities in the developing countries is typically different from that prevailing in the advanced industrialized areas such as the United States and Canada, Western Europe, and Japan, not to speak of the Soviet Union. Despite cyclical ups and downs, the developed countries maintain and can be expected to maintain in the future a high, if not necessarily full, level of employment. Taking account of the age structure, participation rates, and, last but not least, the prevailing technological conditions, the total output can be said to be related in the longer run as directly to the size of the population as it is to the total available stock of productive capital. In developing areas where a substantial part of the labor force does not participate effectively in the production process (in agriculture this situation is often described as disguised unemployment), no such direct relationship between population size and the total level of output can be assumed to exist.

The projected future labor requirements of each sector in every developed region are obtained by multiplying the respective sectoral output—as listed in the solution of the appropriate worldwide set of input-output equations—by the projected sectoral labor input coefficient. Within the framework of the worldwide model, the description of the intersectoral relationships within each of the developed areas contains an equation that states that the sum total of persons employed in all the different sectors must equal the total available labor force, the magnitude of which, in turn, reflects the size and age structure of the total population, taking into account appropriate participation rates.

For the reason described above, no such equation is included in the mathematical description of the operations of the economies of the developing regions. The level of these operations, as measured, say, by the magnitude of their respective gross domestic products, cannot be assumed to bear any direct relationship to the size of their total demographically defined labor force and through it to their total population figures. An additional problem with respect to developing countries is that the absence of sufficiently comprehensive estimates of the true agricultural labor coefficients makes us abstain from projecting agricultural employment in the developing regions. Thus, the aggregate employment figure for each developing region represents the sum total of the labor requirements of all nonagricultural sectors.

The average per capita income—as projected on the basis of a type A scenario—for a developed region bears strong affinity to the projected average output per employed worker. To the extent that the latter reflects anticipated investment and technological improvements in each sector, the projected per capita gross domestic product will also reflect such improvements because these regions are assumed to maintain, in the long run, nearly full employment. By contrast, for the developing countries, total levels of projected gross domestic products are assumed not to depend on the magnitude of the available, but presumably only partly utilized, labor force. They do, however, reflect—as in the developed regions—investment and technological advance in each sector, including agriculture. For all regions, per capita gross domestic product is obtained by dividing the total gross domestic product by the total population figure.

The average per capita gross domestic product affects—within the framework of the complete input-output model—the composition of the total gross domestic product to the extent that it controls the saving and spending pattern of each region.[4]

The data base used in these computations is that compiled for the

[4]Exogenously introduced projections of the size of the urban—as contrasted to the rural—population affect that pattern as well, to the extent that the final bill of goods includes commodities and services, some of which are "public" in nature, destined to satisfy the special needs of urban dwellers.

1977 UN report on *The Future of the World Economy*, except for the more recent UN population projections. A detailed, although by no means exhaustive, description of the methods used to compile and project the thousands of input-output coefficients from 1970 through 1980 and 1990 to the year 2000 is given in that document.

For purposes of the present analysis, the 15 basic regions are combined into three large groups of countries, as follows:

| | |
|---|---|
| Developed countries (DC) | North America, Western Europe (high income), USSR, Eastern Europe, Western Europe (medium income), Japan, Oceania, Africa (medium income) |
| Resource-rich developing countries (LDC-I) | Latin America (low income), Middle East/Africa, Africa (tropical) |
| Resource-poor developing countries (LDC-II) | Africa (arid), Asia (low income), Asia (centrally planned), Latin America (medium income) |

## III. Results

Figure 16-1 traces three alternative UN projections of population growth from 1970 to the year 2000 for the three groups of countries.[5] While the rates of population growth projected for the 15 separate regions differ from each other widely, the three standard variants—high, medium, and low—provided for each region differ from each other within a relatively narrow range. Thus, it is not surprising that the effect of a shift from one of these alternative projections to another (for any given region) on the economy of the same or any other region turns out to be relatively modest. The direction and the relative magnitude of these effects are nevertheless significant. If the same demographic shifts were projected beyond the year 2000, all the percentage figures in terms of which their economic implications are analyzed below would be larger.

A general overview of economic growth from the base year 1970 to the year 2000 as reflected in per capita income figures—projected on alternative assumptions of uniformly high, low, and medium rates of population growth in all regions—is provided in Table 16-1 and Figure 16-2.

[5]Population source: *United Nations World Population Prospects as Assessed as of 1973*, Population Study #60, XIII.4. Matching labor force estimates are provided by the International Labor Office, *Labor Force Estimates 1950–2000*, 2nd edition (Geneva: International Labor Organization, 1977).

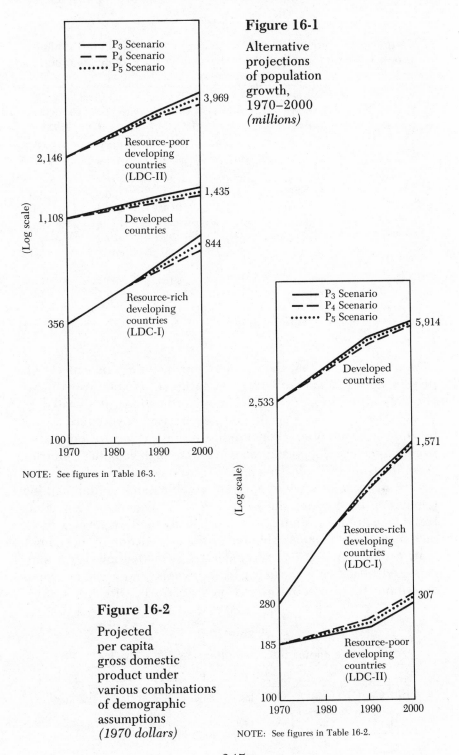

**Figure 16-1**

Alternative projections of population growth, 1970–2000 *(millions)*

P₃ Scenario
P₄ Scenario
P₅ Scenario

Resource-poor developing countries (LDC-II)

Developed countries

Resource-rich developing countries (LDC-I)

NOTE: See figures in Table 16-3.

**Figure 16-2**

Projected per capita gross domestic product under various combinations of demographic assumptions *(1970 dollars)*

NOTE: See figures in Table 16-2.

## Table 16-1

Gross domestic product per capita and rates of growth of gross domestic product per capita under alternative combinations of demographic assumptions

| | World growth rate | GDP per capita (1970 dollars) | | Rate of growth in GDP per capita (percentage) | |
| --- | --- | --- | --- | --- | --- |
| | | 1970 | 2000 | 1970–2000 | Average annual |
| Developed countries | high | 1533 | 5739 | 126.6 | 2.8 |
| | low | 2533 | 6087 | 140.3 | 3.0 |
| | medium | 2533 | 5914 | 133.5 | 2.9 |
| Resource-rich developing countries (LDC-I) | high | 280 | 1534 | 133.5 | 5.8 |
| | low | 280 | 1628 | 481.4 | 6.0 |
| | medium | 280 | 1571 | 461.1 | 5.9 |
| Resource-poor developing countries (LDC-II) | high | 185 | 293 | 58.4 | 1.5 |
| | low | 185 | 324 | 75.1 | 1.9 |
| | medium | 185 | 307 | 65.9 | 1.7 |

To trace the role that the demographic factor can be expected to play in determining the course of future economic growth, five alternative multiregional input-output projections, designated $P_1$, $P_2$, $P_3$, $P_4$, and $P_5$, were carried out, each based on a different combination of assumptions concerning the rate of future population trends in the developed and the two groups of developing countries, as summarized in Table 16-2.

Most of these scenarios represent combinations of high and low population trajectories since comparison of economic projections based on extreme assumptions is more likely to illustrate clearly the influence of the demographic factor than simulation of more moderate assumptions. (Use of a "moderate" scenario, however, can be expected to indicate the most likely events, and a set of figures describing the projection based on scenario $P_5$ with full sectoral

## Table 16-2

Alternative population assumptions used in scenarios $P_1$–$P_5$

| | $P_1$ | $P_2$ | $P_3$ | $P_4$ | $P_5$ |
| --- | --- | --- | --- | --- | --- |
| Developed countries | low | high | high | low | medium |
| Developing countries (I & II) | high | low | high | low | medium |

detail, but aggregated from 15 to 3 regions, is presented in Appendix 16-2.)

By comparing projection $P_4$ with projection $P_2$, or $P_1$ with $P_3$, we can assess the economic implications of a shift, that is, an increase or a reduction, in the projected rates of population growth in the developed countries while population projections for the less developed areas are held constant at either the low or the high level.

By comparing $P_4$ with $P_1$, or $P_3$ with $P_2$, we can assess the economic effects of an upward (or downward) shift in the projected population figures for both groups of developing countries under the assumption that the rate of population growth in the developed countries remains constant at either the high or the low level.

Figures required for carrying out such comparisons of alternative projections of the population increase and corresponding projections of the income growth in the developed countries and the two groups of developing countries are presented in Table 16-3.

A simple method of comparing two figures, or, as in this case, two sets of figures, is to express the difference between the first and the second as a percentage of the second. The results of appropriately selected pairwise comparisons of different rows of figures in Table 16-3 are shown in Table 16-4. The similarity of the numbers in the first and second rows of Table 16-4 indicates that the effects (expressed in terms of percentage changes) of a shift in the projected population level of developed countries are nearly the same, whether the projected level of both groups of developing countries is high or low. Pairwise comparison of figures entered in the third and fourth rows similarly indicates that the effects of shifts in the projected population figures of developing countries are only marginally dependent on the population levels projected for the developed countries. Thus, we need to examine closely only two—say, the first and the third—of the four rows of figures entered in Table 16-4.

The first row of Table 16-4 describes the income effects of a shift from $P_4$ to $P_2$, that is, of a shift in the projected population level of the developed countries from low to high, with the population figures projected for both groups of developing countries remaining the same.

The first three sets of figures entered in the first row of Table 16-4 are translated into a graph in part A of Figure 16-3. In starting to examine it, center your attention on the white bars, disregarding at the outset all the striped bars. In interpreting this and all the subsequent bar charts, keep in mind that they describe changes in

## Table 16-3

Alternative projections for the year 2000 of the total GDP, per capita GDP, and GDP per unit of the labor force in the developed countries

| | Population (millions) | | | | GDP (millions of 1970 dollars) | | | | GDP per capita (1970 dollars) | | | | GDP per unit of employed labor force (1970 dollars) |
|---|---|---|---|---|---|---|---|---|---|---|---|---|---|
| | World | DC | LDC-I | LDC-II | World | DC | LDC-I | LDC-II | World | DC | LDC-I | LDC-II | DC |
| $P_3$ | 6,632 | 1,514 | 895 | 4,223 | 11,299 | 8,688 | 1,373 | 1,238 | 1,704 | 5,739 | 1,534 | 293 | 13,346 |
| $P_1$ | 6,494 | 1,375 | 895 | 4,223 | 10,970 | 8,379 | 1,373 | 1,218 | 1,689 | 6,093 | 1,534 | 288 | 13,321 |
| $P_5$ | 6,248 | 1,435 | 844 | 3,969 | 11,030 | 8,487 | 1,326 | 1,217 | 1,765 | 5,914 | 1,571 | 307 | 13,323 |
| $P_2$ | 5,983 | 1,514 | 777 | 3,693 | 11,161 | 8,680 | 1,265 | 1,217 | 1,865 | 5,734 | 1,628 | 329 | 13,354 |
| $P_4$ | 5,845 | 1,375 | 777 | 3,693 | 10,832 | 8,371 | 1,265 | 1,196 | 1,853 | 6,087 | 1,628 | 324 | 13,330 |

DC = developed countries; LDC-I = resource-rich developing countries; LDC-II = resource-poor developing countries.

## Table 16-4

Pairwise comparison of alternative population and corresponding income projections for the year 2000 (in percentages)

| | Population | | | | GDP | | | | GDP per capita | | | | GDP per unit of employed labor force | | | |
|---|---|---|---|---|---|---|---|---|---|---|---|---|---|---|---|---|
| | World | DC | LDC-I | LDC-II | World | DC | LDC-I | LDC-II | World | DC | LDC-I | LDC-II | World | DC | LDC-I | LDC-II |
| $\dfrac{P_2 - P_4}{P_4}$ | 2.4 | 10.1 | 0 | 0 | 3.0 | 3.7 | 0 | 0 | 0.6 | -5.8 | 0 | 1.5 | 0.8 | 0.2 | 0 | 0.2 |
| $\dfrac{P_3 - P_1}{P_1}$ | 2.1 | 10.1 | 0 | 0 | 3.0 | 3.7 | 0 | 0 | 0.9 | -5.8 | 0 | 1.7 | 0.8 | 0.2 | -0.3 | -0.1 |
| $\dfrac{P_1 - P_4}{P_4}$ | 11.1 | 0 | 15.2 | 14.4 | 1.3 | 0.1 | 8.5 | 1.8 | -8.9 | 0.1 | -5.8 | -11.1 | -0.6 | -0.1 | 2.0 | 0.7 |
| $\dfrac{P_3 - P_2}{P_2}$ | 10.8 | 0 | 15.2 | 14.4 | 1.2 | 0.1 | 8.5 | 1.7 | -8.6 | 0.1 | -5.8 | -10.9 | -0.6 | -0.1 | 1.6 | 0.4 |

DC = developed countries; LDC-I = resource-rich developing countries; LDC-II = resource-poor developing countries.

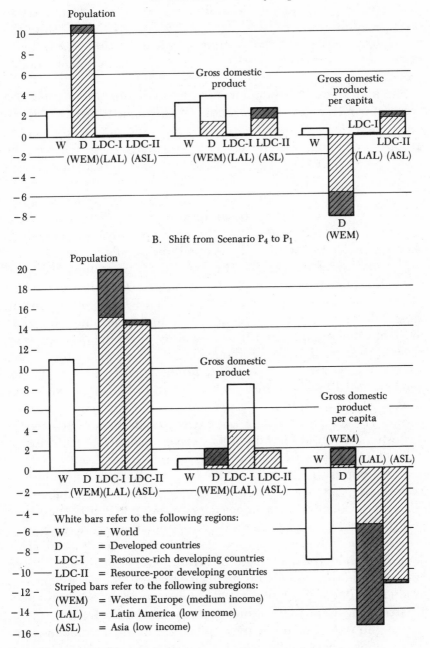

A. Shift from Scenario $P_4$ to $P_2$

B. Shift from Scenario $P_4$ to $P_1$

White bars refer to the following regions:
W          = World
D          = Developed countries
LDC-I    = Resource-rich developing countries
LDC-II   = Resource-poor developing countries
Striped bars refer to the following subregions:
(WEM)   = Western Europe (medium income)
(LAL)    = Latin America (low income)
(ASL)    = Asia (low income)

NOTE: For actual figures, see Table 16-4.

**Figure 16-3**

Alternative population and income projections for the year 2000 *(differences in percentages)* demographic and economic variables, not over time—from 1970 to the year 2000—but rather from one level to another, both in the year 2000, each level corresponding to one of two alternative states of the entire system, under one of two alternative demographic scenarios.

The first block of bars depicts the basic demographic aspects of the shift from scenario $P_4$ to scenario $P_2$: the population in the developed countries increases by 10.1 percent; the population of both groups of developing countries does not change (being kept on the same low level); the world population consequently increases by 2.4 percent.

The second block of bars shows the effect of these demographic shifts on the level of gross domestic product in each of the three regions: in the developed countries it goes up by 3.7 percent, which is only one third as large as the rise in their population level.

The absence of any significant change in the gross domestic product of the resource-rich developing countries (LDC-I) is caused by the fact that this group includes the Middle Eastern oil-producing areas, whose growth prospects are likely to depend much less than those of other countries on the availabiltiy of capital or population growth. Hence, within the framework of our model, the future growth of their total gross domestic product was treated as an independent variable whose future change had to be projected exogenously. That projection, as explained in Appendix 16-1, incorporated a certain assumed rate of future growth of per capita gross domestic product of the Middle Eastern oil-producing countries.

Turning to the third block of bars, we see that a shift from a low to a high population level in the developed countries would lead to a substantial 5.8 percent downward shift in their per capita gross domestic product. This is a necessary consequence of the previous observation that, as a rule, a rise in the population figure of a region brings about a less than proportional increase in its total gross domestic product. Examining the entries in the last column of Table 16-4, we find that, as could have been expected, the gross domestic product produced per unit of the labor force (which constitutes only a part of the total population) changes very little from $P_4$ to $P_2$. Hence, the reduction in the per capita GDP of the developed countries brought about by the shift in the projected population level of these areas from low to high seems to be caused primarily by a change in the age structure—a change that makes the (fully employed) labor force expand proportionally less than the total population.

Since in the transition from $P_4$ to $P_2$ the projected population level of both developing regions stays the same, the spill-over effect of the rise in the gross domestic product of the developed countries is not diluted and, consequently, is translated directly into a proportional rise in the per capita gross domestic product of the resource-poor developing countries. For reasons explained above, the per capita gross domestic product of the resource-rich developing countries does not change.

Disregarding regional distinctions and considering the effects of a 10.1 percent upward shift in the projected population level of the developed countries on the world economy as a whole, we find that while the global population level goes up by 2.4 percent, the world-wide gross domestic product rises by 3.0 percent and the corresponding average per capita income by 0.6 percent.

Part B of Figure 16-3 depicts the economic implications of the demographic shift from $P_4$ to $P_1$. The shift presented by the first group of bars consists of a substantial increase in the projected population level of both sets of developing countries from low to high, with the population projection for the developed countries remaining low.

In worldwide terms, an 11.1 percent increase in the total population figure would be accompanied by a modest 1.3 percent rise in the global gross domestic product and, consequently, a substantial 8.9 percent reduction in the average global per capita income. The per capita income of the resource-poor developing countries would drop by 11.1 percent, and that of the resource-rich developing countries would drop by 5.8 percent, despite the fact that their total income would go up by 1.8 percent and 8.5 percent, respectively. A minuscule spill-over effect can be observed in the developed countries: since their population level remains the same, per capita gross domestic product rises by 0.1 percent.

Under the surface of broad aggregative shifts described above lie changes in the levels of thousands of different but mutually inter-related economic activities. These have actually been traced in our multiregional, multisectoral projections.

As an example of finer regional breakdowns, the striped bars superimposed in Figure 16-3 over the white bars—on which we centered attention up to now—describe the effects of the same basic demographic shift on three subregions, each belonging to a different large region.

Western Europe (medium income) was selected for this purpose among the eight subregions of the developed countries block, Asia (low income) among the four subregions belonging to the resource-poor developing countries block, and Latin America (low income) as one of the three components of the resource-rich developing countries group.

Examining these graphs, we find that, in general, the population figures and the total and per capita gross domestic products of these particular subregions tend to move in the same direction as the corresponding total regional figures, but in different proportions.

As an example of an analysis involving sectoral disaggregation, Figure 16-4 depicts the effects of the same two basic sets of population shifts (one from scenario $P_4$ to $P_2$ and another from $P_4$ to $P_1$) on the output of two particular industries: metals processing and textiles.

The method of graphic presentation is the same as for Figure 16-3. The left-hand block of bars simply provides a concise picture of the particular combination of demographic shifts, the economic implications of which are depicted in the second and third blocks. One of these describes changes in the output levels of the metals processing industries and the other in the textile industries.

In each instance, the first of the white bars refers to global output, the second to output in the developed regions, and the two others to output in the resource-rich and the resource-poor developing regions. For purposes of reference, the corresponding changes in the global and the regional gross domestic products are entered in each instance in striped bars. These are, of course, identical with those of the white bars describing global and regional gross domestic products under the respective shifts in scenarios in Figure 16-3.

Without entering into a detailed interpretation of these figures, one can observe that an upward shift in the projected population level in the developed countries (part A of Figure 16-4) causes the metal industries in these countries to expand more, but the textile industry less, than their total gross domestic product. An opposite relationship between population levels and the two industrial outputs can be observed in the resource-poor developing countries. A higher population level in the developed countries causes the metals processing industries in both groups of developing countries to expand relatively more, and the textile output relatively less, than their gross domestic products. It is also interesting to note that a sharp rise in the population level in the developing areas brings about in the developed areas a greater expansion of the processed metals than of the textile industries. Checking with the computer printout of the corresponding projection of exports from developed countries, we found, as should have been expected, a percentage

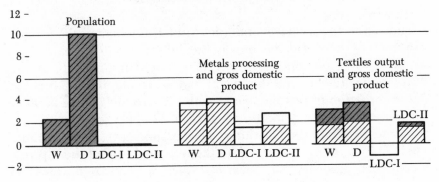

A. Shift from Scenario $P_4$ to $P_2$

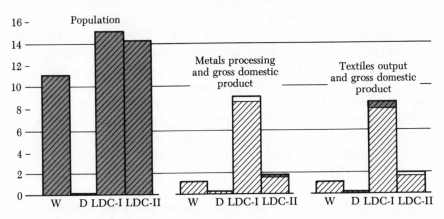

B. Shift from Scenario $P_4$ to $P_1$

White bars refer to the following regions:
and textiles output, respectively.

Striped bars refer to the
following regions:

W     = World
D     = Developed countries
LDC-I  = Resource-rich developing countries
LDC-II = Resource-poor developing countries

NOTE: For actual figures, see Table 16-4.

## Figure 16-4

Alternative projections of population and selected industrial outputs in the year 2000 *(differences in percentages)* rise in the export of metal products four times as large as that in textiles.

Turning to the larger overall picture, let us examine the growth prospects of the world economy in the light of various combinations of alternative assumptions concerning population trends in the developed countries and the two groups of developing countries.

A comparison of prospective growth rates from 1970 to 2000 of the per capita gross domestic product in the three groups of countries under each of the five different scenarios is presented in Table 16-5. The figure 1.85 entered on the left-hand side of the top row means that, according to scenario $P_1$ (where population growth is low in the developed countries and high in both groups of developing countries), the global per capita income projected for the year 2000 is 1.85 times higher than it was in the year 1970. The bracketed number 5 entered to the right of that figure means that if all entries in that row were arranged in order of their decreasing magnitudes, 1.85 would occupy the fifth, that is, the lowest, position. In other words, the average growth rate of per capita income in the world under scenario $P_1$ is lower than under any other scenario.

The highest average rate of growth of per capita income for the world economy as a whole is attained under scenario $P_4$, characterized by a low rate of population growth in both the developed countries and the developing countries. The developed countries, taken by themselves, fare best under scenario $P_1$. Both groups of developing countries, however, fare worse under this scenario than under any others.

The resource-rich developing countries (LDC-I), whose per capita income promises, under any conditions, to rise much faster than that of any other group, does best under scenario $P_5$, that is, the medium rate of population growth in all parts of the world.

In contrast with the developed countries, the developing countries belonging to the resource-poor group (LDC-II) show the greatest growth in per capita income under scenario $P_2$ when their own population increases slowly while that of the developed countries grows fast.

The divergent economic effects of alternative combinations of rates of population growth projected for different regions have obvious implications with reference to the concept of optimal population and the related concept of an optimal rate of population growth. Here, as in many other instances, the attempt to use the notion of optimality in dealing with some particular aspect of social welfare is frustrated by the necessity to reconcile it with the existence of conflicting interests.

## Table 16-5

Average growth rates of per capita gross domestic product, 1970–2000, under alternative combinations of assumptions concerning future population growth

| Scenarios of population growth | | World | Developed countries | Resource-rich developing countries (I) | Resource-poor developing countries (II) | Column 5 / Column 3 |
|---|---|---|---|---|---|---|
| $P_1$ | DC low / LDC high | 1.85 (5) | 2.45 (1) | 5.47 (5) | 1.56 (5) | 0.64 (5) |
| $P_2$ | DC high / LDC low | 2.04 (2) | 2.27 (5) | 5.81 (3) | 1.78 (1) | 0.78 (1) |
| $P_3$ | DC high / LDC high | 1.86 (4) | 2.27 (4) | 5.48 (4) | 1.58 (4) | 0.70 (4) |
| $P_4$ | DC low / LDC low | 2.25 (1) | 2.40 (2) | 5.81 (2) | 1.75 (2) | 0.73 (2) |
| $P_5$ | DC medium / LDC medium | 1.95 (3) | 2.33 (3) | 6.32 (1) | 1.66 (3) | 0.71 (3) |

*Note*: Each entry represents a ratio of the per capita GDP projected for the year 2000 and the actual per capita GDP in the year 1970. Each bracketed number indicates what place the corresponding scenario occupies when all five figures entered in that column are arranged in the order of decreasing magnitude.

As far as the question of closing or even significantly reducing the income gap between the resource-poor developing countries and the developed countries is concerned, the picture emerging from these figures is not encouraging.

The entries in the right-hand column of Table 16-5 are ratios of the average growth rate of per capita income of the resource-poor developing countries to the average growth rate of per capita income of the developed countries, both projected on the basis of the same scenario. All of these ratios are less than 1; in no case is there a tendency toward narrowing the income gap over the time interval 1970–2000.[6]

Turning back to Figure 16-2, with the three groups of curves tracing the growth of per capita income from 1970 to the year 2000 through 1980 and 1990, we note, however, for all population projections a slowdown in the rate of growth in the developed and the developing resource-rich countries and marked acceleration of the rate of growth in the less developed resource-poor areas. This implies that in the last of the three decades spanned by these projections the gap would indeed begin to diminish.

The input-output model of the world economy on which the projection described above is based is being gradually improved both in its analytical structure and its data base. The analysis of the relationship between demographic changes and economic growth will be carried further in the direction of more refined modeling of the relationship between demographic structure and the composition of the labor force described in terms of skills, training requirements, income levels, and household structures. A better understanding of these relationships would, of course, be hardly possible without the completion of an appropriately enlarged and refined data base that would permit the completion of the missing link of the present model: quantitative description of relationships through which various economic variables exert their influence on the demographic structures of the individual regions and the corresponding rates of population growth.

---

[6]As explained earlier, the A version of the world model used in all of the projections presented here is essentially pessimistic; it incorporates the assumption that the balance of trade of the less developed resource-poor countries will, for some time to come, be subjected to the same structural, in this case essentially institutional, restriction that prevails under the present "old economic order." According to *The Future of the World Economy* and the forthcoming "preliminary U.N. study of worldwide economic and social implications of a limitation on military spending," should these developing areas be able to sustain and absorb a much larger and steadily rising import surplus, the pace of their economic growth could be accelerated greatly.

## Appendix 16-1

### Alternative scenarios

| | $P_1$ | $P_2$ | $P_3$ | $P_4$ | $P_5$ | $A_1$[a] |
|---|---|---|---|---|---|---|
| GDP | | Middle East: adjusted to same GDP per capita as in Scenario A. Others: endogenous | | | | Middle East: B[b] Others: endogenous |
| Employment | DC: ILO/L Others: endogenous | DC: ILO/H Others: endogenous | DX: ILO/H Others: endogenous | DC: ILO/L Others: endogenous | DC: ILO/M Others: endogenous | DC: equal to estimated labor force. Others: endogenous |
| Investment | LDC-1 (excluding Middle East) and Central Planned Asia: limited by borrowing and saving Others: endogenous | | | | | |
| Balance of payments | LDC-II (excluding Centrally Planned Asia): set equal to zero Others: endogenous | | | | | |
| Foreign trade | Import and export share coefficients change with regional total per capita income | | | | | |
| Population | DC: low LDC: high | DC: high LDC: low | high | low | medium | B[b] |

[a]The A scenario is taken from *The Future of the World Economy*. While not discussed in this chapter, it is included here for purposes of comparison.

[b]The letter B represents both the GDP and the population levels used in the A scenario. These correspond to medium estimates based on published UN data. The A scenario uses medium ILO labor force estimates, which appear in *Labor Force Estimates, 1960–1985* (Geneva: International Labor Office, 1971). ILO/L, ILO/M, and ILO/H correspond, respectively, to low, medium, and high population estimates taken from the updated document *Labor Force Estimates, 1950–2000*, 2nd edition (Geneva: International Labor Office, 1977). The low, medium, and high population estimates used in scenarios $P_1$ through $P_5$ are taken from the UN document *World Population Prospects as Assessed as of 1973*, Population Study No. 60, 76, XIII.4.

# Appendix 16-2

## Scenario P₅ (medium projections of population growth for all regions)

| | World | | | | Developed | | | | Developing (LDC-I) | | | | Developing (LDC-II) | | | |
|---|---|---|---|---|---|---|---|---|---|---|---|---|---|---|---|---|
| | 1970 | 1980 | 1990 | 2000 | 1970 | 1980 | 1990 | 2000 | 1970 | 1980 | 1990 | 2000 | 1970 | 1980 | 1990 | 2000 |
| *Consumption and population* | | | | | | | | | | | | | | | | |
| GDP[a] | 3305 | 4984 | 7807 | 11030 | 2807 | 4171 | 6408 | 8487 | 100 | 268 | 634 | 1326 | 398 | 545 | 765 | 1217 |
| Personal consum.[a] | 2137 | 3228 | 4848 | 6975 | 1786 | 2676 | 3929 | 5293 | 64 | 152 | 379 | 839 | 287 | 400 | 541 | 843 |
| Gov. (civilian)[a] | 601 | 905 | 1417 | 2000 | 510 | 757 | 1162 | 1538 | 18 | 49 | 115 | 241 | 73 | 99 | 140 | 222 |
| Gov. (military)[a] | 0 | 0 | 0 | 0 | 0 | 0 | 0 | 0 | 0 | 0 | 0 | 0 | 0 | 0 | 0 | 0 |
| Population[b] | 3610 | 4370 | 5276 | 6248 | 1108 | 1217 | 1331 | 1435 | 356 | 474 | 638 | 844 | 2146 | 2680 | 3307 | 3969 |
| Urban population[b] | 1323 | 1824 | 2446 | 3234 | 695 | 835 | 985 | 1129 | 95 | 166 | 262 | 397 | 532 | 823 | 1199 | 1707 |
| Employment[c] | 703 | 872 | 1132 | 1426 | 485 | 548 | 601 | 637 | 53 | 101 | 187 | 321 | 165 | 222 | 343 | 468 |
| GDP/head[d] | 915 | 1140 | 1480 | 1765 | 2533 | 3427 | 4815 | 5914 | 280 | 566 | 993 | 1571 | 185 | 203 | 231 | 307 |
| Consumption/head[d] | 592 | 739 | 919 | 1116 | 1612 | 2199 | 2952 | 3688 | 180 | 322 | 594 | 994 | 134 | 149 | 163 | 212 |
| Calories/day/head[e] | 2.4 | 2.4 | 2.4 | 2.5 | 3.0 | 3.1 | 3.1 | 3.2 | 2.2 | 2.3 | 2.5 | 2.9 | 2.1 | 2.1 | 2.1 | 2.2 |
| Proteins/day/head[f] | 67 | 69 | 71 | 76 | 90 | 94 | 101 | 106 | 57 | 63 | 73 | 88 | 57 | 58 | 59 | 63 |
| *Investment and capital* | | | | | | | | | | | | | | | | |
| Investment[a] | 519 | 803 | 1465 | 1951 | 472 | 701 | 1231 | 1445 | 9 | 56 | 154 | 378 | 38 | 47 | 81 | 128 |
| Equipment[a] | 233 | 316 | 563 | 776 | 210 | 265 | 454 | 532 | 4 | 26 | 67 | 149 | 19 | 25 | 42 | 95 |
| Plant[a] | 281 | 484 | 898 | 1171 | 260 | 434 | 776 | 912 | 4 | 29 | 87 | 228 | 16 | 21 | 36 | 31 |
| Irrigation (area)[g] | 3 | 2 | 3 | 3 | 1 | 1 | 1 | 1 | 0 | 0 | 0 | 0 | 2 | 1 | 2 | 2 |
| Land (area)[g] | 12 | 8 | 10 | 10 | 2 | 1 | 2 | 2 | 3 | 2 | 3 | 3 | 7 | 4 | 5 | 5 |
| Inventory changes[a] | 41 | 38 | 66 | 91 | 33 | 26 | 44 | 42 | 2 | 6 | 14 | 24 | 6 | 6 | 9 | 25 |
| Capital stock[a] | 5895 | 9555 | 16307 | 25181 | 5359 | 8585 | 14290 | 20798 | 96 | 324 | 973 | 2659 | 439 | 646 | 1045 | 1724 |
| Equipment[a] | 2050 | 3086 | 5052 | 7573 | 1800 | 2639 | 4167 | 5696 | 43 | 145 | 400 | 974 | 207 | 301 | 485 | 902 |
| Plant[a] | 3845 | 6469 | 11255 | 17608 | 3560 | 5946 | 10123 | 15102 | 53 | 179 | 573 | 1685 | 233 | 345 | 560 | 821 |
| Inventory stock[a] | 735 | 1044 | 1562 | 2272 | 587 | 807 | 1165 | 1527 | 31 | 68 | 153 | 315 | 116 | 169 | 244 | 430 |
| Land/yield index | 100 | 131 | 175 | 276 | 100 | 118 | 162 | 205 | 100 | 169 | 306 | 570 | 100 | 134 | 187 | 279 |
| Surplus savings[a] | 18 | 75 | −59 | 54 | 11 | 69 | −37 | 140 | 3 | −10 | −39 | −112 | 4 | 17 | 18 | 27 |
| *International transactions* | | | | | | | | | | | | | | | | |
| Imports[a] | 345.8 | 554.7 | 1015.8 | 1585.5 | 289.0 | 448.9 | 800.8 | 1138.8 | 22.2 | 55.2 | 137.2 | 313.3 | 34.6 | 50.7 | 77.8 | 133.4 |
| Exports[a] | 345.1 | 553.7 | 1013.8 | 1583.8 | 287.4 | 450.8 | 831.9 | 1296.0 | 28.2 | 60.8 | 109.0 | 156.3 | 29.5 | 42.1 | 72.9 | 131.5 |
| Payments surplus[h] | −0.7 | −1.7 | −0.0 | 0.6 | −4.1 | −9.0 | 152.3 | −251.8 | 2.8 | 7.9 | 153.5 | 253.1 | 0.6 | −0.6 | −1.2 | −0.7 |
| For. investment[h] | 0 | −8 | 0 | .3 | 0 | −9 | −676 | −2414 | 0 | 9 | 684 | 2387 | 0 | −8 | −7 | 32 |
| For. income[h] | 0.0 | −0.7 | 0.0 | 0.3 | 7.9 | 7.2 | −46.2 | −185.3 | −5.6 | −4.9 | 49.1 | 185.3 | −2.3 | −3.0 | −2.9 | 0.3 |

*Level of pollution abatement activities[j]*

| | | | | | | | | | | | | | | | | |
|---|---|---|---|---|---|---|---|---|---|---|---|---|---|---|---|---|
| Air | 54.3 | 97.2 | 126.6 | 167.1 | 54.3 | 95.8 | 125.8 | 152.1 | 0.0 | 0.8 | 0.0 | 12.7 | 0.0 | 0.6 | 0.8 | 2.4 |
| Primary water | 11.02 | 22.06 | 39.10 | 54.60 | 11.02 | 21.72 | 38.80 | 48.72 | 0.0 | 0.11 | 0.0 | 4.10 | 0.0 | 0.23 | 0.30 | 1.78 |
| Secondary water | 0.65 | 1.26 | 3.67 | 5.18 | 0.65 | 1.24 | 3.65 | 4.85 | 0.0 | 0.01 | 0.0 | 0.23 | 0.0 | 0.01 | 0.02 | 0.10 |
| Tertiary water | 0.13 | 0.55 | 0.80 | 1.14 | 0.13 | 0.54 | 0.80 | 1.06 | 0.0 | 0.00 | 0.0 | 0.05 | 0.0 | 0.01 | 0.00 | 0.02 |
| Solid waste | 534.9 | 902.1 | 1208.5 | 1977.2 | 534.9 | 836.9 | 1129.9 | 1497.8 | 0.0 | 17.1 | 0.0 | 200.3 | 0.0 | 48.1 | 78.6 | 279.1 |

*Net total emissions[i]*

| | | | | | | | | | | | | | | | | |
|---|---|---|---|---|---|---|---|---|---|---|---|---|---|---|---|---|
| Pesticides | 2.60 | 5.43 | 13.51 | 16.47 | 2.16 | 4.04 | 9.11 | 6.87 | 0.18 | 0.65 | 2.16 | 4.96 | 0.25 | 0.73 | 2.24 | 4.65 |
| Particulates | 17.20 | 13.52 | 22.94 | 16.27 | 13.71 | 7.64 | 8.57 | 7.70 | 0.61 | 2.14 | 8.79 | 2.54 | 2.89 | 3.74 | 5.58 | 6.02 |
| Biological oxygen | 30.57 | 36.34 | 44.56 | 55.82 | 25.84 | 28.20 | 30.22 | 33.65 | 0.72 | 1.77 | 5.41 | 7.60 | 4.83 | 8.32 | 13.49 | 19.21 |
| Nitrogen (water) | 0.72 | 0.96 | 1.41 | 1.87 | 0.68 | 0.87 | 1.24 | 1.55 | 0.00 | 0.01 | 0.04 | 0.11 | 0.03 | 0.07 | 0.12 | 0.21 |
| Phosphates | 0.41 | 0.58 | 0.84 | 1.09 | 0.38 | 0.52 | 0.72 | 0.88 | 0.00 | 0.01 | 0.04 | 0.08 | 0.02 | 0.05 | 0.08 | 0.14 |
| Suspended solids | 19.30 | 21.49 | 26.39 | 31.22 | 17.14 | 17.63 | 18.33 | 18.61 | 0.33 | 1.13 | 3.95 | 6.22 | 1.88 | 2.72 | 4.11 | 6.38 |
| Dissolved solids | 131.97 | 183.70 | 268.89 | 364.71 | 116.80 | 149.33 | 203.03 | 246.51 | 1.52 | 4.57 | 16.46 | 32.32 | 13.74 | 30.24 | 50.75 | 87.65 |
| Solid waste | 312.41 | 353.44 | 653.02 | 727.51 | 91.93 | 26.73 | 44.49 | 0.0 | 38.14 | 62.90 | 156.21 | 90.21 | 182.34 | 263.81 | 452.31 | 637.31 |

*Resource outputs[i]*

| | | | | | | | | | | | | | | | | |
|---|---|---|---|---|---|---|---|---|---|---|---|---|---|---|---|---|
| Copper | 6.4 | 9.5 | 16.7 | 23.3 | 3.9 | 5.3 | 7.1 | 9.4 | 1.4 | 2.5 | 6.3 | 8.0 | 1.1 | 1.7 | 3.3 | 5.9 |
| Bauxite | 11.4 | 17.1 | 28.5 | 38.1 | 5.2 | 6.9 | 11.2 | 25.6 | 5.3 | 8.6 | 15.4 | 8.8 | 0.9 | 1.6 | 1.9 | 3.8 |
| Nickel | 668 | 970 | 1618 | 2088 | 461 | 665 | 1031 | 906 | 13 | 17 | 16 | 60 | 194 | 288 | 572 | 1122 |
| Zinc | 5.4 | 7.7 | 12.7 | 17.8 | 4.1 | 5.7 | 10.8 | 14.6 | 0.7 | 1.1 | 1.5 | 1.3 | 0.6 | 0.8 | 0.4 | 1.9 |
| Lead | 3.5 | 5.5 | 9.7 | 14.5 | 2.6 | 4.0 | 9.3 | 11.3 | 0.4 | 0.7 | 0.0 | 1.7 | 0.5 | 0.7 | 0.4 | 1.6 |
| Iron | 425 | 666 | 1117 | 1586 | 295 | 498 | 725 | 1008 | 45 | 52 | 127 | 177 | 85 | 115 | 264 | 402 |
| Petroleum | 3004 | 5094 | 9464 | 14192 | 1262 | 2084 | 3420 | 5184 | 1531 | 2851 | 5835 | 8706 | 211 | 159 | 210 | 302 |
| Natural gas | 1427 | 2388 | 4266 | 5787 | 1328 | 2024 | 3287 | 4289 | 48 | 314 | 929 | 1448 | 51 | 50 | 50 | 50 |
| Coal | 2165 | 3358 | 5292 | 8440 | 1670 | 2692 | 4213 | 6817 | 8 | 17 | 35 | 56 | 487 | 648 | 1044 | 1566 |

*Cumulative resource output at end of period[k]*

| | | | | | | | | | | | | | | | | |
|---|---|---|---|---|---|---|---|---|---|---|---|---|---|---|---|---|
| Copper | 0 | 79 | 210 | 411 | 0 | 46 | 108 | 190 | 0 | 20 | 64 | 135 | 0 | 14 | 39 | 85 |
| Bauxite | 0 | 143 | 371 | 704 | 0 | 61 | 151 | 335 | 0 | 69 | 190 | 311 | 0 | 13 | 31 | 59 |
| Nickel | 0 | 8189 | 21130 | 39660 | 0 | 5632 | 14112 | 23794 | 0 | 148 | 311 | 688 | 0 | 2409 | 6707 | 15177 |
| Zinc | 0 | 65 | 167 | 320 | 0 | 49 | 132 | 259 | 0 | 9 | 22 | 37 | 0 | 7 | 13 | 24 |
| Lead | 0 | 45 | 121 | 242 | 0 | 33 | 100 | 203 | 0 | 6 | 9 | 18 | 0 | 6 | 12 | 22 |
| Iron | 0 | 5454 | 14368 | 27881 | 0 | 3967 | 10086 | 18752 | 0 | 486 | 1384 | 2904 | 0 | 1001 | 2898 | 6225 |
| Petroleum | 0 | 40488 | 113280 | 231562 | 0 | 16730 | 44249 | 87269 | 0 | 21910 | 65338 | 138043 | 0 | 1848 | 3692 | 6251 |
| Natural gas | 0 | 19074 | 52343 | 102609 | 0 | 16764 | 43322 | 81203 | 0 | 1807 | 8019 | 19903 | 0 | 503 | 1003 | 1503 |
| Coal | 0 | 27616 | 70865 | 139522 | 0 | 21812 | 56340 | 111492 | 0 | 126 | 389 | 845 | 0 | 5678 | 14136 | 27185 |

359

# Appendix 16-2 (Cont.)

| | World | | | | Developed | | | | Developing (LDC-I) | | | | Developing (LDC-II) | | | |
|---|---|---|---|---|---|---|---|---|---|---|---|---|---|---|---|---|
| | 1970 | 1980 | 1990 | 2000 | 1970 | 1980 | 1990 | 2000 | 1970 | 1980 | 1990 | 2000 | 1970 | 1980 | 1990 | 2000 |
| *Output levels* | | | | | | | | | | | | | | | | |
| Animal products[i] | 209.8 | 277.6 | 372.6 | 498.9 | 149.3 | 184.3 | 233.4 | 276.9 | 11.0 | 22.3 | 39.2 | 69.2 | 49.5 | 71.1 | 100.0 | 152.8 |
| High-protein crops[i] | 137.7 | 183.5 | 260.0 | 368.1 | 70.3 | 90.7 | 124.1 | 158.4 | 12.3 | 19.5 | 34.0 | 66.5 | 55.1 | 73.3 | 101.9 | 143.3 |
| Grains[i] | 1221.4 | 1534.1 | 2175.7 | 3004.8 | 640.4 | 742.6 | 1040.5 | 1321.2 | 50.9 | 78.2 | 137.8 | 249.3 | 530.0 | 713.3 | 997.4 | 1434.3 |
| Roots[i] | 458.6 | 542.1 | 712.0 | 919.3 | 231.6 | 258.2 | 325.2 | 369.2 | 63.9 | 89.2 | 129.5 | 207.0 | 163.1 | 194.8 | 257.3 | 343.2 |
| Other agriculture[i] | 208.9 | 259.2 | 299.8 | 479.7 | 161.5 | 178.8 | 177.8 | 227.5 | 12.2 | 25.9 | 50.5 | 93.8 | 35.2 | 54.5 | 71.4 | 158.4 |
| Other resources[a] | 16.3 | 26.0 | 46.1 | 66.5 | 13.7 | 21.1 | 36.2 | 47.8 | 0.8 | 1.8 | 4.6 | 9.9 | 1.8 | 3.1 | 5.3 | 8.8 |
| Food processing[a] | 176.3 | 305.6 | 432.9 | 620.7 | 166.2 | 288.2 | 399.1 | 513.9 | 1.8 | 5.1 | 17.1 | 65.4 | 8.3 | 12.3 | 16.6 | 41.4 |
| Petroleum refining[a] | 47.4 | 72.3 | 123.5 | 178.1 | 42.8 | 57.2 | 82.7 | 101.2 | 1.2 | 11.5 | 35.7 | 68.0 | 3.4 | 3.6 | 5.1 | 8.9 |
| Primary metals[a] | 106.3 | 173.5 | 315.7 | 461.4 | 101.3 | 159.6 | 282.8 | 376.0 | 0.7 | 5.3 | 18.0 | 51.4 | 4.4 | 8.5 | 14.9 | 34.1 |
| Textiles, apparel[a] | 185.1 | 263.0 | 358.1 | 525.1 | 144.6 | 203.1 | 258.5 | 356.7 | 5.9 | 12.7 | 30.5 | 60.8 | 34.5 | 47.3 | 69.2 | 107.6 |
| Wood and cork[a] | 43.5 | 65.2 | 98.8 | 129.5 | 39.2 | 58.2 | 86.1 | 103.7 | 0.7 | 1.9 | 4.8 | 11.8 | 3.6 | 5.1 | 7.8 | 14.1 |
| Furniture, fixtures[a] | 84.3 | 117.3 | 108.1 | 166.0 | 72.7 | 96.5 | 67.6 | 81.3 | 2.3 | 7.7 | 21.2 | 48.7 | 9.3 | 13.2 | 19.2 | 36.0 |
| Paper[a] | 55.6 | 89.5 | 150.1 | 218.4 | 52.5 | 84.8 | 141.3 | 198.2 | 0.2 | 0.6 | 2.0 | 5.8 | 2.9 | 4.1 | 6.7 | 14.3 |
| Printing[a] | 56.2 | 95.0 | 170.8 | 255.9 | 53.9 | 90.9 | 160.4 | 226.2 | 0.4 | 1.3 | 5.3 | 20.0 | 2.0 | 2.9 | 5.1 | 9.7 |
| Rubber[a] | 36.7 | 60.8 | 111.4 | 164.2 | 35.1 | 58.1 | 105.6 | 147.0 | 0.1 | 0.5 | 2.1 | 8.6 | 1.6 | 2.2 | 3.7 | 7.7 |
| Industrial chem.[a] | 79.5 | 119.4 | 188.9 | 286.6 | 70.5 | 104.5 | 161.8 | 226.9 | 1.1 | 2.9 | 8.6 | 24.6 | 7.9 | 12.0 | 18.6 | 35.0 |
| Fertilizers[i] | 67.4 | 107.5 | 173.0 | 263.7 | 55.4 | 70.4 | 92.8 | 115.2 | 1.0 | 3.6 | 17.7 | 31.8 | 11.0 | 33.6 | 63.3 | 116.8 |
| Other chemicals[a] | 61.9 | 95.5 | 160.9 | 230.3 | 57.0 | 88.0 | 148.8 | 203.2 | 0.5 | 1.1 | 3.0 | 7.6 | 4.5 | 6.4 | 10.0 | 19.6 |
| Cement[a] | 5.9 | 9.9 | 18.9 | 28.1 | 5.5 | 9.2 | 17.3 | 23.9 | 0.0 | 0.2 | 0.8 | 2.6 | 0.3 | 0.5 | 0.8 | 1.6 |
| Glass[a] | 55.6 | 92.3 | 167.7 | 240.8 | 51.7 | 85.2 | 152.4 | 204.2 | 0.6 | 2.4 | 7.6 | 23.7 | 3.4 | 4.7 | 7.6 | 12.9 |
| Motor vehicles[a] | 98.3 | 157.2 | 299.1 | 427.1 | 97.5 | 155.4 | 291.9 | 400.9 | 0.0 | 0.7 | 4.3 | 20.2 | 0.8 | 1.1 | 2.9 | 6.1 |
| Aircraft[a] | 28.3 | 42.4 | 73.5 | 103.2 | 26.4 | 39.0 | 65.9 | 84.6 | 0.2 | 0.9 | 3.9 | 12.2 | 1.7 | 2.4 | 3.7 | 6.4 |
| Other transp. equip.[a] | 22.5 | 31.7 | 51.0 | 76.9 | 20.4 | 27.6 | 42.4 | 58.2 | 0.3 | 1.8 | 4.8 | 10.7 | 1.7 | 2.4 | 3.8 | 8.0 |
| Metal products[a] | 154.4 | 246.0 | 445.7 | 636.4 | 143.0 | 226.1 | 403.8 | 526.8 | 1.4 | 5.9 | 20.0 | 67.6 | 10.0 | 14.0 | 21.9 | 42.0 |
| Machinery[a] | 163.6 | 229.9 | 398.2 | 581.5 | 153.1 | 211.7 | 357.8 | 475.0 | 0.4 | 4.5 | 17.0 | 53.1 | 10.1 | 13.7 | 23.5 | 53.5 |
| Electrical mach.[a] | 108.7 | 169.3 | 304.5 | 435.1 | 104.1 | 161.8 | 288.9 | 394.0 | 0.1 | 1.3 | 5.2 | 20.6 | 4.5 | 6.2 | 10.4 | 20.6 |
| Instruments[a] | 26.7 | 39.5 | 69.0 | 99.1 | 25.4 | 37.2 | 64.1 | 86.4 | 0.1 | 0.6 | 2.0 | 5.9 | 1.2 | 1.7 | 2.8 | 6.9 |
| Other manufactures[a] | 40.9 | 60.3 | 91.6 | 140.1 | 34.8 | 50.4 | 73.5 | 103.8 | 1.1 | 2.8 | 7.1 | 16.1 | 5.0 | 7.1 | 10.9 | 20.2 |
| Utilities[a] | 80.2 | 153.5 | 293.5 | 414.9 | 75.2 | 142.5 | 265.2 | 346.0 | 1.0 | 3.9 | 15.0 | 48.4 | 4.1 | 7.1 | 13.3 | 20.6 |
| Construction[a] | 399.2 | 666.2 | 1205.8 | 1653.3 | 362.1 | 590.4 | 1035.4 | 1281.4 | 7.9 | 36.8 | 108.0 | 292.2 | 29.1 | 38.9 | 62.4 | 79.7 |
| Trade[a] | 578.3 | 909.3 | 1474.4 | 2097.6 | 531.5 | 825.3 | 1301.0 | 1717.5 | 9.1 | 30.8 | 94.0 | 241.3 | 37.6 | 53.2 | 79.5 | 138.7 |
| Transportation[a] | 194.1 | 290.1 | 436.9 | 634.5 | 170.0 | 247.0 | 354.4 | 476.1 | 3.8 | 13.4 | 37.1 | 79.7 | 20.2 | 29.8 | 45.5 | 78.7 |
| Communications[a] | 58.4 | 92.2 | 167.1 | 241.3 | 53.2 | 83.1 | 149.4 | 201.2 | 1.0 | 3.0 | 8.4 | 22.7 | 4.2 | 6.2 | 9.3 | 17.4 |
| Services[a] | 845.3 | 1364.4 | 2423.3 | 3712.6 | 764.2 | 1215.0 | 2096.5 | 2946.5 | 16.1 | 50.2 | 153.4 | 438.4 | 65.0 | 99.2 | 173.3 | 327.7 |
| *Fish[i]* | | | | | | | | | | | | | | | | |
| Fish catch | 66.0 | 66.0 | 66.0 | 66.0 | 31.5 | 31.5 | 31.5 | 31.5 | 14.5 | 14.5 | 14.5 | 14.5 | 19.9 | 19.9 | 19.9 | 19.9 |
| Nonhuman use | 22.0 | 22.0 | 22.0 | 22.0 | 7.6 | 7.6 | 7.6 | 11.9 | 11.9 | 11.9 | 11.9 | 14.5 | 2.4 | 2.4 | 2.4 | 2.4 |
| Fish imports | 4.0 | 4.0 | 4.0 | 4.0 | 3.4 | 3.4 | 3.4 | 3.4 | 0.2 | 0.2 | 0.2 | 0.2 | 0.4 | 0.4 | 0.4 | 0.4 |
| Fish exports | 4.1 | 4.1 | 4.1 | 4.1 | 3.4 | 3.4 | 3.4 | 3.4 | 0.2 | 0.2 | 0.2 | 0.2 | 0.5 | 0.5 | 0.5 | 0.5 |

*Exports*

| | | | | | | | | | | | | | | | |
|---|---|---|---|---|---|---|---|---|---|---|---|---|---|---|---|
| Livestock | 9.7 | 12.5 | 16.6 | 20.8 | 8.6 | 10.9 | 14.5 | 18.2 | 0.2 | 0.2 | 0.3 | 0.4 | 0.9 | 1.4 | 1.8 | 2.3 |
| High-protein crops | 25.1 | 33.5 | 48.1 | 62.1 | 18.8 | 26.6 | 38.2 | 49.3 | 2.8 | 2.9 | 4.2 | 5.4 | 3.5 | 4.0 | 5.8 | 7.4 |
| Grains | 103.3 | 126.3 | 185.5 | 251.6 | 88.5 | 108.8 | 159.9 | 216.8 | 1.1 | 1.0 | 1.5 | 2.1 | 13.7 | 16.4 | 24.1 | 32.7 |
| Roots | 13.2 | 15.0 | 18.9 | 22.8 | 10.9 | 12.3 | 15.6 | 18.8 | 0.7 | 0.8 | 1.1 | 1.3 | 1.6 | 1.8 | 2.2 | 2.7 |
| Other agriculture | 27.6 | 30.8 | 36.0 | 52.9 | 14.2 | 15.9 | 18.6 | 27.3 | 5.2 | 5.8 | 6.7 | 9.9 | 8.2 | 9.1 | 10.7 | 15.7 |
| Food processing | 13.1 | 15.8 | 20.6 | 30.3 | 9.5 | 11.5 | 15.1 | 22.0 | 1.0 | 1.2 | 1.5 | 2.3 | 2.6 | 3.1 | 3.9 | 6.0 |
| Textiles, apparel | 23.5 | 51.8 | 107.8 | 208.8 | 19.3 | 43.1 | 89.0 | 166.3 | 0.3 | 0.9 | 2.5 | 6.6 | 3.9 | 7.8 | 16.3 | 35.9 |
| Wood and cork | 4.8 | 9.0 | 17.4 | 26.4 | 4.1 | 7.8 | 14.8 | 21.9 | 0.2 | 0.3 | 0.6 | 1.2 | 0.6 | 1.0 | 1.9 | 3.4 |
| Furniture, fixtures | 1.5 | 2.6 | 2.9 | 4.2 | 1.5 | 2.6 | 2.8 | 4.1 | 0.0 | 0.0 | 0.0 | 0.0 | 0.0 | 0.1 | 0.1 | 0.1 |
| Paper | 8.4 | 17.8 | 38.4 | 68.9 | 8.3 | 17.5 | 37.5 | 66.1 | 0.1 | 0.1 | 0.1 | 0.6 | 0.1 | 0.3 | 0.7 | 2.1 |
| Printing | 1.9 | 4.2 | 9.8 | 17.9 | 1.8 | 4.0 | 9.3 | 16.0 | 0.0 | 0.1 | 0.1 | 0.2 | 0.1 | 0.2 | 0.4 | 1.0 |
| Rubber | 2.1 | 4.0 | 8.7 | 17.1 | 2.0 | 3.8 | 8.3 | 16.0 | 0.1 | 0.1 | 0.3 | 0.4 | 0.1 | 0.1 | 0.3 | 0.7 |
| Industrial chem. | 15.2 | 25.2 | 44.3 | 71.3 | 14.8 | 34.6 | 42.9 | 67.6 | 0.2 | 0.3 | 1.0 | 0.7 | 0.3 | 0.5 | 1.2 | 3.1 |
| Fertilizers | 6.6 | 11.6 | 23.3 | 34.8 | 6.0 | 10.5 | 20.8 | 29.9 | 0.1 | 0.2 | 0.5 | 2.1 | 0.5 | 0.8 | 1.6 | 2.8 |
| Other chemicals | 6.9 | 13.7 | 28.1 | 51.3 | 6.5 | 13.0 | 26.4 | 47.4 | 0.0 | 0.1 | 0.3 | 1.2 | 0.3 | 0.6 | 1.2 | 2.7 |
| Cement | 0.3 | 0.6 | 0.6 | 3.6 | 0.2 | 0.4 | 1.0 | 2.3 | 0.0 | 0.0 | 0.5 | 0.8 | 0.0 | 0.1 | 0.2 | 0.5 |
| Glass | 3.9 | 8.7 | 20.6 | 36.3 | 3.8 | 8.4 | 19.8 | 34.6 | 0.1 | 0.1 | 0.3 | 0.4 | 0.1 | 0.2 | 0.6 | 1.3 |
| Motor vehicles | 27.1 | 42.2 | 83.3 | 141.5 | 26.9 | 41.8 | 82.2 | 138.2 | 0.1 | 0.1 | 0.2 | 0.7 | 0.2 | 0.3 | 0.8 | 2.6 |
| Other transp. equip. | 4.9 | 7.2 | 12.1 | 19.1 | 4.9 | 7.1 | 12.0 | 18.9 | 0.0 | 0.0 | 0.2 | 0.0 | 0.0 | 0.0 | 0.1 | 0.3 |
| Aircraft | 5.6 | 9.2 | 17.4 | 25.9 | 5.6 | 9.1 | 17.2 | 25.4 | 0.0 | 0.1 | 0.1 | 0.2 | 0.1 | 0.4 | 0.7 | 1.3 |
| Metal products | 7.7 | 12.0 | 19.6 | 26.6 | 7.4 | 11.5 | 18.8 | 25.1 | 0.1 | 0.1 | 0.2 | 0.3 | 0.3 | 0.5 | 1.3 | 4.0 |
| Machinery | 35.9 | 60.2 | 112.1 | 180.7 | 35.6 | 59.6 | 110.6 | 176.2 | 0.1 | 0.1 | 0.2 | 0.5 | 0.3 | 0.9 | 1.9 | 4.3 |
| Electrical mach. | 17.0 | 33.0 | 67.8 | 125.7 | 16.4 | 32.0 | 65.7 | 121.0 | 0.0 | 0.0 | 0.2 | 0.5 | 0.5 | 0.1 | 0.3 | 0.7 |
| Instruments | 6.2 | 10.9 | 21.5 | 35.0 | 6.1 | 10.8 | 21.2 | 34.1 | 0.0 | 0.0 | 0.0 | 0.1 | 0.1 | 0.1 | 0.3 | 5.7 |
| Other manufactures | 8.7 | 13.9 | 22.9 | 34.5 | 7.0 | 11.5 | 19.0 | 28.0 | 0.3 | 0.4 | 0.5 | 0.8 | 1.4 | 2.0 | 3.3 | 5.7 |
| Services | 20.0 | 28.8 | 43.5 | 58.7 | 16.9 | 24.3 | 36.8 | 49.6 | 0.8 | 1.2 | 1.8 | 2.5 | 2.3 | 3.2 | 4.9 | 6.6 |
| Transport | 27.0 | 41.9 | 71.7 | 106.7 | 24.3 | 37.8 | 64.6 | 96.1 | 1.1 | 1.7 | 2.9 | 4.3 | 1.6 | 2.4 | 4.2 | 6.2 |
| Aid inflow[h] | 27.4 | 41.4 | 66.1 | 97.6 | 15.2 | 22.3 | 35.7 | 54.6 | 3.2 | 5.1 | 8.1 | 11.4 | 8.9 | 14.0 | 22.4 | 31.6 |
| Capital inflow[h] | 26.9 | 45.3 | 86.1 | 125.7 | 21.9 | 32.0 | 55.3 | 58.3 | 1.9 | 9.8 | 25.2 | 59.1 | 3.2 | 3.5 | 5.5 | 8.3 |

*Imports*

| | | | | | | | | | | | | | | | |
|---|---|---|---|---|---|---|---|---|---|---|---|---|---|---|---|
| Livestock | 9.7 | 12.5 | 16.6 | 20.8 | 8.5 | 10.4 | 13.1 | 15.0 | 0.5 | 1.1 | 2.0 | 3.6 | 0.6 | 1.0 | 1.4 | 2.1 |
| High-protein crops | 25.1 | 33.5 | 48.1 | 62.1 | 22.1 | 29.1 | 41.3 | 51.0 | 1.1 | 1.9 | 3.4 | 6.2 | 1.9 | 2.5 | 3.5 | 4.9 |
| Grains | 103.3 | 126.3 | 185.5 | 251.6 | 72.8 | 83.8 | 120.5 | 150.5 | 8.6 | 13.2 | 23.0 | 39.5 | 21.8 | 29.3 | 42.0 | 61.6 |
| Roots | 13.2 | 15.0 | 18.9 | 22.8 | 10.6 | 11.4 | 13.8 | 15.3 | 0.9 | 1.5 | 2.1 | 3.4 | 1.7 | 2.1 | 2.9 | 4.1 |
| Other agriculture | 27.6 | 30.8 | 36.0 | 52.9 | 24.5 | 25.3 | 26.4 | 33.3 | 0.8 | 2.2 | 5.2 | 9.9 | 2.3 | 3.4 | 4.4 | 9.8 |
| Food processing | 13.1 | 15.8 | 20.6 | 30.3 | 10.6 | 11.4 | 13.0 | 15.9 | 1.0 | 2.3 | 4.8 | 9.0 | 1.5 | 2.1 | 2.8 | 5.4 |
| Textiles, apparel | 23.5 | 51.8 | 107.8 | 208.8 | 19.5 | 42.4 | 88.9 | 171.0 | 1.7 | 4.4 | 11.3 | 26.4 | 2.3 | 5.0 | 7.6 | 11.4 |
| Wood and cork | 4.8 | 9.0 | 17.4 | 26.4 | 4.3 | 7.8 | 14.3 | 18.3 | 0.2 | 0.8 | 2.6 | 7.4 | 0.2 | 0.4 | 0.5 | 0.7 |
| Furniture, fixtures | 1.5 | 2.6 | 2.9 | 4.2 | 1.4 | 2.3 | 2.2 | 2.8 | 0.1 | 0.2 | 0.6 | 1.3 | 0.0 | 0.1 | 0.1 | 0.1 |
| Paper | 8.4 | 17.8 | 38.4 | 68.9 | 7.0 | 14.7 | 31.0 | 49.4 | 0.6 | 1.8 | 5.5 | 16.3 | 0.8 | 1.3 | 1.8 | 3.2 |
| Printing | 1.9 | 4.2 | 9.8 | 17.9 | 1.5 | 3.4 | 7.9 | 12.5 | 0.2 | 0.5 | 1.5 | 4.8 | 0.2 | 0.3 | 0.4 | 0.6 |
| Rubber | 2.1 | 4.0 | 8.7 | 17.1 | 1.6 | 3.0 | 6.0 | 9.1 | 0.3 | 0.6 | 2.2 | 7.1 | 0.2 | 0.3 | 0.5 | 0.9 |

# Appendix 16-2 (Cont.)

| | World | | | | Developed | | | | Developing (LDC-I) | | | | Developing (LDC-II) | | | |
|---|---|---|---|---|---|---|---|---|---|---|---|---|---|---|---|---|
| | 1970 | 1980 | 1990 | 2000 | 1970 | 1980 | 1990 | 2000 | 1970 | 1980 | 1990 | 2000 | 1970 | 1980 | 1990 | 2000 |
| Industrial chem. | 15.2 | 25.2 | 44.3 | 71.3 | 12.2 | 19.6 | 33.8 | 51.0 | 0.9 | 2.2 | 5.3 | 11.6 | 2.1 | 3.4 | 5.2 | 8.7 |
| Fertilizers | 6.6 | 11.6 | 23.3 | 34.8 | 4.1 | 5.1 | 7.0 | 9.2 | 0.6 | 1.6 | 4.8 | 7.3 | 1.9 | 5.0 | 11.5 | 18.3 |
| Other chemicals | 6.9 | 13.7 | 28.1 | 51.3 | 4.9 | 9.1 | 17.0 | 25.7 | 0.9 | 2.9 | 8.5 | 21.2 | 1.1 | 1.8 | 2.6 | 4.4 |
| Cement | 0.3 | 0.6 | 1.4 | 3.6 | 0.1 | 0.3 | 0.7 | 1.0 | 0.1 | 0.3 | 0.6 | 2.4 | 0.1 | 0.1 | 0.2 | 0.3 |
| Glass | 3.9 | 8.7 | 20.6 | 36.3 | 3.2 | 6.8 | 15.7 | 22.3 | 0.3 | 1.3 | 4.1 | 12.9 | 0.3 | 0.6 | 0.7 | 1.0 |
| Motor vehicles | 27.1 | 42.2 | 83.3 | 141.5 | 22.7 | 38.3 | 72.4 | 111.5 | 2.2 | 2.1 | 8.0 | 24.4 | 2.2 | 1.8 | 3.0 | 5.7 |
| Other transp. equip. | 4.9 | 7.2 | 12.1 | 19.1 | 4.2 | 5.9 | 10.1 | 15.8 | 0.2 | 0.5 | 0.9 | 1.5 | 0.5 | 0.7 | 1.1 | 1.8 |
| Aircraft | 5.6 | 9.2 | 17.4 | 25.9 | 4.9 | 8.0 | 15.3 | 21.2 | 0.3 | 0.5 | 1.2 | 2.5 | 0.4 | 0.7 | 1.0 | 2.2 |
| Metal products | 7.7 | 12.0 | 19.6 | 26.6 | 5.7 | 8.0 | 12.5 | 13.6 | 1.0 | 2.8 | 5.8 | 11.3 | 0.9 | 1.1 | 1.4 | 1.7 |
| Machinery | 35.9 | 60.2 | 112.1 | 180.7 | 20.5 | 42.4 | 76.3 | 111.2 | 3.0 | 11.9 | 26.5 | 52.4 | 4.4 | 6.0 | 9.3 | 17.1 |
| Electrical mach. | 17.0 | 33.0 | 67.8 | 125.7 | 13.4 | 24.8 | 49.0 | 77.3 | 1.5 | 5.1 | 13.8 | 39.3 | 2.1 | 3.1 | 5.0 | 9.1 |
| Instruments | 6.2 | 10.9 | 21.5 | 35.0 | 5.2 | 8.6 | 16.4 | 24.0 | 0.3 | 1.4 | 3.7 | 8.0 | 0.6 | 1.0 | 1.5 | 2.9 |
| Other manufactures | 8.7 | 13.9 | 22.9 | 34.5 | 7.4 | 11.4 | 18.7 | 27.6 | 0.3 | 0.8 | 1.8 | 3.1 | 1.0 | 1.6 | 2.4 | 3.8 |
| Services | 20.0 | 28.8 | 43.5 | 58.7 | 18.4 | 26.0 | 38.5 | 49.3 | 0.7 | 1.6 | 3.5 | 6.8 | 1.0 | 1.2 | 1.5 | 2.7 |
| Transport | 27.0 | 41.9 | 71.7 | 106.7 | 22.2 | 33.4 | 56.1 | 78.5 | 2.1 | 4.8 | 9.8 | 18.3 | 2.7 | 3.8 | 5.8 | 9.9 |
| Aid outflow[h] | 27.4 | 41.4 | 66.1 | 97.6 | 23.2 | 32.9 | 48.7 | 62.5 | 1.9 | 5.3 | 13.0 | 28.2 | 2.4 | 3.3 | 4.4 | 6.9 |
| Capital outflow[h] | 26.9 | 45.3 | 86.1 | 125.7 | 24.4 | 40.2 | 72.8 | 97.2 | 0.8 | 1.9 | 5.6 | 12.6 | 1.8 | 3.2 | 7.7 | 15.9 |
| *Net exports of resources* | | | | | | | | | | | | | | | | |
| Copper | -0.0 | -0.0 | -0.0 | -0.0 | -1.9 | -3.4 | -8.1 | -10.6 | 1.3 | 2.4 | 5.8 | 6.7 | 0.6 | 1.0 | 2.4 | 3.9 |
| Bauxite | -0.0 | -0.0 | -0.0 | -0.0 | -5.0 | -8.7 | -14.8 | -7.2 | 5.0 | 8.4 | 14.7 | 6.9 | -0.0 | 0.3 | 0.0 | 0.3 |
| Nickel | 0 | 0 | 0 | 0 | -102 | -181 | -407 | -839 | 11 | 11 | 3 | 33 | 92 | 171 | 404 | 806 |
| Zinc | -0.0 | -0.0 | -0.0 | 0.0 | -0.6 | -1.1 | -0.5 | 0.0 | 0.6 | 1.0 | 1.1 | 0.0 | 0.0 | 0.1 | -0.6 | -0.0 |
| Lead | -0.0 | -0.0 | 0.0 | -0.0 | -0.4 | -0.8 | 0.9 | 0.0 | 0.3 | 0.6 | -0.5 | 0.0 | 0.1 | 0.2 | -0.5 | -0.0 |
| Iron | 0.0 | -0.0 | -0.0 | -0.0 | -74.7 | -93.4 | 257.2 | -290.5 | 32.3 | 38.9 | 90.8 | 76.8 | 42.4 | 54.5 | 166.3 | 213.7 |
| Petroleum | 0 | 0 | 0 | 0 | 1341 | 2097 | 3951 | -4396 | 1417 | 2329 | 4329 | 5160 | -74 | -230 | -376 | -762 |
| Natural gas | -0.0 | 0.0 | -0.0 | 0.0 | -8.2 | -4.18 | -49.4 | -71.7 | 3.1 | 57.6 | 111.2 | 224.2 | 5.1 | -15.9 | -61.9 | -152.5 |
| Coal | -0.0 | 0.0 | -0.0 | -0.0 | 5.2 | 5.7 | 13.2 | 65.2 | -1.1 | -7.4 | -27.4 | -77.3 | -4.1 | 1.7 | 14.2 | 12.1 |
| Other resources | -0.0 | -0.0 | -0.0 | -0.0 | -0.9 | -1.4 | -2.5 | -2.9 | 0.6 | 0.8 | 1.5 | 1.7 | 0.3 | 0.6 | 1.0 | 1.2 |
| Petroleum refining | -0.0 | 0.0 | -0.0 | -0.0 | -0.2 | -7.4 | -25.2 | -41.3 | 0.4 | 9.0 | 28.3 | 48.4 | -0.2 | -1.6 | -3.0 | -7.2 |
| Primary metals | -0.0 | -0.0 | -0.0 | 0.0 | 2.8 | -0.0 | -3.5 | -7.2 | -0.7 | 1.2 | 4.2 | 4.7 | -2.1 | -1.2 | -0.7 | 2.5 |

a 1970 U.S. dollars, billions  
b Millions  
c Millions of man-years  
d 1970 U.S. dollars, billions  
e Thousands  
f Grams  
g Hectares, millions  
h Current year, U.S. dollars, billions  
i Metric tons, millions

# 17

## *The distribution of work and income*

## (1982)

### I

"My Lords: During the short time I recently passed in Notting-hamshire not twelve hours elapsed without some fresh act of violence; . . . I was informed that forty Frames had been broken the preceding evening. These machines . . . superseded the necessity of employing a number of workmen, who were left in consequence to starve. By the adoption of one species of Frame in particular, one man performed the work of many, and the superfluous labourers were thrown out of employment. . . . The rejected workmen in the blindness of their ignorance, instead of rejoicing at these improvements in art so beneficial to mankind, conceived themselves to be sacrificed to improvements in mechanism."

With these words Lord Byron in his maiden speech to the House of Lords in February 1812 sought to explain, and by explaining to excuse, the renewal of the Luddite protest that was shaking the English social order. Nearly a generation earlier Ned Ludd had led his fellow workers in destroying the "frames," the knitting machines that employers had begun to install in the workshops of the country's growing textile industry. The House had before it legislation to exact the death penalty for such acts of sabotage. The Earl of Lauderdale sharpened Byron's thesis that the misled workers were acting against their own interests: "Nothing could be more certain than the fact that every improvement in machinery contributed to the improvement in the condition of persons manufacturing the machines, there being in a very short time after such improvements were introduced a greater demand for labour than ever before."

History has apparently sustained the optimistic outlook of the early exponents of modern industrial society. The specter of involuntary technological unemployment seems to remain no more than a specter. Beginning with the invention of the steam engine, successive waves of technological innovation have brought in the now industrial, or "developed," countries a spectacular growth of both employment and real wages, a combination that spells prosperity and social peace. Thanks as well to technological innovation, more than half of the labor force in all these countries—70 percent of the U.S. labor force—has been relieved from labor in agriculture and other goods production that employed substantially everyone before the industrial revolution. It is true that the less developed countries are still waiting in line. If the outlook for the future can be based on the experience of the past 200 years, those countries too can expect to move up, provided their governments can succeed in reducing their high rate of population growth and desist from interfering with the budding of the spirit of free private enterprise.

There are signs today, however, that past experience cannot serve as a reliable guide for the future of technological change. With the advent of solid-state electronics, machines that have been displacing human muscle from the production of goods are being succeeded by machines that take over the functions of the human nervous system not only in production but in the service industries as well. The relationship between man and machine is being radically transformed.

## II

The beneficence of that relationship is usually measured by the "productivity" of labor. This is the total output divided by the number of workers or, even better, by the number of man-hours required for its production. Thus, 30 years ago it took several thousand switchboard operators to handle a million long-distance telephone calls, 10 years later it took several hundred operators, and now, with automatic switchboards linked automatically to other automatic switchboards, only a few dozen are needed. Plainly the productivity of labor—that is, the number of calls completed per operator—has been increasing by leaps and bounds. Simple arithmetic shows that it will reach its highest level when only one operator remains and will become incalculable on the day that operator is discharged.

The inadequacy of this conventional measure is perhaps better illustrated if it is applied to assess the effects of the progressive replacement of horses by tractors in agriculture. Dividing the successive annual harvest figures first by the gradually increasing number of tractors and then by the reciprocally falling number of horses yields the paradoxical conclusion that throughout this time of transition the relative productivity of tractors tended to fall while the productivity of the horses they were replacing was rising. In fact, of course, the cost-effectiveness of horses diminished steadily compared with that of the increasingly efficient tractors.

In the place of such uncertain abstractions it is more productive to try to bring the underlying facts into consideration and analysis. Technological change can be visualized conveniently as change in the "cooking recipes"—the specific combinations of inputs—followed by different industries to produce their respective outputs. Progress in electromechanical technology enabled the telephone company to replace the old technological recipe calling for a large number of manual switchboards having many operators with a new recipe combining more expensive automatic switchboards having fewer operators. In agriculture technological progress brought the introduction of successive input combinations with smaller inputs of animal and human labor and larger and more diversified inputs of other kinds—not only mechanical equipment but also pesticides, herbicides, vaccines, antibiotics, hormones, and hybrid seed.

New recipes come into service in every industry by a constant process of "costing out." Some inputs included in a new recipe are at the outset too expensive, and it takes some time before improvements in their design or in the method of their manufacture bring sufficient reduction in their price and consequently in the total cost of the recipe to allow the adoption of the new technology. The decline, at the nearly constant rate of 30 percent per year for many years, in the cost per memory bit on the integrated-circuit chip has brought solid-state electronics technology first into expensive capital equipment such as telephone switchboards, automatic pilots, machine tools, and computers; then into radio and television sets and powerful, low-cost computers as an entirely new category of consumer goods; then into the control systems of automobiles and household appliances and even into such expendable goods as toys. Thus, the adoption of a new recipe in one industry often depends on replacement of the old by a new technology in another industry, as the vacuum tube was replaced by the transistor and its descendants in the transformed electronics industry.

# III

Stepping back and contemplating the flow of raw materials and intermediate products through the input-output structure of an industrial system and the corresponding price structure, one can see that prices more or less faithfully reflect the state of technology in the system. With the passage of time, price changes can be expected to reflect long-run technological changes going on in the various sectors. In this perspective human labor of a specific kind appears as one, but only one, of the many different inputs whose price must be reckoned in the costing out of a given technological recipe. Its price, the wage rate, enters into the cost comparisons between competing technologies in the same way as the price of any other input.

In the succession of technological changes that have accompanied economic development and growth, new goods and services come on the stage, and old ones, having played their role, step off. Such changes proceed at different rates and on different scales, affecting some sectors of economic activity more than others. Some types of labor are replaced faster than others. Less skilled workers, in many instances but not always, go first, more skilled workers later. Computers are now taking on the jobs of white-collar workers, performing first simple and then increasingly complex mental tasks.

Human labor from time immemorial played the role of principal factor of production. There are reasons to believe that human labor will not retain this status in the future.

Over the past two centuries technological innovation has brought an exponential growth of total output in the industrial economies, accompanied by rising per capita consumption. At the same time, until the middle 1940s the easing of labor was enjoyed in the progressive shortening of the working day, working week, and working year. Increased leisure (and, for that matter, cleaner air and purer water) is not counted in the official adding up of goods and services in the gross national product. It has nonetheless contributed greatly to the well-being of blue-collar workers and salaried employees. Without increase in leisure time, the popularization of education and cultural advantages that has distinguished the industrial societies in the first 80 years of this century would not have been possible. The work week in manufacturing industries of the United States shortened from about 67 hours in 1860 to about 42 hours in

1950 and has remained constant since then. (See Figure 17-1). Such reduction in the average number of working hours per week per employee amounts to the withdrawal from work of more than a third of the manufacturing labor force. The work week actually fell below 40 hours in the great depression of the 1930s with "sharing of unemployment" in part-time jobs and climbed well above 40 hours with overtime work in war production in the 1940s. Since the end of World War II, however, the work week has remained almost constant. Waves of technological innovation have continued to overtake each other as before. The real wage rate, discounted for inflation, has continued to go up. Yet the length of the normal work week today is practically the same as it was 35 years ago. In 1977, the work week in the U.S. manufacturing industries, adjusted for the growth in vacations and holidays, was still 41.8 hours.

Personal income per capita in the United Stated, plotted in Figure 17-2 in constant 1972 dollars, has more than doubled since 1929. The change in percentage shares of income accruing from property, transfer payments, and labor (or to people receiving such income) reflects the evolution of the values and institutions of American society. The curves show that income from property has declined from about 40 percent to not much more than 15 percent of total per-

**Figure 17-1**

Work week in manufacturing industries (the discontinuity in the curve over the period 1910 through 1925 reflects a change in the statistical time series kept by the country's bookkeepers, involving principally changes in their accounting of the time of part-time and seasonal workers)

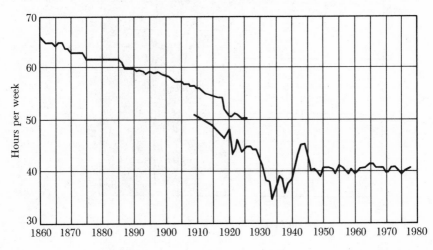

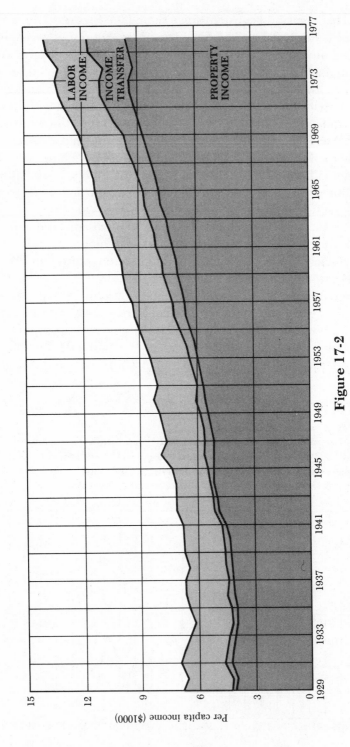

**Figure 17-2**

Personal income per capita in the United States, plotted in constant 1972 dollars

sonal income. Some of that decline reflects the exchange of profit
and interest from small businesses (notably in trade and distribution
and the services) for wages in large business enterprises (income
from labor). It also reflects increased retention of earnings in corporations and increased financing of investment by such deflection
of savings from personal income. Income from labor has increased
from about 60 percent of the total to about 70 percent. Income from
transfer payments (social security, medical benefits, unemployment
compensation, etc.) was negligible in 1929 but now is about 15 percent of total.

Concurrently, the U.S. economy has seen a chronic increase in
unemployment from one oscillation of the business cycle to the
next. The 2 percent accepted as the irreducible unemployment rate
by proponents of full-employment legislation in 1945 became the 4
percent of New Frontier economic managers in the 1960s. The
country's unemployment problem today exceeds 9 percent. How
can this be explained?

## IV

Without technological change, there could, of course, be no technological unemployment. Nor would there be such unemployment
if the total population and the labor force, instead of growing, were
to shrink. Workers might also hang on to their jobs if they would
agree to accept lower wages. Those who are concerned with population growth are likely to proclaim that "too many workers" is the
actual cause of unemployment. Libertarians of the "keep your
hands off the free market" school urge the remedy of wage cuts
brought about by the systematic curtailment of the power of trade
unions and the reduction of unemployment and welfare benefits.
Advocates of full employment have been heard to propose that
labor-intensive technologies be given preference over labor-saving
ones. A more familiar medicine is prescribed by those who advocate
stepped-up investment in accelerated economic growth.

Each of these diagnoses has its shortcomings, and the remedies
they prescribe can be no more than palliative at best. A drastic general wage cut might temporarily arrest the adoption of labor-saving
technology, even though dirt-cheap labor could not compete in
many operations with very powerful or very sophisticated machines.
The old trend would be bound to resume, however, unless special
barriers were erected against labor-saving devices. Even the most
principled libertarian must hesitate to have wage questions settled

by cutthroat competition among workers under the pressure of
steadily advancing technology. The erection of Luddite barriers to
technological progress would, on the other hand, bring more men-
ace to the health of the economic and social system than the disease
it is intended to cure.

Increased investment can certainly provide jobs for people who
would otherwise be unemployed. The value of capital stock
employed per man-hour in manufacturing industries in the United
States—plotted in Figure 17-3 in the form of a constant 1967-dollar
index—has almost doubled since the end of World War II. (See Figure 17-1.) Given the rate of technological advance, the creation of
one additional job that 20 years ago might have required an investment of $50,000 now demands $100,000 and in 20 years will
demand $500,000, even with inflation discounted. A high rate of
investment is, of course, indispensable to the expanding needs of a
growing economy. It can make only a limited contribution to alle-
viating involuntary technological unemployment, however, because

## Figure 17-3

Value of capital stock employed per man-hour in manufacturing industries
in the United States (index in constant 1967 dollars)

the greater the rate of capital investment, the higher the rate of introduction of new labor-saving technology. The latest copper smelter to go into service in the United States cost $450 million and employs fewer than 50 men per shift.

Americans might have continued to absorb potential technological unemployment by voluntary shortening of the work week if real wages had risen over the past 40 years faster than they actually have, allowing the expectation of increase not only of total annual pay but also of total lifetime take-home pay. Because of the greatly expanded opportunities to replace labor by increasingly sophisticated technology, it appears that the impersonal forces of the market no longer favor that possibility. Government policies directed at encouraging a steady rise in real wages sufficiently large to induce workers to resume continuous voluntary reduction in the work week could once have been considered. Under present conditions such policies would require such a large increase in the share of total national income going to wages that it would bring decline in productive investment, which is financed largely by undistributed corporate earnings and the savings of the upper-income group. This would result in an unacceptable slowdown of economic growth. There remains the alternative of direct action to promote a progressive shortening of the work week combined with income policies designed to maintain and to increase, as increases in total output allow, the real family income of wage earners and salaried employees.

Recent studies sponsored by the U.S. Department of Labor seem to indicate that the total number of working hours offered by the existing labor force might be reduced in exchange for a more flexible scheduling of work time. Indeed, some workers, depending on their age group, family status, occupation, and so on, would even be prepared to forgo a certain fraction of their current income, some by extension of their annual vacation, some by earlier retirement or sabbatical leave, and some by working four and a half days per week instead of five. Reducing the work day by 15 minutes proves, incidentally, to be one of the less desirable alternatives. Tentative and obviously somewhat speculative computations based on the most desirable tradeoff choices for different groups developed in these studies indicate that the average U.S. worker would be willing to forgo some 4.7 percent of earnings in exchange for free time. On the basis of the 1978 work year, the average employee's work time would be reduced from 1910 work hours to 1821, or by more than two working weeks in a year.

## V

Although such measures certainly deserve serious consideration and, if at all possible, practical implementation, they cannot provide a final answer to the long-run question of how to enable a modern industrial society to derive the benefits of continued technological progress without experiencing involuntary technological unemployment and resulting social disruption. Sooner or later, and quite probably sooner, the increasingly mechanized society must face another problem, that of income distribution.

Adam and Eve enjoyed, before they were expelled from Paradise, a high standard of living without working. After their expulsion they and their successors were condemned to eke out a miserable existence, working from dawn to dusk. The history of technological progress over the past 200 years is essentially the story of the human species working its way slowly and steadily back into Paradise. What would happen, however, if we suddenly found ourselves in it? With all goods and services provided without work, no one would be gainfully employed. Being unemployed means receiving no wages. As a result, until appropriate new income policies were formulated to fit the changed technological conditions, everyone would starve in Paradise.

The income policies I have in mind do not turn simply on an increase in the legally fixed minimum wage or in the hourly wage or other benefits negotiated by the usual collective bargaining between trade unions and employers. In the long run, increases in the direct and indirect hourly labor costs would be bound to accelerate labor-saving mechanization. This, incidentally, is the explicitly stated explanation of the wage policies currently pursued by the benevolently authoritarian government of Singapore. It encourages a rapid rise in real wages in order to induce free domestic enterprise to upgrade the already remarkably efficient production facilities of this city-state. It is perhaps needless to add that these policies are accompanied by strict control of immigration and encouragement of birth control.

## VI

What I have in mind is a complex of social and economic measures to supplement by transfer from other income shares the income received by blue- and white-collar workers from the sale of their services on the labor market. A striking example of an income transfer of this kind attained automatically without government intervention is there to be studied in the long-run effects of the mechanization of agriculture on the mode of operation and the income of, say, a prosperous Iowa farm. Half a century ago, the farming family worked from early morning until late at night assisted by a team of horses, possibly a tractor, and a standard set of simple agricultural implements. Their income consisted of what essentially amounted to wages for a 75- or 80-hour work week, supplemented by a small profit on their modest investment.

Today the farm is fully mechanized and even has some sophisticated electronic equipment. The average work week is much shorter, and from time to time the family can take a real vacation. Their total wage income, if one computes it at the going hourly rate for a much smaller number of manual-labor hours, is probably not much higher than it was 50 years ago and may even be lower. Their standard of living, however, is certainly much higher. The shrinkage of their wage income is more than fully offset by the income earned on their massive capital investment in the rapidly changing technology of agriculture. The shift from the old income structure to the new one was smooth and practically painless. It involved no more than a simple bookkeeping transaction because now, as 50 years ago, both the wage income and the capital income are earned by the same family.

The effect of technological progress on manufacturing and other nonagricultural sectors of the economy is essentially the same as it is on agriculture. So also should be its repercussions with respect to the shortening of the work day and the allocation of income. Because of differences in the institutional setup, however, those repercussions cannot be expected to work through the system automatically. That must be brought about by carefully designed income policies. The accommodation of existing institutions to the demands and to the effects of labor-saving mechanization will not be easy. The setting aside of the Puritan work ethic, to which Max Weber so convincingly ascribed the success of early industrial society, is bound to prove even more difficult and drawn out. In popular and political discourse on employment, full employment, and unemployment, with its emphasis on the provision of incomes rather than the production of goods, it can be seen that the revision of values has already begun.

The evolution of institutions is under way as well. In the structure of the tax system and through social security, medical insurance, unemployment benefits, and welfare payments, the country is find-

ing its way toward necessary income policies. A desirable near-term
step is to reduce the contrast between those who are fully employed
and those who are out of work. This is the effect of the widespread
European practice of paying supplemental benefits to those who
work fewer than the normal number of hours per week. In the long
run, responding to the incipient threat of technological unemployment, public policy should aim at securing equitable distribution of
work and income, taking care not to obstruct technological progress
even indirectly.

Implementation of such policy calls for close and systematic cooperation between management and labor carried on with government
support. Large-scale financial transfers inevitably generate inflationary pressure. The inflation that dogs all the market economies, some
more than others, does not arise from mere technical economic
causes but is the symptom of deep-seated social problems. In this
country it is basically the incessant wrangling between management
and labor that keeps the cost-price spiral climbing.

West Germany, a country celebrated for its successful stabiliza-
tion policies, is also touted as an example of the unregulated enterprise economy. In reality, the success of the Schmidt government's
anti-inflation measures rests on the firm foundation of institutional-
ized labor-capital cooperation in the management of German industry. The "codetermination" law requires that half of the board of
directors of each large corporation be elected by labor, with the
stockholders represented by the other half. Among the labor members, some are "outside" directors representing the national trade
unions. Since wage and employment questions constitute only one
problem in the broad range of problems on the agenda of these
boards, their deliberations bring employers and employees into
working contact at the grass-roots level of German industry. That
relationship must, of course, be of crucial importance in determining the nature of agreements reached in collective bargaining conducted between the parties at the national level.

Austria is another country that has up to now successfully resisted
inflationary pressure. Relations between management and labor are
mediated by institutional arrangements very similar to those in Germany. The government plays a larger and more active role in the
national across-the-board wage negotiations. It does so by contributing projections, drawn from the input-output data bank of the
country's bookkeeping system, that link decisions affecting the
industry in question to the situation of the country as a whole. This
approach was employed, for example, to model and project the

impact of the new text-processing and printing technologies on the Austrian newspaper industry. That technological revolution, the occasion for months-long disputes and work stoppages in Britain, the United States, and other countries, was carried out smoothly and expeditiously in Austria by close cooperation between management and labor in accordance with detailed plans developed by the government. Until 1980, when the tidal wave of the second oil crisis, reinforced by the recession in the U.S. economy, reached Austria, the annual rate of inflation had been held below 4 percent and unemployment below 2 percent.

Although current business publications, trade papers, and the popular press abound with articles about automation and robotics and speculation on the economic impact of these developments, only the governmental and scientific agencies of Austria have produced a systematic assessment of the prospective consequences of the present revolution in labor-saving technology in a modern industrial economy and society. That study, conducted for the government by the Austrian Academy of Sciences and the Austrian Institute for Economic Research, employed the country's input-output data bank to construct a model of the Austrian economy as of 1976. The model was then used to develop, in the words of Minister for Science Hertha Firnberg in her introduction to the report of the study, "instead of unconditional prognostications—of either jubilation or horror—projections in the form of alternative scenarios . . . to analyze in quantitative terms the combined effects of economic, social, and educational policy measures."

## VII

In input-output analysis the interindustry transactions that go into the production of the output of an economic system are arrayed in a matrix, with the allocational outputs of each industrial sector to sectors that absorb it displayed along its row and the inputs it draws from other industries displayed in its column. The ratio of each input to the output of the sector—the input-output coefficient— reflects the technological requirement for that input, which, although it is usually expressed in monetary value, is best visualized in the physical units appropriate to it, whether tons, bushels, barrels, kilowatts, or man-hours. The entire column of input-output coefficients therefore presents the recipe of inputs required by the prevailing state of the technology involved in the production of that industry's product. At the foot of the column the human input is specified by the different kinds of labor supplied by the households sector.

For the Austrian study, new sets of input-output coefficients had to be constructed reflecting changes in the input structure of all sectors of the economy prospectively dictated by the adoption of new labor-saving technology. In the simulation runs, the effects of these changes could be gauged by comparison with the figures derived from actual interindustry transactions for 1976. Information for construction of the new coefficients was procured by comprehensive questionnaires circulated to technologists in each field and interviews with responsible technical directors of major industrial and service enterprises.

With all these data installed in the model, five alternative projections were run, describing in great detail the prospective state of the Austrian economy in the years 1985 and 1990. The sets of assumptions governing the projections differ from one another with respect to the rate of adoption of labor-saving technology, the extent of reliance on domestic as opposed to foreign suppliers of the new equipment, the more or less optimistic appraisal of the state of the world economy, and, last but not least, the length of the work week for its effect on the distribution of employment among different sectors and the rate of unemployment.

Impact of mechanization on jobs in Austria as projected, industry by industry, from estimates made by engineers and other experts for an input-output study of the effects of mechanization on the Austrian economy, is described in Table 17-1. The first column, under both the blue-collar and the white-collar headings, shows the percentage of jobs potentially affected by technology demonstrated as of 1980 although not yet installed on the production line or in the office; the second column shows the percentage of reduction of labor input in those functions potentially affected by such new technology; the third column shows the estimated percentage of jobs that would be displaced by 1990 if there were full application of the technology; and the fourth column shows the prospective percentage reduction in employment in 1990 that is the result of the other three percentages. Note the large percentage of blue-collar jobs potentially affected compared with the almost invariably small number of white-collar jobs affected, and the larger (in most cases) prospective reduction of labor input in blue-collar production functions compared with the uniform 50 percent reduction in white-collar office functions expected to result from the application of essentially the same technology to clerical and stenographic jobs in all industries and services.

Out of the wealth of thought-provoking indications for the future to be found after close inspection of the several projections that are summarized in Table 17-1, it suffices for the purposes of the present discussion to cite just a few. The projections that carry the present state-of-the-art labor-saving technology into full application everywhere in the Austrian economy by 1990 lead in all cases to the largest increase in gross domestic product—but also to the highest lev-

### Table 17-1

Projected impact of mechanization on jobs in Austria

| | Blue-collar | | | | White-collar | | | |
|---|---|---|---|---|---|---|---|---|
| | Jobs affected | Reduction in labor input | Jobs affected 1990 | Reduction in employment | Jobs affected | Reduction in labor input | Jobs affected 1990 | Reduction in employment |
| Agriculture and forestry | — | — | — | — | .01 | .50 | .200 | .001 |
| Mining | .68 | .50 | .072 | .025 | .10 | .50 | .038 | .019 |
| Petroleum | .60 | .50 | .235 | .059 | .20 | .50 | .076 | .008 |
| Glass | .60 | .50 | .069 | .021 | .12 | .50 | .059 | .008 |
| Food processing | .55 | .50 | .114 | .031 | .10 | .50 | .154 | .008 |
| Textiles | .85 | .67 | .390 | .222 | .10 | .50 | .208 | .010 |
| Clothing | .89 | .67 | .210 | .125 | .07 | .50 | .177 | .004 |
| Chemicals | .55 | .67 | .300 | .111 | .20 | .50 | .206 | .021 |
| Basic metals | .73 | .50 | .369 | .135 | .13 | .50 | .182 | .012 |
| Machinery | .70 | .77 | .480 | .259 | .13 | .50 | .219 | .014 |
| Metal products | .80 | .67 | .215 | .115 | .13 | .50 | .195 | .013 |
| Electrical industry | .65 | .67 | .700 | .305 | .13 | .50 | .220 | .014 |
| Transportation equipment | .50 | .67 | .352 | .118 | .13 | .50 | .219 | .014 |
| Forest products | .75 | .67 | .075 | .038 | .10 | .50 | .118 | .006 |
| Woodworking | .75 | .67 | .075 | .038 | .10 | .50 | .118 | .006 |
| Paper manufacture | .85 | .67 | .400 | .228 | .12 | .50 | .464 | .028 |
| Paper products | .85 | .50 | .429 | .182 | .12 | .50 | .374 | .022 |
| Construction | — | — | — | — | .07 | .50 | .200 | .007 |
| Electric, gas, water utilities | .23 | .50 | .235 | .027 | .22 | .50 | .200 | .022 |
| Trade | .53 | .80 | .100 | .042 | .18 | .50 | .200 | .018 |
| Information industry | .41 | .67 | .020 | .005 | .11 | .50 | .200 | .022 |
| Banks and insurance | — | — | — | — | .70 | .50 | .400 | .140 |
| Hotels and restaurants | — | — | — | — | .02 | .50 | .200 | .002 |
| Other services | — | — | — | — | .12 | .50 | .200 | .012 |
| Housing | — | — | — | — | — | 1.00 | 0 | — |
| Government | — | — | — | — | .64 | .50 | .180 | .058 |

els of unemployment, to unemployment of 10 percent, a level not experienced in Austria since the dark days of the 1930s. With curtailment in the length of the work week at the maximum degree of mechanization, the direction of both the positive and the negative changes remains the same, but their absolute magnitudes are reduced. Unemployment in this case comes closer to the civilized Austrian experience of 2 percent.

No comparable study has yet been completed for the U.S. economy. Fiscal starvation of the federal statistical agencies has them currently sorting out interindustry-transactions data for 1977, with publication scheduled for not sooner than 1984. The Austrian study presents the best model available for projection of conditions in the United States for 1990. The Austrian economy is a mere 3 percent the size of the U.S. economy, but it too is highly industrialized and diversified. With some stretch of the imagination the Austrian projection of a high degree of mechanization supported by rapid expansion of domestic manufacture of all kinds of electronic products can be interpreted as indicating the structural changes the U.S. economy is likely to undergo in the next 10 or 15 years.

The time span covered by these projections is short. Moreover, they reckon with the consequences of the application of the state of the art of mechanization only as of 1980 at the latest, a state soon to be made obsolete by rapid advance in all the relevant technologies. These figures nonetheless throw some light on the quantitative dimensions of the profound challenge that an advanced industrial society must now begin to face under the impact of the continuing industrial revolution. History, even recent history, shows that societies have responded to such challenge with revision of their economic institutions and values conducive to the efficient use of changing technology and to securing its advantages for popular well-being. History shows also societies that have failed to respond and have succumbed to economic stagnation and increasing social disorder.

# 18

## The growth of maritime traffic and the future of world ports

### ( 1 9 7 9 )

To provide a basis for general discussion of the great variety of forces that can be expected to determine the development of seaborne commodity traffic over the next two decades, my collaborators at the Institute for Economic Analysis at New York University and I have prepared a preliminary projection of the future growth of maritime traffic up to the year 2000 and an even cruder assessment of the magnitude and structure of investment in additional port facilities that will be required to handle it.

A report prepared for and published by the United Nations in 1977 contained a number of rather detailed projections of the economic growth of the world economy from 1970 to the year 2000.[1]

The world economy was subdivided for purposes of these projections into 15 regions (see Table 18-1)—8 developed and 7 less developed—and the economy of each region was described in terms of 6 agricultural, 28 manufacturing and service sectors, and 9 primary resource sectors producing oil, ores, coal, and other minerals. These latter make up the bulk of seaborne traffic. The levels of regional outputs, exports, and imports of all these goods and services were projected from 1970 through 1980 and 1990 to the year 2000.

[1]The English version of *The Future of the World Economy* is published by Oxford University Press, New York, 1977; the French is *L'Expertise de Wassily Leontief*, Dunod, Paris, 1977; the German, *Die Zukunft der Weltwirtschaft*, Deutsche Anstalt, Stuttgart, 1977; the Spanish, *El Futuro de la Economia Mundial*, Siglo Veintiuno Editores, Madrid, 1977; and the Italian, *Il Futuro dell'Economia Mondiale*, Mondadori Editore, Milan, 1977. Other editions have been published in Japanese, Romanian, and Portuguese.

This article elaborates the content of a keynote address given by Professor W. Leontief at a meeting of the International Association of Ports and Harbours, May 1979. From *Ports and Harbors* (IAPH Journal), 24, 9 (September 1979).

## Table 18-1

Geographical classification of countries included in the nine regions

| Region | Principal component countries |
| --- | --- |
| North America | Canada, Greenland, U.S.A.<br>(world model region 1) |
| USSR, Eastern Europe | USSR, Albania, Bulgaria, Czechoslovakia, German Democratic Republic, Hungary, Poland, Romania<br>(world model regions 4 and 5) |
| Western Europe | All other European countries<br>(world model regions 4 and 5) |
| Japan | Japan, Ryukyu Islands<br>(world model region 9) |
| Middle East | Algeria, Bahrain, Democratic Yemen, Gabon, Iran, Iraq, Kuwait, Libya, Nigeria, Qatar, Saudi Arabia, United Arab Emirates, Yemen<br>(world model region 11) |
| Africa | All African countries not included in Middle East region above<br>(world model regions 12, 13, and 14) |
| Asia | All Asian countries not included above<br>(world model regions 8 and 10) |
| Latin America | All of Central and South American countries<br>(world model regions 2 and 3) |
| Oceania | Australia, New Zealand<br>(world model region 15) |

Based on applications of the input-output approach, these projections are internally consistent, in the sense that the production of each good in each region is balanced against the consumption, allowing for that good's exports and imports. On the global level, the projected sum total of the 15 regions' exports of each good is equal to the sum total of the projected imports. Moreover, in each region the allocation of the total annual supply of each good takes account of the capital accumulation—that is, the investment in additional productive capacity—that will be required to support the anticipated rise in output. As we will see below, this includes construction of new port facilities to handle increases in oceanborne traffic.

An overall view of the projected growth of the world economy is provided by the three curves (plotted on a logarithmic scale) in Figure 18-1a. One traces the rise of the combined gross domestic products of the developed countries; another the growth of the combined GDPs of the resource-poor less developed areas, and the third the increase in the aggregate GDP of that small group made up of the Middle Eastern and other resource-rich less developed areas.

The corresponding changes in the levels of per capita income are shown in Figure 18-1b.

In the UN publication referred to above, emphasis is laid on what might be called optimistic scenario X, which is based on the assumption that in order to accelerate their growth, both the developed and the resource-rich less developed countries will be ready to provide a very substantial amount of economic aid to the resource-poor less developed areas. The alternative scenario A used for the present study is based on the more conservative assumption that economic assistance granted to the poor less developed regions will, in the coming years, continue to be governed by the same essentially commercial considerations that have determined its level in the past. Hence, while all economies will continue to expand, it can be seen in Figure 18-1b that the gap between the per capita income of the resource-poor less developed and the developed areas will not diminish appreciably. The curve representing the projected per capita GDP of the small group of resource-rich less developed areas

**Figure 18-1**

Projected gross domestic product—*Future of the World Economy*
scenario A *(logarithmic scale)*

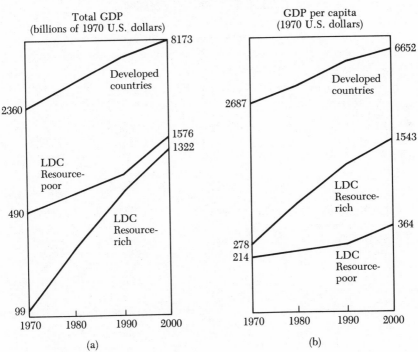

(a)                                        (b)

is seen, as could have been expected, to be rising faster than the other two.

For purposes of this study, the 15 regions, in terms of which the analysis of the future growth of the world economy was conducted and in terms of which its results were presented, have been consolidated into the essentially continental regions listed in Table 18-1.

The combined *total exports* and *total imports* of countries included in each region in the year 1970 and their levels as projected in the aforementioned study for the year 2000 are shown in Table 18-2. For purposes of comparison, each region's gross domestic product is entered alongside these regional foreign trade figures. The units of measurement are billions of dollars in base-year (i.e., 1970) prices.

Only a part of the external commodity trade of the countries included in each region moves by sea. On the other hand, some seaborne traffic originates and terminates in the same country. By comparing the 1970 base-year tonnages of various cargos that actually

## Table 18-2

Gross domestic product, total imports, and total exports—
*Future of the World Economy* Scenario A
*(billions of 1970 U.S. dollars)*

|  | GDP | Imports | Exports |
|---|---|---|---|
| **1970** |  |  |  |
| USSR, Eastern Europe | 599 | 30 | 30 |
| North America | 1059 | 69 | 67 |
| Western Europe | 804 | 162 | 159 |
| Middle East | 36 | 8 | 14 |
| Asia | 257 | 22 | 18 |
| Japan | 150 | 18 | 21 |
| Latin America | 154 | 18 | 18 |
| Africa | 68 | 13 | 12 |
| Oceania | 63 | 7 | 8 |
| Totals | 3190 | 347 | 347 |
| **2000** |  |  |  |
| USSR, Eastern Europe | 2752 | 133 | 174 |
| North America | 2374 | 192 | 219 |
| Western Europe | 2298 | 664 | 739 |
| Middle East | 989 | 234 | 103 |
| Asia | 874 | 85 | 83 |
| Japan | 865 | 107 | 139 |
| Latin America | 558 | 90 | 71 |
| Africa | 230 | 57 | 42 |
| Oceania | 136 | 27 | 19 |
| Totals | 11076 | 1589 | 1589 |

## Table 18-3

### Factors of conversion from trade value to freight tonnage[a]

| World model sector | Metric tons per 1970 $1000 | |
| --- | --- | --- |
| | Low | High |
| Other agriculture | 2.30 | 5.40 |
| Food processing | 2.10 | 3.80 |
| Textiles | 0.20 | 0.45 |
| Furniture, fixtures | 0.40 | 0.70 |
| Paper | 3.70 | 7.40 |
| Printed matter | 0.35 | 0.85 |
| Rubber | 0.45 | 0.90 |
| Chemicals, industrial | 2.35 | 4.95 |
| Chemicals, other | 0.35 | 0.50 |
| Cement | 25.0 | 50.0 |
| Glass | 2.80 | 5.50 |
| Motor vehicles | 0.45 | 0.60 |
| Other transportation equipment | 0.70 | 1.05 |
| Aircraft parts | 0.03 | 0.05 |
| Metal products | 3.00 | 7.80 |
| Machinery, electrical | 0.15 | 0.50 |
| Machinery, other | 0.15 | 0.35 |
| Instruments | 0.05 | 0.12 |
| Other manufactures | 1.20 | 3.50 |

[a]Calculated on the basis of detailed commodity trade data in *Yearbook of International Trade Statistics*, United Nations, 1971.

moved through the ports of each region with the corresponding total export and import figures, we were able to construct nine sets of conversion ratios—each set covering the cargos of one region. These ratios were then used in turn to translate projected regional import and export figures into the corresponding estimates of incoming and outgoing seaborne traffic. This is the traffic that the port facilities of each region should be capable of handling in the year 2000.

For manufactured goods, the calibration procedure referred to above was accomplished in two steps since, unlike raw materials, manufactures are generally measured in value terms. On the basis of the available trade statistics, a set of "weight per 1970 dollar value" ratios was computed that permitted us to translate both the 1970 and the projected 2000 dollar figures of each type of cargo into metric tons. These ratios, or ranges of ratios, used to convert dollar values to metric tons are given for 19 groups of manufactured goods in Table 18-3. Next, these derived base-year (1970) import

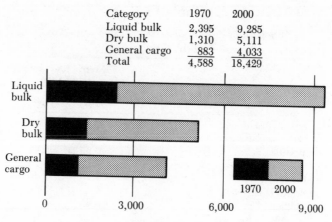

| Category | 1970 | 2000 |
|---|---|---|
| Liquid bulk | 2,395 | 9,285 |
| Dry bulk | 1,310 | 5,111 |
| General cargo | 883 | 4,033 |
| Total | 4,588 | 18,429 |

**Figure 18-2**

Total international oceanborne traffic—Sum of imports and exports of all regions *(millions of metric tons)*

and export tonnage figures were related to the corresponding quantities actually passing through the ports of each region. From this second comparison we calculated sets of regional conversion ratios like those described above.

Thus, we arrived at a tentative estimate of the tonnage of each type of cargo that will have to be handled by world ports in the year 2000. The projected increases from 1970 to 2000, grouped as liquid bulk, dry bulk, and general cargo, are represented by the three bars in Figure 18-2. As can be seen from Table 18-4, the combined total tonnage can be expected to more than quadruple over a period of 30 years.

As explained above, the projection of oceanborne traffic flows was actually calculated separately for over 30 specific commodity groups, and only afterward were these combined to form the three cargo classifications. Table 18-5 shows, for instance, the breakdown of the projected rise in the dry bulk traffic by eight commodity groups.

The projected increase from 1970 to 2000 in the total tonnage of general cargo, broken down into containerized and noncontainerized parts, is presented in Table 18-6.

The projections just described, broken down by regions, by types of cargo, and by specific commodity groups, provide the basis of our assessment of the additional port facilities of particular types that will be needed to load and unload the increased tonnages of the year

## Table 18-4

Port traffic—sum of imports and exports
*(millions of metric tons)*

| | | Bulk cargo | | | |
| | Liquid | Dry mineral | Other dry | Total bulk | General cargo |
|---|---|---|---|---|---|
| **1970** | | | | | |
| Middle East | 920 | 0 | 4 | 924 | 14 |
| Western Europe | 680 | 162 | 80 | 922 | 380 |
| Japan | 211 | 195 | 72 | 478 | 62 |
| North America | 196 | 136 | 98 | 430 | 180 |
| Latin America | 210 | 91 | 32 | 333 | 48 |
| Asia | 86 | 45 | 42 | 173 | 70 |
| Africa | 22 | 74 | 5 | 101 | 48 |
| USSR, Eastern Europe | 47 | 21 | 27 | 95 | 63 |
| Oceania | 23 | 67 | 9 | 99 | 18 |
| Totals | 2395 | 791 | 369 | 3555 | 883 |
| **2000** | | | | | |
| Middle East | 3928 | 176 | 41 | 4145 | 392 |
| Western Europe | 2020 | 389 | 229 | 2638 | 1721 |
| Japan | 1119 | 925 | 375 | 2419 | 359 |
| North America | 520 | 578 | 305 | 1403 | 594 |
| Latin America | 706 | 429 | 85 | 1220 | 228 |
| Asia | 590 | 291 | 213 | 1094 | 239 |
| Africa | 135 | 278 | 49 | 462 | 177 |
| USSR, Eastern Europe | 144 | 72 | 110 | 326 | 267 |
| Oceania | 123 | 163 | 24 | 310 | 56 |
| Totals | 9285 | 3301 | 1431 | 14017 | 4033 |

## Table 18-5

Composition of dry bulk traffic—sum of imports
and exports[a]
*(millions of metric tons)*

| | 1970 | 2000 |
|---|---|---|
| Iron ore | 393 | 1545 |
| Coal | 206 | 863 |
| Timber | 155 | 908 |
| Grains and feedstuffs | 222 | 599 |
| Fertilizers | 123 | 526 |
| Bauxite and alumina | 68 | 208 |
| Scrap and nonferrous ores | 53 | 210 |
| Other dry bulk | 111 | 272 |
| Totals | 1331 | 5131 |

[a]Includes some traffic not counted in regional totals.

## Table 18-6

Estimated increase in international general cargo from 1970 to 2000—
imports plus exports[a]
*(millions of metric tons)*

|  | Containerized | Noncontainerized | Total increase |
|---|---|---|---|
| Western Europe | 1090 | 251 | 1341 |
| North America | 308 | 106 | 414 |
| Middle East | 318 | 60 | 378 |
| Japan | 246 | 51 | 297 |
| USSR, Eastern Europe | 169 | 35 | 204 |
| Latin America | 146 | 34 | 180 |
| Asia | 143 | 26 | 169 |
| Africa | 107 | 22 | 129 |
| Oceania | 30 | 8 | 38 |
| Totals | 2557 | 593 | 3150 |

[a]Figures may vary up to ± 25% with changes in the composition of trade within world model sectors.

## Table 18-7

Cost profiles of ports—cost per berth
*(thousands of 1970 U.S. dollars)*

| Type of port 1 | Region type 2 | Construction costs 3 | Equipment costs 4 | Total costs 5 | Annual throughput 6 | Cost per ton 7 |
|---|---|---|---|---|---|---|
| General cargo | | | | | | |
| Break-bulk | developed | — | — | 2,825 | 125 | 22.6 |
|  | less developed | 1,870 | 550 | 2,420 | 120 | 20.2 |
| General cargo | | | | | | |
| Container terminal | developed | — | — | 14,000 | 750 | 18.60 |
|  | less developed | — | — | 5,115 | 500 | 10.23 |
| Liquid bulk | | | | | | |
| Berth only | developed | 36,300 | 70,100 | 106,400 | 147,000 | 0.72 |
| VLCC | less developed | — | — | 7,000 | 14,700 | 0.48 |
| Terminals[a] | developed | 249,600 | — | 364,700 | 147,000 | 2.48 |
| Dry bulk | | | | | | |
| Minerals[b] | | | | | | |
| Loading terminal | | | | | | |
| Low efficiency | | — | — | 8,000 | 3,500 | 2.29 |
| Medium efficiency | | — | — | 60,000 | 36,000 | 1.67 |
| High efficiency | | — | — | 50,000 | 60,000 | 0.83 |
| Unloading terminal | | | | | | |
| Low efficiency | | — | — | 13,000 | 5,000 | 2.60 |
| Medium efficiency | | — | — | 17,000 | 12,000 | 1.40 |
| High efficiency | | — | — | 22,000 | 24,000 | 0.92 |
| Dry bulk | | | | | | |
| Multipurpose | | 14,000 | 10,000 | 24,000 | 2,000 | 12.0 |

[a]Terminals designed to accommodate very large crude petroleum carriers. These include offshore terminals and deepwater piers.
[b]Three levels of efficiency are distinguished for dry bulk terminals according to the rated capacity of cargo-handling equipment installed at the port, the maximum size of ships that can be berthed, and the annual throughput corresponding to the cargo-handling equipment.

2000. The magnitude and composition of this traffic will determine the amount of capital that will have to be invested in construction of the new facilities.

If the projection of future traffic flows is difficult to make, the task of specifying the technical characteristics of future port facilities and of deriving the corresponding construction costs is still more complex. Without even attempting to describe in detail the procedure by which we have arrived at the final figures about to be presented, I limit myself to outlining the principal steps.

The amount of capital required for the construction of a modern port depends on the natural conditions of the site in which it is to be located, the annual throughput of different types of cargo to be handled, and the degree of mechanization of handling techniques to be adopted. It is, of course, this last factor that will largely determine the equipment costs for the facility.

To arrive at the appropriate range of investment costs per ton for each of several different types of new ports, we have examined actual investment figures for a great variety of recently constructed or enlarged ports. In doing so, we availed ourselves of the opportunity to consult some of the leading engineering firms engaged in planning and construction of large ports.

The cost profiles we derived for the various types of ports that will have to be built in the nine developed and less developed regions over the next 20 years are shown in Table 18-7. Each line of the table presents what might be called the profile of a typical port of one particular kind—a port that handles a certain kind of cargo or a particular cargo mix—and operates at a particular level of mechanization. The first column of the table specifies the type of port facility by the kind of cargo it handles and by its degree of mechanization. The definition of what is meant by low, medium, and high efficiency is given in Table 18-8. Column 2 in Table 18-7 indicates whether the typical port in question is located in a developed or a less developed region. The total dollar investment (valued in 1970 dollars) required to construct such a port—one of the particular type and region location—is entered in column 5. Whenever information was available, that figure was split into construction costs and equipment costs, which are shown, respectively, in columns 3 and 4. The annual throughput, that is, the total tonnage that the particular facility is designed to handle, is given in column 6. Finally, by dividing the total costs by annual tonnage handled, we arrive at an estimate of investment per ton of annual throughput, valued in terms of 1970 dollars.

## Table 18-8
### Classification of mineral dry bulk ports

| Category | Type | Capacity of equipment (TPH) | Maximum ship size (DWT) | Annual throughput (1000 metric tons) |
|---|---|---|---|---|
| High efficiency | Loading terminal | 20,000 | over 250,000 | 60,000 |
| | Unloading terminal | 6,000 | | 24,000 |
| Medium efficiency | Loading terminal | 12,000 | 80,000–250,000 | 36,000 |
| | Unloading terminal | 3,000 | | 12,000 |
| Low efficiency | Loading terminal | 4,000 | under 80,000 | 3,000–5,000 |
| | Unloading terminal | 1,000 | | |

## Table 18-9
### Investment expenditure in port facilities per ton of annual throughput
*(1970 U.S. dollars per ton)*

| | Liquid bulk | Dry bulk | | General cargo | |
|---|---|---|---|---|---|
| | | Minerals | Other | Noncontainerized | Containerized |
| North America | 2.48 | 1.54 | 12.00 | 22.60 | 18.60 |
| Western Europe | 0.72 | 1.40 | 12.00 | 22.60 | 18.60 |
| Japan | 2.48 | 0.92 | 12.00 | 22.60 | 18.60 |
| USSR, Eastern Europe | 0.72 | 1.67 | 12.00 | 22.60 | 18.60 |
| Oceania | 0.72 | 1.67 | 12.00 | 22.60 | 18.60 |
| Latin America | 0.48 | 1.67 | 12.00 | 20.20 | 10.23 |
| Asia | 0.48 | 1.67 | 12.00 | 20.20 | 10.23 |
| Africa | 0.48 | 1.67 | 12.00 | 20.20 | 10.23 |
| Middle East | 2.48 | 0.92 | 12.00 | 22.60 | 18.60 |

## Table 18-10
### Increase in seaborne traffic from 1970 to 2000[a]
*(millions of metric tons)*

| | Liquid bulk | Dry bulk | | General cargo |
|---|---|---|---|---|
| | | Minerals | Other | |
| North America | 324 | 442 | 207 | 414 |
| Western Europe | 1340 | 227 | 149 | 1341 |
| Japan | 908 | 730 | 303 | 297 |
| USSR, Eastern Europe | 97 | 51 | 83 | 204 |
| Oceania | 100 | 96 | 15 | 38 |
| Latin America | 496 | 338 | 53 | 180 |
| Asia | 504 | 246 | 171 | 169 |
| Africa | 113 | 204 | 44 | 129 |
| Middle East | 3008 | 176 | 37 | 378 |

[a]Figures derived from Table 18-4.

The information contained in Table 18-7 was used, in combination with our detailed projections of the volume and composition of additional cargo that will have to pass through the new port facilities in the year 2000, to estimate the investment per ton for each of the five principal kinds of cargo in each of the nine continental regions. These regional investment cost per ton figures are shown in Table 18-9.

Multiplying these per ton investment figures by the corresponding projected increases in annual traffic tonnage, for which figures are shown in Table 18-10, we finally arrive at estimates of the total amount of capital that will be needed in each region, and in the world as a whole, to provide the additional port facilities capable of handling the projected increase from 1970 to the year 2000 in international seagoing traffic. The figures, stated in 1970 dollars, are shown in Table 18-11. These investment requirements can be interpreted more meaningfully if expressed as percentages of the total investment that will have to be carried out over that 30-year period, in each region and in the world as a whole, according to the general growth scenario described at the beginning of this chapter. The highest percentage figure is shown for Africa, the smallest for the USSR and Eastern Europe. For the world as a whole, according to

### Table 18-11

Projected regional investment in additional port facilities to handle increase in seaborne traffic from 1970 to 2000, by region and type of port
*(millions of U.S. dollars)*

| | Type of port | | | | Total investment in ports | Investment in ports as a percentage of total investment[b] |
|---|---|---|---|---|---|---|
| | | Dry bulk | | | | |
| | Liquid bulk | Minerals | Other | General cargo[a] | | |
| North America | 804 | 681 | 2,484 | 8,248 | 12,217 | 0.30 |
| Western Europe | 965 | 318 | 1,788 | 26,383 | 29,454 | 0.75 |
| Japan | 2,252 | 672 | 3,636 | 5,828 | 12,388 | 0.72 |
| USSR, Eastern Europe | 70 | 85 | 996 | 4,002 | 5,133 | 0.09 |
| Oceania | 72 | 160 | 180 | 751 | 1,163 | 0.26 |
| Latin America | 238 | 565 | 636 | 2,330 | 3,769 | 0.49 |
| Asia | 242 | 411 | 2,052 | 2,128 | 4,833 | 0.51 |
| Africa | 39 | 341 | 528 | 1,649 | 2,557 | 1.14 |
| Middle East | 7,460 | 162 | 444 | 7,399 | 15,465 | 0.73 |
| World total | 12,142 | 3,395 | 12,744 | 58,718 | 86,999 | 0.44 |

[a]General cargo port includes container-handling materials.
[b]Total investment is the value of the incremental capital stock over the given period.

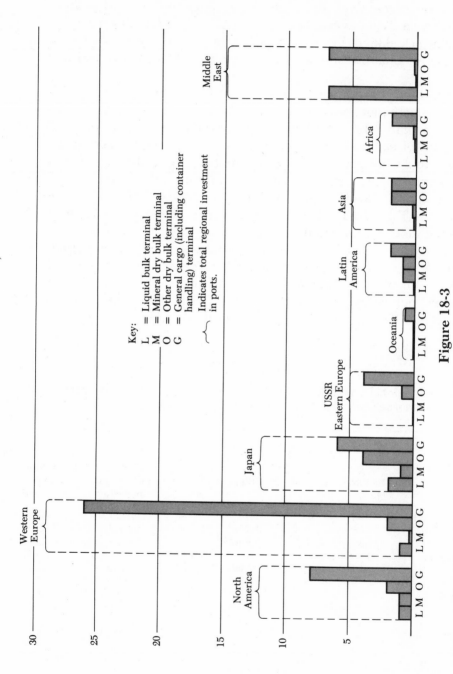

**Figure 18-3**

Projected investment in additional port facilities—total investment and investment by type of port in principal regions (*millions of 1970 U.S. dollars*)

Key:
L = Liquid bulk terminal
M = Mineral dry bulk terminal
O = Other dry bulk terminal
G = General cargo (including container handling) terminal
⎰ = Indicates total regional investment in ports.

these preliminary projections, construction of additional port facilities can be expected to absorb 0.44% of aggregate capital investment projected from 1970 to the year 2000. In Figure 18-3, the structured projection of port investment is presented region by region in graphic form.

# 19

## Technological change, prices, wages, and rates of return on capital in the U.S. economy

### (1985)

This chapter describes a refined version of the basic input-output price model and presents the results of the model's practical application to empirical economic analysis of the new wave of technological change that can be expected to affect profoundly the structure of the U.S. economy over the next two decades. This is precisely the kind of task for which input-output analysis was originally developed and to which it was first applied nearly 50 years ago.[1]

Thirty-five years later, Ann Carter[2] demonstrated how the reach of input-output analysis can be extended through more sophisticated theoretical interpretation of an enlarged data base. Further progress in that direction, however, was stymied by the lack of indispensable empirical data. Instead of rolling up their sleeves and engaging in the back-breaking task of factual inquiry, the great majority of investigators chose to take the much smoother path of pure theorizing. The Dorfman-Samuelson-Solow monograph, "Linear Programming and Economic Analysis"[3] marked the beginning of that phase. Pasanetti's "Lectures on the Theory of Production"[4]

[1]"Quantitative Input and Output Relations in the Economic System of the United States," *Review of Economics and Statistics* 18 (1936):105–25.

[2]A. Carter, *Structural Changes in the American Economy*, (Cambridge, Mass.: Harvard University Press, 1970).

[3]R. Dorfman, P. Samuelson, and R. Solow, *Linear Programming and Economic Analysis* (New York: McGraw-Hill, 1958).

[4]L. Pasinetti, *Lectures on the Theory of Production* (New York: Columbia University Press, 1977).

In conducting the research some of whose results are presented in this chapter, the author was assisted by the staff of the Institute for Economic Analysis of New York University. He is particularly indebted to Dr. Glenn-Marie Lange and George Papaconstantinou for programming and carrying out most of the computations.

provide a comprehensive picture of the present state of such theoretical inquiry.

Successful efforts to enlarge the necessary data base permit us now to step back from simply tracing the direct and indirect repercussions of given structural change toward factual explanation of the choice processes leading to replacement of the old by a new technology.

A concise description of the technology governing the operations of a given industry and in particular its relations to other sectors of the economy can be visualized as a "cooking recipe," specifying the amounts of all current inputs—such as raw and intermediate materials, labor of various types, and so on—as well as the stocks of buildings, machinery, and inventories of different kinds required for production of its output. As in a kitchen cooking recipe, both the input flows and the stocks of implements needed to handle them are measured per unit of output. A change in technology can thus be described as a change in the cooking recipe. If an entirely new good is introduced, its position within the technological structure of the economy has to be specified in terms of the cooking recipe used in producing it and also in terms of the introduction of that good into the cooking recipes of sectors that will utilize it.

Given such technical recipes, one for each producing sector, the following $n$ equations—in which prices, wage rates, and the rate of return on the stock of capital appear as variables—can describe the balance between the revenue received and the total outlays—including wages and returns on the capital invested—incurred per unit of its output by each sector $i$.

$$(19\text{-}1) \quad P_i - \underbrace{(a_{1i}P_1 + a_{2i}P_2 \cdots + a_{ni}P_n)}_{\substack{\text{costs of current} \\ \text{material inputs}}} - \underbrace{(b_{1i}P_1 + b_{2i}P_2 + \cdots + b_{ni}P_n)}_{\substack{\text{returns on} \\ \text{capital invested}}}$$

$$- \underbrace{(l_{1i}w_{1i} + l_{2i}w_{2i} + \cdots + l_{mi}w_{mi})}_{\substack{\text{costs of} \\ \text{labor inputs}}} = 0$$

where

$a_{ij}$ = the input coefficient describing the amount of the output of industry $i$ required to produce one unit of output of industry $j$

$l_{hj}$ = the labor coefficient describing the amount of labor services of type $h$ employed to produce one unit of the output of industry $j$

$b_{ij}$ = the capital coefficient describing the stock of goods that industry $j$ has to employ per unit of its output

$P_i$ = the price of the product of industry $i$

$r$ = the long-run rate of return on capital (same in all industries)

$w_{hj}$ = the wage per unit of labor of type $h$ employed by industry $j$

$$i, j = 1, 2, \ldots, n \qquad h = 1, 2, \ldots, m$$

Current flows of goods and labor services required to maintain and to replace the stocks of goods described by the capital coefficients $b_{ij}$ are included in the corresponding flow coefficient $a_{ij}$ and $l_{hj}$ (see below).

This system of $n$ equations describing the relationship among the prices of all the different goods, the wages of all different types of labor, and the rate of return on capital maintained within the framework of a given technology, or rather a given set of technologies—one for each producing sector—can be summarized by means of compact matrix notation in the following simple form.

(19-2)                          $(I - A' - \hat{r}B')P - \overline{W} = 0$

$$A = \begin{bmatrix} a_{11} & \cdots & & & a_{1n} \\ & & & & \\ \vdots & & & & \vdots \\ & & & & \\ a_{n1} & \cdots & & & a_{nn} \end{bmatrix}$$

$$B = \begin{bmatrix} b_{11} & \cdots & & b_{1n} \\ & & & \\ \vdots & & & \vdots \\ & & & \\ b_{n1} & \cdots & & b_{nn} \end{bmatrix} \qquad \hat{r} = \begin{bmatrix} r & 0 & \cdots & & 0 \\ 0 & r & & & 0 \\ \vdots & & & & \\ & & & & r \\ 0 & 0 & \cdots & & \end{bmatrix}$$

$$P = \begin{bmatrix} P_1 \\ P_2 \\ \vdots \\ P_n \end{bmatrix} \quad \overline{W} = \begin{bmatrix} W_1 \\ W_2 \\ \vdots \\ W_j \\ \vdots \\ W_n \end{bmatrix} \quad \text{where } W_j = \sum_{i=1}^{m} l_{ij}w_{ij} \quad I = \begin{bmatrix} 1 & 0 & \cdots & & 0 \\ 0 & 1 & & & \\ \vdots & & 1 & & \\ & & & & 0 \\ 0 & \cdots & & 0 & 1 \end{bmatrix}$$

Solving for the price vector $P$, considered to be a function of the rate of return on capital $r$, and the wage rates (computed per unit of output) $\overline{W}$, the above equation yields

(19-3)                          $P = (I - A' - rB')^{-1}\overline{W}$

This formula is essentially an elaboration of the often used simpler input-output relationship between prices and the column vector $V$ of values added per unit of output in different industries:

$$P = (1 - A')^{-1}V \text{ with } V = \hat{r}B'P + \overline{W}$$

The introduction of the matrix $B$ of capital coefficients and of the rate of return on capital $r$ permits inclusion of both into the bracketed square matrix that is being inverted. Each element of column vector $\overline{W}$ represents the average wage costs per unit of its output in each industry, that is, averages of money wage rates earned by different skills weighted by appropriate labor input coefficients.

With all technical parameters fixed, the expression on the right-hand side of equation (19-3) can be interpreted as a function of $r$ and $\overline{W}$; in other words, the prices represented by vector $P$ can be considered to be dependent on the rate of return on capital and the money wages paid for various types of labor in different industries.

If all elements of the inverse $(I - A' - rB')^{-1}$ are positive, an increase in any of the wage rates must necessarily lead to an increase in some, and most likely all, prices. Moreover, if all wage rates were multiplied by the same positive factor, say $\lambda$ (which might be smaller or larger than 1), while $r$ is kept constant, all prices would obviously change in the same proportion, $\lambda$. That means that the real wages would remain the same as they were before; so, of course, will the total real returns on investment.

With unchanged technology and given money wage rates, an increase in the rate of return on capital $r$ must necessarily be accompanied by an increase in prices, that is, a reduction in the real wage rates, and vice versa, a rise in the real wage rates by a reduction in the rate of return on capital. But prices are not likely to change in the same proportions. The measurement of changes in real wages requires, because of that, the use of a somewhat arbitrarily defined cost-of-living index, $\overline{P}(r)$, which would, of course, reflect price changes caused by any upward or downward shift in the rate of return to capital $r$. The conventional index formula used in computations described below is

(19-4)                           $$\overline{P}(r) = P'(r)y^0$$

where $y^0$ is a column vector of weights $(y_1^0, y_2^0 \cdots)$, each representing the base-year fraction of total household expenditure devoted to the purchase of the products of one particular industry.

Since the inverse of the bracketed expression on the right-hand side of equation (19-3) is a nonlinear function of $r$, the price vectors $P(r)$ and ultimately the levels of real wages corresponding to different values of $r$ (10%, 12%, etc.) had to be computed one by one. Each such computation began by inversion of that matrix after the particular value of $r$ had been inserted into it. Next, the corresponding price vector $P(r)$ was computed by multiplying that inverse into the column vector $\overline{W}$ whose elements represent the money wage paid out—per unit of their respective outputs—by different industries in the base year 1979. Next, the cost-of-living index $\overline{P}(r)$ was computed by multiplying the row vector $P'(r)$ by the column vector of base-year weights according to equation (19-4).

Even as the rate of return on capital $r$ was assigned different values, all *money* wages, that is, all elements of matrix $W$, were kept constant at their base-year values. Hence the effects of changes in $r$ on the *real* wage rates were transmitted in our computations via corresponding changes in prices—more specifically, via upward or downward shifts in the cost of living index $\overline{P}(r)$. If money wages are fixed, real wages, up to the arbitrary definition of their base-year level, must shift directly proportionally to the inverse, $1/\overline{P}(r)$, of the cost-of-living index.

So that the computationally convenient assumption of constant money wages will not be interpreted as an additional constraint on the operational properties of the system, it can be shown that both the relative prices of different goods and the level of real wages, that is, the purchasing power of money wages, depend within this framework only on the relative, not the absolute, levels of money wage rates paid in different sectors.

Without entering into detailed analysis of the physical input-output flows, of which the price-cost income system we deal with now represents a "dual" counterpart, it suffices to observe that the internal consistency of the entire system is such that any redirection of income flows, from returns on capital to labor earnings or vice versa, will be accompanied by corresponding shifts in physical commodity flows and price changes.

Having described the interdependence of the rate of return on capital, real wage rates, and prices within the framework of a given technological structure, we can now turn to the analysis of the relationship between these variables and technological change. That relationship is described below within a concrete empirical context.

The recently completed report on *The Future Impact of Automation on Workers*[5] involved construction of a dynamic input-output

[5] W. Leontief and F. Duchin, *The Future Impact of Automation on Workers* (New York: Oxford University Press, 1985).

model of the American economy and compilation of two data bases consisting of two different sets of technical coefficients, one describing the old "cooking recipes" employed by the 85 producing sectors into which the U.S. economy was broken down for that purpose in the base year 1979, and the other describing in the same way the technologies that, according to expert—mainly engineering—judgments and actual experience with newly constructed plants, can be expected to replace present methods of production by the year 2000. Each of these two data sets consists of a matrix of current non-labor inputs coefficients, a matrix of labor coefficients describing the labor requirements of each of the 85 industries in terms of 53 different occupations, and a matrix of capital coefficients, that is, of stock-flow coefficients specifying the capital structure of each industry. Input coefficients, describing the flows needed to maintain and to replace the requisite capital stock after having been estimated separately, were, as stated above, incorporated into the matrices specifying other current input requirements. In the analysis that follows, the set of matrices describing the 1979 input requirements will be referred to as representing the "old technology," while the other set will specify the "new technology."

The tradeoff between the rate of return on capital $r$ and the level of real wages, reflecting the requirements and capabilities of the old technology that controlled the operations of the U.S. economy in the year 1979—computed by the method described above—is presented in Figure 19-1 by the solid sloping line. Different rates of return on capital are plotted along the vertical axis, while the corresponding levels of real wages are measured along the horizontal axis. In this particular computation, intersectoral difference in the money and consequently real wages of different skills were assumed not to change. As the rate of return on capital $r$ goes up or down and the relative prices of different goods shift accordingly, relative money and consequently also real wages of different skills are assumed not to change.

Point $a$ marks approximately the position occupied by the U.S. economy in the base year 1979. The average rate of return on capital invested in different industries is about 12.5 percent. The corresponding level of the index of real wages measured along the horizontal axis is set equal to 1.0. Moving upward from that point, we find that a drop of real wages to 0.75 percent of that base-year level would permit a rise in the rate of return on capital to 22 percent.

As explained before and as can be seen by examining both ends of the curve, the relationship traced by it is nonlinear. However,

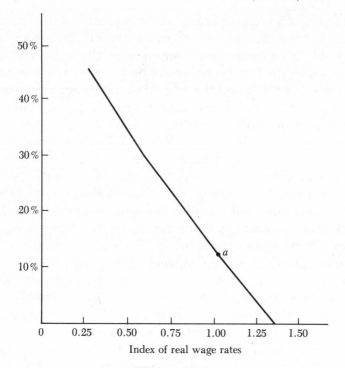

**Figure 19-1**

Tradeoff between the rate of return on capital *r* and real wage rates under the old technology

within the practically relevant range of rates of return on capital lying, say, below 30 percent and above 10 percent, it is nearly linear.

In interpreting the meaning and significance of this curve, it is important to realize that the relationships between the changes in the rates of return on capital and the level of real wage rates described by it hold for each industry regardless of the technology it employs, the output it produces, and the inputs it uses. The reason is that the specific quantitative relationship between the rate of return on capital or the level of real wages must in the long run be the same for all industries regardless of what they produce and what inputs and technology they use. The operation of a more or less competitive (i.e., a more or less uniform) price system accounts for that.

Shifts in the relative prices of different goods reflecting changes in the comparative costs of production brought about by a rise or a reduction in the rate of return on capital and a corresponding rise or fall in real wage rates are plotted in Figure 19-2. As in Figure 19-1, the rate of return on capital $r$ is measured on this graph along the vertical axis (the corresponding changes in real wages can be read off on Figure 19-1). Relative prices, that is, money prices divided by the cost-of-living index $\bar{P}(r)$, are measured along the horizontal axis with all units calibrated so as to make the base-year price of each good equal to 1. Hence all price curves intersect each other at that point.

These curves, plotted only for a few selected goods, show that a rise in $r$ (accompanied by a corresponding fall in real wages) would, for instance, cause the relative prices of steel, communication (except radio and television), and health services to go up, and the prices of wood containers and retail trade services to fall.

**Figure 19-2**

Relationships between the general rate of return on capital $r$ and the relative prices of the outputs of selected industries

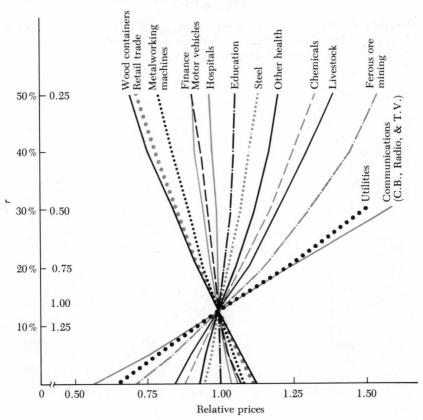

This is obviously caused by the fact that the manufacture of the first three types of goods requires—directly and indirectly—comparatively more capital than the production of the last two types, which, on the other hand, require relatively larger labor inputs. Complete listing—in descending order—of figures describing such price changes for all 85 groups of goods and services is given in the Appendix 19-1.

To examine the possible effects of a complete changeover from the old to the new technology, we turn to Figure 19-3. The solid curve here is identical to that shown on Figure 19-1; however, both the vertical and the horizontal scales are changed. As explained above, the figure describes the tradeoff relationship between the rate of return on capital and the level of real wages existing under the old technology. The broken line describes that relationship as it would be if new technological "cooking recipes" had replaced the old in all industries.

### Figure 19-3

The tradeoff between the rate of return on capital *r* and the real wage rate under the old technology (————), the new technology (— — — —), and the "myopic" steel industry new technology (————)

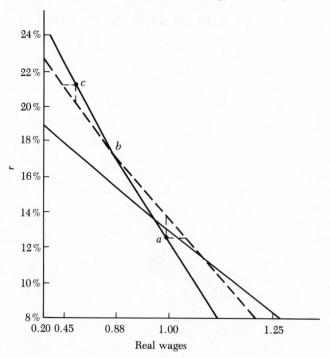

Real wages

Consider a situation in which the choice is being made from the original position described by point *a* on the old curve. An upward move toward the broken curve along the vertical dotted line would mean an increase in the rate of return on capital with the level of real wages remaining the same as it was before. A move to the right along the horizontal dotted line would, on the other hand, signify a rise in real wages with the rate of return on capital remaining unchanged. A choice of an intermediate position between these two means that the benefits brought about by adoption of the new technology would be shared by wage earners and those who receive income on capital.

If, however, the initial position of the U.S. economy on the old curve were located, say, at point *c*, adoption of the new technology would demand income sacrifices on the part of either one or another group or by both of them.

Below the intersection of the two curves at point *b* (rate of return on capital 17.5%, real wage rates 0.88), the new set of technology is obviously more "cost-efficient" than the old; above that point the old technology can, however, hold its own.

The computation of the cost of living index and the corresponding real wage level—as has already been observed above—must, as with any other aggregative procedure, contain certain elements of arbitrariness. This becomes particularly obvious if under conditions of technological change some of the old commodities or services are eliminated and some new items are added to the list of consumer purchases. In this context, however, it is important to note that many, if not most, of the new products and services presently being introduced as a result of new technologies are essentially intermediate outputs absorbed by various productive processes, rather than finished consumer goods. In the system of input-output equations whose solution permits us to compare the relationship between the rate of return on capital and the level of real wage rates, the introduction of new and the elimination of old, intermediate goods is accounted for concisely, without resorting to any kind of index number computations.

Examining how a replacement of the old by the new technology in all industries would affect the relative prices of their respective outputs, we found that the products of Hospitals (81), Health Servies Except Hospitals (82), and Educational Services (83) will rise in prices more than the output of any of the other sectors.

This prompted us to explore what would happen if new technologies were introduced throughout the entire economy except in these three sectors, which would continue to use the old technologies. The results of these computations are shown in Figure 19-4.

The solid and corresponding broken lines describe, here as they do in Figure 19-3, the effect of general changeover from the old to new technologies. The dash-dot line shows the income frontier that could be reached if the new "cooking recipes" were introduced in all but the education and health care industries. Comparing this line's position with that of the two other curves, one must conclude that introduction of new technologies in the education and health sectors hampers rather than advances the income-generating capacity of the economy, if income is measured in terms of the rate of return on capital and the corresponding level of real wage rates. This is not surprising.

Replacement of the old by the new technology obviously tends to

### Figure 19-4

Relationship between the rate of return on capital $r$ and the real wage rates under old technology in all industries (————), new technology in all industries (— — —), and new technology in all but the health and education industries (— · — · — ·)

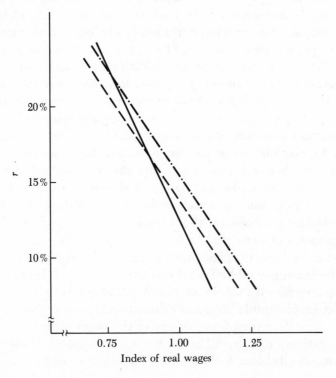

Index of real wages

increase rather than reduce the costs of producing educational and . health service. Under the present institutional setup, it is being heavily subsidized by financial transfer, via government budget, of capital and wage income earned in other sectors. A sharper theoretical formulation explicitly taking into account taxes and subsidies[6] implemented by a more differentiated data base should make it possible to trace the underlying input-output relationships in greater detail. In the meantime, it suffices to observe that in education and particularly in health care, the introduction of new technologies can definitely be expected to improve the quality of the final product and, with it, the benefits accruing to its consumers. To the extent to which these benefits accrue from entirely new goods, they can be legitimately included neither in the cost-of-living index nor in the measure of real wages and consequently of real income as used in the present formulation of the input-output model. As a matter of fact, one can observe that the payment of the opportunity costs of such benefits, in terms of either reduced real wage rates or a diminished rate of return on capital, is controlled by essentially political decisions; so, of course, would be any move in the direction of fiscal retrenchment resulting in delayed introduction of new technologies in these fields.

Having visualized up to now the process of technological change as an elimination contest between two teams, we have assessed their comparative strengths and examined the conditions and consequences of the eventual victory of the new over the old team, treating each of them, except in the last computation, as an indivisible set.

At the risk of placing too great a burden on a fragile data base that might not sustain it, we will proceed now to apply the same selection criteria to formation of a mixed team representing an optimal combination of players picked from both groups.

Formulated from this in a sense less restrictive point of view, the question to be answered is what combinations of technologies—old in some sectors, new in others—would be capable of yielding the highest rates of return on capital for various given levels of real wage rates, or, essentially an equivalent question, what combinations would secure the highest levels of real wages for given alternative levels of the rate of return on capital.

The procedure for selecting an optimal combination of "cooking recipes," described in terms of corresponding input vectors, is, of

---

[6]The role of taxes and subsidies can be made explicit by introduction of corresponding negative or positive terms in the price-income equations of system (19-1).

course, linear programming. As a matter of fact, the Simplex method—the algorithm most often used for this purpose—was invented by George D. Dantzig some 30 years ago in connection with one of the early practical applications of the input-output method.[7] In accordance with the approach used above, this programming procedure was applied step by step to trace the effects of changes in the given rate of return on capital $r$ on the choice of technologies and consequently also of the relative prices that would maximize the general level of real wage rates.

Each step involves fixing in the set of basic equations (19-2) the rate of interest $r$, keeping constant the money wage rates represented by the rectangular matrix of all $w_{hj}$'s, and then finding, by means of the simplex algorithm, the optimal combination of old and new "cooking recipes" to be used in different industries that would minimize the cost-of-living index $\overline{P}(r)$ as defined in equation (19-4). Each industry has a choice between the old and the new technology. Although in the situation considered below, this does not actually happen, the optimal combination of technologies could involve liquidation of some old industries and introduction of some entirely new ones. In the case of final consumer goods, as has been said above, this can create an essentially insoluble index number problem.

The mathematical linear programming problem stated above is as follows. Minimize $\overline{P} = (Y_1 P_1 + Y_2 P_2 + \cdots + Y_n P_n)$ subject to $2n$ constraints:

$$(1 - g_{11}^0)P_1 - g_{21}^0 P_2 - \cdots \qquad - g_{n1}^0 P_n \geq \overline{W}_1^0$$

(19-6)
$$-g_{1n}^0 P_1 - g_{2n}^0 P_2 - \cdots (1 - g_{nn}^0)P_n \geq \overline{W}_n^0$$
$$(1 - g_{11}^1)P_1 - g_{21}^1 P_2 - \cdots \qquad - g_{n1}^1 P_n \geq \overline{W}_1^1$$

$$-g_{1n}^1 P_1 - g_{2n}^1 P_2 - \cdots (1 - g_{nn}^1)P_n \geq \overline{W}_n^1$$

$$g_{ij} = (1 - a_{ji} - r b_{ji})$$

The superscripts 0 and 1 indicate the old and new technologies, respectively.

In the solution of the minimization problem, the $2n$ inequalities

[7]G. D. Dantzig, *Linear Programming and Extensions*, report prepared for U.S. Air Force Project Rand 1967, Rand Corporation.

are reduced to $n$ equations, each reflecting the preferred technology for one of different producing sectors. These equations yield a set of $n$ prices that minimize the magnitude of the cost-of-living index $\bar{P}$ and thus maximize the corresponding real wage rates with all money wages, $w_{hj}$, considered as fixed.

The "dual" (maximizing) problem to the minimizing problem presented above is as follows. Maximize the wage bill, $Z = W_1^0 x_1^0 + W_2^0 x_1^0 \cdots W_n^0 x_n^0 + W_1^1 x_1^1 + W_2^1 x_2^1 + \cdots + W_n^1 x_n^1$, subject to:

$$
\begin{aligned}
[(g_{11}^0 - 1)x_1^0 + g_{12}^0 x_2^0 + \cdots + g_{1n}^0 x_n^0 + (g_{11}^1 - 1)x_1^1 + g_{12}^1 x_2^1 & \\
+ \cdots + g_{1n}^1 x_n^1] & \leq y_1 \\
g_{21}^0 x_1^0 + (g_{22}^0 - 1)x_2^0 + \cdots + g_{2n}^0 x_n^0 + g_{21}^1 x_1^1 + (g_{22}^1 - 1)x_2^1 & \\
+ \cdots + g_{2n}^1 x_n^1 & \leq y_2
\end{aligned}
$$

(19-7)

$$
\begin{aligned}
g_{n1}^0 x_1^0 + g_{n2} x_2 + \cdots + (g_{nn}^0 - 1)x_n^0 + g_{n1}^1 x_1^1 + g_{11}^1 x_2^1 & \\
+ \cdots + (g_{nn}^1 - 1)x_n^1 & \leq y_n
\end{aligned}
$$

where $x_i^0$ = the output of industry $i$ using old technology

$x_i^1$ = output of industry $i$ using new technology

The maximizing solution will contain not more than $n$ nonnegative outputs, either $x_i^0$ or $x_i^1$ for any industry $i$. While the relative magnitudes of the levels of outputs of different industries naturally depend on the relative magnitude of the elements of the final demand, say, $y_1, y_i, \ldots, y_n$, the optimal selection of technologies is independent of either.

The dash-dot curve in Figure 19-5 traces the best possible combination of the rate of return on capital $r$ and the level of real wages that could have been attained if an appropriate optimal mix of old and new technologies were used at each point of that line. The optimal mix of the old and new technologies yields naturally a higher value added than straight lineups of either one of the two. The corresponding changes in relative prices of all goods and services are listed in Appendix 19-2.

Table 19-1 provides a deeper insight into the role of the levels and changes in the level of the rate of return on capital $r$ and the corresponding real wage rates in the ongoing process of replacing the old technologies used by various U.S. industries in the year 1979

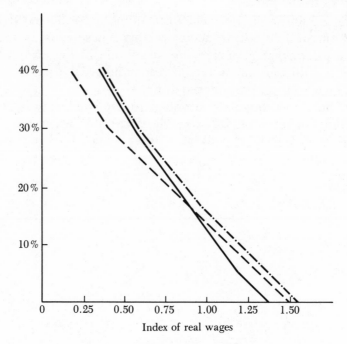

**Figure 19-5**

Tradeoff between the rate of return on capital $r$ and real wage rates for old technology in all industries (———), new technology in all industries (— — — —), and the mix of old and new technologies determined by linear programming (— · — · — ·)

by fairly well-known new technologies. It is based on detailed industry-by-industry comparison of the eight different solutions of the linear programming problem described above each corresponding to one of the following combinations of the rate of return on capital and the corresponding real wage rate levels:

> 40%, 0.36
> 30%, 0.57
> 21.%, 0.78
> 18.56%, 0.84
> 15.00%, 0.96
> 12.50%, 1.00
> 10.00%, 1.07
> 5.00%, 1.20
> .00%, 1.35

The distribution of sectors among the nine parts of the table is

## Table 19-1

Tabulation of sectors according to the highest rate of return on capital and lowest level of real wages at which the old technology is replaced by the new technology[a]

| Real wage index | | | | |
|---|---|---|---|---|
| 0.36 | 0.56 | 0.78 | 0.84 | 0.93 |
| **Rate of return on capital** | | | | |
| 40% | 30% | 21% | 18.56% | 15% |
| Computers (50) | Lumber products (19) | Nonferrous metals mining (6) | Iron and ferroalloy mining (5) | Livestock (1) |
| Semiconductors (58) | Wood containers (20) | Coal mining (7) | Household furniture (21) | Forestry and fisheries (3) |
| Government enterprises (85) | Petroleum refining (30) | Stone and clay mining (9) | Printing and publishing (25) | Agricultural, forestry, and fishery service (4) |
| | Real estate (75) | Chemical and fertilizer mining (10) | Primary iron and steel (36) | Crude petroleum and natural gas (8) |
| | | Construction (11) | Metal containers (38) | Fabrics (15) |
| | | Food (13) | General industrial equipment (48) | Misc. fabricated textile products (18) |
| | | Tobacco (14) | Electronic components n.e.c. (59) | Other furniture and fixtures (22) |
| | | Paper (23) | Misc. manufacturing (66) | Leather tanning (32) |
| | | Paper containers (24) | | Heating, plumbing, other metal products (39) |
| | | Chemicals (26) | | Screw machine products (40) |
| | | Plastics (27) | | Other fabricated metal products (41) |
| | | Drugs (28) | | Farm and garden machinery (43) |
| | | Paints (29) | | Special industrial equipment (47) |
| | | Stone and clay products (35) | | Electrical industrial equipment (53) |
| | | Engines and turbines (42) | | Radio, TV, and communications equipment (56) |
| | | Construction machinery (44) | | Electron tubes (57) |
| | | Materials handling equipment (45) | | |
| | | Service industry machinery (52) | | |
| | | Other transport equipment (63) | | |

## Table 19-1 (Cont.)

| Real wage index | | | | |
|---|---|---|---|---|
| 0.36 | 0.56 | 0.78 | 0.84 | 0.93 |
| | | Transportation and warehousing (67)<br>Radio and TV broadcasting (69)<br>Wholesale trade (71)<br>Finance (73)<br>Insurance (74)<br>Misc. textiles (16)<br>Apparel (17) | | Misc. electrical machinery (60)<br>Scientific and controlling instruments (64)<br>Communications, except radio and TV (68)<br>Other fabricated metal products (41) |

| Real wage index | | | | |
|---|---|---|---|---|
| 0.99 | 1.06 | 1.20 | 1.35 | All other |
| **Rate of return on capital** | | | | |
| 12.5% | 10% | 5% | 0 | All other |
| Footwear (33)<br>Glass products (34)<br>Primary nonferrous metal manufacture (37)<br>Household appliances (54)<br>Aircraft and parts (62)<br>Retail trade (72) | Ordnance (12)<br>Rubber and misc. plastics (31)<br>Misc. machinery except electric (49)<br>Motor vehicles (61)<br>Electric, gas, water service (70)<br>Nonprofit organizations (84) | Metalworking machinery (46)<br>Electric lighting and wiring (55)<br>Optical and photo equipment (65)<br>Auto repair (79) | Other agricultural products (2)<br>Business services (77) | Office machines (51)<br>Hotels, personal and repair service (76)<br>Eating and drinking places (78)<br>Amusements (80)<br>Hospitals (81)<br>Health services, excluding hospitals (82)<br>Educational services, private (83)<br>Robotics manufacture (86)<br>Instructional TV (87)<br>Computer based instruction (88)<br>Public education (89) |

aFor example, the new technology will be adopted by the livestock sector (1) if the rate of return $r$ is less than or equals 15% (the level of real wages $W$ is equal to or is higher than 0.93) but not if it is as high as 18.56%. Thus, this sector appears in the 15% column.

governed by the following rule. The industries listed in a particular column would find it advantageous to use the new technology if the rate of return on capital equals or is lower (and the level of wages is accordingly equal or higher) than that shown in that column's heading. For instance, computer manufacturing (50), semiconductors (58), and government enterprises (85), listed in the left-hand column, would use the new instead of the old technology if the general rate of return on capital were as high as 40 percent or lower and the wage index as low as 0.36 or higher. If the rate of return on capital were 30 percent, not only the three sectors mentioned above but also lumber products (19), wood containers (20), petroleum refining(30), and real estate (75) would convert to the new technology. With the rate of return being 21 percent or below, 24 additional sectors, listed in the third column from the left, would join the procession, and so on. On the other end we see metalworking machinery (46), electrical lighting and wiring (45), optical and photographic equipment (65), auto repair (79), and finally other agricultural products (2) and business services (77) that would modernize only if the return on capital, that is, the cost of capital, approached zero.

Industries falling into the "all other" column on the right-hand side of the table would—according to the results of these computations—continue to rely on the old technology even if capital were practically free. Hospitals, health services excluding hospitals, and educational services, as was observed above, do actually introduce the new expensive technology because they are being heavily subsidized. Except for Office Machines (51), all sectors in this group produce consumer services of different kinds and deliver them directly to Households. Adoption of a new technology involves in this instance mostly introduction of new, more sophisticated, and more expensive products. As has been observed above, the standard description of consumer goods delivered to Households employed in this study tends to register price increases while neglecting quality improvements. It is no wonder that the linear programming procedure aimed at minimizing costs rejects the new and chooses the old technology.

This preliminary investigation had to stop at this point because factual information needed for more detailed systematic (as contrasted to casual and illustrative) analysis of the nature of consumer demand is still lacking.

Because of the fundamental weakness of our data base, which might not be accurate enough to satisfy the rigorous requirements of linear programming applications, conclusions based on these computations are very likely to be subject to a high degree of error.

The linear programming formulation and the results of its empirical implementation presented above should contribute to settlement of the switching and reswitching controversy that for many years pitted the sharpest minds of Cambridge, Massachusetts, against the brightest theoretical lights of Cambridge, England.

A numerical test example can be easily constructed of a simple—say, three-sector—input-output system described by equations (18-6) in which the "cooking recipes" included in the optimal solutions of the linear programming problem are such that some recipes would drop out if the rate of return $r$ goes up from 5 percent to, say, 10 percent, but would reappear again in the optimal solution when $r$ rises further to 15 percent. Examination of Table 18-1 shows that within the range of rates of return on capital between as low as 0 percent and as high as 40 percent, the choice between the old and the new technologies now confronting the U.S. economy actually does not, however, contain even a single instance of reswitching.

Cost comparisons between the old and the new technology are in fact not being carried out by means of computations involving systematic use of an empirically implemented, detailed model of the entire national economy. As a rule, they are made by managers of independent profit-making businesses on the basis of much more restricted sets of data available to them. These decision makers can, of course, be expected to possess a thorough knowledge of the old technology actually used in their particular industries as well as pretty good information on the new technology that could replace it. The prices, in terms of which the cost comparisons are made between these two alternatives, are typically those observed at the time when the critical choice is being made, that is, prices reflecting the dominance of the old method of production not only in the industry in question but in all other industries as well.

The tradeoff between the rate of return on capital and the wage level estimated in such a simple but myopic manner for the U.S. steel industry (industry 36) is represented in Figure 19-3 by the thin solid line.

The computation of that relation between $r$ and $\lambda$ (the general level of wages) is based on the following slightly rearranged form of the 36th equation pertaining to the steel industry in system (19-1).

$$(19\text{-}5) \qquad P_{36} - \sum_{j=1}^{j=n} (a_{j36}P_j) - r \sum_{j=1}^{j=n} (b_{j36}P_j) = \lambda \sum_{h=1}^{h=m} (1_{h36}W_{h36})$$

The scalar $\lambda$ is an index of the general level of wage rates. No distinction can be made in this case between the money and real wage rates. The wage level λ must move up, of course, when $r$ goes down, and vice versa.

The numerical values of technical coefficients, that is, of all $a$'s and $b$'s, describe the "cooking recipe" that the steel industry would use after introduction of the new technology. The prices, the $p$'s, inserted in that equation, however, are those observed before the shift from the old to the new technologies has actually taken place. Instead of being observed directly, these old prices, of course, could be computed indirectly by solving a system of simultaneous equations (19-1), after inserting in them the appropriate set of *old* technical coefficients as well as the appropriate (base-year) values of the rate of return of capital and money wage rates $w$.

The costing out of the new technology, in terms of prices reflecting the state of all industries under the old technologies, is bound to be biased, except, of course, in the unlikely case in which even after the steel industry had adopted the new technology all other industries actually continued to stick to the old.

Examining Figure 19-3, we find that, so long as the managers in the steel industry base their assessment of the new technology on the simple but myopic cost computation whose results are described by the thin solid line, they have to rule against its introduction if the rate of return on capital is expected to exceed 14% and the corresponding index of wage rates falls below 0.9, which marks the point at which that line intersects the heavy solid line.

A more comprehensive and correct assessment of the effect of the introduction of new technology would recommend replacement of the old technology so long as the rate of return on capital does not exceed 17.5 percent and the wage index does not fall below 0.88, at which point the solid line is intersected by the broken line.

Similar comparison between unbiased and what one might call biased computation carried out for the other industries shows that the bias can turn out to be in the opposite direction.

To assess the overall effects of the difference between the technology mix resulting from reliance on observed base-year prices and that determined through application of the linear programming procedure, one can compare the corresponding tradeoff curves between the rates of return on capital and real wage rates.[8]

Such comparision has shown that, while deviating from each other

[8]The shape of the tradeoff curve computed on the basis of the technology mix obtained through biased assessment of the new technology in terms of the "old" prices must of necessity depend on the rates of return and wage rates that acttually prevailed in the base year during which they actually have been observed.

on their upper and their lower ends, the two tradeoff curves nearly coincide in the practically important range of interest rates lying above 12% and below 21%. This seems to demonstrate that, at least in the case under consideration, technology choice guided by the interactive operations of conventional competitive market mechanisms will not differ greatly from that made on the basis of a formal linear programming approach.

Further utilization of methodological procedures developed and the factual findings presented in this chapter can be pursued in many different directions. Detailed descriptions of the mutual interdependence of prices, real wages, and the rate of return on capital incorporated in the large dynamic input-output models now employed in studies of economic growth would contribute to a deeper explanation of the role played in that process by technological change. Another, immediate application of these findings could consist of explicit introduction of the comparative cost principle in the formulation and empirical implementation of multiregional input models such as the large multiregional UN model of the world economy.[9]

[9]W. Leontief, A. Carter, and P. Petri, *The Future of the World Economy* (New York: Oxford University Press, 1977).

## Appendix 19-1

Relationship between the relative prices of different goods, real wages rates, and the general rate of return on capital under the old technology

| Rate of return on capital | | 15.0% | 18.56% | 21.0% |
|---|---|---|---|---|
| Level of real wage rates | | 0.933 | 0.841 | 0.783 |
| | Sector | | | |
| Electric, gas, water, and sanitary services | 70 | 1.080 | 1.185 | 1.259 |
| Communications, except radio and TV | 68 | 1.076 | 1.185 | 1.267 |
| Crude petroleum and natural gas | 8 | 1.059 | 1.136 | 1.190 |
| Iron and ferroalloy ores mining | 5 | 1.051 | 1.116 | 1.163 |
| Petroleum refining and allied industries | 30 | 1.046 | 1.104 | 1.147 |
| Chemical and fertilizer mineral mining | 10 | 1.040 | 1.093 | 1.132 |
| Nonferrous metal ores mining | 6 | 1.038 | 1.087 | 1.122 |
| Forestry and fishery products | 3 | 1.037 | 1.085 | 1.120 |
| Other agricultural products | 2 | 1.035 | 1.082 | 1.116 |
| Livestock and livestock products | 1 | 1.032 | 1.073 | 1.104 |
| Amusements | 80 | 1.029 | 1.065 | 1.098 |
| Chemicals and selected chemical products | 26 | 1.027 | 1.062 | 1.088 |
| Stone and clay mining and quarrying | 9 | 1.026 | 1.060 | 1.086 |
| Plastics and synthetic materials | 27 | 1.024 | 1.055 | 1.079 |
| Transportation and warehousing | 67 | 1.021 | 1.048 | 1.070 |
| Health services, excluding hospitals | 82 | 1.021 | 1.047 | 1.067 |

## Appendix 19-1 (Cont.)

| Rate of return on capital | | 15.0% | 18.56% | 21.0% |
|---|---|---|---|---|
| Level of real wage rates | | 0.933 | 0.841 | 0.783 |
| | Sector | | | |
| Paper and allied products, except containers | 23 | 1.015 | 1.034 | 1.050 |
| Radio and TV broadcasting | 69 | 1.013 | 1.028 | 1.042 |
| Food and kindred products | 13 | 1.012 | 1.026 | 1.039 |
| Primary iron and steel manufacturing | 36 | 1.012 | 1.026 | 1.038 |
| Primary nonferrous metals manufacturing | 37 | 1.009 | 1.020 | 1.030 |
| Tobacco manufactures | 14 | 1.009 | 1.020 | 1.030 |
| Miscellaneous textile goods and floor coverings | 16 | 1.009 | 1.018 | 1.028 |
| Educational services | 83 | 1.008 | 1.016 | 1.024 |
| Stone and clay products | 35 | 1.007 | 1.015 | 1.023 |
| Fabrics, yarn, and thread mills | 15 | 1.007 | 1.014 | 1.023 |
| Hotels, personal and repair services, except auto | 76 | 1.007 | 1.014 | 1.021 |
| Leather tanning and finishing | 32 | 1.007 | 1.013 | 1.021 |
| Office, computing, and accounting machines | 51 | 1.006 | 1.013 | 1.020 |
| Paints and allied products | 29 | 1.005 | 1.009 | 1.016 |
| Metal containers | 38 | 1.005 | 1.009 | 1.015 |
| Glass and glass products | 34 | 1.004 | 1.008 | 1.014 |
| Rubber and miscellaneous plastic products | 31 | 1.004 | 1.008 | 1.014 |
| Paperboard containers and boxes | 24 | 1.001 | 1.001 | 1.004 |
| Electronic computing equipment | 50 | 1.000 | 0.998 | 1.000 |
| Drugs, cleaning and toilet preparations | 28 | 1.000 | 0.997 | 0.999 |
| Optical, ophthalmic, and photographic equipment | 65 | 1.000 | 0.997 | 0.999 |
| Nonprofit organizations | 84 | 1.000 | 0.996 | 0.997 |
| Hospitals | 81 | 0.999 | 0.994 | 0.994 |
| Coal mining | 7 | 0.998 | 0.994 | 0.995 |
| Miscellaneous fabricated textile products | 18 | 0.998 | 0.992 | 0.992 |
| Electronic components, nec | 59 | 0.997 | 0.990 | 0.989 |
| Lumber and wood products, except containers | 19 | 0.996 | 0.989 | 0.987 |
| Agricultural, forestry, and fishery services | 4 | 0.996 | 0.988 | 0.986 |
| Printing and publishing | 25 | 0.995 | 0.986 | 0.983 |
| Screw machine products and stampings | 40 | 0.994 | 0.984 | 0.980 |
| Semiconductors and related devices | 58 | 0.994 | 0.983 | 0.980 |
| Engines and turbines | 42 | 0.994 | 0.983 | 0.979 |
| Motor vehicles and equipment | 61 | 0.994 | 0.982 | 0.978 |
| Eating and drinking places | 78 | 0.993 | 0.982 | 0.978 |
| Insurance | 74 | 0.993 | 0.982 | 0.979 |
| Miscellaneous electrical machinery and supplies | 60 | 0.993 | 0.981 | 0.976 |
| Automobile repair services | 79 | 0.993 | 0.981 | 0.976 |
| Other furniture and fixtures | 22 | 0.992 | 0.980 | 0.974 |
| Household appliances | 54 | 0.992 | 0.978 | 0.972 |
| Construction and mining machinery | 44 | 0.992 | 0.978 | 0.972 |
| Heating, plumbing, and structural metal products | 39 | 0.992 | 0.978 | 0.972 |
| Electron tubes | 57 | 0.991 | 0.977 | 0.971 |
| Farm and garden machinery | 43 | 0.991 | 0.977 | 0.971 |
| Other fabricated metal products | 41 | 0.990 | 0.975 | 0.968 |
| Finance | 73 | 0.990 | 0.975 | 0.969 |
| Miscellaneous manufacturing | 66 | 0.989 | 0.971 | 0.963 |
| Electric industrial equipment and apparatus | 53 | 0.989 | 0.971 | 0.963 |
| General industrial machinery and equipment | 48 | 0.989 | 0.971 | 0.962 |

## Appendix 19-1 (Cont.)

| Rate of return on capital | | 15.0% | 18.56% | 21.0% |
|---|---|---|---|---|
| Level of real wage rates | | 0.933 | 0.841 | 0.783 |
| | Sector | | | |
| Wholesale trade | 71 | 0.988 | 0.969 | 0.960 |
| Aircraft and parts | 62 | 0.988 | 0.968 | 0.959 |
| Electric lighting and wiring equipment | 55 | 0.987 | 0.966 | 0.956 |
| Ordnance and accessories | 12 | 0.987 | 0.966 | 0.956 |
| Service industry machines | 52 | 0.986 | 0.965 | 0.955 |
| Household furniture | 21 | 0.986 | 0.965 | 0.954 |
| Radio, TV, and communications equipment | 56 | 0.985 | 0.963 | 0.951 |
| Metalworking machinery and equipment | 46 | 0.985 | 0.961 | 0.949 |
| Apparel | 17 | 0.985 | 0.961 | 0.948 |
| Footwear and other leather products | 33 | 0.984 | 0.961 | 0.948 |
| Materials handling machinery and equipment | 45 | 0.984 | 0.959 | 0.945 |
| Special industrial machinery and equipment | 47 | 0.983 | 0.956 | 0.942 |
| Miscellaneous machinery, except electrical | 49 | 0.982 | 0.956 | 0.941 |
| Other transportation equipment | 63 | 0.982 | 0.955 | 0.940 |
| Scientific and controlling instruments | 64 | 0.982 | 0.955 | 0.940 |
| Retail trade | 72 | 0.978 | 0.945 | 0.927 |
| Real estate and rental | 75 | 0.977 | 0.943 | 0.924 |
| Wooden containers | 20 | 0.976 | 0.941 | 0.922 |
| Business services | 77 | 0.976 | 0.942 | 0.922 |
| Construction | 11 | 0.976 | 0.941 | 0.921 |
| Government enterprises | 85 | 0.975 | 0.939 | 0.918 |

Each column shows the relative prices of different goods corresponding to the rate of return on capital and the level of real wage rates entered at the head of that column. The relative prices are calculated relative to a rate of return $r = 12.5$ and a real wage rate equal to one.

The relative price of good $i$ is computed according to the following formula:

$$[P_i(r)/\overline{P}(r)]:[P_i(r^0)/\overline{P}(r^0)]$$

## Appendix 19-2

Percentage changes in relative prices and real wage rates brought about by replacement of old technologies (*percentages*)

| | Shift from old technology into: | | | | | | | |
| | All new technologies | | | | Optimal mix of old and new technologies | | | |
| Sector  Rate of return on capital (r) | 12.5 | 15.0 | 18.0 | 21.0 | 12.5 | 15.0 | 18.0 | 21.0 |
|---|---|---|---|---|---|---|---|---|
| 0 Real wage index | *6.362* | *1.995* | −0.839 | −3.576 | *10.12* | *8.360* | *6.658* | *4.853* |
| 1 Livestock and livestock products | −3.667 | −4.344 | −5.214 | −5.753 | −4.934 | 1.786 | 1.469 | 1.329 |
| 2 Other agricultural products | −5.543 | −5.905 | −6.339 | −6.584 | −6.635 | 0.273 | 0.410 | 0.578 |
| 3 Forestry and fishery products | −6.177 | −6.521 | −6.963 | −7.239 | −7.437 | −0.389 | −0.268 | −0.137 |
| 4 Agricultural, forestry, and fishery services | −3.535 | −4.215 | −5.178 | −5.835 | −5.289 | 2.065 | 1.645 | 1.377 |
| 5 Iron and ferroalloy ores mining | −5.483 | −5.954 | −6.612 | −7.059 | −6.739 | 0.225 | 0.121 | 0.069 |
| 6 Nonferrous metal ores mining | −5.164 | −5.835 | −6.741 | −7.336 | −6.726 | 0.354 | −0.016 | −0.228 |
| 7 Coal mining | −3.871 | −4.725 | −5.958 | −6.814 | −5.852 | 1.538 | 0.825 | 0.337 |
| 8 Crude petroleum and natural gas | −6.280 | −6.620 | −7.140 | −7.523 | −7.646 | −0.477 | −0.437 | −0.419 |
| 9 Stone and clay mining and quarrying | −6.321 | −6.723 | 7.252 | −7.587 | −7.577 | −0.586 | −0.556 | −0.489 |
| 10 Chemical and fertilizer mineral mining | −6.532 | −6.821 | −7.186 | −7.409 | −7.581 | −0.692 | −0.487 | −0.299 |
| 11 Construction | −5.714 | −6.153 | −6.838 | −7.349 | −7.021 | 0.022 | −0.111 | −0.231 |
| 12 Ordnance and accessories | *−5.185* | *−4.731* | *−4.051* | *−3.558* | *0.884* | *1.530* | *2.868* | *3.840* |
| 13 Food and kindred products | −5.611 | −6.056 | −6.659 | −7.052 | −6.973 | 0.071 | 0.025 | 0.032 |
| 14 Tobacco manufactures | −5.344 | −5.856 | −6.562 | −7.030 | −6.937 | 0.330 | 0.175 | 0.102 |
| 15 Fabrics, yarn, and thread mills | −4.803 | −5.392 | −6.198 | −6.727 | −6.607 | 0.812 | 0.550 | 0.410 |
| 16 Miscellaneous textile goods and floor coverings | −5.387 | −5.872 | −6.531 | −6.960 | −7.024 | 0.308 | 0.203 | 0.170 |
| 17 Apparel | −3.786 | −4.503 | −5.569 | −6.329 | −6.098 | 1.770 | 1.237 | 0.853 |
| 18 Miscellaneous fabricated textile products | −4.814 | −5.330 | −6.059 | −6.553 | −6.610 | 0.815 | 0.617 | 0.502 |
| 19 Lumber and wood products, except containers | −5.626 | −6.200 | −7.025 | −7.596 | −7.312 | −0.038 | −0.324 | −0.511 |
| 20 Wooden containers | −5.795 | −6.589 | −7.808 | −8.705 | −8.143 | −0.439 | −1.145 | −1.684 |
| 21 Household furniture | −5.148 | −5.618 | −6.317 | −6.814 | −6.817 | 0.571 | 0.422 | 0.314 |
| 22 Other furniture and fixtures | −7.501 | −7.227 | −6.812 | −6.510 | −8.430 | −1.172 | −0.147 | 0.599 |

## Appendix 19-2 (Cont.)

| Sector Rate of return on capital (r) | Shift from old technology into: | | | | | | | |
| --- | --- | --- | --- | --- | --- | --- | --- | --- |
| | All new technologies | | | | Optimal mix of old and new technologies | | | |
| | 12.5 | 15.0 | 18.0 | 21.0 | 12.5 | 15.0 | 18.0 | 21.0 |
| 23 Paper and allied products, except containers | −6.084 | −6.521 | −7.097 | −7.462 | −7.583 | −0.377 | −0.398 | −0.363 |
| 24 Paperboard containers and boxes | −5.865 | −6.430 | −7.224 | −7.758 | −7.658 | −0.276 | −0.528 | −0.675 |
| 25 Printing and publishing | −6.871 | −7.172 | −7.596 | −7.882 | −8.753 | −1.072 | −0.934 | −0.816 |
| 26 Chemicals and selected chemical products | −6.560 | −6.881 | −7.298 | −7.559 | −7.808 | −0.786 | −0.622 | −0.477 |
| 27 Plastics and synthetic materials | −6.231 | −6.659 | −7.209 | −7.549 | −7.675 | −0.536 | −0.532 | −0.473 |
| 28 Drugs, cleaning and toilet preparations | −7.112 | −7.402 | −7.817 | −8.103 | −8.537 | −1.357 | −1.222 | −1.113 |
| 29 Paints and allied products | −7.515 | −7.802 | −8.214 | −8.497 | −8.968 | −1.751 | −1.606 | −1.490 |
| 30 Petroleum refining and allied industries | −6.541 | −6.881 | −7.382 | −7.739 | −7.898 | −0.758 | −0.700 | −0.656 |
| 31 Rubber and miscellaneous plastic products | −4.076 | −4.186 | −4.320 | −4.394 | −2.229 | 2.075 | 2.535 | 2.890 |
| 32 Leather tanning and finishing | −5.418 | −5.918 | −6.616 | −7.086 | −7.033 | 0.245 | 0.097 | 0.022 |
| 33 Footwear and other leather products | −3.942 | −4.542 | −5.438 | −6.081 | −3.179 | 1.730 | 1.380 | 1.124 |
| 34 Glass and glass products | −4.396 | −4.621 | −4.922 | −5.114 | −1.990 | 1.638 | 1.922 | 2.151 |
| 35 Stone and clay products | −7.517 | −7.370 | −7.151 | −6.993 | −8.457 | −1.282 | −0.455 | 0.143 |
| 36 Primary iron and steel manufacturing | −7.461 | −7.052 | −6.456 | −6.035 | −7.680 | −0.946 | 0.285 | 1.168 |
| 37 Primary nonferrous metals manufacturing | −5.830 | −5.257 | −4.443 | −3.882 | 0.223 | 0.967 | 2.444 | 3.487 |
| 38 Metal containers | −9.695 | −8.909 | −7.759 | −6.946 | −8.800 | −2.932 | −1.120 | 0.179 |
| 39 Heating, plumbing, and structural metal products | −7.973 | −7.456 | −6.679 | −6.115 | −8.030 | −1.385 | 0.036 | 1.070 |
| 40 Screw machine products and stampings | −8.249 | −7.137 | −5.486 | −4.303 | −7.765 | −1.056 | 1.301 | 3.005 |
| 41 Other fabricated metal products | −8.706 | −7.974 | −6.885 | −6.104 | −8.730 | −1.933 | −0.180 | 1.088 |
| 42 Engines and turbines | −11.123 | −10.833 | −10.404 | −10.098 | −11.030 | −4.972 | −3.942 | −3.199 |
| 43 Farm and garden machinery | −7.960 | −7.384 | −6.524 | −5.904 | −8.041 | −1.296 | 0.218 | 1.316 |
| 44 Construction and mining machinery | −10.344 | −9.922 | −9.287 | −8.826 | −10.772 | −4.001 | −2.744 | −1.829 |
| 45 Materials handling machinery and equipment | −10.676 | −10.415 | −10.024 | −9.739 | −11.441 | −4.524 | −3.531 | −2.809 |
| 46 Metalworking machinery and equipment | 0.426 | 2.147 | 4.735 | 6.609 | 14.489 | 8.866 | 12.294 | 14.795 |
| 47 Special industrial machinery and equipment | −9.446 | −8.660 | −7.479 | −6.623 | −9.767 | −2.652 | −0.801 | 0.548 |
| 48 General industrial machinery and equipment | −9.798 | −9.006 | −7.827 | −6.980 | −10.007 | −3.022 | −1.175 | 0.161 |
| 49 Miscellaneous machinery, except electrical | −5.883 | −4.724 | −2.960 | −1.668 | 4.057 | 1.544 | 4.046 | 5.885 |
| 50 Electronic computing equipment | −50.987 | −49.788 | −48.098 | −46.950 | −51.290 | −46.490 | −44.359 | −42.884 |

| | | | | | | | | |
|---|---|---|---|---|---|---|---|---|
| 51 Office, computing, and accounting machines | 4.919 | 4.043 | 2.836 | 0.310 | −2.554 | −2.952 | −3.504 | −3.874 |
| 52 Service industry machines | −1.341 | −2.440 | −3.961 | −10.740 | −8.372 | −9.003 | −9.884 | −10.478 |
| 53 Electric industrial equipment and apparatus | 2.040 | 0.995 | −0.449 | −7.438 | −5.231 | −5.798 | −6.588 | −7.120 |
| 54 Household appliances | 2.652 | 1.643 | 0.252 | −2.090 | −4.650 | −5.183 | −5.922 | −6.417 |
| 55 Electric lighting and wiring equipment | 8.023 | 6.370 | 4.098 | 4.282 | 0.343 | −0.770 | −2.311 | −3.338 |
| 56 Radio, TV, and communications equipment | −1.957 | −2.576 | −3.434 | −10.635 | −8.929 | −9.117 | −9.381 | −9.560 |
| 57 Electron tubes | 2.028 | 0.998 | −0.421 | −7.517 | −5.246 | −5.799 | −6.565 | −7.077 |
| 58 Semiconductors and related devices | −39.637 | −40.863 | −42.608 | −47.578 | −43.937 | −44.840 | −46.147 | −47.059 |
| 59 Electronic components, n.e.c. | −1.004 | −1.883 | −3.105 | −9.980 | −8.052 | −8.478 | −9.077 | −9.484 |
| 60 Miscellaneous electrical machinery and supplies | 1.500 | 0.613 | −0.618 | −7.120 | −5.706 | −6.132 | −6.730 | −7.135 |
| 61 Motor vehicles and equipment | 6.432 | 4.870 | 2.717 | −0.085 | −1.143 | −2.175 | −3.612 | −4.576 |
| 62 Aircraft and parts | 2.131 | 1.320 | 0.221 | −0.662 | −5.135 | −5.486 | −5.953 | −6.252 |
| 63 Other transportation equipment | −1.312 | −1.632 | −2.079 | −9.119 | −8.348 | −8.252 | −8.121 | −8.037 |
| 64 Scientific and controlling instruments | −0.156 | −0.916 | −1.970 | −9.281 | −7.246 | −7.560 | −8.000 | −8.297 |
| 65 Optical, ophthalmic, and photographic equipment | 5.843 | 4.548 | 2.751 | 1.583 | −1.606 | −2.404 | −3.522 | −4.277 |
| 66 Miscellaneous manufacturing | −0.117 | −0.935 | −2.073 | −9.048 | −7.157 | −7.532 | −8.060 | −8.422 |
| 67 Transportation and warehousing | 0.114 | −0.031 | −0.174 | −6.933 | −7.025 | −6.759 | −6.334 | −6.008 |
| 68 Communications, except radio and TV | −0.948 | −1.283 | −1.782 | −9.621 | −8.010 | −7.927 | −7.843 | −7.813 |
| 69 Radio and TV broadcasting | −0.156 | −0.185 | −0.194 | −7.552 | −7.270 | −6.899 | −6.349 | −5.957 |
| 70 Electric, gas, water, and sanitary services | 0.023 | −0.009 | −0.021 | −6.226 | −7.110 | −6.740 | −6.191 | −5.791 |
| 71 Wholesale trade | −2.532 | −3.049 | −3.791 | −11.640 | −9.482 | −9.575 | −9.728 | −9.849 |
| 72 Retail trade | 1.042 | 0.193 | −0.994 | −3.646 | −6.162 | −6.550 | −7.103 | −7.483 |
| 73 Finance | −8.531 | −10.211 | −12.546 | −20.761 | −15.051 | −16.253 | −17.941 | −19.080 |
| 74 Insurance | −8.041 | −9.209 | −10.832 | −18.564 | −14.456 | −15.180 | −16.200 | −16.889 |
| 75 Real estate and rental | −5.638 | −5.766 | −5.984 | −13.276 | −12.357 | −12.099 | −11.775 | −11.584 |
| 76 Hotels, personal and repair services, except auto | 4.660 | 4.878 | 5.194 | −1.034 | −2.805 | −2.184 | −1.299 | −0.693 |
| 77 Business services | 4.548 | 4.474 | 4.362 | −4.065 | −2.910 | −2.561 | −2.080 | −1.763 |
| 78 Eating and drinking places | 2.729 | 3.221 | 3.920 | −3.464 | −4.531 | −3.669 | −2.444 | −1.606 |
| 79 Automobile repair services | 3.263 | 3.177 | 3.084 | −2.150 | −4.102 | −3.769 | −3.278 | −2.932 |
| 80 Amusements | 3.056 | 3.242 | 3.595 | −2.932 | −4.284 | −3.699 | −2.792 | −2.110 |
| 81 Hospitals | 1.576 | 2.609 | 4.055 | 29.541 | 29.056 | 29.915 | 31.151 | 32.009 |
| 82 Health services, excluding hospitals | 1.073 | 1.851 | 3.011 | 19.688 | 18.249 | 19.536 | 21.513 | 22.987 |
| 83 Educational services | 1.243 | 2.191 | 3.550 | 11.612 | 15.810 | 14.407 | 12.444 | 11.125 |
| 84 Nonprofit organizations | 2.387 | 2.107 | 1.692 | 0.380 | −4.752 | −4.625 | −4.472 | −4.387 |
| 85 Government enterprises | −8.276 | −7.888 | −7.439 | −14.669 | −14.809 | −14.081 | −13.144 | −12.569 |
| Total | | | | | | | | |

# 20

## An information system for policy decisions in a modern economy

### (1979)

The design of a statistical or any other data system should obviously be controlled by specification of the purposes it is intended to serve. In the course of their historical development, the contents and organization of government statistics gradually adjust themselves to change in the use being made of them. As in any other political or administrative process, this adjustment occurs, however, with a considerable lag. Thus, it is not surprising that users of official statistics both within and outside the government tend to view even the latest facts and figures offered to them as already obsolete. To keep an information system up to date, one has to look ahead.

In this chapter, I endeavor to describe the demands that the U.S. government statistical service should be expected to meet over the next five or ten years, and to suggest some of the steps that would have to be taken in the immediate future to enable it to satisfy these crucial long-term needs.

I center my attention on economic statistics. The same considerations, however, apply to population, health, environment, and all other areas of social statistics as well.

Without the driving force of private enterprise operating within the flexible setting of a free market economy, this country could never have attained the high level of economic well-being that it enjoys today. The invisible hand of competitive price mechanisms cannot, however, maintain the balance of the system and secure the satisfaction of rapidly expanding social needs without the guiding and supporting action of that other, highly visible public hand.

From *Business Disclosure: Government's Need to Know*, Harvey J. Goldschmid, ed. (New York: McGraw-Hill, 1979), pp. 203–11. © 1979. Reprinted by permission.

Over 27 percent of the GNP now passes directly through federal, state, and local government budgets, and most, if not all, private economic activities are subject to direct or indirect government control. The extension of public involvement in all aspects of economic and social life represents a natural and unavoidable response to the rise of modern large-scale technology, the rapid growth of the demand for public as contrasted to private goods, and, last but not least, the increasing concern for social and economic equity as contrasted with simple efficiency.

The present patchwork pattern of government action in the economic field grew step by step out of the necessity to provide immediate remedies to particular exigencies. Only in the case of regularly recurring or persistent problems such as cyclical unemployment or stubborn inflationary trends has there been a semblance of systematic anticipatory policies. The present government involvement in the operation of the economy presents a confusing picture of a sprawling labyrinth rather than a blueprint of a rationally designed edifice.

In an advanced industrial economy, any action intended to meet a problem confronting one particular industry, one particular geographic area, or one particular group of citizens is bound to affect, whether intended or not, many other industries, regions, and groups of citizens. Moreover, many decisions, private as well as public, arrived at today can be expected to affect the economy and the state of our society not only next year but five, ten, and even twenty years from now.

The troubleshooting approach to formulation of government policies, at least in the economic field, is bound to be ineffectual and inordinately costly under such conditions. Measures devised to meet one particular problem turn out to create new problems or to aggravate already existing ones. An alternative to the troubleshooting, trial-and-error approach is one in which the country's economy is viewed as a system of interrelated activities (which it actually is) and the economic policies of the federal, state, and local governments are conceived as a combination of well-coordinated rules and actions designed to facilitate the day-to-day operation and, to some extent, steer in a desired direction the development of the system as a whole.

Some recent legislative reforms and administrative changes can be interpreted as tentative moves in this direction. The time has come to take a decisive step. A strong, autonomous research organization should be established to provide all branches and agencies of the government with technical support required for developing a systematic, coordinated approach to development, evaluation, and practical implementation of national, regional, and local economic policies, both general and sectoral. The proposed organization could also strengthen the quality and compatibility of privately gathered data (i.e., by associations and research groups) by providing suggested statistical standards and guidelines.

The organization should also be responsible for monitoring in great detail developments in all parts of the U.S. economy, with emphasis on changes in their interrelationships and, whenever necessary, on their dependence on anticipated changes in the structure of the world economy. In doing so, it should be able to identify and perhaps anticipate potential trouble spots. In looking ahead, the analytical capabilities of that organization should be engaged not so much in crystal ball predictions of the future but rather in systematic elaboration of alternative scenarios, each describing, with emphasis on sectoral and regional detail, the anticipated effect of a particular combination of national, regional, and local economic policies. This is, in fact, the only means by which the government and the electorate at large will be able to make an informed choice among alternative policies.

While providing research support to legislators and administrators engaged in the overall direction of national economic policies and assisting in the choice of appropriate methods for their practical implementation, the proposed technical organization should not be directly involved in either process any more than is, for instance, the Bureau of Labor Statistics (Department of Labor) or the Bureau of Economic Analysis (Department of Commerce). In order to be able to discharge effectively the responsibilities assigned to it, the organization should, however, have a decisive voice in determining the direction and scope of the data-gathering activities of the federal and, in some instances, even the state and local governments.

## I. The modeling approach

The scientific tool best suited to the task of analyzing the operations of large economic systems is a model. A model is not so much a small-scale replica of the real thing as it is a surveyor's map, a blueprint of its structure and of the interrelationships among all its different parts. The modeling approach can be considered today to be practically indispensable for systematic understanding of the functioning or, as the case may be, the malfunctioning of a modern economy, for tracing the potential or actual sources of trouble, and for deciding what adjustments should be made, what actions could be taken, to set it right.

The model-building approach is widely used by both government and private business. It has been recognized as an effective monitoring device and decision-making aid in dealing with complex production, transportation, or distribution systems, as well as in market analysis. Large government agencies, such as the Department of Energy, the Environmental Protection Agency, and the Department of Transportation, and their state and local counterparts, resort to model building. Large oil corporations and chemical concerns, both in the United States and abroad, use economic models to assess alternative patterns of corporate development. Several hundred economic models are operated in the government, and certainly a much larger number are used by members of the private sector.

Formally, a model is a system of equations. Some of the variables entering into it describe inputs, outputs, and prices of different goods and services, and the levels of income and of employment in various industries and regions; others represent, for example, the levels of investment in new productive capacities or the quantities of exports and imports. The parameters entering into the description of individual equations describe the structural characteristics of the various parts of the economy. Large sets of *technical coefficients* describe, for example, the "cooking recipes" of the individual industries, relationships between the quantities of labor, materials, or energy used and the amounts of finished goods produced. Others reflect the composition of the typical shopping basket of different income groups or the breakdown of various kinds of government expenditures. Still others describe the tax rates determining the level of government revenues.

As time goes on, the magnitude of these relationship parameters must be expected to change, reflecting new methods of production, shifts of consumer tastes, or, for example, the introduction of new environmental regulations.

## II. Large or small models

Models differ in the scope of their coverage and detail. There are models of particular sectors of production, such as U.S. agriculture or the petrochemical industry; there are models of particular geographic areas, such as the state of Texas or the city of Philadelphia; and, of course, there are models of the U.S. economy as a whole.

Detailed methods such as those used by commercial market analysts may have one variable representing coarse gray cotton fabric
and another for printed cotton cloth. In a highly aggregative model,
on the other hand, all types of cotton goods or even all kinds of textiles may be lumped together and represented by a single annual
sales variable. The size of a model (i.e., the total number of equations, variables, and parameters it contains) depends, not unlike the
complexity of a road map, on the magnitude of the geographic area
it covers and the level of detail with which it is depicted.

A model describing the U.S. economy can be very simple if the
picture it represents is drawn sketchily in terms of a small number
of aggregative variables such as the total GNP, investment and consumption, total employment, total government revenues and outlays, the total money supply, and the average levels of wages and
prices. The total number of equations describing such a system
might be as small as ten. On the other hand, a detailed model of a
single sector, say, petroleum refining, can contain several hundred
variables identifying separately each one of the different types of
crudes and of the immediate and finished products. The system of
equations describing in minute detail the structure of production
would, in this case, contain a separate description of each one of the
alternative processes that might be used to produce the same good.

Models used for management purposes in the private sector, and
more recently in the public sector as well, are mostly of the second
type, detailed but offering narrow coverage. Those used for the
description of general economic conditions and projection of business trends belong mostly to the first, aggregative kind. They are
broad in coverage but short on detail. This is largely because most
of the theoretical thinking in this area for many years has been and
still is dominated by the aggregative Keynesian approach, according
to which the economy can be controlled effectively through skillful
manipulation of a few strategic aggregate variables, such as total
government revenue and outlays, the total money supply, and the
rate of interest. A small aggregative model could be expected to
contain all the information required for managing as large and as
complex an economy as that of the United States.

The experience of past years has shown that this is not the case.
Moreover, a small aggregative model cannot possibly incorporate
the factual information and provide the analytical understanding
required for the handling of innumerable problems with which the
government has to cope from day to day, from year to year, from
one decade to the next. Questions raised by the energy crisis, poten-

tial shortages of some basic raw materials, and the problems of environment cannot be treated or even posed in aggregative terms.

Hence, it is not surprising that specialized models, narrow in coverage but rich in details, are now being used not only in the private corporate sector but by governmental agencies as well. Such "departmental" models, while helping an individual agency to organize and interpret facts and figures pertaining to the limited area lying within its immediate purview, obviously cannot be used for purposes of interagency coordination. In fact, "adversary fact finding" is being replaced nowadays with "adversary model building."

The more complex the economy, the greater the mutual interdependence of its parts. The greater such interdependence, the more complete and detailed the model must be. An integrated model of the U.S. economy must consist of a large, detailed set of equations. Far from discouraging the construction of other models, it would facilitate it by providing model developers with large sets of well-organized, calibrated data.

## III. Predictive models and operational models

Most of the existing large models of the U.S. economy are used mainly, although not exclusively, for forecasting purposes, for anticipation of what might be loosely referred to as the general state of business three, six, or twelve months ahead. The primary data employed in construction of such predictive models come in the form of time series, most of them highly aggregative, showing the past behavior and relationships of the economic variables that enter into an equation. The forecasts are obtained through extrapolation of past statistical relationships among those variables that enter into an equation. The forecasts are obtained through extrapolation of past statistical relationships among these variables estimated on the basis of their observed behavior in the past with emphasis on apparent leads and lags. While some of these relationships could be interpreted unequivocally as describing direct observable connections between cause and effect, in most instances this is not the case.

Models of the operational type depend to a lesser extent on formal extrapolation of statistical relationships observed in the past. Since they are generally more detailed than predictive models, they can assimilate directly large sets of detailed factual information of a technical and organizational kind. For instance, the estimate of the use of fertilizers or pesticides per acre by different cultures on different soils can be obtained from agronomists, estimates of the capital requirements of the copper mining industry might involve a survey of operating or projected mines, and an estimate of the demands for primary school teachers would require a systematic study of teacher-pupil ratios in selected school districts.

To be sure, such information can be of little use for the purposes we have in mind unless it is combined with the framework of the model with other data of similar specialized kinds. To know how much fertilizer is required per acre of corn or how much investment is necessary to bring out an additional ton of copper in a particular type of mine does not suffice for estimating the total amount of fertilizer used for corn production or the investment requirement of the copper mining industry at some future point in time. The missing total output figures can be determined only within the framework of a large model covering all sectors of the national economy. Moreover, to be capable of absorbing concrete specific information of the kind described above, that model has to be not only comprehensive but detailed. In spite of their size, such models, or at least the results of computations based on them, will be more comprehensible to those familiar with growing corn, mining copper, teaching school, and so on.

Some corporate users of an aggregative model of the U.S. economy, do indeed undertake the task of disaggregating that part of it in which they happen to be particularly interested, using additional specialized information that the builders of the model could not handle. Some builders of aggregative models supply their customers with what might be called special disaggregation kits as optional equipment. Needless to say, the results of such makeshift operations are bound to be inferior to those that would have been obtained if all details had been incorporated in the original analytical design.

## IV. Facts and figures

One of the great advantages of choosing the modeling approach is that it would provide an impetus and at the same time the means for modernizing and streamlining the entire statistical system.

The lack of effective coordination in the general area of policy formulation and implementation is matched by the absence of a clear overall design in gathering, organizing, and presenting the facts and figures on which both public and private decision making so critically depend. While the Bureau of the Census might have been originally intended to function as a central statistical office, there is now hardly any department or federal agency that has not been put in charge of collecting and publishing statistics pertaining to its particular domain. The Department of Labor is mainly, but not entirely, in charge of employment, wage, and cost-of-living statistics. Information on railroad and trucking freight is collected by the Interstate Commerce Commission, and information on air shipments is collected by the Federal Aviation Administration. The Federal Power Commission is the principal collector of data for the electrical and power companies, while the Department of the Interior is the primary gatherer of coal and oil output data. While the Standard Industrial and Commodity Classifications are commonly adhered to, each agency feels free to use its own classification and definitions and to determine on its own the frequency and timing of its statistical operations.

As every user of government statistics knows, to secure a modicum of comparability and compatibility between figures emanating from different agencies or even from different offices within the same agency is a trying task, absorbing an inordinate amount of time and money. Much valuable information inevitably falls by the wayside. The time elapsing between collection and actual release of urgently needed figures is, in many instances, too long. An official input-output table describing the flow of goods and services between all sectors of the American economy in the year 1972, a table used mainly on census figures, was, for example, ready for release only in 1979, and the 1977 table was still not available in 1982.[1] In the absence of a comprehensive statistical plan, data-gathering crash programs are initiated which are both inefficient and costly. Much more complete and reliable information would be on hand at the time of a crisis if the need for it were anticipated and detailed basic data were collected year in and year out.

Construction of a large integrating model of the national economy, while serving the immediate needs of analysts and policymakers, would also make an important contribution by transforming our obsolete statistical services into a modern, well-integrated information system. According to preliminary estimates (supported, incidentally, by some of the most outspoken opponents of national economic planning), the sum total of present federal budgets should be increased by some $450 million. The modeling approach can be used as a device for securing a reasonable order of priorities in allocating these additional funds.

Most of the well-deserved criticism of the existing large economic models used by the government, and in private sectors as well, is

[1]By contrast, in Japan the Government Administrative Management Agency published their 1975 input-output tables with 544 row sectors of goods and services and 407 column sectors of the production activities of goods and services in March 1979.

directed not at their potential capabilities but at the rather obvious weaknesses of their data base. Even when the analytical design is criticized, this is because it often reflects a desperate attempt to compensate for the lack of reliable factual information by recourse to sophisticated but nevertheless very dubious estimating procedures. Instead of permitting the technical advice that the policy-maker needs so badly to be distorted by the lack of indispensable data, determined efforts should be made to upgrade the national statistical system so that it would be capable of meeting the legitimate demand for complete, reliable figures.

Most of the difficult problems confronting the country—energy, environment, natural resources—are partly economic, partly technical, and partly social. The conventional distinctions among economics, engineering, geology, and even biology are gradually disappearing. This is bound to be reflected in the structure of the model and the data requirements as well. It is also the reason why agencies possessing technical competence in certain areas should continue to collect specialized information pertaining to these areas. They should do so, however, in strict compliance with standards established by the organization charged with the responsibility for construction and maintenance of the master model.

Much emphasis has been placed in recent years on summary indices, such as the general price level, total level of unemployment, and so on. Not to be outdone by the economists, other social scientists are pressing for compilation and publication of summary measures of environmental disruption and even of a number describing the "general qualify of life." Such figures might assist an individual researcher to summarize the subjective impression gained from careful examination of long arrays of heterogenous data. They should, however, not be interpreted as meaningful objective measures of observed facts, and, certainly, such broad indices cannot be used as viable substitutes for large sets of detailed data which they are often supposed to represent. Reliance on broad index numbers is more often than not a sure sign of missing analytical insight or of a lack of detailed factual information and, in most instances, of both.

## V. Functional organization

The limited success of numerous reorganization schemes for increasing the efficiency of the government seems to result, in part, from the fact that too little attention has usually been paid to specification of methods and techniques by which the function assigned to different units shown on fancy organization charts could actually be accomplished. This is particularly true of legislative and administrative functions pertaining to economic questions. Dealing with the formal institutional and legal aspects of a new setup is not enough.

The magnitude and complexity of the task involved in constructing and running a comprehensive computerized model of the largest economy in the world should not be underestimated. It is bound to be a formidable task comparable not so much to that of the research department of the Federal Reserve Board or the National Bureau of Economic Research but rather to that of a major scientific-technical facility such as the Linear Accelerator Center at Stanford.

Economic research is usually carried on like traditional handicrafts. Each analyst works on his or her own assignment, employing with greater or lesser skill a kit of standard hand tools. A large economic model is, on the contrary, one single complex piece of equipment; its operation and maintenance involve systematic division of labor and, at the same time, disciplined cooperation among members of a large, differentiated crew. One team takes charge of the formal design of the model, another handles mathematical programming and computation, and still another organizes and stores the numbers fed into the machine. By far the largest part of the professional staff, however, has to be concerned with substantive economic and technical problems involved in collection and interpretation of these data.

The entire field covered by the model has to be mapped out thoroughly and evenly. The most recent input-output table describes its structure and its operation in terms of 496 different sectors. For general monitoring purposes, these can be consolidated into 60 to 80 groups with at least one expert in charge of each. Moreover, regional, metropolitan, environmental problems or questions of employment or capital functions that cut across the entire sectoral spectrum will have to be tended by separate teams. Staff members working on special sectoral and cross-sectoral problems can be expected to maintain close working relationships with experts in other parts of the government, in the business sector, and in various public and private research institutions as well.

A special section, corresponding to the Statistical Policy Division of the Office of Management and the Budget, will have to be made responsible for the establishment of statistical standards for all data-gathering activities throughout the government, for initiation of new programs, and for integration of all data flows.

The activities and responsibilities of the proposed research organization will thus comprise:

1. Serving the research needs of the Economic Development Board, to be established in the Executive Branch of the federal government
2. Preparing special research reports at the request of congressional committees and various departments and committees in the Executive Branch
3. Monitoring the state of the U.S. economy and its relationship to the rest of the world; preparing and publishing, on its own initiative, technical reports on problems confronting it
4. Coordinating data-gathering activities throughout the government

The size of the professional staff needed to carry out such a program can be estimated to be between 200 and 250 persons. The very nature of the operation requires that it be performed on a sufficiently large scale.

# Index